DEFENDING TAIWAN

Advance Praise for *Defending Taiwan*

"The future of Taiwan may decide the shape of global geopolitics for the next hundred years and beyond, and yet academic scholarship has been slow to catch up. Eyck Freymann is at the forefront of an emerging group of scholar-strategists turning their minds to this problem—and doing so with great skill. In *Defending Taiwan*, he shows expertly how military approaches alone will not suffice and lays out a four-pillar concept of deterrence to help guide policy thinking."
—John Bew CMG, Professor of History and Foreign Policy, King's College London

"A magnificent intellectual achievement. Eyck Freymann has crafted one of those rare scholarly works that offers readers both a deep well of knowledge and a thrilling read. As tensions with the People's Republic of China mount, American government officials and military officers will want to keep copies of this book spring-loaded for emergencies. I was particularly struck by the remarkable clarity, realism, and actionability of the military analysis. The conflict scenarios read like the scripts of tier one war games, and the strategy discussions will make you feel like you have a seat in the White House Situation Room. I didn't want to put it down!"
—Ian Easton, author of *The Chinese Invasion Threat: Taiwan's Defense and American Strategy in Asia*

"Within his time in power, Xi Jinping is determined to assert control over Taiwan if he can possibly find a viable opportunity. The stakes could scarcely be higher: PRC subjugation of the capitalist democracy would devastate global supply chains, trigger economic shocks, hamstring U.S. alliances, and threaten nuclear proliferation. Atop a consummate analysis of these critical dynamics, Freymann offers innovative recommendations regarding a credible U.S. threat to engage in 'avalanche decoupling'—a battery of preplanned economic separation measures—to deter PRC aggression."
—Andrew S. Erickson, Professor of Strategy, U.S. Naval War College's China Maritime Studies Institute

"If the U.S. and China go to war, the catalyst is likely to be Taiwan, a vibrant democracy and technological powerhouse that is coveted by Beijing. America needs a strategy to deter China from coercing or attacking Taiwan as well as a contingency plan to safeguard American interests should deterrence fail. In *Defending Taiwan*, Eyck Freymann offers an innovative, multi-dimensional strategy integrating military, political, economic, and technological tools to enhance deterrence and defeat China if war occurs. Drawing on historical lessons, prior research, and incisive analysis, Freymann unpacks three key pillars of deterrence: the U.S. 'One China' policy, a stable conventional military balance, and integrated strategic deterrence comprising nuclear weapons, cyber, space, and artificial intelligence. Across all these pillars, the crucial role of alliances in preserving peace is a central theme, particularly in Freymann's creative proposal for an allied approach, inspired by the Marshall Plan, to ensure economic security in peacetime and in the event of a rupture with China. This is an essential book for policy practitioners and scholars seeking innovative and feasible ways to protect Taiwan's democracy and secure America's interests in the Indo-Pacific."

—Bonnie Glaser, Managing Director, Indo-Pacific Program, German Marshall Fund of the United States

"*Defending Taiwan* compellingly argues that peace in the Taiwan Strait depends not only on military deterrence but on an integrated strategy combining diplomacy, economics, and technology. Clear-eyed and pragmatic about Taiwan's defense needs, this book offers a valuable path toward sustainable peace. A must read for understanding contemporary strategic challenges."

—Admiral Lee Hsi-min (Ret.), 26th Chief of the General Staff, Republic of China Armed Forces

"Freymann skillfully dismantles trendy theories for how to deter Beijing. There is no one magic bullet—but we may yet save Taiwan and the rest of the free world if we marshal our political, military, geostrategic, and economic advantages in the ways Freymann prescribes. Freymann's knowledge of history imbues the book with a refreshingly broad and authoritative scope. I hope it is widely—and urgently—read."

—Matt Pottinger, former U.S. Deputy National Security Advisor (2019–2021), and editor of *The Boiling Moat: Urgent Steps to Defend Taiwan*

"If we've learned anything over the last century, it is that we should always take statements by authoritarian leaders at face value. Thus, it is not a matter of whether China will move to subdue Taiwan, but when and how. In *Defending Taiwan*, Eyck Freymann offers a comprehensive tutorial on every aspect of this most complex of potential geopolitical cycle-ending crises as well as a compelling approach to how to deter it."

—Admiral James "Sandy" Winnefeld (Ret.), former Vice Chairman of the Joint Chiefs of Staff

"Eyck Freymann has written a seminal, timely, and readable book on how to deter war with China. Based on my discussions with senior officials and experts in Beijing, Taipei, and Washington, I can confirm his four-pillar framework addresses the strategic realities we face: military deterrence alone will fail without unprecedented allied coordination across economic, technological, and diplomatic domains. This is precisely the kind of challenge that Japan—positioned at the forefront and at the strategic heart of the First Island Chain—must take the lead in addressing. It is an essential read for anyone committed to preserving peace."

—Katsuya Yamamoto, Rear Admiral (Ret.), Japan Maritime Self-Defense Force, and Director, Strategy and Deterrence Program, Sasakawa Peace Foundation

"Taiwan is the most dangerous flashpoint in the world and Eyck Freymann's book is the most comprehensive analysis of what can be done about it. It is the first account that integrates economic analysis with national defense to address, as he puts it, 'how to restructure the global economy if the world's manufacturing superpower goes rogue.'"

—Philip Zelikow, Botha-Chan Senior Fellow, Stanford University's Hoover Institution

DEFENDING TAIWAN

A STRATEGY TO PREVENT WAR WITH CHINA

EYCK FREYMANN

OXFORD
UNIVERSITY PRESS

Oxford University Press is a department of the University of Oxford.
It furthers the University's objective of excellence in research, scholarship,
and education by publishing worldwide. Oxford is a registered trade mark of
Oxford University Press in the UK and in certain other countries.

Published in the United States of America by Oxford University Press
198 Madison Avenue, New York, NY 10016, United States of America.

CIP data is on file at the Library of Congress

ISBN 9780197823842

DOI: 10.1093/oso/9780197823842.001.0001

Printed by Sheridan Books, Inc., United States of America

The manufacturer's authorized representative in the EU for product safety is
Oxford University Press España S.A. of Parque Empresarial San Fernando de Henares,
Avenida de Castilla, 2 – 28830 Madrid (www.oup.es/en or product.safety@oup.com).
OUP España S.A. also acts as importer into Spain of products made by the manufacturer.

Contents

Note on Authorship   x
Note on Terminology   xi

Introduction   1
Argument   7
Pillars of Deterrence   8
Outline of the Book   13

I. THE CHALLENGE

1 **The Cross-Strait Dispute**   17
What Is Taiwan?   20
Beijing's Position   23
The One China Policy   24
Views from Taiwan   27
Interpreting Xi   30
China's Interests   34
Why Might Xi Choose to Fight?   38
U.S. Interests in Peacetime   42
U.S. Interests in a Crisis   46
Conclusion   50

II. SCENARIOS

2 **The Gray Zone**   55
The All-Domain Pressure Campaign   57
Quarantine Scenarios   62
Coercive Mobilization   72
The Decision to Break the Glass   81
Conclusion   84

3 **Amphibious Invasion and Blockade**   86
   Basic Requirements for Invasion   88
   Taiwanese Resistance and Allied Choices   95
   The Air–Naval Fight   100
   Blockade as a Part of War   107
   Would Blockade Be Checkmate?   112
   Economic and Political Implications   113
   Conclusion   117

III. THE PILLARS OF DETERRENCE

4 **Political Deterrence**   123
   Engage Taiwan   126
   Manage China   133
   Establish the Core Coalition   142
   Conclusion   145

5 **Strengthening Conventional Deterrence**   147
   by Eyck Freymann and Harry Halem
   Surveillance and Reconnaissance   151
   Long-Range Strike   153
   Logistics   154
   Surface Fleet   155
   The DIB   157
   UAS   161
   Submarines   163
   Space Power   165
   Conclusion   166

6 **Preserving Strategic Stability and U.S. Technological
   Leadership**   170
   The Theory of Strategic Coercion   174
   Interpreting Xi's Strategic Buildup   177
   Miscalculation Risks   183
   Reassuring U.S. Allies   185
   Modernizing the U.S. Nuclear Deterrent   187
   AI and Strategic Stability   190
   Toward an American AI Strategic Deterrent   195
   Conclusion   199

7 **Rethinking Economic Deterrence**   202
   by Hugo Bromley and Eyck Freymann
   "Strategic" Economic Threats   206
   The Neutral Problem   212
   China's Role in the Global Economy   217
   PRC Resilience   223
   The Illusion of "Economic Mutually Assured Destruction"   233
   Conclusion   235

8 **Avalanche Decoupling**   237
   by Hugo Bromley and Eyck Freymann
   Policy 1: National Decoupling   242
   Policy 2: The Economic Security Cooperation Board   249
   Partial Avalanche Decoupling   259
   Imagining a World after Avalanche Decoupling   261
   Conclusion   265

Conclusion: Living History   268

Acknowledgments   278
Appendix A: Four Perspectives from Taipei   280
Appendix B: The Currency Intervention   293
Notes   298
Index   396

Note on Authorship

This book would not exist without my co-authors and collaborators and the presses and journals that granted us permission to adapt previously published work. Chapter 5 is co-authored with Harry Halem, drawing on ideas developed in our book *The Arsenal of Democracy: Technology, Industry, and Deterrence in the Indo-Pacific*. Chapters 7 and 8 are co-authored with Dr Hugo Bromley, adapted from our longer and more detailed study "On Day One: An Economic Contingency Plan for a Taiwan Crisis" and various scholarly articles. The economic analysis also draws on work that Calvin Heng and I have done on Beijing's financial contingency planning for crisis scenarios.

Note on Terminology

The debate over Taiwan's political status is legally complex, fiercely contested, and highly consequential. The governing authorities of the Republic of China (ROC), founded in 1912, refer to their political entity as "ROC (Taiwan)" or simply "Taiwan." The governing authorities of the People's Republic of China (PRC), founded in 1949, view themselves as the only legitimate rulers of a single undivided China, asserting that Taiwan is a part of China. The PRC labels Taiwan as "Taiwan province" and the "Separate Customs Territory of Taiwan, Penghu, Kinmen, and Matsu." Politicians in Taiwan have traditionally referred to the PRC as the "Beijing authorities." President Lai Ching-te calls it "China."[1] Confusion over terms like "Chinese" and "Taiwanese" adds complexity since these adjectives can refer to identity, culture, language, or political entities. Taiwan has a Chinese cultural heritage but also has unique cultural traits. It is also home to Indigenous peoples with no historical connection to the other side of the Strait. Many residents of Taiwan self-identify as both "Chinese" and "Taiwanese," while some recognize just one identity.[2]

This book is mindful of these sensitivities and does not use language games to advance a political agenda. My aim is to be clear without being pedantic. I interchangeably refer to the PRC as "Beijing" or "the Mainland" in cross-Strait contexts, and as "China" in broader contexts. I do not use "Chinese" as an adjective when "PRC" is more precise. I interchangeably refer to the ROC as "Taiwan" and "Taipei."

Introduction

On the windswept grasslands of Inner Mongolia, about four hours north-west of Beijing, stands a replica of Taiwan's Presidential Office Building. Across the dusty street is a replica of Taiwan's Ministry of Foreign Affairs, along with other official structures from downtown Taipei. Nearby, a highway cloverleaf interchange mirrors the entrance to the Taiwanese Air Force's Ching Chuan Kang Air Base, alongside a replica of one of Taiwan's key military airfields. This is not a movie set. It is a training ground for invasion. People's Liberation Army (PLA) motorized infantry brigades use it to practice "decapitation" attacks on Taiwan's political leadership (see Figure 0.1).[1]

In July 2017, China's leader Xi Jinping visited for a dramatic inspection. Riding in an open-top jeep, dressed in military fatigues, Xi addressed thousands of troops in combat garb (see Figure 0.2). "Always listen to and follow the party's orders," he ordered. "And march wherever the party points."[2] This was the first time Xi had reviewed troops in the field, symbolizing his deep personal commitment to military modernization. "Today, we are closer to the goal of the great rejuvenation of the Chinese nation than at any other time in history," Xi said as bombers and fighter jets flew overhead. Yet, beneath Xi's swagger lies uncertainty. "We need to build a strong people's military more than any other time in history," he added, betraying lingering doubts about the PLA's readiness to meet his ambitious goals.[3]

Xi's emphasis on military modernization is part of a broader vision for China's "national rejuvenation," a term he uses to encapsulate the domestic and global ambitions of the Chinese Communist Party (CCP).[4] By 2049, the centennial of the People's Republic of China, Xi aims to solidify CCP control, transform China into the dominant power in the Indo-Pacific, and restructure the global economy to serve CCP interests.[5] He also aims to dominate the development, manufacturing, and deployment of emerging

Figure 0.1 Replica of Taiwan's Presidential Office used in a Zhurihe exercise

Source: Chinese Central Television (CCTV), reprinted in Victor Robert Lee, "Satellite Imagery: China Staging Mock Invasion of Taiwan?," *The Diplomat*, August 9, 2015, https://thediplomat.com/2015/08/satellite-imagery-from-china-suggests-mock-invasion-of-taiwan/.

technologies—including AI, which the CCP insists must "adhere to the core values of socialism."[6] While Xi's project could also lead to crises in the South China Sea, Korean Peninsula, and elsewhere, Taiwan is the most dangerous potential flashpoint. Taiwan occupies a unique position in Xi's grand strategy—a litmus test for U.S. resolve, a production hub for the world's most important technological hardware, and a gateway to regional and ultimately global dominance. As Xi describes it, "reunification" with Taiwan is not only essential to national rejuvenation, but it is "inevitable."[7] (The term "reunification" is PRC propaganda since Taiwan has never been unified with the PRC. I therefore put it in quotation marks.)

Xi's desired endgame is "peaceful reunification."[8] By "peaceful," he means a largely bloodless but coerced settlement in which Taiwan submits fully to CCP rule under a fig leaf called "One Country, Two Systems." In the meantime, he is likely to keep escalating pressure in the "gray zone"—a space between peace and war that includes tactics like economic coercion, cyberattacks, disinformation, and military intimidation. Gray-zone operations allow Beijing to erode

Figure 0.2 Xi at Zhurihe, July 2017

Source: "Reform of China's Army Enters a New Phase," *The Economist*, August 3, 2017, https://www.economist.com/china/2017/08/03/reform-of-chinas-army-enters-a-new-phase.

Taiwan's resolve and redefine the status quo without triggering a conventional military response.[9] This book discusses two crisis scenarios short of war that would test U.S. and Taiwanese resolve. The first is a "quarantine": a PRC move to seize indirect control of Taiwan's international trade under the guise of legitimate customs enforcement, without cutting off food, fuel, and other essential civilian goods.[10] The second is a coercive mobilization of PLA air-naval forces for a potential invasion. This would dare other countries to evacuate their citizens from Taiwan and give Xi the option to strike quickly and forcefully if Taiwan and the United States responded weakly.

Meanwhile, Xi is preparing a more bellicose backup plan: a fully developed military option for a "joint blockade operation" to starve Taiwan out during an outright war, possibly culminating in an amphibious invasion.[11] He is systematically building a defense industrial base, strategic stockpile system, financial system, and domestic police state capable of waging war with the United States.[12] In recent years, he has used dark language that strongly hints to his CCP compatriots to be ready for such a scenario.[13]

The United States does not seek conflict over Taiwan. Its longstanding One China Policy, guided by the Three Joint Communiqués, the Six Assurances, and the Taiwan Relations Act, opposes Taiwan's independence while maintaining an abiding interest in peace and stability in the Taiwan Strait.[14] The United States supports the resolution of cross-Strait differences peacefully and without pressure and intimidation, with any outcome acceptable to the people of Taiwan.[15] More broadly, Washington and its allies believe that the Indo-Pacific region must remain free and open.[16] There is a place for a powerful and prosperous China in this U.S. and allied vision of regional order—so long as China abides by international law and refrains from coercing its neighbors with threats of violence.

However, aspects of Xi's strategy are fundamentally incompatible with vital U.S. interests.[17] These include his efforts to undermine the security of U.S. allies, seize the lead in key AI applications that could threaten strategic stability, and reshape the international economic order to serve China's interest at the expense of the United States. A failure to defend Taiwan would signal a U.S. retreat and embolden China to resolve future disputes in the region through coercion. Taiwan's role as a leading semiconductor producer, producing 99 percent of the most advanced AI chips, raises the economic and strategic stakes.[18] But the most profound concern is the precedent that would be set if China were to be allowed to dictate how its neighbors engage with the global economy. A forced takeover of Taiwan—whether by blockade, quarantine, or invasion—would damage or destroy the international economic system, undermine key U.S. alliances, and risk instability and challenges, including but not limited to nuclear proliferation.[19]

The stakes extend far beyond Taiwan itself. If Xi subjugates Taiwan while the United States falters, China will be on a clear path to achieving its broader global ambitions by 2049. If Xi moves against Taiwan in any way, and fails, the result could be a prolonged conflict that threatens his grip on power but also risks vital U.S. interests. Either way, the consequences will reverberate globally. Simply abandoning Taiwan isn't an option. There is no way for America to escape catastrophic consequences should Taiwan fall.[20]

Despite his aggressive posturing, Xi has likely not made up his mind to risk everything in a full-scale war with the United States. Notably, during his thirteen years in power, Xi has avoided fomenting any crisis that could seriously risk such a war. This suggests that—for now—he views the potential costs as prohibitively high. According to former CIA Director Bill Burns, Xi has instructed the PLA to develop the capability to seize Taiwan by 2027.[21] This is an alarming assessment, but it also confirms that Xi thinks the PLA isn't yet ready for a full-scale invasion. There is no credible evidence in open sources that Xi has decided whether or when to move. He has twice said that the Taiwan issue "cannot be handed down to the next generation."[22] This implies that he would like to achieve "reunification" in his lifetime. However, Xi will be ninety-six years old in 2049. This means the 2049 deadline will most likely become a problem for Xi's successor. The deadline can also probably be fudged if the CCP fails to meet it. Moreover, if Xi can build robust invasion and blockade capabilities, he doesn't have to implement them to get coercive value out of them.

It therefore isn't too late to shore up deterrence—but the United States must still brace itself for a crisis. China undeniably has an advantage in momentum. Over the next several years, China is likely to gain ground in key areas of the military balance relative to the combined forces of Taiwan, the United States, and their other potential partners, which include Japan, Australia, and the UK. On current trends, the United States and China are therefore barreling toward a major brinkmanship event, if not an outright war. Washington should seek to deter both a crisis and a war. But it must also prepare for both.

There are many superb studies of specific aspects of the deterrence challenge. Steve Tsang, Olivia Cheung, Kevin Rudd, and Elizabeth Economy have insightfully analyzed Xi Jinping's worldview, while Rush Doshi has brilliantly shed light on the CCP's broader grand strategy.[23] Ryan Hass, Bonnie Glaser, and Richard Bush have authored seminal works on U.S.–Taiwan relations,[24] while Shelley Rigger, Hsiao-ting Lin, Sulmaan Khan, and Lev Nachman have explored Taiwan's rich political and social history.[25] Thomas Christensen, Scott Kastner, and Timothy Crawford offer key perspectives on political deterrence,[26] and Robert Blackwill and Philip Zelikow have highlighted the quarantine or "indirect control" scenario.[27] Andrew Erickson, Conor Kennedy, Ryan Martinson, Ian Easton, Joel Wuthnow, Oriana Skylar Mastro, and others have written trenchantly on PLA modernization and invasion scenarios.[28] Chris Miller's work on semiconductors, Richard Danzig and Jeffrey Ding's work on AI, and Dale Copeland and Mariya Grinberg's work on economic interdependence are essential.[29] Many others have illuminated China's nuclear strategy, cross-domain deterrence, and other topics.[30] My own collaborations with Hugo Bromley, Harry Halem, and Calvin Heng have explored issues in economic contingency planning and emerging defense technology.[31]

However, this enormous body of analysis has never been brought together into a single framework. As a result, key gaps remain in our understanding. The U.S. government has no coherent public strategy to deter China's gray-zone aggression. It is insufficiently sensitive to domestic politics in Taiwan, a fact that could create serious problems as tensions grow. It has failed to communicate effectively about the concept known as "strategic ambiguity" or, more precisely, "dual deterrence." These communication failures could tempt Xi to create crises to test U.S. resolve. Washington has failed to institutionalize its coalition of regional allies and articulate a vision that would attract support from developing countries in a crisis. The Department of Defense (DoD)— also known by its secondary title, the Department of War—is improving its ability to defeat an invasion, also known as "deterrence by denial," but it is moving too slowly, misallocating resources, leaving key gaps in the force structure, and failing to mobilize the U.S. and allied defense industrial bases. DoD has not publicly articulated a credible plan to deny China victory over Taiwan if it imposes a wartime blockade. It is also failing to respond effectively to China's nuclear buildup. Administrations of both parties have promoted AI and semiconductor policies without a doctrine for how they contribute to strategic deterrence.[32] When it comes to economic deterrence, the United States is waging a trade war with the vague goal of "decoupling" U.S. dependence on China—but still has no clear plan to secure its interests if relations truly break down.

Perhaps most importantly, the U.S. government lacks a coherent concept of how the political, military, and economic aspects of deterrence connect to one another. Washington and Beijing both talk about the importance of "integrated deterrence" to align all the tools of national power to support a single grand strategy.[33] The difference is that China actually has such a strategy, while the United States does not.[34]

This book outlines the first comprehensive strategy to deter war with China over Taiwan, integrating political, military, strategic, and economic tools. It is primarily aimed at policymakers, but I have written it to engage a global audience of scholars, technologists, investors, and concerned citizens. I have tried to keep the main text as jargon-free as possible. The endnotes provide a thorough guide to further reading. In the following pages, I intervene in many analytical debates, offering novel arguments about Xi Jinping's strategy, U.S. interests in peacetime and conflict, quarantine and blockade scenarios, political deterrence, and the role of emerging technology and economic tools in deterrence. Some of these assessments will inevitably be overtaken by events. However, the book as a whole aims to transcend analytical debates about particular issues. The core argument is that the United States needs a more coherent grand strategy to prevent war.[35]

Argument

Military superiority is essential to deterrence, and the United States and its allies must begin a crash effort to maintain their military advantages. Superior technology will not rescue the allies if they lack the industrial capacity to produce essential munitions and platforms. American forces defeated Japan in the Pacific War largely because America enjoyed a decisive industrial advantage. Today, China's military-industrial machine benefits from a head start, enormous momentum, and backing from like-minded authoritarians like Russia's Vladimir Putin. Carl Vinson, the Georgia congressman who sounded the alarm and forced the United States to start rearming in the late 1930s, is rightly remembered as a visionary and an American hero. However, the lesson for today is alarming. Mobilizing the U.S. and allied defense industrial base to fight a great power war during peacetime takes *years*. Even the Vinson buildup, which proved invaluable in the ultimate American victory in World War II, failed in its primary purpose: to deter Japanese aggression in the first place.

At the same time, it is not clear that China cannot be deterred through military means alone, or through threats of nuclear or economic mutually assured destruction. The United States must make a range of targeted investments to sustain conventional and strategic deterrence. But these efforts must be understood as part of a broader strategy that includes political and economic pillars. Even though the United States has the tools to keep Xi deterred, it may fail to use them effectively. That means a Taiwan crisis may well be coming. Washington's deterrence strategy must therefore extend beyond threats of "denial" and "punishment." It must include a clear and credible *affirmative contingency plan* that focuses not on how to defeat or destroy China, but on how to protect vital U.S. interests and preserve a favorable world order during and after a rupture. The key issue is how to restructure the global economy if the world's manufacturing superpower goes rogue.

In essence, political and economic deterrence are inseparable issues, and Washington must rethink them both. It should not lecture other countries about why Taiwan matters, assume that it could bully other countries into picking sides, or draw red lines it will not back up. Everyone knows that a war between the United States and China would be economically devastating. Indeed, emphasizing this point is more likely to deter Americans than Xi Jinping. Instead, the United States should show that it could use a crisis to secure its interests through bold steps that would be impossible in peacetime.

This framework for crisis response must be able to attract broad support among Democrats, Republicans, key interest groups, allies and partners, and neutral countries. This contingency plan should be about guiding principles, not particulars. What countries would comprise the core coalition? What interests would they have at stake? How would they work together to resist China's aggression and preserve their economic security during and after the crisis? What commitments would they make to the rest of the world in the process?

Pillars of Deterrence

There are four essential pillars for building a robust deterrence policy for China in Taiwan.

The first pillar is political. Washington must deepen its engagement with Taiwan. This starts by improving its understanding of Taiwan's politics and society and by supporting Taiwan's democracy. Washington should also build contingency plans to deepen cooperation with Taiwan swiftly in a crisis, especially in trade, technology, and energy. It should push Taiwan relentlessly, but privately, to improve its resilience. The United States must also continue to make clear that it opposes unilateral changes to the status quo in the Taiwan Strait. In accordance with its longstanding One China Policy, it must refrain from treating Taiwan as a formal treaty ally. It must never pressure Taiwan to engage in cross-Strait negotiations. It must resist Beijing's attempts to move the goalposts by limiting longstanding forms of U.S.–Taiwan engagement. Washington should also retain its de facto policy of "strategic ambiguity" about the precise nature of its defense commitments to Taiwan.

While U.S. policy should not change, Washington should consider changing the way it communicates its ambiguous position. It can use a new concept that I call "structured ambiguity" to remind Beijing of some obvious facts. Any offensive move against Taiwan would flagrantly violate Beijing's commitments under the Three Communiqués, which form the basis of the One China Policy. Thus, if the U.S. intelligence community concludes that Beijing intends to unilaterally alter the status quo, the president will inevitably need to re-evaluate the One China Policy at a fundamental level. This reevaluation may include reinterpreting the policy in a limited and proportionate way to protect U.S. national interests while signaling a commitment to peace and stability. It may also include recalibrating longstanding limits on the U.S.–Taiwan political and military relationship. In other words, Xi Jinping must be warned that indefinite gray-zone aggression against Taiwan will carry significant risks. If he provokes a brinkmanship crisis, Washington may act decisively to defend its interests *before* American lives are lost.

Structured ambiguity is a subtle position that will need to be communicated carefully. The United States is not seeking an excuse to abandon the One China Policy; it is seeking to deter Xi from fomenting gratuitous crises. Structured ambiguity will not deter full-scale invasion or blockade, but it might help provide crucial advance warning if Xi does decide to move against Taiwan. Thus, it could potentially offer Washington and Taipei vital days or weeks to prepare. Washington should seek to align this political deterrence strategy with its core allies, particularly Japan, Australia, the UK, and Canada. It should institutionalize this coalition and move toward joint contingency planning and strategic communication. It should prepare a playbook to respond to China's lawfare in the UN and the court of international public opinion, appealing to neutral countries' self-interests without demanding that they adopt the U.S. political position.

The second pillar is conventional military "deterrence by denial."[36] China has various military options for moving against Taiwan. These include bombardment, amphibious invasion, and blockade. An invasion would be a massively complex and large-scale joint operation—a high-risk affair for a military without deep combat experience. The weakest links in the PLA's invasion force are its logistics chain and amphibious ships. There are relatively low-cost ways in which the United States and Taiwan can complicate the PLA's invasion planning. Since China enjoys quantitative advantages in key aspects of the military balance, including aircraft, surface ships, and missiles, maintaining deterrence will partly be an exercise in psychological warfare against Xi himself. Xi must be made to ponder plausible reasons why his military would be unlikely to win if he chose to escalate or prolong a conflict. Maximizing U.S. technological superiority in outer space, cyberspace, and undersea will be essential to this effort, particularly over the longer term. But the allies must also maintain a baseline level of defense industrial capacity.

Deterrence by denial must also extend to the blockade scenario. Starting a conflict with a blockade is probably not the best opening move for Xi—but he may disagree. In any invasion of Taiwan, China would almost certainly try to stop Taiwan's supporters from resupplying the island with munitions, spare parts, energy, and food. Blockade is also a fallback option if an invasion fails.

Persuading Xi that a protracted blockade would not be "checkmate" is the hardest part of conventional military deterrence. If there is no credible allied plan to resupply Taiwan, Taiwan's leaders might calculate that eventual defeat is certain and thus may capitulate quickly. Breaking a blockade by force may require striking targets inside mainland China and mining China's harbors, among other escalatory steps. Whether this would be advisable is a political decision for the U.S. president that this book does not answer. Still, the U.S. president should have an *option* to operationally defeat both a simultaneous invasion and a blockade without nuclear escalation.

The third pillar of deterrence is strategic. China is engaged in the fastest nuclear buildup since the early Cold War. China's strategic deterrence doctrine is deliberately fuzzy, but it clearly believes that strategic deterrence now extends beyond the nuclear domain to include space, cyber, and economic threats. To maintain strategic stability, the United States must continue to embrace its robust, cross-domain strategic deterrence system.[37] Across the range of plausible peacetime, crisis, and conflict scenarios, the U.S. president must have flexible options that signal both credible resolve and credible restraint. Practically speaking, this means the United States should keep modernizing its nuclear forces and delivery systems. It must also reestablish the capability to build new warheads quickly. The United States must remain strongly opposed to nuclear proliferation, but it may consider NATO-style "nuclear sharing" to involve South Korea and Japan in American nuclear deterrence operations, if these two countries continue to request it for reassurance purposes.

Strategic deterrence extends across domains and is no longer just about nuclear weapons. The United States must also act decisively to maximize its advantages in outer space. It should accelerate the transition to resilient satellite constellation architectures for command-and-control, communications, computers, intelligence, surveillance, and reconnaissance (C4ISR)—and build and covertly display capabilities to hold China and Russia's C4ISR at risk. Maintaining U.S. advantages in key AI capabilities and signaling them effectively to China could also strengthen strategic deterrence. Finally, the United States can make various economic threats that may or may not count as strategic deterrence, including tariffs, sanctions, attacks on the PRC financial system, and interdiction of trade. However, economic mutually assured destruction (EMAD) is not interchangeable with nuclear MAD. It likely has a much weaker deterrent effect. Threatening EMAD—let alone attempting it—also undercuts the political pillar of deterrence.

The fourth pillar of deterrence is an affirmative economic contingency plan for a crisis. If supply chains in and out of China and Taiwan were to be disrupted even temporarily, the impact on global financial and macroeconomic stability would be enormous. As the bipartisan House Select Committee on the Chinese Communist Party concluded bluntly in December 2023, "The United States lacks a contingency plan for the economic and financial impacts of conflict with the PRC."[38] Even if Washington had the power to stop other countries from trading with China—a dubious assumption—rapid economic decoupling would not be politically realistic or strategically productive. The sanctions playbook that Washington has become accustomed to using against smaller economies such as Iraq, Venezuela, Iran, and even Russia must be fundamentally reimagined. In practice, this means the baseline economic contingency plan should not include sanctions on China that shut down global supply chains on day one of a crisis.

The best way to communicate resolve in a crisis—and in the gray zone—is to communicate how the United States would act to defend its own economic interests. Effective economic contingency planning must punish China only as a welcome byproduct of policies that advance other U.S. interests, which are shared by allied countries and neutrals alike. It is near-certain that China would keep trading with many U.S. trading partners during and after a potential Taiwan crisis. America should focus on breaking critical dependencies first and addressing noncritical dependencies over time as part of a wider program of economic leadership.[39] Minimizing the economic pain for the United States and protecting the vital interests of key partner countries would require Washington to commit to leading economic recovery and reconstruction. Pulling millions of manufacturing jobs out of China would be a worthy long-term goal, but achieving this goal would be politically sustainable only if shortages and inflation in the rest of the world could be managed.

Economic and political deterrence are thus essential pillars of integrated deterrence. Political deterrence remains central up to the brink of a conflict, shaping Beijing's perception of U.S. resolve and forcing it to weigh the long-term risks of aggression. If China escalates toward a Taiwan crisis, the effectiveness of U.S. military deterrence will depend less on sudden demonstrations of strength than on China's assessment of U.S. resolve. Similarly, we should not understand economic deterrence merely as cost imposition. Economic deterrence is about shaping China's net assessment of who would gain more in the long term if economic ties with the United States and its allies are severed. Extreme economic threats such as sanctions and blockades contribute to deterrence, even if they are left implicit. However, these threats face both credibility challenges and practical limitations. The goal of U.S. and allied economic statecraft cannot simply be to punish Beijing. It should be to show that the United States could use economic tools to shape the post-crisis international system in ways that hold Xi's national rejuvenation project at risk.

During a crisis, managing economic coordination with allies and other countries would be essential, but extremely challenging. The best approach would be to establish an Economic Security Cooperation Board (ESCB) and invite all nations except Russia, North Korea, Iran, and China to join. The ESCB could perform several key functions. Led by the United States, and partially funded by allies, it could help all its member countries manage the economic fallout of a crisis and build the data collection and border enforcement infrastructure needed to secure key supply chains. The ESCB would allow nations to protect their economic interests without triggering a global trade war. If desired, it could also expand to provide other functions, such as collective insurance against China's economic retaliation. The best time to establish the ESCB is *now*. It could help coordinate joint allied decoupling from China in critical products like rare earth magnets and medicines—and show China that the allies can work effectively together on economic security if a crisis comes.

All four pillars of deterrence must recognize that any conflict with China over Taiwan could become protracted, and U.S.–China relations might never recover. This is why Taiwan's will to protect its autonomy is essential. No one knows how Taiwan's society would react in a crisis. Prewar public opinion polls in Ukraine showed little willingness to resist Russian aggression—yet the full-scale invasion suddenly transformed Ukrainian society into a determined and cohesive fighting force. Taiwan's future resilience may similarly depend on its leaders' ability to inspire patriotic resistance in the perilous early days. The situation with U.S. resolve is actually quite similar. Current U.S. war planning focuses on defeating a Chinese amphibious invasion within weeks or months. Xi must also understand that he could not win simply by escalating a conflict or dragging it out until the U.S.-led coalition cracked. A key purpose of political and economic deterrence is to show that Washington could harness the initial global reaction to the outset of a crisis, build a durable coalition, keep up morale in Taiwan, and structure the conflict on favorable terms for a potential long-term struggle.[40]

Outline of the Book

Part I: "The Challenge" establishes the strategic context. Chapter 1 examines Taiwan's ambiguous status, Xi Jinping's goals for "reunification," and potential triggers for conflict. It also analyzes relevant U.S. national interests in peacetime and after a potential rupture with China over Taiwan.

Part II: "Scenarios" explores pathways into a Taiwan crisis. Chapter 2 analyzes China's gray-zone strategy, focusing on quarantine and coercive mobilization scenarios. Chapter 3 examines how a full-scale amphibious invasion would work operationally, including the possibility of a simultaneous blockade, and discusses the political, economic, and strategic implications.

Part III: "The Pillars of Deterrence" shifts to prescriptive strategies for deterring conflict. Chapter 4 on political deterrence discusses how Washington should engage Taiwan, manage China, and establish its core coalition. Chapter 5 on conventional military deterrence highlights the urgent need for U.S. military reform, investment, and, most importantly, allied cooperation. Chapter 6 discusses strategic deterrence, including nuclear weapons, space, cyber, and AI. Chapter 7 argues that threats of economic mutually assured destruction have limited strategic deterrent value and that the United States needs an affirmative economic contingency plan. Chapter 8 proposes an alternative economic approach for Day One, based on the idea of avalanche decoupling.

The Conclusion calls for a more integrated strategy of U.S. political, military, and economic deterrence—and an affirmative vision of how to protect U.S. interests and build a better world after a U.S.–China rupture.

PART I

The Challenge

I

The Cross-Strait Dispute

In November 2024, Xi Jinping and Joe Biden met for the last time in Lima. They spoke for around two hours, covering a range of topics including North Korea, the ongoing war in Ukraine, the status of U.S. citizens detained in China, climate change, and the role of AI in the handling of nuclear weapons. Notably, despite these numerous areas of growing tension, Xi described the broader U.S.–China relationship as "stable on the whole."[1]

Xi's parting message was a warning to the incoming Trump administration that revealed much about his thinking about Taiwan. According to the PRC readout, Xi told Biden that "it is important not to challenge red lines and paramount principles." The "Taiwan question" is one of these red lines. "The One-China Principle and the three China-U.S. joint communiqués are the political foundation of China-U.S. relations. They must be observed," Xi told Biden. "These are the most important guardrails and safety nets for China-U.S. relations."

Xi then added a warning. "If the U.S side cares about maintaining peace across the Taiwan Strait, it is crucial that it sees clearly the true nature of [Taiwan President] Lai Ching-te and the [Democratic Progressive Party] DPP authorities in seeking 'Taiwan independence,' handles the Taiwan question with extra prudence, unequivocally opposes 'Taiwan independence,' and supports China's peaceful reunification," Xi said.[2] Xi's explicit mention of Lai Ching-te by name in the PRC readout of the meeting was unprecedented. Xi was never quoted as referring to Lai's predecessor by name. This was a deliberate signal of China's deep concerns about Lai's intentions. Beijing has long accused the United States of coming close to crossing China's red lines. Now, Xi is more pointed than ever in warning Washington not to go any further.

Whereas Xi characterizes the Taiwan issue as a domestic dispute with DPP-led "separatists," American leaders frame the issue as a PRC threat to the international order. In Lima, Biden "emphasized the United States' commitment to upholding international law and freedom of navigation, overflight, and peace and stability in the South China Sea and East China Sea." Biden "underscored that the United States' one China policy remains unchanged, guided by the Taiwan Relations Act, the Three Joint Communiqués, and the Six Assurances. He reiterated that the United States opposes any unilateral changes to the status quo from either side, that we expect cross-Strait differences to be resolved by peaceful means, and that the world has an interest in peace and stability in the Taiwan Strait. He called for an end to destabilizing PRC military activity around Taiwan."[3] These, too, are standard talking points that U.S. officials have repeated countless times. According to Washington, China's coercive approach to Taiwan is part of a broader "destabilizing" effort to undermine the U.S.-led international economic system, including by threatening lawful transit through important air and maritime spaces. The implicit warning is that if China disrupts regional peace and stability, it would force a decisive U.S. response.

This chapter unpacks these ideas to provide a high-level introduction to the Taiwan dispute in the context of the broader U.S.–China relationship. It does not offer a detailed history of the cross-Strait relationship or the evolution of U.S. policy.[4] Instead, it introduces the essential contextual information that all readers must understand to follow the book's arguments. It also offers assessments of the key actors' interests and strategies that underpin discussions in later chapters.

China cares about the Taiwan issue for reasons that go beyond Taiwan itself. For Xi in particular, the dispute is less about the "status of Taiwan" than the definition of "China." Xi thinks that the United States is trying to derail China's march toward "national rejuvenation." Xi seeks to deter U.S. intervention because Taiwan's permanent separation would call into question the legitimacy of both his leadership and the CCP's claim to have restored China's unity.[5] Taiwan holds additional value as a potential forward base for China's navy.[6] Full-scale war with the United States would put China's national rejuvenation at risk—but if Xi concludes that war with the United States is inevitable, his priorities will shift toward ensuring victory and shaping the conflict in China's favor.

Xi's strategy is systematic and highly coherent. Winning the legitimacy argument about Taiwan's status is a key priority. Beijing wants the entire international community—including the United Nations, the United States, and political leaders in Taiwan—to accept its "One China Principle." It wants to resolve the "Taiwan question" in accordance with PRC law, which of course gives Xi virtually unlimited discretion to use force. Beijing's position is that the political and legal process of "reunification" began in 1992, when Taiwan allegedly acknowledged its status as a province of "One China." (Taiwan disputes this claim).[7] For Xi, so long as the United States does not interfere, "peaceful reunification" will eventually be achieved once Taiwan formally accepts its subordinate status through a "One Country, Two Systems" arrangement.[8] Xi's statements reflect a consistent and credible preference for this coercive but largely bloodless pathway to unification, though he and his predecessors have never ruled out overt military action if red lines are crossed. Of course, China could also move against Taiwan unprovoked for various reasons. These could include domestic political pressures, perceived closing windows of opportunity, and miscalculations about the U.S. and Taiwanese resolve. The United States must rigorously prepare for these possibilities. Still, if we take Xi's statements at face value, we should assume that his "Plan A" is to achieve "reunification" through gray-zone tactics rather than outright force.[9]

China's strategy of gradually redefining the status quo, without a clear-cut phase change of peacetime to wartime, is a major challenge for U.S. interests. For Washington, Taiwan matters mainly for reasons relating to regional and global order. U.S. peacetime interests include maintaining a free and open Indo-Pacific, protecting U.S. technological security through AI primacy, fostering regional alliances, preserving global geopolitical stability, and, to a significant but lesser extent, preserving Taiwan's democracy. China's coercive gray-zone campaign against Taiwan undermines all these interests. If it continues, the United States will eventually have to choose between capitulation and confrontation. Furthermore, China's aggression against Taiwan could spark crises that destabilize the region, creating moments of profound uncertainty about regional and global order. During and after such a crisis, the United States would have additional strategic interests that blend politics and economics. It would want to preserve financial and macroeconomic stability, break U.S. and allied dependence on China's market (and thus vulnerability to China's economic coercion), preserve the trading system and the international position of the dollar, and punish China as part of a long-term strategy to force a favorable resolution.

This chapter's first section provides a very basic introduction to Taiwan: its geography, economic and political system, and international position.

The next three sections introduce the competing political and legal frameworks for understanding the cross-Strait dispute in Beijing, Taipei, and Washington. Then, we explore a framework for understanding China's strategy through Xi's actions and public statements, the CCP's structural interests in Taiwan, and various hypotheses about why Xi might initiate a war. The final two sections analyze the U.S. peacetime interests and additional interests that would become relevant during a crisis.

What Is Taiwan?

Taiwan is a vibrant democracy formally known as the Republic of China (ROC). It is one of the freest societies in the world—not quite as "free" as Japan, according to the nonprofit Freedom House, but "freer" than France, the UK, and the United States.[10] It has more than 23 million citizens. It has a main island and 167 smaller islands that are altogether roughly the size of the Netherlands (see Figure 1.1).[11] It issues its own currency, the New Taiwan Dollar, and its own passports, which give its citizens visa-free access to 144 countries. It is one of the most open and cosmopolitan places on earth, with nearly 1 million foreigners on its soil at any given time, not counting PRC nationals, and daily direct flights to New York, Beijing, London, New Delhi, and beyond. It has a military—the Republic of China Armed Forces (ROCAF)—with 165,000 active personnel, 1.6 million reserves, and a defense budget roughly the same as Spain's and Turkey's.[12,13] The ROCAF is a formidable fighting force, even though the People's Liberation Army (PLA) across the strait has a budget roughly fourteen times larger. Taiwan is also the epicenter of the digital and AI revolutions.[14] The Taiwan Semiconductor Manufacturing Company (TSMC) alone produces over 50 percent of the world's semiconductors over 90 percent of advanced chips used for devices like smartphones and missile systems, and over 99 percent of the chips used for cutting-edge AI training.[15] TSMC is closely linked to U.S. and allied supply chains. It fabricates U.S. designed chips with Dutch photolithography machines and Japanese chemicals and components, among many other inputs.[16] The United States has exploited this fact by banning some advanced chips produced in Taiwan with U.S. technology from being exported to China.

China and the United States are both working strenuously to break their dependence on Taiwan's chips, but thus far neither is succeeding. China has

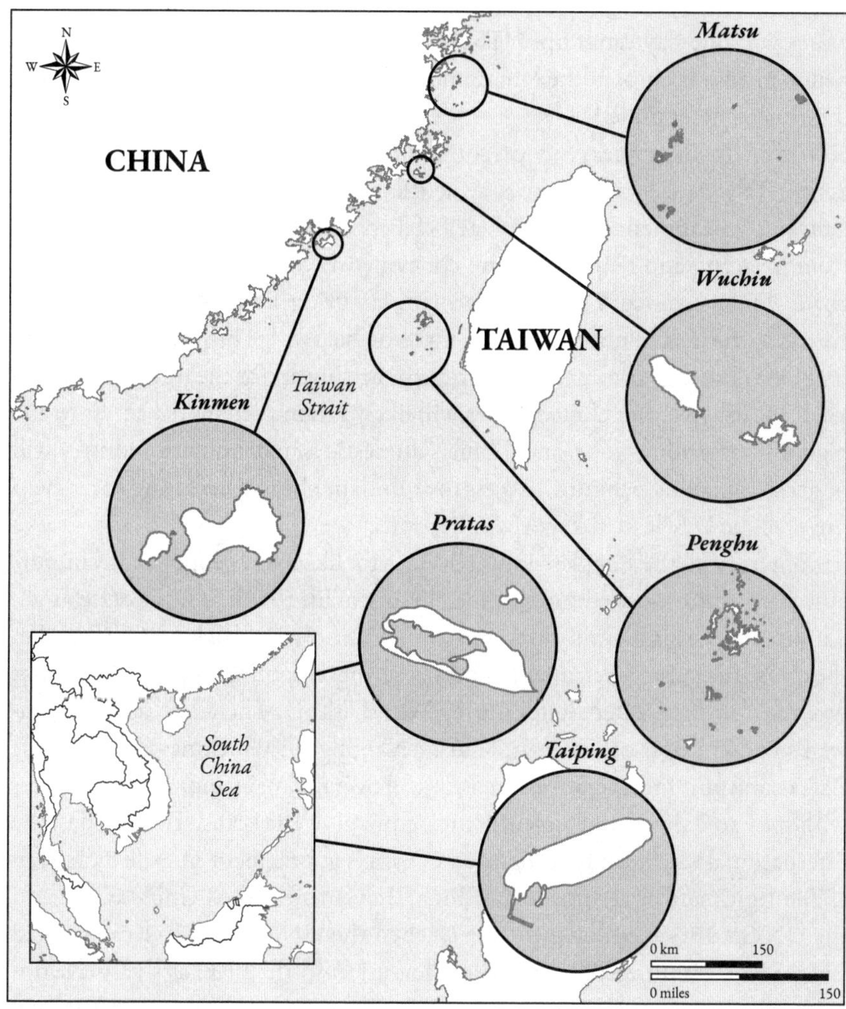

Figure 1.1 Map of Taiwan's Territories

Source: Adapted from Andrew Chubb, "Taiwan Strait Crises: Island Seizure Contingencies," *Asia Society Policy Institute*, February 2023, https://asiasociety.org/policy-institute/taiwan-strait-crises-island-seizure-contingencies-0.

used relentless industrial espionage to steal TSMC technology, poach its engineers, and subsidize domestic competitors.[17] The United States passed the CHIPS and Science Act in 2022, offering TSMC tens of billions of dollars in subsidies to build new manufacturing facilities (known as "fabs") in the United States. Washington has given billions more to domestic firms that it hopes will one day catch up.[18] TSMC has built a fab in Kumamoto, Japan, which produces chips at the 6-nanometer node, and in Arizona, producing at the 3-nanometer node.[19]

Within this complex web of competition, cooperation, and interdependence, Taiwan seems likely to stay at the cutting edge of chip production. Taiwan's government sees TSMC as a "Silicon Shield" that both deters China from invading and helps to ensure continued U.S. support.[20] In November 2024, Taipei banned TSMC from manufacturing its most advanced chips abroad—those at the 2-nanometer node or below.[21] This move will ensure that bleeding-edge production will remain in Taiwan for the next few years at least. Meanwhile, the United States will likely retain preferential access to the highest-performing chips, and China's domestic semiconductor industry will be at risk of falling behind.[22] Access to abundant cheap computing could help preserve the U.S. lead in key AI applications.[23]

Seen from all these angles, Taiwan looks a lot like a very geopolitically important state—but most countries officially maintain that it is not a state at all. Taiwan's governing authorities and constitution trace back to Chiang Kai-shek's Nationalist government (known as the Kuomintang, or KMT) that was allied to the United States during World War II. The KMT adopted Taiwan's constitution on the mainland in Nanjing on Christmas Day, 1946.[24] As Communist forces consolidated control over the mainland, Chiang's forces withdrew to Taiwan and violently took control of the island. For decades, the international community recognized Chiang's government-in-exile in Taiwan as the legitimate government of China. Taiwan held the "Chinese" seat on the UN Security Council until 1971, when the UN General Assembly voted in UN Resolution 2758 to transfer recognition to the PRC as the sole legitimate government of China.[25] Today, Taiwan is shut out of every international institution that requires statehood for membership.[26] It has formal diplomatic relations with just twelve countries, mostly small island states.[27] The United States is not among them, and Beijing is systematically trying to flip those that remain.[28]

Despite its diplomatic isolation, Taiwan has thrived. Its success can largely be attributed to the ingenuity, hard work, and bravery of its people, who built a flourishing society and achieved a peaceful transition to democracy. But Taiwan's security rests on the United States' enduring commitment to maintaining regional peace and stability.

The key question at the heart of the cross-Strait dispute is whether Taiwan is part of a single divided nation known as "One China." The PRC and KMT say yes. The United States takes an ambiguous position: "acknowledging" the claim that Taiwan is part of China without "recognizing" it, while asserting that Taiwan's status is unresolved. The Democratic Progressive Party (DPP), which has governed Taiwan since 2016, says no. According to the DPP, the PRC is not only a distinct country, but also a distinct national community.[29] The next three sections will explore these positions in more detail.

Beijing's Position

Beijing's position is captured in its "One China *Principle*" (一中原则), which is different from the U.S. "One China *Policy*." The principle states that there is only one China in the world, Taiwan is part of China, and the PRC is the only legitimate government.[30] Beijing alleges that the "Taiwan authorities" accepted the One China Principle at a contested meeting in Hong Kong known as the "1992 Consensus." (Both of Taiwan's major political parties—the KMT and the DPP—dispute Beijing's interpretation of this meeting.) Beijing maintains that the consensus began a negotiation process that will lead inexorably to Taiwan's full capitulation. This is how Beijing justifies its strategic patience: since Taiwan is already part of China, and PRC law prohibits independence, there is no particular rush to achieve formal unification.[31] Beijing claims that it has refrained from using force because it does not wish to harm the loyal "compatriots" suffering under the illegitimate authorities on Taiwan.[32]

Beijing has long said that it aspires to achieve "peaceful reunification" through a Hong Kong–style framework of "One Country, Two Systems."[33] Of course, these are weasel words.[34] Beijing's definition of "peaceful" does not imply that Taiwan would accept unification freely, let alone through a democratic process free of coercion. Hong Kongers never got a vote on their return to China as a Special Administrative Region in 1997. Beijing's promise of "One Country, Two Systems" is similarly suspect. The terms of the handover promised that Hong Kongers would continue to enjoy civil liberties and representative government under their preexisting Basic Law. However, under Xi Jinping, Beijing took over Hong Kong's Legislative Assembly and violently compelled Hong Kongers to accept a National Security Law that neutered what remained of the territory's political autonomy and its citizens' civil rights.[35] In 2019, Xi called for exploration of a "Two Systems' Taiwan Plan," implicitly acknowledging that the original One Country, Two Systems conceit created for Hong Kong and Macau may need to be tailored specifically for Taiwan.[36] Xi's directive was reiterated in an August 2022 white paper, resulting in over forty published proposals on possible permutations of a China–Taiwan "Two Systems" arrangement. Conservatives favored a model closely resembling Hong Kong's post-2020 governance,[37] while progressives proposed options ranging from broad democratic consultation on Taiwan's autonomy to restructuring of China's institutions to accommodate Taiwan.[38] As of this writing, the CCP has not formally endorsed any of these proposals.[39] Clearly, if Taiwan ever submits to the principle of the "One Country, Two Systems" arrangement, it will be vulnerable in the same way that Hong Kong was. Beijing could gradually coerce Taipei to accept the PRC's interpretation of the term.

Successive PRC leaders have warned that if all pathways to "peaceful unification" are exhausted, Beijing will not renounce the use of force.[40] Meanwhile, China's growing military power has made the threat increasingly credible.[41] The PRC's 2005 Anti-Secession Law specifies three conditions for using "non-peaceful" methods:[42]

- If "Taiwan independence" forces, under whatever name and method, achieve de facto Taiwanese separation from China.
- If a "major incident" occurs that would lead to Taiwan becoming separated from China.
- If all possibility of peaceful unification disappears.

These red lines are deliberately vague. Leaving key terms like "de facto separation" and "major incident" undefined could allow Beijing to redefine them more expansively in the future, while also allowing future CCP leaders flexibility for potential compromises. So far, from Beijing's perspective, the Anti-Secession Law has succeeded in its intended purpose.[43] Taiwan has not declared independence, and Washington has not recognized Taiwan as a sovereign country. Meanwhile, Beijing steadily gained leverage.

The One China Policy

America's One China Policy is, in many respects, unique in the canon of U.S. foreign policy. It is also a mouthful to recite, since it comprises several interlocking elements that have accumulated through time. According to the State Department:

The United States has a longstanding one China policy, which is guided by the Taiwan Relations Act, the three U.S.-China Joint Communiques, and the Six Assurances." Specifically, "we oppose any unilateral changes to the status quo from either side; we do not support Taiwan independence; and we expect cross-Strait differences to be resolved by peaceful means. We continue to have an abiding interest in peace and stability across the Taiwan Strait."[44]

Since Taiwan democratized, U.S. policymakers have often added that any resolution must be acceptable to the people of Taiwan. The U.S. position on Taiwan's status has long been that it is undetermined.[45] However, the One China Policy downplays the matter of Taiwan's status. It is more interested in *how* the issue of Taiwan's status is resolved. The One China Policy is more than a policy; it is a symbol of the U.S. commitment to peace and stability in the region. The longer it survives unchanged, and the more times U.S. officials reiterate it, the stronger a precedent it becomes, and the more costly and destabilizing it would be to revise. The U.S. policy on Taiwan is also important as a bellwether. A total of 129 other countries take ambiguous positions with respect to Taiwan's status. Many of them are closely modeled on the One China Policy.[46]

The One China Policy emerged incrementally starting in the 1970s, as Washington sought to establish diplomatic relations with the PRC. The First Joint Communiqué, also known as the "Shanghai Communiqué," was negotiated by Henry Kissinger and Zhou Enlai in 1972.[47] The key passage is that "The United States acknowledges (*renshidao* 认识到) that all Chinese on either side of the Taiwan Strait maintain there is but one China and that Taiwan is part of China. The United States does not challenge that position. It reaffirms its interest in a peaceful settlement of the Taiwan question by the Chinese themselves."[48] This legalistic statement unlocked the entire future relationship between the United States and PRC. Washington conceded nothing substantive in it. It did not *accept* Beijing's interpretation that Taiwan was a rebel province. It simply *acknowledged* that this was Beijing's view. Obviously, "Chinese" people in China and Taiwan disagreed about which of their governments was legitimate. Washington's claim that it supported a "peaceful settlement" also implied that it would resist a nonpeaceful settlement.

The Second Communiqué paved the way for diplomatic normalization, while the Third Communiqué was notable for language on Taiwan independence and arms sales.[49] In the former, the United States "recognize[d] the Government of the People's Republic of China as the sole legal Government of China," but noted that "within this context, the people of the United States will maintain cultural, commercial, and other unofficial relations with the people of Taiwan."[50] Notably, the critical passage in the Second Communiqué has different meanings in the Chinese and English versions. This is why Beijing asserts, however implausibly, that Washington acceded to its One China Principle.[51] In the Third Communiqué, the United States ruled out support for Taiwan independence and promised to wind down arms sales to Taiwan over an unspecified period.[52] Notably, the Third Communiqué again implied that restrictions on U.S. arms sales to Taiwan were contingent on China's continued restraint.

The normalization of U.S.–PRC relations in 1979 also led to a change in U.S.–Taiwan relations. Washington agreed to abrogate its mutual defense treaty with Taiwan, but pledged to otherwise keep an essentially unrestricted "informal" relationship with Taiwan.[53] Concerned that the Communiqués might pave the way to abandoning Taiwan, Congress passed a law to tie the hands of future presidents.[54] The Taiwan Relations Act (TRA) of 1979 made it U.S. law to treat the "governing authorities on Taiwan" the same as other "foreign countries, nations, states, governments, or similar entities."[55] It stated that the United States would not oppose the *peaceful* (nonmilitary and noncoercive) unification of China and Taiwan. Yet it warned that the United States would "consider any effort to determine the future of Taiwan by other than peaceful means, *including by boycotts or embargoes*, a threat to the peace and security of the Western Pacific area and of grave concern to the United States [emphasis mine]."[56] This language emphasized the importance that the United States placed on Taiwan's continued ability to trade and participate in the global economy. The TRA also stated that "the United States will make available to Taiwan such defense articles and defense services in such quantity as may be necessary to enable Taiwan to maintain a sufficient self-defense capability." The term "sufficient" was not defined. Finally, the TRA established that the United States "shall maintain the capacity . . . to resist any resort to force or other forms of coercion that would jeopardize the security, or social or economic system, of the people of Taiwan." Beijing does not like the TRA, but it has maintained diplomatic relations with Washington since 1979. This shows that Beijing sees no irreconcilable contradiction between the TRA and the Communiqués.[57]

The final component of the One China Policy is the Six Assurances, which the Reagan administration offered privately to Taiwan in 1982. Their basic idea is that, in the context of the Communiqués, Washington pledges not to conspire with the PRC to allow a coercive unification.[58] Minor wording differences exist between the U.S. government version and the version announced publicly by Taiwan, but the thrust is the same: they represent Washington's self-imposed constraints on its actions regarding Taiwan and cross-Strait relations. Since the first Trump administration, the U.S. government has begun to call more attention to the Six Assurances. It has even incorporated them into the standard litany used to explain the One China Policy. Beijing has complained, calling the Assurances "illegal and invalid." Yet, the shift in emphasis does not imply any change in U.S. policy. It simply emphasizes that Washington is resolved not to break its commitments to Taiwan.[59]

The Six Assurances, 1982

The United States:[60]

- Has not agreed to set a date for ending arms sales to Taiwan.
- Has not agreed to consult with the PRC on arms sales to Taiwan.
- Will not play a mediation role between Taipei and Beijing.
- Has not agreed to revise the Taiwan Relations Act.
- Has not altered its position regarding sovereignty over Taiwan.
- Will not exert pressure on Taiwan to enter into negotiations with the PRC.

Because the One China Policy developed through accretion, it has no single, fixed meaning. This abbreviated history leaves out many important twists and turns of how it has been used and reinterpreted. Nevertheless, decades of diplomatic practice have shown that invoking the One China Policy is a highly effective way to communicate American resolve and restraint. In the end, the policy can be boiled down to two key points. First, the United States wants to see a peaceful and noncoercive resolution to cross-Strait differences, and it does *not* support unilateral "Taiwan independence."[61] Second, the United States does not formally commit to defending Taiwan from an unprovoked attack or restriction on its ability to trade—but it strongly implies that it would.

Views from Taiwan

The KMT, Taiwan's main center-right party, strongly supports "One China." This position may seem surprising. After all, the KMT fought the CCP for two decades during the Chinese civil war, held power during all three Taiwan Straits crises, and still dominates Taiwan's armed forces. The explanation is that the KMT's position is that the Chinese civil war remains unresolved. Taiwan is all that remains of the "free area of the Republic of China," which has not included the mainland since 1949.[62] KMT candidates who support the 1992 Consensus often emphasize that they support it only in accordance with the Republic of China's constitution. Many KMT supporters identify as Chinese or a combination of Chinese and Taiwanese—but their definition of "China" differs from Beijing's.[63]

The KMT supports cross-Strait dialogue for both explicit and implicit reasons. Many KMT politicians believe Beijing is less likely to attack Taiwan if a diplomatic resolution seems viable. Some doubt the reliability of U.S. support in a crisis. Others argue that Washington is provoking Beijing, using Taiwan as a pawn.[64] Personal or business ties to the mainland also lead some to view "reunification" as a desirable goal. The KMT coalition spans from unificationists to pro-business moderates. Thus, KMT politicians often rely on vague or coded language, including references to Xi Jinping's rhetoric about shared "blood" ties across the Taiwan Strait.[65] Critics argue that these statements undermine Taiwan's self-determination. They brand the KMT as the party of "appeasement," or even as "pro-China" and "pro-Communist."[66] The charge of appeasement is accurate. The charge that the KMT is "pro-China" is also accurate—though it is meaningless, since the KMT identifies as the legitimate government of China. The charge of being "pro-Communist" is generally unfair.

The KMT maintains that the Republic of China must preserve its autonomy until CCP rule on the mainland eventually collapses and the KMT can resume its position as the national party of a unified China. This position has gotten harder to maintain as U.S.–China tensions have risen. KMT politicians have struggled to articulate a compelling strategy for enhancing Taiwan's national security without leaning too heavily on the United States.[67] Privately, KMT leaders often reassure American counterparts of their support for a significant U.S. role in Taiwan. They urge Washington not to interpret their public statements as anti-American. However, unable to shake their reputation as a "pro-China" and "anti-U.S." party, KMT presidential candidates have been defeated in the last three general elections.

The DPP, Taiwan's ruling center-left party, has become caricatured as a "pro-independence" party, though its actual position is more complicated.[68]

The problem with the "pro-independence" label is that it conflates two possible meanings that Beijing interprets very differently. As we have seen, Beijing maintains that Taiwan is currently part of China. It seeks to prevent a formal declaration of independence or similar action that would change this status quo. The DPP's official position is that if a declaration is what China fears, it has nothing to worry about. The status quo is that Taiwan is *already* an independent and sovereign country called the Republic of China. Thus, Taiwan does not need to "declare independence" and it never will.[69] The DPP platform explicitly rules out a unilateral declaration of independence.[70] In polls, just 5 percent of voters, representing a small fraction of the DPP base, are in favor of immediate independence.[71]

It is not clear how much the DPP's hairsplitting actually reassures Beijing. China has always resented DPP opposition to the "One China Principle" and dismisses its claims that Taiwan is already independent as both illegitimate and absurd.[72] As a result, Beijing finds little comfort in the DPP's promises not to declare independence in the future. Over the years, various DPP politicians such as Presidents Chen Shui-bian and Lai Ching-te have been somewhat cavalier in talking about independence.[73] Under pressure from Washington, the DPP's language became more disciplined after Tsai Ing-wen took over the party in 2008.[74] Taiwan's current president, Lai Ching-te, has pledged to uphold the "status quo" and to continue Tsai's policies.[75] Like Tsai, Lai maintains that Taiwan does not need to declare independence, since it is already independent.[76] However, Beijing views Lai as a more provocative and inflammatory figure.[77]

Citing Lai's past self-description as a "pragmatic worker for Taiwanese independence," Beijing contends that Lai is a diehard separatist.[78] During Taiwan's general election in 2024, Beijing ran a ferocious information campaign aimed at discouraging Taiwanese voters from supporting him.[79] (The campaign failed to stop Lai from winning the presidency, though it may have played a role in the DPP's loss of control in the legislature.) Beijing's anxieties have only deepened following Lai's election.[80] Lai's inaugural address contained no substantive policy changes from the Tsai administration. Yet his terminology changed in subtle ways that infuriated Beijing.[81] The PLA responded with two days of blockade-style military exercises around Taiwan.[82] Recent history suggests that Lai and other DPP leaders understand Beijing's red lines and choose their words carefully.[83] While outright pro-independence statements are unlikely, they remain theoretically possible.

In summary, the KMT and DPP in a sense agree much more about the substance of cross-Strait policy than they claim. The two sides disagree about whether the right way to frame that status quo includes the words "One China," and whether dialogue with the PRC is necessary or desirable. However, for most politicians in Taiwan across the party spectrum, the practical goal of cross-Strait policy is to prevent a conflict. Pretty much everyone wants to preserve as much autonomy for Taiwan as possible. They simply disagree about how to achieve this goal.

Interpreting Xi

Since 1949, the CCP has shown great patience on the Taiwan issue. "Peaceful unification" has been the official PRC policy since 1981.[84] Meanwhile, the CCP has skillfully used carrots, sticks, psychological warfare, and credible deterrent threats to present Taiwan with a binary choice between standing still or moving toward political and legal "reunification." Of course, just because China has been patient in the past does not mean that its patience is infinite. Just because Beijing has dangled carrots in the past does not mean that it would not attempt an invasion if it thought one could succeed. The power to decide lies in the hands of a single man.

Since Xi took power in 2013, Beijing has increasingly emphasized the consanguinity of the Chinese and Taiwanese people.[85] Xi speaks of "one family across both sides of the strait."[86] His favored term is the "Chinese nation" or "Chinese race" (*zhonghua minzu* 中华民族). This term includes historical and cultural elements, but it is primarily racial in nature, rooted in an idea of common ancestry and "blood" (*xue* 血).[87] As Xi explained to former Taiwanese President Ma Ying-jeou in Beijing in April 2024:

> Both sides of the Taiwan Strait belong to the Chinese nation. The Chinese nation is one of the greatest nations in the world, having created the longstanding, brilliant, and unparalleled Chinese civilization, which sons and daughters of the nation feel proud of and honored for.... The Chinese nation's history of over 5,000 years has witnessed successive generations of ancestors move and settle down in Taiwan, their lives and procreation there, and saw the compatriots from both sides of the Strait fight side by side in the defense against foreign aggression and the recovery of Taiwan. Along the way, the Chinese nation has written the history that Taiwan and the mainland are inseparable and engraved the historical fact that people across the Strait are connected by blood.[88]

When Taiwanese politicians use the "one family" metaphor, they sometimes typically liken Taiwan and the mainland to brother and sister, with neither subordinate to the other.[89] But Xi means that anyone with Chinese blood must be loyal to the CCP and the "core" leader.[90] His references to common blood eerily echo Vladimir Putin's argument in his 2021 essay "On the Historical Unity of Russians and Ukrainians," which argues that Russians and Ukrainians are bound by "blood ties."[91] Rhetoric that treats Taiwanese civilians as compatriots suggests that Xi prefers to take Taiwan through "peaceful unification"—but as Vladimir Putin proved in Ukraine, this does not rule out a bloody war by accident or design.

In 2022, CIA Director William Burns revealed intelligence assessments that Xi has ordered the PLA to be ready to conduct an invasion of Taiwan by 2027.[92] In his most detailed explanation, given in an interview on CBS News' *Face the Nation*, Burns framed it this way:

> We do know, as has been made public, that President Xi has instructed the PLA, the Chinese military leadership, to be ready by 2027 to invade Taiwan, but that doesn't mean that he's decided to invade in 2027 or any other year as well. I think our judgment at least is that President Xi and his military leadership have doubts today about whether they could accomplish that invasion. I think, as they've looked at Putin's experience in Ukraine, that's probably reinforced some of those doubts as well. So, all I would say is that I think the risks of, you know, a potential use of force probably grow the further into this decade you get and beyond it, into the following decade as well. So that's something obviously, that we watch very, very carefully.[93]

According to Burns, the U.S. intelligence community believes that Xi has not committed to a date. Nor has he made a decision to invade at all. Burns carefully emphasized this point every time he discussed the topic. Other U.S. officials appear to have seen the same intelligence, but their references to it have been less precise and may reflect personal views.[94]

The year 2027, which will mark the one-hundredth anniversary of the PLA's founding, is significant for multiple reasons. At the 19th CCP Central Committee's Fifth Plenary Session in October 2020, the party promulgated a "Centennial Military Building Goal." First, it seeks to accelerate the PLA's integration of mechanization, "informatization," and "intelligentization," with a strong emphasis on AI. Second, it aims to modernize military doctrine, organization, personnel, and equipment. Third, it calls for improving efficiency and quality in resource allocation. Finally, it calls for strengthening China's national defense and economic power together through a program of military–civil fusion. The 2027 building goal is no secret; Xi has spoken about it in public on many occasions.[95] It has no explicit link to Taiwan, even though the process of achieving the goal would inevitably make the PLA more lethal and effective in a Taiwan-related fight.

The year 2027 is also a crucial date for Xi personally. It will correspond to the 21st National Party Congress, where he is expected to win a fourth term as China's paramount leader. Notably, 2027 is still an intermediate goal in the PLA's long-term strategy. The goal of establishing "basically complete national defense and military modernization," for example, is not scheduled to be met until 2035. In addition, the goal of possessing a "world-class military" is not expected to be achieved until "midcentury."[96]

Xi is also the first PRC leader to articulate a *public* deadline for achiev- ing "reunification": 2049, the hundredth anniversary of the founding of the PRC. Past CCP leaders have held that as long as a viable political and legal pathway toward future "reunification" can be kept open, future generations can figure out the details. As PRC President Yang Shangkun said in 1990: "It is possible that people of my age may not live to see the day when China is reunified. But it will not be good if the people here today fail to see China reunified. A popular saying in China goes: 'A long night is fraught with dreams.'"[97] But Xi expresses more confidence that a resolution is in sight. In San Francisco in December 2023, Xi told Biden that "reunification" would take place, but that the timing had not yet been decided. He also said in front of a group that he would prefer to take Taiwan peacefully.[98] Xi has called "reunification" an "inevitable requirement for realizing the great rejuvena- tion of the Chinese nation"[99] As he concluded in the Taiwan section of his 2022 Party Congress Work report: "The historical wheels of national reuni- fication and national rejuvenation are rolling forward and will certainly be achieved."[100]

While Taiwan is a CCP core interest, it seems to be just one of Xi's many priorities. "National rejuvenation" is a staggeringly ambitious program that encompasses nearly every aspect of human endeavor: ranging from the revital- ization of the CCP, to the project of "building a moderately well-off society" and "socialist market economy" through world-leading industrial and tech- nological capacity, the construction of "ecological civilization" to create "har- mony between mankind and nature," the creation of a flourishing and patriotic Chinese culture, and the construction of a "community of common destiny for mankind" to bring traditional "Chinese wisdom" into global governance, among many other goals.[101] "Reunification" could either support or hinder this broader project.

This is probably why Xi has articulated the 2049 deadline so that it can be fudged, if necessary. If a future leader of Taiwan is willing to sign a purely symbolic statement on the basis of the "1992 Consensus," Beijing could potentially declare that "reunification" has been achieved while deferring "integration" to a later date. Given that Xi will most likely be retired by 2049, if he is still alive at all, this timeline is quite convenient. Xi surely aspires to make "reunification" the capstone of his legacy, but he can safely hand the Taiwan issue off unresolved to his successor sometime in the 2030s or even early 2040s. So long as Taiwan has not declared independence in the meantime, Xi's successor can bear the blame if national rejuvenation is not achieved on schedule. Indeed, the fact that Xi has not pledged to personally achieve "reunification" suggests that his threats might be partly bluster. Xi's most high-profile statements on the issue—his "Work Reports" at the National Party Congresses held every five years—call for "peaceful unification" and make no mention of deadlines.[102]

Indeed, Xi's argument in all his public statements is not that China must accelerate its "reunification" timeline, but rather that the United States must be deterred from using Taiwan to obstruct China's national rejuvenation. As a key addition to Xi's 2022 Work Report, Xi made repeated references to "interference by external forces" (外部势力干涉) in Taiwan affairs, which he called "serious provocations" (严重挑衅).[103] In 2023, Xi told European Commission President Ursula von der Leyen that Washington was trying to provoke him into attacking Taiwan.[104] While Xi's depiction of U.S. "provocations" is exaggerated—both the Biden and Trump administrations have adhered to the One China Policy, and Taiwan's leaders have respected China's red lines—his statements invite two interpretations. He could be laying the groundwork for an unprovoked offensive against Taiwan. Or, he might genuinely view U.S. actions as aggressive, seeing himself as exercising restraint.

There is at least a plausible case for the "defensive Xi" hypothesis. Xi's reaction to Nancy Pelosi's August 2022 visit to Taiwan is one revealing example. The Biden administration initially privately asked Pelosi not to go ahead with the trip. However, when the press reported on her plans, the administration did not publicly demand that she cancel. It was an extremely sensitive time in China's political calendar. Just two months remained before the all-important 20th Party Congress. Xi personally asked Biden to stop Pelosi from going, but Biden told him there was nothing he could do.[105] Did Xi believe this, or did he think Biden was trying to undermine him? Either way, Xi had to show that he was in control. The PLA responded to Pelosi's visit with coordinated exercises, firing missiles into the sea on all sides of Taiwan and sending ships and planes across the median line in the Taiwan Strait for the first time.[106] Notably, however, the PLA telegraphed the locations of the tests in advance and concluded the exercise at the promised time.[107] It was a performance of strength alongside a signal that Xi did not want escalation.

To conclude, the most plausible theory is that Xi has both defensive and offensive interests at stake in Taiwan. The top defensive goal is security in retirement. This is far from assured as Xi enters his eighth decade.[108] After all, it was Xi who established the precedent that retired CCP elders can be humiliated, purged, and even prosecuted and expropriated.[109] Any move Xi makes on the Taiwan issue must be informed to some degree by fear of being the leader who lost Taiwan. For the same reason, Xi has an offensive reason to seize Taiwan if he can: it would be a legacy-defining achievement that would likely make him untouchable by rivals in his old age.

China's Interests

CCP propaganda frames Taiwan as central to Chinese history and national identity, but its significance to the party is primarily geostrategic.[110] Taiwan sits at the heart of the First Island Chain. This series of archipelagos extends from Japan to Indonesia and restricts China's access from its marginal seas—the Yellow Sea, East China Sea, and South China Sea—to the broader Pacific. The seabed's topography further limits passage to a few critical chokepoints (see Figure 1.2). These include the Miyako Strait and Bashi Channel, located just north and south of Taiwan. By positioning forces along the First Island Chain, the United States can threaten to contain China's navy, including its submarines, within these marginal seas (see Figure 1.3).

China views the U.S. military presence in the First Island Chain as a threatening "containment" (遏制) strategy.[111] While the U.S. homeland lies safely across an ocean, out of range of China's conventional weapons, the U.S. military maintains tens of thousands of forward-deployed troops and advanced air and naval platforms just hundreds of miles from China's coast. In contrast, China has no naval bases or formal facilities further out in the Pacific. PLA aircraft can operate beyond the First Island Chain only with access to friendly

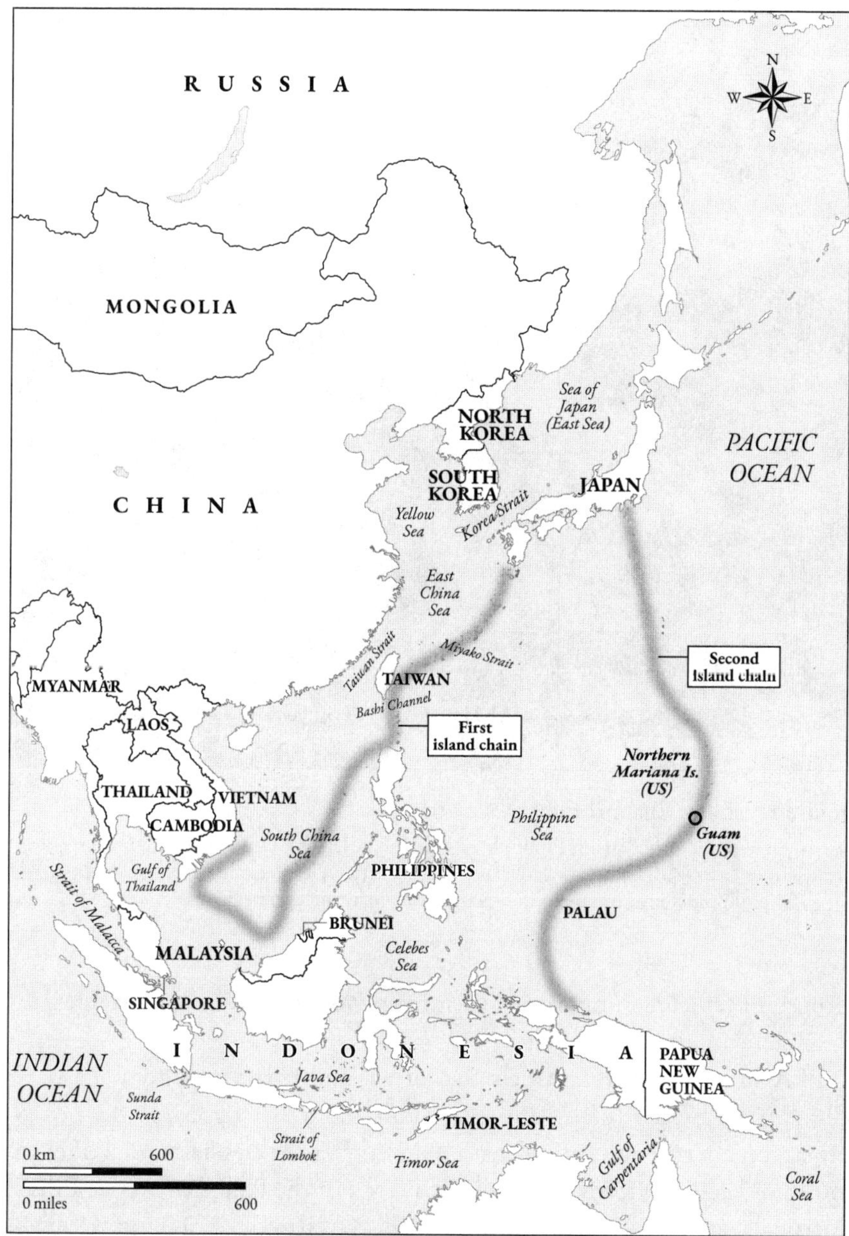

Figure 1.2 The First and Second Island Chains

Source: U.S. Department of Defense, *Annual Report to Congress: Military Power of the People's Republic of China 2009* (2009), 18.

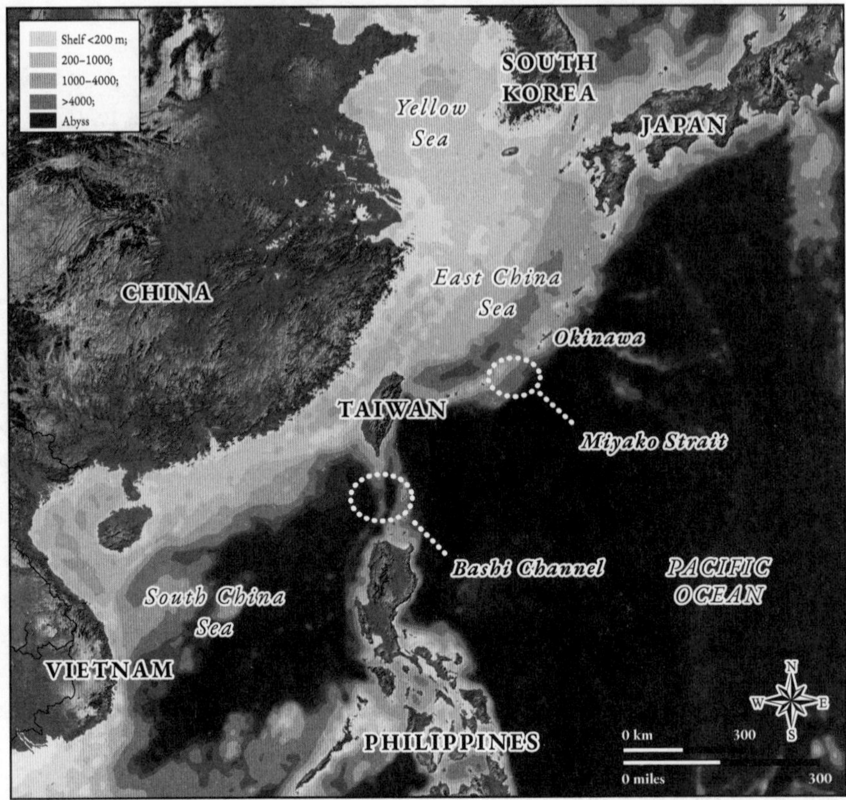

Figure 1.3 Bashi Channel and Miyako Strait

Source: Jean-Paul Burdy, "Bashi (Philippines) et Miyako (Japon), Deux Détroits Maritimes Stratégiques," *Les Mots de Taïwan*, March 15, 2023, https://lesmotsdetaiwan.com/2023/03/15/bashi-philippines-et-miyako-japon-deux-detroits-maritimes-strategiques.

airports or refueling support, but their range would be severely constrained in a conflict with the United States.

PLA strategists therefore view the First Island Chain as both a "barrier" China must breach for maritime freedom and a "springboard" for power projection after "reunification" with Taiwan.[112] They emphasize that Taiwan must not become a formal U.S. ally like Japan or the Philippines. The PLA's doctrinal text, *The Science of Military Strategy*, warns that if Taiwan is "alienated from the mainland," China would lose access to vast waters and resources, remaining trapped west of the First Island Chain. This language echoes Douglas MacArthur's description of Taiwan as an "unsinkable aircraft carrier."[113]

If China's long-term goal is to expel U.S. forces from the region, splitting the U.S. presence in the First Island Chain would be the first step. The next would be to dominate the Second Island Chain, which spans Japan's Bonin and Volcano Islands, the Mariana Islands (including Guam), and New Guinea, and is key to U.S. staging and supply lines. The PLA's "Near Seas Defense and Far Seas Protection" strategy envisions striking as far as the Second Island Chain.[114] China has prioritized weapons like the DF-26 "Guam-killer" missile to target the region's strategic hub. Ultimately, Beijing's interest in Taiwan has always been—and always will be—deeply tied to its military rivalry with the United States.

Another key strand of China's national rejuvenation agenda is reshaping the regional and global order around Taiwan to advance its interests at the expense of the United States.[115] At the G20 in Brazil in November 2024, Xi outlined a vision to "improve global governance and promote an equal and orderly multipolar world and a universally beneficial and inclusive economic globalization."[116] China supports many of the multilateral institutions that anchor the current international system, including the United Nations and World Trade Organization. China presents itself as a responsible steward of the system. In practice, however, China aims to build international consensus around a fundamentally revisionist vision of world order. China is promoting perverse reinterpretations of concepts like "international law," "free trade," "human rights," and "democracy."

Xi envisions a central role for China in global security. As he told the G20 in 2024: "security governance is part and parcel of global governance." His slogan for this vision of world order, the "community of common destiny for mankind" (人类命运共同体), critiques the U.S.-led order and pitches China as a better alternative to third countries.[117] In September 2025, Xi announced a new "Global Governance Initiative" to promote a "fairer" international order.

As China's power has grown, its critiques of the existing order have sharpened, and its assertions of an alternative have become more confident and more specific. Early in Xi's tenure, PRC commentators denied that initiatives like One Belt One Road had a global governance agenda.[118] Over time, China began engaging in global governance discussions but avoided weighing in on security issues, citing its policy of "noninterference" in the internal affairs of other countries. Now, Xi openly advocates reshaping global security governance. The "community of common destiny" concept, too, is likely to evolve as the CCP's power increases, and it may involve a more prominent role for U.S. adversaries such as North Korea, Russia, and Iran.[119] If Xi achieves "reunification," he could pursue a regional and global order that more directly serves CCP interests over those of the United States.[120]

Xi's lofty rhetoric about China striving for a peaceful, fair, and benevolent world order contrasts sharply with the CCP's actions. Xi and his predecessors have consistently exploited every tool of national power to achieve their aims in international disputes. For example, after the Oslo-based Nobel Committee awarded the 2010 Peace Prize to imprisoned Chinese dissident Liu Xiaobo, China imposed significant diplomatic and economic sanctions on Norway. China restricted Norwegian salmon imports, suspended high-level diplomatic contacts, and tightened visa rules for Norwegians until Norway reaffirmed its commitment to the One China Policy in 2016.[121] Xi also promotes Orwellian definitions of "democracy" and "human rights" in international fora while exploiting the free trade regime through industrial espionage and large-scale dumping.[122] He has flouted international law and sovereign rights, seizing Philippine maritime spaces and forcibly building villages on Bhutanese soil.[123] Xi's goals of achieving "reunification" and advancing this malign global order are closely linked. China will not grow more benign as it grows more powerful.

Why Might Xi Choose to Fight?

The discussion above suggests Xi prefers to absorb Taiwan peacefully, allowing the "wheels of national rejuvenation" to turn uninterrupted. But what if he is more risk-tolerant? Why might Xi launch a premeditated effort that risks war, even without a clear violation of China's red lines? The costs and risks of conflict with the United States would be immense. War could devastate China's integration into the global economy, derail its order-building ambitions, and, in the worst case, threaten CCP rule and Xi's personal security. Theories for why Xi might accept these risks fall into three categories: misperceptions of U.S. intentions prompting preemptive action; domestic political insecurities; and opportunistic judgments that U.S. deterrence lacks credibility.

The concept of the "security dilemma" helps explain the potential for a defensively motivated preemptive war.[124] The security dilemma arises when one state's defensive actions are perceived by a rival as offensive, creating a spiral of escalation. We can see this dynamic in the U.S.–China relationship. China views U.S. military activities, alliances, and policies like export controls as systematic efforts to contain its rise. It accuses Washington of a "Cold War mentality" and of "zero-sum thinking," assuming Americans are intent on thwarting China's development and denying its rightful status.[125] As former Prime Minister of Australia and China scholar Kevin Rudd has shown, these beliefs about the United States are deeply held within China's leadership and are not mere propaganda.[126] Meanwhile, the United States interprets China's coercive actions, military modernization, and economic practices as signs of potential aggression.

Whether or not one or both sides are acting defensively, they appear locked in a spiral of eroding trust and escalating risk of miscalculation. In the Taiwan Strait in particular, China and the United States both claim to be defensively upholding the status quo. Each accuses the other of revisionism and "salami-slicing"—trying to achieve major gains through a series of small, incremental steps that individually fall below the threshold of provoking a strong response.[127] Of course, the status quo is fluid. Beijing understands this fact, but not all U.S. analysts do.[128]

The security dilemma is one reason that rising and ruling powers often struggle to achieve "grand bargains" to resolve their differences. Graham Allison calls this dynamic the "Thucydides Trap." Fear, interest, and honor can drive great powers toward conflict rather than negotiation.[129] Xi has shown a strong interest in Allison's concept, hosting him in Beijing and frequently referencing the Thucydides Trap.[130] As he told Joe Biden in 2024, "It is important to have a correct strategic perception. The Thucydides Trap is not a historical inevitability. A new Cold War should not be fought and cannot be won. Containing China is unwise, unacceptable, and bound to fail."[131] These statements seem to invite a grand bargain in which the United States peacefully accedes to China's national rejuvenation. Of course, Xi's implicit threat is that unless the United States accepts China's national rejuvenation, war could become unavoidable.

Xi also presumably has to deal with domestic pressure.[132] China's leaders don't have to compete in elections, but nationalist sentiment still constrains their choices.[133] A failure to act decisively on Taiwan, especially if the island appeared to be moving toward formal independence, could weaken Xi's standing among party elites and enable rivals to challenge his authority. Xi isn't generally responsive to popular unrest, but he has shown flexibility in adjusting policies in response to public outcry. His embrace of a "war against pollution" in 2014 and his U-turn on the "zero-COVID" strategy in December 2022 are two notable examples.[134] These precedents suggest that Xi might feel domestic pressure to act if Taiwan is perceived as slipping away, even if he would prefer to avoid direct conflict.[135] For now, however, this isn't much of a concern. Surveys suggest that only around half of PRC citizens favor the use of outright violence to take Taiwan, and most PRC elites are probably more worried about the stagnant economy.

The possibility of a diversionary war—where a leader initiates a foreign conflict to distract from an unrelated domestic crisis—cannot be discounted, though most scholars think the risk is relatively low in Xi's case.[136] Absent a Taiwan crisis, Xi's hold on power looks secure. He has eliminated factions in the party, crushed private-sector interests that might threaten the party's hold on power, and purged younger officials rumored to be potential successors.[137] In general, authoritarian regimes start fewer diversionary wars than democracies because they have alternative ways to deal with dissent.[138] Finally, if Xi needed to provoke a diversionary conflict due to an economic crisis, social protest, or some other reason, it would be much less risky to provoke skirmishes over disputed border regions or islands with India, Vietnam, or even the Philippines.[139] It would make little sense for Xi to initiate a war with the United States to divert attention from an economic crisis, since any conflict would almost certainly worsen China's economic woes. In short, the probability of a diversionary war is not zero, and domestic pressures could constrain Xi's ability to back down without losing face. But he is unlikely to risk conflict unless he is confident that victory is attainable at an acceptable cost.

A related argument is the "peaking China" hypothesis.[140] According to this view, China's relative power is nearing its zenith, and demographic, economic, and geopolitical factors will drive its decline by the 2030s. This could create a "closing window of opportunity" for China to achieve unification with Taiwan before it loses the ability to challenge the United States. Some analysts have drawn the analogy to Japan's decision to attack the United States in 1941. Faced with an oil embargo that threatened its military, Japan gambled on a short and intense war to secure its strategic objectives.[141] Xi might reason similarly. If the United States is poised to gain compounding relative advantages, maybe the longer Xi waits, the harder it will be to force Taiwan's unification.

But there is *zero evidence* that Xi subscribes to the peaking power narrative.[142] On the contrary, confidence in the superiority of China's political, economic, and social system—and the inevitability of its rejuvenation—is the foundational idea of Xi Jinping's political thought.[143] Even if Xi perceives a narrowing window of opportunity to seize Taiwan, would achieving this one goal be worth jeopardizing all others? Unlike Japan in 1941, Xi does not face the prospect of starvation or collapse from embargo if he exercises restraint. U.S. export controls may slow China's technological progress, but they don't pose an immediate or existential threat to its political system. This logic might shift if Xi were to believe that the United States was on the brink of acquiring superintelligent AI. This seems unlikely today, given China's distinctive conception of AI, but this scenario represents a plausible risk in the future. We will revisit this issue later in this chapter and again in Chapter 6.

A final possibility is that Xi, influenced by imperfect information from fearful or opportunistic advisors, might underestimate the U.S. and Taiwanese publics' capabilities or resolve. This is a significant risk that deserves careful consideration. U.S. public opinion still strongly favors maintaining robust alliances and military superiority, including to deter war over Taiwan. Historical experiences from the Spanish-American War, World Wars I and II, the Korean War, the Gulf War, and the War on Terror suggest that American public opinion can swing quickly in favor of war when foreign policy elites conclude that war is a national security necessity—particularly but not exclusively when Americans are killed.[144] Still, Xi could point to other data points. For example, there are (dubiously worded) polls suggesting that only one-third of Americans would support "sending troops" to defend Taiwan from attack. U.S. resolve has also waned over time in other protracted conflicts, notably Vietnam, Iraq, and Ukraine (though not Korea).[145] Economic interdependence could also play a crucial role in Xi's calculations. A war over Taiwan would almost certainly lead to severe economic disruptions, including sanctions, supply-chain failures, and potential financial crises in China. However, political science research suggests that economic interdependence alone does not prevent conflict.[146] What matters more are perceptions of which side would suffer more and which has a greater tolerance for pain.[147] Xi might believe the United States is a bourgeois society unwilling to bear the economic costs of a protracted conflict. Alternatively, he could conclude that U.S. economic statecraft is incompetent and that U.S. economic retaliation would backfire by driving third countries closer to China.[148]

The United States must closely monitor Xi's domestic context and calibrate its messaging to prevent misperceptions. While it is critical to convince Xi that U.S. and allied forces could thwart a PLA effort to seize Taiwan, he might still act out of desperation or opportunism if he believed Washington was forcing his hand or lacked the resolve to bear the costs of war. Effective deterrence, therefore, requires an integrated strategy that links political and economic preparations to traditional military "denial" and "punishment" frameworks. Xi must be persuaded not only that the United States can defeat him militarily but also that Washington does not intend to use Taiwan to undermine his personal hold on power and is prepared to respond decisively to aggression.

U.S. Interests in Peacetime

Why should Americans be willing to expend blood and treasure—and possibly risk nuclear war—to stop Xi from seizing Taiwan? The United States has extremely important national interests at stake, many of which extend beyond Taiwan itself. Losing a conflict would be disastrous for these interests, and any conflict would endanger them.

A Free and Open Indo-Pacific

The United States has political and economic interests in keeping the Indo-Pacific free and open. This region accounts for two-thirds of global GDP and 60 percent of maritime trade. It is the fastest growing in both population and economic output. The United States must prevent the key economies in this region from falling under China's hegemonic control.[149]

The United States derives enormous strategic benefits from the current regional order in the Indo-Pacific.[150] Nations across the region are free to determine their own political and economic destinies, including by maintaining alliances with the United States that protect them from aggression by China, North Korea, and Russia. Thanks to the robust U.S. military presence in the region, all regional economies are free to decide how they participate in the global economy. U.S. adversaries cannot bring smaller countries—including in the Western Hemisphere—under their control through military and economic coercion. Nor can they rewrite the rules of commerce in the region to disadvantage the United States and its allies. These strategic and material benefits underpin U.S. economic prosperity at home and facilitate U.S. action to protect its sovereign rights and strategic interests. Keeping the Indo-Pacific free and open also matters because a collapse of the current order would likely be followed by a sudden collapse of international trade. This would immediately devastate U.S. prosperity.

There is a place for a strong and prosperous China in a free and open Indo-Pacific. After the Soviet Union collapsed, the United States pursued a vision of globalization that involved integrating former adversaries into the system. Russia and then China were invited to accede to the WTO, on the assumptions that history had repudiated Communist economics, that integration would make these countries more responsible stakeholders, and that ultimately these societies would experience political liberalization.[151] In the process, the United States and its allies and partners became economically dependent on Russia and even more so on China. This strategic bet has failed with respect to Russia, but it has not yet failed in China's case. The United States has an interest in keeping China as at least a quasi-responsible stakeholder rather than a rogue state. Unfortunately, any PRC attempt to seize Taiwan by force would prove that the bet had failed entirely. It would demand a fundamental reevaluation of American strategy for the region and the world.

If the Indo-Pacific is not free and open, the Western Hemisphere and American homeland cannot be kept secure. It is essential to stress this point. The global economy is organized around the principle that all countries should be able to use international waters and airspace without fear or favor, and that powerful states cannot coerce weaker ones by denying them access to the commons or interfering with their ability to trade. The Indo-Pacific is a maritime region, and most of its nations are small states that rely on maritime trade for their lifeblood. If China can stop these countries from organizing to enforce these principles and can block the United States from intervening, it could wield economic coercion directly against the United States. It could manipulate market access to the region, threatening to limit exports of goods and services or denying U.S. firms access to one of the world's largest markets. The Indo-Pacific would effectively become China's sphere of influence. Americans would suffer vastly diminished prosperity and economic security.

After reshaping the region to suit its preferences, China would subsequently extend its influence into South Asia, the Middle East, and Africa, and try to strike a grand bargain with a weak and divided European Union. Other adversaries like Russia, North Korea, and Iran would be empowered to challenge U.S. interests in multiple theaters. The future of the global economic order would likely turn in China's favor as well. Once China could establish a presence in the Arctic, Atlantic, Central Pacific, and Latin America, the vulnerabilities of the U.S. homeland would become increasingly evident.

Technological Security and AI Primacy

The AI revolution has profound implications for global governance, the economy, society, and national security. In the coming years, AI could transform the services sector, which accounts for 80 percent of U.S. GDP, disrupting entire industries and affecting tens of millions of jobs. In the military sphere, AI has the potential to revolutionize operations and deterrence. It could threaten nuclear command-and-control systems, enhance target identification, and enable sophisticated cyberattacks, making AI leadership essential for homeland defense. Predictions of "artificial general intelligence" and even "superintelligence" emerging within the next few years remain speculative.[152] Still, given the stakes, these trends warrant serious attention.[153]

The CCP's pursuit of AI dominance poses a unique threat. The CCP is a Leninist organization that seeks to maximize its power and survival. It rejects individual liberty, freedom of conscience, and freedom of expression as legitimate values. We should all fear a future in which the CCP monopolizes advanced AI and uses it for societal control.[154] The United States therefore cannot let the semiconductor fabrication plants, or fabs, that monopolize the production of essential AI hardware fall under CCP control. If China managed to take control of Taiwan's fabs and industrial know-how, it would not automatically seize the commanding heights of chip production. Taiwan's fabs need continued access to equipment and technology that the United States and its allies could restrict. Still, it would take a big step toward parity and eventually leadership in chip production.

If Beijing took the lead in chipmaking, it could coerce the United States and its allies by restricting the supply of advanced chips.[155] At the same time, the United States must deter Beijing from sabotaging Taiwan's fabs out of fear of falling badly behind in AI, since this too would be an economic disaster.[156] Navigating between these two risks is challenging. Either side could easily disable, damage, or destroy Taiwan's fabs—and few conflict scenarios would see them survive intact.[157]

Survival and Health of U.S. Alliances

The United States has five treaty allies in the Indo-Pacific. China is working assiduously to undermine these alliances.[158] Taiwan is not a treaty ally, but its geographic position at the nexus of this alliance network means that U.S. allies would be far harder to defend if Taiwan fell. U.S. treaty alliances in the region would probably not dissolve, but they would be hollowed out. Doubting the credibility of U.S. security guarantees, Japan, South Korea, and potentially other countries might seek to acquire their own nuclear weapons and form their own alliance groupings without the United States.[159]

Global Geopolitical Stability

While Washington foreign policy analysts are often mocked for their obsession with U.S. "credibility," a U.S. humiliation over Taiwan could have disastrous, cascading consequences for global geopolitical stability. U.S. treaty allies are already losing confidence that Washington would fulfill the treaty commitments it extended decades ago. If Washington allowed Taiwan to fall, its adversaries would have new reasons to test the boundaries of American commitments globally. Russia, North Korea, and Iran might coordinate their aggression during and after a Taiwan crisis, testing America's ability to respond to multiple simultaneous crises globally. North Korea might aggress against South Korea. Russia would have reason to doubt that Washington would fight for the Baltic states, which are largely indefensible by conventional means. Iran may ramp up proxy attacks on merchant shipping in the Red Sea and U.S. forces in Iraq, Syria, and Bahrain. If Washington failed to respond effectively to these tests, it would lose further credibility. A failure of deterrence over Taiwan could open Pandora's box.

A Free and Democratic Taiwan

Taiwan's democracy represents a beacon of liberal governance amid rising authoritarianism. It is no accident that the United States' most trusted and important allies in the region are democracies. Allowing Beijing to extinguish Taiwan's democracy would mark a symbolic and strategic defeat.

Taiwan also represents an alternative pathway for China. Taiwan's very existence as a prosperous, innovative, stable, and orderly liberal democracy rebukes the CCP's claims that the Chinese people are not ready for democracy and that the Communist revolution is inexorably bound toward victory.[160] The CCP's hold on power looks solid for now, but this may not be true forever. The CCP has historically struggled with succession planning and has faced severe internal challenges during leadership transitions, most recently in 1989. Indeed, one reason to keep the One China Policy is that the best possible way to resolve the dispute may be cross-Strait unification *in the context of a free and democratic China*.[161] We can only imagine how the PRC may change after Xi Jinping eventually exits the stage.

To be clear, the U.S. interest in Taiwan's democracy is important but not vital. The United States had interests in peace and security in the Taiwan Strait before Taiwan transitioned to democracy in the 1990s. These interests will abide even if Taiwan's democracy falters. For now, however, Taiwan has become a litmus test of the U.S. commitment to supporting democracy under pressure.

U.S. Interests in a Crisis

If deterrence fails and China moves against Taiwan by force, the United States will retain all four of its key peacetime geopolitical interests, but it will also acquire new interests. In a crisis, some of these interests may be in tension with one another. U.S. policymakers would need to strike a balance between them.

Financial and Macroeconomic Stability

Managing the economic fallout from any crisis would be priority number one. Major economies often grow rapidly during wartime.[162] However, a great power conflict over Taiwan could be different. The sudden rupture of supply chains in and out of China and Taiwan could result in sharp economic downturn, shortages and inflation, and a sharp jump in global unemployment.[163] The United States and its allies and partners would have a common interest in limiting the economic damage—regardless of how China moved, and whether or how the U.S. government wanted to intervene militarily. The president and Congress would face considerable pressure to maintain domestic financial stability and prevent an economic depression. Maintaining financial and macroeconomic stability would be a strategic concern, not just a political one.

A global economic crisis would make it harder to maintain allied unity during a prolonged conflict.

Breaking U.S. and Allied Dependence on PRC Production

Economic dependence leaves countries vulnerable to coercion that undermines their ability to protect their sovereign interests. It is therefore against U.S. strategic interests to remain reliant on a systemic national security threat—or a country with which it is at war. Similarly, the United States in a crisis would need to help its regional allies break their economic dependence on China. Regardless of how a Taiwan crisis unfolded, there would be no return to the old status quo. Beijing's use of force would starkly demonstrate its willingness to disregard the Three Communiqués. From Day One, breaking U.S. and allied dependence on China would become a lasting and urgent priority.

The International Economic System

After a Taiwan crisis, the international trading system would face a significant risk of collapse. Skepticism toward free trade is already growing in the United States, and both political parties could push for isolationist policies.[164] Many other countries might follow suit. The WTO was not designed to manage disputes involving rogue great powers. Its Appellate Body, the board that settles disputes between members, is already paralyzed.[165] Countries can now cite Article XXI of the General Agreement on Tariffs and Trade (GATT) Charter, which allows open-ended national security exemptions, to justify virtually any protectionist trade or industrial policy.[166] If many countries did this at the same time in a crisis, international trade could collapse, as it did during the Great Depression. The result could be a prolonged global economic cataclysm that would degrade U.S. prosperity and economic security.[167]

A blockade or quarantine of Taiwan would pose a different but equally grave threat to the system. These tactics are less bloody than an invasion, but they are just as coercive.[168] As the American economist Thomas Schelling once noted, "the power to hurt is bargaining power." In fact, the threat of "latent violence" can be even more effective than physical force.[169] A blockade would force an ultimatum: submit to Beijing's authority or face starvation. If Taiwan succumbed, other regional economies—such as Vietnam, South Korea, Japan, Malaysia, and the Philippines—would be left vulnerable to similar tactics in the future. China would claim Taiwan as a unique case, but the dark precedent would be established. None of China's neighbors could ever forget it.

Regardless of how America and its allies responded to a blockade or quarantine, the international economic system would face profound challenges. If Washington opted to leave the system unchanged, the rogue, emboldened authoritarian power bent on territorial expansion could redouble its use of economic coercion. If the United States abandoned the system entirely in favor of isolationism, this too would harm long-term U.S. economic interests, since China would now have untrammeled power to dominate its neighbors through military and economic threats.

Revitalizing the system for a post-crisis era would therefore be the only acceptable option. This path would require protecting the system from collapse while reshaping it to serve American interests under new geopolitical circumstances. Trade could no longer be truly "free." The United States and its allies would need to protect themselves from China's predatory, anticompetitive economic behavior. Yet the United States would not be anti-trade. America would need to stand for a *fair and honest trading system* that respects the sovereignty and national interests of all nations. The United States and its allies would have an imperative to pursue strategic decoupling. The message to third countries would be simple: "America has a problem with China, not you. If you are honest and help us secure our borders against mislabeled Chinese products, we will treat you fairly. As we decouple from China, you can compete for manufacturing jobs being reshored."

Fortunately, in a crisis, preserving a functional international trading system would be a common interest between the United States, allies, partners, and neutral states. Everyone would lose from a sudden breakdown in global trade, particularly industrialized economies like the EU and South Korea, and industrializing nations like Brazil and Indonesia. Reimagining the system for a post-crisis era would take bold American leadership, but most of the global economy would prefer a *fair and honest trading system* over no system at all. Many might even prefer it to the status quo ex ante.

Dollar Hegemony

The United States has a vital national interest in maintaining the dollar's status as the global reserve currency. Dollar hegemony gives American families more buying power, and it also grants the U.S. government unparalleled enforcement power, enabling extraterritorial sanctions and export controls. These tools play a critical role in holding back the economic, technological, and military development of adversaries like Russia, Iran, and North Korea. The United States also benefits from unique enforcement capabilities tied to the dollar's dominance. Most international trade is invoiced in dollars. Most international payment messaging and settlement uses the SWIFT (Society for Worldwide Interbank Financial Telecommunication) and CHIPS (Clearing House Interbank Payment System) systems. The U.S. government therefore enjoys significant oversight over financial transactions that occur beyond its borders.[170]

The dollar's position is holding for now, but it is increasingly tenuous.[171] The United States has a unique ability to supply large quantities of currency through its substantial current account deficit. Potential competitor currencies like China's RMB face structural hurdles, including trade surpluses and capital flow restrictions, that make them unsuitable for replacing the dollar entirely. A Taiwan crisis would more likely than not reinforce dollar hegemony, at least temporarily, as investors sought safety in U.S. assets.[172] Yet much would depend on how the United States responded in the medium to longer term. Market reactions since the 2025 trade war reignited reflect shaking confidence in the reliability of the dollar.

Relatedly, China, Russia, and Iran are slowly undermining the Treasury's ability to wield sanctions effectively. U.S. sanctions on Russia have amplified calls for de-dollarization in the developing world, with China now conducting nearly half its trade in RMB and rogue states adopting alternative payment systems. Even close U.S. partners like France and India may welcome a diminished role for the dollar. After a rupture with China, careless use of economic tools could erode the efficacy of the dollar weapon and accelerate the shift toward a multicurrency system, weakening U.S. influence. During and after a Taiwan crisis, policymakers must carefully balance the use of economic statecraft to avoid hastening this transition and undermining U.S. power.[173]

Punishing China

After a violent move against Taiwan, the United States would have a strategic interest in punishing China to preserve the credibility of future deterrence against China and other rogue actors. Economic punishment—and the potential for easing punishment after a settlement—could pressure China to moderate its political aims for Taiwan and the broader region. Additionally, the United States might seek to weaken China economically in order to undermine the regime, exhaust the PLA, and deprive China of resources to challenge U.S. interests elsewhere. If U.S.–China relations were to completely collapse, economic pressure would become a tool to push for long-term regime change, echoing current strategies against Venezuela, Iran, Russia, and North Korea.

Depending on the outcome of the crisis, the United States might need to sustain economic pressure on China indefinitely. However, Washington should not assume punishment will easily lead to victory. In World War II and other conflicts, including the Russia–Ukraine war, strategic bombing and tough sanctions have rarely forced quick capitulation.[174] Moreover, few countries would willingly prioritize punishing China over their own national interests. U.S. policymakers must keep these facts in mind.

Conclusion

The goal of this chapter has been to bring all readers up to speed by characterizing the political challenge in the Taiwan Strait and discussing potential triggers for a conflict. While it hasn't offered a comprehensive history of cross-Strait dispute, it has presented the fundamental background information and analysis that will ground the rest of the book. We have seen that China regards Taiwan as part of China under the temporary illegitimate control of DPP separatists who seek to separate Taiwan from China, but they are doomed to fail. China also claims that the United States and UN have accepted this "One China Principle," even though they have not. We have seen that the United States, by contrast, has a "One China Policy" that opposes unilateral changes from either side but is ambiguous about what Taiwan's status actually is since it remains undetermined. The American position is that the United States will accept any resolution of the cross-Strait dispute that is reached by peaceful means, free of coercion, and agreed to by the people of Taiwan. The U.S. focus is on *how* the resolution would be achieved, and it firmly opposes behavior by either side that threatens "peace and stability." In this long-running dispute, both sides' positions are designed to be compelling in the eyes of third countries. China defines "peaceful unification" as Taiwan's capitulation without a war. The United States similarly presents itself as the side defending regional "peace and stability" against PRC aggression. If a conflict broke out, each side would likely try to engineer the political optics so that the other looked like the aggressor.

The assessment of Xi's strategy in this chapter grounds the rest of the book. Xi is undertaking a massive military buildup, hoping that military threats can coerce the United States into standing aside and Taiwan into capitulating. Xi would probably attack if his red lines are flagrantly crossed. He may or may not attack if his red lines are *not* flagrantly crossed. The lines are vague enough that he could interpret many U.S. and Taiwanese actions either way, depending on his preferences. There are several plausible catalysts that might induce Xi to move without a clear provocation. They include domestic pressure that pushes him to start a diversionary war, fear of a closing window of opportunity (the "peak China" hypothesis), and opportunism based on assessments of U.S. and Taiwanese capabilities and resolve. The United States must prepare for all possibilities, including invasions and blockades. Still, Xi probably wants to avoid outright war. He will therefore employ a combination of gray-zone pressure, bluffs, and deterrent threats to shape the situation to advance his interests.

The United States must deter and if necessary defeat Xi's project of seizing Taiwan by force. Taiwan matters because of its strategic location, critical semiconductor industry, and democracy. It matters because its loss would embolden other adversaries, weaken U.S. alliances, and accelerate nuclear proliferation. Above all, Taiwan matters because if it fell, the international economic order could collapse or fall under China's control. In a crisis, the United States would therefore need to manage economic fallout, preserve financial stability, break dependencies on China, and protect dollar hegemony, even as adversaries pursued de-dollarization. Punishing China may be necessary to restore U.S. credibility and degrade Beijing's future capacity for aggression. But punishment could not be an end in itself and would have to be balanced against other interests. The stakes of preventing conflict over Taiwan—and effectively managing a crisis, if deterrence fails—are nothing less than American prosperity and homeland security.

PART II

Scenarios

2

The Gray Zone

In February 2024, six Chinese Coast Guard (CCG) officers boarded a Taiwanese tourist boat off Kinmen, one of Taiwan's offshore islands. They checked the route plan, as well as certificate and crew licenses, and then departed.[1] Four months later, CCG officers violently boarded Philippine resupply boats off the coast of Second Thomas Shoal, a disputed feature in the South China Sea. They used tear gas, blinding strobe lights, and deafening sirens, ramming the Filipino boats so hard that one sailor lost a thumb.[2] Then they confiscated the crew's rifles and personal cell phones, destroyed the outboard motor and communication and navigation equipment, and used sharp metal objects to puncture the boat's side. Altogether, 190 PRC ships entered the Philippine exclusive economic zone during the operation, including twenty-eight CCG cutters and People's Liberation Army Navy (PLAN) warships.[3] Later that year, another enormous CCG fleet took part in "Joint Sword 2024B," a blockade-simulation exercise to intimidate the Taiwan "separatists."[4]

These incidents reflect a broader pattern. Under the guise of defending its territorial claims and related "core interests," China is undermining the lawful rights of its neighbors through real or threatened violence and overwhelming physical presence.[5] In both cases, China is using "law enforcement" vessels for these operations, not just traditional military ships.[6] In both cases, China is using non-lethal force to establish dangerous new norms and test Washington's willingness to react. The United States is probably willing to go to war if China escalates to outright military force against either Taiwan or the Philippines. But the precise red lines that would provoke a decisive U.S. response are not clear. Above all, both cases show that when it comes to China's self-described "core interests" in the Taiwan Strait and South China Sea, the status quo is fluid and contested.[7]

Gray-zone operations are a defining feature of China's approach toward Taiwan. Air and naval incursions across the median line in the Taiwan Strait draw the most attention. But the all-domain pressure campaign against Taiwan also includes economic, legal, cyber, and sociocultural avenues of attack. These matter even more for Taiwan's long-term survival as a free society. China's intermediate goals are to create a pervasive, ambiguous threat environment that weakens Taiwan's resolve to protect its autonomy, to coerce businesses and other third parties into falling in line with Beijing's dictates, and to create new facts on the ground while deterring the United States and its allies from intervening. Its long-term goal is to achieve "peaceful reunification" without war with the United States. While China uses similar gray-zone tactics in its territorial disputes with its other neighbors, the campaign against Taiwan is particularly insidious. Unlike India, Japan, and the Philippines, Taiwan can't seek recourse through international organizations or explicit assurances from formal treaty allies.

So far, the pressure campaign has failed to force Taiwan to submission. Indeed, it has provoked a backlash in Taiwan's domestic politics. Yet, it poses an acute challenge to U.S. interests and U.S. deterrence strategy because it can be ramped up significantly.[8] China's gray-zone activity blurs the line between peace and war. It blurs the definition of blockade, a category that American analysts tend to define too rigidly as a total stoppage of trade flows. It also blurs the lines between military, economic, and political aggression, raising difficult questions about what constitutes a proportionate response. If the gray zone contains the entire universe of potential PRC actions against Taiwan that stop short of lethal force, then we can imagine many Taiwan crisis scenarios much graver than the episode in Second Thomas Shoal. Gray-zone scenarios include threats, ultimatums, and brinkmanship crises extending up until the minute actual war breaks out. The essential problem for the United States (and Taiwan) is that at some point along the gray-zone escalation ladder, it is necessary to draw lines in the sand and start activating crisis contingency plans.

The goal of this chapter is to provoke readers to imagine some of Beijing's options for ramping up pressure in the gray zone and to ponder why they might be tempting. First, it characterizes China's all-domain pressure campaign to date. Then it discusses two particularly worrying pathways for gray-zone escalation. The first option is what foreign policy analysts Robert Blackwill and Philip Zelikow have called a "quarantine" or "indirect control" scenario.[9] In this approach, China uses "law enforcement" operations like the ones described above to squeeze and screen the flow of goods and people in and out of Taiwan. As we will see, the line between the status quo and a quarantine is fuzzy. So is the line between a quarantine and a traditional military blockade. Still, it is analytically useful to distinguish between wartime and nonwartime forms of economic coercion. A quarantine need not be a coercive diplomacy exercise designed to force Taiwan's immediate capitulation. Instead, it might aim to *incrementally establish the norm* that Taiwan no longer has full practical control over its economic interactions with the outside world.

After discussion of quarantine, the chapter explores how China might mobilize for war as a form of coercion. Such a move would be ambiguous. It might be a prelude to conflict, or it might be a routine exercise designed to rattle financial markets, temporarily disrupt supply chains, and sow terror. A coercive mobilization would test the resolve of Taiwan, the United States, and other countries. It would force them to make tough decisions such as whether to mobilize their own forces and evacuate foreign nationals from Taiwan. Beijing could thereby discover critical information about Taipei's willingness to fight and the U.S.'s ability to rally its coalition. The final part of the chapter discusses the politics of these scenarios. It will likely be much harder to mobilize bipartisan support in the United States to react decisively to gray-zone aggression than against an invasion. Nevertheless, some gray-zone scenarios will require U.S. responses in the military, economic, and political domains. We will discuss strategies for deterring gray-zone aggression in Chapter 4.

The All-Domain Pressure Campaign

Under Xi, China's gray-zone aggression against Taiwan has broadened and intensified to become a whole-of-government and whole-of-party effort. Gabriel Collins and Andrew Erickson have aptly termed it an "all-domain pressure campaign."[10] The campaign involves the PLA, CCG, paramilitary groups such as the People's Armed Forces Maritime Militia (PAFMM), the domestic PRC legal system, and the diplomatic corps. The United Front Work Department (UFWD) also plays a key role, operating covertly through civil society groups, supposedly private enterprises, and internet personas. The campaign integrates military, economic, legal, cyber, and sociocultural elements. It is carefully calibrated across domains.[11] It aims to apply persistent pressure on Taiwan across multiple fronts, creating a continuous atmosphere of low-intensity conflict to exhaust Taiwan's resources and morale. China can dial pressure up to express displeasure or dial pressure down to reward submissive behavior.

China uses its domestic law to justify the pressure campaign and conduct "lawfare"—the use of legal instruments as a means of coercion—against Taiwan at home and abroad.[12] China's 2005 Anti-Secession Law and 2015 National Security Law assert supremacy over Taiwanese law.[13] In September 2024, a PRC court sentenced a Taiwanese activist to nine years in prison on a charge of "separatism."[14] So far, Beijing has enforced these laws relatively narrowly, but it could theoretically charge any DPP member with the crime of separatism.[15] Beijing has begun to pressure Taiwanese citizens visiting or working on the mainland to acquire PRC local identity cards, in a direct challenge to Taiwanese law.[16] Taiwanese citizens already know they are not entirely safe when they travel abroad. Hundreds have been extradited from third countries to China to face trial.[17] Over sixty countries have extradition treaties with China that cover political offenses, and Taiwan's government has warned citizens against traveling there.[18] Taipei has warned its citizens about the risk of taking connecting flights through China, even if China is not the final destination.

China has many options to ramp up the lawfare campaign going forward. For example, it could demand that Taiwanese companies with business in China share information on their employees and customers. Or it could try to curtail direct flights between Taiwan and third countries by pressuring airlines or foreign governments to stop on the mainland first. The mere threat to take these steps would have a chilling effect on Taiwan's democracy and undermine Taiwan's ability to interact freely with the outside world.

China's pressure campaign extends to foreign companies and countries that engage with Taiwan.[19] Since 2016, the number of countries that maintain diplomatic relations with Taiwan has nearly halved, from twenty-two to twelve. Multinational corporations—airlines, technology firms, and even fashion brands—are also feeling the pressure.[20] Companies that operate in China are vulnerable to reprisals if they resist demands to comply with Beijing's policies, such as listing Taiwan as part of China on their websites or avoiding references to its autonomy. Thus, it is difficult for even the most liberal-minded companies to justify principled stances on Taiwan to their shareholders. Even companies that do not do business directly in China can be targeted if they depend on subcontractors or suppliers in China.

Meanwhile, China is using offensive lawfare around the world to delegitimize Taiwan's claim to protection under international law. Central to this effort is Beijing's attempt to redefine UN General Assembly Resolution 2758. This is the 1971 text in which the UN recognized the PRC as "the only legitimate representative of China to the United Nations," thereby transferring the "Chinese" seat in the UN from Taipei to Beijing. The language of Resolution 2758 unambiguously refrained from taking a position on the sovereign status of Taiwan.[21] However, Beijing has recently launched a major propaganda effort claiming otherwise. Beijing even argues, baselessly, that the UN has accepted the "One China Principle."[22]

China seeks to exclude Taiwan from all international organizations, even those that do not require statehood for membership.[23] For example, sustained diplomatic pressure from Beijing has led to Taiwan's exclusion from the International Civil Aviation Organization (ICAO) and the World Health Assembly (the World Health Organization's decision-making body). These efforts have limited Taiwan's ability to engage globally on critical issues such as COVID-19 response, where Taiwan was the undisputed world leader. Instead, the World Health Organization has promoted PRC propaganda, including by failing to adequately investigate the pandemic's origins.[24]

Beijing's gray-zone work in international institutions is insidious and effective. If international institutions fear acknowledging Taiwan's existence, Taiwan will have no pathways to seek recourse from them, even if China acts against Taiwan in violation of international law. Under Article 51 of the UN Charter, member states have the right of self-defense against armed attack. The UN Charter also includes an open-ended concept of "collective self-defense," which the United States could cite to justify intervention in a cross-strait conflict. But Taiwan is not a UN member state, so this argument would have to be based on customary international law. China is preparing to contest this interpretation.[25]

Meanwhile, China is running a multifaceted political pressure campaign inside Taiwan to destabilize and divide the island's politics and society. The United Front Work Department (UFWD), the arm of the CCP responsible for influence and ideological operations, plays a key role in this effort.[26] The UFWD seeks to foster pro-Beijing sentiment by building connections with political figures, media organizations, business leaders, and local communities sympathetic to unification. It has likely penetrated most large civil society groups on Taiwan, including unions and temple organizations.[27] The UFWD also reportedly has deep ties with organized crime groups in Taiwan.[28] In January 2025, Taiwanese police arrested seven retired military officers who were allegedly funded by the PRC to take pictures of sensitive military facilities and form "assassination squads," presumably to menace pro-independence politicians.[29]

The UFWD also practices what PLA analysts call "cognitive domain operations" (认知域作战), hybrid warfare tactics that involve spreading disinformation.[30] The UFWD runs these operations through Confucius Institutes, scholarship programs, television and radio programs, and personal engagement with Taiwanese citizens who visit the mainland.[31] It targets key constituencies like young people and business leaders.[32] Ultimately, the UFWD aims to sow division within Taiwanese society, undermine public trust in Taiwan's government and the United States, and promote pro-Beijing narratives.

The UFWD could become extremely important in a crisis. Suppose that Taiwanese politicians who oppose "One China" start receiving blackmail or death threats or even are physically attacked or assassinated. Alternatively, suppose that Taiwanese politicians friendly to China claim to be targeted by similar tactics. In Hong Kong in 2019, the UFWD promulgated disinformation on social media blaming the "black hand" of the United States and UK for coordinating civil unrest.[33] Beijing then used this false narrative to justify mobilizing law enforcement and masked thugs who terrorized and brutally beat protesters.[34] In all plausible civil unrest scenarios in Taiwan, China's ability to mobilize paramilitary forces and manipulate the information environment will be useful. From Beijing's perspective, this was a key lesson of its savage pacification of Hong Kong in 2019.[35]

Beijing also uses economic coercion. It has offered carrots, such as allowing Taiwanese businesses to invest in PRC industries like 5G telecoms and theme parks, while also wielding sticks, such as suspending imports of Taiwanese pineapples, grouper fish, and sugar apples.[36] China has also extended generous incentives to attract Taiwanese IT specialists to relocate. However, Beijing has been cautious about applying broad economic pressure. Most PRC imports from Taiwan are semiconductors and related electronics that China cannot yet produce domestically. Beijing likely fears that restricting bilateral trade would drive Taiwan to strengthen economic ties with the United States and Japan. As a result, future gray-zone tactics are likely to focus on increasing Taiwan's dependence on the PRC market while obstructing its trade with other countries.

Under the pretext of routine "law enforcement" operations, the CCG continues to ramp up its coercive presence in the maritime space around Taiwan, particularly Taiwan's outlying islands. China has also assembled an irregular paramilitary maritime force that U.S. analysts have termed the People's Armed Forces Maritime Militia (PAFMM).[37] Official texts describe these forces as "helpers of the PLA" (解放军的助手), particularly for carrying out "joint military, law enforcement, and civilian defense" (军警民联防) alongside the CCG and PLA.[38] The PAFMM operates under direct military command but masquerades as an uncoordinated fleet of civilian vessels. PAFMM operations have included large-scale sand dredging just off Taiwan's outlying islands, GPS interference targeting Taiwanese fishing operations, and cutting of undersea cables that connect Taiwan to the outside world.[39]

While remaining in the gray zone, these activities have created a constant state of tension and uncertainty for Taiwanese vessels operating in Taiwanese waters. They also threaten vessels flying the flags of third countries.[40] The PAFMM could be useful for harassing resupply ships during quarantine and blockade scenarios. It could also conduct reconnaissance and surveillance during conflict, or even sabotage.

China's military pressure against Taiwan has also escalated sharply. The PLA has massively ramped up the frequency and extent of operations around Taiwan. Violations of the Taiwan Strait's median line, once rare, have become routine since 2022.[41] PLA fighter jets and bombers now enter Taiwan's Air Defense Identification Zone (ADIZ) daily.[42] While this zone includes areas beyond Taiwan's territorial airspace and even over mainland China, Taiwan's air force currently scrambles each time the zone is violated, straining its aircraft and pilots. (Some argue that this is unnecessary.)[43] In September 2024, China sent long-endurance, unmanned drones to circle Taiwan.[44] With drones operating closer to Taiwan's airspace in larger numbers and denser formations, China likely aims to establish a constant unmanned presence around the island. These drones are primarily used for reconnaissance but could also potentially carry out strikes. Drones are useful for testing Taiwan's response capabilities and imposing psychological pressure.

China uses cyberattacks for both espionage and strategic deterrence, targeting Taiwan's government, financial institutions, and critical systems. Some attacks aim to disrupt operations. Others seek to steal information or create a generalized sense of insecurity. Notable examples include the 2020 attacks on the largest gasoline supplier in Taiwan and the 2021 attacks that temporarily disrupted trading on Taiwan's financial exchanges.[45] China currently has no interest in sabotaging TSMC, since it relies on chips the company produces. However, if China reduces its dependence on Taiwanese semiconductors—or if U.S. actions cut off China's chip supplies—Beijing may feel emboldened to risk actions that could disrupt Taiwan's chip production.[46] No cyberattacks directly targeting TSMC have been publicly confirmed, but it is almost certain they have occurred.

To conclude this initial discussion, China's all-domain pressure campaign is an intricate, multifaceted strategy. It aims to exploit every possible pressure point on Taiwan and give Beijing flexible tools for calibrating coercion. By sustaining constant pressure across multiple domains, Beijing aims to keep Taiwan in a defensive and reactive position. The pressure campaign has not forced Taiwan to capitulate yet. Indeed, it has coincided with a sharp turn in Taiwanese public opinion against China. But the campaign is still in its early innings. For the United States, these gray-zone operations are constantly redefining the nebulous "status quo" in the region, changing facts on the ground while testing U.S. red lines.

Quarantine Scenarios

The most obvious pathway forward for China's gray-zone strategy is to gradually establish de facto control over Taiwan's ability to trade with the outside world. The quarantine or indirect control scenario has many possible variations, but its defining characteristic is that unlike the situation in a blockade, China would permit food and energy supplies to continue flowing freely, as long as certain criteria were met. The goal of a quarantine would not be to force Taiwan's immediate capitulation. Rather, China would be seeking *indirect* control. The goal would be to force Taiwan to accept the principle that it could no longer participate with full freedom in the global economy. A quarantine would probably seek to shut down the U.S. ability to transfer any more arms to Taiwan, but this would not need to happen right away.[47] The key would be to make the extent of Taiwan's economic autonomy—something that the Taiwan Relations Act explicitly commits the United States to protect—an object of gray-zone pressure.

Robert Blackwill and Philip Zelikow, who first posited this scenario in a 2021 report for the Council on Foreign Relations, characterize it this way:

> In a quarantine scenario, the Chinese government would effectively take control of the air and sea borders of Taiwan. It would declare control over Taiwan's airspace so that, in effect, Taipei's Taoyuan International Airport was no longer its own international gateway, and Kaohsiung was no longer its own international port. The Chinese government would run effectively a clearance operation offshore or in the air to screen incoming ships and aircraft. The screeners could then wave along what they regarded as innocent traffic. Or they could request that suspect ships or aircraft divert for full Chinese customs clearance at a neighboring airport on the mainland or in a neighboring port, such as Fuzhou or Guangzhou, or Xiamen or Shantou. . . . The Chinese government could run such a quarantine without actually trying to take effective control of the Taiwanese people themselves. In this scenario, the Chinese government would allow the people in Taiwan to run their own affairs on the island, at least for some time, as China showed that it controlled who came (and perhaps who went).[48]

In other words, "quarantine" actually describes several distinctive scenarios. In one variation, the PRC's customs authority ("China Customs") announces that henceforth *all goods and people entering and exiting* Taiwan must first clear customs on the mainland. Existing PRC law already establishes a plausible basis for this claim.[49] In another variation, Beijing applies the rules to goods and people entering, but not to those leaving. In a third variation, the rules apply only to specific categories of goods and people—for example, to people convicted of a crime in the PRC, or to shipments suspected of carrying "contraband" such as weapons or drugs. From a propaganda perspective, the third option is the most attractive.

Beijing may invent an excuse. For example, it could claim that it is cracking down on fentanyl precursors or even disrupting a Taiwanese plot to build weapons of mass destruction. For the reasons discussed above, private companies would likely comply with PRC legal mandates, however flimsy the justification. The more plausibly deniable Beijing's pretext, the harder it would be for the United States to mobilize itself and coordinate a response with allies.

Beijing could gradually escalate into a quarantine scenario without formally announcing new rules. It is already normalizing a constant military and coast guard presence around Taiwan. Future exercises and missile tests could last longer, for more variable lengths of time, and with less advance notice. An early step might involve requiring private operators entering or exiting "Taiwan province" to submit passenger and cargo manifests to China Customs.[50] Non-compliance could lead to selective interceptions, with vessels searched, delayed, or seized for carrying "contraband." Punishing only a few violators would likely ensure widespread compliance. Over time, Beijing could make key air and maritime spaces unsafe. This would force traffic into specific corridors near Taiwan's main ports, streamlining enforcement. By pressuring private companies to comply, China would effectively outsource enforcement to Taiwanese and foreign operators.

This option is appealing to China because it would shift the burden of resupplying Taiwan onto the United States. If Washington failed to respond decisively to a quarantine, Taiwan's economic autonomy would be effectively extinguished. China would achieve full indirect control over Taiwan's exchanges with the outside world, blocking it from acquiring new arms and materials, hindering its ability to produce weapons, and eventually taking control of its chip production ecosystem. Beijing could also extend its control to the flow of people, goods, and even data.

If the United States and its allies attempted to resupply Taiwan during such a crisis, the situation could unfold in two distinct ways. In the first scenario, Beijing might use lethal force against U.S. vessels. This would risk war and force the U.S. president to choose between escalation and capitulation. In the second scenario, China could avoid direct attacks while still applying pressure—publicly protesting U.S. violations of the customs rules while portraying itself as exercising restraint. This approach would rely on attrition, seeking to erode U.S. and Taiwanese resolve through logistical and psychological strain. Without firing a shot, China could endanger ships and aircraft approaching or leaving Taiwan by surrounding them and maneuvering dangerously close to them. Boarding and searching vessels, rather than outright blocking them, could still disrupt operations and amplify economic pressure. Drawing from historical examples and operational analysis, the following sections imagine what these scenarios would actually entail.

The Berlin Case

The history of the Soviet Union's failed blockade of Berlin in the early Cold War illustrates why a quarantine could be a dangerous gamble for China—especially if it were unwilling to fire on resupply vessels. After Hitler's defeat, Germany was divided into U.S., British, French, and Soviet occupation zones. Berlin, surrounded by the province of Brandenburg in East Germany, was also divided into four zones. The United States, Britain, and France agreed to unify their respective zones of Berlin to form a democratic, capitalist metropolis in the heart of Communist East Germany. By early 1948, Washington still officially sought eventual German reunification, but in practice it supported the status quo. West Berlin was now a de facto island that had to be sustained hundreds of miles inside East Germany. The East German government quite rightly saw West Berlin as a grave threat to its legitimacy.

The Berlin blockade came on gradually and then suddenly.[51] The Soviets first experimented with partial embargoes and harassment. When they met relatively soft resistance, they escalated. On March 25, 1948, they restricted all Western military and passenger traffic between the U.S., British, and French occupation zones and Berlin. In response, General Lucius Clay, the U.S. commander in Berlin, ordered a "little airlift" to resupply his sector. Soviet planes then began to harass Western planes arriving at Berlin airports. On April 5, this led to a collision with a British European Airways Vickers Viking 1B airliner, killing everyone on board both aircraft. The CIA warned President Truman that failing to resupply Berlin would "constitute a political defeat of the first magnitude."[52] Yet, there was little that Truman could do to push back. On June 21, the Soviets stopped a U.S. military supply train. On June 22, they conducted military exercises just outside Berlin. On June 24, they severed Berlin's land, rail, and water connections with the non-Soviet zones. The city had just thirty-six days' worth of food and forty-five days' worth of coal.

America's interest in Berlin had nothing to do with its military value. As Clay wrote in a cable on June 13: "There is no practicability in maintaining our position in Berlin and it must not be evaluated on that basis. . . .Whether for good or bad, it has become a symbol of the American intent."[53] The parallel is striking. One can imagine a U.S. general or admiral writing something similar about Taiwan if a crisis began today—except that, in the case of Taiwan, there is inherent military and substantive value.

A conventional war was not an option. The United States, Britain, and France collectively had fewer than 23,000 troops in Berlin, surrounded by 1.5 million Soviet troops. However, the United States was still the world's sole nuclear power, and it believed it could put this capability to use.[54] General Curtis LeMay, commander of United States Air Forces in Europe, advocated sending potentially nuclear-armed B-29 bombers with fighter escorts to circle Soviet air bases, while Western ground troops marched through East German territory to Berlin.

Truman chose a less confrontational option: coordinated resupply. This too came with risk of nuclear escalation. The Western allies began the airlift on June 24. By July 1, it had scaled up massively. Within six weeks, 1500 flights were delivering 4500 tons of cargo per day. By the peak in 1949, they were delivering nearly 13,000 tons of supplies daily. Moscow was taken by surprise, having assumed that the airlift was too ambitious to pull off. For the next fifteen months—from June 26, 1948, to September 30, 1949—the American and British air forces, with occasional help from Australia, Canada, New Zealand, and South Africa, made over 278,000 deliveries weighing 2.3 million tons to West Berlin. U.S. planes alone flew over 92 million miles. At the peak, flights were landing at Berlin's Tempelhof Airport every thirty seconds. The calculation was that if the Soviets shot the planes down, they would risk nuclear war.

As a result of the airlift, the Soviet blockade failed to achieve its strategic goal. Soviet aircraft harassed the Western planes on at least 733 occasions, using flak, air-to-air fire, rockets, and bombs. However, Moscow was clearly unwilling to shoot the planes down, which revealed that it feared nuclear escalation. As the airlift continued into its second year, the Allied forces signaled their ability and resolve to resupply Berlin indefinitely. Meanwhile, the political optics were a disaster for the East German government. Crowds of Berliners gathered to watch the relentless stream of American C-54 planes landing at Berlin's Tempelhof Airport and the men unloading them with practiced gestures, like a finely engineered watch. Moscow lifted the blockade on May 12, 1949.

The Berlin issue reemerged under Eisenhower and Kennedy when an overconfident Nikita Khrushchev tried again to compel a change to the status quo.[55] By the late 1950s, the Soviets had acquired both nuclear weapons and the ballistic missiles able to deliver them to targets in the United States. Khrushchev thought this gave him leverage, and he demanded Western withdrawal from Berlin. Eisenhower refused. Khrushchev lifted the ultimatum in exchange for a summit with Eisenhower, but the summit never took place. In June 1961, Khrushchev renewed the ultimatum to the new U.S. president, Kennedy, who responded by sending troops to Berlin. Since NATO still couldn't defend the city with conventional forces, Moscow tested him with salami-slicing tactics. In August 1961, East German authorities built a wall in Berlin, formalizing the division of the city. Kennedy sent Vice President Lyndon Johnson and Gen. Clay to Berlin, signaling that war was still on the table if the Soviets tried another blockade. In October 1961, at Checkpoint Charlie, the two sides again found themselves on the precipice of conflict. They deescalated by pulling back from the line of control five meters at a time. For reasons that are still not quite clear, Khrushchev remained persuaded that Kennedy could be stared down, and he resolved to press him further.

In August 1962, Khrushchev decided to force a crisis and regain his credibility. "It's been a long time since you could spank us like a little boy," he warned on September 6. "Now we can swat your ass. . . . We have the advantage. If you want to do anything, *you* have to start a war."[56] In a private letter to Kennedy dated September 28, Khrushchev affirmed that after the U.S. elections he planned to "eliminate this dangerous hot-bed which spoils our relations all the time."[57] Soviet Foreign Minister Andrei Gromyko again told Kennedy on October 18 that unless NATO troops were removed from Berlin, the Soviet Union would sign a defense treaty with East Germany legally binding it to liquidate any Western forces stationed in the country. Berlin was a "rotten tooth which must be pulled out," Gromyko said.[58]

Again, however, the Soviets failed to enforce a change to the status quo by pushing the burden of escalation onto the Americans. In 1948–49, Washington had shown credibly that it was committed to resupplying Berlin at all costs. As recently as October 1961, Kennedy had reaffirmed the U.S. resolve. When Moscow tried yet again to compel a change in the status quo, it did not have credibility. Years of past action and inaction had revealed that it was unwilling to accept a nuclear exchange as the price of taking Berlin.

To show Kennedy that he was serious, Khrushchev broadened the conflict by deploying nuclear-capable missiles in Cuba. However, Kennedy called this bluff too on October 22, 1962, issuing an ultimatum on national television that the missiles be removed. After days of nail-biting brinkmanship, known as the Cuban Missile Crisis, Khrushchev ultimately pulled back.

The United States achieved its objectives—but only through an enormously ambitious resupply operation and a crisis that brought the world to the brink of nuclear Armageddon.

Imagining a Taiwan Resupply Operation

Resupplying Taiwan with an airlift would be vastly more expensive and operationally challenging than resupplying Berlin.[59] The Berlin airlift cost $224 million over fifteen months, equivalent to roughly $2.76 billion in 2023 dollars.[60] No good cost estimates exist for a resupply of Taiwan, but the daily cost would likely be at least two orders of magnitude higher. West Berlin's population in 1948 was 2.5 million, roughly one-tenth of Taiwan's population today. The distances involved were also much shorter, and Taiwan today is a vastly larger and more energy-intensive economy than Berlin in 1948. The United

States still has the world's largest and most effective *air* logistics system.[61] But air logistics cannot substitute for maritime logistics. Not all airfields can support heavy-lift aircraft. Air cargo has natural capacity limits and is much less cost-effective than maritime logistics. Even the largest U.S. airlifter carries less cargo than the smallest U.S. Navy fast transport (see Figure 2.1).

In resupplying Taiwan through a quarantine, Washington would need to bear in mind the risk that Beijing could lose patience and escalate to direct force at any time. Tanker aircraft are large and can be vulnerable targets if they operate within range of enemy missiles.[62] All airfields within the First Island Chain are also vulnerable to PLA precision strikes. It would therefore be imprudent to expose too many U.S. aircraft at once to the risk of a large, coordinated strike.

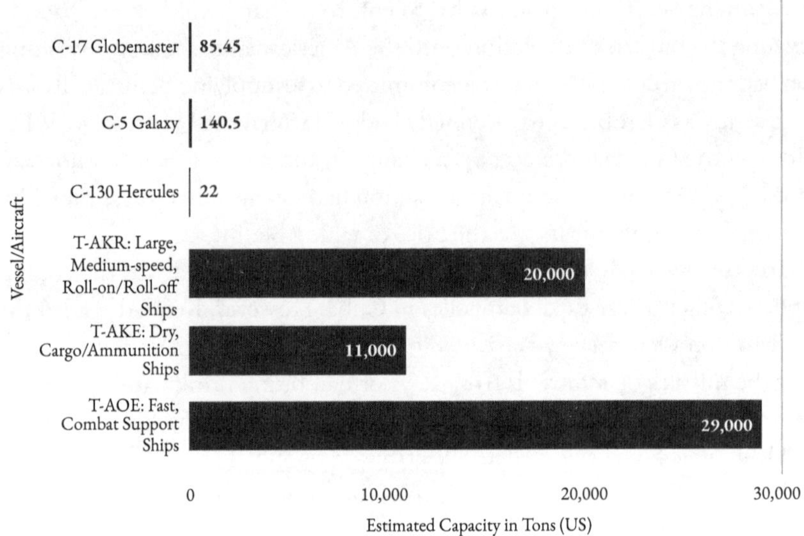

Figure 2.1   Estimated capacity of major U.S. sea/airlifts

Source: Data found at this spreadsheet: *Google Spreadsheet*. "Dataset on Aircraft Fuel Capacity." Accessed January 16, 2025. https://docs.google.com/spreadsheets/d/1-FhnLswJ-52VpRodG-suoEiAo1jqX5RwAeTDuWahZJc/edit?gid=0#gid=0, underlying data found at: *U.S. Air Force*, "Aircraft Fact Sheets," https://www.af.mil/About-Us/Fact-Sheets/Aircraft-Factsheets; *U.S. Navy*, "Fact Files," https://www.navy.mil/resources/fact-files. Estimated capacity in tons assumes that oil is stored at the typical density of around 0.85 kg/l. Thus, it is around 0.135 metric tons per barrel, or 0.145 U.S. tons per barrel; *Chevron Marine Products*, "Conversion Charts," https://www.chevronmarineproducts.com/content/dam/chevron-marine/fuels-conversion-chart/Fuels%20Conversion%20Charts.pdf.

For the reasons we have explored above, privately owned merchant ships would be of little help, as few shipping companies would be willing to sacrifice their business interests in China to support Taiwan. Additionally, the standard "Five Powers Clause" in commercial war-risk insurance policies effectively terminates coverage in any conflict involving the United States or China. To compensate, a government—likely the United States—would need to step in and provide war-risk insurance. However, no such U.S. program currently exists with funding or plans for immediate implementation. The U.S. Maritime Administration (MARAD) claims it could establish such a program quickly, but it would face significant administrative challenges in suddenly becoming one of the world's largest maritime insurers.[63]

Could the U.S. government resupply Taiwan without support from private carriers? It would not be easy. MARAD manages a fleet of inactive, government-owned cargo ships, tankers, and other vessels that can be activated during national emergencies.[64] This includes the Ready Reserve Force (RRF), which is maintained in a higher state of readiness and can typically be activated and deployed within a few days.[65] The RRF primarily includes roll-on/roll-off ships, heavy-lift ships, and other specialized vessels that are crucial for transporting military equipment, supplies, and personnel. However, the average age of RRF ships is over forty years old. Maintenance costs are high and equipment is not fully reliable.[66] Many of these ships may not meet activation deadlines, both because of poor maintenance and because there is no ready supply of mariners to crew them.[67]

The U.S. Merchant Marine would be critical for many Taiwan crisis scenarios, including quarantine.[68] The Merchant Marine is a fleet of privately owned U.S.-flagged commercial vessels crewed by civilian mariners.[69] It operates as a public–private partnership, with government agencies like MARAD providing support, regulation, and financial incentives to sustain the industry. The domestic fleet focuses on moving goods between U.S. ports. The international fleet is small and almost entirely dependent on government contracts.[70] Notably, the U.S. Merchant Marine fleet no longer includes vessels capable of transporting passengers.[71]

Unfortunately, the decline of the U.S. maritime industry has undermined U.S. readiness for any quarantine, blockade, or invasion contingency.[72] In World War II, the United States had over 6,000 merchant ships to supply Allied forces. Today, fewer than 200 U.S.-flagged oceangoing commercial vessels remain—as PRC analysts well know.[73] The entire U.S. maritime industry also faces a human capital crisis. The average age of U.S. merchant mariners is in the mid-fifties and rising.[74] In a protracted blockade scenario or conflict with China, even if additional vessels were available, the United States may struggle to crew them. U.S. firms have long since stopped competing in other key parts of the global maritime ecosystem, while China dominates port management software, gantry crane production, and other key systems essential for commercial maritime operations. Among Beijing's other advantages, its unparalleled insight into global supply chains allows it to pinpoint potential U.S. and allied vulnerabilities.[75] Rebuilding the U.S. maritime enterprise is a multi-decade project.

Given the massive volume of peacetime seaborne trade in the Western Pacific, it is not viable for the United States to fully replace merchant sealift in a crisis. Any operation to resupply Taiwan would be minimally focused on food and the bare minimum of energy to keep the island alive and resupply its armed forces. All countries in the region that depend on maritime trade—particularly Taiwan—should heed the warning. They should massively expand their stockpiles of food, fuel, and other key items like medical supplies, commodities, and machine parts. Regional allies with more robust merchant marine fleets, such as Japan and South Korea, may be called upon to step up in a crisis. However, under the circumstances, they may need to prioritize resupplying their domestic populations. This is why joint logistics planning is essential.

Evaluating the Quarantine Scenario

We've looked at how a blockade could work to China's advantage, but the quarantine option also poses significant risks for China. Taiwan's political resilience under blockade conditions is uncertain. Immediate capitulation is possible, but so is stiff resistance—as we saw in Ukraine after Putin's full-scale invasion. A quarantine could also backfire politically against Beijing. If CCG or PLA ships entered Taiwan's territorial waters or sought to board Taiwanese vessels anywhere, Taiwanese captains could respond in accordance with their standard rules of engagement. This could result in fatal collisions or violent confrontations. Beijing might therefore lose control over the nature and timing of crisis escalation. Meanwhile, regional allies, led by the United States, might mobilize in Taiwan's defense. This would raise the risk of escalation to broader war. If a quarantine results in a disruption of Taiwan's semiconductor exports, whether by accident or intentional actions by any of the relevant governments, a global financial shock could follow. This would undermine China's argument that Taiwan is purely a domestic issue.

The United States would have a legal basis for escalating politically and militarily if China tries to seize indirect control over Taiwan. The Taiwan Relations Act states that "the United States shall maintain the capacity to resist any resort to force or other forms of coercion that would jeopardize the security, or the social or economic system, of the people of Taiwan."[76] A quarantine would clearly fall into the category of "other forms of coercion." The TRA also states that "blockades and embargoes" would count as "grave" threats to U.S. interests. While "quarantine" is a convenient term for distinguishing the scenario where China masks a partial blockade as a law enforcement exercise, there would be an extremely strong argument that China had crossed U.S. red lines under the TRA. This would legally require a decisive U.S. response.

Washington could pursue several avenues of response that would together make a future conflict harder for China to win. If private insurers refused to cover shipping to Taiwan, the U.S. president could order the Merchant Marine to resupply the island, and Congress could authorize government-backed insurance for private carriers.[77] Resupplying Taiwan's outlying islands could prove challenging, but the United States could focus on sustaining the main island. If China refrained from attacking U.S. vessels, a partial resupply operation could potentially continue for months or years, buying time for Taiwan to accelerate preparations for potential escalation. Meanwhile, the United States and allied countries could begin a crash mobilization to prepare for a possible general war with China.

The United States would also take the opportunity to mobilize its core coalition. Key U.S. allies such as Japan, Australia, and the Philippines are currently ambiguous on how they would respond to a quarantine.[78] In a crisis, they would quickly have to make decisions that would reveal their level of resolve. Of course, this risk cuts both ways. If these countries' signals of commitment fell short of expectations, U.S. credibility would suffer and Beijing could gain an advantage. However, neither side can be entirely sure of how decisively the U.S. allies would respond. Beijing must plan for the worst-case scenario in which the U.S.-led coalition rapidly pulls together.

During the first days and weeks of a quarantine, the emerging allied coalition would likely signal its resolve. For example, it could send high-profile delegations to Taiwan, ignore the quarantine to airlift in advanced weapons and military advisors, or even issue joint political statements threatening to declare

Taiwan's independence.[79] It is impossible to know which of these measures Washington and its allies would take—if any. Yet, Beijing cannot discount the possibility that U.S. actions would force it to choose between a war and an unfavorable change in the status quo. China therefore should not attempt a quarantine unless it is fully prepared for both these possibilities. We will return to this issue in Chapter 4 when we discuss political deterrence.

The United States and its partners could also retaliate economically against China. This retaliation could include targeted sanctions against PLA-linked organizations and key individuals (which would likely have little immediate effect on China's warmaking capabilities). It could also include broader sanctions, asset seizures, tariffs, and more. It is uncertain how much economic pain the American people would be willing to accept in responding to a quarantine of Taiwan. The answer would depend largely on the politics of the moment. At minimum, the United States and allied nations would probably accelerate efforts to break economic dependence on China. We will return to these issues in Chapters 7 and 8.

In sum, the quarantine or indirect control scenario is fraught with analytical uncertainty. China faces significant risks, but Taiwan would be harder to resupply than Berlin. The United States may lack the resolve and preparation to prevail in a protracted crisis. Xi might also calculate that salami-slicing its way to a quarantine over several years could achieve his goals without triggering a sudden rupture. The United States needs to prepare for these possibilities. The Defense Department should develop capabilities for naval convoys and airlifts to resupply Taiwan with critical imports, coordinating with Japan and other regional partners. Congress should craft an economic contingency plan that would be appropriate to trigger in a scenario in which China begins without using lethal force. Maintaining a robust Merchant Marine fleet is also essential, even as Taiwan grows its stockpiles. Resolving these logistical vulnerabilities must be a top priority.

Coercive Mobilization

In March and April 2021, up to 100,000 Russian military personnel and large quantities of military equipment began to mass along the Ukrainian border. Russian Defense Minister Sergei Shoigu claimed that Russia's mobilization was a "response to threatening activities" by NATO.[80] However, this excuse strained credibility. NATO's exercise was long-planned, and Moscow was obviously not engaged in standard deterrence behavior.[81] Satellite imagery showed movements of Russian armor, missiles, and heavy weaponry, including some transported all the way from Siberia.[82] Russia took other unusual steps, including moving ships between the Caspian Sea and Black Sea and firing mortars at Ukrainian positions in the Donbas. On the night of April 14, a naval confrontation took place in the Sea of Azov between Ukrainian artillery boats and Russian coast guard vessels.[83] Thereafter, Russia closed parts of the Black Sea to foreign vessels. Russia withdrew some of the troops in June but left infrastructure for a potential invasion in place.[84]

Thus, even months before Russia finally launched its frontal invasion of Ukraine, U.S. intelligence suspected that a major operation was coming. In July, Putin published an essay, "On the Historical Unity of Russians and Ukrainians," in which he claimed that Russians and Ukrainians were "one people."[85] Putin had made similar statements before, but "his rhetoric began to change quite markedly in public," U.S. National Security Advisor Jake Sullivan later recalled. "At that point, our antennae went up higher. Something was shifting in his mindset." By September, Russia was planning a new exercise, called *Zapad*, and the U.S. military knew something was wrong. "They came to me with this map, and laid it out on my table," Chairman of the Joint Chiefs of Staff Mark Milley recalled. "They explained, 'this was different, sir, this looks different, this is bigger in size and scale and scope, the disposition, composition of the force, etc.' We talked for maybe an hour. I gave them a bunch of questions. Next day, they come back [sic]. They drilled down in a lot of detail."[86] By the time Russia began its second buildup in October, with more soldiers on more fronts, the Biden administration was very confident that Putin was planning a major operation.

While every war is different, the point of this anecdote is that countries generally cannot mobilize for war in secret. Mobilization involves moving hundreds of thousands of people and millions of tons of equipment and supplies. It also involves difficult political work to prepare the population and state institutions for the strains of wartime. In the modern era, it is almost impossible for any state to hide these activities from its adversaries. Popular narratives of history tend to forget this point. Even Japan's attack on Pearl Harbor in 1941, which came as an *operational* surprise to U.S. forces in Hawaii, was not a *strategic* surprise. The Roosevelt administration was aware that Japan was likely to strike first, but it suspected that it would begin by attacking the

Philippines or Guam, rather than attacking all U.S. forces in the Pacific in a single coordinated strike.[87] As Secretary of War Henry Stimson wrote in his diary on November 25—twelve days before Pearl Harbor—FDR expected "that we were likely to be attacked perhaps next Monday [December 1], for the Japanese are notorious for making an attack without warning." According to Stimson, FDR believed that "the question was how we should maneuver them into the position of firing the first shot without allowing too much danger to ourselves."[88]

Far from falling out of the blue, the outbreaks of great power wars typically mark the culmination of prolonged *political* processes in which both sides try to prepare themselves while projecting strength, probing each other for weaknesses, and exploring the possibility of a negotiated off-ramp. For example, before Pearl Harbor the United States had imposed an escalating trade embargo to pressure imperial Japan to end its war in China. In 1940, President Roosevelt ordered the Pacific fleet to deploy to Pearl Harbor to strengthen deterrence against Japan. Congress hiked naval spending by 70 percent. In July 1941, five months before Pearl Harbor, FDR froze Japanese assets in the United States. In August, he embargoed exports of gasoline to Japan, cutting off 80 percent of Japan's oil supply.[89] Negotiations continued through the day of the Pearl Harbor attack. U.S. strategists miscalculated, but they knew the risks.[90]

While China could not invade Taiwan out of the blue, it could absolutely mobilize for war as a form of political coercion. Along the way, several key early warning signals would flash red. Beijing could take some preparatory actions in secret, some in ways that only military professionals would truly understand, and others ostentatiously for signaling purposes. PLA preparations for a full-scale invasion might be visible in open sources at least three months before maximum readiness was achieved. China would also likely send signals through private channels to communicate its resolve. However, it would not be clear at first whether these were preparations for war or were simply exercises with a coercive intent. Just as Russia initially did in Ukraine, Beijing may partially or completely mobilize under the guise of routine exercises to test its adversaries' resolve and pressure Taiwan toward negotiations. To understand the deterrence challenge Washington faces in the gray zone, it is therefore essential to understand what the pathway to war might look like. The following sections discuss the key early warning indicators and the choices Washington would face as tensions grew.

Early Warning Indicators

Preparing for an amphibious invasion of Taiwan would require the PLA to concentrate a range of assets within the Eastern Theater Command (ETC), the military jurisdiction that includes the East China Sea and the Strait of Taiwan.[91] Most PLA missiles are mobile and could be repositioned under the guise of standard military exercises, but their movement might also be revealed intentionally for political signaling. The PLA would need to bolster air defenses around key ETC installations. Beijing could deny the intentions behind a gradual buildup, but a large-scale effort would eventually become undeniable. Amphibious and airborne units, as well as numerous aircraft, would need to converge in the ETC, since a Taiwan invasion would require nearly all of the PLA's amphibious and airborne capacity.[92] Additionally, China's civilian roll-on/roll-off (RO/RO) mega-ferries, mostly stationed in northern China, would need to move south toward the Taiwan Strait. These movements would be detectable via commercial satellite imagery.[93] A clear signal would be the repositioning of refueler aircraft (Y-20Us), which would need to operate out of specific coastal air bases. In response, Washington would probably reposition some of its own forces within the First and Second Island Chains.

Meanwhile, the PLAN, China's Navy, would deploy surface combatants and carriers in the waters around Taiwan. The PLAN would want both of its aircraft carriers and their battle groups deployed east of Taiwan, to conduct anti-submarine reconnaissance and potentially strike U.S. submarines as they approached the narrow corridors connecting the East China Sea to the wider waters of the Pacific. The Type-055 cruisers that the PLAN deployed east of Taiwan in the August 2022 crisis are not enough for this purpose. These operations would also be visible from open-source satellite imagery. Washington would respond by convoying merchant vessels to Taiwan and shadowing these ships. Japan might also respond by deploying naval power to the Ryukyu Islands north of Taiwan.

As these surface vessels mobilized, conventional and nuclear-armed submarines would leave their bases for war patrols. PLAN nuclear-armed submarines might try to break out into the Pacific to get into missile range of the U.S. homeland. The submarines that carry China's nuclear second-strike, armed with longer-range submarine-launched missiles, would deploy to secure bastions in the Bohai and South China Seas (see Figure 2.2).[94] In response, the United States, Taiwan, and Japan might set up an anti-submarine cordon

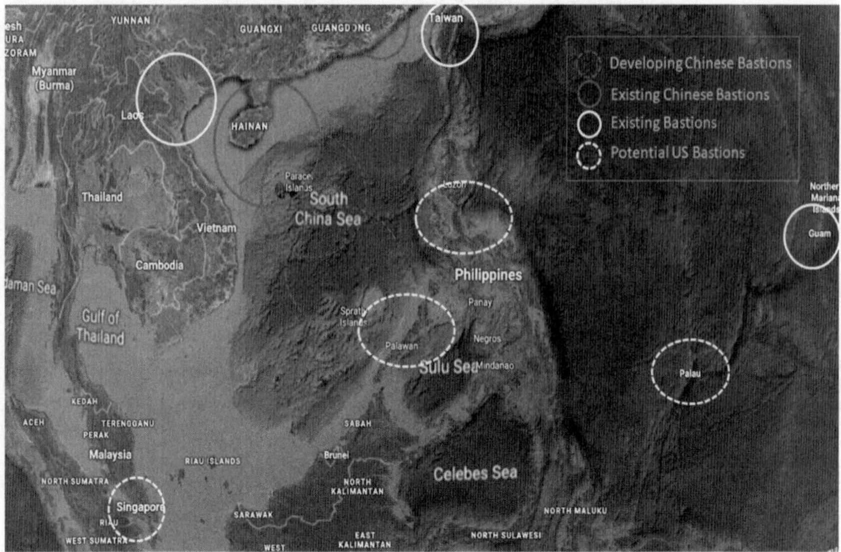

Figure 2.2 Potential U.S. and PLA submarine bastions around Taiwan

Source: Adapted from James Lacey, "Battle of the Bastions," *War on the Rocks*, January 9, 2020, https://warontherocks.com/2020/01/battle-of-the-bastions/. Image credit: Allison Lacey.

along the First Island Chain. Washington might surge submarines to the South China and Bohai Seas to threaten the bastions where the PRC keeps its nuclear second-strike. If China's nuclear second-strike were to be put at risk, Beijing would be at a severe disadvantage if a conflict escalated. PLAN warships would have to secure the bastions in advance of submarine deployment. They could not do this stealthily. Then, the submarines themselves would probably leave port for war patrols weeks before a crisis began.

The PLA could also target Taiwan's outlying islands, including Kinmen, Matsu, and the Penghu archipelago, which were key flashpoints in previous Taiwan Straits crises. They are tempting targets because they are largely indefensible—China could seize them within the first day or two of a full-scale war. The United States would probably offer no direct resistance.[95] However, seizing these islands outright could gravely harm Beijing's chances of getting the main prize. A move against the outlying islands would give Washington a pretext to modify or abandon the One China Policy and bolster military ties with Taiwan.

Another indicator of an impending crisis would be China's accelerated stockpiling of oil, food, chips, and blood. Blood is one of the most important resources during large-scale armed conflict. Rapid transfusions keep wounded soldiers alive. In the high-casualty combat that China would have to be prepared to face during an amphibious assault, blood would be crucial. Major national blood drives would be required to increase China's blood supply. These drives, too, probably cannot be conducted stealthily—though the PLA might be able to rely to some degree on synthetic plasma.

China's large state-owned shipyards would likely expand and harden repair facilities in anticipation of conflict. While these dockyards significantly outpace Western capacity, a war would strain their resources. Many would remain vulnerable to U.S. missile strikes. To address this issue, China could accelerate the construction of berths, drydocks, and other facilities, while hardening commercial port infrastructure. Dozens of major and medium-sized airports near the Taiwan Strait could serve as staging points for invasion aircraft, but the PLA would need fallback options in case U.S. forces attacked them. Civilian ports that might stage troops for an amphibious assault would require significant upgrades. Additionally, the PLA would need to establish fortified supply depots along key rail and road lines across coastal regions. Efforts to conceal these preparations would extend the mobilization timeline. Images of these construction progress would be reported day to day on Western social media.

Put simply, the world would know that China was preparing something big. In addition to commercial satellite data and other open sources, Western intelligence agencies might choose to declassify some information, as the U.S. and UK governments did to great effect before Putin's full-scale invasion of Ukraine. (Some U.S. and allied preparations would be similarly visible.) Financial markets would also take notice. When Beijing began to de-clutter the air and sea space around Taiwan—a prerequisite for an effective invasion or blockade, since civilian ships could disrupt operational patterns, clutter radars, and ferry weapons to Taiwan—Beijing's offensive motivations would become undeniable. Supply chains would be immediately disrupted. Markets would crash.

Politics on the Road to War

Beijing would also need to prepare politically, both internally and externally. At home, the CCP's propaganda machinery would need to lay the groundwork for public support for what could potentially be a long and costly conflict.

At a minimum, Beijing would need to manufacture a credible justification for the use of force, just as Deng Xiaoping needed to fabricate an excuse for China's 1979 invasion of Vietnam.[96] China would frame U.S. and allied activity as illegal and illegitimate and seek political statements of support from its partners, particularly in the developing world. China would also probably seek to resolve, freeze, or deescalate disputes with other countries, particularly India, to reduce the risk of unwanted multi-front escalation. China might also strike deals with Russia and Central Asian republics such as Kazakhstan and Turkmenistan to increase supplies of overland oil, gas, and minerals. It would likely seek to improve relations with both North and South Korea.

For all these reasons, Beijing is therefore much more likely to mobilize ostentatiously as a form of political and psychological coercion than to try to mobilize in secret. China could mobilize and demobilize multiple times. Or it could stay mobilized for an extended period before attacking. It could synchronize mobilization with an accelerating tempo of exercises and gray-zone activities in the Taiwan Strait to confuse its adversaries about whether it planned to attack, to impose a blockade, or just to posture. Once it was fully mobilized, it could choose the time and character of the first strike. China could also use psychological and political warfare to throw the United States and its allies off balance. The PLA Information Support Force could conduct coordinated cyberattacks.[97] Beijing might use ICBM and nuclear tests as signaling mechanisms, as it did during the Third Taiwan Straits crisis in 1996.[98]

History also shows that as crises mount, states often escalate with the ultimate goal of deescalating. Leaders use public statements and ultimatums to "tie their own hands," putting themselves in situations where it would be reputationally costly to back down.[99] Sometimes—for example, in the case of the Austrian démarche to Serbia in July 1914—these statements are simply excuses for a premeditated attack.[100] At other times, states are trying to signal resolve or to preserve their freedom of action, and the push toward conflict is unintentional.[101] For example, Tsar Nicholas II decided to mobilize Russian forces on July 30, 1914, because he knew that Russia's vast size and low level of development meant that mobilization would take longer than it would for rival states.[102] Other European states, fearing that they would fall behind in their own mobilizations, rapidly followed. Nicholas's precautionary action therefore accelerated the process that led to the outbreak of conflict.[103] In a U.S.-China political crisis that teetered on the edge of conflict, miscalculations could tip a volatile situation into a conflict that neither side wanted.[104]

To deal with these risks while strengthening deterrence, U.S. planners must think systematically about roads to war. They should consider articulating in advance what they would or might do to strengthen deterrence at each stage of an escalating crisis.

Neither the United States and its allies nor other adversaries would remain passive as China mobilized for an invasion. Some nations might call for dialogue and deescalation. Others—especially Russia, Iran, and North Korea—could exploit U.S. distraction by pressuring their neighbors, potentially triggering simultaneous crises on the Korean Peninsula, in the Middle East, and along NATO's eastern border. Countries fearing U.S. abandonment in a broader conflict might issue their own deterrent threats, including hints at pursuing weapons of mass destruction.[105] Meanwhile, the United States and its allies would scramble to improve readiness and strengthen deterrence. Though ramping up production of advanced armaments would be impossible on short notice, Washington might redeploy forces to the Western Pacific. Political threats, ultimatums, and high-profile visits to Taiwan by prominent U.S. and Japanese figures would likely follow. Pressure would mount to reconsider the One China Policy. Allies and partners worldwide would face pressure to take a stand.

The final weeks before a potential invasion would be critical for pursuing off-ramps while preparing for the possibility that no diplomatic solution could be reached.[106] To maintain deterrence in the gray zone, it is essential to anticipate and plan for these scenarios. A key consideration would be Washington's responsibility to protect U.S. citizens on Taiwan.

The Problem with Evacuating Civilians

The presence of foreign civilians on Taiwan is a key reason why China is unlikely to attack without warning. As of April 2023, there were over 800,000 foreign residents in Taiwan, representing 164 countries, plus an unknown number of PRC citizens.[107] Over 700,000 of the foreigners come from Southeast Asia, but substantial numbers of Japanese (16,000), American (11,000), South Korean (5,000), Indian (5,000), British (3,000), Canadian (3,000), French (2,000), Singaporean (2,000), and German (1,000) citizens are also on the island.[108] If PLA strikes killed or injured large numbers of these civilians or made it impossible for them to be safely evacuated, Beijing would risk all these U.S. allies and partners entering the war against it. For this reason,

Beijing would probably prefer to frighten foreign countries into evacuating their people from Taiwan *before* it made a military move.

A noncombatant evacuation operation (NEO) to remove foreign nationals from Taiwan would be an enormous undertaking. In 2023, the House Armed Forces Committee asked the Pentagon to draw up plans for a potential Taiwan NEO. This suggests that no such plan existed at that time.[109] None of the other countries listed above, including Japan, currently has anything approaching the resources and doctrine to withdraw its own nationals quickly. The United States and its allies do not have a joint doctrine for NEOs.[110]

Any NEO would be a chaotic mess and would play out in full view of the cameras. The U.S. airlift out of Saigon between April 5 and 29, 1975, carried just 45,000 people, including 5,600 U.S. citizens. Thousands of refugees and many U.S. citizens were left behind when the last C-130s departed, including the U.S. ambassador and his staff. An additional 7,800 people had to be evacuated by helicopter on April 29 and 30.[111] As Afghanistan fell to the Taliban in August 2021, just over 122,000 people escaped in the frenzied sixteen-day airlift.[112]

The Kabul evacuation was a political catastrophe for President Biden, whose approval rating never recovered. It was a catastrophe despite the fact that U.S. forces already had a large combat presence in and around Kabul. "I think there may be a misperception that what we saw in Afghanistan is something that the U.S. government can undertake anywhere and everywhere in the world," Ned Price, the State Department spokesman, said. No American "should expect that we may be in a position to undertake something similar to what we saw in Afghanistan."[113] Amidst the chaos, the government in Taipei might collapse, just as South Vietnamese and Afghan governments collapsed during evacuations. Thousands of refugees from Taiwan might also set out by boat for the Japanese Ryukyu Islands, overwhelming local communities.[114]

As tensions rose, the U.S. president would therefore face a difficult decision about whether and when to initiate an NEO. Ensuring the safety of American citizens abroad is a fundamental obligation of the U.S. government, particularly when host nations are unable or unwilling to protect them. Reducing the number of Americans in harm's way decreases their vulnerability to physical harm or hostage-taking. But this must be balanced against the destabilizing effect that a decision to evacuate could have on a crisis. Announcing an evacuation signals an imminent conflict and a loss of control. Beijing could interpret an evacuation as a sign of U.S. hesitancy, encouraging further escalation under the belief that Washington was backing away from confrontation rather than reinforcing deterrence. This dilemma illustrates why NEOs are so difficult to execute effectively.[115] Leaving civilians in place can, paradoxically, serve as a form of deterrence.[116] However, U.S. elected officials have moral responsibilities that need to be taken into account.

It may seem prudent to encourage U.S. citizens to leave Taiwan voluntarily while a conflict still appears weeks or months away, as the Biden administration did before Russia's invasion of Ukraine. On February 11, 2022, eleven days before the attack, President Biden urged Americans to evacuate during an NBC News interview with Lester Holt. "American citizens should leave now," Biden stated. When asked if U.S. forces would conduct a rescue mission in the event of an invasion, Biden replied, "There's not [one]. That's a world war— when Americans and Russians start shooting at one another, we're in a very different world than we've ever been in."[117]

But Washington cannot simply replicate the Ukraine playbook for Taiwan. Unlike Ukraine, where millions fled overland to neighboring countries, Taiwan's island geography makes air evacuation the only viable option for evacuating large numbers of people quickly. Hundreds of thousands—if not millions—of Taiwanese nationals might attempt to flee with their families before hostilities begin, competing with foreigners for a limited number of seats on outbound flights. Ticket prices would skyrocket, and it is unclear how Taiwanese authorities would respond. Even if flights to China were suspended and commercial carriers operated normally—two significant assumptions—it would still take at least a week to evacuate all foreign nationals and probably over a month. Taiwan might declare martial law, banning men of fighting age from leaving, as Ukraine did in 2022. Furthermore, if Taiwan's leaders interpreted the NEO as U.S. capitulation, they would have little incentive to facilitate a smooth evacuation.

The Decision to Break the Glass

In scenarios of gradually increasing pressure, a moment eventually comes when the United States must choose: take actions to secure U.S. interests at the price of triggering regional or even global chaos, or back down. This is why escalating gray-zone pressure is an effective strategy for China. A quarantine, a gradual ramping up of military exercises, and mobilization for amphibious invasion are all ways of pushing the burden of escalation onto the United States. If Washington were to fail to respond effectively to gray-zone pressure, China would succeed in shifting the so-called status quo in its favor, eroding the U.S. ability to defend its interests until the U.S. position in the region became untenable. At some point, the United States would have to make a decision about whether to break the proverbial glass and move decisively to evacuate its civilians and prepare a robust defense or resupply of Taiwan.

The nature of the crisis that forces this choice will shape the domestic response in the United States. Powerful interest groups, including businesses, labor unions, and consumer advocates, may resist escalation due to concerns over economic fallout. Even in the face of blatant PRC aggression, such as an unprovoked attack that results in American casualties, some may quietly argue against actions that disrupt U.S.–China economic ties.

The decision to break the glass is theoretically in the hands of the president alone, but practically it is shared between the president and Congress. Because the decision to accept the costs of a rupture with China is so momentous, economic and political deterrence are fundamentally interconnected. Washington must recognize that defending U.S. interests in gray-zone crisis scenarios could require taking steps that would make it seem to the world that war could be imminent. If the United States lacks credible contingency plans to handle the domestic political and economic response to a crisis, its broader deterrent threats will lack credibility. In such a moment, to put it plainly, China's economic deterrent against the United States could prove more effective than the U.S. economic deterrent against China.

If the United States fails to provide clear guidance to the market about how it is approaching its decision about whether or when to break the glass, financial markets might have a say as to when and how the decisive moment comes. U.S. lawmakers have warned that if U.S.–China relations break down, sweeping sanctions might be the first response.[118] Any Taiwan crisis, even without war, would also cause major disruptions to supply chains. Shipping in East Asia, where nearly half the world's container ships pass through the Taiwan Strait, would be heavily affected. Insurance costs for merchant vessels would skyrocket, and $3 trillion in trade flows could face immediate risk.[119]

Financial markets and businesses do not want to be caught unprepared if a U.S.–China war breaks out, so they might start pricing in the risk before shots are fired. First, investors could try to liquidate assets in China and Taiwan and withdraw their capital to safer countries. Beijing would probably ban or restrict foreign investors from selling assets in China or withdrawing funds. It might also accelerate its ongoing process of liquidating assets in the United States and moving capital to countries that are less likely to freeze them.[120] (This could also be an early warning indicator.) These moves would rattle markets further by indicating that Beijing planned to escalate. Shipping prices could soar, and panic-buying of scarce commodities could begin. Investors would dump risky assets, putting pressure on banks and other systemically important financial institutions. Questions would arise about how the United States might respond if a crisis escalated, including whether strikes on targets inside mainland China would be on the table. Financial markets would focus on predicting and correctly pricing the U.S. response, particularly U.S. economic action and possible PRC retaliation. At any point, the merest hint that Taiwan's semiconductor production could be disrupted would send markets into a tailspin. Technology stocks like NVIDIA and Apple would be among the hardest hit.

Since markets would largely be following the U.S. government's lead, federal government agencies would need to tightly coordinate their communications. In normal circumstances, officials like the U.S. secretary of the treasury give interviews to reassure markets that the U.S. government will preserve financial stability. In a brinkmanship crisis over Taiwan, however, Beijing may read such statements as a sign that Washington lacks resolve—particularly if U.S. economic deterrence before the crises was based on threats of mutual economic devastation.

Washington's strategy for the gray zone cannot simply be to wait for the PLA to fire the first shot before taking action. It must have a plan for what to tell financial markets and business to shape perceptions and communicate resolve *over time* through an evolving crisis. Financial markets are highly sophisticated readers of public officials. They react to news at lightning speed. If the U.S. government is caught unprepared for a financial shock in the gray zone and markets discern that Washington has no plan, they may start to move in ways that Washington will struggle to control. Policymakers and the public must therefore understand that the United States and its allies have an economic plan for the "break-glass scenario," even if not all the details are public.

The analogy to fire safety is helpful. Fire alarms and fire extinguishers are typically placed behind glass. Everyone knows they are there, but we rarely think of them. People don't usually pull the alarm and take away the fire extinguisher when there *isn't* a fire, because breaking glass is dangerous and unpleasant. But if there actually is a fire, it is likely that someone will break the glass. That means when we hear a fire alarm ringing or see someone break the glass to grab the fire extinguisher, we all know to get out of the building as soon as possible, even if it is inconvenient, and wait for the firefighters to arrive. Breaking the glass in the U.S.–China relationship is not a decision that would be taken lightly. Still, if the moment comes, Washington must be prepared, since it would be playing the roles of both glass-breaker and firefighter. Amidst the uncertainty of a crisis, America could not afford to play a passive or reactive role. It must be prepared to take control of events.

Conclusion

Gray-zone pressure is China's main line of effort against Taiwan, and Americans should pay much closer attention. Beijing's all-domain pressure campaign aims to incrementally redefine the status quo, eroding Taiwan's ability and resolve to resist while depriving the United States of a clear and catalyzing reason to intervene. The fact that this pressure has triggered a backlash in Taiwanese public opinion is not a reason for complacency. Beijing has ample room to escalate.

This chapter has highlighted two particularly concerning pathways for gray-zone escalation. The first is a quarantine to seize indirect control over Taiwan's economy. Taiwan's right to control the movement of goods and people across its border is critical to its identity as a WTO member and the integrity of the broader Indo-Pacific economic order. Beijing has already used military exercises and customs enforcement as pretexts to disrupt Taiwan's trade and could escalate these measures over time. Pairing such actions with pressure on private firms and third countries could isolate Taiwan further. China would not need to block all traffic to establish effective control. Even partial disruptions could strain Taiwan's economy and U.S. resupply efforts. A quarantine would be far harder to counter than the Berlin Airlift, since resupplying Taiwan would require sustained operations over vast distances. To deter China from entertaining this scenario, the United States must credibly threaten to resupply Taiwan while imposing costs on Xi and triggering crash preparations for war. These actions may include proportionate reinterpretation or adjustment of the One China Policy.

The second scenario is coercive mobilization for a full-scale invasion. China could not achieve full readiness for a full-scale amphibious invasion through secret preparations. Even amateur analysts could detect the signs. U.S. intelligence agencies might declassify even more information. As the crisis escalated, Washington and Beijing would engage in a tense standoff, signaling their resolve while exploring deescalation options. The U.S. president would face critical decisions, including whether to surge forces, activate military plans with allies, or evacuate civilians from Taiwan. During the brinkmanship crisis, political, military, and economic considerations would be deeply intertwined. History, not game theory, is the best guide for thinking about how these crises could evolve.

Third countries, private firms, and financial markets would react dynamically in the run-up to conflict, with unpredictable ripple effects. If the United States and China approached the brink of war, economic and financial disruptions could begin before any shots were fired. Given the threat of prolonged trade shutdowns in the South and East China Seas, signals of resolve from either side might trigger panic buying, stockpiling, and severe supply-chain disruptions. Financial markets may respond violently, amplifying uncertainty. If the U.S. government seemed to lack resolve and robust preparation, domestic constituencies and less-committed allies might push for capitulation to avoid economic collapse. U.S. officials would face a difficult challenge. They would have to communicate resolve to Beijing without inadvertently sparking a global financial crisis. If sparking a crisis is part of the plan, Washington would need a concept for dealing with the fall-out, including the effects on regional allies. Whatever the U.S. president chose to do, and however the crisis unfolded, Washington would need an integrated strategy to show it could safeguard its vital interests.

3

Amphibious Invasion and Blockade

The strike comes without warning. In the darkness, on the seafloor beneath the Taiwan Strait, PLA underwater drones and frogmen begin to sever the eighteen undersea cables connecting Taiwan to the outside world. A night watchman streaming television dramas on his smartphone tries to refresh the page. A university student scrolling social media assumes there is something wrong with the dormitory Wi-Fi. The bandwidth keeps slowing and slowing, until nothing will load at all. Then, the power plants that service downtown Taipei are crippled by cyberattacks. Neon signs and streetlights go dark. Taipei's broad boulevards are now illuminated only by moonlight and the headlights of passing cars.

Five minutes later, the explosions begin. A salvo of missiles screeches across the night sky and lands on the residences of Taiwan's leaders: the president and vice president, the premier and vice premier (next in the order of succession), and the heads of the armed forces and intelligence services.[1] In a blink, Taiwan's democratically elected government has been decapitated. Hundreds more missiles now begin to rain down: on naval bases and air defense batteries, the tarmac at the Ching Chuan Kang Air Base, military command posts and radar beacons, and telecom infrastructure. PLA forces use lasers to jam American and Japanese satellites, temporarily disrupting communication links. Cyberattacks take down Taiwanese government websites and IT systems. PLA special forces and UFWD sleeper agents on Taiwan then begin a campaign of psychological warfare, hanging red posters on streetlamps declaring that Taiwan's defeat is certain, and resistance will be futile. Hundreds of CCG vessels and China-flagged "civilian" merchant ships and fishing boats change course and begin to sail toward the median line in the Taiwan Strait. Dozens of helicopters, carrying more PLA special forces, take off from mainland bases, heading toward Taiwan.

Taiwan's military is not completely unprepared. PLA forces mobilized in the Eastern Theater Command months before, and U.S. intelligence has been closely tracking their movements. While Taiwan's political leaders did not take these warnings seriously enough to decamp to bunkers, they did place Taiwan's armed forces on high alert and mobilize tens of thousands of reserves. The Taiwan Marine Corps' 66th Brigade, across the river from Taipei, has been training for years to deal with a decapitation strike. It quickly swings into action.[2] Within minutes, the commander has assessed the situation: the president is dead, but a surviving member of the line of succession has been found and is on his way to the presidential bunker in a command vehicle.[3] Teams have been sent out to gather key officials from their homes and escort them out of the city. A secure communications link is set up with the White House switchboard. Over a million more Taiwanese reservists now receive emergency text messages informing them that they should be prepared to be called up.

The president of the United States (POTUS), visiting a school in Atlanta, is 8,000 miles away when the news breaks. Secret Service agents hurriedly escort POTUS into a command vehicle. Immediately, the briefing begins. The secretaries of state, defense, and treasury, the national security advisor, and the chairman of the Joint Chiefs of Staff are dialed in. POTUS immediately orders contingency plans set in motion. At hundreds of facilities at home and across the Indo-Pacific, U.S. military forces mobilize to their highest state of readiness. Minutes later, as the hailstorm of missiles intensifies in Taipei, Air Force One is wheels up.

In the next few minutes, POTUS will have key decisions to make, and only some of them are military in nature. How should the United States respond to China's attacks on U.S. satellites? What rhetorical and substantive support must the United States provide to help Taiwan defeat the invasion? If the PLA escalates to strikes on U.S. bases, how should the United States retaliate? What will happen to Taiwan's semiconductor fabs, and what will be the impact on the global economy if production is disrupted? Are U.S. allies prepared to fight?

This chapter sets the stage for the prescriptive chapters ahead by exploring the challenges both sides would face in an invasion scenario. Of course, the picture sketched out above is just one of many possible variations. Beijing may not try a decapitation attack, and if it does, such an attack may not succeed. Russia failed many times to assassinate Volodymyr Zelensky. The key point is that an amphibious invasion of Taiwan would be the most complex military operation in modern history. It would require the PLA to execute large-scale, multi-domain warfare across land, sea, air, cyber, and space. Taiwan, using its geography, advanced technology, and asymmetric defenses, would aim to delay and disrupt any invasion until international reinforcements could arrive.

The opening hours and days would be critical. The PLA would need to secure air and naval superiority in a heavily defended region, transport tens of thousands of troops across the Taiwan Strait, establish a foothold on a rugged and fortified island, and sustain its forces—all while countering U.S. and allied intervention. These challenges are heightened by the PLA's lack of modern combat experience and the inherent complexity of amphibious operations. Even if China overcame these hurdles, the invasion could devolve into a protracted conflict with guerrilla resistance. A U.S.–China war could break out—and spread.

I do not attempt to predict the exact outcome of an invasion or to declare which side would have the upper hand. War is inherently uncertain. Wargames are useful for exploring path dependencies, not predicting results.[4] They cannot address all the nuanced questions policymakers would face.[5] My goal here is to provide a clear framework for general readers by synthesizing a wide range of open-source literature, including authoritative Chinese-language sources. In this chapter, I assume that the PLA would execute documented war plans, that Taiwan would mount a robust defense, and that the United States, Japan, and Australia would quickly engage.[6] To make this scenario accessible to non-specialists, the analysis focuses on key risk factors and decision points, with detailed references available in the notes. The chapter's main argument is that the U.S.–China military balance is best understood as a dynamic contest of political signaling and risk management, not as a binary calculation in which the side with more ships, planes, drones, or missiles necessarily wins. Militaries are complex systems. While China faces significant challenges and uncertainties, the balance is shifting in favor of China's system.[7] This trend in the balance undermines U.S. deterrence in the gray zone—even if China never actually invades.

Basic Requirements for Invasion

This section examines what the PLA would need to do to invade Taiwan successfully. The PLA would need to coordinate all its forces seamlessly, manage complex supply lines, and maintain intense operations while under attack.

This is extremely difficult. China's military has not fought a major war since the late 1970s. It would be using many untested technologies, and would face weapons systems it may not fully understand. Taiwan's forces are even less prepared for war, but PLA military planners should assume the worst-case scenario. To understand how China is likely thinking about invasion—and how to strengthen deterrence—this discussion assumes Taiwan would mount the strongest possible defense with its current military. The bottom line is that Taiwan could not defeat China alone, but it could very likely disrupt and delay an invasion long enough for the U.S. and allies to intervene.

Taiwan's geography makes it a hard target for an amphibious invasion.[8] The island has few beaches wide enough for an invading force to establish a secure foothold.[9] Much of the west coast, which faces the Taiwan Strait, is either densely developed with residential and industrial buildings or covered by networks of coastal ponds. The remaining shoreline consists of mudflats that stretch for miles at low tide. These are difficult to traverse on foot. For heavy military vehicles, they are nearly impassable. Taiwan's armed forces have spent decades fortifying the island's most viable landing beaches to maximize the complication and risk for potential invaders. Meanwhile, most of Taiwan's east coast, facing the Pacific, is dominated by sheer cliffs and is separated from major population centers by a rugged mountain range.

Beyond the island's topography, the Taiwan Strait's unpredictable hydrography and extreme weather pose further challenges. As Ian Easton has noted, between October and March, civil aviation and passenger ships often avoid the Strait due to harsh weather. Winds can be so strong that on the Penghu Islands in the middle of the Strait, only the very thickest trees avoid getting uprooted.[10] Winter storms can produce waves up to 50 feet high. The sweltering summer months between June and October bring an average of six typhoons per year, along with thick, unpredictable fog. Given these conditions, Easton assesses that only April and October consistently offer suitable weather for an amphibious invasion. Delivering roughly half a million PLA soldiers across the Taiwan Strait and sustaining them over time would therefore not only be the largest combined arms and multi-service operation in the history of modern warfare. It would also have to be executed within a narrow and unforgiving window.

Amphibious operations unfold in multiple phases. First, the attacker must identify and shape the landing zone. This usually begins with bombardment to "soften" the enemy and destroy critical road and rail links to the landing zone, slowing down defensive reinforcements. Airborne units and special forces can also help prepare the ground. Next, the first wave of troops lands and establishes a beachhead. Simultaneously, airborne forces may attempt to secure an airhead where additional troops and supplies can safely be delivered by air. Subsequent waves of attackers then work to expand the beachhead and airhead into lodgments. These are zones with enough space for reinforcements and supplies to mass for eventual breakout. At every stage, the invading force is vulnerable to counterattack. If the beachhead or airhead is destroyed, or if the lodgment collapses, the entire operation can fall apart. Successfully executing such an operation would require China's air, naval, and ground forces to move rapidly and coordinate their efforts with precision.

Air superiority is a nonnegotiable precondition for a successful invasion.[11] Without control of the skies, essential PLA logistics elements such as heavy-lift aircraft and helicopters would be easy targets. Taiwan has an integrated air defense system (IADS), a sophisticated and decentralized network that combines U.S.-provided Patriot interceptors and domestically produced Sky Bow III missiles. Taiwan's air defense systems can intercept ballistic missiles, cruise missiles, and aircraft. Taiwan's IADS is probably at least moderately resilient. It has mobile radar and launcher units designed to evade detection and strike. Taiwan also has F-16V fighter jets, equipped with advanced radar and long-range AMRAAM missiles. At the beginning of any invasion, Taiwan would therefore contest the airspace around the island. Taiwan's fighters are dispersed in hardened shelters and can operate from highway airstrips, complicating PLA targeting efforts.[12]

China would have to neutralize Taiwan's air defenses. The PLA Air Force (PLAAF) would likely rely on ground-based missiles for this purpose, as well as stealth fighters such as the J-20, H-6 bombers armed with precision-guided cruise missiles, and vast numbers of drones. The PLA's electronic warfare units would try to blind Taiwan's radar and disrupt its communications. Still, even a partial failure to suppress Taiwan's IADS would leave PLA naval forces vulnerable to retaliatory strikes. This would delay subsequent operations and expose the PLA's transport ships to attack. Historical precedents underscore the dangers of underestimating a well-prepared adversary with adaptive defenses. In the 1973 Yom Kippur War, Egyptian forces failed to sustain air superiority. Ukraine's air defenses have held up through four years of conflict, denying Russia command of the air.[13]

Once China gained control of the air, the PLA Navy (PLAN) would need to secure control of the surface and subsurface in the Taiwan Strait. The PLAN is the world's largest navy by fleet size (though not by tonnage). It vastly outnumbers Taiwan's navy on the surface. However, Taiwan operates diesel-electric submarines optimized for the shallow, acoustically challenging waters of the Strait, where sonar detection is difficult.[14] These submarines are armed with torpedoes capable of sinking high-value PLAN assets such as Type 071 landing platform docks and Type 075 amphibious assault ships. Taiwan has fast-attack craft armed with Hsiung Feng III anti-ship missiles that could conduct hit-and-run attacks on PLA transport convoys before retreating to the safety of the coastline, though these craft would be targets in any opening bombardment. In addition, Taiwan has a substantial drone program and could probably extensively mine the waters off its western coast. PLAN mine-clearing operations would take time, and China's minesweepers would be vulnerable to Taiwanese missiles, drones, and shore-based artillery. Of course, the PLA might respond with its own offensive mine warfare campaign against Taiwan's major harbors.[15] All these operations would be catastrophic for commercial shipping.

After China achieved air and sea control, it would need to master the landing on Taiwan. Amphibious landings require meticulous preparation and involve vast numbers of men and quantities of matériel.[16] The largest amphibious operation in history remains Operation Neptune, when Allied forces landed in Normandy in 1944.[17] Allied preparation for Normandy combined airpower, naval support, deception, and strategic bombing. By the time D-Day arrived, the Luftwaffe was severely degraded, and the roads and railways Germany needed to redeploy its forces were badly damaged. A massive Allied deception operation successfully confused the German High Command and prevented preemptive reinforcements.[18]

Despite all these advantages, it is worth remembering that Operation Neptune nearly failed. Although 156,000 men hit the Normandy beaches on June 6, 1944, Neptune quickly fell behind schedule. By D-Day+1, the Allies were meant to have linked all their beachheads and captured four major ports, including Caen. In the event, it took them six days to connect their beachheads, two weeks to capture the major port of Cherbourg, and six weeks to solidify the lodgment for the offensive into France. Neptune succeeded because it kept the beachhead secure, allowing more Allied reinforcements to pour in unimpeded.[19] By late July, 1.5 million Allied soldiers were in France. With better fortifications, reserve management, and planning, Germany might have derailed the entire operation.

Because Taiwan can predict the likely landing beaches and track the PLA in real time as it mobilizes, it would have some advantages that the Germans

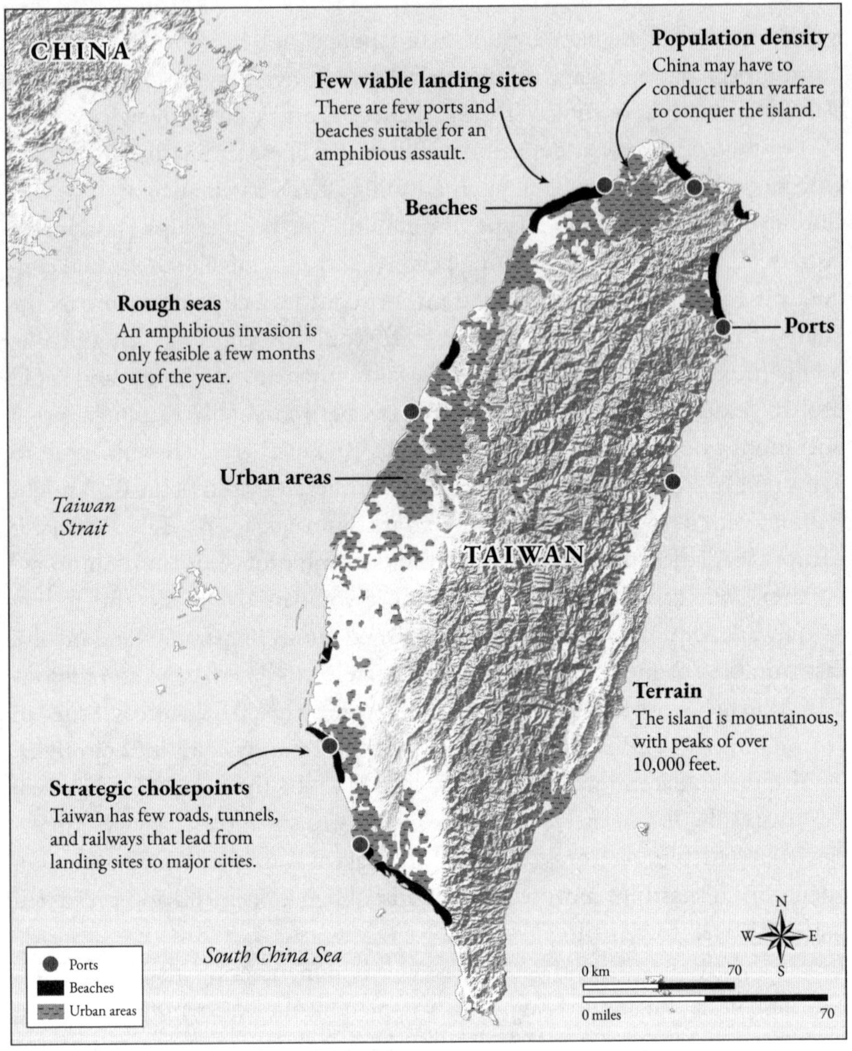

Figure 3.1 Possible landing zones on Taiwan's Western coast

Source: Adapted from Susan Gordon, Michael Mullen, and David Sacks, "U.S.-Taiwan Relations in a New Era: Responding to a More Assertive China," *Council on Foreign Relations*, June 2023, https://www.cfr.org/task-force-report/us-taiwan-relations-in-a-new-era/introduction.

lacked on D-Day (see Figure 3.1).[20] Recent U.S. weapons sales to Taiwan have provided many capabilities helpful for holding beaches, including long-range artillery, anti-tank and anti-air missiles, and anti-ship missiles.[21] Western governments have absorbed lessons from Ukraine and developed counter-drone technology. Taiwan's defenses against amphibious attack could further improve, though they would suffer attrition over time.[22] The PLA could try to attack and seize Taiwan's major ports directly, but this approach would throw its forces into immediate urban combat. This is a slow, high-casualty type of warfare that heavily favors the defender.[23]

The PLA amphibious fleet can deliver only a fraction of the necessary invasion forces to Taiwan in a single wave. In theory, it could initially land around 30,000 troops. However, this estimate does not account for the space required for equipment or the likely need to transport armored vehicles separately on smaller craft.[24] A more realistic figure is closer to 20,000 troops. The PLA's dedicated amphibious ships are limited in number and vulnerable to both mines and anti-ship missiles.[25]

If an invasion took place today, the PLAN would have to rely heavily on requisitioned civilian ferries.[26] China has enormous roll-on/roll-off (RO-RO) civilian cargo ferries, which are much larger than their Western counterparts. But these vessels lack armored hulls or self-defense systems. This makes them easy targets for naval mines, mobile anti-ship missile batteries, or in the future, large numbers of cheap drones. If even one-third of these ferries were destroyed or damaged in the early days of a conflict, thousands of PLA troops could be stranded on Taiwan, potentially facing annihilation.[27] The PLA has conducted joint exercises to incorporate civilian ferries into its logistics network, but this does not mean they are prepared for the demands of combat, when missile and submarine-launched torpedo threats would be omnipresent. The ferries are likely crewed by maritime militia, who have experienced training of variable quality. It is therefore possible that China's ferry crews could panic under pressure. Any amphibious invasion before the early 2030s would probably require help from civilian ships. Any such operation before 2027 would almost certainly require them.

While a force of tens of thousands of PLA troops might be able to seize and hold a beachhead, defeating Taiwan's ground forces and pacifying the population might require a far larger force and many waves of resupply.[28] A full-scale invasion could demand tens of millions of tons of combat matériel, tens of millions of tons of oil, a million vehicles, and thousands of ships and aircraft. Even preparing these supplies for transport would be a significant logistical challenge—let alone delivering them to shore under combat conditions.[29] PLA airborne forces could potentially airdrop some supplies onto target sites if they could neutralize Taiwan's air defenses. However, Russia's failed attempt to seize Hostomel Airport near Kyiv in February 2022 illustrates how vulnerable isolated PLA airborne forces would be to Taiwanese counterattack. The risk is especially great if Taiwanese units can destroy the low-flying helicopters the PLA needs to resupply its airborne units.[30] Ultimately, most of the supplies and fuel would have to be delivered across the Taiwan Strait by sea. PLA planners need to consider how they could keep the amphibious fleet safe in what could involve dozens or even hundreds of back-and-forth crossings of the Strait.

Simultaneously with an amphibious assault, China could launch a heliborne and airborne assault to intensify the pressure on Taiwan's defenders. This action too carries significant complexities and risks. The PLA could try to use Z-20 helicopters, similar to American Black Hawks, to insert troops into critical inland positions such as radar stations, command centers, or infrastructure nodes. Meanwhile, the PLA Airborne Corps could deploy paratroopers in an attempt to seize airfields or ports.[31] The PLA could also deploy special forces to Taiwan by boat, aircraft, or submarine. As discussed in the previous chapter, significant numbers of sleeper agents might already be stationed on Taiwan as part of Beijing's influence campaign.[32] However, the PLA can only "lift" so many troops this way before establishing an airhead. Taiwan's layered air defenses and dense urban terrain would make these operations complicated to pull off at scale.

Even with localized air superiority, heliborne and airborne forces would face high attrition rates and the risk of isolation if follow-on reinforcements were delayed. Operation Market Garden, the 1944 Allied attempt to penetrate the German-occupied Netherlands, is a classic cautionary tale for this type of airborne assault. The Allies underestimated the difficulty of coordinating air, land, and logistical support under fire. They suffered high casualties without achieving their full objective.[33]

In short, achieving near-simultaneous dominance across multiple interdependent domains is possible, but it is no easy task.[34] The PLA's amphibious doctrine—the Joint Island Landing Campaign—recognizes this fact.[35] Achieving air superiority requires neutralizing Taiwan's air defenses, but the suppression of these defenses relies on precision strikes, which themselves depend on air superiority to execute effectively. The PLA is a rigid and overly centralized institution that struggles to delegate operational initiative to lower levels of command.[36] Open-source materials show that overly centralized command-and-control systems would impair smooth coordination with amphibious forces.[37] For instance, PLA airborne forces do not exercise under realistic conditions.[38] Nor does the PLA do large-scale training for logistics operations under fire, which could prove disastrous for its air, naval, and land forces. It has been slow to adopt key capabilities that could make its logistics chain more resilient.[39] Taiwan's defensive strategy aims to exploit these facts.

Given all these moving parts, timing would be a critical factor in the success or failure of the invasion. Delays could result from failure to suppress Taiwan's air defenses, from U.S. or Taiwanese submarine attacks, or from logistical disruptions. Any delay could create cascading operational challenges for the PLA in the next phase of fighting. The PLA's lack of experience and the need to sustain a high operational tempo increase the likelihood of mistakes.[40]

Taiwanese Resistance and Allied Choices

As we have seen above, Taiwan has geographic advantages, but its forces would be greatly outnumbered. That means its ability to withstand an initial bombardment would hinge on its layered air defense systems and carefully rehearsed dispersal strategies. Air defenses would have to deal with thousands of missiles aimed at airbases, radar installations, and critical communication nodes. Taiwan has mobile surface-to-air missile (SAM) systems, including the domestically produced Tian Kung III and U.S.-supplied Patriot missiles.[41] Patriots have proven highly effective in protecting Israel against the salvos of several hundred missiles from Iran, and Ukraine from Russian bombardment, though China would likely launch much larger salvos. Taiwan's decoy systems and radar reflectors would also play a role in confusing China's targeting algorithms. Recognizing that aircraft are most vulnerable while still on the ground, Taiwan's air force would disperse and shelter its key assets if it saw the PLA preparing for an invasion. The PLA's strategy includes using missile strikes to crater Taiwan's air base runways, aiming to ground its fighter force. Repairs could take hours, and repair teams would face the threat of follow-up strikes.[42]

Drawing from Ukraine's experience with Russian missile strikes, Taiwan must integrate decentralized airfield operations to sustain its air force and deny the PLA air superiority. Runway repair kits—including rapid-setting concrete, specialized engineering vehicles, and trained teams—will be essential.

Fighter jets could also launch from secondary airstrips, including highways adapted for emergency use.[43] Mobile missile launchers and command units should be hidden in urban and mountainous terrain. Taiwan has hardened hangars at its mountain air bases. Communications might be disrupted by cyberattacks and kinetic strikes, so Taiwan needs to rely on redundant satellite links and other backup systems to sustain command and control. Taiwan is betting that its command infrastructure, dispersed in hardened bunkers, would remain operational through the initial days. Everything comes down to this bet. How well Taiwan's air defenses and critical infrastructure would weather the initial bombardment is a critical question with an unknowable answer.

The opening bombardment might also be coupled with cyberattacks on Taiwan's civilian infrastructure. It is unclear how resilient Taiwan's infrastructure would prove in the face of these attacks. It is even less clear how Taiwan's civilian population would respond. Taiwan and its foreign supporters may have cyber exploits against China which they could use to restore deterrence and hopefully prevent humanitarian disaster.

Given Taiwan's numerical disadvantages, it would have to focus on repelling the amphibious and airborne assault. Pre-laid naval minefields in the Taiwan Strait could force PLA ships into narrow corridors, exposing them to more concentrated attacks.[44] However, indiscriminate mining before a conflict could cripple Taiwan's economy, so mines would need to be prepositioned but not activated. Smart or remotely activated mines could further enhance flexibility. Once hostilities began, ships, aircraft, and submarines would lay additional mines to slow the PLA advance and disrupt its assault formations. Taiwanese forces could fire mobile anti-ship cruise missiles from concealed mobile launchers dispersed across urban and coastal areas, targeting high-value PLA assets like amphibious ships and logistics vessels. Drones would also play a vital role. Small, expendable drones like the U.S.-supplied Switchblade 300, or repurposed civilian drones armed with explosives as in Ukraine, would target concentrations of PLA personnel and equipment. Larger drones would provide real-time targeting data to Taiwan's missile forces, although they would have to contend with electronic warfare and could struggle to take off if the runways at Taiwan's air bases were damaged.

In the air, Taiwan's forces would focus on neutralizing any helicopters and transport aircraft trying to ferry troops across the Strait. Taiwan would use Man-Portable Air Defense Systems (MANPADS), including Stingers and domestically produced systems, to turn its infantry into a mobile and decentralized air defense network.[45] If Taiwan's outmatched air force wanted to contest China's air superiority—a debated proposition—it would have to plan operations carefully to gain maximum advantages from each sortie. More likely, Taiwan would focus on attacking key PLA assets like transport aircraft and helicopters.[46] Taiwan would probably leave to the United States and its allies the tougher challenge of dealing with China's surface combatant vessels, submarines, fighter aircraft, and support infrastructure.

Rules of engagement would add a layer of complexity. With no common operating picture shared among the Taiwanese, U.S., and Japanese forces, the allies might struggle to differentiate between friends, foes, and neutral actors in the chaotic environment of the Strait. Different types of submarines—American, Japanese, Taiwanese, and even Australian or British—might mistake each other for PLA boats in the congested, shallow waters around Taiwan. Despite pre-crisis consultations and contingency planning with its allies, gaps in communication and interoperability would create significant challenges, particularly under the strain of PLA electronic interference. These facts would provide an additional reason for civilian ships and aircraft to avoid operating around Taiwan, even if the combatants somehow negotiated guardrails that guaranteed safe passage for them.

As PLA forces drew closer to its territorial waters and airspace, Taiwan would focus on rapidly mobilizing reserves and fortifying its coastal defenses. Taiwan's military has long prepared for this scenario by prepositioning weapons and supplies and training rapidly deployable reserve units. Coastal artillery, multiple-launch rocket systems (MLRS), and portable anti-tank guided missiles (ATGMs) would concentrate fire on PLA landing craft and disembarking troops. Taiwanese combat engineers might destroy bridges, roads, and other key infrastructure to slow the enemy's potential inland advance. Managing the mobilization would be a huge challenge for Taiwan's government. Civilian volunteers trained in basic defense and emergency response would need to support the military. Civilians would man checkpoints, provide logistical assistance and prepare urban areas for a prolonged defense that they would still hope would not be necessary.[47] Taiwan's health infrastructure would come under strain, since civilians would be killed in any opening bombardment.

Despite Taiwan's best efforts, the PLA would probably succeed in putting at least some boots on the ground. Assuming the PLA could sustain its position on the ground, it would have two paths to victory: co-opt the local authorities, or make the population submit with overwhelming force. History shows that the former pathway is much easier. This is why China would likely seek to decapitate Taiwan's leadership and replace it with a more pliant, collaborationist government. The PLA's special operations forces (SOF) could be useful for this task.[48] According to the 2020 edition of the *Science of Military Strategy*, the PLA's key doctrinal text, SOF would be used for "asymmetric warfare" operations, including sabotage and "psychological operations involving all types of technologies and means."[49] SOF might also deal with guerrilla resistance on Taiwan. China would need to identify a Taiwanese leader who could serve as a plausible collaborator, though this individual would be at risk of assassination by the defenders.

History provides examples of brutal tactics breaking civilian resistance during insurgencies, but China cannot be confident that these tactics would work quickly. Russia took a decade to subdue Chechnya, and Taiwan's population is seventeen times larger than Chechnya's. Brutality can also backfire, strengthening civilian resolve, as Russia's atrocities in the Ukrainian city of Bucha did in 2022.[50] Even when the population initially greets the invaders, the invaders can quickly lose political legitimacy.[51] Beijing must therefore assume the need for a grisly occupation requiring an open-ended force commitment—and a plan to deal with U.S. and Japanese reinforcements.[52] In Algeria, France failed to subdue an insurgency with 500,000 men. In Indochina, 190,000 French regulars could not defeat the Vietminh's combination of insurgency and conventional tactics. Later, the U.S. and South Vietnamese forces failed to break another hybrid conventional-insurgent threat, despite deploying 543,000 Americans to the country at the peak in 1969.[53] If Taiwan's political and military leadership were to retreat into prepared positions in the mountains, civilians resisted in the cities, and the Taiwanese government stockpiled the light weapons and secured the communications needed to coordinate resistance, China might face a prolonged insurgency.[54] Quelling the insurgency could take months or years and could require 500,000 or more PLA troops.[55] China would have to keep its occupying army resupplied. This could be challenging if it lost many ferries, helicopters, and cargo aircraft in the early stages of the invasion.

Any conventional ground or counterinsurgency campaign in Taiwan would be horrific. Cities like Taipei, Taichung, and Kaohsiung would become the focus of resistance. Taiwan's defenders would rely on ambush tactics, sniper teams, and improvised explosives. Taiwan's urban environments provide key advantages for the defenders. Taipei, for example, is nearly as densely populated as New York City, but its streets are much narrower. Many are lined with terraces, and cars often park perpendicular to traffic. These environments create abundant opportunities for sniper cover and complicate mobility for an occupying army's armored vehicles. Local knowledge of the terrain would further tilt the balance in favor of the defenders. PLA military analysts liken this nightmare scenario to "battling rats in a china shop."[56] Moreover, as combat damaged cities, the rubble of major buildings would create unexpected strongpoints that the defender could leverage, slowing conventional or counterinsurgent offensive operations to a bloody crawl.

Discussion of this scenario is taboo in Taiwan, for understandable reasons. But this does not mean that Taiwan is completely unprepared. Washington and Taipei may already be training together in guerrilla tactics when military personnel from Taiwan visit the United States to train with the U.S. National Guard.[57] Taiwan's armed forces have combat training facilities to train troops for gas attacks, nighttime combat, and urban warfare. Taiwan's Ministry of National Defense has a new All-out Defense Mobilization Agency (全民防衛動員署) designed to prepare for the occupation contingency.[58] Then there is Forward Alliance, a nongovernmental organization led by the charismatic Yale graduate Enoch Wu, which has trained thousands of Taiwanese citizens in emergency survival skills.[59] Until China can develop confidence that it is prepared for this worst-case scenario, the threat of a protracted guerrilla resistance movement significantly enhances deterrence against an invasion.

It is hard to tell just how prepared Taiwan's armed forces are to fight. Although Taiwan has a system of mandatory military service, enlistment currently lasts only one year, recently extended from four months.[60] Recruits do not receive realistic training exercises, and Taiwan's reserve forces lack robust training.[61] Taiwan's forces face shortages of essential equipment, including small arms, ammunition, and helmets, as well as larger munitions, aircraft, and artillery. Taiwan faces a crisis of morale that is both cause and consequence of this lack of preparation. Most likely, the quality of training, readiness, and morale varies widely between units. Thus, while it is impossible to know just how well Taiwan's forces could perform in the event, it is certain that morale and operational adaptability would be essential. Taiwan's military knows that it would have no path to victory without direct American intervention.

In the invasion scenario, everything therefore comes down to the Taiwanese military's morale and willingness to fight. Lessons from Ukraine indicate that national morale can swing wildly in the early days of a war. Highly motivated territorial defense forces and civilian-led resistance movements can significantly complicate an invader's plans. Beijing hopes that psychological operations and economic coercion will erode Taiwan's resolve before a conflict begins. However, Ukraine's experience shows that an adversary's miscalculation of national willpower can lead to strategic failure.

Communicating resolve and maintaining public trust in the U.S.–Taiwan defense partnership would therefore be critical both before and during a crisis. Taiwan's civilian and military leaders would operate out of bunkers in the mountains, coordinating flows of supplies, reinforcements, and information. Public broadcasts and encrypted communications would be essential for maintaining unity and purpose among the population. The mood on social media would be vitally important. In this context, Taiwan's international supporters would need to show ironclad resolve to support Taiwan until victory is achieved. The United States and any allies would therefore face a fundamental choice about their communication strategy at the very outset. Should they continue to espouse the One China Policy, taking the position that Taiwan's status remains "unresolved"? Or would they be supporting an independent country: the Republic of China (Taiwan)? We will return to this question in Chapter 4.

The Air–Naval Fight

Assuming the United States and its key regional allies sprint to Taiwan's defense, an invasion would also trigger a simultaneous air–naval war with China. Beijing's goal would be to keep the allied forces far enough back from Taiwan that they could not resupply Taiwan or attack the invasion force. To do so, Beijing might strike U.S. surface combatants, submarines, aircraft, logistics platforms and infrastructure, and space assets. It would try to screen Taiwan on all sides with warships, submarines, manned aircraft, and drones. The allies, meanwhile, would have to fight their way in. China's "reconnaissance-strike complex" is an integrated combination of sensors and shooters that enables the PLA to detect and attack hostile assets. Allied forces would have to peel back this network layer by layer, focusing first on China's information and reconnaissance systems, and eventually destroy China's offensive air–naval power.[62]

As with the amphibious invasion itself, the early hours and days would be critical for the defenders. A defining principle of air–naval warfare throughout history has been that whichever side attacks effectively first enjoys large, compounding advantages. That means that, unlike the situation in land warfare, once a conflict began both sides would surge all relevant capabilities into the fight, rather than holding key forces back as reserves.[63]

It is unclear, based on open sources, whether or when China might strike U.S. bases across the region to gain an early advantage. PLA doctrinal texts explicitly recommend targeting enemy air bases to prevent aircraft from taking off and to undermine air strike capabilities.[64] The PLA Rocket Force has conducted exercises in western China that appear to simulate strikes on facilities resembling U.S. bases like Kadena Air Base in Okinawa.[65] China's force posture is also well adapted to fit this strategy, with long-range precision strike capabilities, including medium-range missiles capable of reaching U.S. air bases across the region.[66]

Despite the operational military benefits, a preemptive strike against U.S. bases might run counter to China's broader political strategy. As we have seen, China would prefer to push the political burden of deciding whether to get involved onto the United States. If China framed its move against Taiwan as an action short of war, it could portray the United States as the aggressor. This could make it easier to pressure key U.S. allies in Asia and Europe to remain neutral or offer only symbolic support for Taiwan. China also clearly assigns significant value to the UN as a legitimizing force. As we saw in Chapter 1, the CCP's interests in Taiwan are about symbolism and legitimacy, not just the substance of who controls Taiwan's territory and economy.

An unprovoked attack on U.S. forces would amount to a declaration of total war. While anything is possible, historical analogies such as Germany's sinking of the *Lusitania*, Japan's attack on Pearl Harbor, and the September 11 attacks suggest that the American people and elected officials of both parties would rally around the flag if China attacked first. The United States would likely resolve not only to defeat the PLA invasion of Taiwan, but also potentially to remove the CCP from power. Washington might also become more risk-tolerant if the war escalated, including with respect to nuclear use. U.S. allies in Europe and elsewhere would find it hard to stay on the sidelines.

Would the deterrence logic be different if the U.S. president ordered conventional strikes on PLA facilities in mainland China and perhaps also on artificial islands in the South China Sea? Caitlin Talmadge, Fiona Cunningham, Robert Blackwill, and Philip Zelikow are among those who argue that any strikes on PRC territory would run a high risk of escalation to general war, including potentially nuclear escalation. They think the president therefore needs options to deter and if necessary defeat the PLA without such attacks.[67] However, other commentators, including former Pacific Command commander and director of National Intelligence Admiral Dennis Blair, have argued that the probability of conventional U.S. attacks on PLA facilities triggering a nuclear retaliation is "between nil and zero."[68] According to Blair, both sides would clearly differentiate between strikes on conventional facilities and supporting infrastructure and "counterforce" strikes on nuclear assets or command-and-control systems.[69] A 2024 RAND Corporation study implicitly agrees with Blair.[70]

Of course, even with classified information, the answers to these questions are unknowable. No nuclear-armed power has ever launched a large-scale kinetic strike against another. But no matter how clearly these strikes were telegraphed in advance, and no matter how carefully targeters tried to distinguish between conventional and nuclear infrastructure, any exchange would risk miscalculation and strategic (namely, nuclear) escalation. We will return to this issue in more detail in Chapter 6. Since multiple scenarios can be imagined, the rest of this chapter fudges the question of whether U.S. forces would strike inside China and PLA forces would strike U.S. bases. Let us simply assume that the conflict would be contained to the conventional level.

Crucially, nearly all aspects of a U.S.–China war would involve integration across domains: space, cyber, air, ground, maritime, and undersea. Both sides rely heavily on space-based systems for positioning, navigation, and timing (PNT), reconnaissance, and communications.[71] These systems could become targets very quickly, either through kinetic anti-satellite attacks, jamming, or cyberattacks on ground stations.[72] Early warning aircraft and UAS would play an essential role and would be vulnerable to electronic warfare. All surface assets could potentially be targeted by missile or drone strikes in any weather and in any time of day or night, placing a premium on mobility and stealth. The undersea domain would also play a critical role; and for now it represents the most important area of U.S. advantage.

The two most important aspects of air–naval warfare—scouting and strike—rely fundamentally on cross-domain integration. Assessing the conventional military balance is therefore much more complicated than simply counting ships, planes, or missiles. The question is which side's overall military system is more resilient and robust. PLA doctrine understands this fact. China characterizes modern war as conflict between systems, not conflict between specific capabilities.[73]

China's extensive missile arsenal has created a high-risk zone extending roughly 600 kilometers off its coast.[74] Within this zone, American ships (and to a lesser extent aircraft) face significant threats from PLA anti-ship and anti-air missiles. The United States, by contrast, has limited stockpiles of cruise missiles capable of striking beyond 600 kilometers. China continues to refine its targeting capabilities and expand its arsenal of anti-ship ballistic missiles (ASBMs) and anti-ship cruise missiles (ASCMs).[75] As China gains the ability to spot and strike targets from greater distances, high-value U.S. surface ships and strike aircraft must either operate farther away from contested zones, field longer-range aircraft and missiles, or use new techniques to mitigate their vulnerabilities. This is a particular problem for aircraft carriers and long-range heavy bombers.

Many U.S. assets that are based within striking range of Taiwan in peacetime would therefore be at risk. Kadena Air Base on Okinawa, for example, has been described as "uniquely ill-positioned for permanently basing large numbers of American aircraft" due to its proximity to China.[76] One analysis found that the PLA could fire 252 missiles at Kadena in a single salvo, and 26 at Misawa Air Base in northern Japan.[77] Even Andersen Air Force Base on Guam, the logistical linchpin for U.S. airpower in the region, is within range of China's DF-26 missiles.[78] Recognizing this reality, the United States has already withdrawn two fighter squadrons from Okinawa. Basing aircraft further away keeps them safer but makes them less relevant. The F-16 has a combat radius of less than 600 kilometers and cannot influence the aerial balance around Taiwan from Guam, which is 2,700 kilometers away. Bombers have longer ranges, but U.S. Air Force fighter squadrons outnumber bomber squadrons eight to one.[79]

The Air Force cannot quickly engineer a new generation of fighter jets with much longer ranges, but it can house them in hardened shelters and disperse them geographically to make the force more resilient. The Air Force has developed a new operational concept to describe its efforts in this area. Agile Combat Employment (ACE) emphasizes the resilience and flexibility of operations, rapid deployment, and dispersal of forces across a network of smaller, more agile bases, rather than relying on large, fixed installations.[80] It also involves classified counter-scouting techniques. Increasing the redundancy and resilience of U.S. facilities in the region is a key element of conventional military deterrence.

The growing importance of range and precision has also made the U.S. bomber fleet an increasingly crucial element of war planning for the invasion scenario.[81] The Air Force has 141 bombers. Each can carry sixteen to twenty-four long-range precision-guided weapons and operate globally with the aid of aerial refueling. Deployed beyond the PLA's reach—including on U.S. soil—bombers can refuel out of interception range, strike key PLA assets with long-range missiles, and return to secure bases to refuel and rearm. Ranges on the most sophisticated air-launched missiles vary from around 500 to 1,000 kilometers. Boeing also produces kits that can transform simple Joint Direct Attack Munition (JDAM) bombs into guided "Powered JDAMs" (PJDAMs) with a range of over 500 kilometers and decoy PJDAMs with ranges of over 1,000 kilometers.[82] If about one-third of the U.S. bomber force were deployed daily, it could deliver around 800 missiles against the PLA assault forces each day.[83] China could in principle target and shoot down these bombers and refuelers, but not easily.[84]

The Marine Corps would play a critical role in facilitating the cross-domain effort to deter an invasion. The Corps is transforming itself into a maritime organization capable of conducting reconnaissance, drawing enemy fire away from the Navy and Air Force, and delivering lethal force against enemy ships.[85] Marine units are training to deploy from small ships to islands in the First Island Chain, well within China's weapons engagement range. These units have a light logistical footprint to avoid detection and move quickly between firing positions. The Marines would force China to divert resources away from attacking Taiwan or U.S. bases and carriers, among other essential missions.

Meanwhile, the U.S. surface fleet, which has long been the backbone of American naval power, now faces profound uncertainty. The fleet's offensive combat power is concentrated in carrier air wings, which consist of aircraft carriers protected by a screen of destroyers, cruisers, and sometimes submarines. For decades, this configuration has allowed the U.S. Navy to maintain global sea control and project power ashore. The Navy is adapting to emerging threats from drones and missiles with a concept called Distributed Maritime Operations (DMO).[86] The basic idea is to spread out the fleet geographically and use stealth techniques and long-range anti-ship missiles to enable surface ships to deliver lethal punches without being sunk themselves. The United States is developing long-range missiles, unmanned systems, refuelers, and other capabilities that will enable surface ships and carrier-based aviation to engage in a fight across greater distances.[87]

Carriers will remain foundational to U.S. conventional deterrence in the short to medium term, and possibly the long term as well. New defensive systems are being developed for them, including rail guns and directed energy weapons. Still, given the long-term trend of precision strikes at ever-greater ranges, large-surface combatants including carriers will have to keep adapting aggressively to stay relevant. If the U.S. surface fleet can't keep pace—or if China miscalculates about the fleet's vulnerability—deterrence could weaken quickly.[88] The U.S. fleet conducts regular deterrence operations because it needs to show China that DMO actually works.

U.S. and allied attack submarines are a critical complement to the surface fleet. U.S. submarines are extremely stealthy. In a conflict, this would enable them to operate much closer in to the Taiwan Strait than large surface ships, and deliver many lethal strikes quickly against PLA targets. The United States has around fifty operational conventionally-armed attack submarines. These include the newer *Virginia* and the older *Los Angeles* classes, along with three *Seawolf*-class boats.[89] The Navy could probably surge around thirty to thirty-five of them to the region in a crisis. U.S. attack submarines can deploy cruise missiles, torpedoes, and mines. The PLA's anti-submarine scouting capabilities are improving, but they are still underdeveloped. In the shallow waters around Taiwan, sonar signatures are badly scrambled. This fact makes anti-submarine warfare harder.[90]

However, U.S. preeminence undersea is not guaranteed, and the balance is currently moving in China's favor.[91] When submarines fire munitions, they give away their rough location, making it easier for the enemy to hunt them down. The Philippine Sea gets shallower the closer it gets to the First Island Chain.[92] Meanwhile, if PLA submarines can break out beyond the First Island Chain to the far side of Taiwan, they will be able to hold U.S. surface vessels at risk.[93] Hence, U.S. forces will have an acute defensive need to monitor the deep-water channels around Taiwan and maintain a large-scale anti-submarine dragnet around its major naval formations.[94] China's submarine fleet is rapidly growing larger and more sophisticated, thanks in part to Russian support.[95]

As both sides look to the Russia–Ukraine War for clues, drones are becoming increasingly important for air–naval war planning. The Department of Defense (DoD) has announced various programs and initiatives to put drone warfare at the forefront. The most notable is REPLICATOR, a $1 billion effort based on the concept of "All-Domain Attritable Autonomy."[96] DoD intends to buy tens of thousands of unmanned aerial, underwater, and surface drones for rapid deployment to the Indo-Pacific. The U.S. government has made few details public.

In June 2024, Admiral Samuel Paparo, commander of U.S. Indo-Pacific Command, publicly acknowledged a plan called "Hellscape." If China attacks one of its neighbors, "I want to turn the Taiwan Strait into an unmanned hellscape using a number of classified capabilities," Paparo said. "I can make their lives utterly miserable for a month, which buys me the time for the rest of everything." Paparo declined to elaborate, but he promised that the program was "real and it's deliverable."[97] Hellscape might involve naval mines, as well as drones. These threats will make for more credible deterrents if allied industrial capacity can fully back them up. Currently, no single company can produce drones at the scale to meet the mission that Hellscape envisions or to satisfy the requirements that REPLICATOR articulates. Moreover, REPLICATOR is neither a formal program of record nor a defined set of programs. DoD should clarify REPLICATOR's mission and enable U.S. allies to participate in accelerating the program.[98]

It is important to acknowledge that all open-source assessments of the military balance—including this one—must be approached with caution. Classified military programs on all sides may significantly alter real-world operational capabilities. The existence of undisclosed weapons systems, particularly in cyberspace, could make certain battlefield assumptions incomplete or outdated. As programs like Hellscape suggest, U.S. and allied capabilities may be more advanced than is publicly known. China also probably has classified capabilities that could shape a conflict in unpredictable ways. For example, if one side can blind the other and scramble its communications for the opening minutes or hours of a high-intensity fight, it may be able to land the first effective blow and gain compounding advantages. Policymakers must therefore recognize that the most decisive factors in a future Taiwan conflict may not be visible in open-source analyses.

It is also worth noting that just as planners in the United States and China cannot be certain about how a war over Taiwan would play out, they can only guess at how military outcomes might translate into political outcomes. Once a war began, it would end only after both sides agreed that a negotiated peace would be better than continued conflict. Before then, each side might take political steps that would make a peace deal harder to achieve. Each side might plausibly persuade itself that it would improve its position by creating a protracted conflict. One can imagine the two sides eviscerating each other's forces, pausing to reconstitute, and then resuming fighting after months or years. It is also possible that a U.S.–China war over Taiwan could escalate "horizontally" to include conflict on the Korean peninsula, in the South China Sea and Indian Ocean, in the Western Hemisphere, and in cyberspace. Adversaries such as Russia, Iran, and North Korea may not stay on the sidelines in these scenarios. Nonaligned countries across the Indo-Pacific would have to decide whether to offer access, basing, and overflight rights to the United States, China, or both.[99]

What is clear is that any peace deal to end a hypothetical U.S.–China war over Taiwan would likely have to encompass more than just an agreement on the status of Taiwan. It would be more like a grand bargain over the future of the entire Indo-Pacific region, reflecting the prerogatives of the winning side while offering the loser the smallest of face-saving fig leaves. Every country in the region would have a profound stake in the outcome.

To keep up morale in Taiwan during what could be a prolonged crisis, the United States and its allies would probably need to provide explicit and unconditional support, both symbolic and substantive. This might involve the United States adjusting its interpretation of the One China Policy, or even abandoning the policy altogether, severing diplomatic relations with the PRC, and formally recognizing Taiwan independence. U.S. and Japanese forces might not make publicized landings on Taiwanese soil, but U.S. military advisors would probably play a key role in coordinating Taiwan's military response on the ground. U.S.–Taiwan defense cooperation would inevitably deepen over time if a conflict became protracted. U.S. naval and air operations might disrupt China's logistics chains and force it to divert resources away from the main assault. The United States would also leverage its political and military power and its relationships across the broader western Pacific to complicate China's ability to sustain the invasion and pressure it to the negotiating table.

Blockade as a Part of War

In the context of a war, China could also impose a blockade. Unlike a quarantine, which could be framed as a limited law enforcement measure, a blockade would represent a full-scale attempt to cut off Taiwan from essential supplies. A "close," medieval-style blockade, akin to a siege, would restrict or threaten ships and planes bringing essential civilian supplies like food and fuel to Taiwan with lethal force. According to the 2006 *Science of Campaigns*, a key PLA doctrinal text, a "joint blockade campaign" might also include strikes against key facilities in Taiwan, including ports, airfields, and information infrastructure, and the mining of maritime approaches into Taiwan's harbors.[100] As we have seen, the PLA's August 2022 and May 2024 exercises were intended to demonstrate that the PLA can not only harass or obstruct ships or planes approaching Taiwan from all directions, but also destroy them if ordered to do so (see Figure 3.2).[101]

While a close blockade may not be China's most likely opening move, its effects would be devastating.[102] Taiwan's oil refineries, power plants, power distribution systems, and some of its strategic energy reserves are vulnerable to disabling strikes. (So are China's—though Taiwan has only limited ability to strike them in return, and striking PRC civilian infrastructure could be escalatory.) All but one of the eight thermal power stations on Taiwan's main island are on its mainland-facing west coast, and they generate 90 percent of Taiwan's power. Damage to either power stations or transmission lines would cause blackouts. China has also cyberattacked Taiwan's electricity grid.[103]

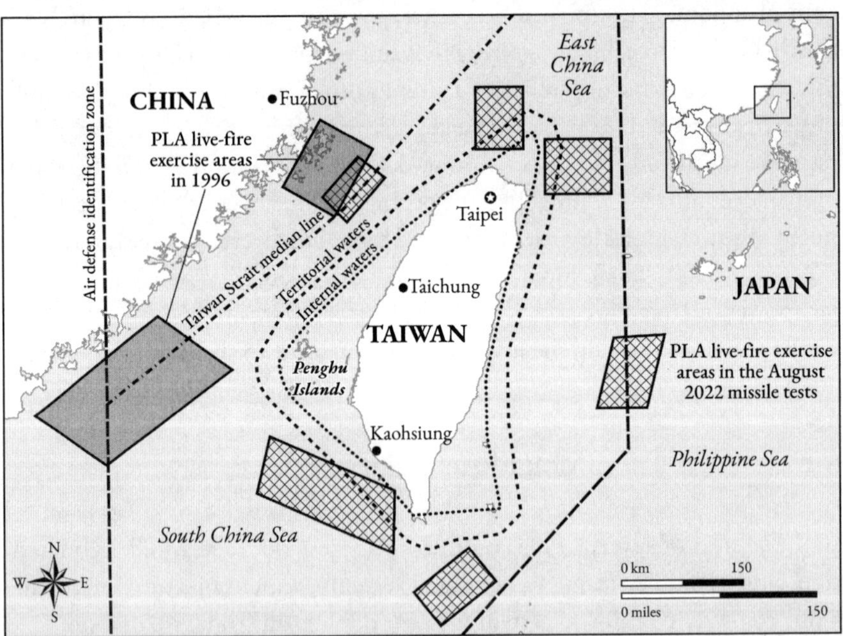

Figure 3.2 Map of Taiwan's internal and territorial waters, median line, and air defense identification zone. Exclusion zones for China's August 2022 missile tests are also noted.

China might even threaten Taiwan's Maanshan nuclear power plant, as Russia has threatened Ukraine's Zaporizhzhia nuclear power plant.[104]

Keeping the lights on in Taipei would soon become a challenge. Most of Taiwan's population lives on the west coast, facing the Taiwan Strait. Most of the island's ports are also located there. A mountain range runs through the middle of the island, bisected by just a few road and rail links that are easily damaged. Taiwan has just three east coast ports—Keelung, Yilan, and Hualien—which are small. In an extreme scenario, the PLA might mine the approaches to *all* of Taiwan's harbors. Taiwan has just eight minesweepers, some of which date back to the 1950s. Lonnie Henley, a retired senior intelligence officer specializing in China security issues, frames the potential challenge this way: "U.S. forces would have to get cargo ships into the west coast ports on a regular basis, in the face of extensive mining and hostile fire, close to China, and under conditions of PRC air superiority." Resupply by air under hostile conditions would be even harder. A large cargo jet is a "fat, slow, and extremely vulnerable target" for PLA surface-to-air missiles, to say nothing of the expense and operational difficulty of meeting Taiwan's energy needs through airlift.[105]

The Taiwanese government has published guidance on how it would prepare for food shortages, but it has provided no equivalent recommendations for energy.[106] As a result, Taiwan's society is psychologically unprepared for a situation in which fuel and electricity are rationed. Taiwan imports 97 percent of its energy supply, with all its imports coming via the Taiwan Strait and the lion's share offloading at the ports of Kaohsiung and Keelung on the southern and northern tips of the island.[107] As of December 2021, Taiwan imported nearly a million barrels of oil per day, as well as around 100,000 barrels of other petroleum products, refining nearly all its own crude. Taiwan also consumes about 2.64 billion cubic feet of gas per day—equivalent to roughly half the capacity of the largest liquefied natural gas (LNG) tanker in the world.[108] It consumes around 170,000 tons of coal per day, which is roughly equivalent to the full load of one Capesize ship, the world's largest dry cargo vessel.

Taiwan's energy reliance is not just about volume—it is also about sectoral concentration. The semiconductor industry alone accounts for a significant portion of electricity consumption. TSMC alone consumed about 8 percent of Taiwan's total electricity in 2024, a figure projected to rise as high as 24 percent by 2030.[109] Even under strict rationing, an advanced economy of 23 million people in a time of war would have significant energy needs. Taiwan's government has pledged to produce 20 percent of its power from renewables by 2026, up from just 2 percent in 2021, but these plans are probably not feasible. The government is also opposed to nuclear power. Taiwan will therefore remain reliant on fossil fuels for the foreseeable future.

A rough calculation based on open sources and baseline assumptions suggests that Taiwan could hold out for anywhere from a few weeks to a few months under conditions of near-total blockade.[110] Assuming Taiwan could seamlessly substitute oil for gas, rationing energy supply to the civilian sector could reduce total energy needs by about 40 percent, which would leave Taiwan with eleven months of oil reserves.[111] But at the same time, Taiwan's military would need more energy during an active conflict. Britain's oil imports doubled from 1939 to 1944, despite aggressive rationing to the civilian sector.[112] Factoring in higher military fuel usage would bring Taiwan's total oil demand back up to around 20 percent below prewar levels in a base-case blockade contingency.[113] Energy rationing would devastate Taiwan's economy, which might undermine the population's motivation to resist in a protracted conflict. Ukraine's energy consumption dropped 35 percent in the first year of war. Rationing energy also means kneecapping the civilian economy: Ukraine's GDP fell 29 percent in the same period, despite massive provision of aid.

Altogether, Taiwan could probably hold out for around six months without energy resupply. (This assumes its power plants are capable of converting from gas to oil and the electricity grid can remain functional—two assumptions that may be dubious.) It could presumably hold on longer if it could bring more nuclear power online.[114] But eventually Taiwan's foreign supporters would have to figure out a resupply strategy. Otherwise, Taiwan's morale might give out long before energy supplies were exhausted.

Taiwan's food situation is relatively more secure. While the island produces only one-third of the calories it consumes, this reliance on imports reflects the preferences of a wealthy, land-scarce nation in peacetime.[115] In wartime, Taiwan could adapt. As of 2021, it had 953,000 metric tons of rice in stock, sufficient to feed its population for eighteen months.[116] It also held six months' worth of fruits and vegetables, 525,000 metric tons of pork, and 510,000 metric tons of chicken products, alongside the domestic capacity to produce one egg per capita daily.[117] Taiwan is self-sufficient in fertilizer, although production is energy-intensive. Taiwan's robust fisheries industry produces over 300,000 tons of seafood annually through aquaculture, enough for basic protein needs.[118] Additionally, Taiwan's fleet of over 2,000 fishing vessels generates 765,000 tons of seafood globally each year. While a PRC blockade could disrupt some of these operations, it would struggle to halt them entirely. Rising protein prices might also incentivize smuggling from regional countries like the Philippines. Contraband flows across borders, even during wartime. Notably, a 2024 memorandum between the American Institute in Taiwan and Taiwan's representative office in the United States suggests that food resilience under blockade has improved since 2022.[119]

As Lonnie Henley has observed, China could impose a blockade at any point:

1. As political coercion against Taiwan's authorities, in a context short of war.

2. As a prelude to a planned invasion.

3. As part of an invasion.

4. As a "Plan B" strategy following a failed invasion.[120]

In practice, the first two scenarios seem unlikely. For reasons discussed in Chapter 2, a narrowly targeted quarantine framed as routine law enforcement is a better strategy. Targeting "separatist" leaders rather than the civilian "Chinese compatriots" would undermine China's political arguments and cause human catastrophe. China would stand accused of atrocities worse than anything Russia has yet to commit in Ukraine. Other countries in the region would be terrified and may support a U.S.-led international effort to resupply Taiwan. Moreover, as Washington could respond to any attempt to curtail Taiwan's economic autonomy by taking steps that dared China to escalate to war. The Pentagon has made this threat explicitly.[121]

Thus, a full-scale blockade is much more likely to accompany an invasion or to be used as a fallback after a failed invasion. Once a war begins—particularly if the United States and Japan intervene—dissuading foreign intervention would no longer be a concern, and public opinion in third countries would matter less than winning the war. Beijing might find a blockade most attractive as a last-ditch measure following a failed invasion, when it may be desperate to avoid a defeat that could imperil the CCP regime's survival.

To conclude this discussion, in a hypothetical scenario of a long and impermeable blockade, the people of Taiwan would suffer great privation, but the island would run out of energy long before it ran out of food.[122] The key question is how Taiwan's politics and society would respond. The answer would depend on political signaling from Beijing and Washington, not just the size of Taiwan's reserves. Civilian life under blockade would be grueling. Morale would be a big problem, if not the single biggest.

Would Blockade Be Checkmate?

While starving out Taiwan's population cannot possibly be Beijing's first-choice strategy, the fact that this "Plan B" exists is a deterrence problem.[123] If Beijing declared total war on the people of Taiwan, the burden would fall on Washington to show that all hope was not lost. Otherwise, Taiwan's leaders, facing mass starvation, might immediately begin negotiating their surrender. The more the blockade scenario seems to represent "checkmate," the more risk-tolerant China may become in other crisis scenarios. Indeed, if Xi thinks he has a guaranteed pathway to force Taiwan to capitulate even if an amphibious invasion fails, he may be more willing to gamble on an invasion even if he is uncertain it will succeed.

To prevent Beijing from thinking this way, Washington must implement robust denial and punishment strategies specifically tailored to counter blockade. Operationally defeating a blockade by breaking through PLA resistance with regular resupply vessels would be an extraordinarily difficult task. It would require Taiwan and its allies to clear naval mines from the approaches to Taiwan's harbors, while simultaneously preventing China from reseeding those waters. (In practice, this might require mining mainland ports to immobilize China's Coast Guard and maritime militia). U.S. forces would also need to suppress or destroy China's reconnaissance satellites and IADS, which would otherwise enable precision targeting of ships and aircraft approaching Taiwan. China's IADS can be likened to an intricate network of sensors and missile systems—its "eyes and ears"—designed to detect and neutralize airborne threats. This system includes ground-based and aerial sensors on the mainland, installations on artificial islands in the South China Sea, and an array of land- and ship-based surface-to-air missiles of varying ranges. China's maritime reconnaissance and targeting rely heavily on satellites, adding another layer of complexity to the challenge.[124] U.S. military planning accounts for this through operations such as "suppression of enemy air defenses" (SEAD) and "destruction of enemy air defenses" (DEAD).[125] However, these would be far harder than simply sinking the PLA Navy's amphibious fleet, requiring sustained and coordinated strikes on a vast, resilient network.

Breaking a blockade would thus require extensive strikes on mainland targets, large-scale mine warfare, and escalation into cyberspace and outer space. All these steps would risk mass civilian casualties on both sides, as well as further escalation, and success would not be guaranteed. Beijing could retaliate directly against the U.S. homeland with cyberattacks or other terrorist acts. Both sides would likely target each other's satellites, disrupting communications, surveillance, and precision targeting. These steps could risk nuclear miscalculation by degrading early warning systems. If the crisis escalated, the use of tactical nuclear weapons by each side could not be ruled out. Clearly, no sane U.S. president would desire such a catastrophic and existentially risky scenario. Neither would a sane PRC leader. Ensuring that China does not regard a blockade as a sure path to checkmate is essential to deterring it from starting a war in the first place. Thus, the United States must build and maintain the capabilities described above, deterring China from attempting a full blockade at any point on the escalation ladder.

Economic and Political Implications

Let's revisit the chapter's opening: the first moments of an amphibious invasion of Taiwan. As reports of explosions and blackouts in Taipei flood social media, financial markets globally enter free fall. Within hours, Apple alone loses nearly $1 trillion in market value. Investors abandon developing economies and flock to safe havens like gold and Swiss francs. Liquidity in the global banking system begins to evaporate, leaving many firms unable to meet overnight obligations. Meanwhile, speculators stockpile rare earths, pharmaceuticals, and other exports from China, anticipating that supplies will soon be cut off. Insurers suspend coverage for cargo traveling through the East and South China Seas. Airlines across Asia cancel flights. The financial system, overwhelmed by uncertainty, starts to fracture.[126]

In this moment of crisis, POTUS would convene the Joint Chiefs of Staff, followed by urgent calls to the New York Stock Exchange, Federal Reserve governors, and treasury secretary. A halt in trading would likely be the first step to stem panic and prevent a run on the banking system. Yet such measures could only slow, not stop, the financial reckoning. Investors would continue pricing in the risk of a U.S.–China war, further accelerating capital flight from vulnerable economies and driving currency collapses in weaker markets.

Oil prices could spiral out of control, surging in some regions while plummeting in others.

These financial and economic tremors would reverberate globally, forcing Washington to manage both the immediate fallout and the strategic consequences of the unfolding crisis. At the heart of the U.S. response would be the Federal Reserve, which would face extraordinary challenges in balancing its dual mandate of price stability and full employment. Slashing interest rates to stabilize financial markets and preserve jobs could exacerbate inflation, which would be poised to skyrocket anyway amidst supply-chain disruptions and resource shortages. The Fed would also likely extend dollar swap lines to allied central banks to prevent liquidity crises in key partner economies, among other emergency measures previously deployed during the COVID-19 pandemic.[127] These efforts would need to be carefully coordinated with fiscal measures from Congress and the Treasury.

To better understand the economic dimension of the invasion scenario, it is worth examining historical precedents, especially the outbreak of World War I. In 1914, investors first dumped all assets perceived as risky. The London Stock Exchange closed for six months, during which time the British government spent the equivalent of one-fifth of its national debt, stabilizing global financial markets.[128] While the pound sterling initially strengthened due to its status as the reserve currency, prolonged conflict undermined sterling's dominance, eventually paving the way for the dollar to rise in its place. A Taiwan crisis might follow a similar trajectory: the dollar could surge as a safe haven initially but risk losing ground if the conflict dragged on and the global financial system realigned.

Unlike the situation in 1914, today's central banks possess a broader array of tools to contain financial panic, from quantitative easing to emergency lending facilities. Yet the interconnectedness of modern markets presents challenges of its own. Sharp currency realignments, supply-chain disruptions, and capital flight would reverberate across industries and regions in ways that even the most coordinated policy interventions might struggle to control.

Even if Washington refrained from full-scale economic warfare, a PRC invasion and/or blockade of Taiwan would disrupt supply chains, leading to rapid, broad-based, and potentially sustained shortages of key goods, as well as inflation and mass layoffs. The economic disruption would be particularly acute if the United States, China, or both sought to weaponize semiconductor supply chains. As markets priced in these risks, the most likely first-order response is that the U.S. dollar, long regarded as the world's most liquid and widely held reserve currency, would surge in value. At the same time, U.S. bond yields would fall as investors sought stability in dollar-denominated assets such as Treasury bonds. Meanwhile, China's currency, the renminbi, would face opposite pressures: significant capital outflows, trade disruptions, and shaken investor confidence.

Beijing's response would likely resemble its actions during the 2015–16 market turmoil. In that crisis, it spent nearly $1 trillion in foreign exchange reserves to stabilize its currency. However, a Taiwan crisis would be vastly more challenging. It would likely require even stricter enforcement of China's capital controls and more aggressive intervention to prevent China's banking system from collapsing.[129]

The effects of these moves on developing economies would be profound. Capital would flee from assets perceived as risky—particularly in countries like South Korea and Malaysia that are deeply dependent on electronics and other supply chains that involve trade with both sides. These countries could face immediate financial distress. They would immediately require access to dollar liquidity to prevent systemic collapse. The entire global financial system would face risks of contagion, putting pressure on central bankers to coordinate.

Yet central bankers would face a difficult choice. With supply chains badly disrupted by the war and potentially exacerbated by U.S. and PRC economic warfare policies, the supply shock would lead to shortages, a drying up of liquidity, and potentially skyrocketing prices. At the same time, however, prices of some key commodities—including oil—might swing wildly. If producers were unable to make deliveries to customers as a result of sanctions or physical obstructions, prices would collapse wherever supply exceeded demand and would spike wherever demand exceeded supply. Governments around the world might complicate the situation further by imposing price controls, export bans, strategic stockpile expansions, and other policies distorting markets and impairing the flow of trade. Marine insurance markets could take time to heal. Replacement of semiconductor manufacturing equipment or facilities damaged during a conflict could take years.

The medium- to long-term effects on consumer behavior, investment, and the like would be very difficult to forecast. In the short term, central banks would face intense pressure to ease monetary policy and provide unlimited liquidity to support financial stability. However, these actions would come with huge longer-term costs and risks. The same monetary policy that would be necessary to preserve stability and macroeconomic collapse would risk letting inflation surge out of control and potentially become entrenched, leading to a crisis in the bond market. Coordination between central bankers and politicians could prove challenging, particularly in countries that had done no pre-crisis contingency planning.

While the immediate shock might last weeks or months, with supply chains beginning to heal after the fighting stopped, the restructuring of global trade and financial flows could persist for years, reshaping the global economy fundamentally. Even if Taiwan's fate were quickly resolved in either direction and a cease-fire achieved, the United States and its major developed country allies would probably seek to permanently curtail their dependence on imports from China. At a minimum, this could involve efforts to break "critical" dependencies, but broader-based sanctions or trade restrictions are also possible. China, meanwhile, might cut off exports of critical minerals, advanced materials, certain electronic components, and other products to disrupt the economic security efforts of the United States and its allies.

Supply chains, once disrupted, might take many years to heal. Even if combat temporarily paused in the Western Pacific, private shipping companies might be cautious about the political and legal risk of operating there. In this context, the market would impose sustained downward pressure on China's exchange rate. China would probably intervene to keep its exchange rate stable. However, Beijing's incentives would be to allow a gradual, managed depreciation of the renminbi over a period of months or years to grant China's exporters a competitive edge.

Over time, as trade flows resumed, cheap made-in-China goods would likely flood global markets to an even greater degree than before the invasion of Taiwan. Over a time horizon of months to years after the outbreak of hostilities, China's dumping behavior would undercut producers around the world. It would likely provoke protectionist responses from industrialized economies, including the European Union. These trends would further destabilize fragile markets in developing nations and throw the international trading system even deeper into crisis.

A key question is what would happen to the dollar. In the short term, as we have seen, the market's typical response in moments of extreme geopolitical crisis is to flee to "safe assets." Assuming U.S. Treasury bonds are in this category, that would push down borrowing costs in the United States, though it would also force the Fed and Treasury Department to ensure that other countries could continue to access dollar liquidity. In the longer term, developing countries and industrialized countries exposed to China-related trade disruptions might need additional support to manage their balance of payments and prevent default. A much stronger dollar would increase the cost of imports for most countries and make dollar-denominated debt more expensive to service, straining government budgets and fueling inflation. The impact could vary by region.[130] However, given the experience of 2025, when the dollar sold off sharply following President Trump's announcement of tariffs on China, it is no longer safe to assume that markets would regard U.S. Treasury bonds as "risk-free" assets.

How Washington planned to retaliate economically against China would therefore become the most important question for global financial markets. In some scenarios, this could work to America's advantage. But there are also conceivable scenarios where Washington overplays its hand and triggers a crisis in the bond market and a full-blown flight from the dollar system. Such a crisis would have seismic implications for the future of global finance—and U.S. geopolitical power.

In summary, an invasion or blockade of Taiwan would represent one of the greatest financial and economic shocks in history. The details are impossible to forecast precisely because of the scale of the crisis and the uncertainties about how governments would respond. However, history and theory suggest that supply-chain disruptions and abrupt movements in capital markets would have transformative consequences for the global economy. In general, trade-dependent Indo-Pacific economies would be the worst-affected, followed by commodity producers. China would suffer a much greater hit to GDP than the United States. However, no country would be spared the economic devastation, which in turn would have seismic political consequences.

In this context, large-scale policy interventions into the economy would be inevitable. Much of the uncertainty centers on how blunt and broad-based these interventions would be and how long they would last. In such a scenario, the top political concern for most countries, companies, institutional investors, and ordinary people would be *uncertainty* about their economic future. They would look to Washington not only to resist China's military aggression, but also to provide economic leadership.

Conclusion

This chapter has shown that it is still possible for the United States, Taiwan, and their partners to deter an invasion and blockade—but the trends in the military balance are worrying. In principle, Taiwan can hold off an invasion long enough for U.S. and allied forces to come to the rescue and decimate the PLA's air and naval power within the First Island Chain. Yet China is rapidly and systematically expanding key capabilities—particularly in long-range precision strike, amphibious lift, and integrated air defense—to improve its prospects. The defenders are not adapting fast enough in response. Partly as a result, Taiwan faces a morale crisis. Everyone in Taiwan knows that the island is quantitatively outmatched and that key trend lines in the military balance favor China. The PLA's increasingly obvious Plan B of a medieval-style blockade is another reason why the balance of risk is shifting in Beijing's favor. Without rapid U.S. and allied intervention and strong leadership within Taiwan, morale could implode. Taiwan could fall—and fall quickly.

Any invasion scenario would therefore require a robust American response starting on Day One. U.S. and allied forces would have to fight their way in through China's reconnaissance-strike complex, using bombers, submarines, surface ships, and drones. China would likely retaliate against U.S. bases in the region. U.S. forces may respond with strikes on mainland targets. Both sides would likely attack each other's reconnaissance and communications systems in outer space and cyberspace. Nuclear threats and other forms of strategic deterrence would shape these choices and escalation pathways. The outcome of this fight is impossible to predict from wargaming and simulation alone, not least because economic and political factors would be essential in shaping Taiwan's morale, U.S. and allied coalition unity, and the responses of the rest of the world. U.S. commanders today signal confidence that they would win decisively. But once a conflict began, peace would come only through negotiation. In the heat of the crisis, this means it would be highly unclear to all sides how long a conflict might go on. The stakes: the shape of global order after the dust settled.

Holding together the U.S.-led coalition would be an essential and challenging task in this perilous moment. U.S. air and naval forces would lead, but Japan's geographic position and logistical capabilities make it a critical partner. Australia's strategic depth and resources could sustain logistics, while South Korea's industrial base could be very helpful in securing key supply chains. Cooperation across the Western alliance network would need to extend far beyond conventional military operations. Washington would have to take account of the domestic political constraints and economic vulnerabilities of each ally.

Meanwhile, the economic consequences of a Taiwan conflict would reverberate across global financial systems in ways without historical precedent. When World War I broke out in 1914, flows of trade and gold were disrupted, leading to immediate financial crisis. In today's even more globalized world, sudden disruptions could easily trigger cascading failures. Central banks would face extraordinary challenges. Allies and nonaligned states would have to navigate pressure from both the United States and China as they struggled to protect their own economic security in the crisis. These dynamics would reshape global trade and power structures. The fight for Taiwan would determine who dominates the broader international economic order.

In short, conventional military "deterrence by denial" is necessary but not sufficient: the United States needs an integrated strategy across all domains to deter an amphibious invasion and blockade. All these elements must reinforce one another. In the next four chapters, we will examine each pillar of this integrated deterrence strategy.

PART III

The Pillars of Deterrence

4

Political Deterrence

On August 1, 1995, President Bill Clinton sent a secret letter to his PRC counterpart, Jiang Zemin.[1] In the weeks previously, Taiwan President Lee Teng-hui had visited his alma mater, Cornell University, to speak at an alumni event. The Clinton administration had initially promised Beijing that it would deny Lee's visa, but Congress had intervened, and Lee ultimately attended the event.[2] To make Washington and Taipei pay a price for these provocations, Jiang launched missiles into the water around Taiwan. Clinton hoped that a personal letter artfully reiterating the U.S. position might help defuse the situation.[3]

The letter was full of assurances—but it was backed by an unmistakable threat. Clinton reiterated that "the policy of the United States with respect to China and Taiwan remains unchanged." He noted that in accordance with the One China Policy, his administration had "resisted calls" for "Taiwan independence," as well as other formulations such as "two Chinas" or "one China, one Taiwan."[4] Having made these assurances, Clinton strongly implied that he would respond decisively if China violated its commitments to resolving cross-strait differences by "peaceful" means. As Assistant Secretary of Defense Joseph Nye reportedly told his PRC counterparts later in the crisis: "We don't know what we would do, because it's going to depend on the circumstances, and you don't know what we would do."[5] Clinton further demonstrated his resolve by sending a carrier battle group to the Taiwan Strait.[6] Beijing continued to launch missiles intermittently through the election, but the crisis ultimately deescalated.

This episode captures the essence of U.S. political deterrence. The One China Policy is a principled position that emphasizes the longstanding U.S. commitment to regional peace and stability. Within this framework, the United States deliberately cultivates ambiguity about how exactly it would respond to a unilateral change in the status quo. The ambiguity allows

Washington to couple credible threats to each side with credible assurances. Taiwan receives reassurance that the United States is likely to defend it from unprovoked attack; Beijing receives assurances that Washington will oppose any unilateral Taiwanese declaration of independence and exercise restraint in its bilateral relationship with Taipei.[7] Dual deterrence imposes enough uncertainty on both sides to discourage reckless action. It also gives Washington the flexibility to respond effectively to new circumstances.[8]

Today, however, ongoing shifts in the regional balance of power are raising questions about whether an ambiguous U.S. policy is sustainable. China's ongoing military buildup has not completely undermined U.S. military primacy in the region, but it has cast doubt on it. The greater the costs and risks U.S. forces would face in an escalating conflict, the less credible ambiguous American threats become. Xi Jinping is trying to signal greater resolve than his predecessors, raising the prospect that he might take more risks in crisis situations. Beijing's all-domain pressure campaign has created a climate of chronic tension below the threshold of open conflict. Meanwhile, domestic changes in Taiwan have introduced new complexity. The ruling Democratic Progressive Party (DPP) favors a stronger assertion of Taiwan's autonomy, and the opposition Kuomintang (KMT) advocates engagement with Beijing. Public opinion in Taiwan increasingly leans toward a distinct Taiwanese identity, and yet surveys and recent election results show that public opinion is fluid, with many voters growing disenchanted with both parties.[9] Taiwan's leaders must navigate a precarious path—pushing back against the all-domain pressure campaign without provoking Beijing and preparing for potential crisis scenarios without undermining public morale or taking blame from voters who charge them with provoking China. U.S. statements and actions can have large and unpredictable effects on Taiwan's domestic politics. Washington lacks an institutionalized Core coalition of regional allies and partners that can speak with a perfectly coordinated voice on key issues.

This chapter explores three categories of action that the United States can take to adapt its political deterrence strategy to these evolving challenges, starting by strengthening engagement with Taiwan itself. There is much work to be done here. The U.S. government must help its own officials—and the American public—deepen their understanding of Taiwan's politics, language, and society. It must defend democracy in Taiwan and beyond, including through robust public diplomacy. It must deepen economic cooperation with Taiwan, particularly in trade, energy, and information technology. It must push Taiwan privately to invest in its resilience, build asymmetric defense capabilities and robust defense supply chains, and expand its strategic stockpiles. Executing this enhanced engagement strategy will require sophisticated diplomacy. Washington has long committed to Beijing that its interactions with Taiwan will be "informal." This commitment by custom precludes many of the traditional engagement mechanisms that two states would use to deepen relations.[10] Taiwan needs to be pushed to do more, but Washington must deliver this message without provoking Beijing or undermining Taiwan's domestic political stability. Washington must also resist showing favoritism toward any political party in Taiwan, focusing instead on building lasting institutional relationships that transcend electoral cycles.

Next, the chapter discusses how Washington can use political signaling to help deter Xi from forcing brinkmanship crises. Since power in Beijing is concentrated in Xi's hands, political deterrence must account for both his potential motivations and his personal incentives to bluff. This chapter evaluates the deterrent logic of "strategic ambiguity" and argues that it remains the best approach, given the uncertainty about Xi's thinking. However, Washington should communicate ambiguity differently. Under a new concept that I call "structured ambiguity," the United States would explicitly warn that destabilizing moves in the Taiwan Strait could prompt it to modify or "clarify" the One China Policy to uphold peace and stability. Structured ambiguity would involve using selective intelligence disclosures, public and private, to signal U.S. awareness of imminent threats, following the model demonstrated before Russia's invasion of Ukraine. For this approach to work, Washington must ensure consistent communication across administrations and convince Beijing that the United States has reliable early warning systems and the resolve to act preemptively if necessary. While this strategy may not deter an invasion if Xi is already determined to invade, it could disrupt gray-zone brinkmanship and force Beijing to reveal its hand before PLA forces fully mobilized.

Finally, the chapter addresses how to institutionalize the Core coalition. The five Core members of the coalition would likely be the United States, Japan, Australia, Canada, and the UK. These countries have shared strategic interests and collectively represent over one-third of global GDP, nearly two-fifths of global demand, and nearly half of global defense spending. Japan's geographic position and Australia's commitment to a free Indo-Pacific make them indispensable partners. Despite recent trade disputes, the United States has an extremely close defense and security relationship with the UK and

Canada. London and Ottawa also have overlapping interests with Canberra and Tokyo, a fact that likely ensures their participation in any Core coalition. By contrast, the extent of support from other major allies like France and South Korea remains uncertain. The United States needs a flexible political framework that can mobilize overlapping circles of military, political, and economic cooperation. While most countries may remain neutral in a Taiwan crisis, the United States should engage them on shared interests, recognizing that they may also maintain ties with China. Broadly speaking, effective political deterrence requires the United States to articulate a clear vision for the post-crisis international system and the role of U.S. leadership within it.

Taken together, this program of jointly engaging Taiwan, managing China, and establishing the Core coalition aims to preserve the delicate balance of dual deterrence. The best way to preserve peace is to communicate the U.S. commitment to regional stability while dissuading both Beijing and Taipei from reckless behavior. As China's power grows and Taiwan's democracy matures, maintaining this balance becomes both more difficult and more essential.

Engage Taiwan

Principled and consistent U.S. engagement toward Taiwan is an essential component of political deterrence. As we have seen in previous chapters, Beijing is pursuing a strategy of political and psychological warfare against Taiwan's democracy. It hopes to drive a wedge between Taipei and Washington and persuade the people of Taiwan that the United States will not come to their aid in a crisis. Taiwan's society, understandably, is caught between nihilism and cautious optimism. If Beijing's relative military power continues to grow, it will be increasingly difficult for the United States to reassure Taiwan that it is not going to be abandoned or used as a pawn in a devastating U.S.–China conflict. Paying close attention to the state of Taiwan's domestic politics—especially perceptions of the United States in the public discourse—is therefore more important today than it was just a few years ago.

In this chapter, we will explore three categories of actions that the United States can take in its relationship with Taiwan: strengthening its reassurances to Taiwan's democracy, deepening defense cooperation, and encouraging Taiwan to improve its resilience by bolstering its energy security, food supplies, cyber defenses, and civil defenses. Washington must take these steps actively and with diplomatic care. While public statements of U.S. support are essential for deterring Beijing, Washington must privately and consistently remind Taipei that it strongly opposes unilateral changes on either side—including statements and actions from Taipei seeking to formalize Taiwan independence. This private messaging should complement public reassurances.

Ensuring that Taiwan's leadership understands the limits of U.S. commitments is critical to preventing miscalculations while maintaining the credibility of deterrence. On the one hand, if Washington fails to act in accordance with the historical understanding of the One China Policy or if it unequivocally suggests that it would defend Taiwan, it risks provoking Beijing and lulling Taiwan's leaders into complacency. On the other hand, it must push Taiwan to do more without being seen as favoring one of Taiwan's political parties over the other. Above all, U.S. officials should be discreet, empathetic, and respectful when speaking about crisis scenarios that might involve the devastation of Taiwan. If the people of Taiwan expect that the United States plans to devastate their island in the name of denying Beijing victory, they may prefer to negotiate peace with Beijing than to fight in their own defense.[11]

Deepen U.S. Understanding of Taiwan

Helping the American people understand what Taiwan is and why it matters for U.S. interests is essential. Informal U.S.–Taiwan contacts in the economic, educational, and cultural spheres should be expanded as much as possible. The U.S. side should ease visa rules for students, businesspeople, researchers, and cultural figures from Taiwan. It should foster a younger generation of Taiwanese leaders who are familiar with and supportive of U.S. values and interests. Meanwhile, both governments should expand scholarship programs for U.S. nationals to visit and live in Taiwan, especially for language study. Americans studying in mainland China face recruitment attempts from PRC intelligence services. The strict political environment in CCP-controlled educational institutions is antithetical to free inquiry and expression. This is why hardly any U.S. students and researchers work and study in China anymore.[12] The United States needs a deep bench of China expertise. Taiwan can help.

U.S. policymakers working on the region also need to spend more time in Taiwan and seek out a broader range of Taiwanese perspectives. English-language media provide only limited coverage of Taiwanese politics and do not reflect the diversity of public opinion.[13] Taiwanese observers are grappling with the same questions as their American colleagues about how to deter China. They know that their democracy is in danger. They know Taiwan needs help. They have strong views but not necessarily perfect answers. They also want to shape public opinion in the United States to support their point of view and advance their vision of Taiwan's future. It is helpful to remember that America and Taiwan are two free and open societies that are highly responsive to one another. Whether Taiwan will prepare adequately to fight in its own defense depends largely on how its people assess America's commitment. Meanwhile, America's commitment depends in part on Taiwan's willingness to defend itself. If the United States hopes to defend Taiwan effectively, it needs to understand the island it is defending.

Notably, polling shows that the Taiwanese public remains skeptical that an invasion or blockade is imminent. In an October 2024 poll conducted by the think tank INDSR, only 24 percent of respondents expected the PLA to attack Taiwan in the next five years, while 61 percent deemed it unlikely or very unlikely. When asked about potential U.S. support in such a scenario, 75 percent expected the United States to airlift food and medical supplies, 74 percent believed it would impose sanctions on China, and 76 percent anticipated military aid in the form of weapons and supplies. However, only 53 percent expected that U.S. troops would assist in Taiwan's defense, and just 40 percent expected the United States to risk a war with China to break a PLA blockade of Taiwan.[14]

All surveys show that Taiwan's willingness to fight depends heavily on its assumptions about whether America will fight and on whether a conflict is winnable. Such surveys have yielded varying results on these questions, which are likely explained by differences in the wording of the questions and the survey design. For example, a Taiwan Foundation for Democracy poll found that 72.5 percent of respondents would "fight" to defend Taiwan, but a Global View Monthly poll reported that only 40 percent would be willing to "fight yourself or let your family members fight on the battlefield."[15]

There is a striking similarity to Ukrainian sentiment before Russia's invasion in February 2022. A CNN poll conducted just before the war began revealed that Ukrainians strongly rejected forced unification with Russia—85 percent believed Ukraine and Russia should remain separate countries, and only 28 percent saw them as "one people," even rising to just 45 percent in the heavily Russophone east. Yet, despite rising tensions, most Ukrainians did not expect an imminent attack: only 42 percent believed Russia was likely to invade, while 43 percent anticipated a peaceful resolution, and 61 percent remained optimistic about the future.[16] These perceptions shifted dramatically after President Volodymyr Zelensky boldly told the Americans "I need ammunition, not a ride," and Russia's initial assault in Kyiv's Hostomel Airport failed. Once the Ukrainian people decided that the war might in fact be winnable, willingness to fight skyrocketed. Prewar public opinion is generally a poor predictor of actual conflict.

The United States must help to strengthen rather than undermine Taiwan's morale. Many people on Taiwan do not trust the United States' motivations. Some Taiwanese voters, disproportionately on the KMT side, are exposed to constant PRC propaganda that presents the United States as an unreliable partner that considers Taiwan as a pawn to be sacrificed. When U.S. politicians such as President Trump observe that Taiwan is dedicating insufficient resources to its own defense, they are undoubtedly correct—but their comments also play into PRC propaganda. Another widespread belief, which CCP propaganda echoes at every opportunity, is that Washington is simply trying to force Taiwan to give up its crown jewels—its chipmaking know-how—and that it plans to abandon Taiwan as soon as it achieves self-sufficiency. As Republican presidential candidate Vivek Ramaswamy said in 2023: "We will defend Taiwan, at least until we have achieved semiconductor independence in this country, at which point we will reevaluate."[17] The more American political figures understand Taiwan, the less likely they will be to make such comments.

Readers interested in getting a taste of the diversity of elite opinion in Taiwan can consult Appendix A in this book. This section presents in-depth interviews with four prominent Taiwanese individuals—two former national security advisers, a major IT executive, and a prominent political commentator—conducted during the course of a single week in the summer of 2023. Two of these individuals can be described as "green" (DPP-leaning), and two as "blue" (KMT-leaning). All four have interacted with American and PRC interlocutors on Taiwan's behalf at a high level over many years and are now in a position to speak freely. Of course, summing up the political discourse in an entire democratic society through the voices of four retired men is impossible. The world has also changed profoundly since the election of Lai Ching-te and the reelection of Donald Trump. Still, in deepening their understanding of Taiwan, readers might find it interesting to study these interviews alongside each other. They reveal that behind Taiwan's disciplined public diplomacy lie debate, disagreement, and profound uncertainty.

Defend Democracy in Taiwan and Beyond

To support Taiwan's democracy, U.S. officials must systematically expose, condemn, and challenge China's psychological warfare and information operations designed to undermine Taiwan's democracy.[18] Washington should selectively disclose intelligence about UFWD activity and offer grants to support scholarly research on the subject. It should also facilitate cooperative partnerships with social media platforms and leading AI labs to help Taiwan's government detect and counter PRC disinformation and malign influence operations. The recent defunding of government-supported media like Radio Free Asia threatens the United States' ability to emphasize and celebrate the resilience of Taiwan's democracy. U.S. diplomats and government-funded media revitalizing America's public diplomacy will help to show Taiwan and the wider world that the PRC's psychological warfare will not weaken either U.S. support or Taiwan's determination to remain autonomous.

Supporting Taiwan's democracy also means respecting the outcome of Taiwan's democratic processes. The United States should communicate candidly in private meetings with Taiwan's elected officials through existing informal arrangements, but it must never publicly show favoritism to any Taiwanese political party. Public alignment with any particular party would erode the credibility of U.S. support for Taiwan's democracy and undermine the trust of Taiwanese citizens who support different parties. Washington should instead emphasize its commitment to the island's democratic processes and self-determination. By focusing on principles, the United States can ensure that engagement will play a unifying role, reinforcing Taiwan's political stability rather than exacerbating internal divisions.

In the international arena, the United States must counter PRC propaganda about UN Resolution 2758, which recognizes the PRC as the lawful "Chinese" representative in the UN. As noted in Chapter 2, Beijing falsely claims that this resolution has settled Taiwan's status, even though the text takes great pains to leave the matter ambiguous.[19] U.S. diplomats could prioritize this issue and work with allies to engage developing countries at the UN to garner broader support for this position. Additionally, Washington and its allies must continue to bolster support for the twelve countries that still recognize Taiwan; not surprisingly, these states face relentless and intensifying pressure from Beijing.[20]

The United States can also prepare to communicate directly with the PRC public during a crisis. Taiwan's thriving democracy is living proof that Chinese people can live lives of abundance and maintain a harmonious society under a political system based on open elections, free speech, and individual liberty. By highlighting Taiwan's democracy, the United States can remind the world that the CCP's hold on power is neither inevitable nor immutable. Increased awareness of Taiwan's democratic model could prompt mainland citizens to challenge their government's legitimacy. While direct engagement with the PRC public should generally be avoided to avoid provoking Beijing unnecessarily, Washington must be ready to counter CCP propaganda and champion Taiwan's democratic achievements everywhere in the world if Beijing resorts to force.

Reaching audiences across the "Great Firewall" is challenging but feasible. Despite Beijing's efforts to control information and suppress dissent, tools such as shortwave radio broadcasts—like the Voice of America—have proven capable of reaching millions.[21] Cyber operations and other information strategies should also be explored. If a crisis arises, Washington must have a *comprehensive information campaign* ready to ensure that the people of China have access to the facts. In moments of peril, America must stand firmly in support of democracy. The CCP fears democracy because it fears its own people.

Deepen Economic and Technology Ties

Meanwhile, the United States should pursue a comprehensive trade and investment agreement with Taiwan.[22] A robust deal should seek to take tariffs and non-tariff barriers as low as possible, promote technology transfer, and ensure investment protections. It would help to reduce Taiwan's economic dependency on China by opening new markets for Taiwanese goods and services in the United States and beyond. As part of this deal, TSMC should expand its investments in the United States. Taiwan should also be allowed to co-produce essential defense components for the U.S. military, particularly for drones.

The United States can also pursue deals to improve Taiwan's long-term energy security.[23] If Taiwan depends heavily on energy imported from neutral countries on foreign-flagged ships, Beijing could potentially coerce Taiwan's third-party suppliers into pausing deliveries without even firing a shot. Moreover, the smaller Taiwan's stockpiles, the more vulnerable it would be in a blockade and invasion scenario. An obvious potential solution is for Taiwan to sign large-scale, long-term contracts to buy liquefied natural gas (LNG) directly from the United States. The gas could be delivered on ships flagged in friendly countries and crewed by mariners from Core allied nations, or on ships that could be quickly re-flagged in a crisis. As part of this cooperative effort, Taiwan and the United States could also ensure that workers from a range of allied countries are physically positioned inside Taiwan's critical energy infrastructure. This would raise the stakes if China tried to sabotage Taiwan's energy system, as Russia has done to Ukraine. Finally, Washington should try to facilitate multi-party deals with Taiwan, Japan, South Korea, and the UK to help Taiwan adopt small modular nuclear reactors.

To counter potential PRC economic coercion, senior U.S. officials can anonymously tell media organizations that if China forces a financial panic, the Federal Reserve will provide dollar swap lines to Taiwan's central bank, ensuring that Taiwan's banking system has guaranteed access to dollar liquidity. This would be a purely symbolic signal of support. (In fact, Taiwan's central bank and commercial banking system are already so dollar-rich that they make money when the domestic currency depreciates.)[24] Still, making this symbolic assurance publicly and in advance would reassure markets that the United States will provide economic leadership if Beijing resorts to force. It would also demonstrate U.S. readiness to defend other key regional partners against China's economic coercion.

Push Taiwan Privately to Improve Its Resilience

The final area of U.S. engagement involves addressing gaps in Taiwan's resilience where it has fallen short and requires a push from Washington. On these issues, the United States must apply unrelenting pressure—but strictly in private. For instance, Washington can insist that Taiwan's resilience be the first agenda item in every informal bilateral discussion. It can present Taipei with quantitative targets for strategic reserves of critical resources like energy, food, and essential industrial machine parts—and it can demand regular progress reports. If Taiwanese leaders fail to meet these benchmarks on schedule, the United States can respond with highly targeted private measures, starting by withholding high-level interactions. Successive U.S. administrations have made their frustration with Taiwan clear, but public ultimatums should be avoided.[25] Public pressure has historically eroded the Taiwanese people's trust in the United States and failed to deliver desired results.[26] Building confidence in U.S. preparedness will help prevent panic in a crisis and strengthen the partnership between Washington and Taipei.

Taiwan should establish a formal territorial defense force modeled on the reserve systems of Israel and Estonia.[27] Such a force would mobilize civilian participation, create a more resilient reserve, and handle auxiliary functions during conflict. Washington should privately offer unofficial advisors and training opportunities in the United States and in allied nations like Australia. While steps in this direction are already underway, political foot-dragging has slowed progress. Washington must demand faster progress. A territorial defense force would enhance Taiwan's defense capacity, boost morale, and demonstrate resolve.

Taiwan's Ministry of National Defense also needs to effect internal reforms that will enhance the country's operational efficiency and preparedness. Washington can encourage Taipei to tackle inefficiencies and streamline bureaucratic procurement processes.[28] While visible U.S. interference can be politically counterproductive, behind-the-scenes pressure is possible. For example, Taiwanese journalists can be guided to cover stories that embarrass officials who are moving too slowly on critical defense issues. Additionally, Taiwan must prioritize asymmetric capabilities—notably, coastal defense systems, anti-ship missiles, and drones—that are cost-effective and directly counter PLA strategies. These reforms would not only strengthen Taiwan's preparedness but also reassure U.S. forces about Taiwan's commitment to its own defense.

Manage China

The aim of political deterrence against China is to convince Beijing that any attempt to seize Taiwan by force will come at an intolerable cost. While political measures alone cannot stop a military operation, they can play a crucial role in both gray-zone conflicts and full-scale invasion scenarios. In abstract terms, political deterrence is about signaling both U.S. resolve and restraint at every level of the escalation ladder. It is how Washington shapes Beijing's calculus by displaying U.S. capabilities and forcing Beijing to think twice about risks and uncertainties. The goal of political deterrence is twofold: first, to make clear that any use of force against Taiwan will provoke a U.S. response that will make Beijing regret its decision, and second, to reassure Beijing that if it refrains from aggression, it will not be left at a strategic disadvantage. On a very practical level, effective political deterrence hinges on clear communication. It is about ensuring that Beijing understands what the United States and key third countries are likely to do both before and after a potential Taiwan crisis.

Ambiguity has long played a key role in the U.S. approach to managing China on cross-strait issues, but the role of ambiguity is sometimes misunderstood. Under the One China Policy, the U.S. position on Taiwan's status is intrinsically ambiguous. Washington's vague position about how it would respond to a violent move against Taiwan—the position that most commentators typically call "strategic ambiguity"—is something else entirely. It is not intrinsic to the One China Policy. In principle, the value of ambiguity is that it forces an adversary to grapple with uncertainty, and therefore potentially offers a way to enjoy the partial benefits of taking multiple positions at the same time. The challenge is that ambiguity supports deterrence only if the underlying threats are credible.

Emphasize the One China Policy

The United States need not overextend itself to "reassure" China in the Taiwan Strait.[29] It simply needs to reaffirm its longstanding principled position: the One China Policy. U.S. officials and members of Congress should be briefed on the symbolic importance of communicating the policy correctly and consistently. Every articulation of the One China Policy must be recited verbatim and in full, as both China and Taiwan closely scrutinize its language.

As long as Washington adheres to the norms defining the policy, this is all the reassurance Beijing needs. Commitment to the One China Policy allows Washington to maintain, deepen, and broaden its unofficial relationship with Taiwan without conceding ground to Beijing. A critical element of China's pressure campaign involves using extreme rhetoric to deter Washington and Taipei from continuing with routine engagements, such as the transiting of Taiwanese officials through the United States. U.S. officials should counter these empty threats by publicly exposing them as bluffs. In July 2025, the Trump administration denied President Lai a planned transit. This was intended as a goodwill gesture to Beijing. But it was a mistake. Signaling that established practices in U.S.–Taiwan relations are negotiable invites China to ramp up future coercion.

Washington can also turn Xi Jinping's rhetoric against him. Xi has called the Three Communiqués the "political foundation" of U.S.–China relations. This statement is true. But it is Xi—not the United States—who is undermining that foundation! As highlighted in Chapter 1, the Communiqués were based on reciprocity: Washington agreed to limit its relations with Taipei in exchange for Beijing's commitment to pursue a peaceful resolution to cross-Strait differences. Relentless military exercises and coercive operations that threaten Taiwan's autonomy and economy clearly violate this pledge. These measures, while bloodless, are acts of violence. A Taiwanese capitulation under such duress would be illegitimate. Beijing's strategy of redefining the status quo through violent actions deemed "peaceful" undermines the credibility of its historic commitments and is destined to fail. Nevertheless, the United States will remain resolute in preserving the spirit of the Communiqués. As China acts, America will respond flexibly and proportionately to safeguard peace and stability. Washington should state this policy clearly and consistently, in both public and private settings.

Understand Strategic Ambiguity and Its Notional Alternatives

The concept informally known as strategic ambiguity is incidental to the One China Policy. The U.S. government does not officially use the term. The question is not *whether* Washington can adapt its current approach while remaining compliant with the Three Communiqués. It can. The question is *how* it should adjust its communications about its defense commitments to Taiwan. For decades, the dominant view was that strategic ambiguity was the optimal communication strategy because it preserved dual deterrence over Beijing and Taipei.[30] The idea was that even though Beijing could not be sure that Washington would come to Taiwan's defense in a crisis, it would have to assume U.S. intervention. Beijing therefore would not move if it believed that U.S. intervention would be decisive. In the meantime, strategic ambiguity gave Washington freedom of action.

The shift in the military balance in Beijing's favor has ignited a debate about strategic ambiguity.[31] Back when Taiwan could repel an invasion with only minimal outside assistance, the United States had little reason not to come to its defense in a crisis. Today, everyone knows Taiwan could not hold out for long without outside help. The question is no longer simply whether the United States *would* intervene to defend Taiwan, but whether it *could* prevent China from winning the prize at an acceptable cost. Thus, the more the military balance tips in Beijing's favor, the more the United States risks looking like it is holding on to strategic ambiguity as a get-out-of-jail-free card, and the more Beijing may be tempted to call the bluff.

In essence, the danger is that far from anchoring strategic stability, strategic ambiguity might lead to a crisis through miscalculation. As tensions approach the line of direct hostilities, strategic ambiguity undermines the credibility of U.S. threats. If deterrence fails and Taiwan falls, punishment alone will not compel China to relinquish Taiwan after the fact, and China could retaliate. Indiscriminate punishment could also lead to a general war without clear and achievable strategic objectives for the U.S. side. Making threats of punishment credible requires the United States to tie its own hands by committing irrevocably to delivering on a threat that would cause great pain and risk to itself. Strategic ambiguity makes it harder for Washington to tie its own hands. In a crisis, when Taiwan is panicked and looking to Washington for reassurance, strategic ambiguity could become untenable.

Consider the following scenario. Sometime after 2027, China finds a pretext to initiate a brinkmanship crisis over Taiwan. Beijing signals a bold assessment of the military balance: it thinks it could take and hold Taiwan, whatever Washington does. Washington responds by surging military forces to the region and preparing a muscular economic response. But China is seemingly unperturbed. It begins to mobilize an amphibious invasion force in the Taiwan Strait and moves quickly toward a quarantine of Taiwan, while signaling that it doubts that Washington would actually follow through on its punishment threats. In any case, Beijing is willing to pay the price. Taiwan's leaders panic.

How could Washington deescalate such a crisis without risking Taiwan's capitulation? Beijing might be bluffing, but Xi may simply have a high tolerance for risk and pain. Or he may also have bad information about the military balance. In this context, piling on increasingly extreme threats of punishment would be unlikely to change Xi's calculus. In fact, it might embolden him if he interpreted the threats as desperate bluffs. Washington could negotiate, but it would have no leverage. Any concessions would gut the Six Assurances, and if Washington failed to offer concessions, Xi could simply go back to turning up the temperature. Washington's last remaining option would be to reinterpret, "clarify," modify, or abandon the One China Policy. (The two sides would surely disagree about which word is most apt.) Washington could signal to China that it was prepared to send uniformed U.S. troops to Taiwan, ship more powerful weapons to Taiwan, or take various other steps up to and including recognizing Taiwan diplomatically and seeking a formal treaty alliance. Of course, taking these steps would make it harder for Xi to deescalate and would make war more likely. Any U.S. president would not want to take these steps as long as it seemed that war was avoidable. But if it became clear that war was inevitable, abandoning some past self-imposed limitations on cooperation with Taiwan might seem to serve U.S. interests, even though doing so would give Xi a more compelling pretext to escalate and make it harder for him to back down.

In essence, strategic ambiguity has been effective in reassuring both China and Taiwan up until now, but it also incentivizes Xi to use gray-zone pressure to test U.S. resolve and undermine U.S. credibility in ways that could risk misperception and miscalculation. If Washington waited until a moment when both sides were maximally invested, and then caught Beijing by surprise by modifying or abandoning the One China Policy, it could potentially trigger a war that neither side wanted.

If Xi backed down *after* the United States had abandoned the One China Policy, he would suffer a major reputational blow. It would appear to all that Beijing had been bluffing all along about its willingness to fight a war to prevent Taiwan's formal separation. Any PRC leader who "loses face" in this way would become vulnerable to internal challenges and might also lose the ability to deter Taiwan independence in the future. Mindful of these scenarios, a growing number of analysts now support reconsidering strategic ambiguity. However, all of the alternatives carry their own challenges.

One alternative is for Washington to send hints about *relative* changes in its ambiguous commitment. This is what Joe Biden was doing when he said explicitly—on four separate occasions—that the United States would defend Taiwan. In July 2021, Biden said: "We made a sacred commitment to Article 5 that if in fact anyone were to invade or take action against our NATO allies, we would respond. Same with Japan, same with South Korea, same with Taiwan."[32] A senior administration official later clarified that U.S. "policy with regard to Taiwan has not changed," suggesting that Biden had misspoken.[33] That October, Biden was again asked if the United States would come to the defense of Taiwan. "Yes, we have a commitment to do that," he said. In June 2022, Biden was asked this question yet again. "Yes," he said, without hesitation. "That's the commitment we made."[34] In September 2022, asked once again, Biden said that he would be willing to deploy U.S. troops if necessary to protect Taiwan. Each time, his administration subsequently clarified that U.S. policy had not changed.[35]

It is unclear how much Biden's statements contributed to deterrence, however. Were Biden's statements gaffes, or did they signify premeditated, definitive changes in U.S. policy? They surely put Beijing on notice that pro-Taiwan sentiment in Washington was hardening, and they strengthened Beijing's assessed probability that the United States would probably intervene to protect Taiwan from attack. At the same time, however, Biden's statements may or may not have weakened deterrence from the other direction. Beijing blamed Biden for emboldening pro-independence elements in Taiwan.[36] Of course, this is spin. But insofar as Xi believes his own rhetoric, he may think that Biden's administration was salami-slicing its way toward revising the One China Policy, and that he must therefore strengthen his own deterrence by ramping up pressure against Taiwan. In short, there are speculative arguments on each side, but it is analytically impossible to tell whether efforts to "strengthen" strategic ambiguity from within accomplish anything for deterrence. (In 2025, Donald Trump refused to state whether he would defend Taiwan, seemingly returning U.S. policy to its previous strategic ambiguity position.)[37]

Some analysts have proposed abandoning strategic ambiguity and unilaterally bringing Taiwan explicitly under the U.S. security umbrella in advance of a crisis.[38] This step could be accomplished with a single written statement from the president. It could be made even more credible if Congress adopted a similar statement. This step would make U.S. threats of punishment more credible by making it harder for Washington to ignore its past promises, even if the PLA managed to seize Taiwan. Perhaps most importantly, a shift to strategic clarity would help to reassure Taiwan. Supporters of strategic clarity argue that Washington should not worry too much about the risk of Taiwan unilaterally declaring independence.[39] Beijing has lots of ways to punish Taiwan that Washington would be powerless to prevent. Others argue that reassuring China should not be a major concern of U.S. policy, since the collapse of Taiwanese morale is a much bigger risk. In this view, Taiwan would fear abandonment no matter how ironclad a defensive pledge Washington makes— just as U.S. allies like Lithuania and South Korea have long wondered about whether an American president would really trade Vilnius or Seoul for San Francisco or Los Angeles.[40] Historically, countries that are sufficiently motivated to avoid being "entrapped" by past commitments nearly always find an excuse.[41]

Some have argued that Washington could split the difference by adopting a form of *conditional clarity*, promising explicitly to defend Taiwan if attacked, but not if Taiwan brings the crisis on itself.[42] However, it is not clear how such a move would strengthen political deterrence. U.S. statements in support of Taiwan are already implicitly conditional. (As President George W. Bush once explained the One China Policy: "If China were to invade unilaterally, we would rise up in the spirit of [the] Taiwan Relations Act. If Taiwan were to declare independence, it would be a unilateral decision that would then change the U.S. equation.")[43] Furthermore, explicitly conditional clarity has its own problems. The proximate trigger of a crisis might be an incident such as a collision in international waters or airspace. In such a scenario, it might be hard to judge—let alone agree on—which side was the aggressor.[44] In any Taiwan crisis, if Washington truly wanted to abandon Taiwan, it would find a way to blame Taiwan. Seen in this light, ostentatiously leaving open the option to abandon Taiwan if it brings a crisis on itself might undermine deterrence even more than the current policy of strategic ambiguity.[45]

Another problem with strategic clarity is that key U.S. allies like Japan and Australia are not comfortable with it. Japan recognizes Beijing as "the sole legal government of China" and avoids taking a clear stance on Taiwan's legal status.[46] Tokyo's 1972 normalization Communiqué is similar to the first U.S.–China Communiqué, but Japan has no equivalent of the Taiwan Relations Act and Six Assurances. Tokyo has historically maintained a more limited relationship with Taipei than the United States, including forgoing arms sales and related "informal" defense cooperation. Japan even typically refrains from criticizing China's coercive tactics against Taiwan.[47] Even Japanese politicians who harbor more hawkish personal views tend to follow this line in public. In 2021, Deputy Prime Minister Taro Aso was quoted as saying at a private event that a Taiwan crisis could pose an existential threat to Japan, but when the story broke, he walked back the remarks.[48] If Washington pursued strategic clarity without aligning with allies, it could risk sowing divisions within the U.S.-led alliance, which Beijing might be able to exploit.

Consider a Policy of "Structured Ambiguity"

America would benefit from a new approach that communicated credible restraint and commitment to the One China Policy, but also a credible resolve to push back against gray-zone coercion and brinkmanship crises. A potential solution lies in the fact that the One China Policy is ambiguous on many points, not just the question of what Washington would do if China invaded Taiwan. As we have seen, the substantive contents of the One China Policy have never been fixed. The nature of the U.S. relationships with Beijing and Taipei has evolved over time. U.S. commitment to the One China Policy serves as an important symbol of its dedication to regional peace and stability. The symbolism matters so deeply to Beijing that it may be in America's interest to maintain the policy even in the event of war. If the United States were to defeat China in such a conflict, continuing to observe the One China Policy could offer Beijing a face-saving pretext to end hostilities. However, the One China Policy can and should be reinterpreted as circumstances demand. China recognizes this. That is why it often complains that Washington is "hollowing out" the One China Policy.

The United States needs *a flexible toolkit for imposing proportionate costs on China when it tries to redefine the status quo unilaterally.* When China attempts to normalize constant military exercises near Taiwan, cyberattacks, interference with undersea cables, and other forms of aggression, it should face proportionate costs in the form of hollowing out the One China Policy. In short, Washington should use its own playbook of political gray-zone pressure to show China that it will face proportionate costs for gray-zone aggression against Taiwan. Beijing must understand that to provoke a brinkmanship crisis to test U.S. resolve would be to tempt fate and gamble with the CCP's legitimacy and survival.

A concept of *structured ambiguity* along these lines can deter gray-zone aggression without abandoning the flexibility of strategic ambiguity. Under this approach, Washington should retain the One China Policy but make it clear that any time Beijing attempts to alter the status quo through force or coercion, the United States may recalibrate its policy proportionately and pre-emptively to stabilize the situation. This could mean deepening military cooperation with Taiwan, strengthening diplomatic ties, or reassessing previous limits on U.S.–Taiwan relations.

Crucially, structured ambiguity is not a preemptive shift in U.S. policy. It is a warning that if China tries to change the rules through coercion, Washington will respond by reinterpreting its own strategy in a proportionate way to maintain a stable overall situation. Unlike strategic ambiguity, which aims to maintain uncertainty across the board, structured ambiguity is targeted and conditional. It is designed specifically to deter actions that risk sparking a crisis.

To illustrate how structured ambiguity might work in practice, consider a hypothetical scenario. Imagine that, sometime after 2027, China decides to escalate tensions by imposing a partial blockade on Taiwan, including on fuel and essential goods. Beijing insists that this is simply routine enforcement of PRC customs law. Under traditional strategic ambiguity, Washington has no clear framework to calibrate its response. Structured ambiguity, however, would already have signaled that if China attempts such a move, the United States might adjust its policy in ways that Beijing finds uncomfortable— perhaps by significantly increasing military aid to Taiwan, expanding official and military engagements with Taipei, or reinterpreting key aspects of the One China Policy. This uncertainty would force Beijing to weigh the risk that its actions might backfire, making it less likely to test the limits of the status quo in the first place.

A key tool for making structured ambiguity credible is selective intelligence disclosure.[49] The United States demonstrated the power of this approach before Russia's invasion of Ukraine, publicly exposing Moscow's war plans and disrupting its ability to justify escalation. A similar strategy could be applied in the Taiwan Strait. If U.S. intelligence detects preparations for a PRC blockade, quarantine, or military mobilization, Washington could make this information public, signaling that it sees these actions as potential precursors to war. The goal would be to create uncertainty for Beijing. If China's leaders believe that Washington might shift its policy in response to their provocations, they must factor this risk into their decision-making.

Structured ambiguity is not without risks, however. If mismanaged, it could be framed by Beijing as an unprovoked shift in U.S. policy, potentially reducing international support for Washington in a crisis. China could claim that the United States, rather than China itself, was responsible for destabilizing the region. Taiwan's leaders might also misread the policy, assuming that structured ambiguity guarantees U.S. military protection. The success of structured ambiguity depends on how well it is communicated in public and private.

Another potential challenge is ensuring consistency across U.S. administrations. If Washington signals resolve one year and backtracks the next, China might conclude that U.S. deterrence lacks credibility. Unlike strategic clarity, which would require Washington to make a firm, long-term security guarantee to Taiwan, structured ambiguity relies on sustained discipline in execution.

Above all, if China is truly committed to invading Taiwan, no amount of dancing around diplomatic ambiguity is likely to stop it. The purpose of structured ambiguity is to prevent the kind of slow-moving crises that could escalate into war if mismanaged. By discouraging both gray-zone coercion from Beijing and reckless independence moves from Taipei, structured ambiguity provides a flexible way for Washington to reinforce deterrence without locking itself into rigid commitments or empty threats. It keeps tensions below a dangerous threshold while preserving U.S. flexibility, ensuring that Beijing always has to calculate the risk that its actions might change the game in ways it cannot control.

Establish the Core Coalition

The third and final pathway to strengthening political deterrence involves establishing an allied coalition for coordinated planning and action before, during, and after any potential rupture with China. Of course, the precise composition of the coalition will depend on the political context of a crisis scenario. It is therefore inherently unpredictable. If even Washington does not know what it would be called to do in a Taiwan crisis, it is unhelpful to pressure allies to pre-commit to specific courses of action.[50] Still, the United States must identify and communicate its close alignment with allies whose national interests overlap on the Taiwan issue.

Japan is central to this effort. Tokyo has vital interests in maintaining regional order. It views Taiwan as a key test of U.S. resolve to ensure peace and stability in the region. Japanese officials have privately told me that U.S. abandonment of Taiwan—even under a quarantine scenario—would irreparably damage the U.S.–Japan alliance. Strengthening the political alignment with Japan would reassure both Tokyo and Taipei while bolstering U.S. commitments to other regional allies. It would also send a strong message to China that Japan would likely take decisive action in Taiwan's defense, including in non-invasion scenarios. It would signal that the United States and Japan would pursue no-limits coordination on economic, military, and political responses to a crisis.

To enhance policy alignment, Japan could adopt its own version of the Taiwan Relations Act and Six Assurances. Doing so would signal that Tokyo would regard a quarantine, blockade, or invasion of Taiwan as a violation of Beijing's commitments under the Sino-Japanese Joint Communiqué of 1972.[51] While this decision is up to Japan, any action in this area would significantly enhance the credibility of U.S.–Japan cooperation.[52] Both nations could also jointly outline rules of engagement for a Taiwan quarantine and develop plans for evacuations, resupply missions, and other key operations.

Today, Japan and other Indo-Pacific countries are not preparing effectively for crisis scenarios because they fear PRC retribution. To involve allies more fully in contingency planning, Washington must credibly promise to defend them against PRC retaliation.

The UK, Australia, and Canada can also play essential roles in political deterrence. These three countries possess economic and military heft; diplomatic savvy; human capital; industrial, technological, and financial expertise; geographic diversity; and key natural resources. All three are close U.S. allies with a long history of fighting alongside the United States. As part of the Five Eyes intelligence sharing group, they are trustworthy with Washington's most sensitive secrets. The Australia–UK–U.S. (AUKUS) partnership supports research and industrial integration with Australia in the most sensitive military-technological areas, the sale of Virginia-class nuclear-powered submarines to Australia, and the eventual joint construction of a new class of highly capable nuclear-powered attack submarine.[53] Again, of course, the UK, Australia, and Canada are sovereign nations. Washington would have to ensure that their participation in any coalition aligned with their interests, needs, and abilities.

The ultimate goal should be to establish NATO-style structures in the Indo-Pacific. Unlike the situation in Europe, where NATO allies have all pledged to defend one another if attacked, the U.S. alliance system in Asia has historically operated on a "hub-and-spoke model," with limited multilateral cooperation between U.S. allies.[54] This has begun to change, thanks to recent efforts by Japan, Australia, the UK, the Philippines, and France to pursue reciprocal basing agreements.[55] The emerging coalition is still informal and lacks a legal mutual defense pact equivalent to NATO's Article V. But the trend lines are clear: a shared political interest in protecting the free and open Indo-Pacific against PRC aggression is driving ever-closer cooperation.

Discussions on deeper security collaboration—especially regarding Taiwan—must be approached with sensitivity to the distinct political and legal considerations in each country, particularly Japan. America should actively support cooperation between these countries and NATO on discrete security issues such as defense industrial production, AI, and cyber.[56] As of this writing, France is blocking NATO's cooperation with Indo-Pacific partners, for no good reason.[57] Washington should impose diplomatic costs on France until it reverses this position. In the meantime, the Indo-Pacific allies should not wait for NATO. The integration of the burgeoning Indo-Pacific alliance and formal NATO structures can take place later, if member states agree. For now, Washington can convene and institutionalize a separate coalition of the willing. A good place to start would be to hold an annual leaders' summit for this group immediately prior to the G7. This "Core" coalition should also lead the coordinating work on economic contingency planning, discussed in Chapters 7 and 8.

Countries such as South Korea, New Zealand, and European NATO allies will likely support U.S. efforts to keep the peace in the Taiwan Strait politically, even if they do not join the core of the emerging U.S.-led regional alliance structure. Cooperation with European partners such as France and Germany would be particularly valuable because Europe could bring significant economic heft to any crisis response. However, Emmanuel Macron's public statements downplaying France's interest in Taiwan have made crystal clear that the United States cannot rely on direct European military participation or even extensive economic coordination in a Taiwan crisis.[58] Fortunately, the five Core allies account for 36 percent of global GDP, more than twice China's share, and make up 45 percent of global defense spending.[59] Together, they have the political and military strength to deter aggression, even without extensive European support. The United States needs a flexible model of coalition management that allows allies to cooperate with the United States on some policy issues and go their own ways on others. Respect for partner countries' distinctive national interests will be even more important if a Taiwan crisis erupts.

Strengthening U.S. partnerships in the developing world is another key element of political deterrence. China portrays itself as the leader of the developing world. It is actively cultivating partnerships there, pitching an alternative vision for a "fairer" world order than the supposedly "hegemonic" and neocolonial international system dominated by the United States.[60] China's strategy is already working to some degree. India, for example, has engaged in the China-led BRICS and the Shanghai Cooperation Organization, even as it has strengthened ties with the United States. Whenever China or the United States tries to pressure India, New Delhi's standard practice is to lean in the other direction.[61] Washington must therefore set realistic expectations. Many if not most countries would remain neutral during a Taiwan crisis. They would hope to maintain productive trade and technology relations with both the United States and China. The United States would not be able to force them to make binary choices. Rather, it would have to compete more actively to counterbalance China's influence.

The broader point is that political and economic deterrence are interconnected. The United States and its Core allies must articulate a positive vision for regional and global order that focuses on economic security and is directed especially toward developing countries. Their message should emphasize the right of sovereign states to safeguard their economic security in a fair and honest way. While China relies on unfettered globalization to sustain its struggling economic model, the United States recognizes that globalization must be balanced with respect for national interests and strong state institutions. We will explore the economic aspects of this vision further in Chapter 8. The key point is that Xi Jinping's vision for a changing world order places heavy weight on partnerships with developing countries. If it seems that a violent move against Taiwan would damage these relationships—especially by driving key countries to deepen economic cooperation with the United States—that strengthens political deterrence.

Conclusion

A political strategy to prevent war with China must extend beyond dissuading Beijing from using force against Taiwan. It aims to align the interests of all parties toward preserving peace and stability in the region. For nearly half a century, the One China Policy, reinforced by strategic ambiguity, has been central to this balance. The One China Policy reassures Taiwan of U.S. support against unprovoked aggression while signaling to Beijing that Washington does not support Taiwan independence. It implies a strong likelihood of U.S. intervention in the event of an unprovoked attack, while maintaining the flexibility to manage crises and safeguard broader interests. However, shifting regional power dynamics and Taiwan's evolving domestic politics are testing the limits of this approach. The risk of miscalculation is rising. America's strategy for political deterrence must evolve in response to these challenges while remaining rooted in the One China Policy.

The first priority is to deepen U.S. engagement with Taiwan to strengthen Taiwan's democracy and resilience. Taiwan must demonstrate not only military preparedness but also an unmistakable societal commitment to resisting aggression. As in Ukraine, Taiwanese public sentiment is shaped by perceptions of U.S. commitment. While some surveys indicate strong willingness to fight, others suggest hesitation. Ensuring that Taiwan's population is psychologically and materially prepared requires steadfast American support for the One China Policy. Within the bounds of this policy, the United States must broaden its understanding of Taiwan and foster closer ties through expanded exchanges, trade agreements, and public diplomacy initiatives. Washington should quietly but relentlessly push Taipei to expand its strategic reserves of critical resources and build more robust defense supply chains. Taiwan's defense establishment also requires reform to prioritize asymmetric capabilities and enhance its readiness. However, such measures must be undertaken with diplomatic care to avoid provoking Beijing or disrupting Taiwan's domestic stability. U.S. officials must ensure their public engagement is nonpartisan and respectful of Taiwan's democratic choices.

Taking the One China Policy as a foundation, Washington also needs new tools to deter Xi from escalating gray-zone pressure indefinitely. A communication strategy of "structured ambiguity" offers one promising approach. By selectively disclosing intelligence and signaling that Washington may modify its policy in response to destabilizing moves by Beijing or Taipei, the United States can impose uncertainty on both sides. Structured ambiguity could serve as a circuit breaker in potential crisis scenarios. It could expand the space for preemptive action and provide early warning of an impending conflict. If implemented effectively, structured ambiguity would deter brinkmanship by both Taipei and Beijing. However, successful implementation would require consistent and precise communication.

Finally, the United States must establish and institutionalize its coalition. Japan, Australia, Canada, and the UK form the natural Core, given their significant military and economic capabilities and their shared interest in preserving a free and open Indo-Pacific. Japan's geographic position and strategic interests make it indispensable. Australia's deepening defense ties with Washington underscore its commitment to regional stability. Canada and the UK bring critical political and economic leverage to the table, and their inclusion would signal the global stakes of a Taiwan crisis. Strengthening these partnerships requires joint planning and joint communications. The United States must treat these countries as core partners in all domains, including trade. At the same time, the United States must engage with neutral countries and developing nations, recognizing their reluctance to take sides while encouraging their cooperation on shared interests. The best way to rally a broad coalition of support while countering Beijing's efforts to isolate Taiwan is to articulate an affirmative vision for regional and global order.

5

Strengthening Conventional Deterrence

by Eyck Freymann and Harry Halem

A pair of drones hover quietly in eastern Ukraine. High above, a fixed-wing reconnaissance drone captures and transmits real-time imagery to a command center. It tracks the telltale shapes of two artillery pieces tucked beneath camouflage nets. A Russian officer gives the order, and a loitering munition flying nearby zeroes in on its target, accelerating to over 300 kilometers per hour. Its explosive payload detonates on impact.

Warfare is undergoing a technological transformation. In some ways, images from the trenches in Ukraine recall the horrors of World War I. But in others, this war is unlike any in history. Due to drones, satellite communications, and precision munitions, enemy targets can be spotted and attacked within minutes, even kilometers behind the front line. To survive, the Russian and Ukrainian militaries are constantly adapting. They've adopted new logistics models, changed how units maneuver, and repurposed existing capabilities for reconnaissance and strike. They've invested in countermeasures like air defenses, decoys, and electronic warfare, and hardened their equipment and fighting positions. The battlefield in Ukraine has become a sandbox of innovation—and a contest of industrial capacity.

To deter a catastrophic conflict with China over Taiwan, the U.S. government must absorb these lessons and apply them through an integrated military and industrial strategy. China, Russia, North Korea, and Iran are sharing advanced defense technologies and selling each other basic items ranging from munitions to drones, effectively building an integrated defense industrial base (DIB). As they shift from dollar networks to Chinese payment systems, they are also building resilience to sanctions, which will make it harder for U.S. policy to impede their future military-industrial cooperation. The more their cooperation deepens, the greater the chance that a conflict in one region could spread.

Amid a growing consensus that U.S. military power is overextended, there is a renewed focus on defending the homeland and the Western Hemisphere. But it is also important to remember that deterring war with China in the Western Pacific is vital for hemispheric defense. As we saw in Chapter 1, Taiwan is a key link in the First Island Chain, the archipelago that contains China's air and naval forces near its coastline. If Taiwan falls, the People's Liberation Army (PLA) could project military power around Japan, the Philippines, and across the Western Pacific. From this position, it could eventually project power across the Pacific to threaten the American homeland—just as Japan did in 1941 (see Figure 5.1).

To deter China from aggressing against Taiwan with an invasion, blockade, or quarantine, America must show it can decisively defeat the PLA in an all-out air–naval war around the First Island Chain. Credible military strength is the necessary foundation for diplomacy to succeed and prevent such a conflict. The best open-source wargames suggest the United States would probably win such a war today, albeit at significant cost. All is not lost, even if China pulls ahead in some quantitative military metrics. However, China has industrial momentum, and U.S. deterrence is operating on ever-narrower margins. Most American citizens, legislators, and national security professionals understand that a collapse of conventional deterrence against China would be catastrophic for American freedom, prosperity, and security. But on the specifics—what to fund, what to divest—the debate lacks clarity, urgency, and consensus. Silicon Valley has one vision, large defense manufacturers another. The Services and the Joint Staff all see the problem slightly differently.

The policy community and public urgently need a conversation about how to stabilize the military balance and secure American conventional military advantages quickly and affordably. In the early 2030s, sci-fi technologies will coexist with 20th-century platforms. How should we evolve the force from what we have today to what we will need in a decade? The further into the future we look, the less consensus there is. Stabilizing the balance is less a matter of dramatically expanding the budget and more about making the hard choices to reallocate resources to core industrial priorities.

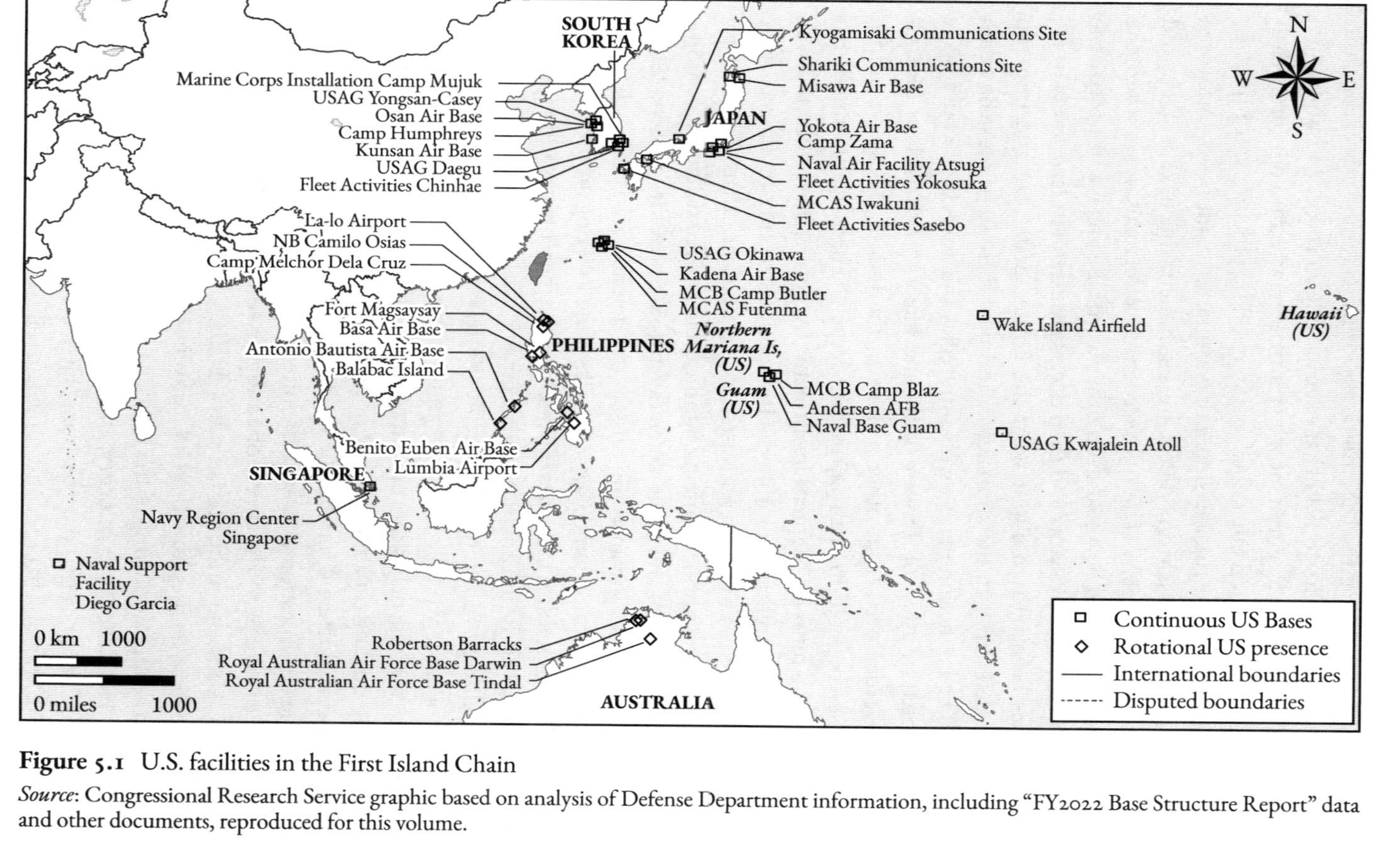

Figure 5.1 U.S. facilities in the First Island Chain

Source: Congressional Research Service graphic based on analysis of Defense Department information, including "FY2022 Base Structure Report" data and other documents, reproduced for this volume.

The problem isn't that the U.S. military is losing its technological edge, but that it is losing the ability to field that edge at scale, at speed, and under fire. The force structure has forgotten how to translate new technology into lethality or integrate legacy and cutting-edge systems. The procurement process is optimized for peacetime risk aversion, not wartime adaptation—despite some encouraging recent steps. Meanwhile, China is modernizing its capabilities and building industrial capacity at an unprecedented scale, focusing on where the U.S. force structure will be weakest. In other words, Beijing wants to seize the advantage in the next five years and then decisively extend its lead.

Much has been written about what the United States can and must do to preserve deterrence in the short term, and why these steps must be taken urgently.[1] The key action items involve strategies and assets that would make any attempted invasion of Taiwan costly and likely to fail. Various capabilities can be redeployed from other regions to the Indo-Pacific, for example. U.S. defense cooperation with Japan can deepen. There is also much that Taiwan can and must do.[2] Urgent investments in mobile, survivable, and scalable defensive capabilities, combined with an infrastructure resilient to siege tactics, would help Taiwan present itself as a "porcupine" that China cannot subdue quickly or without incurring significant losses. Air defenses, including mobile missile systems and short-range defense, are necessary to deny China air superiority. Mines and anti-ship missiles can defend Taiwan's coastline and disrupt an amphibious assault. Coastal artillery and loitering munitions would allow Taiwan to establish kill zones on its shores, further complicating any invasion attempt. Robust information and electronic warfare capabilities can help deceive and disrupt PLA targeting. Resilient infrastructure and expanded fuel and food stockpiles would enable Taiwan to withstand a potential blockade.[3]

Still, steps that will help shore up deterrence in the very short term, mainly by repurposing existing capabilities, may not be sufficient to preserve deterrence against an emboldened China in the longer term. Over a five- to fifteen-year horizon, the key question is how the United States and allied militaries and their DIBs can adapt to the effects of emerging technologies more effectively than the PLA and the authoritarian states' DIBs.[4]

This chapter sketches how the U.S. conventional deterrence system works and how to adapt it, drawing on the key conclusions of our book *The Arsenal of Democracy: Technology, Industry, and American Leadership in the Indo-Pacific*. It focuses on three core questions. First, if deterrence fails, what would a U.S.–China war look like? Second, what capabilities does America struggle to produce and sustain at wartime scale? Third, how can America work with allies and industry to secure our supply chains and bridge the gap between what we have and what we need? Using history as a benchmark, we take a whirlwind tour of the system: scouting (C4ISR), long-range strike, logistics, the defense industrial base, the surface fleet, aerial drones, submarines, and space. Mindful that readers will have varying levels of background knowledge, we discuss each of these issues at a high level, focusing mainly on how each capability interacts with others to shape deterrence across domains. We pay particular attention to how the United States can cooperate with allies to develop key technologies and share the burden of industrial expansion.

Our net assessment is hopeful. Working with allies and the private sector, the United States can revitalize its deterrence system at a reasonable cost. But it doesn't have much time.

Surveillance and Reconnaissance

In an air–naval conflict, surveillance and reconnaissance are key. In the Indo-Pacific theater, air and naval units must operate across vast, open seas. To strike their targets before they become targets themselves, they must be able to detect the enemy from hundreds of kilometers away while evading enemy scouts. Unlike land forces, which can use terrain for concealment, surface ships are both highly visible and dispersed across enormous areas. This makes effective reconnaissance essential for survival and operational success.[5] It also means that whichever side can disrupt the other side's scouting system can potentially deliver decisive strikes in the early engagements that will decide the subsequent course of a war.

As technology has evolved, naval scouting has become increasingly important in warfare. At Trafalgar (1805), scouting enabled British Admiral Nelson to locate the Franco-Spanish fleet, but it had little tactical value during the battle itself.[6] By the Battle of Jutland (1916), the most important naval battle of World War I, scouting had become essential. Approximately one-fifth of both British and German big-gun fleets were dedicated to scouting, helping to contribute to Britain's victory over a numerically superior German force.[7] The advent of naval aviation in the 1930s extended combat ranges from 10–30 kilometers to hundreds of kilometers. This increased both the accessibility and necessity of scouting.[8] For example, at the Battle of Midway (1942), superior

U.S. scouting, coupled with signals intelligence, enabled the decisive sinking of four Japanese carriers.[9] Starting in the 1970s, the advent of satellite communications integrated reconnaissance with weapons targeting for precision strikes.

Meanwhile, ongoing improvements in *counter*-scouting techniques have increasingly become strategically significant.[10] Counter-scouting was vital during the late Cold War, when programs such as Haystack and UPTIDE pioneered technologies like decoys, jammers, and emission control. These innovations extended the evasion time of U.S. ships from two to fifteen hours, enabling them to credibly threaten the flanks of Soviet ground forces and eventually the ballistic missile submarines that safeguarded the Soviet nuclear second-strike capability.[11] Today, China's reconnaissance–strike complex extends beyond the First Island Chain. It incorporates over 490 intelligence, surveillance, and reconnaissance (ISR) satellites equipped with diverse sensor types.[12] U.S. forces must demonstrate to Beijing that they can evade China's scouts effectively enough to operate within around 600 kilometers of China's coastline.

Thus, U.S.–China competition to demonstrate advantages in scouting and counter-scouting is fundamental to deterrence.[13] Both sides are utterly dependent on satellites for peacetime scouting. But satellites can be jammed, blinded, or even destroyed. Both sides' actual and perceived backup strategies therefore play a fundamental role in war planning. Drones, also known as unmanned aerial systems (UAS), are one potential solution. Alarmingly, China has seized an advantage in building the right kind of UAS. Its Wing Loong II costs just $1 to 2 million per unit to build, while an American MQ-9A Reaper with similar specs can cost $10 to 25 million.[14] China's BZK-005 UAS boasts an impressive 40-hour endurance, and the WZ-7 Soaring Dragon HALE UAS offers advanced reconnaissance capabilities comparable to the U.S. RQ-4 Global Hawk.[15] China is rapidly building hundreds of affordable, capable scouting drones, while U.S. platforms remain expensive and limited in number.[16]

To address these disparities, the United States should adopt a two-pronged approach. First, it must invest in an array of resilient, affordable, and scalable scouting assets and communications systems, particularly UAS and small satellites. Recent initiatives like the DoD's REPLICATOR program, which aims to field thousands of UAS within twenty-four months, reflect this need.[17] Second, the United States should prioritize hardening its scouting UAS fleet against PLA disruptions and enhance its counter-scouting capabilities through large investments in electronic warfare, stealth, and decoy technologies.

Long-Range Strike

China's advanced long-range strike capabilities, particularly its extensive missile arsenal, present significant challenges for U.S. forces. China's larger stockpiles and robust production capacity could potentially prove decisive in a prolonged conflict.[18] To counter China's quantitative advantages, and ensure Xi doesn't conclude he could win simply by protracting a war, the United States must expand its stockpiles of long-range precision munitions. These include the Joint Air-to-Surface Standoff Missile (JASSM), Long-Range Anti-Ship Missile (LRASM), Naval Strike Missile (NSM), Harpoon, and Tomahawk, as well as various ballistic and hypersonic missiles.[19] It is also important to field platforms in the region that can use these missiles effectively.

The modern precision strike regime enables combatants to inflict substantial damage from great distances using small but highly accurate munitions. These assets can degrade enemy reconnaissance, neutralize forward-deployed air assets, and disrupt command networks, compounding advantages for the offensive force.[20] China has over 3,500 conventionally armed ballistic and cruise missiles, including the DF-21D "carrier killer," the DF-26D "Guam killer," the DF-27, and the YJ-18, an anti-ship cruise missile designed to overcome U.S. Navy air defenses.[21] Additionally, China has large numbers of DF-17, DF-15, and DF-11 short-range missiles.[22] Collectively, these systems create a high-risk zone extending 600–1,000 kilometers off China's coast at the outset of conflict. U.S. forces operating in this area would face substantial threats, though the risks would diminish over time as China expands its longest-range and most advanced missiles.[23] To counter these challenges, the United States and its allies must develop more flexible long-range strike options. One promising approach is air-launched palletized munitions, which enable cargo aircraft like the C-130 and C-17 to deploy cruise missiles. The Rapid Dragon program significantly increases strike capacity without relying solely on bombers,[24] while the CLEAVER initiative explores modular precision-guided munitions for rapid deployment.[25] These systems could allow Taiwan and its allies to expand their strike options from dispersed locations, reducing reliance on vulnerable air bases and complicating China's anti-access, area-denial (A2/AD) strategy.

The United States must invest urgently in standoff strike capabilities. Key assets, such as JASSM and LRASM, have effective ranges of 370 to 1,000 kilometers, while carrier-based aircraft can operate at ranges of 500 to 900 kilometers.[26] Although highly capable, these systems are in limited supply.

Current U.S. stockpiles include approximately 3,000 JASSMs and only 350 LRASMs.[27] Open-source wargames suggest that these stockpiles could be exhausted within two weeks of a Taiwan conflict, with replenishment taking years.[28] Compounding the challenge, China has achieved what the Pentagon now refers to as "the world's leading hypersonic missile arsenal."[29] Closing this gap will require sustained investment and innovation.[30]

Air defense systems are equally critical to offset China's missile advantage.[31] Recent conflicts, such as Iran's 2024 attacks on Israel, demonstrated the effectiveness of U.S.-designed systems, which intercepted hundreds of drones, cruise missiles, and ballistic missiles.[32] In the Indo-Pacific, protecting U.S. forces and allies requires sufficient air defense coverage. For example, comprehensive coverage of Taiwan would necessitate at least ten Patriot batteries, each costing around $1 billion.[33] U.S. surface ships also need IADS, which create a unified operational picture for all air defense assets.[34]

Expanding production capacity is a critical priority. Defense contractors like Lockheed Martin have begun increasing output, with LRASM production quadrupling from 30 to 120 missiles annually in 2024.[35] Scaling these numbers up further will require major investments in industrial facilities, supply chains, and workforce development.[36] The biggest bottlenecks to missile production are at the subcontractor level, and allied cooperation is the fastest way to secure these supply chains.[37] Frameworks like AUKUS can play a vital role. Ultimately, addressing asymmetries in missile capabilities is less a technological challenge than an industrial one.

Logistics

Logistics is the bridge between a nation's economy and its military operations. Yet U.S. logistics networks in the Indo-Pacific are dangerously unprepared for a prolonged conflict with China.[38] The Philippine Sea, east of Taiwan, is over 11,000 kilometers from San Diego.[39] DoD's shift toward distributed operations will tax the logistics system further, and China can hold the U.S. logistics system at risk. These vulnerabilities not only limit U.S. strategic flexibility but also weaken deterrence.[40] Although the United States has the world's largest and most capable air logistics system, airlift alone cannot meet the demands of a large-scale conflict.[41] Heavy-lift aircraft carry only a fraction of the material a ship can, are vulnerable to enemy missiles, and cannot resupply warships at sea.[42] Meanwhile, as we saw in Chapters 2 and 3, the U.S. Military Sealift Command faces a crisis. Its fleet has dwindled to just 125 ships, and severe personnel shortages have forced it to decommission vessels that it cannot crew.[43] Uncompetitive working conditions relative to the commercial sector further compound the problem, reflecting a broader decline in the U.S. maritime industry. China, by contrast, has strategically positioned itself as a global leader in maritime infrastructure.[44]

To alleviate the strain on U.S. sealift logistics, one solution is to preposition supplies closer to potential conflict zones.[45] The Pacific Deterrence Initiative (PDI) has started funding efforts to harden U.S. military installations in the Indo-Pacific. However, with an annual budget of only $9 billion, PDI pales in comparison to China's extensive investments in its own basing infrastructure.[46] The PDI budget should be significantly increased and the program should be refocused on logistics. U.S. diplomats must also accelerate efforts to establish logistics hubs across Japan, the Philippines, Papua New Guinea, and small islands in the Second Island Chain.

The United States must also launch a comprehensive effort to rebuild its maritime logistics capacity. This should include expanding the Military Sealift Command's fleet, offering competitive pay to attract new mariners, and modernizing the Ready Reserve Force. Building a fleet of smaller logistics vessels, including unmanned platforms, would further enhance the ability to support distributed operations.[47] Rebuilding America's maritime industrial base is a necessary investment. It is also a generational project. In the meantime, Washington must leverage partnerships with South Korea and Japan.[48]

Surface Fleet

The U.S. surface fleet has long relied on the offensive power of the carrier strike group, which consists of a carrier protected by destroyers and cruisers. Despite the growing threat from China's advanced long-range strike capabilities, carriers remain indispensable for U.S. power projection and deterrence.[49] Congress and the Navy are resolute in their commitment to maintaining ten to twelve carriers and fully recapitalizing the fleet by the 2040s.[50] DMO seeks to keep carriers relevant by enabling them to operate from greater ranges and defend against modern threats like drones and unmanned systems.[51] It is too early to tell whether this adaptation strategy will prove effective.

China's rapidly advancing missile arsenal, including the DF-17, DF-21D "carrier killer," and DF-26 "Guam killer"—all of which have ASBM variants—pose a direct challenge to the U.S. fleet's traditional operating model.[52] These missiles can strike targets over 2,150 kilometers away.[53] Closer to China's shores, they are supplemented by other types of submarine-, aircraft-, and surface-launched cruise missiles. The threat is compounded by the proliferation of unmanned systems, such as surface drones and loitering munitions.[54] These systems are still maturing.[55] Still, recent examples, such as Ukraine's use of USVs to sink Russian ships in the Black Sea, make the trend clear.[56]

Since surface ships cost hundreds of millions to billions of dollars apiece and are designed to last decades, Congress and the Navy must critically assess which ship classes can remain viable. DMO offers a promising path by dispersing the fleet and equipping surface combatants with long-range anti-ship missiles.[57] However, implementing DMO faces steep challenges, including maintaining secure communications in contested environments, rearming ships at sea, and supporting a dispersed fleet logistically. It is also unclear how well emerging air defense technologies like directed energy weapons and rail guns can protect large ships against massed attacks of missiles or drones.

History suggests that it is too early to declare the death of the carrier. The advent of the torpedo in the 1860s, for instance, led many to predict the end of battleships.[58] Instead, navies adapted, and battleships remained central to fleets for several more decades.[59] Similarly, during the transition from battleships to carriers in World War II, older ships adapted to support roles or incorporated new technologies.[60] Legacy platforms like the carrier will probably contribute meaningfully during periods of transition. Some might be repurposed to suit a new paradigm of naval warfare over the longer term.[61]

The U.S. Navy is already adapting the surface fleet. It is advancing integrated air and missile defense (IAMD) systems, though these systems remain vulnerable to large-scale, coordinated attacks.[62] Programs like Ghost Fleet Overlord and Orca aim to integrate unmanned systems into fleet operations, though China is making parallel investments.[63] Notably, neither the Navy nor Congress has wanted to compete ship-for-ship with China. The Navy currently fields 296 battle force ships and plans to expand to 355 manned ships and 130 unmanned vehicles by the mid-2030s.[64] Meanwhile, China's fleet has surpassed 370 ships and submarines, with over 140 major surface combatants concentrated in the Western Pacific.[65] The U.S. Navy believes that fleet size alone does not equate to naval power.[66] It is more important to have ships with the surveillance, defense, and strike capabilities to operate in high-threat environments.

Given the fragility of the U.S. shipbuilding industry, the cost of new vessels, and uncertainty about technological trends, the Navy would be wise to pursue a hedging strategy. It should focus on maintaining the industrial capacity to produce both large, manned ships and smaller, unmanned ships. Partnerships with allied shipyards, especially in South Korea, are the best way to maintain this capacity in the medium term. Meanwhile, it must invest heavily in secure communications, electronic warfare, and advanced missile defense technologies. The most vulnerable platforms, like the Littoral Combat Ship (LCS) and potentially the *Constellation*-class frigate, should be retired immediately.[67] Similarly, large amphibious assault ships should be deprioritized.[68]

The DIB

The DIB is the network of facilities, workforce, and supply chains that produce and maintain military resources. A robust DIB enables rapid production during crises and contributes to deterrence by demonstrating that the nation can sustain prolonged military engagements. However, today's DIB is undermining deterrence rather than supporting it. Bureaucratic inefficiencies and the incentive structure of private contractors have caused innovation to stagnate and have produced a brittle force.

The procurement system has struggled to maintain industrial capacity since the end of the Cold War.[69] In the 1990s, over fifty aerospace and defense contractors were consolidated into just six major "primes," such as Lockheed Martin and Raytheon (now RTX). While this model has produced highly sophisticated systems like the F-35 fighter jet, it has brought delays, supply-chain disruptions, horrific underinvestments in capacity, and ballooning costs.[70] These problems were laid bare when Russia invaded Ukraine. U.S. producers struggled to ramp up production of simple items like 155 mm artillery shells, despite their best efforts.[71]

A conflict with China would amplify these challenges. The weapons required would be far more sophisticated than artillery shells, and China might use export bans or even industrial sabotage to disrupt key U.S. supply chains. Compounding the problem, hundreds of thousands of skilled workers in the

DIB are nearing retirement. Contractors have yet to present credible plans for replacing this critical workforce.[72]

The deeper systemic problem is that the U.S. defense procurement system distorts incentives and stifles innovation. The process is riddled with redundant and outdated rules. For example, new products have to be extensively tested, even when they have identical specifications to existing systems.[73] The contract-by-contract nature of defense work creates unpredictable workloads, discouraging skilled workers from returning after layoffs and deterring contractors from maintaining latent production capacity.[74]

Congress and DoD have proposed several reform pathways to address these issues. They fall into four key areas: streamlining the Pentagon's internal procurement processes, reforming contracting practices, reducing regulatory barriers to better integrate allied defense industries, and making direct federal investments in the DIB. There is broad consensus support for these reforms in principle. They should almost certainly be pursued in parallel. However, the specifics remain complex and contentious.

Reforming the procurement system is both a technical challenge and a political minefield. The current system prioritizes consensus-building among the services, theoretically to reduce waste and prevent duplication. In practice, this approach often backfires, disproportionately empowering the Army at a time when geography demands that the Navy and Air Force take the lead in the Indo-Pacific. Moreover, the system makes it politically fraught to take risky bets on exciting new technologies or cancel underperforming programs. Individual officials risk their careers if they are associated with failures. One proposed solution is to empower the chairman of the Joint Chiefs of Staff to oversee force structure development and ensure alignment with strategic priorities, possibly giving this individual license to override objections from the services.[75] Another option is to grant individual services or combatant commanders greater autonomy over their acquisitions. This would foster flexibility and responsiveness but might also lead to duplicative programs. A third option would be a cultural change, coming from the Office of the Secretary of Defense, to give officers more autonomy to take risks.

Either way, a key goal of reform should be to make the DoD more risk-tolerant, enabling it to adapt quickly to emerging technology trends. Beijing is more willing to invest heavily in experimental projects—even if many ultimately fail—on the chance that one succeeds and can be scaled up quickly. In an era of fast-paced technological change, DoD should be able to place strategic bets on promising emerging technologies, reallocate resources quickly as circumstances change, and provide clear, accurate demand signals to private contractors. Realistically, wholesale reforms are unlikely. Progress is more likely to come from gradually cutting red tape and creating special offices with independent funding that can bypass the traditional bureaucracy.

One reform pathway is to align the incentives for defense contractors. For these companies, national security is a business, not a religion. Today, the best way to maximize shareholder value is to lock in a long-term contract for a high-end system that guarantees a consistent cash flow. Persuading companies and their subcontractors to maintain spare capacity to produce items like munitions and drones in high volumes requires a credible promise to buy future output. Currently, DoD limits multi-year contracts to major programs like warships and fighter jets.[76] Long-term contracts for key systems like missiles, drones, and submarine subcomponents would send a clearer demand signal and drive the private sector to expand production capacity.[77] As a last resort, the president can invoke the Defense Production Act (DPA) to compel businesses to fulfill critical defense contracts, but this is no silver bullet.[78] The government can't manage intricate supply chains as well as a specialized company.[79] The optimal role for the U.S. government is to create the right incentives and send the right signals so that private industry mobilizes itself to meet national security goals.

One way to leverage the private sector's ingenuity is to adopt a "productized sales model" for certain defense contracts. Currently, the Pentagon contracts through a "cost-plus" model that limits the potential upside for producers.[80] A productized-sales model (also known as a venture capital or VC model) would allow defense companies to take more risk and potentially capture greater rewards. This could increase competition, drive innovation, reduce overall costs, and leverage Silicon Valley to attract talent into the defense enterprise. DoD has experimented with productized sales at a small level through an office called the Defense Innovation Unit, where it has achieved some notable successes.[81]

Despite the obvious benefits of a productized sales model, reforms to the procurement system need to be taken carefully. For private firms, defense technology is a risky business, since the U.S. government is in many cases the only potential customer. If the government supports companies at an early stage but gives them no pathway to a durable business model, then businesses risk falling into the "valley of death"—with lots of expensive liabilities but no revenue.[82]

In recent years, investor excitement about potential procurement reform has led to a flood of private capital into the defense tech space.[83] However, only two startup companies—Palantir and Anduril—have navigated the transition through the valley of death. Many other companies enjoy bubble valuations and could fold quickly if investors lose confidence that they have a path to profitability. For certain types of systems like submarines and fighter jets that need to be maintained over decades, it makes sense to use the most reliable contractors, not necessarily the most dynamic ones.

Congress and the Pentagon therefore need to communicate honestly and specifically about what procurement reforms are realistic and what capabilities they would like to acquire. Ultimately, at least 10 percent of defense contracting by value should probably follow a productized sales model—and potentially two or three times that amount. However, the model is most appropriate for smaller, cheaper platforms that are produced at scale, or for software systems offered as a service. Hybrid approaches are also possible. Traditional contractors could develop core platforms that can accept modular updates and software updates, while VC-backed companies compete for subsystems, sensors, and software.[84] Striking the right balance is a key challenge.

The United States can also partner with allies to leverage their comparative advantages in defense production.[85] For example, South Korea has air defenses and shipbuilding, while European defense firms are strong in aerospace and naval technologies.[86] Allied shipyards could also help maintain, repair, and expand the U.S. surface fleet.[87] However, the International Traffic in Arms Regulations (ITAR) remains a significant obstacle to these collaborations. Designed to prevent defense technology proliferation to U.S. adversaries, ITAR limits sharing of technology and data with foreign manufacturers.[88] The lengthy ITAR approval process particularly discourages co-production on short-term projects in rapidly advancing technologies. Even the closest U.S. allies are affected by ITAR. The Biden and second Trump administration have issued exemptions designed to cut red tape for the UK and Australia, but undersea stealth technologies and other key defense articles remain restricted.[89] Australian officials have identified ITAR as the "most significant obstacle" to Australia–U.S. defense cooperation.[90] ITAR has also hindered collaboration with Japan in missile production and space technologies.[91] DIB alignment with allies is the most promising of all the reform pathways, though it will take many years to achieve. ITAR reform is therefore essential, though it must be done carefully to prevent U.S. adversaries from acquiring sensitive technology.

Finally, DoD can allocate money directly to contractors to attract, train, and retain workers. At Fincantieri's Marinette Marine shipyard, the Navy offers $5,000 retention bonuses after the first year and another $5,000 upon ship delivery.[92] There have been piecemeal efforts across the DIB to hire veterans and establish pipelines from universities, but they aren't sufficient.[93] Broader structural reforms are necessary to incorporate workforce development and retention funding into initial budget allocation.

All the reforms discussed in this section will require a political mandate. An active president and secretary of defense can do a great deal unilaterally. But allied DIB integration can move ahead only if Congress accepts the idea that protecting domestic defense industries must take a back seat to addressing urgent deterrence needs.

UAS

The war in Ukraine has highlighted the rapid evolution of UAS, with each side using tens to hundreds of thousands per month.[94] This scale of deployment, combined with rapid technological adaptation, presents both opportunities and challenges for the United States. Many kinds of UAS have been used in Ukraine. They range from small copters to large fixed-wing aircraft and loitering munitions. These systems have been used for a variety of purposes, from tactical reconnaissance to strategic bombardment.

Meanwhile, counter-UAS (CUAS) technologies are rapidly evolving. These systems rely on four primary tracking methods: radar, radio frequency analyzers, acoustic sensors, and optical sensors.[95] Once a UAS is detected, there are many ways to counter it. Methods include frequency jammers, cyber takeover methods, directed energy weapons (lasers), and kinetic interceptors. Often, the most effective countermeasures target control stations and central data hubs than individual drones.[96]

The U.S. and allied UAS production ecosystem needs to catch up with the times. Most UAS platforms that the United States and allied militaries operate today are large, expensive fixed-wing drones designed for counterterrorism operations. The MQ-9 Reaper is a consummate example. Unfortunately, these exquisite UAS are vulnerable to kinetic and electronic attacks, which makes them ill-suited for high-intensity conflicts with peer competitors. The United States will need to develop and produce smaller, cheaper UAS at vastly higher volumes.

Industrial capacity is the critical challenge. China's leading UAS manufacturer, DJI, dominates the global commercial drone market with a 76 percent market share.[97] Additionally, U.S. and allied producers depend on China for key components. This dependency became impossible to ignore when China cut off critical components to U.S. dronemaker Skydio in October 2024.[98] Batteries are a particular bottleneck. Because China's drone makers enjoy economies of scale, they can also use more efficient techniques like vacuum injection molding. The only structural solution is for the allies to build an independent ecosystem for the entire drone supply chain.

Even after production bottlenecks are addressed, integrating these UAS and counter-UAS into the force will be a major effort.[99] A good example is collaborative combat aircraft (CCA)—also known as "loyal wingman" aircraft.[100] If CCA can be made to work, they could potentially enhance the capabilities of manned aircraft by providing pilots with expanded situational awareness, information, and analysis, as well as protection from adversary aircraft.[101] The Air Force is investing \$8.9 billion in CCA programs between 2025 and 2029.[102] However, CCA are years away from being combat-ready, in part because their range is limited and communications are not yet secure.[103] Perhaps most importantly, it will take time for pilots to learn to fight alongside CCA and fully trust them in high-stakes situations.

While drone swarming technology is not yet developed to the operational level, it holds significant potential. China is actively working on the technology as well.[104] The Biden administration's export controls on advanced semiconductors aimed to maintain U.S. advantages in edge computing to process sensor data more effectively close to the front line. If China fails to keep up in this area, American and other guided munition technologies could potentially gain accumulating qualitative advantages over the next decade and beyond. However, CCA and swarms are particularly vulnerable to electronic warfare and other forms of disruption. Emerging techniques like spoofing and adversarial (AAI) can compromise UAS navigation systems and decision making by feeding false information or misleading UAS into misidentifying targets.[105] These challenges are difficult to mitigate, and it may turn out that large numbers of "dumb" UAS are more effective than smaller numbers of "smart" ones.[106] Thus, while the U.S. military should invest aggressively in CCA and swarms, it should not overestimate their usefulness, particularly if a war breaks out before 2030. It is also important to buy drones that have modular parts and can be upgraded to work in an ever-adapting electronic environment.

As of this writing, the United States is moving to ban UAS imports from China while investing in domestic and allied production capacity.[107] This approach must extend beyond simple protectionism to include comprehensive supply-chain development and industrial base expansion. The United States and its allies need to work with the private sector to incentivize scaling of production and ongoing investment in software and modular parts. Allied governments also need to jointly develop CUAS capabilities, produce them at scale, and share technology and best practices.[108]

Submarines

The U.S. submarine fleet provides a critical asymmetric advantage over China around the First Island Chain. U.S. submarines can safely operate closer much to China's coastline than surface ships, where they could potentially strike many PLA targets quickly and at short ranges.[109] China's anti-submarine warfare capabilities remain relatively underdeveloped. U.S. war plans generally envision submarines as the door-kicker for the rest of the force, degrading China's scouting and strike assets early in the fight, and enabling U.S. air and surface assets to move further in and gain compounding advantages.

The U.S. Navy maintains fifty-three fast-attack submarines (SSN), fourteen ballistic-missile submarines (SSBN), and four guided-missile submarines, of which twenty-five to thirty are ported in the Indo-Pacific.[110] In theory, up to around forty U.S. attack submarines are deployable at any given time.[111] However, the fleet faces a severe readiness crisis, with maintenance issues radically limiting availability. This maintenance crisis is characterized by significant backlogs and delays. The average submarine waits 1,500 additional days for maintenance during each five-year maintenance cycle, a delay that compounds over time and can take multiple submarines out of commission.[112] These delays effectively reduce the size of the deployable fleet, a situation that would only worsen during wartime due to combat damage and supply-chain disruptions.

Production capacity is the critical challenge to maintaining the U.S. lead undersea. U.S. submarines are built at only two yards: in Groton, Connecticut, and Newport News, Virginia. Together these two facilities can produce just 1.2 boats annually. Neither yard currently has the capacity to scale up production substantially. Meanwhile, ageing boats are being retired. The AUKUS Agreement commits to delivering *Virginia*-class submarines to Australia by the early

2030s, promising significant long-term benefits from cooperation with the UK and Australian submarine fleets. The United States must fulfill its promises to Australia and deliver these boats on schedule, but this commitment emphasizes the need to expand existing yards further.[113] If aging subs are decommissioned as planned, the result will be a net loss of approximately 0.4 submarines per year through 2030.[114] A shortage of munitions for the attack submarine fleet is another, related area of concern.[115]

In contrast, China is rapidly modernizing and expanding both its submarine fleet and its anti-submarine warfare capabilities.[116] China operates six nuclear-powered ballistic missile submarines (SSBN), six nuclear-powered attack submarines (SSN), and forty-eight diesel-powered/air-independent powered attack submarines (SS).[117] Its new Type-095 and Type-096 attack submarines approach the capabilities of advanced Russian submarines in terms of propulsion, sensors, and weapons.[118] More concerning than China's current fleet size is its potential for future growth. The DoD expects China's fleet to increase to sixty-five by 2025 and to eighty by 2035. These numbers could increase further if China keeps expanding its submarine construction capacity.[119] China is also likely acquiring advanced submarine technology from Russia, which will improve its fleet qualitatively.

Given the vital importance of maintaining U.S. dominance undersea, Congress needs to recapitalize the submarine industrial base. Expanding production to three boats per year would cost around $13 billion annually, plus additional funding for industrial base expansion and maintenance, for a total of around $14–16 billion annually. This is no small commitment. It is equivalent to roughly half of the Navy's current shipbuilding budget. But it is a necessary strategic investment to stabilize the military balance in the medium term.[120] Additionally, the United States should pause attack submarine fleet retirements and extend the service life of older *Los Angeles*–class submarines until the mid-2030s. Additionally, Congress must invest in expanding both the U.S. submarine industrial base and the workforce to sustain a robust, high-tech submarine force well into the future. As a stopgap, South Korea might be able to produce conventional submarines to support the U.S. Navy's regional operations for the next decade or so.[121]

Starting in the 2030s, several emerging technologies could revolutionize undersea warfare, including advanced seabed sensors, quantum sensors for detecting magnetic fields and gravitational shifts, unmanned underwater vehicles (UUV), autonomous mines, and advanced torpedoes.[122]

These technologies face significant developmental hurdles and are unlikely to reach operational maturity for at least a decade. Yet, several countries are currently developing extra-large unmanned underwater vehicles (XLUUV).[123] While current technology remains immature, advances in battery technology, materials science, and computing power should significantly enhance XLUUV capabilities over the next two decades. Because submarines remain in service for several decades, any new submarines built today may have to contend with these technologies for much of their operational life. For now, the United States has no choice but to redouble its focus on building more manned submarines, but it must also invest in basic R&D for emerging undersea technology and deepen and broaden research collaboration with allies.

Space Power

Space capabilities have been fundamental to military operations since the Cold War. They enable critical functions across intelligence, surveillance, and reconnaissance (ISR), communications, and positioning, navigation, and timing (PNT).[124] The U.S. military is reliant on the U.S. satellite network, making the protection of space assets essential for maintaining conventional deterrence. Space systems not only support military operations but also undergird key civilian functions, from banking to cell tower operations.[125] While the United States still has the world's leading space program, China has made remarkable progress under Xi. Its number of assets in orbit has increased 560 percent since 2015.[126] By 2023, China now operates over 490 ISR satellites capable of detecting American assets in the Indo-Pacific.[127] The ostensibly civilian BeiDou navigation system also supports PLA missile targeting.[128]

China has heavily invested in anti-satellite (ASAT) systems that would threaten U.S. space assets during a potential conflict.[129] Satellites in Low Earth Orbit (LEO, 1,000–2,000 km) and Medium Earth Orbit (MEO, 2,000–35,000 km) are vulnerable to various forms of interference, from laser dazzling to physical destruction.[130] While large constellations like StarLink (with around 4,500 satellites) are more resilient to individual attacks, they remain vulnerable to cyberattacks and ground station strikes. Alarmingly, China has also demonstrated kinetic ASAT strikes, where surface-to-space rockets smash into satellites, scattering dangerous debris in orbit.[131]

The United States must therefore ensure that its space systems are more resilient than those of its adversaries.[132] StarLink is a good example of the types of constellations needed to create low-cost, replaceable networks.[133] The DoD has already awarded over $900 million in contracts through the Proliferated Low Earth Orbit Satellite-Based Services program to sixteen companies specializing in various space services.[134] If the cost of destroying a U.S. satellite is higher than the cost of replacing it, China is unlikely to attack the network.

Without preventive action, launch infrastructure could become another costly bottleneck. Launch costs have dropped dramatically from $45,000 per kilogram in 1980 to approximately $1,500 per kilogram today. Advances in reusable rocket technology could potentially drive launch costs down towards $500 per kilogram by 2030.[135] As prices have plummeted, demand has soared. Existing facilities like Cape Canaveral and Vandenberg Space Force Base are now approaching capacity limits.[136] This could become a major problem in conflict scenarios if large numbers of satellites need to be rapidly replaced. Cutting red tape to establish new launch infrastructure, including in allied countries, must be a priority.[137]

Finally, DoD should support companies investing in emerging technologies that could help preserve long-term competitive U.S. advantages in space. Nuclear thermal propulsion could potentially improve maneuverability significantly and allow rockets to carry vastly larger payloads.[138] Innovations that support in-space serving, assembly, and manufacturing (ISAM) technologies could extend satellite lifespans and enable on-orbit repairs and upgrades.[139] Finally, the United States should also invest aggressively in its own classified ASAT capabilities, particularly in cyberspace.

Conclusion

In the spring of 1940, the United States faced a world descending into chaos. On April 9, Nazi Germany invaded Norway, and by June, France had fallen. In Asia, Japan's expansionist ambitions had driven Chiang Kai-shek's Nationalist government deep into China's interior. Japan increasingly looked to control the oil-rich British and Dutch territories in Southeast Asia and even the U.S.-controlled Philippines. Having renounced the London Naval Treaty in 1934, which aimed to maintain naval parity among the great powers, Japan was building advanced battleships and aircraft carriers at a breakneck pace. The U.S.

Navy, by contrast, remained underfunded and constrained by treaty limits. Despite officially maintaining neutrality, President Franklin Delano Roosevelt recognized that the United States could not remain on the sidelines indefinitely.[140] While he demanded Japan's withdrawal from China, his focus was primarily on Europe, where he anticipated the greatest threat to U.S. interests. This was why the naval expansions approved in 1938 and early 1940 were relatively modest. Roosevelt was prioritizing preparations for a land war across the Atlantic over an air–naval war in the Pacific.

It was not until France fell that the United States began all-out preparations to fight a two-front war. On June 17, 1940, Carl Vinson, the pugnacious chairman of the House Armed Services Committee, visited Roosevelt at the White House. Abrasive and effective, the congressman from Georgia chewed on cheap cigars in committee hearings and was known for spitting theatrically into a spittoon from across the dais during tedious testimony. He was also a longstanding champion of naval modernization. At the White House, the president asked Vinson to delay his legislation funding a massive naval buildup until after the November election. Vinson nodded politely—and then went straight back to the Capitol to introduce his bill. The House passed it the very next day after less than an hour of debate. Facing a united Congress, Roosevelt reluctantly signed what became known as the Two-Ocean Navy Act. The legislation allocated $8.55 billion (equivalent to over $150 billion today), expanding the Navy by 70 percent and revitalizing the naval industrial base.[141]

The Two-Ocean Navy Act proved essential once the war broke out. Seventeen months after the act's passage, Japan launched a surprise attack on Pearl Harbor. By early 1942, Japan's rapid advances had brought Southeast Asia under its control, cutting off Allied access to the vital Strait of Malacca. American, British, and Dutch naval forces suffered devastating defeats against Japan's battle-hardened fleets. It was not until the U.S. victory at Midway in June 1942 and the arrival of ships commissioned under the Two-Ocean Navy Act that the tide began to turn. By 1943, the U.S. Navy was on the offensive, driving Japan back across the Pacific.

Today, Vinson is rightly remembered as a visionary and an American hero—but the lesson for today is disturbing. Mobilizing the American DIB to fight a great power war during peacetime takes years. The Vinson buildup proved invaluable in the ultimate American victory in World War II. But it failed in its primary purpose: to deter Japanese aggression in the first place.

Conventional deterrence today requires showing that America has the capability and capacity to defeat the PLA in an all-out air–naval war. As this chapter has shown, U.S. forces face challenges—but so do China's. The PLA has never fought a major naval war. Its officer corps is untested and rarely exercises in realistic conditions. Beijing knows the United States enjoys key qualitative advantages, particularly in C4ISR. Before risking a devastating defeat, Beijing will want substantial confidence that it has all-around superiority and is prepared for all scenarios. Strengthening deterrence therefore means increasing China's uncertainty while preventing it from miscalculating. The fastest path to U.S. defeat is the collapse of its scouting and logistics networks. Munitions, drones, and submarines are the most time-sensitive industrial investments, while satellite and drone ISR systems must become more networked and redundant. Addressing these industrial challenges should therefore be a priority. Procurement reform should focus on evolving the force, not searching for disruptive "killer apps." The existing deterrence system must adapt faster, and the engine of that adaptation must be an allied DIB that can produce what an evolving force needs.

Communicating conventional deterrence effectively is ultimately a psychological warfare operation aimed at Xi himself. The U.S. government already appears to understand this. In late 2023, for example, anonymous U.S. officials revealed to the press that corruption in the PLA Rocket Force was so extensive that it included ICBMs filled with water instead of fuel. This was followed by revelations in 2024 that a new nuclear-powered attack submarine had sunk while under construction. A senior U.S. official told the media that this was evidence corruption "may have disrupted the PLA's progress toward its 2027 goals."[142] The point is that establishing superior hardware is not enough by itself to preserve deterrence. Xi must be made to fear U.S. capabilities—and, crucially, to question the reliability of his own forces and advisors.

Members of Congress, who face the ultimate responsibility to make these hard choices, need to better understand the deterrence system, the costs of inaction, and the trade-offs involved. Deterring China to secure the Western Hemisphere does not require a politically impossible doubling of the defense budget. The United States needs to spend more, but more importantly, it must make hard choices to prioritize key programs and spend smarter. This includes a frank re-examination of budgets to align resources with the primary challenge: an air–naval conflict in the Pacific. National security professionals should spend less time admiring specific capabilities and more time debating and fixing the weakest links in the deterrence system. Demanding that allies spend more on defense makes little sense without coordinating those investments to meet shared production needs.

In the end, deterrence is a system of strategic, industrial, and institutional choices. It is not too late to shore up the system, but the clock is ticking, and the margin for error is shrinking. A moment like this requires the broadest possible consensus on what needs to be done and why. We should take inspiration from 1940, when Franklin D. Roosevelt realized a crash effort was needed to arm the democracies against the Axis powers. In his famous "arsenal of democracy" fireside chat, FDR told Americans, "We must discard the notion of 'business as usual.'" [143] The tragic irony is that Roosevelt was right—but he moved too late. Deterrence failed in 1941. The world's democracies must not make the same mistake today.

6

Preserving Strategic Stability and U.S. Technological Leadership

In September 2021, open-source intelligence analysts made a startling discovery: China was constructing more than 250 missile silos across its western plains, each large enough to hold intercontinental ballistic missiles (ICBMs). The U.S. government later confirmed these findings. Adm. Charles Richard, then-commander of U.S. Strategic Command (STRATCOM), described the development as a "strategic breakout" for China. "The explosive growth and modernization of its nuclear and conventional forces can only be what I describe as breathtaking," he said.[1]

Xi has made massive nuclear expansion a key priority of the PLA's modernization.[2] In 2022 alone, China built at least 300 new ICBM silos. Its nuclear arsenal now exceeds 600 operational nuclear weapons, the third-largest arsenal in the world.[3] Just a decade ago, it had fewer than 100 warheads. At its current pace, China is expected to surpass 1,000 warheads by 2030 and reach 1,500 by 2035 (see Figure 6.1).[4] This rapid buildup raises concerns that China's nuclear doctrine may be shifting.[5] For half a century after China acquired nuclear capability in 1964, China maintained a "lean and effective" arsenal of 60 to 150 warheads with limited delivery capabilities.[6] Today, China has a nuclear force capable of surviving a U.S. first strike and delivering a devastating retaliatory blow. China's expansion shows no signs of slowing, and it may aim for parity with the United States.[7] Much information remains classified, and open-source analysis provides only partial insight. However, these developments demand scrutiny, as the risk of nuclear escalation looms over any Taiwan contingency.

The U.S. government's definition of strategic deterrence is deliberately vague. STRATCOM's mission is to "deter strategic attack" on the United States, but it does not specify whether such an attack must be nuclear.[8] Since

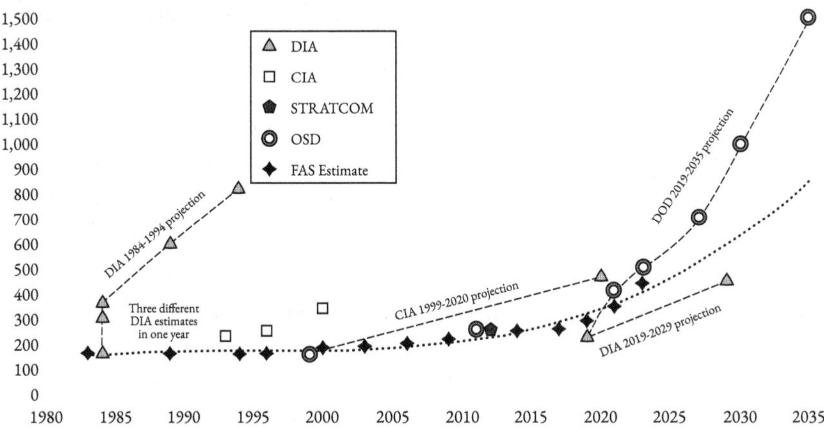

Figure 6.1 U.S. estimates of the PRC nuclear weapons stockpile. Estimates have been revised up sharply during the Xi era.

Source: Adapted from Kristensen et al., "Chinese Nuclear Weapons, 2024."

STRATCOM oversees the U.S. nuclear arsenal and its command-and-control systems, it would likely consider any attack on these assets as "strategic." Advances in cyber, counter-space, and long-range strike capabilities have introduced new threats to these systems.[9] STRATCOM has also sought to deter nonnuclear threats, including chemical, biological, and radiological attacks, as well as state-sponsored terrorism and cyberattacks on U.S. critical infrastructure. This broad scope reinforces the ambiguity surrounding strategic deterrence.

Russia and China similarly view strategic deterrence as encompassing both nuclear and nonnuclear threats. However, their terminology differs. The Chinese and Russian equivalents of the word "deterrence" can also refer to offensive actions aimed at changing the status quo, and are therefore closer in meaning to the English word "coercion."[10] As former STRATCOM Commander, Air Force Gen. John E. Hyten observed in 2019, these trends raise broader questions: "What is deterrence in the 21st century, how do we deter our adversaries and how do we deter strategic attack, which is broader than just the nuclear capability."[11]

In this chapter, I define strategic deterrence broadly and in the way Xi Jinping is most likely to define it: as a direct threat, by any means, to a state's or regime's survival. This definition is not limited to nuclear weapons.

Under certain conditions, chemical, biological, radiological, conventional kinetic, information, cyber, and economic attacks could trigger crises leading to general institutional collapse. Thus, some nonnuclear attacks may qualify as strategic, while some nuclear strikes—such as those on conventional assets in-theater during an active conflict—may not. Defining strategic deterrence this way allows us to skirt the question of how the United States and China might respond to attacks on their soil during a conventional war.

We also need to clarify another key misunderstood concept: the *status quo*. Traditional U.S. nuclear theory assumes that both sides share a common understanding of the status quo.[12] On this basis, scholars since Thomas Schelling in the 1960s have distinguished neatly between deterrence, a "defensive" behavior to defend the status quo, and compellence, an "offensive" effort to revise the status quo. China rejects this distinction. PRC analysts argue that the status quo is often fluid. Furthermore, the first-mover in a crisis is hard to identify. Therefore, deterrence and compellence are effectively the same thing. Beijing also believes that the status quo in the Taiwan Strait is contested, not fixed.

China's nuclear buildup is thus not solely defensive: it is part of Xi's broader strategy to compel the United States and its allies to accept an incremental redefinition of the status quo in China's favor.[13] As previous chapters have established, China is pursuing several instrumental goals in support of this broader goal:

1. Deter Washington from abandoning the One China Policy.

2. Deter Taipei from declaring independence.

3. Compel Washington to limit political and security assurances to Taipei.

4. Compel Taipei to accept gradual encroachment on its autonomy, ultimately leading to "reunification" on Beijing's terms.

A robust, diverse, and survivable PRC nuclear arsenal supports all four goals. In a conflict, China's nuclear forces might also help to deter Washington from using nuclear weapons first or attacking China's nuclear infrastructure through cyber or conventional kinetic means. To bolster deterrence, China is developing a range of other cross-domain strategic threats. These include cyber exploits, containerized missiles, and potentially others that have not been publicly reported. These capabilities enable China to threaten the U.S. homeland with chaos and devastation. They could potentially deter U.S. strategic attacks on China that fall short of general nuclear war.

No matter how large China's arsenal grows, the principle of mutually assured destruction (known in China as *xianghu quebao cuihui* 相互确保摧毁) incentivizes both sides to limit strategic escalation.[14] Even in peacetime, this ever-present risk encourages restraint. In the event of a conventional U.S.–China war, misperception and miscalculation could trigger nuclear escalation. In some scenarios, both sides fight cautiously, avoiding strikes on each other's territory and civilians while refraining from the use of weapons of mass destruction. More plausibly, large-scale attacks occur, but the logic of mutually assured destruction, crisis signaling, and communications helps keep the war "limited." These limits might include restrictions on strikes against others' nuclear forces and command-and-control systems, civilian targets, and possibly certain conventional military targets as well.

In most conflict scenarios, we should assume that U.S. extended deterrence would protect treaty allies like Japan, Australia, and the Philippines from strategic nuclear attack. (Notably, Taiwan remains outside Washington's "nuclear umbrella." Extending U.S. nuclear assurances to Taiwan would be rightly seen in Beijing as a massive escalation. However, since Beijing considers Taiwan its own territory, it is unlikely to use nuclear weapons there.)

The main danger lies not in accidental descent into conflict, but rather in deliberate escalation caused by severe misjudgment of the opponent's capabilities or resolve. The United States considered nuclear strikes on China during the Korean War and the first two Taiwan Straits Crises. In each case, it thought better of it. China has recently fought savage border skirmishes with nuclear-armed India (using clubs and stones, but not firearms).[15] These episodes highlight both sides' awareness of nuclear risks. However, a U.S.–China war would differ fundamentally from past conflicts. The stakes would be so high that, under extreme conditions, both sides might consider nuclear use to avoid defeat in a conventional fight. While wargames and models provide insights into potential crisis behavior, real-world decisions in the "fog of war" remain unpredictable. Compounding this uncertainty, the PLA keeps its strategic deterrence doctrine deliberately vague.[16] Without clarity on Xi's views, the extent of the risk remains unclear—but China's actions warrant a robust and proportionate U.S. response.

This chapter examines U.S.–China strategic deterrence in theory and history. It begins by introducing the fundamental theory of nuclear coercion and explaining the key differences in PRC thinking. Next, it discusses the potential rationales for Xi's ongoing strategic buildup, how this buildup threatens

U.S. interests and alliances, and the growing risk of nuclear miscalculation. The United States must continue to modernize its entire nuclear enterprise, oppose nuclear proliferation, and actively explore new ways to strengthen extended deterrence for regional allies.

The second half of the chapter turns to non-nuclear strategic deterrence, including space and cyber threats, conventional risks to the U.S. homeland, and the growing role of AI. AI potentially has a crucial role to play in nearly every aspect of strategic deterrence. It could plausibly become game-changing if one side pulls far ahead. Since affecting China's perceptions is a key goal, there are potentially valuable lessons to be learned from how the Reagan administration communicated U.S. satellite and computing advantages to the Soviet Union in the late years of the Cold War. However, strategic signaling may work differently for AI capabilities than for nuclear weapons. America must study this issue carefully. Meanwhile, it should assume that China and other adversaries will soon find ways to leverage AI for strategic deterrence. American AI policy, and technology policy more broadly, must therefore be closely aligned with the nation's strategic deterrence doctrine. Neither the Biden nor the Trump administration has grasped this crucial point.

The Theory of Strategic Coercion

Nuclear weapons are powerful tools because they enable states to threaten indiscriminate destruction on an immense scale. This understanding emerged during the Cold War, when nuclear strategy was first formally theorized. As Nobel Prize–winning economist Thomas Schelling noted in his 1966 book *Arms and Influence*: "The power to hurt is a kind of bargaining power, not easy to use, but used often."[17] Schelling argues that the "power to hurt"—when held in reserve—can be used to coerce others into changing their behavior. Nuclear weapons are the ultimate example of this principle, but the same logic extends to other coercive tools. PRC scholars draw from Schelling's foundational work. However, as we will explore below, they seem to disagree with Schelling in significant ways.[18]

Schelling divides coercion into two categories: *deterrence* and *compellence*. Deterrence aims to maintain the status quo by convincing an adversary that the costs of action outweigh the benefits. Compellence, by contrast, seeks to change the status quo by forcing the adversary to act or stop a behavior.

Deterrence is simpler because the defender holds the advantage: merely refusing to move leaves it to the challenger to risk a collision. The challenger can back down while saving face by claiming it never intended to act in the first place. Compellence, however, requires the challenger to create the inevitability of a collision unless the defender yields. This is a far more complex task. If the challenger fails, he risks public loss of face.[19]

To compel change, brinkmanship is necessary. Schelling defines brinkmanship as "a competition in risk-taking . . . initiating a process that carries some risk of unintended disaster."[20] The compeller must convince the adversary of his willingness to accept higher risks, making concession the safer option. But the longer deterrent threats go unchallenged, the more credible they tend to become, because the harder it is for the challenger to assess the defender's risk tolerance. Schelling called this dynamic the "static clarity" of commitment to a long-established status quo.[21]

Subsequent literature has reaffirmed Schelling's core ideas while emphasizing that deterrence is rarely as clear-cut in practice as in theory. In the real world, perceptions and misperceptions, domestic politics and bureaucratic procedure, individual personalities, and misleading or ambiguous signaling all introduce uncertainty.[22] As political scientists Alexander George and Richard Smoke famously observed, deterrence can operate at multiple levels: the "strategic" level, "limited war," and crises short of war. In other words, deterrence is not a law of nature. How or whether deterrence works depends on context.[23]

The historical record basically backs up Schelling's theory. Reviewing over 200 "militarized compellent threats" between 1918 and 2001, involving both nuclear and nonnuclear states, researchers found that compellent threats succeeded just 30 percent of the time.[24] Moreover, compellent threats from nuclear states were even less effective, succeeding just 20 percent of the time.[25] These results held even when accounting for potentially confounding variables. In other words, Schelling was right when he noted that nuclear weapons are "neither useful tools of conquest nor low-cost tools of punishment."[26] If you irradiate the territory you want with nuclear explosions, the territory loses its value to you. Take the example of the India–Pakistan conflict over Kashmir. Pakistan is unlikely to use nuclear weapons to seize the region, as a nuclear strike would kill thousands of Muslims and render parts of the area uninhabitable.[27] Moreover, any nuclear use risks severe consequences—moral outrage, diplomatic isolation, economic sanctions, and even retaliatory strikes aimed at preserving the norm against nuclear warfare. Because of these risks, the road from nuclear use to strategic victory is by no means certain. This is why most states historically have chosen not to take it.

When both sides in a conflict are deterred from launching a nuclear first strike, the resulting equilibrium is known as "strategic stability." When two nuclear-armed countries have survivable *second*-strike capabilities, mutually assured destruction (MAD) takes hold. Both sides know that any first strike would be met with devastating retaliation, and therefore have no incentive to strike first.

Notably, MAD can hold even when one state has a vastly larger arsenal than the other. This logic has guided China's nuclear strategy for decades. From the 1960s until today, China has maintained a much smaller nuclear arsenal than the United States and the Soviet Union/Russia. Today's China has clearly shifted to a different approach.

Strategic stability is not inherently self-sustaining. Through brinkmanship, nuclear-armed states can exploit perceived weaknesses in their adversaries' nuclear forces for political leverage, even under the logic of MAD. Throughout the Cold War, the United States and the Soviet Union repeatedly adjusted their doctrines and invested in new capabilities in the hope of gaining coercive advantages. In the 1950s, the Eisenhower administration adopted a policy of "massive retaliation," threatening nuclear strikes if the USSR attacked Western Europe.[28] When bombers proved vulnerable to Soviet air defenses, both sides shifted to stealthier, second-strike capabilities like ballistic missile submarines.[29] In the 1960s, strategic stability briefly emerged. Both sides achieved credible second-strike arsenals, making a nuclear exchange tantamount to suicide.[30] But soon, advancements like missile defense systems again began to erode stability.[31] Even after the 1972 Anti-Ballistic Missile Treaty tried to restore MAD by ensuring mutual vulnerability, competition persisted in lower-yield warheads, intermediate-range missiles, anti-submarine technologies, and space-based defenses. These innovations created political leverage. But they also increased the risk that in a crisis the more vulnerable side would launch a preemptive strike, driven by the logic of "use it or lose it."

Nuclear competition continues today.[32] China points to U.S. technological advancements as justification for its own buildup, even as it undermines stability to pursue its political objectives. The United States rightly accuses China and Russia of building strategically destabilizing capabilities. For the first time, nuclear rivalry now involves three major players. China's buildup also raises the question of whether Xi's goal is to *deter* U.S. or Taiwanese changes in the status quo or to *compel* a change to the status quo—and whether he clearly perceives the distinction.

Interpreting Xi's Strategic Buildup

The PLA has a clear *defensive* interest in nuclear modernization that precedes Xi Jinping. By the mid-2000s, China recognized that its nuclear arsenal was increasingly vulnerable as U.S. reconnaissance and strike capabilities improved. Leading U.S. scholars predicted that China would take "logical" steps to strengthen deterrence.[33] In 2015, political scientists Fiona Cunningham and Taylor Fravel correctly predicted that this would include building more warheads and missiles capable of reaching the continental United States.[34] China was also using nuclear threats to deter Taiwan independence long before Xi took power. The 2013 edition of the *Science of Military Strategy*, an important textbook for senior PLA officers that likely reflected pre-Xi military thinking, states that China maintains nuclear forces to ensure that its "status as a powerful country does not waver, ensure that its core national interests are not violated," and to "create a secure environment for [China's] peaceful development."[35] As we've discussed, Taiwan is the "core of China's core interests."[36] In short, Xi's thinking about nuclear issues probably partly reflects a broader shift in PRC expert consensus that coalesced before his rise to power.

Xi also has historical reasons to believe that the United States may consider nuclear use if a conflict breaks out over Taiwan. The United States remains the only country to have used nuclear weapons in war—against civilians in the cities of Hiroshima and Nagasaki. During the Korean War and the First and Second Taiwan Straits crises, U.S. generals recommended using nuclear weapons against the PRC.[37] In both cases, Presidents Harry Truman and Dwight Eisenhower rejected these recommendations—but because European allies feared Soviet retaliation in Europe, not for humanitarian reasons.[38] In Vietnam, Washington considered using nuclear weapons on multiple occasions.[39] The United States has repeatedly considered and rejected calls to adopt a "no first use" nuclear policy, most recently in the Obama administration.[40] China's desire for a robust strategic nuclear deterrent is logical.[41]

However, this does not fully explain China's nuclear transformation under Xi, who has clearly taken a personal interest in nuclear modernization. Less than three years after taking power, Xi established the PLA Rocket Force as a separate service equal to the Army, Navy, and Air Force. "The Rocket Force is our country's core strategic deterrent force," Xi said. "It is the strategic support for our country's major power status; and it is an important foundation for safeguarding our nation's security."[42] The 2020 *Science of Military Strategy* describes the Rocket Force as "a strategic service that uses land-launched missile weapons systems operations and that possesses a number of operational capabilities, such as nuclear counterattack and conventional attack."[43] This system deliberately blurs conventional and nuclear capabilities.[44]

Under Xi, the PLA has developed its first credible nuclear "triad," dramatically expanding its capabilities across land, air, and sea. The Rocket Force has built hundreds of new ballistic missile silos and expanded its arsenal to over 600 warheads.[45] On land, the PLA has developed road-mobile ICBMs that can strike regional targets like Hawaii and Guam, as well as over 100 missiles capable of hitting anywhere in the continental United States.[46] In 2021, China demonstrated a significant technological leap by testing a fractional orbital hypersonic delivery system. This system combines the extreme speed of fractional orbital bombardment with the maneuverability of hypersonic glide vehicles, making it particularly challenging for U.S. missile defense systems to intercept.[47] In the air, the PLA Air Force has modernized its H-6K strategic bombers to be able to carry nuclear-capable air-launched ballistic missiles.[48] China is also developing a new stealth bomber (the H-20) that will have a nuclear mission, significantly enhancing its air-based nuclear deterrent.[49] At sea, China has six operational Type 094 Jin-class ballistic missile submarines (SSBNs). These vessels are capable of carrying up to twelve submarine-launched ballistic missiles (SLBMs), including the JL-3 missile with a range of over 5,400 nautical miles.[50] These submarines conduct regular deterrent patrols, allowing the PLAN to threaten continental U.S. targets while still remaining closer to Chinese waters.[51] The next-generation Type-096 submarine, reportedly benefiting from Russian stealth technology transfers, will be even harder to detect and could carry long-range multiple-warhead SLBMs capable of striking the continental United States.[52] Taking these unprecedented advancements together, Xi ought to have allayed any old concerns about the "assuredness" of his nuclear deterrent.

Yet China's nuclear buildup has continued, and it has deliberately blurred the distinction between conventional and strategic capabilities. China has deployed roughly 100 dual-capable DF-26 intermediate-range ballistic missiles (IRBMs), which can carry either nuclear or conventional warheads capable of striking critical U.S. military bases and logistics hubs across the region.[53] This ambiguity would create a dangerous situation in a Taiwan conflict: the United States could not immediately determine if an incoming missile carried a nuclear or conventional warhead until detonation. This might lead Xi to believe he could use low-yield nuclear weapons against key U.S. facilities—such as those on Guam and in Japan—to gain significant conventional advantages while minimizing the risk of a strategic nuclear response from the United States.[54]

China has also diversified its nuclear arsenal, from low-yield warheads to multi-megaton warheads. This expansion provides Beijing with more options and additional rungs on the nuclear escalation ladder.[55] To summarize, China has not only moved well beyond its former "minimal deterrent" strategy, but also built a flexible and dynamic nuclear posture. This reveals a desire for escalation dominance in a potential limited nuclear conflict.

The imbalance in theater capabilities places U.S. forces at a potential strategic disadvantage. U.S. forces lack a diverse arsenal of ground-launched intermediate-range nuclear-capable missiles.[56] Indeed, China now has more land-based ICBMs and IRBM launchers than the United States does.[57] China's growing anti-satellite capabilities further complicate this dynamic. The U.S. relies on roughly two dozen satellites for nuclear early warning and general reconnaissance.[58] If China disabled these satellites, it could leave U.S. commanders uncertain as to whether the attack was aimed at enabling conventional operations or preparing for a strategic nuclear strike on the U.S. homeland.

These developments significantly increase the risk that U.S. commanders may miscalculate and overreact during a fast-paced crisis, leading to general nuclear war. During the Cold War, superpowers used nuclear alert levels to signal risk tolerance and manage brinkmanship crises. For example, the United States raised its nuclear alert to DEFCON 3 during the 1973 Yom Kippur War to deter Soviet intervention.[59] However, in a U.S.–China war, both sides would likely place their nuclear forces on wartime alert. These signaling mechanisms would lose their effectiveness.

Xi has also prioritized nonnuclear strategic deterrence capabilities, including the potential to deliver conventional strikes against U.S. and allied homelands. In 2022, a state-owned missile manufacturer unveiled a self-powered missile system that can fit stealthily into a standard 40-foot shipping container.[60] China is also pursuing possible containerized deployment of the YJ-18 ASCM and YJ-21 ASBM.[61] Although it is not clear whether these containerized missile systems are operational, their strategic threat is evident.

In a conflict, Beijing could weaponize its vast "civilian" maritime enterprise to target critical U.S. and allied infrastructure anywhere near coastal areas. China Ocean Shipping Company (COSCO) is the world's fourth-largest shipper, operating over 500 container ships capable of carrying more than 3 million 20-foot containers, calling at 356 ports in 105 countries. COSCO vessels regularly stop in major U.S. cities and pass near key U.S. military bases.[62] These vessels, each carrying thousands of containers, could conceal missile systems or other weapons.[63] PRC law explicitly requires COSCO to support PLA "strategic projection" efforts, if ordered.[64] China's state-owned enterprises, embedded in global port management software and infrastructure, could potentially load containerized missiles at third-country ports without local authorities' knowledge.[65] Beyond direct attacks, Beijing could exploit this capability to smuggle weapons around the world or trigger false alarms to divert U.S. intelligence resources.

Defending against such tactics poses significant challenges for the United States. Using civilian ships for military operations violates international law, but identifying and neutralizing hidden threats in integrated global supply chains would risk massive economic disruptions. The United States currently lacks effective measures to mitigate this vulnerability without significant consequences for global trade.[66] It would also struggle to threaten China with an equivalent program since PRC firms are more deeply embedded across global shipping networks than American companies. The Trump administration is currently working to crack down on PRC container ships docking at U.S. ports.[67] This effort is necessary, but it will be costly.

Additional threats to the U.S. homeland are already apparent in open sources. PRC entities maintain relationships with Mexican drug cartels, supplying them with fentanyl precursors. In 2024, a PRC crime syndicate was indicted for laundering millions for the Sinaloa cartel.[68] In a Taiwan crisis, Beijing could potentially weaponize these relationships to create chaos on both sides of the U.S.–Mexico border. In the most extreme scenarios, one could imagine China using these criminal connections to smuggle weapons over the U.S. border or help conduct terrorist attacks inside the United States. Additionally, China's integration into global supply chains raises the risk that PRC components in some U.S. industrial systems could be remotely disabled or even detonated.[69]

Cyber threats further amplify these dangers. As former FBI Director Christopher Wray has warned, China has systematically prepositioned cyber exploits across critical U.S. infrastructure, including energy, transportation, telecommunications, and water systems. In Wray's interpretation, Beijing is covertly signaling that it could "wreak havoc and inflict real-world harm" if it wished.[70] The U.S. government's shambolic response to COVID-19—a virus that originated in China, albeit under different circumstances—highlights another potential U.S. vulnerability.[71]

Xi appears to have drawn lessons from the pandemic about the importance of state capacity for regime resilience. For three years, he steadfastly pursued a "zero COVID policy," which was painful for the people but represented a victory for the party-state.[72] Xi has spoken often about the pandemic as a "stress test" that China successfully passed and the West did not.[73] At the 20th Party Congress in October 2022, he emphasized the need to prepare for "extreme-case" scenarios (*jiduan qingkuang* 极端情况).[74] Xi's national mobilization to build up China's "resilience" now extends to all kinds of crises, including not only conventional war, but also "financial war" (discussed in Chapter 7), pandemics, and natural disasters.[75]

The concept of "resilience" is fundamental to Xi's vision for China in an age of intensifying competition with the United States. Xi regularly states that "national rejuvenation" is achieved through "struggle" (*douzheng* 斗争). To succeed in struggle, a nation and its vital systems must be *renxing* (韧性). This term is usually translated as "resilience," but this slightly misrepresents the meaning. In English, the core idea of *resilience* is the ability to recover, adapt, or return to equilibrium after a shock. In Chinese, that would be translated with another word: *huifu* (恢复). *Renxing* means something different: the capacity to endure pressure without breaking. In general, this is how Xi talks about strategic threats: his emphasis isn't on how to recover from a shock but on how to contain risk and preserve the stability of a nation's internal system.[76] In other words, it is all about the party's grip on power. Xi views strategic deterrence as ultimately about regime survival. U.S.–China strategic deterrence is a competition over which system can endure more pressure without breaking—in all possible ways that pressure can be applied.

China's strategic deterrence doctrine provides little insight into Xi's use of his strategic capabilities to pressure the United States. China has formally committed itself to a policy whereby China will not use nuclear weapons first, a policy known as No First Use (NFU). However, this policy appears to be in tension with China's evolving nuclear posture and deliberate ambiguity about its doctrine.[77] The PRC open-source literature also hints at an internal debate about NFU.[78] U.S. military leaders and government officials have consistently expressed skepticism about the credibility of China's NFU pledge, citing potential loopholes and broader interpretations that could justify first use under certain scenarios.[79] The United States must assume that Xi might use nuclear weapons first if he believed he could contain subsequent escalation.

Open-source materials offer some insight into the PRC's strategy, but it is not clear whether they accurately convey Xi's thinking or whether they are merely trying to rationalize actions taken under his leadership.[80] PRC scholars typically speak of strategic stability as the goal. They blame U.S. policies for destabilizing the region, and they justify China's nuclear buildup as a defensive response.[81] They argue that the lines separating conventional and nuclear war, and therefore the definition of strategic deterrence, have blurred not due to China's actions, but because of broad technological trends and U.S. actions.[82] Are these commentators actually knowledgeable? Or are they simply highly credentialed propagandists for a strategic deterrence command walled off within the Central Military Commission?

Adding to the analytical confusion is the PRC analysts' failure to use the word "deterrence" consistently. The term is typically translated as *weishe* (威慑). But like the Russian equivalent, *weishe* can also describe offensive, compellent behavior.[83] Indeed, the prominent analyst Li Bin of Tsinghua University has explicitly criticized U.S. overreliance on Schelling's theories. In Li's view, identifying which side changed the status quo first is often inherently difficult.[84] He defines *weishe* as "the use of force to make the other party perceive fear," suggesting it aligns more closely with Schelling's concept of "coercion" than deterrence.[85] How, then, should we interpret Xi's directive at the 20th Party Congress to develop a "strategic deterrence system" (*zhanlüe weishe tixi*, 战略威慑体系)? Is this system intended to be solely defensive? Or does Xi envision leveraging nuclear threats to *compel* Taiwan's "reunification"?

China's opacity is probably deliberate: an attempt to put psychological pressure on adversaries. Scholars at the Chinese Academy of Social Sciences have acknowledged the strategic value of maintaining "a certain degree of 'fuzziness'" regarding tactics, technical indicators, and deployment specifics, describing the approach as "strategic transparency and tactical secrecy."[86] U.S.–China nuclear dialogues, held regularly, provide limited value. As one

U.S. official with decades of experience in such discussions reportedly put it: "China doesn't want us to understand their deterrence strategy."[87]

Facing these uncertainties, the United States cannot let Schelling's theory breed complacency. China seems to think that strategic deterrence is not separated from conventional conflict in rigid levels, but is rather a continuum extending all the way from what we call "peacetime" to full-scale nuclear war. China is building a "strategic coercion force" to establish escalation dominance *across* this entire spectrum. Its goal may therefore be to conduct attacks that Washington considers "strategic"—such as strikes on U.S. critical infrastructure or low-yield nuclear strikes on military targets—while deterring effective U.S. responses. It may also seek to deter Washington from striking PLA targets in mainland China during a conventional war. In short, Washington must prepare for potential nuclear brinkmanship over Taiwan and strategic attacks on the U.S. homeland. It must also build and signal flexible deterrence capabilities across domains to keep China deterred all the way up the escalation ladder.

Miscalculation Risks

While miscalculations have never resulted in nuclear conflict in the past, several near misses provide critical lessons. One of the most alarming examples is the 1983 Able Archer exercise, when the Reagan administration badly underestimated the risk that it might inadvertently trigger a nuclear war. In November 1983, NATO conducted its annual exercise to simulate conflict with the Soviet Union, but with unprecedented realism. The exercise incorporated coded communications, radio silences, and even personal participation from British Prime Minister Margaret Thatcher and West German Chancellor Helmut Kohl.[88] The scenario envisioned proxy conflicts in Syria, South Yemen, and Iran, escalating into a Soviet invasion of Finland, Norway, and West Germany.[89]

KGB analysts feared Able Archer might be a pretext for a NATO surprise attack against the Soviet Union.[90] Before the exercise, Soviet leaders conveyed their concerns to Reagan's team through backchannels.[91] These warnings went unheeded. When the exercise began, the Soviet leadership was therefore dangerously misinformed and misinterpreted the situation. As NATO forces simulated alert escalation from DEFCON 5 to DEFCON 1, KGB reports convinced the Kremlin that these weren't merely exercises.[92] Several factors heightened their concern: a radio-silent airlift of 19,000 U.S. soldiers to

Europe, NATO's testing of ground-launched cruise missiles, Reagan's recent "Star Wars" announcement, and NATO's demonstrated ability to threaten Soviet nuclear submarines in the Arctic. The Soviet leadership was on a hair trigger and ordered the country's nuclear forces to the highest readiness. Years later, multiple KGB officials confirmed that they genuinely believed a U.S. surprise first nuclear strike was plausible, or even likely.[93]

The true gravity of the situation became clear only after the Soviet Union collapsed and its archives were opened. Given the Soviets' "peculiar and remarkably skewed frame of mind," Deputy Director of National Intelligence Robert Gates later noted, "I don't think the Soviets were crying wolf. They may not have believed a NATO attack was imminent in November 1983, but they did seem to believe that the situation was very dangerous. And U.S. intelligence had failed to grasp the true extent of their anxiety."[94]

Indeed, U.S. officials regularly underestimate other states' fears that America might launch a surprise nuclear attack.[95] Robert S. McNamara, the U.S. secretary of defense during the Berlin and Cuban Missile crises, later reflected: "It is impossible to predict with a high degree of confidence what the effects of the use of military force will be because of the risks of accident, miscalculation, misperception, and inadvertence. . . . In my opinion, this law ought to be inscribed above all the doorways in the White House and the Pentagon, and it is the overwhelming lesson of the Cuban missile crisis. 'Managing' crises is the wrong term. You don't 'manage' them because you can't 'manage' them."[96] Ronald Reagan himself acknowledged this in his memoirs, reflecting on how close Able Archer brought the world to disaster: "The more experience I had with Soviet leaders and other heads of state who knew them, the more I began to realize that many Soviet officials feared us not only as adversaries but as potential aggressors who might hurl nuclear weapons at them in a first strike."[97]

Policymakers today must not forget Reagan's insight. The history of nuclear near misses in the Cold War is marked by accidents and misperceptions. Crises that look clear to historians in retrospect were perceived very differently by those who lived through them.[98] While states strive to act rationally, they can make grave mistakes due to human error and procedural faults. Intelligence agencies also make mistakes and are prone to strategic misperceptions. If Xi forces a brinkmanship crisis, the United States must be prepared to accept some nuclear risk. It must trust in its time-tested theory and doctrine, but it must also remember that Xi sees the world differently, and the real world is not as certain as game theory suggests. The United States must revitalize its own cross-domain strategic deterrence system partly because it should seek to dissuade Xi from forcing a brinkmanship crisis in the first place.

Reassuring U.S. Allies

China's nuclear buildup could stress U.S. alliances, similarly to the Euromissiles crisis of the late 1970s and early 1980s. In 1976, the Soviet Union deployed the SS-20, a road-mobile intermediate-range ballistic missile with multiple independent reentry vehicles that could destroy any target in Europe with little chance of interception.[99] As the Soviets eroded U.S. nuclear superiority, Europeans feared the United States might abandon them in a war.[100] Yet, the European powers were hesitant to let the Americans balance the scales by deploying more intermediate-range nuclear forces in Europe, which they feared would make them targets in a nuclear exchange.[101] In other words, European governments paradoxically sought U.S. nuclear guarantees without expanded nuclear presence on European soil.[102] For nearly a decade, the "Euromissiles" issue severely strained U.S.–Europe relations, even putting the future of NATO itself in jeopardy.[103] The crisis took many years to resolve.[104]

Today, Japan and South Korea face a similar growing nuclear threat from North Korea, China, and Russia. Like the Europeans in the late 1970s and early 1980s, these countries want Washington to provide stronger nuclear assurances. However, the U.S. nuclear posture in Asia has significant limitations. Since withdrawing its nuclear weapons from South Korea in 1991, the U.S. nuclear weapons closest to Taiwan have been based in Guam—and, presumably, on submarines conducting deterrence patrols.[105] Moreover, the United States lacks a diverse arsenal of ground-launched or sea-launched intermediate-range nuclear-capable missiles, the current equivalent of Euromissiles. This gap emerged partly because of the Intermediate-Range Nuclear Forces (INF) Treaty (1987), which prevented the United States (but not China, which never joined) from developing ground-launched theater nuclear weapons. The Trump administration withdrew from the treaty in 2019, but the United States is still playing catch-up.[106]

It is not clear how best to enhance U.S. nuclear assurances. North Korea's expanding nuclear arsenal and unpredictable leadership directly threaten both

South Korea and Japan. Pyongyang has repeatedly conducted missile tests simulating strikes on U.S. regional allies and military bases. South Korea also fears that North Korea might exploit America's distraction during a Taiwan crisis to move against Seoul.[107] A 2022 poll found that 71 percent of South Korean respondents supported developing nuclear weapons, while 56 percent supported the return of U.S. tactical nuclear weapons to the peninsula.[108] In January 2023, then-President Yoon Suk-yeol demanded more specific U.S. promises to defend South Korea against nuclear attack, hinting that Seoul would otherwise have to develop its own nuclear weapons.[109] Biden sought a compromise, sending an *Ohio*-class ballistic missile submarine to visit the South Korean port of Busan in 2023. The idea is that semi-regular visits could strengthen deterrence similarly to ground-based missiles.[110] However, a debate has arisen regarding the strategic wisdom of revealing an SSBN presence, as well as about whether the W76-2 low-yield nuclear warhead aboard an *Ohio*-class SSBN is comparable to larger strategic weapons stationed on the peninsula.[111]

In Japan and the Philippines, public and elite opinion on nuclear topics is complex and contentious. Japan abides by the "three nonnuclear principles"—not possessing, producing, or permitting the introduction of nuclear weapons—which are rooted in the legacy of Hiroshima and Nagasaki. These principles have been central to Japan's national identity since the 1960s, and public opposition to nuclear arms remains strong.[112] In the Philippines, the 1987 constitution explicitly bans stationing nuclear weapons on the nation's soil.[113]

The United States has several programs to stabilize the nuclear balance in the Indo-Pacific, but more needs to be done. Congress has mandated the development of the Nuclear-Armed Sea-Launched Cruise Missile (SLCM-N).[114] New air-launched nuclear-armed Long Range Stand-Off (LRSO) weapons are in development.[115] Still, China's theater-level nuclear delivery systems currently outmatch those of the United States, and both China and Russia are reportedly developing low-yield nuclear weapons that they might consider more usable in theater. Building and deploying more ground-launched ballistic missiles in the region would be an appropriate response.

As a potential solution, some analysts and policymakers have proposed "nuclear sharing" with South Korea and Japan.[116] The United States has nuclear sharing agreements with several NATO allies. Five nations host dual-capability aircraft on their soil. Seven are organized to support U.S. nuclear operations with their own, conventional air tactics.[117]

Nuclear sharing differs from nuclear proliferation because it does not involve allies acquiring *independent* nuclear arsenals. Instead, host nations support and might help deliver U.S.-owned nuclear weapons, but they cannot launch them unilaterally. In NATO, for example, foreign commanders cannot use nuclear weapons without explicit U.S. executive approval and approval from NATO's Nuclear Planning Group.[118] Nuclear-sharing proposals are gaining traction in both Japan and South Korea. In 2022, former Japanese Prime Minister Shinzo Abe suggested that Japan should consider a nuclear-sharing arrangement with the United States. Some hawkish military and civilian officials still agree.[119] Polls conducted in Japan show that support for this position among the general population is rising, too.[120] In South Korea as well, politicians and military leaders have called for nuclear sharing.[121]

Expanding nuclear sharing in the Pacific presents challenges and risks. Training Japanese and South Korean forces to support U.S. nuclear-related operations would largely serve a symbolic purpose, as operational control would remain exclusively with the United States. The only relevant military targets in the region that the United States would be unable to destroy with conventional weapons during a regional security contingency are inside mainland China. A nuclear-sharing agreement with South Korea would violate the 1991 Joint Declaration of the Denuclearization of the Korean Peninsula. This agreement is not enforced and has been extensively violated by North Korea, but it still represents a symbolic U.S. commitment.[122] China, Russia, and North Korea could also retaliate with anything from economic and cyber measures to threats to spread nuclear technology to adversarial states such as Iran.

Still, given that Seoul and Tokyo have shown interest and legitimately need stronger nuclear assurances, it is worth exploring how nuclear sharing could be offered quickly if circumstances demanded.[123] For all its limitations, nuclear sharing would be a sign of U.S. resolve and commitment to peace and stability in the region.

Modernizing the U.S. Nuclear Deterrent

Meanwhile, the U.S. nuclear arsenal must be modernized. This is largely because the United States now faces two nuclear peer adversaries—China and Russia—whose deepening partnership threatens potential aggression in two theaters simultaneously.[124] The nonpartisan Congressional Commission on U.S. Strategic Posture has found that the United States is currently unequipped to address this dual threat. It recommends either expanding or altering current U.S. nuclear capabilities to maintain credible deterrence.[125] A resilient nuclear force must be able to absorb a first strike and still respond powerfully enough to inflict unacceptable damage to the aggressor and maintain deterrent power over any other adversaries.[126] To this end, the Commission recommends modernization of nuclear command, control, and communications and the nuclear industrial base.[127]

Currently, the entire ICBM arsenal is run by a computer system with roughly the processing power of a modern smartphone.[128] These legacy systems have proven reliable for decades, and hardware remains more critical than software sophistication in maintaining deterrence. Still, modernization is eventually necessary to ensure future safety and reliability.

U.S. nuclear modernization is a multi-decade project.[129] Most of the funds are going to replace delivery systems, not warheads themselves. The Minuteman III—the backbone of the ground-launched nuclear force—is being replaced by the Sentinel.[130] The Air Force is procuring the B-21 Raider to replace its B-1 and B-2, while keeping B-52 bombers armed with long-range cruise missiles.[131] The Navy is ordering twelve *Columbia*-class SSBNs to replace its eighteen *Ohio*-class boats. U.S. adversaries characterize the modernization effort as a strategic threat, but this is rhetoric rather than reality. Modernization is about maintaining the current force, not expanding it. All currently proposed nuclear spending—the new platforms identified above, plus new command-and-control and early warning systems—totals $750 billion through 2032. The key question is whether or not the president will spend political capital to secure another large nuclear spending increase. If not, the modernization timeline could be delayed, with potential implications for readiness.

There is also a growing debate over the role of tactical nuclear weapons in U.S. strategy. The SLCM-N, discussed above, will be the U.S. Navy's first nuclear cruise missile since the Cold War and the first nonstrategic nuclear weapon to enter the U.S. arsenal in decades. The United States also maintains an arsenal of "Dial-a-Yield" gravity bombs whose explosive power can be adjusted before launch.[132] It is unclear under what circumstances the United States would want to use these weapons. Delivering them to relevant PLA targets would run a high risk of escalation in a high-intensity combat scenario.[133] It is hard to take a firm position on the tactical nuclear weapons debate from unclassified sources alone.

U.S. nuclear modernization must also address emerging cross-domain strategic threats, particularly in space. China's counter-space capabilities could threaten both nuclear and conventional command-and-control systems during crises.[134] The current U.S. space C2 infrastructure remains overreliant on a small number of key assets, creating dangerous single points of failure. In the short to medium term, nonkinetic attacks such as cyberattacks and jamming may pose even greater risks than physical attacks on satellites. Destroying satellites through kinetic means is difficult, expensive, slow, and easily traced, but Russia has demonstrated GPS jamming techniques that reduce precision-guided munition accuracy without physically destroying satellites.[135] Satellite ground control stations are also vulnerable to cyberattack.

To counter these vulnerabilities, the United States should increase the number and orbital diversity of its satellites, particularly in low Earth orbit (LEO). The trend is toward smaller, more numerous satellites becoming increasingly deployable in constellations to support a variety of applications. The United States and its allies currently lead in satellite production and launch, but sustaining this lead will require concerted policy support. LEO constellations also use smaller, more mobile operating stations, which makes the overall system more resilient to cyberattack.[136] DoD is already awarding contracts for LEO satellite constellations, and so is China. These efforts should be expanded.[137] A key focus should be integrating U.S. government satellite networks with networks operated by U.S. and allied firms. Neutral countries should also be invited to join. This strategy could help the U.S. network benefit from the private sector's innovation and agility, while making the overall network more costly and risky for adversaries to attack.

The ultimate goal should be robust arms control agreements with China and Russia to limit the growth of nuclear stockpiles and restrict strategically destabilizing capabilities. Unfortunately, neither China nor Russia has engaged in good-faith arms negotiations in decades.[138] To establish effective space arms control, Washington needs to rebuild leverage.

Missile defenses such as Golden Dome could be part of this push for leverage, but only in the long term. When the Reagan administration announced the Strategic Defense Initiative (SDI, also known as "Star Wars"), its ambitious plans for lasers and satellite-based missile interceptors were largely speculative. Still, the program bolstered deterrence by convincing Moscow that the United States had decisive technological advantages, which contributed to Gorbachev's retrenchments in the late 1980s.[139] Today, however, U.S. missile defenses focus primarily on threats from smaller states like North Korea and Iran—and China knows this.[140] Despite decades of investment totaling hundreds of billions of dollars, experts in the public domain have questioned whether the system could stop a large-scale ICBM attack or intercept nuclear-armed hypersonics.[141] Fully modernizing U.S. missile defenses, as President Trump has proposed, is an admirable goal. It is also a long-term project that will require trillions of dollars over decades. There is also no guarantee that these systems will be fully effective against emerging threats from hypersonic missiles. In the short to medium term, cheaper, offensive countermeasures—first and foremost missile-based—will therefore be essential for strategic deterrence.

AI and Strategic Stability

Meanwhile, AI is emerging as a disruptive force that introduces both new deterrence tools and new threats to strategic stability. Taiwan looms in the background of this discussion for two reasons. First, it is the primary battleground where the United States and China are using strategic coercion to protect their respective interests. Second, Taiwan's semiconductor industry supplies the critical hardware that underpins the competition for advanced AI. How U.S. policymakers deal with these uncertainties will determine the island's future, which is why America's AI strategy must be aligned with its strategic deterrence strategy.

AI can be viewed in two ways. First, it can be seen as a set of discrete capabilities. This approach focuses on tasks that we know AI can (and can't) do well. As of this writing, AI excels at coding, computer vision, and pattern recognition in large-text datasets. It sometimes exceeds elite human performance on difficult knowledge and reasoning tasks, including international mathematics Olympiad exams. Benchmarks show that performance in these areas is improving with astonishing speed. At the same time, AI models often make "dumb" mistakes. They have a disconcerting tendency to hallucinate and make false statements with high confidence. This unreliability has slowed institutional adoption, particularly for high-stakes applications. Of course, as we will see below, AI systems could have significant strategic implications even if the broader applicability of the technology is highly uneven. Early evidence suggests that China perceives AI mainly as an enabler of discrete capabilities. China is particularly interested in industrial AI applications such as engineering, manufacturing, materials science, and synthetic biology.[142]

In essence, China is betting that it can use AI to win in hardware, even if America leads in software.

The second way of thinking about AI—which is dominant in America—emphasizes its potential value as a general-purpose technology.[143] According to this line of thinking, the most important feature of AI models is that they follow a scaling law: the more compute is put into training them, the more capable they tend to become across all different kinds of tasks. New models routinely display emergent capabilities that even their creators did not anticipate. Analysts who emphasize scaling laws tend to emphasize long-term trends rather than short-term limitations. They note that both computation costs and AI performance per unit of computation are improving exponentially. On this basis, the argument goes, there is a single U.S.–China horse race in AI. Whichever side can field a better frontier model will gain compounding advantages across the board.[144] Put more plainly: software will carry the day.

Prominent industry leaders and analysts who speak about a race for artificial general intelligence (AGI) are in the second camp. Some predict that as soon as 2027, leading AI models could match or exceed human capabilities in most cognitive tasks, offering access to what amounts to a "country of geniuses in a datacenter."[145] If AGI can be achieved, some claim that it will be a short step to AI "superintelligence" that vastly exceeds human capabilities.[146] There is an active debate within the AI community about whether AGI is the right way to think about what AI is and can become.[147] Critics counter that AI models aren't designed to replicate human intelligence.[148] Believers in AGI and superintelligence hypothesize that AI models will eventually reach a tipping point where they can invent new technologies, including algorithmic techniques that recursively improve their own intelligence, unlocking new possibilities that can scarcely be imagined.[149]

While debates over AGI remain speculative, even today's more limited AI capabilities are reshaping the security landscape in ways that demand serious attention. Whether AI advances in an uneven fashion or accelerates broadly toward superintelligence, its integration into military operations, cyber warfare, and nuclear deterrence is already altering the balance of power—and deterrence over Taiwan.

AI could potentially start to affect strategic stability in the very near future. In fast-moving crises, AI could predict adversaries' moves in advance and strengthen cross-domain signaling.[150] It could support cyberattacks on countries' nuclear infrastructures.[151] It could fuse data from various kinds of sensors to identify enemy ballistic missile submarines, which once spotted could be neutralized relatively easily.[152] It could enhance cyber operations through more capable operatives or virtual hacker armies. Offensively, AI could help with espionage, destruction or corruption of sensitive data, and implanting of cyber exploits. Defensively, it could protect IT systems against attack by enemy AIs, while running counter-intelligence operations to confuse the adversary or conduct information operations against an opposing state's civilian population.[153]

If and when these capabilities are developed, we can imagine many scenarios where they lead to grave miscalculation. The thought should be sobering for anyone familiar with past nuclear close calls, such as the 1983 Able Archer crisis. But it is potentially hopeful for the American theory of AI supremacy, in which software-driven capabilities in cyberspace trump hardware-driven capabilities in the physical world.

More speculatively, AI-driven advances could structurally affect strategic stability by inventing new technologies. New advanced materials, chemical compounds, manufacturing processes, and biological engineering techniques could all be applied to weapons systems. AI-augmented robotics could potentially improve the speed, efficiency, and quality of manufacturing for warheads, delivery systems, and related infrastructure. These capabilities could potentially disrupt the balance of nuclear, biological, and chemical weapons over time, giving one side leverage even in the context of MAD.

As AI grows more capable, measuring adversaries' AI capabilities will become increasingly important to assessing the overall strategic balance—but this could prove harder than it sounds. Private businesses that hold sensitive data and the weight of valuable closed models will become increasingly prominent targets for adversaries' intelligence operations. Beyond China, rogue states such as Russia and North Korea will seek to steal cutting-edge AI capabilities. But at the same time, the U.S. government will likely deepen its collaboration with key AI companies to secure their secrets and apply their capabilities to U.S. government operations. And then there is the problem of disinformation. Companies and countries already have commercial incentives to exaggerate their AI capabilities. (In January 2025, for example, Open AI CEO Sam Altman wrote on his blog that "we are now confident we know how to build AGI as we have traditionally understood it," and that the company would now be refocusing on "superintelligence."[154]) Future disinformation and marketing campaigns may aim to confuse adversaries about AI development timelines and capabilities. Signaling these capabilities—and sometimes bluffing—will become an essential part of strategic deterrence.

More broadly, AI will transform intelligence operations. In one scenario, AI makes intelligence agencies much better at their jobs. Vast teams of AI agents acquire and process data at superhuman speeds, becoming invaluable decision support tools for all government functions. In another scenario, AI makes intelligence agencies considerably worse at their jobs. If one intelligence organization can "poison" its adversary's AI during training, or confuse it by laying fake evidence, decision-makers might face paralysis during crises, uncertain about whether they actually understand the situation or are receiving bad advice from the AI. Leaders who are not confident they have good information may be less comfortable engaging in nuclear brinkmanship.

What is clear is that there is no going back to a pre-AI world. Some scholars have called for AI arms control, but restricting AI development on the international level will be harder than restricting the proliferation of traditional weapons of mass destruction.[155] AI models also differ from nuclear weapons in key ways. Nuclear capabilities are relatively straightforward to assess. Fissile material, warheads, and delivery systems are physical items that can be inspected, measured, and monitored through satellite imagery and other means. A clear international taboo against nuclear weapons use has helped deter nuclear use since 1945. AI defies such clear assessment. AI capabilities vary widely, evolve constantly, and once developed can be copied and hidden with relative ease. Additionally, no clear taboos exist at the international level relating to the use of AI for strategic coercion. As AI technology diffuses through institutions and systems, defining what is and is not AI is becoming increasingly fuzzy.

It therefore seems inevitable that AI will become increasingly integrated into states' strategic deterrence forces. Major countries have thus already begun to embed AI within their strategic deterrence enterprises for tasks like intelligence collection and analysis and decision support. Thus, even if all countries with nuclear weapons can agree with the U.S. doctrine that humans should be "in the loop" for all decisions regarding nuclear use, AI will inevitably become a relevant part of many nuclear, cyber, and space deterrence operations.[156]

Bringing AI closer to strategic capabilities could present serious challenges in maintaining human control.[157] Any dangerous technology brings risks of accidents, which can result from mechanical failures, human errors, and misperceptions, or combinations thereof.[158] The risk of disastrous accidents comes not just from the possibility of "misaligned AI"—a disputed concept—but from the interface between this complex ecosystem and individual human decision-makers.[159] Practically speaking, all states need procedures for managing these risks. Deterrence and control over dangerous technologies are not necessarily mutually exclusive concepts.

Indeed, brinkmanship is precisely the art of risking the loss of control. During brinkmanship crises, states sometimes put their nuclear forces under "launch-on-warning" orders. This step deliberately increases the chance of miscalculation and a catastrophic accident in order to deter an adversary.[160] States that believe they are falling behind in strategic competition often become prone to exploiting this fact, since the best way to deter a capable adversary is often to accept more existential risk. As AI models grow more powerful and capable of autonomous action, the question of how thoroughly to vet them for safety before deploying them will become an increasingly important judgment call. Anthropic CEO Dario Amodei has warned about this dynamic. If the United States and China are racing to deploy advanced capabilities, the laggard may face incentives to cut corners on safety.[161]

Lacking clear answers to these questions, the United States and China will likely continue to approach the AI/strategic competition nexus from a position of acute uncertainty. Neither side knows how quickly AI capabilities will advance. Neither fully understands the shifting strategic balance, or how the other side perceives the balance. Even if today's AI prognostications turn out to be hype, rapid AI progress will still increase all countries' *uncertainty* about the future strategic balance. Nuclear-armed states may quickly gain or lose their confidence in the assuredness of their nuclear deterrents.

In conclusion, perceptions and misperceptions of AI competition could potentially make the strategic balance much less stable than in the Cold War. The United States wants to prevent the CCP from being the first to acquire advanced capabilities that could undermine U.S. strategic deterrence. China might well perceive a mirror image of the same interest. No one yet knows what strategic stability looks like in this context because AI could potentially create strategic capabilities beyond the nuclear domain. For example, might a future superintelligent American AI breach the "great firewall" and help to rally the Chinese people to rise up against the CCP regime? It may be premature to hold bilateral dialogues on AI arms control, but the United States must design its own AI policy with one eye squarely focused on strategic deterrence against the CCP. We must achieve a long-term strategic balance that is both stable and favorable to U.S. interests and values.

Toward an American AI Strategic Deterrent

Both the Biden and second Trump administrations have pursued a strategy of maximizing America's lead in AI. In 2023, National Security Advisor Jake Sullivan called for achieving "as large of a lead as possible," and the Trump administration has maintained this goal.[162] The Trump administration calls for cementing "AI dominance."[163] China's leaders, in turn, have expressed fears about "falling behind," though they seem to understand the competition as a large number of parallel horse races, not a single horse race in large language models.[164] This section argues that maximizing the U.S. lead is an appropriate strategy for the short term—but that the United States may ultimately need to pivot toward prioritizing long-term strategic stability.

As of this writing, the United States seems to enjoy a substantial but perishable advantage in frontier AI capabilities. U.S. firms enjoy access to more and cheaper computational power. The most advanced chips produced in Taiwan are U.S. designs that cannot legally be exported to China. The largest AI companies by market capitalization are all American. Their models have the most users worldwide and lead on performance benchmarks. China's leading models like Deepseek lag slightly behind Western competitors and perform far worse on safety tests, though they are much cheaper to run.[165] The United States also enjoys substantial advantages in talent, not least because much of China's top AI talent comes to America for education and employment. This situation may change if U.S. policymakers change immigration rules to block PRC students and researchers.

While America currently holds the advantage in cutting-edge chip production, it is not certain that this advantage will endure. Optimists such as Christophe Fouquet, CEO of the Dutch lithography machine producer ASML, predict that China's ability to produce its own advanced chips will soon lag ten to fifteen years behind the West.[166] Others, such as former Commerce Secretary Gina Raimondo, are less convinced that export controls will prove effective at holding back China's chipmaking ecosystem.[167] China is establishing a large industrial advantage over the rest of the world in producing "legacy chips" with larger transistors. These chips can be useful for some AI applications and many important consumer and military products, even though they are less cost-effective at training models than leading-edge graphics processing units (GPUs). Both sides are ramping up their efforts to retain AI talent.[168]

Even if the United States retains the advantage in compute, that might not translate to sustained leadership in AI applications. It is relatively easy to measure how many GPU chips each side uses to train its models, and how well each side's models perform on standardized tests. But the real question is how well each side can leverage AI for strategic deterrence capabilities. There is no one metric for evaluating the *diffusion* of AI across a government or a country's industrial system, and there is an active debate about whether the United States or China has structural advantages in adopting AI faster and more effectively. Some argue that China's aggressive regulation and rigid governance system will inevitably be a bottleneck for adoption.[169] Others point to contrary evidence that China's institutions are embracing AI with lightning speed, arguing that China's specialty is experimenting to find best practices and then rolling out those practices nationwide.[170] It is far too early to crown a winner in this debate. Without good ways to measure AI diffusion, Washington and Beijing will probably remain uncertain about the precise character of the AI capability gap for some time to come.

Mindful of these uncertainties, the U.S. government should maintain its current policy of helping U.S. companies maintain the *largest possible lead* in foundational AI models. This may involve permitting reform to help the data centers that train cutting-edge models with defense applications to meet their growing energy needs.[171] The federal government can increase issuance of special visas to help the world's top AI talent settle in the United States. So can key allies like Canada, the UK, and Japan. Washington could develop a specific program to poach top AI talent from China, if only to deny China's top AI labs access to this talent, just as the U.S. government poached German rocket scientists after World War II.[172] China is already trying to lure the best talent back home.

Washington must also keep tightening China's access to compute. The goal of current export controls is not to cut off China's access to *all* chips made in Taiwan, merely the most advanced chips. Yet, the definition of "advanced" can and should be expanded. The Commerce Department should also expand restrictions on access to U.S. cloud systems. It should work more closely with key allies such as the Netherlands and Japan to coordinate export controls on advanced chipmaking equipment, including maintenance for existing machines in China, and specialized inputs like wafers and chemicals. The U.S. government needs better procedures to monitor the flow of GPUs beyond U.S. borders and harsher penalties to deter smugglers.[173] It can also work with allied countries to make the chip supply chain more resilient, including by incentiviz-ing TSMC to build additional fabs outside Taiwan and devising an industrial strategy for legacy chips. In the future, it may be appropriate to establish joint allied stockpiles for parts of the chip supply chain.

Meanwhile, the United States must start treating the sensitive data and AI capabilities of American companies as critical national security assets.[174] The Department of Defense should strike ongoing contracts with the major pri-vate AI labs to explore how their products can be integrated into the U.S. strategic deterrence enterprise. The U.S. government should require private labs to report security breaches, and it should levy large fines or even pros-ecute executives responsible for negligent security practices. The U.S. intelli-gence community must also cooperate far more actively with universities and private labs to crack down on PRC espionage.[175] U.S. companies that safe-guard Americans' sensitive financial and healthcare data must improve their cybersecurity. AI clearly has a major role to play in improving the nation's cybersecurity.

Insofar as AI competition boils down to access to the most advanced chips, the United States must appreciate and exploit Taiwan's pivotal role in the strategic balance. As of this writing, 99 percent of NVIDIA's most advanced GPUs are produced in Taiwan.[176] Throughout this book, we have seen that both sides care about Taiwan for reasons that are fundamentally unrelated to chips. Still, so long as both sides depend heavily on Taiwan's chips, and as models trained on Taiwanese chips carry the potential to bring game-changing strategic capabilities, Taiwan's ability to participate freely in the global econ-omy is a vital U.S. national security interest. Today, the United States and China both depend on chips from Taiwan. A key question is which side would be set back relatively more if Taiwan's fabs were disabled or destroyed.

Washington must carefully monitor and manipulate the level of mutual dependence on Taiwan, such that China is incentivized to practice restraint. In the worst-case scenario, Xi might assess that the United States is approach-ing AGI or other critical capability thresholds. Believing this, he might gamble on preemptively seizing or destroying Taiwan's chipmaking ecosystem in a last-ditch effort to deny them to the United States.[177] Alternatively, Xi may become persuaded that China has achieved insurmountable advantages in legacy chips, and calculate that destroying the more advanced chip production in Taiwan might present China with the opportunity to leapfrog the United States in AI. It is essential to ensure that Xi does not think this way. The United States must keep restricting China's access to cutting-edge chips and cloud training, but it must do so carefully. Tech export controls need to be seen as part of a broader concept of strategic deterrence, and Washington must remain carefully attuned to how Beijing perceives its situation.

As Cold War history demonstrates, public announcements of transformational capabilities can provoke dangerous responses from adversaries. The Strategic Defense Initiative (SDI), announced by President Reagan in 1983, offers a cautionary example.[178] Reagan announced SDI while the program was still largely aspirational. The Soviet Union was already deeply insecure about U.S. technological superiority, and we have seen how these fears increased the risk of miscalculation during Able Archer. With this history in mind, an argument can be made for not revealing AI-backed deterrence initiatives until they are fully operational. Even then, the United States may want to maintain deliberate ambiguity about where the cutting edge lies and how fast it is advancing. Covert leaks of outdated or experimental systems could reinforce the perception that U.S. capabilities remain nascent, even as cutting-edge systems are deployed—or vice versa. Such a strategy might take its cue from U.S. strategic signaling efforts in the late Cold War. The U.S. military conducted carefully calibrated operations around Russian bases in Kamchatka and Murmansk to let Moscow know that its early warning systems were ineffective.[179] Of course, this strategy is viable only if China believes that the United States is ahead.

In the long run, the most stable equilibrium will probably involve calibrating China's dependence on Taiwan's semiconductor industry while carefully signaling U.S. AI superiority. This could be achieved through carefully designed export controls that let PRC firms buy limited access to Western cloud systems and certain Taiwanese chips that are downgraded a few generations behind the cutting edge.[180]

This strategy will work only if Washington can effectively manipulate China's overall access to compute. Currently, China can partially circumvent hardware restrictions by downloading and fine-tuning open-source models, avoiding the need for advanced GPUs.[181] Reports that the PLA is already using Meta's open-source Llama model highlight this risk.[182] The PLA can also access Western models remotely through the cloud and via data centers in third countries. Addressing this challenge will require carefully tailored regulations. The United States may need to restrict domestic AI labs from releasing models with certain cutting-edge capabilities in the open-source or making them available in the cloud without robust know-your-customer rules.[183] It may encourage private firms to maintain more capable, closed-source versions, maintaining different safety guardrails for commercial and government use.

It may eventually need to control the supply of the most advanced chips very tightly. As of this writing, it is too early to know the optimal policy design. Washington should start to build up enforcement capacity in anticipation of getting more clarity. It should not underestimate China's ingenuity in adapting and finding ways around restrictions.

Ultimately, maintaining a lead in cutting-edge AI applications potentially offers a pathway to reinforcing U.S. strategic deterrence over Taiwan, but getting the policy mix right will require careful, ongoing calibration. One approach is to keep China dependent on Taiwan's chip ecosystem, while denying China access to the most advanced chips. A second approach is to cut China off almost entirely from advanced chips, deliberately send signals to confuse PRC intelligence analysts, and seek to shake Xi's confidence that he understands the U.S. strategic deterrent capability. A third option involves abandoning controls on the export of finished chips to China and going all-in on preventing China from building a competitive domestic chipmaking base.[184] Other possible strategies may also present themselves. We need more robust theory and wargaming to evaluate these strategies and understand their potential trade-offs. Most likely, maintaining strategic stability in the age of AI will involve multiple tools: some kind of controlled interdependence through semiconductor access, calibrated ambiguity through strategic signaling, and narrowly tailored regulation.

Conclusion

Strategic deterrence is not a Cold War relic, but a rapidly evolving competition with fundamental significance for Taiwan and the fate of the wider world. Xi has made it a personal priority to develop a robust and comprehensive "strategic deterrence system." This system goes beyond the traditional nuclear triad to include dual-capable systems that blur the line between conventional and nuclear deterrence, as well as cross-domain strategic threats in space, cyber, and beyond. Meanwhile, Xi is signaling a high tolerance for pain and risk over Taiwan. China's nuclear community is sowing deliberate vagueness and uncertainty about its nuclear doctrine. The United States must confront these challenges and uncertainties head-on.

The good news from history is that nuclear threats rarely succeed in compelling changes to the status quo. Succumbing to compellent threats sets a dangerous precedent for future coercion.[185] We can be reasonably confident that China will not be able to conquer Taiwan simply by threatening to use nuclear weapons.[186]

The difficulty, as we have seen, is that both sides claim to be defending the status quo in the Taiwan Strait. Potential crises could emerge from disputes in which both sides believe they are defending the status quo. For this reason, it is more accurate to say that Xi is building a "strategic coercion system," not a "strategic deterrence system." Bearing this distinction in mind, the United States must make sure that any preemptive steps to stabilize the status quo communicate restraint as well as resolve. This point matters in particular for structured ambiguity, the idea of crisis reinterpretation of the One China Policy discussed in Chapter 4. Any U.S. reinterpretation of the One China Policy would have to be proportionate to Beijing's provocation. Proportionality would be the key to communicating credible resolve and credible restraint.

China may well use nuclear brinkmanship to test U.S. and Taiwanese resolve. Brinkmanship crises are competitions in risk-taking. The side willing to accept greater risk prevails. As Secretary of State John Foster Dulles put it in 1956: "The ability to get to the verge without getting into the war is the necessary art. . . . If you are scared to go to the brink, you are lost."[187] In the Cold War, nuclear brinkmanship often defied theoretical models. The personalities and psychology of leaders, internal political dynamics, and bureaucratic procedures introduced unpredictability and heightened the risk of errors and misperceptions. Studying past cases can provide insight into high-stakes confrontations today.

To prevent war with China in the Taiwan Strait, the United States therefore needs a strong and flexible strategic deterrent, as well as a credible tolerance for risk. Modernizing the U.S. strategic deterrent system—including but not limited to the nuclear force—is the essential first step. Congress must fully fund the recapitalization of U.S. nuclear forces. Given the rapid expansion of China's arsenal, reestablishing the ability to produce new warheads quickly may also be prudent. Washington should seek arms control agreements in good faith, but China and Russia will come to the table only if the United States has leverage. To maintain and display leverage, the United States must bolster its space-based early warning and reconnaissance systems. It must signal that it can hold China's space-based C4ISR systems at risk, as well as other essential strategic deterrence infrastructure inside mainland China. To the extent possible, the United States must exploit Xi's distinctive concept of regime "resilience." It must tailor its strategic threats to hold Xi personally at risk and threaten the CCP's hold on power, not to impose general pain on the people of China. Few Americans want to re-litigate the pandemic, but American policymakers must understand that our resilience to these kinds of threats matters for our credibility. If Xi believes American society and American institutions aren't resilient, he might be more likely to force a crisis.

Strengthening alignment with regional allies is another key part of strategic deterrence. More frequent and visible deployments of strategic assets, such as *Ohio*-class SSBNs and B-21 bombers, are helpful but insufficient. The United States should offer more advanced missile defense systems, such as Aegis Ashore and Terminal High Altitude Area Defense (THAAD), to regional allies like Japan, South Korea, and the Philippines. It should work towards creating a layered, interoperable regional missile shield and common operating picture that can benefit all allies during crises. Accelerating the development and deployment of ground-launched and sea-launched intermediate-range missiles in the region is another appropriate way to offset China's growing missile arsenal. Above all, Washington should prepare to provide stronger nuclear assurances to Japan, South Korea, the Philippines, and Australia. It should actively discuss pathways to future nuclear-sharing agreements if allies express interest.

Emerging technology will also play a pivotal role in strategic deterrence, though this issue requires further study. AI has broad potential uses across the strategic deterrence enterprise, including for strategic deception, remote disabling of adversaries' nuclear forces, and all manner of cyber and intelligence operations. AI competition creates a cloud of uncertainty over the entire strategic balance. The United States needs to remain in the lead in key AI-enabled capabilities. Tightening export controls on advanced semiconductor technologies and limiting China's access to Western cloud infrastructure are two ways to constrain and ultimately control Beijing's progress in strategic AI applications. However, seeking and displaying maximum AI capability advantages might actually become strategically destabilizing. It may be that the most stable strategic balance involves a significant but steady U.S. advantage in AI. Whatever the answer, the U.S. intelligence community and government offices responsible for economic security must start staffing up for a new era of strategic technology competition. U.S. tech policy is too important to be left to the technologists. It must be aligned with the nation's strategic deterrence doctrine.

7

Rethinking Economic Deterrence

by Hugo Bromley and Eyck Freymann

In the Britain of the early 1910s, the fashionable view was that financial and economic globalization had changed the character of warfare forever.[1] The world's great powers had become so financially interconnected that the cost of waging war no longer justified any possible benefit. If war did break out, the thinking went, the economic costs would be so devastating that hostilities would end quickly.[2] Journalist Norman Angell famously made this argument in 1910 in his book *The Great Illusion*.[3] "Germany's success in conquest," he wrote, "would be a demonstration of the complete futility of conquest."[4] By 1914, the year Archduke Franz Ferdinand was assassinated in Sarajevo, the book had sold over two million copies.[5]

When preparing for potential war with Germany, the British Admiralty put its belief in global economic interdependence at the heart of deterrence and war planning.[6] In late 1908, senior members of the Admiralty briefed Prime Minister H. H. Asquith on how they could weaponize Britain's financial system, British-controlled undersea cables, and Britain's world-leading merchant marine to force Germany's rapid collapse in a total economic war.[7] In 1912, the Committee for the Defense of the Empire pre-authorized the Admiralty to execute the plan if war broke out. Of course, these threats failed to deter Germany. Kaiser Wilhelm II gave Austria-Hungary a "blank check" to punish Serbia, which triggered the conflagration on the continent in late July 1914.

Rather than deterring Germany, interconnectivity deterred Britain from implementing its own strategy. When war came in early August 1914, the Admiralty's economic war plan fell apart in a matter of weeks. The Foreign Office and Board of Trade persuaded the government that the price to the British economy and financial system would be unacceptably high. But the problem with the Admiralty's plan was more fundamental. At a time of such peril, Britain could not afford to antagonize the United States, which remained neutral in the conflict. Acquiescing to U.S. pressure, London decided to impose a "distant blockade" on Germany instead. This was a labor-intensive administrative operation designed to screen merchant shipping. Enforcement softened further over time.[8] As a result, Germany found ways to keep trading with the world via neutral countries like the Netherlands. Some British soldiers, seizing German trenches, even discovered that the enemy was eating food from the same cans as they were. In essence, prewar threats of financial "mutually assured destruction" were largely empty.

Britain's choice to conciliate with neutral nations rather than push economic coercion to its limit turned out to be an enlightened decision. American financing sustained the British war effort. Soon it was *Germany* that was targeting neutral American shipping. Washington ultimately found itself pulled into the war on Britain's side, where it played a major role in defeating Germany.[9]

Today, U.S. economic deterrence against China is based on the same illogical and unrealistic assumptions as the Admiralty's plan over a century ago. The fundamental problem is not just the direct cost of decoupling to the U.S. economy, though that cost is high. It is that it would not be in the U.S. interest to wage an economic war against the entire world while also trying to resist PRC aggression in the Taiwan Strait. This fact has become both more urgent and more obvious since "Liberation Day" in April 2025. A week after the Trump administration launched its attempt to "rewire" the global trading system through massive "reciprocal" tariffs, U.S. Treasury markets melted down. The administration abruptly "paused" most of its tariffs on the rest of the world, while leaving average tariffs on China at 145 percent.[10] Treasury Secretary Scott Bessent insisted this had been President Trump's "strategy all along."[11] In reality, it was just the first step in a longer process of coming to terms with the limits of American economic power. On May 12, tariffs on China were reduced to 30 percent.

As of this writing, the second Trump administration's trade war has reached a fragile truce, but a few key points relevant to Taiwan deterrence have already become apparent. First, the U.S. government clearly wants to "decouple" from China, at least in part. No "deal" or decision to reduce tariffs temporarily can change this fact—and investors, business executives, and China's leaders will respond accordingly. That means some amount of U.S.–China bilateral decoupling is now inevitable, even though total decoupling in peacetime still isn't viable. Second, U.S. allies and neutral countries are not interested in waging economic war against China at high cost to themselves—particularly given their own trade disputes with the United States, which are likely to continue. Many are concerned about China's anticompetitive economic policies. But even close allies like Canada and Japan don't want to follow the United States if its conduct is unpredictable and domineering. This fact has undermined the credibility of U.S. political deterrence and has raised doubts that any U.S.-led coalition can endure in a prolonged confrontation. Third, it is now common knowledge that Washington's ability to achieve decoupling from China is limited by market forces. The market responded to Trump's tariffs with an across-the-board sell-off of U.S. financial assets, causing an abrupt weakening in the U.S. dollar exchange rate. China, working with private firms and third countries, immediately began exploring techniques to transship goods and parts into the U.S. market. It also took extreme economic measures of its own, including limits on rare earth exports. The obvious lesson is that the United States can no longer take dollar hegemony for granted if it wages all-out economic warfare against China. Indeed, more alarmingly, the United States has no way to fully decouple from China *in any scenario* without voluntary support from third countries.

In essence, America has been revealed to be economically unprepared for a sudden rupture with China. This revelation, in turn, makes it more likely that deterrence will fail in the Taiwan Strait. It did not have to go this way. Years before this recent conflagration, in December 2023, the bipartisan House Select Committee on the Chinese Communist Party published an alarming report concluding that "the United States lacks a contingency plan for the economic and financial impacts of conflict with China."[12] We echoed this warning in a July 2024 report entitled "On Day One: An Economic Contingency Plan for a Taiwan Crisis," which is the inspiration for this chapter and the next. And yet the U.S. government still has not communicated any credible economic contingency plan.

The damage to U.S. credibility is particularly problematic in the gray-zone scenarios we explored in earlier chapters. Suppose China moves against Taiwan using a quarantine or other gray-zone action that does not directly disrupt global trade. The burden of economic escalation would fall onto the United States. How can the United States effectively communicate its resolve during such a brinkmanship crisis if it visibly lacks a coherent economic contingency plan?[13] Why would U.S. allies follow the United States to the brink, if they believe that falling over the brink would mean economic calamity for themselves? Washington cannot strong-arm other countries into going against their national interests to prosecute an economic punishment campaign against China.

This chapter argues that America must fundamentally rethink its approach. Economic deterrence has much more in common with political deterrence than with strategic deterrence. If China thinks that U.S. economic threats would be politically unsustainable at home—or would antagonize other countries whose support America would need—then they are not credible. Extreme economic punishment works like a nuclear weapon only if it destroys the opponent *on impact*. If the punishment has to be *sustained over time*, the question becomes political. Which side can tolerate more pain for longer? Which side gets more indirect political benefits from the contest of pain?

The first part of the chapter discusses existing theories on economic deterrence. Most of these theories were developed after the end of the Cold War, in a now-distant era of great power *cooperation*, not competition. The section argues that threats of extreme economic punishment are obvious and implicit, but they face significant credibility challenges and practical limitations in todays' world. There are simply too many large neutral countries for such extreme coercion to work. As long as the United States and China remain economically intertwined with neutral states, trade would continue indirectly—even during a war.[14] If the United States attempted to use blocking sanctions on China, the world would simply move away from the dollar toward a multi-currency system, in which the Euro and RMB would likely play more prominent roles.[15] Thus, sanctions, blockades, and other tools that interfere with third countries' ability with China are likely to backfire.

The second half of the chapter examines China's perspective, drawing on previously untranslated Chinese-language speeches and writings. Beijing is growing more confident in its ability to survive sanctions and absorb economic shocks, even though it remains vulnerable to any sustainable U.S. plan to cut it off from key markets. Yet if America tries to coerce third countries against their will, it risks weakening its coalition and undermining political deterrence. The United States must therefore build an *affirmative contingency plan* that threatens China's economic system over the long term in conjunction with advancing its own and its allies' interests—not sacrificing those interests in the uncertain hope of harming China more. Chapter 8 will explore the shape of such a plan.

"Strategic" Economic Threats

Economic "decoupling" from China has been on the table for several years now, yet no one quite knows what it means.[16] "So when you mention the word decouple, it's an interesting word," President Donald Trump said in September 2020. "We will make America into the manufacturing superpower of the world and will end our reliance on China once and for all. Whether it's decoupling, or putting in massive tariffs like I've been doing already, we will end our reliance on China, because we can't rely on China."[17]

When it comes to critical products like semiconductors, electric vehicles, and drones, there is broad bipartisan agreement that America should break its dependence on China.[18] But even this has proven hard to achieve. Industry has resisted, and neither the U.S. government nor its allies has a coherent definition of criticality. When Biden took office in 2021, his team distanced itself from the word "decoupling," which antagonized U.S. allies.[19] As National Security Advisor Jake Sullivan put it in April 2023, "we are for de-risking and diversifying, not decoupling."[20] The second Trump administration abandoned the term "de-risking" in favor of the undefined "strategic decoupling."[21] Does this mean a full-scale economic divorce, a more limited breaking of U.S. dependence on production that is "critical" for national security? The second Trump administration has not come closer to answering this question. Before "Liberation Day," legislation and executive orders to accelerate decoupling even in highly strategic sectors like drone parts and critical minerals were repeatedly delayed and watered down.[22] As of this writing, the Trump administration claims to be trying to rebalance U.S.–China trade, not to take trade permanently to zero.

In principle, China is extremely vulnerable to decoupling (see Figures 7.1 through 7.5 below).[23] Over 200 million PRC citizens—nearly one-third of the workforce—are employed in manufacturing.[24] Roughly half of China's manufactures are exported. Moreover, the CCP has organized China's economy and society so that the country runs a massive, persistent trade surplus.[25] Thanks to policies known as financial repression, China consistently consumes much less than it produces, exporting the balance. By definition, when the rest of the world buys China's net exports, that comes at the cost of manufacturing jobs in the rest of the world.

China's economy is likely to grow even more dependent on exports going forward. Persistent deflation and an ageing population all mean that China's

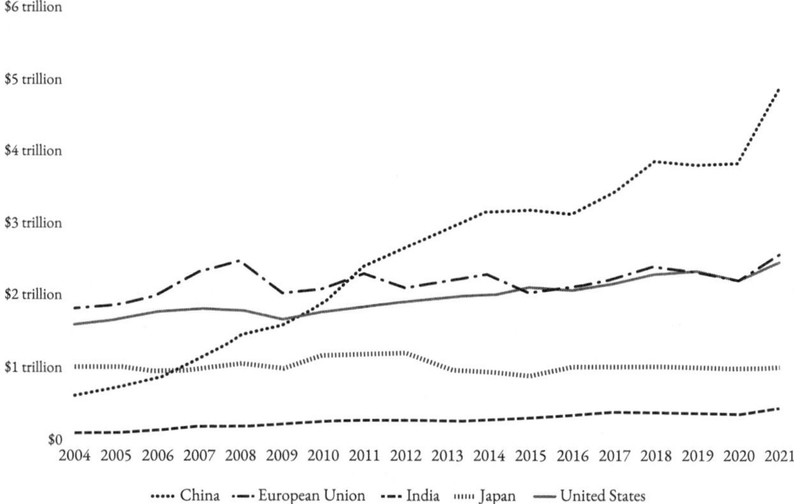

Figure 7.1 Manufacturing value-added, in trillion USD

domestic demand will remain subdued.[26] Meanwhile, China's manufacturers rely on American, European, and Japanese machinery in key sectors, including chemicals, autos, and aerospace.[27] China also remains heavily dependent on imported raw materials, especially fossil fuels. This is why China is so visibly alarmed by talk of "deglobalization."[28] But threats of decoupling will deter China only if the United States has a credible plan to achieve it.

It is not easy to calibrate threats of economic punishment. If China thinks it could move against Taiwan and carry on economically just as before, then threats of *symbolic punishment* will do nothing at all for deterrence. If the United States tries to force *hard decoupling*, which we define as a near-total stoppage of all countries' trade with China, it could theoretically impose enormous pain on China. But the costs of hard decoupling for the United States, U.S. allies, and neutral countries would be huge, with massive political and geopolitical consequences. When the British Admiralty proposed such action, it failed thanks to the opposition of the United States and a small number of north European neutrals. The neutral community today is vastly larger and more diverse. Of course, Washington can keep Beijing guessing. By never closing the door entirely on hard decoupling, it might be able to deter China through uncertainty alone.[29] The problem is that no one knows Xi Jinping's threshold for economic pain, and no one knows how he assesses the United States and its allies' threshold for economic pain.

Policymakers and scholars have developed some alternative approaches that hope to thread the needle.[30] Some look to history.[31] Others focus on economic analysis and modeling.[32] No matter the method, the key idea in this debate is *weaponized interdependence*.[33] Powerful states can leverage chokepoints in interconnected systems—such as the SWIFT system for cross-border payment messaging, or semiconductors produced with U.S. technology—to impose asymmetric costs on an adversary.[34] Because the United States occupies a uniquely central position in the global financial and economic system, it theoretically has more chokepoints to choose from than any potential adversary.[35] Proponents of weaponized interdependence theory have proposed three options: financial sanctions, the weaponization of Taiwan's semiconductor industry, and a "distant blockade" against trade passing through the Malacca Strait. We will explore these proposals in detail below.

The clear lesson from this debate is that there is no such thing as a free lunch. Trying to weaponize interdependence with Beijing would incentivize other countries to move out of financial and technological networks that the United States controls and onto networks China has built specifically to take advantage of such a moment. Among other possibilities, this could put the position of the U.S. dollar in jeopardy.[36] And this sets aside China's resilience and potential counterreactions. As Emily Kilcrease has observed, when it comes to U.S.–China sanctions scenarios, "there are no winners in this game."[37]

Hard Decoupling through Sanctions and Blockades

According to most of the works published before the second Trump administration, sanctions are the default U.S. economic response to a Taiwan crisis. The Council on Foreign Relations' Independent Task Force report on "U.S.-Taiwan Relations in a New Era," endorsed in whole or part by seventeen luminaries, including Michael G. Mullen, former chairman of the Joint Chiefs of Staff, and Ivan Kanapathy, the current National Security Council senior director for Asia, argues that the U.S. public and allied nations should immediately begin "intense consultations" with allies and partners "on the scope of a sanctions package that would be introduced immediately after a blockade or attack, while urgently working to lessen economic dependence on China."[38] Others argue that even if China does not see economic sanctions as a credible deterrent, Washington will likely impose them in any conflict scenario.[39]

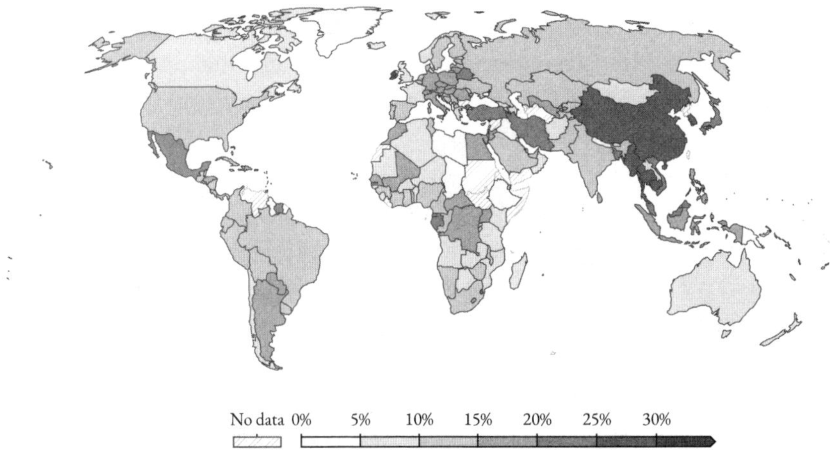

Figure 7.2 Manufacturing as share of GDP, 2021
Source: "Share of Manufacturing in Gross Domestic Product (GDP), 2021," Our World in Data, n.d., https://ourworldindata.org/grapher/manufacturing-value-added-to-gdp.

The president has the authority to impose a range of sanctions on China without congressional approval. The Council on Foreign Relations report recommends using the 2022 Russia sanctions as a baseline. This would probably involve blocking sanctions on China's central bank, the People's Bank of China (PBoC), as well as leading PRC financial institutions and a range of important PRC industrial firms.[40] Many members of Congress on both sides of the aisle believe that this approach is the right one. The bipartisan Sanctions Targeting Aggressors of Neighboring Democracies with Taiwan Act of 2022 would automatically trigger broad sanctions following a congressional resolution finding that China had attacked Taiwan.[41] In 2023, the bipartisan House Select Committee on the CCP endorsed the idea of automatically triggering sanctions.[42] The Office of Foreign Assets Control (OFAC), the agency in the Treasury responsible for enforcing sanctions, could also attempt to block China's access to the dollar system by claiming jurisdiction over Beijing's dollar-denominated assets held abroad.[43]

Some scholars and practitioners also assume that the United States could intensify sanctions pressure with a naval blockade in the Strait of Malacca.[44] This could work like a quarantine, with U.S. Navy ships screening oil tankers bound for China as they passed through the Malacca Straits, between the Indian Ocean and the South China Sea.[45] It could also seek to inspect tankers transiting through other chokepoints, such as out of the Persian Gulf. (In theory, the United States could fire indiscriminately at commercial ships bound for China, or even mine China's harbors, but the latter would be a war crime of an unprecedented scale.[46])

A Malacca blockade could in theory interdict either PRC oil imports specifically or PRC merchant shipping in general. China imports approximately two-thirds of its oil by sea, and its economy is highly dependent on maritime trade. As political scientists Eric Heginbotham and Richard Samuels put it in 2018, "Beijing has only limited capacity to mitigate [this] vulnerability."[47] The attraction of the Malacca blockade proposal is that it would be a way to harm China without striking targets inside China and accepting the resultant risks of nuclear escalation.[48] A counter-blockade of China also sounds—superficially—like a proportionate response to a quarantine or blockade of Taiwan.

Operationally, the U.S. Navy probably *could* execute a Malacca blockade—so long as other Southeast Asian countries and the UK and Australia cooperated, which is far from guaranteed.[49] In parallel, it would also have to screen transit through the Lombok and Sunda Straits and other channels into the First Island Chain. Even naval analysts Gabriel Collins and Andrew Erickson, who argue that a Malacca blockade would take too long to work and would have at best "muddled" strategic benefits, believe that the U.S. Navy is "undoubtedly capable" of executing such an operation.[50] One can also imagine more targeted variations of a Malacca blockade that could create costs for China without shutting down all trade.

China has long seen Malacca as a vulnerability. Communist Party General Secretary Hu Jintao called attention to the "Malacca dilemma (马六甲困境)" at a Central Economic Work Conference in 2003.[51] One prominent PRC scholar even called Malacca the "Achilles heel" of China's energy policy.[52] Some PRC scholars have suggested that the One Belt One Road initiative is an effort to mitigate the Malacca dilemma by building alternative supply lines through Central Asia and over the Himalayas to Indian Ocean ports.[53] Fear of a Malacca blockade probably also explains China's decision to build a vast strategic petroleum reserve, which holds around 1 billion barrels at any given time and has a total capacity of around 1.8 billion barrels.[54] Aaron Friedberg has argued that maintaining the capability to enforce a Malacca blockade

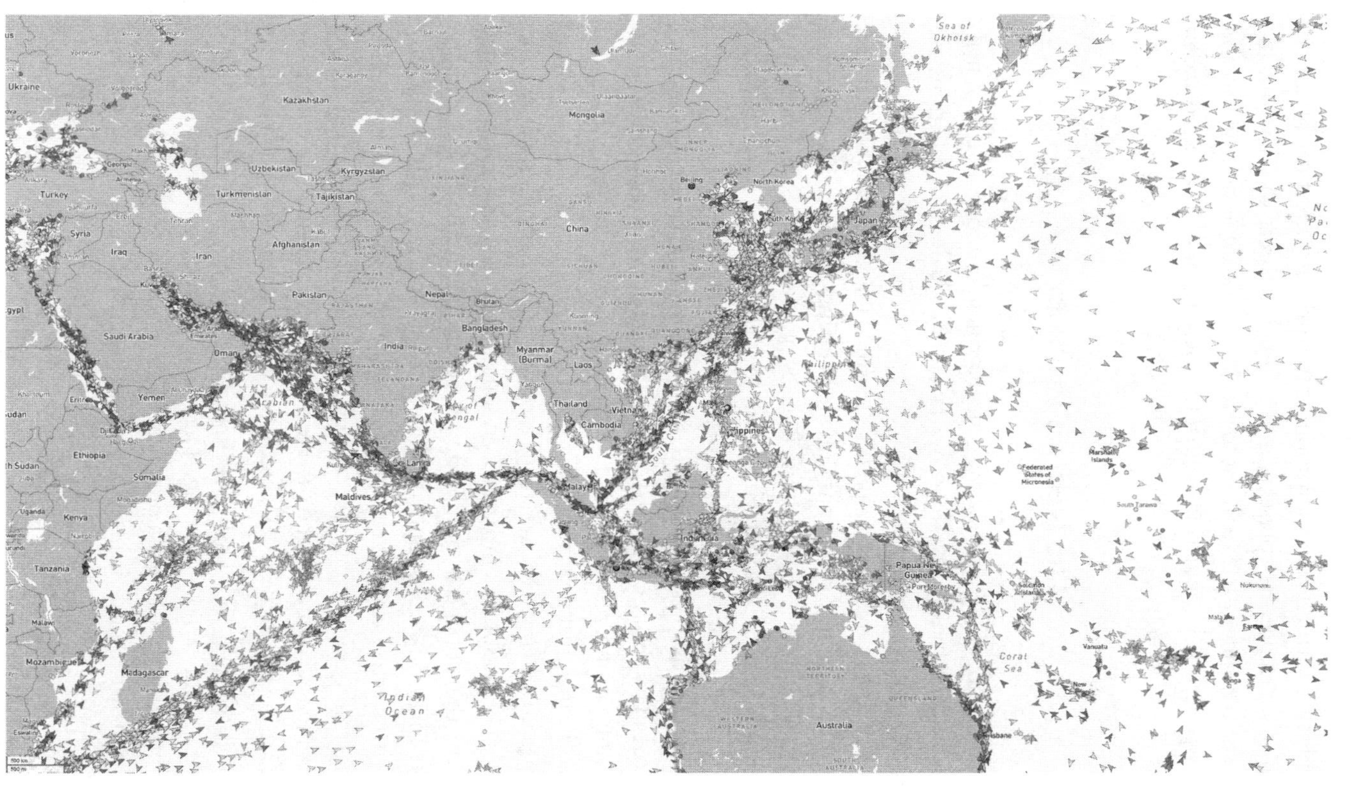

Figure 7.3 Cargo vessels tankers, and other types of ships passing through the Strait of Malacca, January 24, 2024
Source: Courtesy of Marine Traffic.

is good policy even if the threat is only implicit.[55] Since even a successful Malacca blockade would take many months to work, the threat itself is a form of strategic deterrence. It represents not so much a threat to starve out the PLA in a conventional war, as a threat to break China's domestic economy and turn an impoverished population against the CCP during a prolonged war of attrition.

The Neutral Problem

The discussion above highlights some general principles about the role of neutral states in great power economic warfare.[56] Blockades and sanctions are different from embargoes and other forms of trade policy. They don't just limit direct trade between the coercing power's national market and its target. They reach beyond the direct sovereignty of the coercing power to interfere with neutral countries' trade. They do this either by physically blocking trade or by weaponizing infrastructure that is physically located in the sanctioning power's national market. In all cases, neutral countries are self-interested and respond accordingly. Very simply: when great powers wage economic war, third parties do not face binary choices.[57] Indeed, the very concept of neutrality as it exists in modern international relations was developed to allow countries to trade with both sides during great power wars.[58]

Neutral states themselves have strong incentives to undermine sanctions and blockades. The reason lies in basic economic theory. If you arbitrarily draw a line across the global economy, supply exceeds demand on one side of the line, and demand exceeds supply on the other. Price differentials emerge as a result. Neutral actors can make money by buying goods for cheap on one side of the line, trafficking them across, and selling them for inflated prices on the other side. Neutral countries and private firms—which behave like neutrals— therefore arbitrage relentlessly. They comply with the sanctions and blockades only if the potential costs of getting caught and punished exceed the potential profits they could earn by cheating. The War on Drugs failed because when there are buyers willing to pay a premium to get access to a good (in economic parlance: when the price is highly "price inelastic"), disrupting supply just means that prices rise. The prospect of higher profits compensates suppliers for incurring personal risk to meet the demand.[59] It's the same mechanism for sanctions evasion.

A country attempting economic coercion therefore faces an ongoing enforcement headache. Making neutrals comply is costly. Neutrals can resist unilaterally, including limiting their own trade with the sanctioning power. (This is how Thomas Jefferson responded in 1807 when Britain and France attempted to use naval warfare to interrupt American shipping.) They can form clubs with other neutrals. They can even join the opposition, or at least threaten to do so. Turning a blind eye to even a single neutral country's cheating comes with the risk that vast quantities of illicit trade could be rerouted through that country. The strategic, political, and economic costs of getting all the neutrals to comply at the same time need to be tallied as part of the total cost of economic coercion. Ultimately, the only way to make economic coercion successful is to get the neutral community as a whole to cooperate in a sustained way.

The bigger the market being sanctioned, and the bigger the neutral community, the more costly it is to enforce sanctions and blockades.[60] It is no accident that sanctions and blockades were most effective during the first half of the twentieth century, when a small number of empires dominated most of the global economy, and during the post–Cold War "unipolar moment" of the 1990s and early 2000s, when U.S. power was supreme and China and Russia supported sanctions on countries like Iraq and North Korea.[61] Sanctions are a tool of globalism. They work best when the great powers work together and the neutral community is small and weak. But today, the neutral community is larger, more diverse, and collectively more powerful than ever. Across South and Southeast Asia, Africa, the Middle East, and Latin America, most countries would almost certainly prefer to continue trading with both sides in a U.S.–China conflict. Nor can the United States count on support from most of the other major economies if it declares economic war on China. Russia would likely back China. India would likely stay neutral, as it has done in the Russia–Ukraine War. Even the European Union would probably hedge, though some member states would probably want to take a stronger line.

With such profound economic interests at stake, moralizing and persuasion would be unlikely to move the neutrals to compliance. Among U.S. planners, there is sometimes a temptation to assume that countries would go along with hard decoupling in a crisis simply because the economic situation would already be extremely bad.[62] But this assumption makes no sense. Plunged into a global economic crisis, most countries would try to *preserve* what they could, not to aggravate the crisis. Even if the United States persuaded other countries to make the sanctions automatic, a general economic crisis would provide both a reason and an excuse for countries to renege on past commitments.

Could the United States *force* the allies and neutrals alike to go along? As Jude Blanchette and Gerard DiPippo argue, "if U.S. forces were engaged" in a war over Taiwan, "the sanctions [on China] would be severe" and "Washington would probably coordinate with—or even compel—major allies to join such sanctions."[63] They contend that major European allies would likely "support Washington's efforts to punish China economically" because European countries' "economic and financial ties to the United States are far deeper than those with China." They also note that if allies resist, Washington might "present European leaders with a binary choice they might otherwise hope to avoid." Presumably, this would mean threatening secondary sanctions against European companies and banks that facilitate trade with China.

These threats are not remotely credible. Imposing secondary sanctions on Europe would deepen the economic crisis in the United States and put dollar hegemony at risk. The EU and China combined account for close to 40 percent of global GDP. If they wanted to shift their trade into euro or RMB settlement networks beyond Washington's control, they could do so quickly. The market reaction to Liberation Day has already revealed how quickly investors may flee the U.S. financial system if they lose confidence that the U.S. government is reliable. Furthermore, if Donald Trump was unwilling to impose 25 percent tariffs on trade with the European Union at his moment of maximum political strength, why would Brussels believe any American president capable of bringing all transatlantic trade to a halt during a crisis with China?

If European cooperation is uncertain, support from non-Western countries that refused to support sanctions on Russia would be even less forthcoming. Countries like India, Brazil, the Gulf States, and the export economies of Southeast Asia would prefer to live in an integrated global economy than a permanently bifurcated one. These countries have also just seen clear evidence that Washington cannot sever its largest trading relationships all at once without an unacceptable political cost. They may therefore expect that America will eventually acquiesce to a situation where trade with China resumed. Commodity producers in Africa, Oceania, Central and Southeast Asia, Latin America, and the Middle East could experience economic collapse if China were struck out of the global economic system and no longer able to buy their exports. These countries might not resist U.S. sanctions overtly, but they could use foot-dragging, lackluster enforcement, and other passive techniques to continue with business as usual.

Countries wishing to break from the U.S. coalition would also have an easy political excuse. A total of 181 countries already recognize Beijing as the sole legal government of China. And 51 of them accept Beijing's "One China Principle." (The other 130, including the United States, hold some sort of ambiguous position on Taiwan's status.[64]) Only twelve countries recognize Taiwan as a sovereign state, and Taiwan is not a UN member. In terms of international politics, a PRC move against Taiwan would therefore be quite unlike Russia's full-scale invasion of Ukraine, which was widely acknowledged to be a conflict between two sovereign states. China could argue that any military action against Taiwan was an internal matter. Other states might accept this argument even if they didn't fully agree with it, if they hoped that giving Beijing a quick victory would reduce the chances of devastating U.S.-led economic warfare. Thus, it's unclear whether a majority of the UN General Assembly would condemn or even oppose an invasion of Taiwan, let alone a blockade or quarantine.[65] As more countries backed China or joined the neutral bloc, the costs for others to follow suit would diminish.

In other words, if the United States went into a Taiwan crisis threatening secondary sanctions, it would start with a divided coalition that would almost certainly fracture further over time. In the process, U.S. actions would shatter the international trading system, devastate the U.S. economy, and put dollar hegemony in jeopardy. China would be left with more influence in global affairs than it enjoys today. In short, deterrent threats that involve economic war against neutrals undermine the credibility of America's political deterrence.

The neutral problem also casts a long shadow over deterrence strategies based on export controls, especially those involving Taiwan's semiconductor industry. One proposal that has gained traction in Washington is that Taiwan could respond to a quarantine or limited blockade by cutting off China's access to TSMC chips.[66] In principle, Washington could use the Foreign Direct Product Rule (FDPR), which asserts U.S. jurisdiction over foreign-made goods that incorporate U.S. technology. (Of course, this threat will retain its deterrent power only if China remains dependent on TSMC chips.) Another proposal is that the United States and its allies should pursue a broader export control regime to cut off vital chokepoints for China's high-tech industrial base.[67]

In practice, export controls present two serious problems. The first is enforcement. Once goods leave the jurisdiction of a cooperating country, they are difficult to track. Even under existing rules, sensitive items—especially small and valuable ones like semiconductors—are routinely routed through third countries like Malaysia, where they are repackaged or re-exported to China.[68] Short of a naval blockade, enforcement depends on documentation audits and threats of secondary financial sanctions. These mechanisms are already proving insufficient, and they are unlikely to withstand the pressure of a crisis. The second problem is that export controls require deep and sustained buy-in from key allies and firms whose economic futures are tied to China's market. While most TSMC chips are made with U.S. intellectual property, the United States is far less central to the global production of precision tools and machinery. In 2023, China accounted for 32 percent of global metal-working tool production and 33 percent of consumption. The next largest producers were Europe at 32.7 percent and East Asia—mostly Japan—at 25.9 percent. North America's share was only 8 percent.[69] The foreign firms that China relies on most in this sector are based in Europe and Japan. If these companies were suddenly unable to sell to China, their balance sheets would be badly damaged and their home economies could face recession. (It is also not clear how fast China could adapt, building inferior substitutes and breaking its remaining reliance on Western supply chains.) As with sanctions, without a sustainable economic contingency plan that is attractive to these firms, the United States would be faced with a choice between symbolic action and an attempt to force the collapse of the global economy, bringing it into direct conflict with neutrals.

Both problems are acute in the case of TSMC, a private firm with complex incentives. China is TSMC's largest single market. Despite U.S. export controls, TSMC has continued to produce for dubious PRC customers. As of this writing, the company faces a risk of penalties of $1 billion or more for producing millions of chips that ended up inside advanced Huawei AI processors.[70] Since both Washington and Beijing could unilaterally shut down TSMC's manufacturing operations in Taiwan, the company has neither a commercial nor a strategic reason to be seen picking sides.

In sum, export controls offer a more targeted alternative to hard decoupling, but they are no silver bullet. Without reliable enforcement, intensive allied coordination, and incentive structures to win compliance from neutral countries like Malaysia and firms like TSMC that seek to avoid picking sides, export controls are unlikely to impose sustained costs on China. If they do, they will probably also impose sustained costs on the U.S.-led alliance. Deterrence cannot rely on chokepoints and licensing regimes alone. It must be embedded in an affirmative strategy that promotes allied economic resilience while steadily constraining China's room to maneuver.

China's Role in the Global Economy

In case the theory is not persuasive by itself, it is worth considering some data points that illustrate why a unilateral American move to expel China from the global economy overnight would be the boldest act of economic coercion in world history. No victorious great power has ever attempted to sanction half of global demand for key commodities and more than half of global supply of numerous essential goods. On the eve of the 2022 Ukraine invasion, Russia represented just 13 percent of global oil production and 1.3 percent of total global imports; yet Washington still held back from imposing across-the-board sanctions, for fear of disrupting markets. To take just two examples, China accounts for 55 percent of global copper demand and 79 percent of the world's lithium-ion battery production.[71] Its manufacturing base is sophisticated and staggeringly diverse. It took decades and tens of trillions of dollars of public and private investment to build. Decoupling too quickly would therefore disrupt supply chains that depend on China, imposing enormous economic pain on the entire world—including the United States. In the meantime, China is a much larger and more sophisticated economic adversary than Russia. It would have more tools to fight back.

The U.S. economy's dependence on China runs deep, and the Trump administration's trade war has made this fact common knowledge. China dominates the production of critical minerals, representing 60 percent of global production and 85 percent of processing capacity as of this writing.[72] Three of the four factories in the world that produce the active pharmaceutical ingredient for benzathine penicillin G are in China. Global value chains for pharmaceuticals—especially generic drugs—and medical goods and devices are also highly dependent on chemicals, materials, and electronic components produced in China.[73] China has already begun to lay the legal groundwork for its own sweeping export controls. In a crisis, China would probably have difficulty enforcing these controls, but they could still lead to shortages and inflation and threaten lives and livelihoods worldwide. Whatever the situation in the Taiwan Strait, the United States needs to act *now* to address these shocking vulnerabilities.

The fallout of Trump's "Liberation Day" tariffs has also shown that American small businesses are highly vulnerable to even partial decoupling. As of 2023, small and medium-sized enterprises accounted for 41.2 percent of U.S. imports from China, but just 29.8 percent of imports from Canada and

23.6 percent of imports from Mexico.[74] Large corporations have diversified access to multiple markets and consultants who can help them fine-tune their supply chains. But most small businesses rely on a small number of suppliers, many of whom source their goods from China. Many small businesses experienced a rude awakening when Trump suddenly imposed high tariffs on China, learning just how dependent they are on products and parts from China—and how hard they are to replace. Media coverage of supply risks tends to focus on "critical" products. But as the Trump trade war has shown, shortages of more mundane goods are also deeply painful.

Shutting China out of the global market would also devastate the U.S. agricultural industry. China imported $35.5 billion of U.S. agricultural products in 2022, or 18.4 percent of U.S. agricultural exports. After Trump imposed tariffs in 2025, these figures plummeted. Within months of China's decision to withhold purchases of U.S. soybeans, many soybean farmers faced financial ruin. This was one reason Trump sought a trade truce. More importantly, PRC demand supports *prices* for these agricultural products. China imports 60 percent of the world's soybeans, for example. Soybean prices rise and fall on the back of PRC demand. If China were suddenly unable or unwilling to import soybeans from anywhere, then the 300,000 American farms that grow soybeans would face a devastating blow—even if China's purchases of U.S. soybeans had already fallen to zero. Over 89 million acres of farmland in the United States—an area the size of Montana—are currently dedicated to growing soybeans. If these acres were used for other crops instead, those prices would fall, too.[75] Unlike the first Trump administration's tariffs, which generated revenue to partially compensate soybean farmers for their lost sales, a hard decoupling from China would be a pure deadweight loss. Farmers would have no time to adapt. Other U.S. export industries, such as aerospace, would face a similar fate.

Rapid decoupling from China would therefore cause prices of some products to collapse, but in general it would trigger shortages and inflation. Numerous efforts have been made in recent years to calculate the precise impact of any Taiwan crisis. All rest on debatable assumptions. Economic models are not designed to understand exogenous shocks of this nature and scale. However, they offer useful ballpark estimates. Recent experience from the COVID-19 pandemic also provides another point of reference. At the peak of the pandemic supply-chain crisis in October 2021, the average time for PRC goods to travel from factory to warehouse rose from the pre-COVID average of 40–50 days to 76.[76] That month, U.S. inflation jumped to 6.2 percent. Supply chains ultimately healed because factories in China came back online. A hard decoupling would have a much greater effect on prices and would impact a much broader array of goods.

America's closest allies are vastly more vulnerable to rapid decoupling. According to one study, if Japan's imports from China were reduced by 80 percent for two months, Japan's total production would decline by 15 percent, for a total annualized loss of nearly 10 percent of GDP.[77] Roughly a quarter of Japanese imports of intermediate products come from China.[78] In a different paper, calculating using a more elaborate methodology, the same authors found that a hard decoupling from China could reduce Japan's total value added manufacturing output by up to 39.5 percent.[79]

Australia is similarly vulnerable. China buys nearly one-third of Australia's exports, and trade is directly responsible for 1 in 5 Australian jobs.[80] In Western Australia, exports are 56 percent of GDP, and the largest export segment is iron ore destined for China. Australia's Department of Foreign Affairs and Trade and Treasury Department have conducted three classified studies to explore the potential for hard decoupling from China. All three studies found that it would be "impossible," according to two sources with knowledge of the matter. "No other markets could replace China as a market for Australian commodity exports," one of the sources told the *South China Morning Post*.[81] The Treasury secretary ordered that the reports not be publicly released. The reality is probably not quite so dire. If Australia lost the China market, it would eventually find other customers for its exports. Still, the transition would be extremely painful.

All European countries would be badly affected, and Germany, which counts China as its largest trading partner, would be among the hardest hit. According to one study, hard decoupling would cause a 5% contraction in German GDP in the first year, roughly the same as the COVID shock of 2020. Unlike the COVID crisis, however, this would be a *permanent* loss to prosperity if China remained a pariah.[82] The effects on German workers and industry would be catastrophic. Volkswagen, for example, sells 40% of its cars in China.[83] As German Finance Minister Christian Lindner noted in January 2023, with some understatement, "decoupling our economy from the Chinese market would not be in the interest of jobs in Germany."[84] Perhaps more importantly, a U.S. attempt to forcibly cut off China-Germany trade could lead to a resurgence of extreme anti-U.S. and pro-Russian parties in Germany, on both the far left and far right.

For major oil exporters like Saudi Arabia, the story is much the same. China currently imports 11.3 million barrels of crude oil per day.[85] If the United States somehow blocked China from importing oil for an extended period, prices could collapse.[86] Saudi Arabia requires oil prices above $86 a barrel to balance its budget.[87] The Kingdom is also exposed, like all other countries, to a disruption in imports of goods from China. Saudi consumers, like those around the world, are accustomed to a high standard of living and rely on "Made in China" products in their daily lives. They would surely not appreciate shortages and rationing—and Saudi ruler Mohammed bin Salman would prefer to avoid a discontented population. This is one reason why Saudi Arabia signed a "comprehensive strategic partnership" with China in 2022.[88] The story is similar for most of the Persian Gulf's other major oil exporters.

If the hard decoupling effort involved financial sanctions, Malacca blockade, a kinetic war, or a combination thereof, the economic crisis for third countries could be greater still. Physical disruption of trade flows out of Taiwan alone could cause over $2 trillion in lost economic activity globally.[89] War or blockade-style operations short of war could also disrupt supply chains by making it expensive or impossible for shippers to insure their cargoes. According to a Bloomberg analysis, in such a scenario, U.S. GDP would decline 6.7 percent in the first year, and nearly every U.S. ally would suffer a greater shock: Canada (6.9 percent), Australia (7.4 percent), India (8 percent), the EU (9.6 percent), Japan (13.5 percent), China (16.7 percent), Southeast Asia (20.1 percent), and South Korea (23.3 percent).[90] These are eye-popping figures. If this crisis came to pass, it could be the worst global economic crisis since the Great Depression.

In conclusion, there may be scenarios where the U.S. president is willing to accept this kind of extreme economic devastation in order to punish China—but in general these threats strain credibility.[91] Beijing is aware of this. When the House China Select Committee war-gamed a Taiwan invasion scenario in April 2023, the "blue" team playing the United States chose to use only "moderate" sanctions against PRC state banks.[92] Meanwhile, Beijing has every reason to believe that even close U.S. allies would resist the imposition of sanctions, and third countries would actively seek to circumnavigate sanctions to continue to trade—and indeed, profit from Beijing's continued demand for raw materials and need to export its manufactured goods. If China's economy and financial system were so fragile that they would collapse instantaneously under sanctions, there might be an argument for accepting acute short-term economic pain and long-term political risk, to end a conflict quickly. Unfortunately, as we will see next, this is very far from a sure bet.

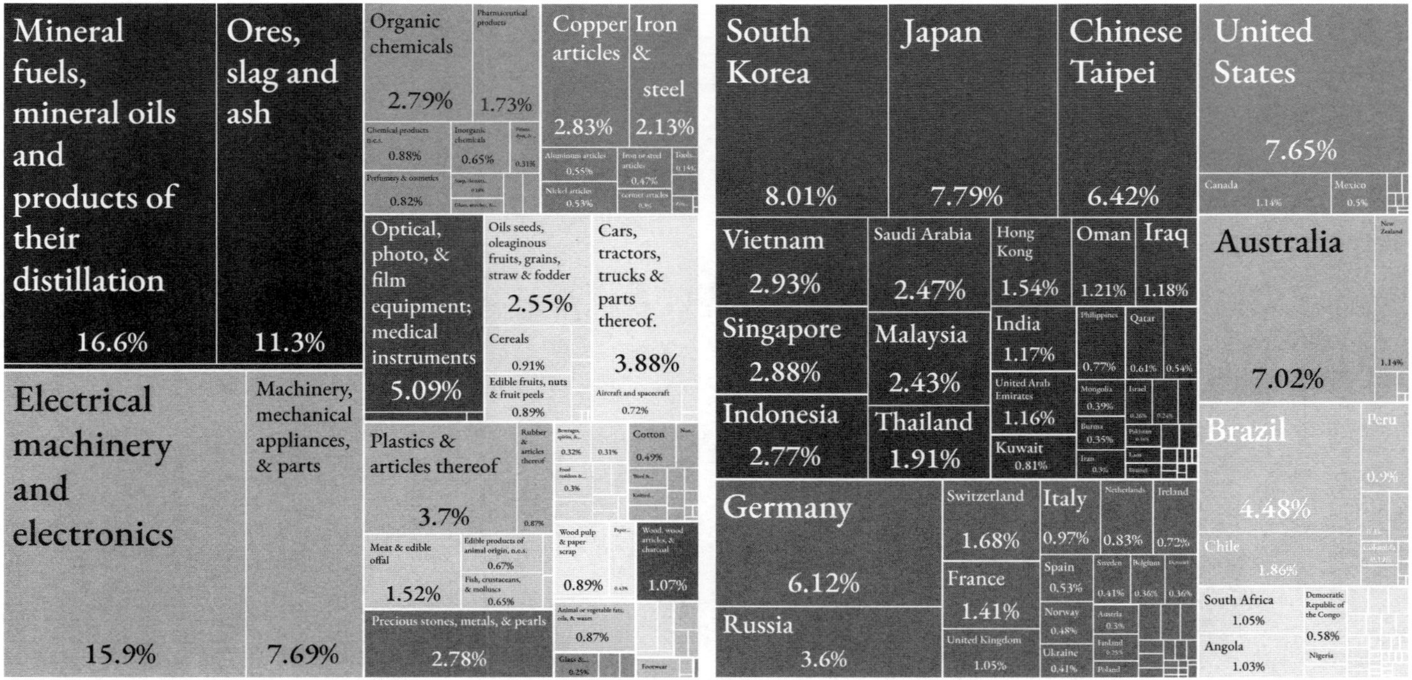

Figure 7.4 Composition of China's imports by category and country of origin, 2021

Source: "OEC Profiles: China," *Observatory of Economic Complexity*, accessed January 19, 2024, https://oec.world/en/profile/country/chn?depthSelector1=HS2Depth&yearlyTradeFlowSelector=flow1.

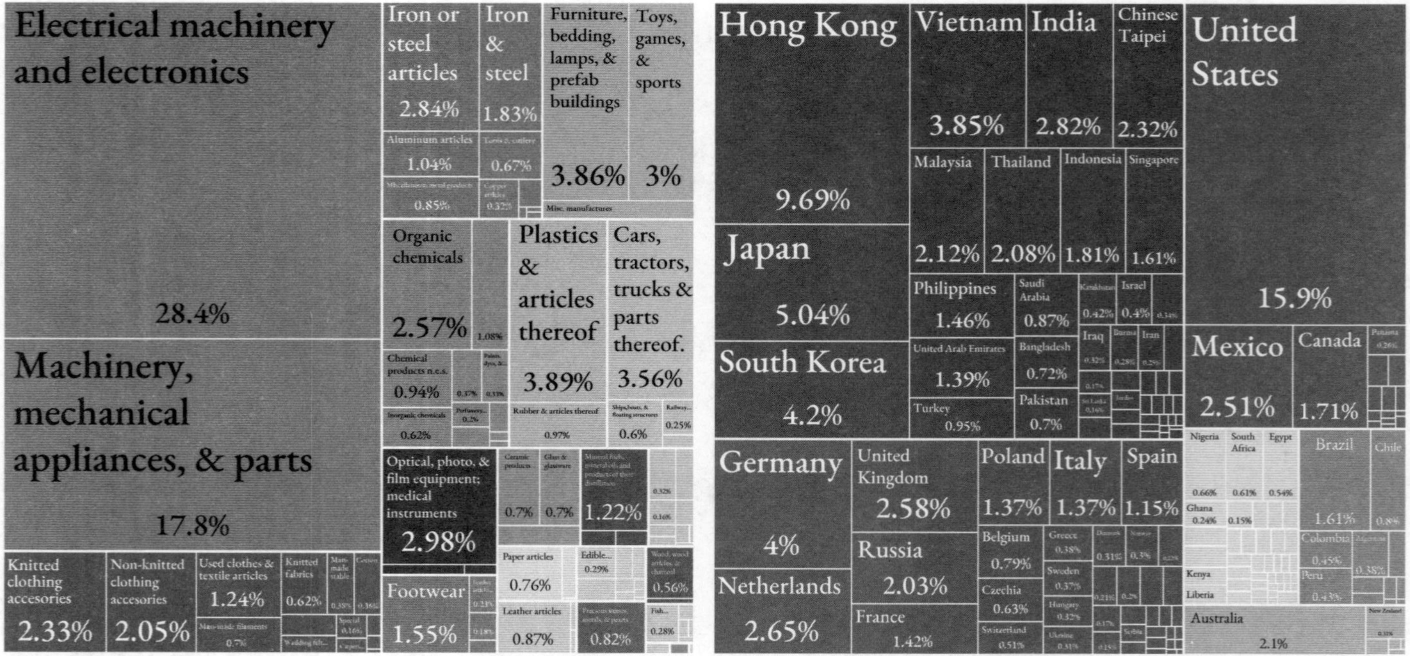

Figure 7.5 Composition of China's exports by category and country of origin, 2021

Source: "OEC Profiles: China," *Observatory of Economic Complexity.*

PRC Resilience

After more than a decade of assiduous effort, China has become far more resilient to rapid decoupling than many U.S. analysts recognize. Financial sanctions or physical blockades would not meaningfully impair the PLA's warfighting capacity for many months, if not years. Moreover, untranslated PRC sources show that Beijing likely believes that it would be resilient even if Washington acted on these threats, so the threats themselves may not deter aggression.[93]

Overall, PRC scholars appear to have thought more carefully about the hard decoupling scenario than their American counterparts.[94] Their academic and policy literature on financial warfare exhaustively references American authors and officials, including some of the same sources cited in this book. In addition to understanding the legal and political basis of the U.S. financial warfare toolkit, PRC scholars have mined the historical record for clues about likely U.S. actions and counter-reactions, going all the way back to the privateer Francis Drake in the 16th century.[95] These sources shine a light on China's strategy for dealing with the worst-case scenario: a "financial war" with the United States.

Beijing is sufficiently worried about the risk of U.S. sanctions that it has determined not to liberalize its capital account.[96] This means China's onshore currency, the CNY, cannot become a truly international currency. However, China can encourage other countries to hold its offshore currency, the CNH, and use China-controlled payment systems to settle bilateral trade with China. It can also offer swap lines with the central banks of friendly countries to conduct trade in CNY under controlled conditions. China also uses swap lines to issue CNY-denominated loans to developing countries and invoice import purchases in CNY. Xi Jinping himself has made it a personal priority to accelerate the expansion of swap lines and the development of the offshore CNH market.

Beijing's strategy is to pursue partial currency internationalization, persuading China's key trading partners to settle particular transactions in CNY and using cross-border payment mechanisms that China controls. The linchpin of this system is the Cross-border Interbank Payments System (CIPS), established in 2015. CIPS is both a messaging and settlement system. It represents an alternative to systems that the U.S. government effectively controls (the Belgium-based SWIFT for messaging and the New York-based CHIPS for settlement). Evading U.S. sanctions is one of CIPS's explicit goals.

Gao Xingwei of the Central Party School, writing in 2019, predicted that CIPS's first adopters would be Iran and other countries already under U.S. sanctions.[97] Not having to rely entirely on SWIFT for messaging would "significantly improve China's financial security and autonomy," he added.[98] In plain language, CIPS can be understood as an alternative plumbing system for global payments. If Washington closes off the pipes that allow China to trade in dollars, China and its trading partners can switch at least some of their trade settlement to CIPS.

China's effort to expand the overseas adoption of CIPS is making rapid progress. As of March 2024, it was used by around 1,500 financial firms worldwide, compared to 11,000 for the American alternative, CHIPS. The total transaction value was much smaller: less than $100 billion for CIPS compared to $1.8 trillion for CHIPS.[99] However, these figures are not indicative of how usage rates would change during conflict. Today, nearly all of China's partner countries can settle payments in USD on established channels, so they have no particular reason to use CIPS unless they are evading sanctions or doing a political favor for China.[100] The situation would be different if Washington shut down the alternatives and CIPS became the *only* way to transact with China. U.S. sanctions against Russia have accelerated Moscow's adoption of the CNY and CIPS for international payments.[101] In the first half of 2023, Russia used RMB to settle 75 percent of its trade with China and 25 percent of its transactions with other countries.[102]

China is actively enlisting developing countries in its strategy for currency internationalization. The share of China's overseas lending denominated in dollars has dropped significantly, from 93 percent in 2013 to 44 percent in 2021. In contrast, the proportion of loans denominated in RMB surged from 6 percent to 50 percent over the same period. Most of these new RMB loans are emergency loans to countries in financial distress.[103] Additionally, China is rolling over its existing portfolio of dollar-denominated loans to Belt and Road Initiative countries into RMB loans. These moves signal China's strategy for dealing with developing countries that took on debt during the Belt and Road boom and are now struggling to repay. Rather than collaborating with the United States and other Western creditors to restructure these countries' debts and help them achieve financial stability, China appears to be keeping these nations on the edge of default. By doing so, it leverages their vulnerability to draw them into the RMB system. The more long-term demand for RMB China can secure in the developing world, the more resilient it becomes to dollar sanctions.[104]

With tight capital controls plus CIPS, PRC authorities could probably weather the initial financial reaction to the outbreak of war, even if Washington imposed sweeping dollar sanctions. PRC regulators and monetary authorities would have to intervene decisively to prevent financial collapse. But the 2015 stock market crash and the outbreak of COVID-19 in January 2020 proved that Beijing has a viable playbook for managing a sudden panic.[105] The PBoC could offer enormous liquidity facilities to banks and corporations, guarantee bank deposits and holdings in wealth management products held by shadow banks, and slash interest rates. Securities regulators could restrict the selling of real estate and more liquid financial assets. The State Council could issue special bond quotas to local governments to manage an anticipated fiscal crunch. Other economic planners could deal with the logistics of rationing and industrial policy for the wartime economy, setting quotas on key goods and perhaps imposing price controls. Monetary authorities could intervene in the CNH market if foreign investors dumped their holdings. If China's financial system survived this initial shock, the U.S. government would be essentially out of ammunition in the financial war.

Most importantly, China has every reason to believe that its trading partners, if necessary, would find ways to help it keep trading through sanctions. This may involve trade through CIPS, if China could successfully internationalize its currency during a crisis; through cryptocurrency; or through proxies that access the U.S. dollar system on behalf of PRC enterprises. As Zhou Hanmin of East China University of Political Science and Law puts it, China could "make use of international offshore financial centers to conduct offshore financial business and continue to clear in dollars by concealing our own information, as Iran has done."[106] Unlike Iran, China has close relationships with Gulf nations that would be happy to play this role. India, too, wants to promote its currency for international trade settlement, in coordination with China.[107] This is why, as Zhou has noted, "U.S. foreign financial sanctions are indeed very severe and complete, but they are not invulnerable."

Sanctions Lessons from Russia

Russia's response to the imposition of U.S. and EU sanctions in February 2022 provides a playbook for China to weather the initial shock. On January 31, 2022, President Joe Biden threatened "swift and severe" economic responses if Russia attacked Ukraine.[108] The threat did not deter Putin.[109] The Biden administration telegraphed that it would only impose sanctions that could win widespread support from European allies and avoid increasing energy prices for Americans.[110] Ironically, after Putin invaded, the G7 decided to sanction Russia's oil and gas sector, a step that would have been inconceivable before the war. Now, however, sanctions were no longer relevant to deterrence. Their goal was simply attrition: to starve Russia's economy and undermine Putin's regime over the long term.[111] In the run-up to the invasion, it was not clear that Vladimir Putin was entirely forthright with Xi Jinping about his thinking and plans. Nevertheless, the two leaders are personally close, having met more than forty-five times as of this writing, and they speak regularly of their common view of the "great changes" to the world order and stress that they are "moving forward" together.[112] Xi has had a front-row seat as Russia has battled sanctions, and he has certainly learned his own lessons from this experience.

To be sure, Russia's case illustrates the challenge that China's financial system might expect on Day One if the United States imposed dollar sanctions or similar trade restrictions. Four days after Russia's full-scale invasion of Ukraine, the United States and its allies froze some $300 billion in assets held abroad by the Central Bank of Russia (CBR) and Russian Direct Investment Fund, the sovereign wealth fund.[113] On the same day, the U.S. Treasury prohibited U.S. entities from transacting with the CBR. Other sanctions followed. The goal was to destroy Russia's banking system by forcing a tsunami of capital outflows, debasing the ruble, and triggering rampant inflation. It was an unprecedented exercise in financial warfare—"a kind of financial nuclear bomb," as former Russian Deputy Finance Minister Sergei Aleksashenko put it at the time.

Markets reacted violently.[114] The ruble fell from 84 to the dollar on February 24 to 139 to the dollar on March 12. Russian inflation jumped to over 2 percent per *week*. Russian households withdrew $9.8 billion worth of foreign currency from their bank accounts in March alone.[115] The sanctioning countries did not want to shut Russian oil and gas out of the global market altogether, fearing a sharp rise in prices. They therefore did not impose dollar sanctions on Russia's entire financial system, allowing the country to continue to settle its energy trade in dollars and euros. Nevertheless, Russian authorities tried to shift trade into other currencies. Before the war, 86 percent of Russia's foreign transactions by value were settled in dollars or euros. Nine months later, that figure had fallen to 54 percent.[116] Russia began to settle trade in CNY, Indian rupees (INR), and Emirati dirhams (AED) instead.

Russian financial authorities steadied the economy by acting decisively to stabilize the exchange rate. These steps reduced the pressure on the banks and contained inflation. On February 28, the day the sanctions were imposed, CBR Governor Elvira Nabiullina raised interest rates from 9.5 to 20 percent. This move dramatically increased the incentive for households and firms to keep their rubles deposited in Russian banks, rather than withdrawing them and exchanging them for foreign currency. In the following days and weeks, Moscow took several additional steps to increase global demand for rubles and reduce Russian demand for dollars, including capital controls and limits on bank withdrawals.[117]

Essentially, Russia's government created incentives for market participants to buy and hold rubles rather than sell them. The United States and other sanctioning powers did not respond with additional policies to keep the ruble weak. So, starting in late March, the exchange rate began to snap back toward its fundamental value. In April 2022, the ruble was the world's best-performing currency. By June, thanks to rising oil prices and reduced imports, the ruble strengthened to between 50 and 60 to the dollar—stronger than its prewar average.

The same policies kept the sanctions from triggering out-of-control inflation in Russia (see Figure 7.6). True, inflation rose higher than the prewar average because of difficulties acquiring essential imports. But high interest rates kept prices under control. As of this writing in autumn 2025, over three years after the war began, Russia is paying a high price to sustain its war effort, and inflation is again creeping up, but its overall economic and financial system seems far from collapse. A key reason is that Russia's supply chains have re-routed over time. Firms in Central Asia, the Caucasus, and Middle East bought up essential goods from the sanctioning countries and re-sold them to Russia, albeit at marked-up prices.[118] The governments of these countries turned a blind eye, or even encouraged these activities.[119]

China has much larger reserves of foreign currency than Russia, which means its financial system is potentially much more resilient to the sudden imposition of sanctions. In February 2022, Russia's government controlled $630 billion of foreign currency and gold. Even though more than half of this total was frozen in foreign accounts by March 1, Moscow successfully righted the ship.[120] As of April 2023, China's State Administration of Foreign Exchange (SAFE) held $3.2 trillion in foreign currency reserves. China likely has up to $3 trillion of *additional* undeclared dollar assets, though it is not

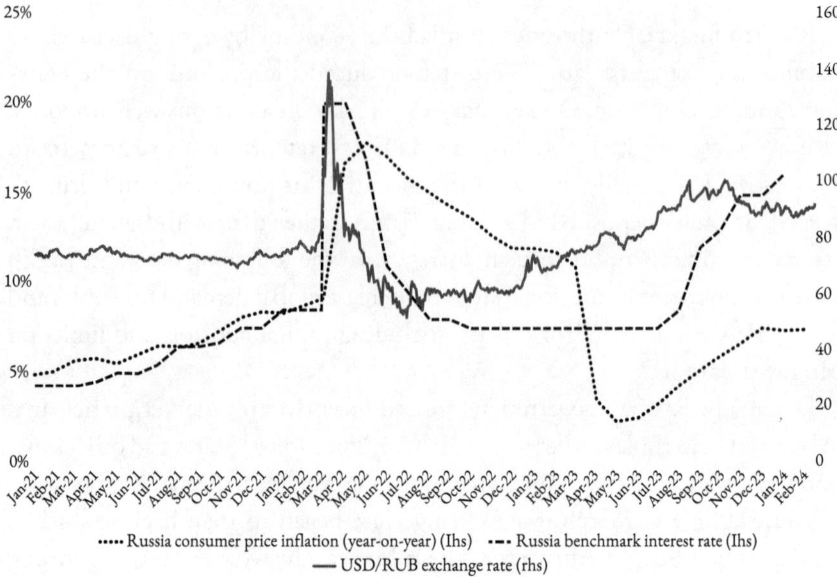

Figure 7.6 Russia's exchange rate, inflation, and benchmark interest rate, January 2021–March 2024

Source: Bloomberg.

clear how liquid these holdings are.[121] In short, Beijing has ample reserves to prevent a default on external debt and copy the Russian playbook if a Taiwan crisis caused a financial shock.

As of this writing, three years into the war, Russia's economy has proven much more resilient than financial analysts expected. While sanctions have limited long-term growth and hurt household finances, its economy is still expanding, with real GDP growth expected to come in around 1 percent in 2025. Unemployment remains near multi-decade lows, largely due to war mobilization and a shift toward military production. Meanwhile, Russia's public finances remain sound. The country has the lowest debt-to-GDP ratio of all G20 countries, with deficits throughout the war running below 3 percent of GDP annually.[122] Moscow therefore has plenty of room to run larger deficits indefinitely—and if necessary also to bail out corporations that have taken on hidden debts to finance the war machine.[123] Oil and gas revenues have declined, but Russia is still running current account surpluses and preserving a basically stable exchange rate. Its banks are well capitalized. Shortages of advanced technology and industrial equipment have driven up production costs, but Russian firms have found workarounds, buying components through third countries. For example, auto production declined in 2022 and 2023, but rebounded in 2024.[124] Some of these data may be falsified, but financial market behavior suggests that they are not wildly distorted.

At present, our best evidence is that the Russian state believes the current economic situation is difficult but manageable. Nor is there evidence that Russian elites, let alone ordinary citizens, are so unhappy with the state of the economy that they are pressuring Putin to sue for peace. Russia's economy is undoubtedly performing below the trend that would have been expected without sanctions—but it is also performing far above the trend that most Western analysts predicted when sanctions were imposed.

It is worth emphasizing how badly wrong many highly capable analysts were about the effect of sanctions. In July 2022, a team at the Yale School of Management led by Jeffrey Sonnenfeld performed a "comprehensive" analysis of the Russian economy. They concluded that it was "reeling" in the face of "catastrophically crippling" sanctions and that "there is no path out of economic oblivion."[125] Many other esteemed commentators have made similar predictions throughout the war.[126] At the time, these expert predictions served a political purpose by maintaining morale. However, the analytical community has not yet fully reckoned with why it got these forecasts so badly wrong, and what lessons the Russia case may hold for China. If Russia is resilient and adaptable, China is surely vastly more so.

This discussion highlights some important lessons for China. First, U.S. threats to trigger a rapid financial crisis using sanctions or other tools will deter China only if they can be made very credibly in advance. Taiwan is not Ukraine, of course, but Putin never thought U.S. sanctions would existentially threaten Russia's financial stability. Second, China can draw lessons from Russia's rescue of its financial system. It might well conclude that it is in a stronger position to absorb an initial blow. Third, market participants and third countries would react opportunistically and dynamically to U.S. economic punishment and China's reactions. These moves might support China's short-term economic and financial resilience. Even the imposition of sweeping dollar sanctions would not permanently shut down China's ability to trade with the world, and there would be substantial leakage, rerouting, and other evasion in third markets. Even in extreme scenarios, fully decoupling the U.S.–China trade relationship would be a long-term process that would profoundly affect third countries and require their cooperation. Finally, Americans should assume that China's economy, with its far more capable state and sophisticated industrial base, is at least as adaptable to sanctions-related disruptions as Russia's. Large, resource-rich economies can adapt to external shocks—especially when they remain partly integrated into global trade.

Malacca Reconsidered

This discussion may help explain why, despite the significant risk of a Malacca blockade for China, some credible PRC analysts have long argued that the threat is exaggerated. Zhao Hongtu of the China Institutes of Contemporary International Relations (CICIR) put it this way in 2007: While a U.S. blockade or embargo "cannot be completely ruled out, this possibility is not very likely," and "the overall impact of such risks on China's energy security is relatively limited."[127] CICIR is the in-house think tank of China's Ministry of State Security and likely the country's most influential institution for wargaming economic conflict with the United States. Zhao emphatically concludes that "there basically is no Malacca dilemma."[128] Western scholars have almost entirely overlooked these perspectives.[129]

In the last two decades, China has expanded stockpiles and diversified its import streams to greatly reduce its vulnerability to blockade.[130] China now produces 4.1 million barrels of oil per day domestically, roughly a quarter of its total consumption. Its petroleum reserves now hold roughly two billion barrels of oil and continue to grow rapidly.[131] China could build new pipelines to Russia and Kazakhstan within a year—that is, unless the United States sabotaged them. The PLA itself would need only around 500,000 barrels per day for the war effort—around 12 percent of *domestic* production. "The energy needs of a country in wartime are very different from those in peacetime," Zhao observes. "China, as a major energy and oil producer, has sufficient domestic energy supplies to meet its wartime energy needs, especially its military needs."[132] China's food system is similarly adaptable. As of 2022, China had 69 percent of global maize reserves, 60 percent of global rice reserves, and 51 percent of global wheat reserves.[133] China derives most of its protein from soybeans imported from the United States and Brazil, or from meat (imported, or produced domestically with soybean-based feed). However, China was self-sufficient in protein until the early 2000s. It imports protein now not because it needs foreign protein to survive, but because the population is now rich enough to afford it.[134] Beijing would respond decisively if protein supplies are cut off. In a 2021 speech, Xi called China's food security a top-priority national security issue and called for research into "alternative proteins" from "plants, animals, and microorganisms."[135] China has been stockpiling critical metals, semiconductors, and other important resource inputs, as well as food and energy.

We also need to consider how global commodity markets would adapt if the United States tried to shut down China's imports. A blockade of China would create an unprecedented arbitrage opportunity for merchant shippers from around the world, in the midst of a general economic crisis. The greater China's need for oil, the higher a price it would be willing to pay for the marginal barrel. This means a profit motive for producers to send extra barrels around the blockade, anticipating that those that made it through would pay for those that the Americans confiscated. Supply chains would adapt. Russia and the Central Asian republics would export (or transship) surplus barrels to China by rail or even by road. Smaller quantities might well be smuggled in via Thailand, Myanmar, and Pakistan, or by ships sailing across the Pacific, ostensibly bound for other markets.[136] "The goal of containing China's economy through an oil embargo is difficult to achieve in an integrated global energy market," notes Zhao. "The world has only one oil market, and any disruption in oil supply anywhere will have an impact on the global oil market."[137]

Preventing cheating would be extremely difficult. As Zhao notes, "intercepting or attacking China-bound tankers at sea would present difficulties in determining whether they are China's own or chartered by another country."[138] Even if the United States demanded that all ships passing through Malacca provide GPS tracking, shippers (and their governments) are no more likely to participate willingly than the United States was to disclose shipping manifests to Britain during its blockade of Germany during World War I.[139] Merchant vessels could plausibly re-sell their cargoes to China after passing through the blockade. If GPS tracking rules made it infeasible to dock in mainland ports, they could illicitly transfer cargoes to PRC ships on the high seas, as Russian and Iranian tankers regularly do to evade sanctions.[140] As Xue Li of the Chinese Academy of Social Sciences noted in a 2010 essay on the scenario: "tankers could change their destinations during the course of their voyage, rendering U.S. inspections in the Straits meaningless."[141] Because of these factors, simple calculations probably underestimate how long China could hold out under blockade.

The supply-chain disruptions and financial market dislocations caused by a Malacca blockade would also have *political* effects in neutral countries. Even if neither Washington nor Beijing wanted to disrupt China's exports, an onerous inspection regime that created delays at Malacca would disrupt all other supply chains.[142] The result would be shortages, inflation in manufactured goods, and a collapse in the global price of key commodities, even beyond the impact of any sanctions. All countries that depend economically on stable commodity prices and stable international trade would suffer acutely.

Beyond the wider economic impacts which will be discussed below, any Malacca blockade would be bitterly contested by key countries in the region. It is to prevent precisely this kind of action that the trade-dependent countries that geographically border the Malacca Straits—Malaysia, Indonesia, and particularly Singapore—have historically been some of the most committed to the UN Convention on the Law of the Sea (UNCLOS). This commitment lies at the heart of their relationship with the United States, which has acted as the primary guarantor of the Convention since 1945, despite not being a signatory.[143]

If neutral countries sent naval vessels to convoy merchant ships, which refused to comply with inspection orders, would the U.S. Navy engage them with force? Would they sink them? Where would they impound them? Britain faced this problem repeatedly in the Napoleonic Wars, ultimately declaring war against neutral Denmark, Sweden, and Russia. As Lord Jackie Fisher, First Sea Lord, noted during Britain's blockade of Germany in 1915: "The prolongation of war at sea tends to raise up fresh enemies for the dominant naval power in a much higher degree than it does on land, owing to the exasperation of neutrals."[144] In essence, it is impossible to enforce a blockade of a major country without a credible threat to use military force against neutrals.

China understands this. As Xue notes, "the countries along the Malacca Strait are very much opposed to two 'elephants' fighting in their 'meadow'" because their interest lies in unencumbered trade.[145] Yet a Malacca blockade could not succeed without the active participation of neighboring countries. Otherwise, where would the noncompliant ships bound for China be impounded?[146] A "discriminatory inspection would not be legal and would be difficult to implement fully due to the opposition of many countries," Xue concludes.[147]

Importantly, the same principles would not apply in reverse if China blockades or quarantines Taiwan. A Malacca blockade would be a *far blockade*: a naval operation that aimed to control commercial traffic to China at a significant distance from China's coast.[148] Rather than closing off China's key harbors, it would seek to manage China's international trade as it moved through key sea lanes. A blockade of Taiwan would be a *close blockade*, which involves policing waters immediately off Taiwan's coast to control its access to the sea. Close blockades against small islands are far more common in history and have a far better track record of success.[149] Close blockades can cause spillover problems in relations with other states. But because they are geographically bounded around the target state's territorial waters, they only rarely escalate to outright conflict with neutrals. If both sides turn to scorched-earth tactics, China can almost certainly hold out longer than Taiwan could. As Lonnie Henley has put it: "We are not on the winning end of that cost-imposition contest."[150]

The Illusion of "Economic Mutually Assured Destruction"

Based on the previous discussion, we need to reevaluate how economic threats fit into the broader concept of integrated deterrence. Threats of extreme economic punishment—such as sweeping sanctions, blockades, or even shut-offs of Taiwan's semiconductor production—are all forms of what we might call "economic mutually assured destruction" (EMAD). The logic behind EMAD is that if China crosses U.S. red lines, the U.S. president could unilaterally shatter the global trading system upon which all countries depend. The potential consequences for global macroeconomic and financial stability make the comparison to nuclear MAD seductive.

The threat of EMAD looms over all U.S.–China interactions, whether or not it is explicitly stated. Indeed, the most plausible explanation for Xi's actions to insulate China's financial system from external shocks, build enormous strategic stockpiles, and make economic decisions that go beyond what would be economically prudent is that he thinks there is a nonzero chance that the United States might unleash this threatened destruction.

However, while implicit threats of EMAD serve as a supplement to strategic deterrence, they are not a sustainable strategy for economic deterrence in their own right. There are crucial differences that make EMAD a much weaker basis for strategic deterrence than nuclear MAD. First, MAD involves unilateral threats. The president can credibly commit to using nuclear weapons without the need to coordinate with third countries or even Congress. By contrast, sanctions—such as expulsion from the dollar system—require broader political support and some level of third-party compliance or transparency. Given China's importance to the global economy, enforcing sanctions effectively would require active European and global cooperation. Over time, third parties could adapt by developing alternative payment systems, and OFAC might be overwhelmed with monitoring compliance. Even close U.S. allies could oppose the imposition of sanctions on China before a crisis, undermining the deterrent threat. Thus, third-party reluctance to fully commit to EMAD in advance could diminish its deterrent power, even if "Day One" triggers a shift in thinking, as was seen in Europe after Russia's 2022 invasion of Ukraine. In such scenarios, U.S. economic leadership would face a fundamental challenge.

Second, MAD threatens immediate, catastrophic, and irreversible damage to both sides. In contrast, economic statecraft is an ongoing process of policy implementation and is responsive to domestic pressure. The imposition of dollar sanctions can cause short-term financial crises. But even the most severe sanctions influence an adversary's behavior only if they can sustain long-term pressure on an adversary's ability to trade. In the case of China, both the U.S. and allied economies would endure great pain during this prolonged process. Xi may come to believe that if China can survive the initial shock and achieve a political or military victory over Taiwan, the United States or its allies might eventually be pressured to lift sanctions or create loopholes, accepting that U.S. economic power is fundamentally limited.

The differences between MAD and EMAD become particularly pronounced in gray-zone scenarios. A quarantine, for instance, might not cause any significant economic disruption by itself. China could frame its actions as a continuation of the status quo or a defensive response to U.S. or Taiwanese "escalation," allowing goods to flow freely in and out of Taiwan in the short term. In this context, it would be up to the American president to draw the red line, either causing or threatening to cause a global economic crisis. At the height of a brinkmanship crisis, U.S. voters and third countries might be swayed toward China's position, for fear of EMAD. Of course, if China decided to trigger active conflict, maritime supply chains would be automatically disrupted. In such a scenario, both sides would suffer significant economic consequences. However, even in the most extreme conflict scenarios, the United States and China would keep trading with neutral countries. At any point, both sides would pay a strategic price if they tried to interfere with neutral trade.

Conclusion

Hard decoupling makes for a superficially tempting threat, but conventional threats of sanctions and blockades contribute to integrated deterrence less than one might expect. Any attempt to enforce an immediate and lasting hard decoupling would devastate the U.S. economy and the economies of allies. They would also undermine coalition unity.

In times of great power competition, third countries do not face binary choices.[151] Any attempt to bifurcate the global economy by force would trigger organized resistance. It would incentivize neutral countries to develop workarounds, including overland smuggling routes and trade settlement in currencies other than dollars. It would shatter the international trading system. It would undermine America's long-term sources of structural economic leverage over China. Existing export controls and sanctions on Russia, North Korea, Iran, and other rogue states would begin to lose their effectiveness at the very moment when they were most needed. In other words, hard decoupling would be so costly and so risky that it would not be a realistic option even in many extreme scenarios.

Xi has the right idea: to undermine the credibility of these deterrent threats, he just needs to build enough of a buffer to withstand the initial financial shock, followed by a few months of a near-total collapse in trade. Beijing is making progress on both fronts. In reality, of course, even the most extreme U.S. efforts to curtail PRC imports would be only partially effective. Considering adaptation, China may be able to hold out for a year or more with close to zero international trade before its political system faced collapse. Beijing has reason to believe that other countries would not wait that long before finding ways to get trade flowing again. In short, the threat of an acute financial and macroeconomic shock is unlikely to deter Xi unless he thinks the Western coalition could sustain high pressure on China *indefinitely.*

It is therefore essential to develop an alternative plan for achieving full decoupling over time, in a manner that would better support key U.S. interests. The next chapter therefore turns to the following questions: *Suppose China moves against Taiwan and the United States reaches a bipartisan consensus that decoupling is necessary but hard decoupling is unacceptable. What principles and policies should guide the U.S. economic response?* How could the United States complete its own decoupling from China, and help its willing allies and partners do the same, in a way that advanced their political interests while imposing long-term pain on China? How could U.S. economic contingency planning work with market forces rather than against them, winning compliance through incentives rather than threats? How could Washington neutralize China's most potent retaliatory tactics and minimize the chance of a protracted, uncontrolled, and unwinnable economic conflict? How could it combine actions that the president could and likely would take unilaterally on Day One with a convincing framework for why most countries would want to accept U.S. economic leadership on Day One, Day 100, and Day 1,000?

While the U.S. government cannot hold together an allied coalition through bullying and threats, it can articulate a positive vision for how it would preserve the global economy and align coalition interests at China's expense. Most countries would prefer to prevent the collapse of the trading system and have little interest in seeing China wrest control of it. Many countries can see that a forcible seizure of Taiwan would undermine norms that maintain peace in the Indo-Pacific and concentrate power in the hands of a totalitarian regime that rejects the rule of law and insists on CCP control over people and economic assets. In the long run, this outcome would be catastrophic for free markets and the interests of all free countries, as well as small countries that would be powerless to resist Beijing's dictates. But countries will not join the United States in such an effort for principled reasons alone.

8

Avalanche Decoupling

by Hugo Bromley and Eyck Freymann

On August 4, 1941, Winston Churchill and the Chiefs of Staff embarked on a risky trans-Atlantic voyage on the battleship HMS *Prince of Wales*.[1] Between August 9 and 12, off the coast of Newfoundland, Churchill held meetings with U.S. President Franklin D. Roosevelt about the world system they hoped to create should the Allies triumph in the war. The result was the Atlantic Charter: eight succinct "common principles" that described their "hopes for a better future for the world."[2] Among them were commitments to self-determination for all nations, the renunciation of territorial expansion, economic cooperation, and disarmament. Another commitment was to a fair international trading system. Both sides committed to "endeavor, with due respect for their existing obligations, to further the enjoyment by all States, great or small, victor or vanquished, of access, on equal terms, to the trade and to the raw materials of the world which are needed for their economic prosperity."[3]

The principles of the Atlantic Charter helped to hold the Allies together throughout the war. They guided the creation of the Bretton Woods agreement, the United Nations, the Marshall Plan, and the GATT, the predecessor to the WTO. These institutions, whatever their flaws, formed a system that helped to secure American prosperity, security, and leadership of the free world for three generations. Notably, allied and neutral countries alike were invited to enjoy the benefits of these institutions, though the Soviet Union and its Communist allies were eventually excluded from much of the U.S.-led economic order.

Today, amidst widespread doubts about U.S. reliability, Washington and its allies should begin consultations on an economic contingency plan for a Taiwan crisis. Like the Atlantic Charter, the plan should address both the immediate challenge of crisis response and the long-term challenge of how to organize the world after a rupture with China. The watchword of these plans should be *economic security*: a vision for a fair and honest international trading system that respects all countries' need to balance their vital national interests with the benefits of market integration. This contingency plan should then be enacted when the president and Congress determine that China has either violated the current status quo in the Taiwan Strait or left the United States unable to respond effectively to gray-zone aggression.

The plan should ground itself in four fundamental principles:

1. Avoid breaking noncritical supply chains on Day One. Provide firms sufficient time to reshore production out of China.

2. Sustain dollar hegemony at all costs and prevent the rapid internationalization of the RMB.

3. Do not require any country to decouple from China. Instead, incentivize cooperation by integrating U.S. decoupling into a broader program of economic support in response to a Taiwan crisis.

4. Enforce anti-PRC trade policies against third countries in a fair and honest manner, with avenues for appeal and adjudication.

These principles would be essential to instilling confidence in the chaotic context of a Taiwan crisis. The bilateral trading relationship between the United States and China remains uncertain, following the Trump administration's initial, partially reversed effort at decoupling. However, U.S. allies almost certainly will remain extremely exposed. In the immediate aftermath, Washington would have to lead the immediate crisis response to protect global financial stability, safeguard other countries from the fallout, and secure the position of the dollar. At the same time, Washington would have to communicate a credible commitment to sustaining a functional international economic system, even as major economies decoupled bilaterally from China. Lastly, the United States would have to commit to supporting not only any allies that chose to decouple through the process but also third countries caught between the United States and China. It would have to organize the system so that these countries could benefit economically at China's expense if they helped to enforce the Core's trade policies.

If Washington could stay true to these four principles, it could trigger *avalanche decoupling*—a process that caused no more economic disruption than necessary on Day One but inexorably gained momentum over time.

Washington could trigger the avalanche unilaterally, on a timeline of its choosing, to complete whatever bilateral decoupling it had not already achieved. Of course, avalanche decoupling would be vastly more beneficial for the United States—and harmful for China—if U.S. allies went along. Allies that have proven unable or unwilling to pursue rapid decoupling during the Trump trade war may choose to pursue partial or total avalanche decoupling on Day One of a Taiwan crisis. But this would be a momentous choice. They would need robust assurances that the United States would respect their vital interests along the way.

Avalanche decoupling does not depend on wishful thinking. It does not assume that any country would cut its economic ties with China for high-minded moral reasons. All negative actions against China could be taken unilaterally by the United States and a small number of Core allies. All coalition-building would be built on incentives and organized through institutions established, funded, and guided by the United States. Because the point of the plan would be to align the economic interests of third countries with U.S. and allied goals, China would struggle to disrupt decoupling with threats or retaliation. The exodus of production from China would gain momentum over time, much like a mass of snow sliding down a mountain.

Avalanche decoupling is a flexible mechanism. It can be used in peacetime, for partial "strategic" decoupling in specific critical products or sectors. Or it can be used in crisis, to cover the full suite of trade. The export controls introduced by China in response to the "Liberation Day" tariffs have highlighted numerous areas where China is the only or dominant supplier of industrial inputs critical to the functioning of American society. However, any effort to break that dependence leaves the United States vulnerable to PRC economic coercion. Avalanche decoupling represents a potentially viable pathway to pursue the original vision of "strategic decoupling." In that sense, it speaks to key areas of continuity and consensus between the Biden and Trump administrations.

The avalanche decoupling mechanism has two policy pillars. First, the United States and any other Core allies that wanted to join would use ratcheting tariffs or quotas to decouple bilaterally from China. They could decouple by product, by sector, or across the board. They would implement decoupling in the name of national security. (This is legal under WTO rules—a point that will likely matter greatly to Japan, the UK, and other allies). Second, the Core allies would establish an Economic Security Cooperation Board (ESCB).

The ESCB would have two primary mandates: (1) provide aid and economic support to member states, and (2) support the enforcement of national trade policies passed under the national security exemption against nonmembers.

In the United States, Congress would have to take the lead in implementing avalanche decoupling. On Day One of a Taiwan crisis, Congress would need to coordinate with the Federal Reserve, the Treasury, and the White House to preserve the world's access to dollar liquidity and prevent global financial contagion. If the United States has not yet achieved strategic decoupling in those areas where PRC export controls risk catastrophic harm to American society, it may spend a substantial amount of money to reshore a few critical supply chains into Core countries as fast as possible.

The harder part would involve achieving consensus on how noncritical dependencies on China should be phased out. To the extent possible, the United States would want to coordinate this effort with allied countries. A two-year decoupling window would be much more ambitious than a ten-year window, for example. Once the right policy incentives were enshrined in law, most of the avalanche would occur organically through market-based mechanisms as firms and consumers responded to changing relative prices.

For the reasons described in Chapter 7, without the cooperation of neutral countries it would be impossible to stop Chinese goods from being transshipped into the U.S. market. Washington would therefore need all U.S. trading partners to report accurate data on their imports and exports of PRC goods and parts. This is already a major focus for the Trump administration, given its own intention to pursue discriminatory trade policies. Building on whatever steps are taken to enhance compliance over the course of this administration may be easy at first. But the higher the trade barriers rose, the greater the incentives for private firms and foreign governments to mislabel and transship PRC products.[4] National governments might have neither the ability nor necessarily the will to stop firms from profiting through this transshipment activity. Without a robust plan to prevent mass transshipment, it would be decoupling in name only. U.S. consumers would pay higher costs, but they would remain nearly as dependent on PRC products as before. The U.S. border would remain fundamentally out of control.

In the wake of a Taiwan crisis, the United States would need to make a sustained strategic investment in its long-term economic security. Simply giving money to businesses or other countries with no strings attached would be politically impossible and strategically unwise. But bluntly transactional *quid pro quo* deals would not work either. The United States would need key countries to collaborate with it in a sustained way. The solution to this challenge is to take America's two most important policy objectives in the crisis—robust trade enforcement and global economic stability—and intertwine them over time to serve America's key economic security interests.

A full-scale reordering of the global economy after a rupture with China would be very expensive, particularly upfront. But it would also present enormous long-term opportunities. The challenge in the wake of the crisis would be to set up institutions and frameworks that would allow the global trading system to evolve in a way that benefited the United States, its allies, and neutral countries. U.S. spending up front would be an investment in avoiding an economic depression and structurally reshaping the trading system at China's expense. The alternative to collaboration would be ongoing, simultaneous trade disputes with all its major trading partners.

The ESCB would help keep the trading system fair and honest in a post–Day One world. All countries, except rogue states like China and Russia, would be invited to join. The ESCB would *not* be empowered to punish its members. Rather, it would provide them with regular tranches of financial aid and technical support with customs enforcement. Member states would be given some leeway at first. But soon, further aid would become conditional on honest trade reporting. Over time, the main incentive to cooperate with the United States would increasingly be market access, not direct payments. If member states were found to be acting as transshipment points, the ESCB would support the United States and its allies in enforcing discriminatory trade policy against them also, subject to clear guidelines. As the Core markets phased out their direct imports from China, millions of manufacturing jobs would need to move from China to other countries. Trillions of dollars of private investment would be needed to build the new factories, roads, power infrastructure, and so on. For many third countries, the reshoring avalanche would be the most important economic opportunity of the 21st century.

Washington would not try to command and control where these supply chains moved. All ESCB members could compete on a level playing field. This would ensure that market forces guided the avalanche in the most efficient possible direction, ensuring that consumers everywhere could maintain access to safe and affordable noncritical products. For any country hoping to attract these new investments and manufacturing jobs, it would be up to the government to persuade the private sector and the ESCB that they could be trusted to report accurate customs data now and in the future, and therefore retain access to Core markets. As the avalanche proceeded, countries trying to benefit from the reshoring process would increasingly face incentives to respect U.S. and allied economic security interests. The ESCB would monitor global value chains and investigate cases of transshipment. If the ESCB found that third countries were failing to cooperate in securing the borders of Core countries against products from China, the Core countries would be free to treat *their* products as if they came from China.

The inspiration for this vision is the reconstruction of an economic order for the free world after World War II. The 1941 Atlantic Charter articulated an Anglo-American consensus that the postwar economic order would be based on incentives and inclusive international economic institutions. Because that consensus had already been established, it was possible to set up robust institutions quickly between 1944 and 1947. This swift action proved critical in preventing important countries like West Germany, France, and Italy from falling under Communist domination. The postwar international economic order and its leading initiatives, such as the Marshall Plan, had a geopolitical rationale. But the anti-Soviet logic was always implicit. The United States focused on laying the structural foundation for shared prosperity, extending a hand to all countries, including neutrals. In conceptualizing the economic response to a Taiwan crisis, American lawmakers should take their inspiration from this history.

Policy 1: National Decoupling

The first pillar of the Day One Plan is a discriminatory trade policy—tariffs or quotas—to phase out trade with China over a politically negotiated timeline. Beyond this, all aspects of national decoupling are negotiable. The future of the United States' trading relationship with China is highly uncertain and is likely to remain so throughout the Trump administration. Regardless of the bilateral relationship, the United States needs to provide key allies in the region, above all Japan and Australia, with a viable pathway to lessen their economic dependence on China over time. Beyond those two nations, the strategic, political, and economic conditions on Day One would inform which countries chose to decouple and how they chose to do it. The details would emerge through negotiations between the key parties at the time. We cannot predict them in advance.

Even in extreme Taiwan crisis scenarios, only a very small group of Core allies would probably join the United States in broad decoupling from China. As discussed in Chapter 4, the Core group may include the UK, Canada, Australia, and Japan. All four of these countries stand to suffer terribly if the existing economic order in the Indo-Pacific disintegrates. Each would also have additional reasons for participating. The UK, America's closest ally, is highly exposed to financial stability risks in the region. It is also a technology superpower that would benefit from increased access to U.S. consumer and capital markets. Canada, another historically close ally, is economically interdependent with the United States, which buys 73 percent of its exports. Canada is also very close to the UK.[5] Australia has more diversified trading relationships, but it leans heavily on the United States for security and would become even more dependent on U.S. security assurances in a post–Day One world. The AUKUS partnership symbolizes the ironclad strategic alignment between these countries. Japan, the second-largest economy in the Core group, would play a pivotal role. Japan relies on the United States for security and would become even more dependent in the context of a revanchist China. Japan is deeply integrated economically with the United States and more than any other major country needs a fair and honest regional trading system. Untangling Japan from China's market would be an enormous and challenging project. Yet Japan could also see the upside in decoupling: as the Core's manufacturing powerhouse, it would stand to gain significantly if it retained preferential access to the other Core markets as they wound down their economic relationships with China.

The Core allies would not undertake the enormous cost and risk of decoupling from China simply to do the United States a favor. Nor would they do so as part of a handshake "deal" that the United States could easily abandon. All of these countries are deeply economically linked to China. All are more vulnerable to China's military, political, and economic retaliation. All would be sacrificing something valuable in a time of great power competition: the ability to play both sides. Now that the United States has decided that its alliances are transactional, it would need to be prepared to make big commitments to secure the Core allies' cooperation in trade, defense, and potentially other areas. It would need to enshrine those commitments so that future presidents could not easily walk away from them.

Membership in the Core could be flexible. Countries like South Korea, New Zealand, and even Taiwan itself might seek very close policy alignment, depending on their political leadership at the time. From a burden-sharing perspective, it would be ideal if European nations joined the Core. However, the structure of the European Single Market and Customs Union makes it impossible for some member states to join the Core while others opt out.[6] Trade policy is a competency reserved for Brussels, and achieving unanimous support among the "EU 27" for full decoupling is unlikely. Core members would not need to adopt identical policies. Some countries might participate in a joint industrial policy for some critical products, but not for others. Over time, the Core might evolve into overlapping coalitions of the willing, united by a shared commitment to decoupling from China in a gradual, coordinated, and market-driven way. This is probably the best-case scenario for alignment with Europe.

In the chaotic context of a Taiwan crisis, the Core allies would need to prioritize breaking their *critical* dependencies first. At the top of the list would be advanced semiconductors, components and machine tools for building essential defense platforms, active pharmaceutical ingredients and medical devices, and batteries. (Hopefully, they would break these dependencies in advance of a crisis, but they might not do so in time.) The Core would aim for maximum policy alignment across all domains, but critical goods would be by far the most important. The Core might use industrial policies, export controls, joint stockpiles, and other approaches. To break the critical dependencies as quickly and efficiently as possible, they would try to exploit complementarities in natural resource endowments, institutions, and capital markets. The Core countries might also impose export controls on dual-use technologies to China, as part of a strategy of technological dominance. The allies would have to collaborate intensively to align their policies. Establishing a formal dispute resolution mechanism for the group would be impractical. Washington would need to offer increased market access to Core allies to secure their long-term commitment. This is a key lesson from the postwar reconstruction of Europe.[7]

The greater challenge lies in achieving decoupling from China in noncritical goods, however noncritical is defined. As a first step, Core allies would need to revoke China's permanent normal trading relations (PNTR) status, which grants trade partners the same benefits offered to WTO members.[8] In the United States, this would require a majority vote in the House, sixty votes in the Senate, and presidential approval. This is a high political hurdle under normal circumstances, but not necessarily in a break-glass scenario. Revoking PNTR would also be an appropriate first response to a quarantine of

Taiwan, and Congress could show credibility by passing legislation to automatically revoke PNTR if China imposes a quarantine.[9] After revoking PNTR, the legal authority for U.S. decoupling measures would derive from Section 232 of the Trade Expansion Act of 1962.[10]

The Core would pursue decoupling consistent with WTO rules. It would issue a joint declaration labeling China's initiation of a Taiwan crisis as a "systemic national security threat." This declaration would provide legal justification for subsequent tariffs or quotas imposed on imports from China under Article XXI of the GATT Charter.[11] The Core might also consider extending similar measures to North Korea, Russia, or other rogue states if they coordinated with China during an attack on Taiwan.[12] Washington should not demand that other countries join it in labeling China a national security threat—or even condemn China's actions against Taiwan. It would ask third countries just to acknowledge its own actions as lawful. Third countries would be motivated to adopt this position, as it would be necessary to qualify for ESCB support.

Beijing would accuse the United States of attacking the international trading system, but this claim would be demonstrably false. The Core allies would be taking significant pains to *uphold* a functional trading system in the face of China's aggression. Indeed, they would be taking proportionate and lawful action to defend their economic security against China's aggression.[13] In practice, China would have no meaningful legal recourse. With a strong U.S. legal case and the current paralysis in the WTO's dispute settlement process, resolving such a case could take years, and neither side could be compelled to comply with the ruling. Beijing's objections would amount to political theater, aimed at developing countries.

As we write these words in 2025, the international trading system is in precarious straits. The WTO had already been hollowed out before the second Trump administration took office in 2025. Since then, President Trump's coercive trade measures against Canada, Mexico, the European Union, and other allies have raised fundamental questions about what kind of international economic order America actually wants.

We will not speculate here about how ongoing trade negotiations will play out, but we can say that America's interests during and after a Taiwan crisis would differ fundamentally from its interests today, in peacetime. During a crisis, America would face much greater constraints. It would need to protect its most vital national interests first, while countering a PRC attempt to hijack or destroy the international economic order. It would need to keep its most important alliances from disintegrating. In this context, the administration's goal of rebalancing trade with allies would have to take a back seat to preventing the imminent collapse of the dollar system and the architecture of U.S. national security in the Western Hemisphere and around the world. Meanwhile, America would have to break its remaining vulnerabilities to economic coercion as fast as possible and help its allies do the same.

Keeping allies and neutral countries on board with this effort—and proving to financial markets that the United States was all-in—would be no small task. Washington would be asking allies to make a generational commitment to partnership. Much more than speeches calling America's alliances "ironclad," this would require new legal procedures that ensured future presidents would treat allies fairly, honestly, and consistently.[14] The president would need to lead, and Congress would need to step up. The first step would be to modify Section 232 of the Trade Expansion Act of 1962 to clarify the separation of powers on trade policy between the legislative and executive branches.[15] The president should maintain the power to enforce U.S. trade policy. Congress must maintain the power to set the policy in the first place. Bipartisan legislation along these lines already exists. In essence, Congress would take control over the avalanche decoupling process.

Ratcheting Tariffs or Quotas

The Core allies would achieve bilateral decoupling through coordinated ratcheting trade policies against China: either tariffs that moved up or quotas that moved down. The specific design and pace of the ratchet would be determined by elected officials based on the circumstances. It is less important that the ratchet move quickly than that, once triggered, the ratchet is visibly difficult to reverse. The objective of the policy is to provide clarity and predictability for capital markets and businesses about the future pathway of trade friction between the Core markets and China. If market participants viewed the ratchet as credible, they would begin to price in the inevitability of eventual full decoupling. Thus, while supply chains remained open, private enterprise would find the most cost-effective way to reshore production out of China. Capital markets would reward firms that proactively reshored supply chains to safer countries while penalizing those that delayed or resisted.

A ratcheting regime offers several key advantages. Because tariffs or quotas would impose no restrictions on noncritical trade on Day One, supply chains would remain largely untouched at first. U.S. policy would cause no immediate shortages or sudden price hikes for consumers, though China might decide to break supply chains at any time. Additionally, a ratcheting regime that provided clarity for markets would reduce trade policy uncertainty, which could be paralyzing for businesses. An automatic ratchet is therefore highly preferable to an ad hoc system in which tariff rates are set arbitrarily by elected officials. The experience of spring and summer 2025 illustrates why a format of "tariff forward guidance" would be more effective. When businesses lack certainty about future trade policy, their incentive is not to shift production. It is to shut production down and wait for more predictable market conditions. This leads to unemployment, supply-chain disruptions, and inflation—and none of the benefits of an American manufacturing renaissance.

Potential PRC Countermeasures

Washington should assume that China would retaliate if the United States or its allies attempted avalanche decoupling in any form, just as China has retaliated against tariffs in the past. China depends on foreign markets for its manufactures, just as Russia needs foreign buyers for its oil. In the long term, the rest of the world could substitute for both. But in the short term, cutting off supply would cause shortages, inflation, and other problems.

As we have seen, China's retaliation could cause economic pain and political division in the Western alliance, though not without considerable cost to China. Beijing recognizes this fact. It could weaponize the Core countries' remaining critical dependencies by cutting off exports of products like critical minerals or lifesaving drugs. China's economic actions could have many goals, including persuading the United States to capitulate totally over Taiwan. However, as discussed in Chapter 7, China's most extreme options for strategic economic coercion suffer from the same credibility problems as those of the United States. China's retaliating in response to avalanche decoupling would only confirm that avalanche decoupling was the right decision in the first place.

Alternatively, China may respond by flooding global markets with cheap products to counteract the effects of tariffs. China could do this by letting its exchange rate weaken and by expanding subsidies for exporters. Unfortunately for China, a surge of low-cost goods from China would undercut domestic production in countries without protective tariffs—that is, the neutrals. The more egregiously China dumped its products, the more pressure neutrals would face to join the Core allies in imposing their own trade restrictions on China's products. The Core could try to leverage this trend by striking trade deals with key partners such as India, Brazil, Vietnam, and the EU.

It is therefore possible that China would *not* respond to avalanche decoupling with punitive measures. In some scenarios, particularly in a quarantine, China may take a softer approach, betting that it could isolate the United States politically by painting Washington as an agent of instability and chaos. If China wanted to split the U.S.-led coalition, it could use positive economic incentives like trade deals and investments. This approach might work on the European Union—another reason why America cannot base its economic contingency planning on the assumption of unanimous European support. China might also lobby foreign businesses to ask their governments to pause or slow down the ratcheting tariffs.

Enforcement Challenges

As we have seen in Chapter 7, dealing with transshipment is always the hardest part of decoupling. As the Core countries restricted the legal entry of PRC products into their markets, importers would face growing incentives to misrepresent the origin of goods. Even before the Trump administration dialed up tariffs in April 2025, extensive fraud networks for laundering Chinese goods and parts already existed to send PRC goods and parts into the United States.[16] According to some estimates, the value of this trade exceeded $100 billion annually—more than total U.S. imports from Japan or Germany.[17] Arbitrageurs will always try to profit by smuggling products across borders.

Executing avalanche decoupling would therefore require a comprehensive overhaul of customs enforcement and border security in all U.S. trading partners.[18] Decades of agreements aimed at minimizing barriers to trade have hollowed out the customs enterprise, to the point that only a small fraction of goods crossing borders are physically inspected. Predictive analytics and other technologies could reduce the need for inspections, but customs enforcement would still demand substantial increases in funding and staffing. Identifying mislabeled PRC products and components would pose an enormous challenge. The long-term solution would lie partly in renegotiating rules of origin to provide greater transparency in supply-chain pathways. These reforms are overdue anyway.

For the reasons we discussed in Chapter 7, tough enforcement of rules of origin would have political implications. In some cases, they could disrupt supply chains. Some amount of cross-border leakage of PRC goods would also be unavoidable. Perfection is unnecessary to achieve broad decoupling, but a generally effective customs regime would be essential to sustaining decoupling over the medium to long term. The Core would therefore have to incentivize third countries to accurately report when PRC products and components were being transshipped through their markets. This is where the ESCB would play a pivotal role.

Policy 2: The Economic Security Cooperation Board

While the United States could unilaterally trigger avalanche decoupling, ensuring that it serves long-term U.S. interests would require broader actions to sustain a fair and honest trading system. The first step: addressing the immediate global economic crisis, which would probably ripple far beyond Taiwan. The Core would need a vehicle for collective resilience against PRC retaliation. All these goals would involve interaction with neutral states. The ESCB would be where this interaction took place.

The Core allies should ideally establish the ESCB *now*, before a Taiwan crisis occurs—but any crisis would require that it be scaled up as fast as possible. In peacetime, the ESCB would build on measures already taken by the United States to coordinate allied decoupling in critical products. In a crisis situation, the ESCB would need a secretariat (which would grow over time) and a substantial budget. All countries other than rogue states would be invited to join.

Decoupling from China or opposing China's actions against Taiwan would *not* be conditions of membership in the ESCB. Indeed, for non-Core members, ESCB participation would carry no political or financial obligations whatsoever. The ESCB's primary purpose would be to support the global economy through the economic fallout from any Taiwan crisis while managing avalanche decoupling in a way that upholds a fair and honest trading system for the benefit of all. It would use financial incentives to encourage neutral countries to cooperate with the Core during the decoupling process. Politically, the ESCB would allow the Core to frame avalanche decoupling as part of a larger global economic recovery effort.

The inspiration for the ESCB is the Marshall Plan. The ESCB, like the institutions that distributed Marshall aid, would offer financial, material, and technical support to its members. Initially, aid would come with minimal strings attached, to help countries weather the financial shock and maintain political stability. (This would be especially important if China exploited procedural tactics to paralyze the IMF and World Bank during the crisis.) Over time, the ESCB would provide a framework for collective resilience against China's economic coercion. Member states would gain the confidence and capacity to resist China's demands, contingent on the Core allies' willingness to back them. As avalanche decoupling progressed, the ESCB's focus would gradually shift from economic recovery to trade enforcement. Its goal would be to ensure third countries complied with Core countries' trade policies, hold together the broader U.S.-led coalition, and reinforce global economic stability during a new period of economic conflict with China.

As the avalanche gained momentum, the ESCB would become increasingly critical for addressing the leakage problem. In the first months after Day One, the transshipment problem would be relatively minor because U.S. and allied trade barriers on Chinese imports would remain low. However, as trade barriers ratcheted higher, the financial incentives for transshipment would increase. Customs enforcement would grow progressively more challenging. The ESCB's administrative capabilities would accordingly have to scale up. Trade disputes between Core allies and third countries would inevitably arise as firms were caught transshipping goods from China into Core markets. Many countries would find it increasingly difficult to trade with both China and the Core in some complex products. The ESCB would play a pivotal role in supporting these countries and maintaining the integrity of the decoupling process.

The ESCB would serve as an honest broker for supporting and monitoring the customs enterprise. Working with the national governments of member states, it would collect, compile, analyze, and publish data on the global flow of goods and components from nonmembers to ESCB markets. It would have inspectors that it could deploy to investigate disputes. When it identified cases of large-scale transshipment, the ESCB would enable the Core to pressure offending countries to toughen enforcement. If violations persisted, the ESCB could authorize proportionate retaliation. In extreme cases, the ESCB could reach a finding that a member state was completely unwilling or unable to stop functioning as a transshipment point. This could give the Core justification to treat the offending country's exports as a systemic national security threat, whether in a particular product, sector, or overall.[19] In short, while the ESCB's members would hopefully contain most of the global economy, its enforcement efforts would target rogue nonmembers like China, Russia, and Iran.

By establishing the ESCB, the United States would be sending an important signal to other countries and the private sector. To major neutral countries like India, Indonesia, and Brazil, the message would be that decoupling is narrowly focused on China and rogue states, not a guise for indiscriminate U.S. protectionism that could collapse the global trading system. Indeed, Washington's commitment to preserving the system would offer these countries significant opportunities to benefit from cooperation with the Core. As supply chains withdrew from China, countries like India and Brazil could attract investment and expand manufacturing employment. For firms grappling with the challenge of exiting the China market, the ESCB would provide assurance that the trading system would survive, enabling efficient decisions about where to reshore production. In the long run, this would create widespread benefits for shareholders, workers, and consumers.

Thus, the ESCB would begin primarily as a mechanism for distributing aid but would gradually evolve into an institution with a broader structural role in the global economy. It would evolve the system beyond the current gridlock in the WTO and open a pathway for structural reform. The ESCB would establish the principle that states can safeguard their economic security against systemic national security threats. It would ensure that most states could benefit economically from reshoring from China while preserving a fair and honest international trading system and dollar hegemony. Far from replacing or undermining the WTO, the ESCB could enhance its functionality by taking back control over trade with nonmarket economies—economies that never belonged in the system to begin with.

Lessons from the Marshall Plan

The Marshall Plan (1948–1952) illustrates why American aid would be essential for institutionalizing the coalition. Under the Plan, officially known as the European Recovery Program (ERP), the United States transferred

$13.3 billion (around $173 billion in 2023 dollars) to Europe over four years to eighteen European countries. This was equal to less than 3 percent of the recipient countries' combined national income during this period.[20] Even though Washington appropriated less than half of the $29 billion that the Europeans had requested, the Plan still succeeded in its objectives.

The economic logic of the Marshall Plan was that it encouraged the transition from wartime to peacetime economic structures that would sustain the capitalist economic system in Western Europe. During wartime, Western European governments had taken control of industrial production and resource allocation. Marshall funding and technical support gave Europeans the confidence to dismantle these wartime controls and re-liberalize their economies. Marshall aid was more than a handout. It was backed with administrative capacity, technical support, and a coherent agenda for encouraging European market integration. The Economic Cooperation Administration (ECA), which Congress established to administer the Plan, was a fully U.S.-run agency that had broad discretion to deploy Marshall funds, as well as "matching funds" that European states provided themselves. By combining technical assistance with aid, the ECA established functional partnerships with governments, industry, and labor groups.[21]

The ECA had such an outsized influence on a limited budget because it let recipient countries choose how to spend the money. For example, France used Marshall funds to buy machinery and raw materials.[22] In addition, the ECA allowed France to maintain many state controls on production, knowing that it was charting its own course within the Western coalition. France, Germany, and Italy all imposed tight national controls on agriculture that contradicted Marshall's free-trade goals. Britain used most of its Marshall funding to pay down debt. "It was undesirable," the UK Cabinet Economic Policy Committee noted in January 1948, "that any opening should be given for excessive interference by United States representatives in our domestic affairs."[23] The ECA exercised restraint in criticizing the Europeans for these actions. Washington was playing a longer game.

Instead of demanding specific and controversial changes to European countries' domestic economic structures, the Marshall Plan emphasized practical cooperation in areas like customs enforcement. The Customs Cooperation Council (CCC), established in 1950, aimed to encourage "the highest degree of harmony and uniformity in their Customs systems and especially to study the problems inherent in the development and improvement of Customs technique and Customs legislation."[24] In 1994, the CCC changed its name to the World Customs Organisation. It is still operating today.[25]

Of course, Washington's ulterior motive was to rebuild Western Europe into a U.S.-aligned bloc opposed to Soviet influence.[26] Moscow recognized this intent, which is why it forced the Eastern Bloc countries to reject U.S. support. In China today, schoolchildren are taught that the Marshall Plan is the paradigmatic success story of American capitalist imperialism.[27] These interpretations are partially correct, but the Marshall Plan was far from imperialist. For the United States, the Marshall Plan was an expression of hard-nosed self-interest, even though Washington never pitched the Plan to its allies as a geopolitical scheme or demanded that countries choose sides. America offered aid to former Axis countries like Austria that remained neutral in the emerging Cold War, and even to Warsaw Pact countries. This decision was far-sighted. It prevented key neutral countries such as Austria from falling under Soviet influence at a time when Communist parties were on the rise, and forced the Soviet Union to expose the fact that it was offering a rotten, coercive deal to its partners. From beginning to end, the explicit purpose of the Marshall Plan was to drive European economic recovery. Punishing the USSR and defeating Communism were beneficial effects and central to the logic, which is why the Plan got enough Republican votes to pass. But these goals were always implicit.

Following a Taiwan crisis, the United States would adopt different policies, but it would need to maintain a similarly long-term perspective that saw economics as part of a broader political strategy. Unlike the situation that existed after World War II, it would not face the task of rebuilding an entire war-torn continent. Core allies could share some of the financial burden. However, China's wealth today far exceeds that of the Soviet Union in 1945, giving Beijing the capacity to engage in competitive aid distribution if it chooses, and the neutrals would be more numerous and collectively more influential than in 1945. America's long-term goal should be to keep as much of the global economy as possible within a fair and honest trading system anchored by the dollar. It should therefore frame its efforts not as "sanctions" or "economic warfare," but as economic leadership and reconstruction. As George Marshall put it, the objective should be both political and economic: to restore "the confidence of people in the economic future of their own countries and of the [global] economy as a whole."[28]

Budget and Mandates

The size of the ESCB budget would ultimately depend on how much the Core countries were willing to contribute. There is no minimum funding level below which the ESCB would fail entirely. However, the more financing it had at its disposal, the easier it would be to sustain the global economy and hold together a broad-based community of states to cooperate with the United States during avalanche decoupling. A larger, more stable budget would enable the ESCB to offer stronger incentives to third countries to support Core trade policies and resolve disputes within a fair and transparent framework. Conversely, limited or unstable funding would likely see higher levels of transshipment and closer collaboration between China and key neutral states. Since the purpose of the ESCB is to build direct, political support for the new settlement, aid should be transmitted through the national governments of member states, not directly from the ESCB to businesses or multilateral or supranational institutions. The scale of emergency funding required at the very outset of a crisis would also vary, depending on the context of the Taiwan crisis and China's ability and willingness to offer competing aid. However, the *formula* for determining the distribution of aid should be negotiated in advance, by countries that are willing to pre-commit to participation. The formula might include metrics such as GDP per capita, population, state capacity, and geographic proximity to and scale of trade with China and Russia. Countries closer to China would be more vulnerable in a crisis and might therefore require more support.

The ESCB's first mandate would be emergency aid distribution. In the immediate aftermath of Day One, the Board would provide unconditional support to all members, allowing them to use aid as they see fit—for infrastructure, education, health care, or other priorities. The purpose of this aid would be to create a stable financial and political environment for private firms to begin relocating supply chains out of China. Additional aid would go to states facing PRC coercion or those states needing resources to improve customs enforcement due to geography, poverty, or other challenges. Conversely, states found transshipping PRC goods in large quantities without addressing the issue would quickly be cut off from aid. Inspired by the Marshall Plan, the Board would distribute aid in tranches to member states, with disbursements guided by consultations between recipient governments and Board advisors.[29] Before releasing each subsequent tranche, Board administrators would evaluate the country's use of the aid, its adherence to WTO rules, and its efforts to prevent transshipment.

The ESCB's second mandate would focus on supporting the enforcement of member states' trade policies toward nonmembers. The Board would manage disputes arising when Core countries accused other members of facilitating illegal transshipment of PRC goods. Its role would be administrative, not legal. It would be aimed at resolving such disputes while avoiding broader involvement in member-state conflicts. The Board would prioritize generating detailed, transparent data on trade flows between members and nonmembers, particularly China. By collaborating with customs authorities and publishing exhaustive trade data, it would ensure accountability and, if necessary, would assist in arbitrating disputes about the origins of products or components.[30]

If the ESCB Secretariat found that a member state was consistently transshipping PRC goods into the Core market, it would first offer help to improve customs enforcement. If the problem persisted, the ESCB could take two steps. First, it could withhold aid until the country showed progress. Second, its governing body could rule that the state had systematically violated rules of origin without making reasonable efforts to comply. Since the Core had declared trade with China a systemic national security threat, this finding would justify discriminatory trade measures against the transshipping country in the name of national security.

The United States, as the Board's largest donor, would have significant influence, but the organization's operational independence would give its decisions greater legitimacy. The ESCB would thus integrate the enforcement of discriminatory trade policy into a broader framework. It would establish a norm that the United States would apply its trade policies fairly, avoiding their misuse as leverage on unrelated issues. The Board would also safeguard norms governing the use of the national security exemption, maintaining market confidence in the survival and growth of a fair and honest trading system after Day One. Its design reflects the historical lesson that withholding aid is often a more effective tool of statecraft than imposing sanctions.[31]

Beyond the cash on the table, non-Core states would have another compelling reason to join the ESCB and support the Core allies' anti-China trade policy: they would need to retain access to Core markets. Together, the Core allies (the United States, Canada, Australia, UK, and Japan) account for 40 percent of global consumption, compared to China's 15 percent. Their consumption is poised for future growth, whereas China's consumption is stagnant. Most importantly, the Core markets collectively run a large trade deficit, whereas China runs large structural trade surpluses. For industrializing countries like Indonesia and Brazil, losing access to Core markets would be an unmitigated disaster. The alternative would be to become a deindustrialized dumping ground for cheap PRC goods. In contrast, joining the ESCB would allow countries like Indonesia and Brazil to compete for over $1 trillion in annual Western consumer demand as this production moves out of China. It would be a path to development for countries around the world that have lost the opportunity as a result of China's predatory economic model. Small states would also likely find the promise of collective insurance against PRC economic retaliation to be appealing.

Establishing Structure and Membership

The ESCB would be operationally independent of the United States but substantially influenced by it. It would *not* have legal jurisdiction over the United States or any other country. Unlike the WTO, it would *not* have an arbitral tribunal that could make binding judgments. Membership would theoretically be open to any country not deemed a systemic security threat by the United States. The Core countries could set more specific rules for accession, but the basic principle would be to start with the broadest possible membership and maintain it over time.

Key aspects of the ESCB's structure and authorities would have to emerge through negotiation. One potential model is the International Monetary Fund (IMF), whose member states receive voting shares proportional to their financial contributions. Given that Core allies would likely provide the bulk of the ESCB's funding, countries committed to decoupling would dominate decision making. As in the IMF, key voting thresholds could give the United States a de facto veto over major decisions. Non-U.S. Core allies could gain influence by making comparable contributions. This point is particularly relevant for the European Union, for reasons discussed below. Other voting frameworks might also be considered.

Several critical questions would need resolution in the ESCB's Articles of Agreement. These include how much autonomy ESCB staff would have in investigating trade disputes and publishing findings, what process would exist for staffing and leadership selection, how data would be controlled, and so forth. The United States would likely favor a structure maximizing its control over finances and administration. Core allies would seek safeguards to ensure the United States could not unilaterally halt the ESCB's functions once avalanche decoupling began. They would also want assurances against non-Core countries gaining control in the future. Non-Core members would require credible guarantees that the ESCB would not punish states simply for trading with China. Ultimately, any architecture for a new international trading system without China would require compromises from all sides. The most sensible approach is to develop an initial framework in advance, to ensure that crisis response could be swift and decisive. Following the founding principles, details could be negotiated later, in the period immediately after any crisis. The ESCB would succeed only if it could foster broad confidence in its impartiality and effectiveness.

A key question is what role EU member states and the EU itself would play in the ESCB. Precisely because it is unlikely that the EU would fully join the Core, Europeans would be incentivized to join the ESCB to secure their ability to trade with both China and the Core countries. Since Europe has a common market, it would need to determine whether membership in the ESCB would be led by Brussels or whether individual states would need to join independently. In any case, a Taiwan crisis that resulted in broad decoupling would introduce trade disputes between the Core allies and the EU. In this crisis context, both sides would share an interest in preventing a structural breakdown in transatlantic trade relations.

Given the political challenge of designing a new multilateral institution from scratch, the United States should begin consulting with key stakeholders well in advance of a crisis. States interested in participating in these dialogues can weigh in on foundational issues. Central bankers, international economists, trade lawyers, historians, and elected officials should be involved. Beijing should be made aware of the negotiations, but their substance can remain confidential. Public statements should focus on emphasizing consensus around guiding principles.

No matter how the ESCB is designed and scoped, scaling up such an organization from nothing would take years and require tackling many difficult challenges. Setting aside questions of funding, staffing such an organization would not be easy. Officials might need to be poached from member states' governments or the private sector. Ensuring accountability and efficient operations would be another challenge. The ESCB's most important task would be to help countries modernize their customs regimes. Developing countries with weak state capacity and land borders with

China or Russia would struggle the most, since significant quantities of goods might be smuggled past customs inspectors. Some of these countries might eventually be forced out of the ESCB and lose access to the Core market—not for lack of willingness, but because their capacity challenges prove insurmountable. Over time, such nations could become de facto members of China's trading bloc. Despite these difficulties, the ESCB's architects should aim to build the broadest possible coalition.

Collective Resilience against PRC Countermeasures

Recognizing the threat to its interests if the ESCB succeeded, the PRC would likely use every tool at its disposal to pressure neutral countries not to join. China might offer aid, debt relief, market access, discounted goods, or even arms deals.

More ominously, China could escalate to economic warfare. Under its 2021 Anti-Foreign Sanctions Law, Beijing could freeze or seize foreign assets within its jurisdiction or prevent foreign investors from liquidating their holdings, as Russia did in 2022.[32] However, such drastic measures would likely follow only if G7 countries froze PRC assets first, as China's $2.8 trillion net foreign asset position gives it more to lose in a competitive asset freeze scenario.[33] China could also restrict exports of strategic goods, a tactic it has used before. As we have seen, China is building the legal basis for a sweeping export control regime, building on its successful weaponization of critical minerals and drone parts.[34] These restrictions would cause shortages, price spikes, and significant political fallout. The ESCB could play a vital role in coordinating a response to PRC economic warfare. Without such trust, member states might turn inwards, undermining the fair and honest trading system the ESCB is designed to protect.

Fortunately, export controls are a blunt instrument, and their indiscriminate use may undermine China's strategic goals. Aggressive export controls could accelerate avalanche decoupling as foreign firms lose trust in China's supply chains and rush to reshore production. The United States and Core allies could highlight China's arbitrary and damaging actions in contrast with their own aid and support programs. Markets would also adapt over time. While rationing might be necessary in the short term, private industry would work to develop substitutes, technological solutions, and alternative sources of supply.[35] In the medium to long term, Beijing's economic leverage would diminish. China appears to understand this risk.[36]

Import restrictions would probably be China's most effective economic tool for splitting the U.S.-led coalition and undermining the ESCB. Beijing has a history of using import restrictions for geopolitical coercion. It often disguises them as technical customs-related measures or "grassroots" boycotts.[37] Countries targeted by such restrictions could face severe economic consequences. Many commodity exporters depend heavily on China for tourism, debt financing, or other economic ties.[38] Exporters of finished goods like South Korea, Japan, and northern European countries also need China's market. U.S. backing would likely be essential for stiffening these countries' spines to resist China's retaliation. The good news is that China's import restrictions have backfired in the past when used against South Korea, Taiwan, Australia, and the Philippines. In 2015, only 37 percent of South Koreans held a negative view of China. By 2017, after Beijing used import restrictions against South Korea, that number had climbed to 61 percent, and it has continued to rise.[39]

China could also procedurally undermine the IMF and World Bank to undermine the United States' ability to provide crisis response. Whether or not the Day One plan is adopted, a Taiwan crisis might render IMF emergency lending unviable. The ESCB could offer an alternative mechanism for providing emergency loans, though this would require expanding its mandate beyond what is discussed here. In a worst-case scenario, the United States might need to step in directly, offering bilateral dollar loans to support important countries on the verge of capitulating to China's coercion.

To conclude, China's responses to the formation of the ESCB, as a large and resourceful country, could pose significant challenges—yet all economic warfare tools China might deploy reinforce the case for the ESCB. The greater the economic disruption caused by PRC retaliation, and the more evident China's disregard for international trade rules and norms, the stronger the incentive for smaller countries to seek protection through ESCB membership.

Partial Avalanche Decoupling

Partial avalanche decoupling could serve as a pre-crisis strategy for Core allies to test and refine the mechanism in targeted critical products or sectors, as well as demonstrating the credibility of the deterrent threat to China. Discussions are already ongoing among allied governments and may yield public agreements by the time this book appears in print. For instance, the United States and its allies might initiate avalanche decoupling on specific pharmaceutical imports from China while establishing a "Healthcare Security Cooperation Board" to support production and enforce rules of origin. Quotas wouldn't need to reach zero during peacetime; even a partial decoupling would be an important proof of concept. Although creating an ESCB-like structure for a single sector might be politically challenging outside a crisis, a scaled-down version focused on a few critical supply chains could still prove valuable. It would help identify and address gaps in existing enforcement infrastructure. It would also lay the political and institutional groundwork for a bigger and more robust ESCB if needed later.

Partial decoupling could also be the U.S. and allied crisis response to PRC aggression, if consensus for full decoupling is politically unattainable. Several factors could hinder consensus. U.S. consumers might resist paying higher prices for lower-quality goods. Congress could balk at funding the ESCB. The Core might not be prepared to deny market access to noncompliant third countries. Exporters of noncritical goods might argue that trade restrictions unfairly deny them market access without sufficient national security justification. Core allies might not offer full-scale cooperation. In these scenarios, the president may be advised to begin the avalanche in key sectors—for example, more advanced manufacturing—while retaining the option to escalate to broad-based decoupling. This approach would allow the United States to maintain escalation dominance during a crisis in the gray zone.

While full decoupling would be strategically optimal in most crisis scenarios, any serious contingency plan needs a flexible mechanism for decoupling and a resolute focus on border security and rules of origin. The more accurate the trade data, the more effectively the avalanche mechanism can be calibrated down to the level of specific products and sectors. As a result, setting up a minimum viable ESCB is in some ways *more* important in a partial decoupling scenario. If political factors foreclose a robust economic response, having an adaptable mechanism that allows for political horse-trading would make it much easier for the Core allies to align policy. Partial decoupling would still achieve key U.S. objectives in a crisis: sustaining the coalition, limiting vulnerability to PRC economic coercion, preserving the trading system, and punishing China by clawing back manufacturing jobs.

Imagining a World after Avalanche Decoupling

Full decoupling by the Core countries would not exclude China from the global economy. China could continue trading with neutral countries, including non-Core ESCB members in good standing. China would therefore avoid the severe economic isolation threatened against Japan and Germany in the 1930s. Additionally, Congress could design the avalanche mechanism so that the ratcheting trade policy could be paused or even reversed if China changed its behavior. To regain access to Core markets, China would need to provide credible assurances that it no longer posed a systemic security threat. Keeping the door open to potential future economic reintegration could provide strategic leverage, even as avalanche decoupling proceeded. However, after a major geopolitical rupture, the United States would want to approach any economic reintegration from a dominant position.

A critical question is how the Core can deter China from acting like a rogue state during and after avalanche decoupling. Since 2014, Western efforts to marginalize and economically punish Russia have inadvertently lowered the costs of its rogue behavior. From chemical weapon attacks in English cities to incendiary devices in DHL shipments and nuclear provocations with potential implications in outer space, Russia has exploited its pariah status, knowing that adversaries are running out of options for further punishment.[40] China today is more cautious, but it is also learning lessons from the Russia playbook. For example, credible reports suggest that China-flagged ships deliberately severed undersea cables in the Baltic Sea in December 2024.[41] In worst-case scenarios after a Taiwan rupture, China might escalate to catastrophic actions, targeting vulnerable nodes of the global commons, such as satellites, undersea cables, cyberattacks on financial infrastructure, pipelines, or datacenters. These risks underline the importance of designing a deterrence framework that can counter such extreme behavior *in the context* of avalanche decoupling.

Although this point warrants further study and debate, a global economic order where the United States and China continue trading with the neutral community—but not with each other—might be the most stable arrangement under the circumstances. Neutral countries hold leverage during great power economic conflicts because both adversaries rely on their cooperation. In a post–Day One world shaped by avalanche decoupling, China would be more dependent on neutral markets to absorb its excess production. While neutral countries would have diverse interests, they would share an interest in maintaining a functional trading system that allows them to trade with both sides. They would also strongly oppose acts of terrorism targeting the global commons and might unite to impose costs on either power that violated these shared interests. The same logic would apply to the United States, which would be relying heavily on imports from the neutral community to limit the inflationary effect of decoupling.

Because both the United States and China would depend on neutral trade, the neutral community would gain economic leverage to discourage conflict that disrupts global trade. The ESCB framework would enhance coordination between the Core countries and the neutral community, fostering a more stable global economic system.

Thus, in a hypothetical post-avalanche world, China could still incur significant costs for acting like a rogue state—but only if much of China's foreign trade remained dependent on central nodes that the United States controlled and neutral countries relied upon. During and after avalanche decoupling, the United States would need to present itself as a responsible steward of these critical nodes. It would need to build trust with third countries and reinforce the costs China would face if it attacked them. Shared dependence on these nodes would foster a form of what we might call "community deterrence."

Since expelling China from the dollar system outright would be neither realistic nor prudent, as discussed in Chapter 7, U.S. policy should seek to *lock China inside the dollar system while avalanche decoupling proceeds*. This approach would minimize the ability of rogue states to violate existing sanctions and export controls. Meanwhile, locking China into the dollar system would degrade its terms of trade and erode its long-run competitiveness, undermining its internal social stability. Keeping China inside the dollar system would require not pushing other countries off the dollar system. It would mean refraining from sanctions against China's trade in noncritical goods. In multiple ways, successful avalanche decoupling requires restraint in the use of sanctions on China.

But if sanctions threats were largely taken off the table, how could the United States use economic threats to deter China from further bad behavior after avalanche decoupling began, should community deterrence prove insufficient? This is a crucial question.

One way to maintain strategic deterrence in a post–Day One world would be to threaten to intervene in global currency markets to attack China's currencies: the CNY (Chinese Yuan) and HKD (Hong Kong dollar). Such an operation would be operationally complex and involve enormous risks to both sides. It would not be viable outside the context of avalanche decoupling and may not even be advisable within it. Still, the threat would be to deal a severe short-term blow to China's financial stability and commit the United States to destroying China's terms of trade over the long term. A currency intervention would be executed by the Treasury, with authorization from Congress. The details of how it would work, how it would achieve its strategic goals, and how it would manage Beijing's retaliatory tactics are technical. Interested readers can consult Appendix B for more detail. If successful, the proposed operation would force Beijing to expend a large amount of its foreign currency reserves to stave off a crisis, while making a profit for the U.S. taxpayer.

The threat, in essence, would be to leverage global financial markets to join the U.S. Treasury in breaking China's currency system. If the Treasury actually executed the operation, and did so with credibly communicated resolve, private market participants might effectively leverage the U.S. Treasury's short trade. This would multiply the amount of foreign currency that China would have to spend to defend its exchange rate and prevent a systemic financial crisis. Washington cannot guarantee these favorable effects, but by signaling its resolve in advance, it could potentially make these effects more likely.

The current uncertainty over the future of the dollar would make any currency intervention existentially risky for the United States. However, if China had already moved against Taiwan and production was already visibly moving out of China, the situation would be fundamentally different from the peacetime situation today. It is only the unique character of the crisis context that would make such a threat credible.

Although this proposal may seem radical, the United States has long used currency markets as a foreign policy tool. A notable example is the Suez Crisis of 1956, when the pound sterling, pegged to the dollar under the Bretton Woods system, depreciated as the UK's position in Egypt faltered.[42] Hoping for emergency support, Chancellor of the Exchequer Harold Macmillan turned to the United States or the IMF. However, Washington opposed the UK's aggression against Egypt. Instead of supporting sterling, Treasury Secretary George Humphrey directed the Federal Reserve Bank of New York to sell its sterling holdings. The reason was ostensibly to protect U.S. reserves, but in practice this move massively increased the downward pressure on the sterling exchange rate.[43] Macmillan accused Washington of "viciously orchestrating" sterling's depreciation, and the United States vetoed IMF support unless the UK accepted a UN resolution demanding withdrawal from Suez.[44] With 15 percent of its foreign currency reserves depleted and under pressure from financial markets, Soviet opposition, and domestic divisions, London ultimately backed down.[45] "This was blackmail," said senior Conservative politician R. A. Butler, "but we were in no position to argue." A currency intervention against the RMB might not prompt such a dramatic policy shift in Beijing, but the underlying principle remains the same.

The key difference from the Suez case is that attacking China's currency would require sustained, indefinite intervention. A one-time U.S. financial operation would have little long-term impact on China's economy. While exchange rates fluctuate, currencies retain a fundamental value tied to the demand for the goods and services produced in the issuing country. As long as global consumers value PRC products, the CNY will maintain a fundamental value. To prevent the exchange rate from rebounding after an initial shock, the U.S. Treasury would need to continue intervening in markets indefinitely— a potentially costly endeavor that would have to survive several presidential administrations and election cycles. To offset these expenses and minimize the risk of financial losses, Washington would need a credible strategy for achieving broad economic decoupling over time, eroding the fundamental value of the CNY by ruining China's terms of trade. China would be paying for its imports denominated in dollars with a debased currency, but China's largest overseas markets would be steadily closing their doors to China's exports.

Thus, avalanche decoupling is a necessary precondition for currency intervention. If Washington successfully carried out the operation, U.S. taxpayers might ultimately profit significantly at China's expense. However, failing to follow through on avalanche decoupling could turn the intervention into an unlimited financial liability, potentially undermining the full faith and credit of the U.S. government. Currency intervention would not function as a standalone tool for punishing China economically. In essence, executing such an intervention would commit the United States fully to making avalanche decoupling permanent and inflicting severe damage on China's economy. As a result, the threat of currency intervention might serve as a powerful form of strategic deterrence.

Unlike EMAD, which poses a binary choice between peace and mutual destruction, currency intervention would be entirely zero-sum. The threat, in essence, would be that if China crosses further U.S. red lines while avalanche decoupling is proceeding, Washington will force an economic fight to the death.

Conclusion

After the Cold War, the United States and its allies, aiming to create integrated global markets, chose to incorporate Russia and China into the international economic system. This decision was a calculated gamble that trade and engagement could transform former rivals into responsible stakeholders that would resolve disputes through negotiation rather than violence. Vladimir Putin's full-scale invasion of Ukraine demonstrated that this bet had failed with Russia, but the bet has not entirely failed with China. While China's WTO accession caused significant economic shocks that were not fully addressed at the time, trade with China continues to provide many benefits. China provides affordable goods for American consumers, helps to hold down inflation, and supports U.S. employment by offering a large market for American technology, products, and services. Close U.S. allies have reaped even greater benefits from trade with China. China's repeated violations of WTO rules, its erosion of international norms, and its ambitions to coopt or replace key multilateral institutions cannot be ignored. But these malign activities demand responses within the framework of the current trading system.

If China were to use force against Taiwan, the situation would change fundamentally. Washington would need to reassess whether it could coexist within the system with a powerful and sophisticated rogue state that the system was not designed to handle. Because hard decoupling is unrealistic in most foreseeable crisis scenarios, the Core allies need a credible plan for breaking their dependence on China for critical goods as fast as possible, and breaking all other forms of economic dependence later, as necessary.

The feasibility of executing any economic contingency plan depends on whether the United States has the strategic interest, political will, and capability to act when the moment arises. None of the steps discussed in this chapter would be plausible except under extraordinary political and geopolitical circumstances. Establishing the ESCB would demand bipartisan support in the U.S. Senate and significant, ongoing financial commitments from the United States and its Core allies, in a marked break from policy norms over the last several decades of peacetime. It is, to put it mildly, a big deal. A shift in U.S. political priorities could jeopardize the entire endeavor, since the ESCB's success would require sustained multilateral coordination long after the acute phase of a Taiwan crisis ended.

Given these uncertainties, any crisis economic contingency plan must be based on a flexible mechanism rather than a rigid blueprint. The United States and its allies cannot safely assume that any particular countries will join the Core coalition or that U.S. policymakers will pursue total decoupling. This makes it critical for the avalanche decoupling mechanism to function at any scale, from sectoral or product-level decoupling to full decoupling, and to operate at varying speeds.

Despite the challenges of implementation, it is strategically and politically advantageous for the U.S. government and its allies and partners to develop plans for avalanche decoupling publicly and in advance. Such planning would demonstrate Washington's ability to respond flexibly and decisively if China crosses its red lines in the gray zone, ensure that economic factors strengthen rather than weaken its political deterrent, and hold Xi Jinping's economic and political interests at risk.

Avalanche decoupling provides a flexible framework for addressing gray-zone aggression that crosses U.S. red lines. It shows that a calibrated economic response is possible, proportional to the severity of China's actions. By allowing decoupling to proceed at the sectoral or product level, the plan offers a way to target critical vulnerabilities without causing immediate and unnecessary disruption to the broader global economy. This adaptability ensures that the United States and its allies can respond decisively to provocations such as blockades or coercive actions against Taiwan without overcommitting resources or alienating neutral countries. Importantly, the plan creates a credible deterrent by demonstrating that the Core allies can quickly escalate decoupling if China crosses additional red lines, giving Beijing clear incentives to moderate its behavior.

The plan also strengthens political deterrence by fostering collaboration among Core allies and building bridges with neutral countries. The ESCB would position the United States as a leader of global economic recovery, providing a mechanism for cooperation that prioritizes the stability of the global trading system. This approach reduces the risk of U.S. isolation by ensuring that the Core allies remain united in their commitment to a collective economic response. Additionally, the plan reassures neutral countries that their interests will be safeguarded. It offers them a path to benefit from the reshoring of supply chains and a buffer against economic coercion. By presenting a credible, inclusive alternative to hard decoupling, the plan makes it harder for China to exploit divisions within the international community.

Finally, avalanche decoupling directly threatens China with economic and political punishment that strikes at the foundations of CCP legitimacy and Xi Jinping's political vision. Xi's vision for national rejuvenation requires not only China's continued economic development, but also China's growing stature in the global economy and global governance. Avalanche decoupling targets China's Achilles' heel: its dependence on export manufacturing to maintain employment and social stability. By denying China access to Core markets and exacerbating China's growing trade frictions with developing countries, avalanche decoupling would erode China's terms of trade over the longer term, undermining China's economic strength and social cohesion. It would also shift the center of international governance away from the old multilateral institutions that China has spent the last thirty years entrenching itself inside. These pressures would work slowly. They would not force China's capitulation on a timescale of months to a few years. But they would set China on a course of permanently diminishing influence in the global economy. Meanwhile, they would ensure that China faced credible threats of additional punishment if it lashed out against third countries or acted as a terrorist in the global commons.

Given the American public's reluctance to commit to direct military intervention in Taiwan's defense, the Day One plan provides a comprehensive strategy that leverages U.S. diplomatic, economic, and technological strengths to deter aggression without relying solely on military force. Developing the Day One plan strengthens U.S. integrated deterrence by forcing China to confront the risks of aggression. Even if Beijing doubts Washington's ability to fully execute the plan in a quarantine scenario, it cannot be certain about this assessment. By outlining a framework for gradual, orderly decoupling, the plan forces China to reckon with the long-term costs of overturning regional peace and stability. It undermines Xi's confidence in China's ability to outlast U.S. resolve or weather a financial crisis triggered by a Day One scenario. Crucially, the Day One plan is the only economic strategy yet devised that sets out how China could face indefinitely escalating economic pain if it moved against Taiwan—regardless of the military outcome.

Conclusion
Living History

In November 2023, I visited Beijing, perhaps for the last time. China's Ministry of Foreign Affairs, apparently unaware that I was working on this book, had invited me and seven other American scholars and policy thinkers to attend a dialogue on the state of U.S.–China relations. On my final morning I took the subway to Tiananmen Square, which was somber and orderly as ever in the crisp autumn air. The National Museum of China, which stands opposite the Great Hall of the People, houses a vast collection with exhibits spanning China's paleolithic origins to Xi Jinping's "New Era." Under different circumstances, I might have spent days exploring the collections. But since time was short, I went directly to the museum's centerpiece: *Road to Rejuvenation*, a vast exhibit that tracks the story of the CCP's rise and rule.

Road to Rejuvenation is history as the Party wishes to tell it. It begins with China's "century of humiliation," turns a corner in 1949 with the CCP takeover, and crescendos in a triumphalist vision of Xi's leadership. In 2012, just weeks after being elevated to general secretary, Xi brought the Politburo Standing Committee here. Standing in one of the exhibits, he spoke of the new chapter they would write together. "Achieving the rejuvenation of the Chinese nation has been the greatest dream of the Chinese people since the advent of modern times," he declared. "The goal of building China into a modern socialist country that is prosperous, strong, democratic, culturally advanced and harmonious can be achieved by 2049 . . . and the dream of the rejuvenation of the Chinese nation will then be realized."[1] It remains the most-quoted speech Xi has ever given. In 2018, Xi expanded *Road to Rejuvenation* to include a glitzy new annex devoted entirely to celebrating his achievements in the so-called New Era.

While other exhibits were packed with visitors from across China, *Road to Rejuvenation* was quiet, and Xi's annex was deserted. The silence was striking. The meticulously curated exhibit on the dear leader seemed to hold little allure compared to the Han vases, Yuan coins, and Qing porcelains downstairs. Maybe my fellow museum-goers had heard the CCP's origin story too many times before. Or maybe they knew that even the Party itself can't fully commit to a consistent version of events. *Road to Rejuvenation* frequently closes for "renovations," a euphemism for revisions that undermine its claim to objectivity.

Taiwan, so central to Xi's story of national rejuvenation, is conspicuously absent from the exhibit. The only significant mention of Taiwan appears in the Deng Xiaoping room, where a series of large wall photos depict a revisionist history of the Hong Kong handover. While there are no labels to spell out the story, the subtext is clear enough: Deng proposing "One Country, Two Systems," the PLA conducting military exercises and testing enormous missiles, and British Prime Minister Margaret Thatcher signing the Joint Declaration to formalize Hong Kong's imminent return to Chinese rule, seemingly under duress. Beneath these images is a 1981 copy of the *People's Daily*, the party mouthpiece, with a headline reading: "A Message to Our Compatriots on Taiwan." The threat is unmistakable: that China will one day become militarily powerful enough to coerce Taiwan's foreign supporters to stand out of the way while "reunification" is achieved. But the fact that this threat is communicated in a veiled way and is buried in a part of the exhibit dedicated to Xi's deceased predecessor speaks to the CCP's fundamental problem. There is no way to achieve "reunification" with Taiwan—the keystone in the arch of national rejuvenation—without jeopardizing the Party's broader ambitions. The lack of mention of Taiwan also says something profound about Xi's effort to write his own history in real time. For all of Xi's bluster, he has not left any empty space in his own annex where "reunification" will one day be commemorated.

What *Road to Rejuvenation* does capture persuasively is the staggering scope of Xi's ambition. Dioramas of missiles, tanks, and aircraft carriers celebrate China's military advancements. Displays of surveillance cameras, offshore drilling platforms, and semiconductor factories depict a CCP striving for comprehensive modernization and control. The Party's insistence on pursuing all of its goals "comprehensively" makes it a formidable strategic competitor. It warns that the CCP will deploy every tool at its disposal—military, economic, political, and strategic—to pursue "reunification." But ambition is a double-edged sword. Xi knows that if he rolls the iron dice, he will put his entire rejuvenation project in jeopardy.

To deter Xi, the United States needs its own integrated strategy that draws on every source of national power to preserve the peace. While hard power is fundamental, this book has argued that America also needs a compelling and credible story to tell to the American people, its allies, and Xi himself. Much of Xi's vision for national rejuvenation is compatible with U.S. interests. America in principle has no problem with a strong, proud, and wealthy China. Yet any violent attempt to seize Taiwan or act against a U.S. treaty ally would cross a line, and may force America to take actions that would irreparably shatter Xi's legacy. Xi may already know this. He has shown restraint during his time in power, proving in the process that he can live with the status quo. Washington must convince Xi that the dream lives on, but that patience is the surest path to achieve it. This is the way to keep him in check—one day at a time.

We began this book by evaluating Xi's strategy. For the CCP, Taiwan is an age-old issue of regime legitimacy. Taiwan proves that a society whose majority is people of Chinese heritage, people with a shared colonial history, can embrace democracy, human rights, and individual liberty while achieving prosperity and transitioning peacefully from autocracy to democracy. It therefore offers an alternative vision of what a future Mainland China could become, which the CCP correctly finds extremely threatening. Xi seems to see additional personal interests at stake in Taiwan. He seems to view Taiwan as central to the ultimate completion of his national rejuvenation project and as a focal point in the broader U.S.–China rivalry. Xi's predecessors knew they could not take Taiwan by force, so they settled for blocking its formal independence and gradually trying to steer it toward "peaceful reunification." Xi clearly perceives more urgency.

While it is impossible to know Xi's true thinking, he likely has both offensive and defensive motivations. On the one hand, seizing the prize would cement his legacy and secure his personal security in retirement. On the other hand, his numerous comments on the matter may not be bluffs: he may believe that Washington is supporting Taiwanese "separatists" because, fundamentally, America cannot tolerate China's national rejuvenation. Achieving the capability to seize Taiwan by force, which Xi has tasked the People's Liberation Army with achieving by 2027, is therefore only an intermediate step in an ongoing series of milestones. His grand strategic project is ultimately about much more than Taiwan. It is about compelling America to stand aside while China completes its national rejuvenation and becomes a superpower in its own right, if not the leading power in the world.

Xi's strategy threatens several vital U.S. interests. Taiwan occupies a critical geographic position in the region, it plays a key role in the global high-tech economy, and it has become the single most important litmus test of U.S. resolve to uphold a free and open Indo-Pacific. A forceful takeover of Taiwan could open Pandora's box. It would embolden adversaries like Russia, North Korea, and Iran, destabilize and potentially break the international economic system that underpins American prosperity and geopolitical power, and hollow out key U.S. alliances globally. Of course, American policy toward Taiwan must take heed of the message the American people have sent in the last several presidential elections. No one wants to be dragged into foreign wars. Few Americans believe that Taiwan's democracy is a cause worth potentially sacrificing thousands of American lives to defend. There are widespread misperceptions about America's readiness to fight and win a war, if one broke out in the near future. However, the need to defend Taiwan is not just a matter of principle; it is a matter of U.S. national interests and the defense of the homeland. Simply abandoning Taiwan is not an option. America needs both a strategy to deter Xi from aggressing and a contingency plan to secure its interests should deterrence fail.

For now, the struggle for Taiwan's future is playing out in the "gray zone," where China is using aggressive pressure tactics to advance its aims in every domain. Beijing is seeking to undermine Taiwan's institutions, demoralize its population, disrupt its economic ties, and weaken the credibility of U.S. security assurances. Xi's public statements—and, indeed, the implicit narrative in his cherished *Road to Rejuvenation* exhibit—indicate that Plan A is to keep incrementally redefining the status quo while deterring decisive U.S. intervention. Two gray-zone crisis scenarios are particularly concerning. The first is a quarantine, distinct from a blockade, which would gradually restrict Taiwan's access to goods and people under the guise of routine law enforcement actions. The second involves military brinkmanship. In both scenarios, Xi would be leveraging the ambiguity of U.S. red lines to push the burden of escalation onto Washington. As long as Washington lacks a coherent strategy to deter such moves, Xi will keep doubling down on this relatively low-risk, high-reward strategy. He will also be incentivized to create brinkmanship crises to test U.S. and Taiwanese resolve. These crises could come on suddenly and escalate quickly. Like the crises over Berlin and Cuba in the Cold War, they would be shaped by explicit and implicit nuclear threats.

Xi's fallback plan is an amphibious invasion of Taiwan. An invasion would rank among the most complex military operations in modern history, requiring the PLA to dominate the air, sea, cyber, and land domains while overcoming Taiwan's adaptive defenses. Success would require precise joint integration, robust logistics, and sustained high-tempo operations in a contested environment.[2] Xi can think what he likes about American resolve, but he must assume that the United States and its key regional allies would intervene. Given the PLA's limited combat experience and the reliance of both sides on technologies that have never before been used in combat, no one can know how an amphibious invasion would play out. No amount of wargaming and simulation can bring certainty. The key point is that, even though China faces significant obstacles and vulnerabilities, the balance of risks is shifting in its favor. This fact may make Xi more risk-tolerant in the gray zone—particularly if he believes that some variation of the invasion scenario, such as a scorched-earth blockade, could guarantee him victory.

This is why the United States must remain committed to the first pillar of deterrence: the One China Policy. The United States has a principled position that cross-Strait differences must be resolved peacefully, without coercion, and in a manner democratically acceptable to the people of Taiwan. The fact that Washington has maintained this policy for decades, resisting opportunities from both sides to revise it under pressure, is a great source of credibility. In brinkmanship crises, the party defending the status quo usually enjoys an advantage over the party trying to revise it, even though the definition of the status quo is contested in this case. The United States should never be deterred from maintaining and broadening its relationship with Taiwan within the bounds of longstanding norms. These include informal engagements that support Taiwan's democracy and defensive military capabilities, expanded economic and technological cooperation, and private pressure and support for Taiwan in building resilience. U.S. officials also need to better understand how Taiwan's elites and political parties think. Taiwan's political system is volatile, and it does not respond predictably to external pressure.

Without changing the One China Policy, the United States can pursue a communication strategy of *structured ambiguity* to remind Beijing that while U.S. commitments to Taiwan are ambiguous today, they would not be ambiguous in a crisis. Washington should privately explain to Xi that if U.S. intelligence concludes that he is planning a major move against Taiwan, the United States will not wait for him to use lethal force before sprinting to Taiwan's defense. Emphasizing the U.S. commitment to the One China Policy, Washington can explain that it will regard an effort to constrain Taiwan's ability to trade as a PRC violation of the Joint Communiqués, and that reinterpreting or clarifying the One China Policy may be a necessary and proportionate response to communicate U.S. resolve and restraint. Washington can also prepare contingency plans to evacuate U.S. nationals from Taiwan, respond to economic and financial shocks resulting from a crisis, and resupply Taiwan under conditions of quarantine. These steps won't deter Xi if he is otherwise prepared to accept general war with the United States, but they ought to deter him from escalating against Taiwan without limit in the gray zone.

The second pillar of deterrence is conventional military "deterrence by denial." By the late 2020s or early 2030s, the PLA is expected to achieve significant quantitative advantages in surface ships, aircraft, missiles, drones, and industrial capacity. To sustain deterrence to 2030 and beyond, the United States and its allies must therefore convince Xi that these numerical advantages are not decisive. Competing with China ship-for-ship or plane-for-plane is neither necessary nor practical. Instead, the United States should prioritize helping Taiwan rapidly deploy asymmetric capabilities such as air defenses, electronic warfare, and naval mines. Simultaneously, the United States must shore up its own asymmetric toolkit across domains. It must build more long-range munitions and drones, modernize its maritime logistics enterprise, harden its regional bases, double its production of attack submarines, and perhaps most importantly extend its relative advantages in command and control. More money is needed, but simply throwing money at defense contractors won't stabilize the military balance. Both the Pentagon and the defense industrial base need substantial reforms. The long-term path to countering China's military coercion is to build a robust joint allied defense industrial base for the world's major democracies, working closely with countries like Japan, South Korea, Australia, the UK, and where possible the European Union.

The third pillar of deterrence is strategic, encompassing nuclear weapons, cyber, space, and the emerging cross-domain field of AI. The United States must counter Xi's unprecedented nuclear buildup by modernizing its nuclear arsenal, command-and-control systems, and delivery platforms. It must demonstrate that U.S. strategic deterrence far exceeds China's in precision, flexibility, destructive power, and resilience. China's strategic deterrence doctrine is deliberately vague, extending beyond nuclear weapons to include space and cyber. The United States should seek to undermine Xi's confidence in the reliability of his own strategic forces through covert actions and selective intelligence disclosures. To reassure allies alarmed by threats from China and North Korea, Washington should consider deploying nuclear-capable intermediate-range delivery systems in the Indo-Pacific and explore NATO-style nuclear-sharing arrangements with South Korea and Japan.

AI development and integration must be recognized as a crucial part of strategic deterrence. In particular, the United States must harness AI to maintain and extend its advantages in cyberspace. It should work with allies and the private sector to maintain leadership in advanced AI hardware and software, defend against espionage, and signal emerging AI capabilities effectively. Xi must understand that the United States has a significant edge in using AI for strategic deterrence purposes, but he should not be led to believe that he faces a rapidly closing window to strike before the United States achieves AI superintelligence. Across the entire U.S. federal government, technology policy therefore needs to be aligned systematically with America's strategy for deterring war with China.

Finally, even if the United States successfully implements political, conventional, and strategic deterrence, it still faces a credibility challenge in the economic domain. In theory, America has various ways to impose extreme punishments on China. But China's size and integration into global value chains means that a sudden break would wreak havoc on the U.S. economy, devastate allied economies, and trigger financial panic and supply-chain disruptions. Such actions would be a perilous gamble and would probably undermine U.S. national interests, even in extreme scenarios. China might also assume, based on its experience negotiating with the Trump administration, that the United States is bluffing. Indeed, the more America brandishes such extreme threats, the more it risks dividing its coalition and further undermining its credibility.

Rather than threatening that the cost of enforcing U.S. red lines would be automatic economic Armageddon, the United States should offer an affirmative vision for the international economic system. Inspired by the Marshall Plan, which helped create a stable and prosperous free world under American leadership after World War II, the United States should propose an allied agenda for protecting economic security in peacetime, as well as a contingency plan for broadening and accelerating that program during and after a potential rupture with China. The driving force behind that vision should be respect for the right of sovereign states to safeguard their economic security and prosperity, within a fair and honest international framework. America's public messaging should be that China needs unfettered globalization to sustain its own broken economic model and that, by contrast, the United States understands that globalization is not an end in itself. All countries should have the right to protect their economic security.

The U.S. affirmative vision for the global economy after a rupture should have four guiding principles. First, the United States would not break non-critical supply chains on Day One and would give producers an appropriate amount of time to pull out of China. Second, it would maintain dollar hegemony at all costs. Third, it would not demand that other countries decouple from China. Instead, it would incentivize decoupling through a wider program of economic support in response to the Taiwan crisis. Finally, the United States would commit to enforcing its anti-China trade policy against third countries in a fair and honest manner, subject to appeal and external adjudication.

In accordance with these principles, the American economic contingency plan should be to work with its allies to ensure that as much of the global economy as possible begins avalanche decoupling from China. Mindful that every country will follow its own interests, the United States should plan to lead the response to the resulting economic and financial crisis. It should work with allies to reshore critical supply chains as fast as possible, pulling back noncritical supply chains gradually over time.

A credible U.S. commitment to this kind of economic leadership would not only help stabilize the international economic system in a moment of crisis, but also potentially transform it in a way that would benefit most countries at China's expense. The United States would lead the creation of an Economic Security Cooperation Board (ESCB), a new institution with membership open to all countries other than a handful of rogue states. The ESCB would ensure decoupling took place in a fair, honest, and market-driven way that respected the distinctive interests and economic security needs of all its members. The United States would encourage all countries to decouple from China in critical products and sectors. But it would accept that inevitably most countries would continue to trade with China in some form.

The power of avalanche decoupling is that it harnesses market forces to create a process that gains momentum over time. As Core countries ratcheted up trade barriers against products from China, firms producing in China would face growing incentives to move production elsewhere. The predictable schedule would allow them to allocate capital as efficiently as possible during this transition. Meanwhile, countries seeking to attract this new investment and manufacturing employment would have reason to strengthen customs enforcement to maintain access to Core markets. Once firms had made investment decisions based on the expectation of the ratchet, they would gain strong incentives to lobby against repealing or modifying the ratcheting tariff. They would also put pressure on third countries to meet rules-of-origin requirements.

China may try to disrupt the avalanche by retaliating against the most vulnerable ESCB members. The ESCB would therefore need some ability to support and compensate China's victims. But China's retaliatory power would be limited. If it used import or export controls against ESCB member states, it would only serve to accelerate the avalanche. In all these respects, this is the opposite approach to the one the Trump administration took in spring 2025: slow, steady, and inclusive, rather than fast, erratic, and confrontational.

As a deterrent, avalanche decoupling targets China's real vulnerability—not its financial system but its export manufacturing base, which employs nearly 100 million workers and constitutes nearly one-sixth of its GDP. China's economy faces structural headwinds, including industrial overcapacity and deflation. China can survive bilateral decoupling with the United States. But Beijing is not prepared for a rewiring of the trading system in which other countries pursue partial decoupling for their own interests. Avalanche decoupling could aggravate China's mounting challenges from aging demographics and debt, undermining the foundation of the country's prosperity and social stability and potentially putting Xi's vision for "national rejuvenation" out of reach. Such broad-based decoupling is politically unimaginable as long as China refrains from outright aggression. But the mechanism is flexible, designed so that each country can target specific critical products or sectors. Demonstrating a proof of concept of the mechanism in peacetime would enhance deterrence.

In the end, the target of U.S. deterrence is Xi himself, not the CCP or China in general. The precise details of Xi's thinking are unknowable. It is therefore too risky to hang deterrence on any one capability or threat. America needs an integrated strategy that counters Xi's strategy and threatens everything he might care about. Put another way, integrated deterrence is ultimately a psychological warfare operation directed against a single man. Communicating the message must be a task for the entirety of the U.S. government, including Congress, as well as allied and partner governments and the private sector. Xi must be made to see his fears corroborated wherever he looks.

To walk the halls of the National Museum is to understand that it is in everyone's interest—including Xi's—to handle the Taiwan issue in a way that preserves an honorable peace. Xi is more determined than his predecessors to extinguish Taiwan as a free society. He thinks China is an ancient civilization with the wind of history at its back, destined to be rejuvenated and "reunified" under the Party's leadership. He knows that the conquest of Taiwan would be both a triumphant symbol and a practical guarantee of rejuvenation. He yearns to be the man who delivers this promise and earns his place forever in the museum, alongside China's greatest emperors. But he is not a madman. Xi has many remarkable achievements that he would like to protect. He knows just how much he, his Party, and his country have to lose if he moves against Taiwan in the wrong way and at the wrong moment. This is why nowhere in the museum can you find the merest whisper or suggestion of a promise that China and Taiwan will be unified in Xi's lifetime. Xi has found glory in other achievements, as he will surely continue to do.

The United States, its allies, and the freedom-loving people of Taiwan therefore should not despair. We can sustain the honorable peace for another generation. This moment calls not for panic but for courage, preparation, and a steady hand.

Acknowledgments

All books are the work of many hands. This one particularly so.

Thanks are due, above all, to my friends and co-authors Hugo Bromley, Harry Halem, and Calvin Heng. Without their erudition, creativity, and work ethic, this book could never have been written.

Many others deserve special mention. Niall Ferguson and Rana Mitter supported the project from its inception. Bob Graham, Jaya Chatterjee, David McBride, and Gabriel Kachuck offered editorial guidance and helped to make this a better book. The five anonymous reviewers at Oxford and Yale University Presses spotted errors and offered insights that improved every chapter. Alexcee Bechthold guided me through the production process.

One of the joys of writing a book is the opportunity to work with research assistants who are smarter and more detail-oriented than you—and know things you don't. Many RAs contributed to this project over several years. Most I can't name publicly, due to the political sensitivity of the work. To each one of you: I salute your intelligence and dedication, and I am grateful.

Dozens of members of the Hoover community contributed to the project in ways both large and small. Glenn Tiffert, Frances Hisgen, and Larry Diamond edited work in progress and sponsored its publication. Philip Zelikow offered detailed feedback. Darrell Duffie, Matt Pottinger, and John Cochrane and John Taylor's Economic Policy Working Group provided crucial feedback on the economic analysis. The Hoover Maritime Security Working Group—including Adm. Gary Roughead, Steve Carmel, Edlyn, Jim Timbie, and Mike Brown—provided multiple rounds of detailed feedback and supported the publication of *The Arsenal of Democracy*, from which much of the military analysis in this book is derived. Adm. Jim Ellis and David Fedor led that effort, with support from Lindsay Hendershott. Niall's Applied History Working Group co-sponsored *Arsenal* and hosted workshops on related research. Stephen Kotkin and Joseph Ledford made the Hoover History Lab into an extraordinary academic home. Elizabeth Economy and H.R. McMaster supported my work in many ways, both direct and indirect. Kharis Templeman taught me about Taiwan; Jacquelyn Schneider taught me about wargaming. Gen. Jim Mattis offered feedback and encouragement. Among many on Hoover's press, marketing, policy outreach, and administrative teams, special thanks are due to Barbara Arellano, Danica Hodge, Ruth Eileen Sakata Corley, Rachel Moltz, Shana Farley, Victoria Guzman, Sarah Delahunty, Jeff Marschner, Jacquelyn Johnstone, Lillian Boog, Kim Zermeño, and Julianne Caballero. It is a true privilege to have such brilliant, effective, and generous colleagues.

Hugo and I have many people to thank for help in formulating our ideas on economic deterrence and contingency planning. In addition to the Hoover colleagues named above, we are grateful to Richard Danzig, Barry Eichengreen, Roz Engel, Andrew Sinclair, Erik Woodhouse, Emily Kilcrease, Beth Baltzan, Chris Gorman, Jake Carney, Angel Ubide, Brad Setser, Andy Grotto, Adam Posen, James Schott, Martin Chorzempa, Meg Hogan, Frank Gavin, Michael McFaul, Matt Turpin, Eddie Fishman, Martin Daunton, Kori Schake, Jude Blanchette, Aaron Friedberg, Michael Forscey, Peter Harrell, Nels Nordquist, Joshua Stinson, Josh Zoffer, Nazak Nikakhtar, Brendan Simms, Bill Hurst, Paul Tucker, Alex Bick, John Bew, Hal Brands, and Adm. Sandy Winnefeld. Many of these read drafts in progress, and all offered trenchant feedback. Chris Miller offered relentlessly constructive reactions to the work and made dozens of introductions. Anonymous reviewers at *International Security* and the *China Quarterly* also provided essential feedback.

Among those who shaped my thinking on the military analysis, I owe a particular debt to the team at the U.S. Naval War College's China Maritime Studies Institute. Andrew Erickson, Chris Sharman, Ian Easton, and their former colleagues, including Peter Dutton and Isaac Kardon, represent the gold standard of analytical excellence in the study of the PLA. It has been a privilege to learn from their work over the past five years. I am also grateful to Derek Solen, Reed Simmons, Bryce Mitchell, Tarun Chhabra, Oriana Skylar Mastro, Mike Loftus, Gabriel Collins, K.R. Reinhold, Emile Simpson, and Jason Hansberger, among others, for graciously tutoring me on various aspects of military affairs.

The Indo-Pacific is a vast and complex region, and I am indebted to the many friends and colleagues who have helped me try to understand it. At Harvard and Columbia, Alistair Iain Johnston and Tom Christensen taught me about Taiwan. Bonnie Glaser, Zack Cooper, and the Sasakawa Peace Foundation offered me an eye-opening trip to Japan. Suzuki Kazuto has assembled an extraordinary group of talent in the Institute of Geoeconomics. My Greenmantle colleagues have also taught me much about the history, markets, and politics of this region, including Nicholas Kumleben, Will Taylor, Joon Yang, Sophie Coste, John-Clark Levin, Sebastian Orbell, and Ava Kelley.

Many other friends and trusted colleagues must go unnamed here, but they are remembered and appreciated. Particularly thanks to those in the United States and allied and partner countries who provided anonymous feedback on drafts and workshopped ideas in this book.

Finally, I would like to thank my family—including Marc and Andrea Chafetz, my second family in Washington, who kept their doors open on my countless visits. Stephanie Kerry sat by my side and offered encouragement on many late nights. I love you all.

Appendix A

Four Perspectives from Taipei

I conducted the four following interviews in Taipei in August 2023. At the time, the United States and Taiwan were both in election season. Joe Biden was on track to win the Democratic nomination. The Republican primary was in its early stages, with Donald Trump and Ron DeSantis the two leading candidates. In Taiwan, President Tsai Ing-wen (DPP) was retiring. Her vice president, Lai Ching-te, was favored to win but was engaged in a three-way contest with KMT candidate Hou You-ih and the maverick mayor of Taipei, Ko Wen-je, who had formed his own third party.

My goal in these conversations was to focus not on the election horse race and other short-term political stories, but on broader dynamics in Taiwan's relationship with the United States and PRC. Each conversation lasted around two hours, and the transcripts have been edited for clarity and length. Each interviewee has approved the text. The conversation with Chang Jung-feng was conducted in Chinese; he has approved my translation. I framed each conversation as an attempt to help Americans improve their understanding of Taiwan. Given the subjects' various perspectives and experiences, each conversation developed organically.

Su Chi

Su served as secretary-general of Taiwan's National Security Council from 2008 to 2010 and is one of Taiwan's most prominent—and controversial—national security intellectuals. He is closely associated with former KMT President Ma Ying-jeou (2008–2016), the only leader of Taiwan since democratization who maintained cordial ties with the Mainland. While working in Ma's administration, Su popularized the term "1992 Consensus" and remains a leading advocate of cross-Strait diplomacy.

* * *

What do Americans need to understand about the situation here in Taiwan?
Public opinion here is not what they say. President Tsai has one "face" for the world, and another for her domestic audience. Her message to the United States and Japan is that Taiwan is in danger, that we are threatened by the big bad wolf, and that we need help. Internally, her message is completely different: we are completely safe, so don't worry. We don't need to build our food and fuel reserves. China will not strike—and if it does, the United States will come to our aid. But she is wrong. China may strike. The United States may not come. We need to take these possibilities into consideration. Before 2022, I was in the minority in Taiwan when I said that we couldn't count on the United States. But then Russia invaded Ukraine, and America never put boots on the ground. Now I think I am in the majority.

What is the nature of China's interest in Taiwan?
Three things. The first and most obvious is nationalism. The second is naval strategy. China has a larger navy than the United States and many times the shipbuilding capacity, but its whole fleet is stuck inside the First Island Chain. The PLA Navy must feel like a bird in a cage. If it can seize Taiwan, it can project itself far into the Pacific. The third consideration is U.S.–Taiwan relations.

Most public discussion in the West focuses on nationalist sentiment as the reason that China wants to control Taiwan. But I think the second and third reasons are equally if not more important for Beijing's thinking. Reason one is for people on the street. Reasons two and three are for the strategists and elites.

What has changed in recent years to make the situation more dangerous?
The doves in China have long argued that China is rising and Taiwan is stagnating, so China can wait, because someday Taiwan could fall into their hands like a falling apple. In Taiwan, we used to say that Beijing is filled with hawks, Shanghai is filled with doves, and Xiamen [in Fujian Province across the Taiwan Strait] is full of "surrenderists" who like Taiwan so much that they want to become Taiwan. Now even in Xiamen, they are all hawks! What changed? Taiwan's public opinion changed, so the PRC position changed, and vice versa. The two interact. Now, the DPP government is pushing closer ties with the United States in a way that makes Taiwan part of America's anti-China strategy. So the argument that the doves used to make—that China could rise first and do reunification later—has become hard to sustain. It now seems, from Beijing's vantage point, that if they let current trends in U.S.–Taiwan relations continue, it could damage China's rise. So the order of action must be reversed. China should take care of reunification first and complete its rise later.

In your view, what are the red lines that, if crossed, would lead China to attack?
Don't think in terms of red lines. President Tsai Ing-wen was right when she said China's red lines can move.

If that is the case, why are you so concerned that the election of Lai Ching-te may trigger China to attack? Lai has said many times that he will retain the status quo.
Tsai is a covert Taiwan independence supporter who allows China to save face, but Lai's past remarks suggest that he is an overt Taiwan independence supporter. If Xi Jinping can't rein Lai in, he will be under severe pressure at home for letting Taiwan drift out of China's sphere of influence. From Beijing's perspective, Taiwan is like an egg, with a hard shell composed of China's red lines. The eggshell looks solid and still, but China believes that a chick is hatching inside. The chick is *taidu* (台独)—the project of Taiwan independence. Following Lai's election, I fear that Beijing will think that the egg is ready to hatch, and will strike first before it does.

Is there anything Taiwan could do politically to reassure Xi Jinping?
Dialogue is the only way to avoid military conflict. To deter Beijing by itself, Taiwan would need capabilities that it does not have and cannot acquire. Think about it from Beijing's perspective. There are only two ways to achieve unification: peaceful and non-peaceful. Within the peaceful approach, you have two options. One is U.S.–China dialogue, the other is China–Taiwan dialogue. Today, the paths to negotiation with Washington and Taipei seem almost entirely closed off. If and when China decides that it has exhausted its peaceful options, unilateralism is the only option left. It will pick its time and method, and Taiwan will bear the blow. I believe it would be a terrible outcome for Taiwan to "marry" China. But we can promise at least that Taiwan will

not "marry" someone else, and that we will marry them some other time, so please be patient and wait. That's the best we can hope for.

How do you expect Beijing would attack?
I don't *know* how China would attack Taiwan, but if they did, why wouldn't they use all the tools available, in rapid succession? Decapitation of Taiwan's political leadership, to limit the physical damage and risk to civilians, which could lead to resistance. Cyber and drone attacks against critical infrastructure. Blockade for sure. Direct missile strikes. Invasion is the last move, to be attempted only after they have air superiority and Taiwan's will to resist is very low. We are so unprepared to deal with all of these measures at once, it's incredible.

Would the Taiwan people fight?
Taiwan is not like Ukraine or South Korea. It has not seen war for hundreds of years. Taiwan itself was never invaded in World War II.

What can Taiwan do to prepare militarily?
It is too late for us to do anything meaningful. Military preparation takes years. We are so low on ammo that we don't even use live rounds when we do exercises, when we can avoid it. But more importantly, our training and doctrine are out of date. Now, English-speaking members of the military, particularly the Navy people, are more confident. They think we can handle an amphibious attack. But the Army and Air Force personnel have extremely low confidence—especially those who do not speak English.

What message should the next Taiwan president communicate to the Taiwan people about the nature of the threat and the importance of preparedness?
Even if Taiwan had a world-class military, it might not be able to deter China. We need a political approach—to reassure China that we will not declare independence.

Many people in Taiwan think the KMT wants dialogue with the Mainland because it actively seeks unification. What you are proposing sounds different—dialogue as a tactic for buying time to preserve Taiwan's autonomy. Do others in the party agree with you?
I don't speak for the party, but from my perspective, the KMT wants *autonomy* for Taiwan under the concept of "One China." The crucial difference between the KMT and the DPP, which many Americans ignore, is that KMT people like me believe that Taiwan is part of China historically and culturally. We speak Chinese, we eat Chinese food, our folklore and everything is Chinese. We believe we are ethnically Chinese. Many DPP people deny this. China considers that position absurd, as well as intolerable. How dare we deny our identity?

If I understand you correctly, the message you are proposing to send to Beijing is a bit insincere. You are evoking your common history and blood to create a narrative that the CCP can sell back on the Mainland, which hopefully allows it to justify not attacking Taiwan. But your plan is, in fact, to keep Taiwan autonomous indefinitely. Is that right? How could that strategy possibly work?
I don't know if it is going to work or not—but it has worked so far. Take the example of the 1992 Consensus. The 1992 Consensus is just a political symbol. Many people ask us to define the 1992 Consensus. I believe that this is the wrong question. You don't have to define it. You take it or you leave it. In Taiwan, if you say you agree with the 1992 Consensus, you indicate you are more inclined to cross-Strait dialogue. If you say that the 1992 Consensus doesn't exist, it shows you are not inclined to dialogue. It is a choice, and either way you have some responsibility.

What would have to happen for cross-Strait dialogue to resume?
There needs to be some basic degree of trust for cross-Strait dialogue to resume. The 1992 Consensus is not "Open Sesame," some magic incantation that unlocks cooperation. If a future president of Taiwan says they support the 1992 Consensus, China will not open dialogue solely for that reason. It is a necessary but insufficient condition. Similarly, if Tsai Ing-wen really wanted a dialogue and just didn't like the concept of the 1992 Consensus, she should have come up with a replacement concept. But she never did. Doves always have a hard time among hawks. Right now, both great powers are run by hawks. I hope that we can reach a place where both the United States and China feel confident enough to parley. The problem today is that each side believes it cannot trust the other to fulfill an agreement.

Jou Yi Cheng

Jou Yi-cheng is an entrepreneur, public intellectual, and former leader of the Wild Lily student movement that catalyzed Taiwan's movement toward democratization in the late 1980s and the 1990s. In his student days, Jou was an activist organizer calling for the end of martial law and an aspiration for Taiwan independence. He retired from politics in 2007 and now owns a tea house that serves as a hub for Taipei's political and cultural elite.

* * *

What must the United States do in the Taiwan Strait, and what do Americans need to understand about Taiwan?
A clear U.S. commitment to support Taiwan democracy is essential. American leaders need to push back against the conspiracy theories. A clear message of support will help to strengthen the Taiwanese people's resolve to defend themselves. The clearer the U.S. is, the lower the risk that war will break out. Strategic clarity will not encourage Taiwanese leaders to take risks, because they observe the reality. If there is no U.S. commitment, other Taiwanese leaders may go the Chinese way.

What is China's political strategy for Taiwan?
China's fundamental strategic goal is to take over Taiwan at its lowest cost. That is, political strategy is above military strategy. China is trying to influence Taiwan's domestic politics by every means available. Over decades, the CCP has established business relationships with many private businesses and local governments in Taiwan. They have access down to the township level, and with powerful interest groups like agricultural and fisheries associations. For years, China's strategy has been to influence Taiwan's society via the KMT. They put a lot of money into studying Taiwan and putting their messages into Taiwan's media. Some of this is working, but of course there has also been a backlash.

When Chinese leaders talk about "peaceful reunification," what exactly do they mean?
They mean taking Taiwan without waging a major war with the United States. But this is a euphemism. It is not possible to "reunify" peacefully. Even if Taiwan's leaders acceded to "reunification," the Taiwanese people would resist. Beijing would have to be repressive, even brutal. People would be killed. "Peaceful reunification" might cost even more lives than a limited military conflict.

So by "peaceful reunification," Beijing doesn't mean unification with Taiwan's consent, or even without bloodshed—they mean unification without war with the U.S.?
Yes. "Peace" by their definition. The CCP has never been shy from using armed force against their own people, let alone the Taiwanese people who have never been governed by them. Deep in their minds, the Chinese do not trust Taiwanese people, and vice versa. It's not possible to imagine a scenario in which the PRC could rule Taiwan without using force.

What does that scenario look like, from Beijing's perspective?
First, when the U.S. gives up its commitments to its allies in the Western Pacific, and second, when a certain number of Taiwanese people give up their determination to defend their democracy. Whether this scenario is going to happen depends mainly on the balance of power between China and the U.S. and its allies.

So their preferred outcome is to avoid World War III if possible—to persuade the U.S. that it cannot win a war with China, then coerce Taiwan to "democratically" accept some version of "One Countries, Two Systems"?
Mostly but not totally. They do not need to persuade the U.S. that it *couldn't* win in a war with China. They just want the U.S. to step aside because it is unwilling to pay the cost of a war. Washington and Beijing both understand that they have mutual interests in the short term, but they will be in conflict in the long term. Both sides are currently trying to fix the short-term relationship to support their preparations for more competition and confrontation in the future. The Chinese Communists do not rule out any scenario.

How important is it that Taiwan's younger generation is growing more hostile to China? What do Americans need to understand about the role of young people in Taiwan's politics?
At every major turning point, Taiwan's democratization was driven by young people. At the height of KMT repression in the "February 28 incident" of 1947, it was young people who rose up to resist. In the "Meilidao (Formosa) incident" of 1979, it was the courage of demonstrators in their twenties and thirties who revealed the brutality of martial law. In the late 1980s and early 1990s, it was my generation, the so-called Wild Lilies, who held sit-ins to call for democracy. Since 2014, it has been the "Sunflower Movement Generation," who are now in their thirties. The youngsters believe that Taiwan must not make itself more dependent on China. That might change in the future. Those in their teens or twenties are complacent. Some take Taiwan's democracy for granted, just like youngsters in other free countries. Some assume they will not need to defend it and might not support the political leaders who ask them to defend it. These youngsters are subject to cognitive manipulations and political illusions. American decision makers must pay attention to Taiwan's younger generation if the U.S. is to maintain popular support in Taiwan. More efforts must be taken to strengthen trust and good feeling between the Americans and Taiwanese.

With the young generation of Taiwanese turning against them, how does China plan to break their will to resist?
I am not sure how rational China's leaders are. Xi could be like Putin, and get distorted information. My guess—and this differs from conventional wisdom—is that most CCP leaders see Taiwan as already going their way. The Chinese are very fond of history. They take a very long-term view. Most have no doubt that one day there will be unification. Of course, before unification, I think Chinese leaders foresee an intense power struggle—if not a war—with the United States.

How do you think Xi Jinping himself is thinking about this issue?
If I were Xi Jinping, I would push to the very edge of a war to test the Americans' mettle and
boundaries. If the U.S. doesn't respond to the PRC's sending fighter jets across the Taiwan Strait,
I would keep pushing and pushing. Testing and provoking would cost me nothing, or very little.
Of course, crises bring risks of mistakes and accidents. But I don't think the U.S. would see it as
in its interest to wage a war. For China, the best scenario is to keep pushing until eventually the
U.S. makes an agreement not to intervene.

What are Beijing's red lines?
Their bottom line is that the CCP doesn't want to lose power. Other than that, there is no fixed
red line. They will keep pushing for more as long as their power is not threatened.

*But surely it's unwise to gamble on that. As Taiwan's society turns away from China, why shouldn't
the United States be worried that some future leader of Taiwan would trigger a war by declaring
independence?*
If Taiwan offered its people a plebiscite, most voters would choose independence. But this would
not happen. Why? Because there is a threat from China, and because the U.S. government is
always preaching to Taiwan's leaders that they *shouldn't* do it. Taiwan's leaders observe the international situation very well. There will not be a declaration of independence. In the foreseeable
future, Taiwanese leaders will try not to disrupt the status quo. So don't worry about a Taiwanese
president provoking a crisis.

*Beijing has signaled that tensions would ease if Taiwan's leaders accept the so-called 1992 Consen-
sus. Why does the current government resist using the term?*
The 1992 Consensus was not "discovered" until the 2000s. Ma Ying-Jeou wanted a cross-Strait
dialogue, so he had Su Chi invent the term. The "consensus" has no concrete meaning. That's
why it's so seductive. Talking about it is an olive branch to the Chinese side. Because nobody can
say what it is, it is tempting to treat it just as empty words. The problem is that, precisely because
it has no concrete meaning, the stronger side gets to define it. It is not a consensus. It is a hollow
statement and its nature is China's consent.

*The DPP's position is that China and Taiwan are separate independent countries. The "1992 Con-
sensus" implies some kind of understanding that there is only "One China" that includes Taiwan.
Is that ideological disagreement the reason that the DPP rejects the "1992 Consensus"? Or is there
something else going on?*
It is not just about ideology. You are correct that the DPP is opposed to "One China." It's also
true that Taiwan had not yet fully democratized in 1992, so the people's elected representatives did not have a say when the "consensus" was supposedly agreed. But the DPP's position
is also opposed to the "1992 Consensus" for practical reasons. It believes that handing over the
discourse about the future of Taiwan to the 1992 Consensus is fundamentally dangerous: it is
ceding Taiwan's autonomy and self-determination to the so-called One China.

*It certainly seems like there can be no cross-Strait dialogue so long as the DPP is in power and doesn't
accept the "1992 Consensus." Does the DPP think this situation is sustainable?*
The DPP's fundamental position is that more interaction with China is not necessarily good for
Taiwan. For example, China has long wanted a services trade agreement with Taiwan. The DPP
rejected it—and is now actively trying to diversify Taiwan's trade with other markets.

How do you see the state of the KMT today?
Old KMT elites like Ma Ying-Jeou and Su Chi think the KMT can play a balancing game
between the U.S. and China. But the old KMT elites cannot get elected with this message any-

more. They need the party to go a more populist way, so they can try to direct from behind the scenes. Perversely, the KMT needs a U.S.–China crisis to get back to power, because the party's message is that they are the only ones who can manage a crisis. So, the KMT politicians are spreading messages across the ocean and across the straits that there is a crisis.

What lessons is Taiwan learning from Ukraine?
Many people in Taiwan today believe that we should not become a U.S. tool like Ukraine. According to this view, the U.S. is using Taiwan to fight with China. Some politicians on the blue [KMT] side even flirt with the conspiracy theory that the U.S. *wants* a war before China gets too strong, and that Taiwan is the excuse. The counterargument is that we should learn from Ukraine, and we should have very strong determination to defend ourselves.

While the world's largest navy has built up across the strait, Taiwan's military has languished. Many people in Washington think that Taiwan is being naïve about its vulnerability. How do you explain Taiwan's foot-dragging on this existential issue?
It is natural that a democracy doesn't want to spend more on defense and that its families do not want their children to be conscripted. I give Tsai Ing-wen great credit for extending conscription under pressure from public opinion. Even lawmakers from her own party do not like this idea, since their constituents are opposed. The DPP does not want to spend more on defense.

Perhaps you think this is naïve. But is it prudent to terrify the public? If the whole society were so worried about the war, if they faced a real death threat, they may conclude that the situation is hopeless and want to surrender. Before the real military conflict, perhaps more important, is the political and psychological war, the information war. This is fundamental to China's strategy to take Taiwan without a military conflict.

How do you rate the Taiwan government's effectiveness at countering information warfare?
Not good enough. Our government ministries are insufficiently coordinated. Every day on social media we see Chinese propaganda and disinformation. Beijing has it easy. We use the same language. They have essentially infinite manpower to conduct their information war. Our young people are using PRC apps like Xiaohongshu and TikTok. But, in our defense, how *should* our government respond? Free speech is protected in our society. It doesn't help that Taiwan's own media has become so partisan. Both parties accuse the other of spreading misinformation. There aren't really any universally trusted news sources in Taiwan. This should be an important part of your story. China's war on minds may be even more important than the war on our bodies.

Edward Lee*

Over the past four decades, Edward Lee—not his real name—has played a pivotal role in Taiwan's transformation into the world's high-tech manufacturing base. He is the co-founder of one of Taiwan's largest IT companies, producing products used in edge computing, robotics, and missile technology. He oversaw his firm's rapid expansion into the China market in the 2000s and 2010s. But more recently, as the geopolitical winds have shifted, Lee has changed his mind about the wisdom and future prospects of cross-Strait cooperation. Lee requested that I anonymize his comments, so that there would be no risk of retaliation against the company.

* * *

What opinion do most people in Taiwan hold, but not dare to express?
Until I was in high school, I didn't know much about Taiwan's history. I didn't know that the KMT military came to Taiwan as invaders and killed many Taiwanese. I did not have a Taiwanese identity, since we were taught that Taiwan is China. My parents told me not to ask questions. Not until the end of martial law, and then democratization in the 1990s, did we in Taiwan become fully free to face our history. As Taiwan gained this freedom to talk and debate, and especially after the DPP took power [in 2000, under President Chen Shui-bian], we started to understand that we are not Chinese just because our ancestors came from the Mainland to Taiwan, just as you Americans are not British because your ancestors and political institutions came from there. You are an independent country. So why can't Taiwan become an independent country?

China started to ramp up pressure. I myself lived in China for ten years, on and off. I met a lot of Chinese people and I respect them as individuals. We did our best to help China develop. Since Xi Jinping took power [in 2012], China's path has changed, but its economy has continued to grow, and Taiwanese have started to lose confidence. The KMT represents this view: that we shouldn't challenge China, that China is much stronger than Taiwan, and that in fact we should belong to China.

I think this is ridiculous. My ancestors came to Taiwan 200 years ago. We have our own currency and military. The People's Republic of China has never ruled Taiwan for a single day. Yet China has issued many laws relating to Taiwan, even claiming the right to arrest Taiwanese anywhere. On what basis can the CCP claim that Taiwan belongs to China?

If the Americans said tomorrow that they would support an independent Taiwan and treat it like an ally, would the politics of Taiwan change?
Yes. Around 40 percent of Taiwanese believe that Taiwan should be independent, and are firmly committed to defending it. Another 30–40 percent of people are in-between. They may support independence if the United States promises to defend Taiwan's sovereignty.

As a prominent Taiwanese businessman who is known to support Taiwan independence, how did your experience living in China evolve over time?
It used to be that when I visited Beijing, all our local managers would come to my desk for lunch and ask questions about the democratic elections of Taiwan. At that time, they could still get information about Taiwan by using virtual private networks (VPNs) to read foreign news. They knew that the DPP won the legislative elections and that Chen Shui-bian was president. They knew a lot of details. But after 2012, they lost access to this information. The propaganda became all about how China is better than the West. They started to become brainwashed.

How do you see the balance of power between the U.S. and China evolving?
The balance has moved toward the United States in the last three to four years, due to economic and technological factors. For a while, I think Xi got wrong information from his think tanks and advisors. They told him that China was very strong, so Xi thought that the East is rising while the West is in decline. But from my understanding—and I have many friends in China—the view there is that China is still quite far behind the United States in terms of military capability. They have a lot of hardware, but in terms of intelligence and precision, they are way behind.

How effective do you think the United States export controls on semiconductors will be in widening the competitive gap in emerging areas like edge computing and AI?
Very important. China is good at adopting Western technology in manufacturing and internet applications, like Alibaba. But without the chipset, they cannot compete. Similarly, with AI, if

you cut off their access to the chipset, their progress will stop. Who knows what this means for geopolitics, of course. China is a big country with a crazy leader who wants to challenge the U.S. It may be that no matter how many sanctions and punishments you impose to prevent China from getting the technology, Xi Jinping will not surrender.

Should our mental model be that if this is Cold War II, China is the Soviet Union, and is eventually going to lose?
Yes. If they cannot access advanced chips, they will fall far behind technologically.

Given your optimism about the structural trend in the balance of power, what advice would you give to the U.S. government about how to avoid a war with China?
The United States must show its military muscle. China has two aircraft carriers, but they are very low-tech. They have a Dongfeng 17 hypersonic missile which they claim can hit U.S. carriers from over 1,000 miles away. But it has never been tested. You should put strategic pressure on them, just like President Reagan put pressure on the Russians in the 1980s. Don't be afraid. Prepare and push.

While the United States applies this strategic pressure, do you think it should be a priority to reassure Xi that a Taiwanese declaration of independence won't happen?
Taiwan has been an independent country since 1949, so there is no need for Taiwan to declare independence. But if Xi Jinping thinks the United States will find other ways to destroy him if he does *not* attack Taiwan, then he may attack even if Taiwan does not change any policy. America must create a way for the CCP to save face. It is not just about Xi. If the CCP doesn't change their mindset or strategy, Xi will face the same internal pressure, and if he retires or falls, you'll just get another, younger Xi Jinping.

What message would you communicate to the American people if you had the chance?
For the past fifty years, strategic ambiguity has seemed effective at keeping the peace, but this was because China was weak. But now China thinks it is strong enough to challenge the U.S. China is a tyrant, and it is your great American duty to confront it. Why are you so afraid of a country that claims it is number one, but is actually not? You should show your muscle! You should tell China in no uncertain terms: if you dare to cross *my* red lines, I will fight!

Chang Jung-feng

Chang started working with President Lee Teng-hui (KMT) in June 1988 and was responsible for cross-Strait matters during Lee's presidency from 1992 to 2000. He led the government's crisis management team during the Third Taiwan Straits Crisis of 1995–1996, including the backchannel negotiations with Yang Shangkun, former president of the PRC and vice chairman of its Central Military Commission. After the election of Chen Shui-bian in 2000, he was appointed deputy secretary general of the National Security Council, retiring in 2003. He now runs a private consulting firm.[1]

* * *

What do Americans tend to misunderstand about Taiwan?
For decades, American policymakers were in thrall to the idea of "engagement." They ignored Taiwan, thinking that when China democratizes, it will be fine if Taiwan is swallowed or reunified. In the 1990s and 2000s, whenever Taiwan tried to claim diplomatic space or participate in

international organizations, it was labeled as a "troublemaker." U.S. national security officials told us that America was Taiwan's best security guarantee and that we shouldn't interfere with their engagement policy. However, based on our long-term understanding of the CCP, we never believed that China would democratize under CCP rule. We understand why the United States might adopt a diplomatic strategy of "engagement" toward China, but Taiwan must also consider its own national security. It is unfair to treat Taiwan as a "troublemaker."

The U.S. Navy has always understood that Taiwan matters for U.S. interests for fundamental geographic reasons. The Bashi Channel between the south of Taiwan and the Philippine island of Luzon, and the Miyako Strait to the north are deep enough for submarine access. If China seizes Taiwan, they could deploy Su-21 aircraft on the east coast and control the waters and airspace in those straits. Major oil supply routes pass around Taiwan. Many undersea cables pass through Taiwan.

What is China's main reason for wanting to take Taiwan?
It is unlikely to have anything to do with national identity. Why hasn't China tried to retake other historic territory lost in the 19th and 20th centuries, like Mongolia and parts of Siberia? The belief that China must claim Taiwan at all costs, even if it has to kill everybody on the island, can be justified only by geopolitical logic.

If you are right, then how should the U.S. government interpret China's statements about Taiwan?
In the end, the Taiwan independence issue is just an excuse for Beijing. If they have the capabilities, they can create any excuse to do what they want. That's why it is essential for Taiwan to have the power to resist these excuses. The CCP is good at playing with language, both to make threats and to save face. For example, in 2022, when Nancy Pelosi visited Taiwan, they described her "sneaky visit" using a derogatory term and allusively compared her to a slinking rat.[2] When the CCP cannot win by way of substance, it uses language and rationalization to save face, like the character Ah Q in Lu Xun's famous story. [Chang is alluding to the eponymous hero of the famous Chinese novella "The True Story of Ah Q" by Lu Xun. Ah Q is a poor and uneducated man who often finds himself in situations where he is humiliated or defeated. In colloquial Chinese, the term "Ah Q mentality" (Ā Q jingshen 阿Q精神) is a derisive term used to describe someone who has such delusions of grandeur that he can persuade himself that he has succeeded—even in defeat.]

In your experience, how does China use these sorts of psychological and language games in private diplomacy?
Most scholars and policymakers in Taiwan who work on cross-Strait issues are very courteous, and they are treated respectfully in China. But you must understand two themes in the CCP's behavior in such interactions: tributary dynamics and organizational discipline.

When large groups visit China, the key is tributary dynamics. Beijing arranges for the visitors to meet with very prominent people. Guests are not immediately introduced to the highest-ranking official. Instead, meetings begin with lower-ranking officials and gradually progress to higher levels. Besides, they treat their guests to sightseeing tours, lavish dinners with fine alcohol, and so forth. All these are meant to shape a sense that the guests are coming to pay tribute to the "celestial empire." The hope is that when the guests go home, they will feel warm, important—and indebted.

When interaction takes place in smaller groups, it is a story of organizational discipline, which is more important than everything—above and beyond personal relationships. It is a very different experience from the large delegations mentioned earlier. They will try to buy your loyalty by offering you whatever you might be interested in. They may arrange for women to accompany you. They will use the words "old friend" (*lao pengyou* 老朋友) to build rapport with you. They will use ritual practices to show off how great China is and evoke feelings of brotherhood in you. I think it is important to keep our goal of the engagement in mind, to remember who we are, and to follow our own protocol even if the Chinese have a different protocol. But many Taiwanese fall for such tactics.

In your experience, how does the CCP's negotiation playbook work?
The first stage of negotiations involves setting a very friendly atmosphere. At the same time, they make you feel that time is on their side and that you are the one in a hurry. They set the agenda for the meeting in a very unique way. Typically, in negotiations, the two sides negotiate over agendas. Each side agrees to discuss certain issues and to leave others aside. But China does not negotiate when setting an agenda. They identify what they want to talk about and generalize the list into abstract principles. They insist that both sides reach a consensus on the principles before starting the negotiation. Because the principles tend to be very vague, they seem harmless. Foreign negotiators often fall for this. Later, the Chinese negotiators use the frame to constrain your negotiating position. If you resist, they will remind you that "we have agreed on the principles" and "you are my friend," and that if you do not continue the discussion or comply, the friendship will end. But you must remember that they are not your friends and that they are simply following Party procedure. When dealing with China, always remember: organizational principles come before everything else.

Once they turn to threats, how do you tell when they are bluffing?
Ultimately, China's "red lines" depend on how much leverage the two sides have. I will give you an example of how this principle applies to small-scale brinkmanship. In the Asia-Pacific Economic Cooperation (APEC) 2001 meeting, hosted in China, the pass they issued to Taiwan's Minister of Economy had no title and signature. Our Foreign Ministry complained, but the Chinese diplomats claimed that the decision was made by "higher ups" and was out of their control.

But Taiwan knew that China was applying to host the 2008 Olympic Games and needed one more vote to win. We also knew that this particular issue mattered more to China than denying Taiwan access to APEC. So we warned China that it would stage a protest at APEC and tell the International Olympic Committee (IOC) that China was unfit to host an international event if a proper pass was not issued. When no change in attitude was forthcoming, we canceled the minister's flight to Shanghai—though we told the airline to save a few seats, in case China changed its mind. At the last minute, China changed its mind and issued the pass. Negotiations continued until 3 a.m. Eventually we reached a consensus that China would invite the "Minister of Economy of Chinese Taipei" to attend the ministerial meeting.

Similarly, during the Taiwan Straits Crisis (1995–1996), I held a backchannel discussion with the commander-in-chief of the PLA's military exercises at a third-party location. They said that if we crossed the median line in the strait, there would be very serious consequences. I told them that if *they* crossed the median line, we would definitely shoot them down. As I was the youngest in the negotiating team, the president asked me to be the "bad cop" while the senior officers spoke more decorously. The dispute was extremely intense; the CCP people constantly resorted to threats and intimidation, showing their "willingness to go to war." It was only toward the end that they softened their stance, suggesting that both sides should exercise restraint to avoid accidents. Ultimately, China was bluffing in that crisis. We got hold of their training plans and their post-training review report, which revealed that they knew they lacked the ability to conduct an amphibious landing and that coordination between the PLA Air Force and Navy was lacking. This is why it is particularly important to have good intelligence about China. Their red lines depend on the balance of power between you. To discover their red lines, you have to look at their actual power, rather than listen to their statements.

How concerned should we be that Xi Jinping is getting inaccurate information about cross-Strait relations and about the balance of power in general? Is there any way the United States and Taiwan can influence his thinking?
It seems that Xi does not delegate enough, which creates organizational problems. There are limits to how much information he can digest. He has isolated himself and his country to a high degree. As a result, Xi's perception of threat is probably very high, and it is difficult to influence his thinking from outside. China has collected a lot of information on Taiwan, but his underlings might only send up information that they think the boss wants. Furthermore, the only Taiwanese people who take advantage of state-sponsored opportunities to go to China tend to be the minority who truly support "reunification," so I suspect he may think that a lot of people in Taiwan actually want that outcome.

So is your advice to the United States to "speak softly but carry a big stick" in its dealings with China?
Very much so. The CCP is organizationally obsessed with "face." Whenever they may not have sufficient strength to win, if they think they can save face, they are often willing to back down from conflict. Back when our Air Force was stronger than theirs, we used to fly regularly across the median line. You never heard any public protests or observed any counter-actions from them. President Li Teng-hui taught me this lesson when I first went to work for him: When China cannot do something, they tend to turn it into a slogan. If a CCP slogan says "do not spit on the sidewalk," it means a lot of people are spitting, and the government is unable to stop it. That being said, the CCP believes in power. If they have enough power, they can always find a way to save face.

How do you feel about Taiwan's state of preparedness for conflict? Not just to fight, but to survive privation or a blockade?
Taiwan is not well prepared. Many Taiwanese are not even aware of the need to prepare. They just do not think a war will occur. Taiwan needs to prepare not just in terms of military matters, but also in background planning. If rockets fly into Taiwan, and we lose electricity and water, there could be panic. Taipei has around fifty emergency water wells dug in parks. They are tested once a month. Preparations can be made to ensure adequate water supply. Taiwan is too dependent on imported food, but becoming self-sufficient in food is not so hard. The most important task is to ensure we have adequate stockpiles of energy. In terms of food, Taiwan is too dependent on imported food, but becoming self-sufficient in food is not so hard. When it comes to energy, if the electrical grid infrastructure itself is destroyed, households could lose access to natural gas for cooking, cities might shut down and communication would be chaotic. More preparation needs to be done in these areas. The most important task is to ensure we have adequate stockpiles of energy.

What message should Taiwan's political leaders send to the public?
Taiwan has been at peace for a long time. We only have one air raid exercise a year. Instead of showing people where to find the nearest air raid shelter, we just ask people to stay inside. This is not enough. We need more realistic exercises that teach citizens what to do if the worst-case scenario happens. A responsible political leader should be honest to the public that a hostile military operation from China is possible, and the best way to prevent it from happening is to prepare ourselves both physically and psychologically. We should let our people know that peace comes with a cost.

The Currency Intervention

A CLOSER LOOK AT A STRATEGIC DETERRENT THREAT

The currency operation is a threat that the United States might hold in reserve against China in the context of avalanche decoupling. As discussed in Chapter 8, it would not be viable outside that scenario. Given the potential expense and risks to the U.S. economy, it is more effective as a deterrent than as a punishment to implement.

I have moved this discussion out of the main text for two reasons. First, the technical mechanics of the operation are unlikely to interest most readers in the United States and allied countries. (Of course, it may be of keen interest to readers in China, who have no say in Xi Jinping's decisions about Taiwan but could be greatly harmed if it is implemented. To these readers: I sincerely hope the plan below will never be necessary.) Second, and more importantly, this currency intervention is a conditional threat—a form of strategic deterrence tailored to a specific post-crisis context in which the United States chooses *not* to impose large-scale financial sanctions on China.

The currency intervention would have four proximate goals:

1. Break the 1:1 relationships between the CNY and CNH, and between the HKD and USD.

2. Drive down the value of HKD and CNH as far as possible.

3. Keep HKD and CNH weak and volatile for an indefinite period, raising transaction costs and currency risk to disincentivize third parties from holding it.

4. Tempt Beijing to waste liquid FX reserves defending the CNY exchange rate.

Following a break-glass scenario in U.S.–China relations, it is impossible to predict in advance exactly how far and fast the CNH and CNY might depreciate, or how quickly and far they might rebound later. The CNY exchange rate is protected by capital controls. If the capital control regime broke, a tsunami of capital could flow out of China, causing a collapse of the banking system. This is not the base case, as PRC authorities would likely act decisively to tighten capital controls. Still, the fact that senior PRC policymakers and financial experts fear "currency sniping" suggests that they are not perfectly confident about how well capital controls would hold up in a crisis.

The CNH market is also joined at the hip with the Hong Kong financial system, which presents an additional PRC vulnerability that Washington could exploit. Hong Kong has always been the main settlement hub for offshore transactions. The Hong Kong Monetary Authority (HKMA) is a vital provider of CNH liquidity. If the peg between the Hong Kong dollar and the U.S. dollar broke, capital would flood out of the territory, and Hong Kong's financial institutions could quickly become insolvent. Beijing would lose its most important clearing center for RMB transactions, and a banking crisis on the mainland might follow. If it had to, Beijing would probably intervene to preserve financial stability in Hong Kong.[1] This could be a very expensive proposition.[2]

Attacking the CNH and HKD at the same time would involve higher risks and higher potential rewards. It would put U.S. taxpayer money on the line, and if successful it would cause far greater collateral damage to the global financial system. At the same time, it would further undermine the CNH capital market and increase the probability of a crisis in China's domestic banking system. The CNH market is quite small, which makes it a relatively easy target for a speculative attack. As of July 2021, just $200 billion worth of CNH was deposited offshore. The derivatives market is even smaller and shallower, which would give speculators an additional tool to wreak havoc.[3] Anticipating this vulnerability, China is trying to expand the market. Unfortunately for China, allowing the CNH market to grow comes with a trade-off. The bigger and deeper the market gets, the more FX China might have to spend to keep the exchange rate stable in a crisis. The smaller and shallower the CNH market is, the less costly it would be to attack. Total currency in circulation, demand deposits, and other liquid deposits of HKD are worth roughly $325 billion. Washington should prepare in advance to attack both currencies at once, with the final decision resting with the president.

If the CNY and CNH exchange rates to the dollar began to move independently, China's capital controls would come under extreme pressure. Today, PRC authorities currently allow regulated financial institutions to make 1:1 conversions of CNH to CNY under controlled conditions. This arrangement would become problematic if a peg could no longer be maintained because PRC entities could profit through arbitrage. Multinational companies operating in China would seek excuses to buy dollars with CNY, perhaps under the pretext of buying foreign components; use those dollars to buy CNH; and then convert them into CNY for a profit.[4] PRC firms receiving payment from foreign customers might also have incentives to seek payment in dollars, hide those earnings overseas from their own authorities, and convert them later after the CNH had weakened further. These activities would be highly likely to cause the CNY to weaken, exacerbating pressure on capital controls and causing domestic inflation. In the long term, these potential risks would be highly problematic for China. To prevent China from re-pegging the CNH to the CNY in the future, the Treasury would simply double down on its short selling.

Most likely, Beijing would abandon the CNH—and potentially the HKD peg as well—and return to its pre-2015 model of a single currency (CNY) behind capital controls. In this scenario, China's economy would continue normally. Beijing would conserve its FX reserves for a rainy day. However, Beijing's trading partners would no longer be interested in taking payment in CNH. Nor could Beijing offer large swap lines of CNY to foreign partners, since the Treasury might borrow CNY from them and short it, too. PRC firms would therefore have to conduct international trade in dollars or other FX, using payment and clearing systems that Beijing did not control. Existing U.S. sanctions and export controls on rogue states would retain their efficacy.

Most of China's retaliatory options involve spending FX to persuade the market that it can overpower or outlast Treasury action. Beijing would have two basic strategies. It could increase demand for CNH, CNY, and HKD. The main way to do this would be to spend dollars to buy China's currencies on the open market, in the mirror image of what the Treasury was doing. Alternatively, China could raise interest rates to make the currency intervention more costly for the Treasury.

Both strategies would have downsides for China. China officially declares $3.2 trillion of FX reserves, which it could hypothetically use to support both exchange rates. Beijing may also be able to mobilize up to $3 trillion more through the sovereign wealth fund and state banks, though it is not clear how much of these "leveraged" FX holdings are liquid.[5] However, if Beijing spent FX trying to defend the currency but lost control of the exchange rate anyway, it might face a balance-of-payments crisis in the future if avalanche decoupling took place and its terms of trade became unfavorable. China could also try to follow the Russia playbook discussed in Chapter 7.[6] This would mean adopting policies to increase external demand for CNH and shrink the CNH money supply. The problem is that efforts to shrink the CNH money supply would contradict Beijing's goal of expanding trade in CNH. Once PRC banks and other entities had bought up CNH, they could not return it to circulation without selling or lending it, which would weaken the exchange rate.[7] Sharply raising interest rates, as Russia did in 2022, would also create new financial stability risks in China's highly leveraged shadow banking system.

To help support the currency, China could sell dollar-denominated assets such as U.S. Treasury and Agency bonds. Doing so would temporarily drive up U.S. interest rates, but the risk to U.S. financial stability and public finances is exaggerated.[8] China held a reported $782 billion of Treasurys in November 2023.[9] If Beijing abruptly liquidated this position, U.S. government bond prices would fall, and yields would spike. However, the Federal Reserve could in principle buy up the surplus Treasurys to stabilize the market. There is precedent for such action: the Fed bought up over $1 trillion in Treasury securities between March and April 2020.[10] Even if China's true holdings of dollar assets are several times higher than reported—which is possible—the Fed could in principle respond in the same way.[11] Prominent PRC scholars have acknowledged that a sudden sale of dollar assets would be a weak to useless economic weapon. This finding explains why China's State Administration of Foreign Exchange (SAFE) reduced its holdings of dollar assets by 40 percent between 2013 and 2023.[12] Moreover, the currency intervention would make it risky for China to divest itself of all its dollar assets. If the CNY/CNH peg broke, China would need FX to conduct its international trade. Most of that trade would still be denominated in dollars.

Alternatively, China could try to stabilize the CNH/CNY exchange rate at some weaker level. There is no reason in principle why the CNH and CNY must be pegged 1:1. So long as they are freely convertible at some exchange rate—such as 2:1, or even 10:1—China could maintain the purchasing power of the CNY, while limiting the incentives for arbitrage. If the two exchange rates could be re-pegged at another level, third parties would once again have incentives to hold it. However, having abandoned the first peg, China would have to persuade the market that the new peg could be relied upon.

Other PRC counter-strategies would probably not work.[13] China could ban conversion between CNH and dollars, requiring that all CNH transactions take place on CIPS. However, the Treasury could respond by selling CNH in exchange for euros, yen, or any other currency for which CNH conversion was not banned. If necessary, the Treasury could conduct its currency intervention through proxies. China could try to establish a cryptocurrency pegged to the dollar. However, the Treasury could simply short the cryptocurrency, draining FX reserves in the process. China could hypothetically create a blockchain-enabled e-CNH that automatically demonetized itself when taken off the CIPS platform. However, it is not clear that such a solution is technically possible. Even if it were, foreign central banks and private actors might not want to hold a currency that Beijing could render worthless at any moment.

Intervening in global currency markets would carry risks for the United States. The risks fall into two categories: fiscal losses, and effects on the monetary base that affect prices.

The Treasury's short trade would be a bet that the value of the shorted currencies would fall rather than rise. If the currency intervention turned out to be a self-fulfilling prophecy, the Treasury would make a profit on behalf of the taxpayer. However, if the trade failed for any reason, and the CNH and HKD exchange rates to the dollar rose *above* the level rate at which the Treasury had shorted them, then the taxpayer would face significant and theoretically unlimited fiscal liability. The Treasury would also lose money if the exchange rate held constant because it would have to pay interest (possibly denominated in CNH) on the CNH that it borrowed. In a sense, the currency intervention could therefore be understood as a non-refundable down payment on future trade decoupling. The United States would now have a powerful fiscal interest in eroding the long-term fundamental value of China's currencies by destroying its terms of trade.

No matter what the Treasury did, the value of the CNH would be unlikely to fall to zero. Indeed, the exchange rate would probably continue to fluctuate wildly for as long as the Treasury's currency intervention lasted.[14] CNH would have some value as long as PRC exporters were willing to accept it as payment.[15] CNH would also retain some value as a "war option."[16] Even if China ran out of FX, it would still be able to purchase essential imports by issuing IOUs denominated in FX.[17] The U.S. government would therefore have to show credibly that it could sustain the short trade for as long as necessary.

Importantly, the point of the currency intervention would not be to destroy the CNH altogether, but to render it a poor store of value. At any given market price and set of exchange rates, firms and countries prefer to be paid in a stable and secure currency, rather than the same amount in a devalued, highly volatile, and/or nonconvertible one. This preference explains why all oil exporters today prefer to take payment in dollars rather than Bitcoin—except for Venezuela and Iran, which are subject to dollar sanctions and are therefore forced to sell their oil at a discount.[18] The goal of the currency intervention would not be to shut down trade with China. Indeed, the U.S. government would *encourage* China to continue to trade in dollars with the rest of the world by letting China keep using dollar payments networks: SWIFT and CHIPS. The goal, rather, would be to make it so that foreign countries and firms selling to China preferred to take payment in dollars, euros, or other currencies—anything other than CNH. Major central banks and institutional investors would also reduce or even eliminate their allocations of CNH, driving down the value further. Insofar as Beijing wanted to pay for its imports in a currency that had only speculative value, it would have to pay a premium above the global market price.

In this context, currency intervention would be highly likely to succeed if—but only if—the Treasury enjoyed an iron-clad and open-ended mandate from Congress. Congress can in theory authorize the Treasury to deploy an unlimited number of dollars for the purpose of shorting the CNH. On the other side of the trade, Beijing has and can theoretically acquire only a limited quantity of dollars to support the exchange rate by buying CNH and HKD. Thus, the goal of the operation would be to persuade both Beijing and the market that the CNH and HKD were indefensible. The surest way for Congress to prove this commitment would be to give the Treasury *unlimited* authorization to deploy dollars for the currency intervention. This would signal that Washington was staking the credibility of its own currency on its ability to destroy the CNH.

The effect of currency intervention on dollar prices is less clear, but it would not necessarily be inflationary. The Treasury would be *deploying* trillions of dollars to execute a financial operation. It would not be *spending* them or injecting them into the economy as a fiscal stimulus. In fact, shorting the CNH by borrowing CNH and selling it for dollars would *reduce* the dollar money supply. This on its own would cause the dollar to strengthen. The aggregate effect of the currency intervention on the dollar price level would depend largely on what happened to the value of the CNH and other peer currencies. This in turn would depend on how Beijing and financial markets responded to the Treasury's actions. If the currency intervention succeeded quickly and the CNH exchange rate collapsed, the impact on U.S. prices would probably be mildly deflationary. If the currency intervention took longer to work, because Beijing spent vast quantities of FX to buy CNH, the inflationary outlook could be uncertain for some time. It is possible that the dollar money supply could increase, with mildly inflationary results. The Federal Reserve would have to manage the effects of the Treasury's currency intervention. The Fed is by law an independent and nonpolitical entity. However, if the dollar money supply abruptly expanded or contracted as a result of the Treasury's currency intervention or PRC fire sales of dollar assets, the Fed would have to act accordingly to maintain macroeconomic and financial stability.

A successful currency intervention would incentivize capital outflows from China, creating a large and enduring financial stability risk for Beijing to manage. Capital controls would be like a dam, drained on the outside. If cracks ever opened in the dam, the CNY would sharply depreciate and depositors would empty their onshore accounts, risking a financial crisis in China. If the CNY depreciates, China would experience inflation, since key imports such as energy are priced in dollars. Over the longer term, inflation may threaten the legitimacy of the regime, as it did in the lead-up to the 1989 Tiananmen protests.[19] In the meantime, the steps that Beijing would have to take in response would make it much more cumbersome for foreign entities to do business using CNH. This would hamstring Beijing's efforts to internationalize its currency rapidly after Day One. A weakening CNH—by itself—would not be all bad for Beijing. A weaker currency would not necessarily make China's exports more competitive if these goods had to be shipped through a war zone. But in a quarantine scenario without kinetic conflict, or after a hypothetical war, a weak CNH would greatly boost the competitiveness of PRC exports. This would pose a challenge for the United States and its partners, but also an opportunity.

Notes

PRELIMS

1. "Inaugural Address of ROC 16th-term President Lai Ching-te," *Office of the President, Republic of China (Taiwan)*, May 20, 2024.
2. The most thoughtful discussion of the nomenclature debate is Richard Bush, *Difficult Choices: Taiwan's Quest for Security and the Good Life* (Washington, DC: Brookings Institution Press, 2021), xv–xviii.

INTRODUCTION

1. Elsa B. Kania and Ian Burns McCaslin, *The PLA's Evolving Outlook on Urban Warfare: Learning, Training, and Implications for Taiwan* (Washington, DC: Institute for the Study of War, April 2020), 1–43, https://understandingwar.org/wp-content/uploads/2025/04/The20PLA20Outlook20on20Urban20Warfare20ISW20April202022_0.pdf.
2. "Zhurihe Base," *South China Morning Post*, 2017, https://multimedia.scmp.com/2017/graphics/ZhuriheBase/index.html.
3. Michael Martina and Ben Blanchard, "China's Xi Calls for Building Elite Forces during Massive Military Parade," *Reuters*, July 30, 2017, https://www.reuters.com/article/us-china-defence-idUSKBN1AF0oJ.
4. On the CCP's grand strategy, see Rush Doshi, *The Long Game: China's Grand Strategy to Displace American Order* (New York: Oxford University Press, 2021); Kevin Rudd, *On Xi Jinping: How Xi's Marxist Nationalism Is Shaping China and the World* (Oxford: Oxford University Press, 2024); Steve Chang and Olivia Cheung, *The Political Thought of Xi Jinping* (Oxford: Oxford University Press, 2024).
5. Xi Jinping, "习近平: 承前启后继往开来 朝着中华民族伟大复兴目标奋勇前进," *Xi Jinping: Carrying on the Past and Forging Ahead into the Future, We Will Forge Ahead Courageously Toward the Goal of the Great Rejuvenation of the Chinese Nation*, 中国共产党新闻网 (*Chinese Communist Party News Network*), November 30, 2012, accessed June 1, 2024, http://cpc.people.com.cn/n/2012/1130/c64094-19746089.html; "关于实现中国梦的时间节点," On the Timeline for Realizing the Chinese Dream, 新华网 (*Xinhua News*), July 7, 2015, http://www.xinhuanet.com/politics/2015-07/07/c_127994345_2.htm; Elizabeth Economy, "China's Alternative Order," *Foreign Affairs*, April 23, 2024, https://www.foreignaffairs.com/china/chinas-alternative-order-xi-jinping-elizabeth-economy.
6. 中共中央网络安全和信息化委员会办公室 [Officer of the Central Cyberspace Affairs Commission], "生成式人工智能服务管理暂行办法," *Interim Measures for the Administration of Generative Artificial Intelligence Services*, July 13, 2023, https://www.cac.gov.cn/2023-07/13/c_1690898327029107.htm.
7. See 中国共产党第十九次全国代表大会 [CCP 19th Party Congress Report]. (English version "Secure a Decisive Victory in Building a Moderately Prosperous Society in All Respects and Strive for the Great Success of Socialism with Chinese Characteristics for

a New Era: Delivered at the 19th National Congress of the Communist Party of China," *Center for Strategic and International Studies (CSIS), Interpret: China*, October 18, 2017; "Hold High the Great Banner of Socialism with Chinese Characteristics and Strive in Unity to Build a Modern Socialist Country in All Respects—Report to the 20th National Congress of the Communist Party of China," *Center for Strategic and International Studies (CSIS), Interpret: China*, October 25, 2022; Matt Pottinger, *The Boiling Moat: Urgent Steps to Defend Taiwan* (Stanford, CA: Hoover Institution Press, 2024), 4.

8. 中华人民共和国外交部 [Ministry of Foreign Affairs of the People's Republic of China], "习近平在《告台湾同胞书》发表40周年纪念会上的讲话," *Xi Jinping's Speech at the Commemoration of the 40th Anniversary of the Publication of the Message to Compatriots in Taiwan*, January 2, 2019, accessed October 15, 2024, https://www.mfa.gov.cn/web/ziliao_674904/zt_674979/dnzt_674981/qtzt/twwt/xjpzsjstzyjh/202206/t20220606_10698873.html.

9. Isaac Kardon, "Combating the Gray Zone: Examining Chinese Threats to the Maritime Domain," *Carnegie Endowment for International Peace*, June 4, 2024, https://carnegieendowment.org/posts/2024/06/combating-the-gray-zone-examining-chinese-threats-to-the-maritime-domain?lang=en.

10. Robert D. Blackwill and Philip Zelikow, *The United States, China, and Taiwan: A Strategy to Prevent War* (New York: Council on Foreign Relations, 2021), 30–41.

11. Lonnie D. Henley, *China Maritime Report No. 26: Beyond the First Battle: Overcoming a Protracted Blockade of Taiwan* (Newport, RI: China Maritime Studies Institute, 2023), 1–11.

12. The term "joint blockade operation" (联合封锁战役) comes from the 2006 *Science of Campaigns* textbook published by China's National Defense University. See China Aerospace Studies Institute, *In Their Own Words: PLA's Science of Campaigns* (Montgomery, AL: China Aerospace Studies Institute, December 2, 2020), 329–350, https://www.airuniversity.af.edu/CASI/Display/Article/2421219/in-their-own-words-plas-science-of-campaigns/. On China's preparations for war, see *China's Stockpiling and Mobilization Measures for Competition and Conflict*, Hearing before the U.S.-China Economic and Security Review Commission, 118th Cong., 2d sess., June 13, 2024.

13. "习近平：加强顶层设计和底线思维，积极开展大国外交," *Xi Jinping: Strengthening Top-Level Design and Bottom Line Thinking, Actively Advancing Major Power Diplomacy, China.org*, December 2013, accessed November 15, 2024, http://henan.china.com.cn/news/china/201312/H084770T3Q.html; Nectar Gan, "Xi Jinping Tells China's National Security Chiefs to Prepare for 'Worst Case' Scenarios," *CNN*, June 1, 2023, https://edition.cnn.com/2023/05/31/china/china-xi-national-security-meeting-intl-hnk/index.html.

14. Richard Bush, *A One-China Policy Primer* (Washington, DC: Brookings Institution Press, 2017), https://www.brookings.edu/wp-content/uploads/2017/03/one-china-policy-primer-web-final.pdf.

15. "Background Note: Taiwan," *U.S. Department of State*, September 2008, https://2001-2009.state.gov/r/pa/ei/bgn/35855.htm.

16. *A Free and Open Indo-Pacific: Advancing a Shared Vision* (Washington, DC: U.S. Department of State, 2019), 5, https://www.state.gov/wp-content/uploads/2019/11/Free-and-Open-Indo-Pacific-4Nov2019.pdf.

17. "Remarks by Vice President Pence on the Administration's Policy toward China," *Trump White House Archives*, October 4, 2018, https://trumpwhitehouse.archives.gov/briefings-statements/remarks-vice-president-pence-administrations-policy-toward-china; "The Administration's Approach to the People's Republic of China," *U.S. Department of State*, May 26, 2022, https://www.state.gov/the-administrations-approach-to-the-peoples-republic-of-china.

18. David Sacks and Seaton Huang, "Onshoring Semiconductor Production: National Security Versus Economic Efficiency," *Council on Foreign Relations*, April 17, 2024, https://www.cfr.org/article/onshoring-semiconductor-production-national-security-versus-economic-efficiency.

19. Gabriel B. Collins, Andrew S. Erickson, and Matt Pottinger, "Taiwan: The Stakes," in *The Boiling Moat: Urgent Steps to Defend Taiwan*, ed. Matt Pottinger (Stanford, CA: Hoover Institution Press, 2024).

20. Pottinger, *The Boiling Moat*, 11–12.

21. Thompson Chau, "China Could Threaten War in 2023 to Force Talks: Taiwan Official," *Nikkei Asia*, October 20, 2022, https://asia.nikkei.com/Politics/International-relations/Taiwan-tensions/China-could-threaten-war-in-2023-to-force-talks-Taiwan-official.

22. "China's Xi Says Political Solution for Taiwan Can't Wait Forever," *Reuters*, October 6, 2013, https://www.reuters.com/article/us-asia-apec-china-taiwan/chinas-xi-says-political-solution-for-taiwan-cant-wait-forever-idUSBRE99503Q20131006; "Xinhua Headlines: Xi Says 'China Must Be, Will Be Reunified' as Key Anniversary Marked," *Xinhua*, January 2, 2019, accessed November 12, 2024, http://www.xinhuanet.com/english/2019-01/02/c_137714898.htm.

23. Steve Tsang and Olivia Cheung, *The Political Thought of Xi Jinping* (Oxford: Oxford University Press, 2024); Rush Doshi, *The Long Game: China's Grand Strategy to Displace American Order* (Oxford: Oxford University Press, 2021); Elizabeth Economy, *The World According to China* (Cambridge: Polity, 2022).

24. Ryan Hass, Bonnie Glaser, and Richard Bush, *U.S.-Taiwan Relations: Will China's Challenge Lead to a Crisis?* (Washington, DC: Brookings Institution Press, 2023); Richard Bush, *Difficult Choices: Taiwan's Quest for Security and the Good Life* (Washington, DC: Brookings Institution Press, 2021); Richard Bush, *At Cross Purposes: U.S.-Taiwan Relations Since 1942* (Abingdon, UK: Routledge, 2004).

25. Shelley Rigger, *The Tiger Leading the Dragon: How Taiwan Propelled China's Economic Rise* (Lanham, MD: Rowman & Littlefield, 2021); Hsiao-ting Lin, *Accidental State: Chiang Kai-shek, the United States, and the Making of Taiwan* (Cambridge, MA: Harvard University Press, 2016); Hsiao-ting Lin, *Taiwan, the United States, and the Hidden History of the Cold War in Asia* (Abingdon: Routledge, 2022); Sulmaan Wasif Khan, *The Struggle for Taiwan: A History of America, China, and the Island Caught Between* (New York: Basic Books, 2024); Jonathan Sullivan and Lev Nachman, *Taiwan: A Contested Democracy under Threat* (Newcastle: Agenda Publishing, 2024).

26. Thomas J. Christensen, "The Contemporary Security Dilemma: Deterring a Taiwan Conflict," *The Washington Quarterly* 25, no. 4 (2002): 5–21, https://doi.org/10.1162/016366002760252509; Bonnie S. Glaser, Jessica Chen Weiss, and Thomas J. Christensen, "Taiwan and the True Sources of Deterrence," *Foreign Affairs*, November 30, 2023, https://www.foreignaffairs.com/taiwan/taiwan-china-true-sources-deterrence; Thomas J. Christensen, M. Taylor Fravel, Bonnie S. Glaser, Andrew J. Nathan, and Jessica Chen Weiss, "How to Avoid a War over Taiwan," *Foreign Affairs*, October 13, 2022, https://www.foreignaffairs.com/china/how-avoid-war-over-taiwan; Thomas

J. Christensen, *The China Challenge: Shaping the Choices of a Rising Power* (New York: W. W. Norton, 2015); Scott L. Kastner, *War and Peace in the Taiwan Strait* (New York: Columbia University Press, 2022); Timothy W. Crawford, *Pivotal Deterrence: Third-Party Statecraft and the Pursuit of Peace* (Ithaca, NY: Cornell University Press, 2003).

27. Blackwill and Zelikow, *The United States, China, and Taiwan.*

28. Andrew S. Erickson, Conor M. Kennedy, and Ryan D. Martinson, eds., *Study No. 8, Chinese Amphibious Warfare: Prospects for a Cross-Strait Invasion* (Newport, RI: China Maritime Studies Institute, 2024), https://www.andrewerickson.com/wp-content/uploads/2024/11/Chinese-Amphibious-Warfare_Prospects-for-a-Cross-Strait-Invasion.pdf; Joel Wuthnow, Derek Grossman, Phillip C. Saunders, Andrew Scobell, and Andrew N.D. Yang, eds., *Crossing the Strait: China's Military Prepares for War with Taiwan* (Washington, DC: National Defense University Press, 2022), https://ndupress.ndu.edu/Portals/68/Documents/Books/crossing-the-strait/crossing-the-strait.pdf.

29. Dale C. Copeland, *Economic Interdependence and War* (Princeton, NJ: Princeton University Press, 2015); Mariya Grinberg, "Wartime Commercial Policy and Trade Between Enemies," *International Security* 46, no. 1 (2021): 9–52.

30. On China's nuclear policy, see Kaufman and Waidelich, *PRC Writings on Strategic Deterrence*; Henrik Stålhane Hiim, M. Taylor Fravel, and Magnus Langset Trøan, "The Dynamics of an Entangled Security Dilemma: China's Changing Nuclear Posture," *International Security* 47, no. 4 (Spring 2023), https://doi.org/10.1162/isec_a_00457. On cross-domain deterrence, see Gartzke and Lindsay, *Cross-Domain Deterrence*. On economic deterrence and sanctions, the three most essential works are Daniel Drezner, Henry Farrell, and Abraham L. Newman, *The Uses and Abuses of Weaponized Interdependence* (Washington, DC: Brookings Institution Press, 2021); Henry Farrell and Abraham L. Newman, *Underground Empire: How America Weaponized the World Economy* (New York: Henry Holt and Co., 2023); Edward Fishman, *Chokepoints: American Power in the Age of Economic Warfare* (New York: Penguin, 2025).

31. Hugo Bromley and Eyck Freymann, *On Day One: An Economic Contingency Plan for a Taiwan Crisis* (Stanford, CA: Hoover Institution Press, 2024); Hugo Bromley and Eyck Freymann, "The Malacca Myth," *International Security*, forthcoming; Eyck Freymann and Calvin Heng, "The Logic of Partial RMB Internationalization: PRC Perspectives on 'Financial War,'" *China Quarterly* (2025), 262, 429–444; Eyck Freymann and Harry Halem, *The Arsenal of Democracy: Technology, Industry, and American Leadership in the Indo-Pacific* (Stanford, CA: Hoover Institution Press, 2025).

32. Pence, "Remarks by Vice President Pence on China"; "The Administration's Approach to the People's Republic of China," *U.S. Department of State*, May 26, 2022, https://www.state.gov/the-administrations-approach-to-the-peoples-republic-of-china/.

33. U.S. Department of Defense, *2022 National Defense Strategy of the United States of America: Including the 2022 Nuclear Posture Review and the 2022 Missile Defense Review* (Washington, DC: U.S. Department of Defense, 2022), 8, https://media.defense.gov/2022/Oct/27/2003103845/-1/-1/1/2022-NATIONAL-DEFENSE-STRATEGY-NPR-MDR.PDF.

34. China's concept is referred to as "integrated strategic deterrence." Authoritative PRC texts interchangeably use the terms *zonghexing zhanlüe weishe* 综合性战略威慑 and *zhengti weishe* 整体威慑. See Peng Guangqian and Yao Youzhi [彭光谦, 姚有志], eds., *The Science of Military Strategy* [战略学] (Beijing: Military Science Press [军事科学出版社], 2001), 236, 238, 243; Peng Guangqian and Yao Youzhi, eds., *The Science of Military*

Strategy, official English translation of the 2001 Chinese edition (Beijing: Military Science Press, 2005); *The Science of Military Strategy* (Beijing: Academy of Military Science, 2013). Cited in Michael S. Chase and Arthur Chan, *China's Evolving Approach to "Integrated Strategic Deterrence"* (Santa Monica, CA: RAND Corporation), footnote 7, 3–4, https://www.rand.org/pubs/research_reports/RR1366.html.

35. Other books with similar ambition include Graham Allison, *Destined for War: Can America and China Escape Thucydides's Trap?* (Boston: Houghton Mifflin Harcourt, 2017); Kevin Rudd, *The Avoidable War: The Dangers of a Catastrophic Conflict Between the US and Xi Jinping's China* (New York: Hachette, 2022); and Elbridge A. Colby, *The Strategy of Denial: American Defense in an Age of Great Power Conflict* (New Haven, CT: Yale University Press, 2021).

36. Colby, The Strategy of Denial, 1.

37. The best study of cross-domain deterrence is Erik Gartzke and Jon R. Lindsay, eds., *Cross-Domain Deterrence: Strategy in an Era of Complexity* (New York: Oxford University Press, 2019). Successive administrations have pointed to the need for this form of deterrence. See Erik Gartzke and Jon Lindsay, "The U.S. Department of Deterrence," *War on the Rocks*, July 22, 2024, https://warontherocks.com/2024/07/the-u-s-department-of-deterrence.

38. *Reset, Prevent, Build: A Strategy to Win America's Economic Competition with the Chinese Communist Party* (Washington, DC: Select Committee on the Strategic Competition Between the United States and the Chinese Communist Party, December 12, 2023), https://selectcommitteeontheccp.house.gov/sites/evo-subsites/selectcommitteeontheccp.house.gov/files/evo-media-document/reset-prevent-build-scc-report.pdf.

39. Eyck Freymann and Hugo Bromley, "The Case for 'Avalanche Decoupling' from China," *Foreign Affairs*, January 29, 2025, https://www.foreignaffairs.com/china/case-avalanche-decoupling-china.

40. Iskander Rehman, *Planning for Protraction: A Historically Informed Approach to Great-Power War and Sino-US Competition* (Abingdon: Routledge, 2023).

CHAPTER I

1. Rehman, *Planning for Protraction*.

2. "President Xi Jinping Meets with U.S. President Joe Biden in Lima," *Ministry of Foreign Affairs of the People's Republic of China*, November 17, 2024, https://www.fmprc.gov.cn/mfa_eng/xw/zyxw/202411/t20241117_11527672.html.

3. "Readout of President Joe Biden's Meeting with President Xi Jinping of the People's Republic of China," *U.S. Mission China*, November 17, 2024, https://china.usembassy-china.org.cn/readout-of-president-joe-bidens-meeting-with-president-xi-jinping-of-the-peoples-republic-of-china-3.

4. Scott L. Kastner, *War and Peace in the Taiwan Strait* (New York: Columbia University Press, 2022). See also Richard C. Bush, *At Cross Purposes: U.S.-Taiwan Relations Since 1942* (Armonk, NY: M. E. Sharpe, 2004); Richard C. Bush, *Untying the Knot: Making Peace in the Taiwan Strait* (Washington, DC: Brookings Institution Press, 2005); Richard C. Bush, *Uncharted Strait: The Future of China-Taiwan Relations* (Washington, DC: Brookings Institution Press, 2013); Ryan Hass, Bonnie S. Glaser, and Richard C. Bush, *U.S.-Taiwan Relations: Will China's Challenge Lead to a Crisis?* (Washington, DC:

Brookings Institution Press, 2023); Shelley Rigger, *Why Taiwan Matters: Small Island, Global Powerhouse* (Lanham, MD: Rowman & Littlefield, 2021); Shelley Rigger, *Politics in Taiwan: Voting for Democracy* (Abingdon: Routledge, 2002).

5. Jun Tao Yeung, "Why Is Taiwan So Important? The Manipulation of Nationalism in Legitimizing One-Party Rule in China," *The Yale Review of International Studies*, October 29, 2019, https://yris.yira.org/asia/why-is-taiwan-so-important-the-manipulation-of-nationalism-in-legitimizing-one-party-rule-in-china. See also Hardina Ohlendorf, "The Taiwan Dilemma in Chinese Nationalism: Taiwan Studies in the People's Republic of China," *Asian Survey* 54, no. 3 (2014): 471–491, https://doi.org/10.1525/as.2014.54.3.471; James Palmer, "Why China Won't Back Off Taiwan," *Foreign Policy*, October 13, 2021, https://foreignpolicy.com/2021/10/13/china-taiwan-xi-jinping-tsai-ing-wen-speech.

6. Danielle Maguire, "Why Does China Want Taiwan When It's Already So Big and Rich? The Answer Is about More Than Land and Money," *ABC News*, August 12, 2022, https://www.abc.net.au/news/2022-08-12/why-does-china-want-taiwan-military-strategic-location/101321856. See also "White Paper: The Taiwan Question and China's Reunification in the New Era," *Embassy of the People's Republic of China in the United States of America*, August 10, 2022, http://us.china-embassy.gov.cn/eng/zgyw/202208/t20220810_10740168.htm; Joshua Espena and Chelsea Bomping, "The Taiwan Frontier and the Chinese Dominance for the Second Island Chain," *Australian Institute of International Affairs*, August 13, 2020, https://www.internationalaffairs.org.au/australianoutlook/taiwan-frontier-chinese-dominance-for-second-island-chain.

7. "Questions and Answers Concerning the Taiwan Question (2): What Is the One-China Principle? What Is the Basis of the One-China Principle?," *Mission of the People's Republic of China to the European Union*, August 15, 2022; Yu-Jie Chen and Jerome A. Cohen, "China-Taiwan Relations Re-Examined: The '1992 Consensus' and Cross-Strait Agreements," *University of Pennsylvania Asian Law Review* 14 (2019): 1–40; Interview with Su Chi, August 15, 2023; Alan D. Romberg, "The '1992 Consensus'—Adapting to the Future?" *China Leadership Monitor* 49 (2016): 1–17; Austin Wang, Charles K. S. Wu, Yao-Yuan Yeh, and Fang-Yu Chen, "What Does the 1992 Consensus Mean to Citizens in Taiwan?" *The Diplomat*, November 10, 2018; Austin Horng-En Wang, Yao-Yuan Yeh, Charles K. S. Wu, and Fang-Yu Chen, "The Non-Consensus 1992 Consensus," *Asian Politics & Policy* 13, no. 2 (2021): 212–227; Dean P. Chen and Kiely Paris-Rodriguez, *The Role of the 1992 Consensus and Taiwan's 2024 Presidential Elections* (East-West Center, 2024).

8. Xin Liu and Lingzhi Fan, "Scholars Outline Conditions to Be Met for China's Peaceful Reunification," *Global Times*, August 13, 2022, https://www.globaltimes.cn/page/202208/1272868.shtml.

9. Jacob Stokes, *Resisting China's Gray Zone Military Pressure on Taiwan* (Washington, DC: Center for a New American Security, 2023), https://www.cnas.org/publications/reports/resisting-chinas-gray-zone-military-pressure-on-taiwan.

10. "Global Freedom Status," *Freedom House*, accessed December 9, 2024, https://freedomhouse.org/explore-the-map?type=fiw&year=2024.

11. These are Kinmen, Matsu, Wuchiu, Penghu, Pratas, and Taiping.

12. All costs discussed in this book are in U.S. dollars unless otherwise noted.

13. Ministry of National Defense, Republic of China, "112年國防報告書," *2023 National Defense Report* (Taipei: Ministry of National Defense, Republic of China, 2023).

14. Department of Statistics, Ministry of Economic Affairs, "半導體業全年產值可望續創新高," *Semiconductor Industry's Annual Output Expected to Reach New Highs*, October 5, 2022.

15. Taiwan Institute of Economic Research, "2025台灣總體經濟預測," *2025 Taiwan Macroeconomic Forecast*, November 7, 2024, https://www.tier.org.tw/forecast/macro_trends_annual.aspx. On the 99 percent figure, see Lauren Faith Lau and Annabelle Droulers, "TSMC Supplier's CEO Dismisses AI Concerns after Nvidia Wipeout," *Bloomberg*, September 4, 2024, https://www.bloomberg.com/news/articles/2024-09-04/tsmc-supplier-s-ceo-dismisses-ai-concerns-after-nvidia-wipeout.

16. Chen-Yuan Tung, *Taiwan and the Global Semiconductor Supply Chain* (Singapore: Taipei Representative Office in Singapore, 2023), https://roc-taiwan.org/uploads/sites/86/2023/12/December-2023-Semi-Report.pdf.

17. Yimou Lee and Sarah Wu, "'Tip of the Iceberg': Taiwan's Spy Catchers Hunt Chinese Poachers of Chip Talent," *Reuters*, April 8, 2022, https://www.reuters.com/world/asia-pacific/tip-iceberg-taiwans-spy-catchers-hunt-chinese-poachers-chip-talent-2022-04-08; Pan Che, "Tech War: China Pumps Up State Subsidies for Chip Industry to Counter US Sanctions," *South China Morning Post*, September 25, 2024, https://www.scmp.com/tech/tech-war/article/3274599/tech-war-china-pumps-state-subsidies-chip-industry-counter-us-sanctions?module=perpetual_scroll_0&pgtype=article.

18. Marie Boran, "Joe Biden Just Trump-Proofed His Hallmark CHIPS Act," *Newsweek*, November 20, 2024, https://www.newsweek.com/biden-chips-act-taiwan-tsmc-trump-1988924.

19. Yuri Kageyama, "Taiwan Giant Chipmaker TSMC Opens First Plant in Japan as Part of Key Global Expansion," *Associated Press*, February 24, 2024, https://apnews.com/article/tsmc-semiconductor-chips-taiwan-sony-japan-toyota-2b42cfe27047f68c5edc5228eb27e0c1.

20. Joyce Huang, "Can Taiwan's Silicon Shield Protect It Against China's Aggression?" *Voice of America*, May 10, 2021, https://www.voanews.com/a/east-asia-pacific_can-taiwans-silicon-shield-protect-it-against-chinas-aggression/6205660.html; Jieh-min Wu, "Silicon Shield 2.0: A Taiwan Perspective," *The Diplomat*, September 14, 2024, https://thediplomat.com/2024/09/silicon-shield-2-0-a-taiwan-perspective; "'Silicon Shield' Not Taiwan-Centric: Academic," *Taipei Times*, August 26, 2024, https://www.taipeitimes.com/News/taiwan/archives/2024/08/26/2003822780.

21. Chris Miller, *Chip War: The Fight for the World's Most Critical Technology* (New York: Scribner, 2022); Chris Miller, "Transcript: Who Is Winning the Chip Wars? With Chris Miller," interview by Soumaya Keynes, *Financial Times*, August 26, 2024, https://www.ft.com/content/42bde830-ad35-4b3a-b13b-03390aceee25; Lisa Wang, "TSMC Cannot Make 2nm Chips Abroad Now: MOEA," *Taipei Times*, November 8, 2024, https://www.taipeitimes.com/News/biz/archives/2024/11/08/2003826545.

22. Stephen Ezell, *How Innovative Is China in Semiconductors?* (Washington, DC: Information Technology and Innovation Foundation, 2024), https://www2.itif.org/2024-china-semiconductors.pdf; Jonathan O'Callaghan, "Who's Making Chips for AI? Chinese Manufacturers Lag Behind US Tech Giants," *Nature*, May 3, 2024, https://www.nature.com/articles/d41586-024-01292-1; Jordan Schneider, Arrian Ebrahimi, and Chris Miller, "To Win the Chip War, the U.S. Must Prioritize Revolutionary Research," *The Washington Post*, May 30, 2024, https://www.washingtonpost.com/opinions/2024/05/30/semiconductor-industry-china-research-development.

23. "Global AI Power Rankings: Stanford HAI Tool Ranks 36 Countries in AI," *Stanford Institute for Human-Centered Artificial Intelligence*, November 21, 2024, https://hai. stanford.edu/news/global-ai-power-rankings-stanford-hai-tool-ranks-36-countries-ai.

24. "Legislative History—Constitution of the Republic of China (Taiwan)," *Laws and Regulations Database of the Republic of China (Taiwan)*, accessed December 9, 2024, https:// law.moj.gov.tw/Eng/LawClass/LawHistory.aspx?pcode=A0000001.

25. United Nations General Assembly, *Restoration of the Lawful Rights of the People's Republic of China in the United Nations*, A/RES/2758 (October 25, 1971), https://undocs.org/ en/A/RES/2758.

26. According to longstanding policy, Beijing will not conduct diplomatic relations with any country that recognizes Taiwan: Yu-Jie Chen and Jerome Cohen, "Why Does the WHO Exclude Taiwan?," *Council on Foreign Relations*, April 9, 2020, https:// www.cfr.org/in-brief/why-does-who-exclude-taiwan; Sigrid Winkler, "Taiwan in International Organizations: New Road Ahead or Dead End?" in *Political Changes in Taiwan Under Ma Ying-jeou*, ed. Jean-Pierre Cabestan and Jacques deLisle (London: Routledge, 2014).

27. As at June 2024, these are Belize, Guatemala, Haiti, Holy See, Marshall Islands, Palau, Paraguay, St Lucia, St Kitts and Nevis, St Vincent and the Grenadines, Eswatini and Tuvalu. "Diplomatic Allies," *Ministry of Foreign Affairs, Republic of China (Taiwan)*, accessed June 1, 2024, https://en.mofa.gov.tw/AlliesIndex.aspx?n=1294&sms=1007.

28. Zongyuan Zoe Liu, "What the China-Solomon Islands Pact Means for the U.S. and South Pacific," *Council on Foreign Relations*, May 4, 2022, https://www.cfr.org/in-brief/china-solomon-islands-security-pact-us-south-pacific; Joel Atkinson, "China–Taiwan Diplomatic Competition and the Pacific Islands," *The Pacific Review* 23, no. 4 (August 13, 2010): 407–427, https://www.tandfonline.com/doi/abs/10.1080/09512748.2010. 495998.

29. Russell Hsiao, "President Lai's Inauguration Speech: Resurrecting 'Two Sides, Two Constitutions'," *Global Taiwan Institute*, June 12, 2024, https://globaltaiwan.org/2024/06/ president-lais-inauguration-speech-resurrecting-two-sides-two-constitutions.

30. Ministry of Foreign Affairs of the People's Republic of China, "一个中国的原则与台湾问题," *The One-China Principle and the Taiwan Issue*, February 2000, https:// www.mfa.gov.cn/web/ziliao_674904/zt_674979/dnzt_674981/qtzt/twwt/twwtbps/ 202206/t20220606_10699030.html.

31. Yu-Jie Chen and Jerome A. Cohen, "China-Taiwan Relations Re-examined: The '1992 Consensus' and Cross-Strait Agreements," *Asian Law Review* 14, no. 1 (2019). See also Qi Su and Anguo Zheng, eds., *Yi ge Zhongguo, ge zi biao shu gong shi de shi shi [One China, with Respective Interpretations: A Historical Account of the Consensus of 1992]* (Beijing: Guo jia zheng ce yan jiu ji jin hui, 2002).

32. "Xi Jinping: Working Together to Realize Rejuvenation of the Chinese Nation and Advance China's Peaceful Reunification Speech at the Meeting Marking the 40th Anniversary of the Issuance of the Message to Compatriots in Taiwan," *Wikisource*, January 2, 2019, https://en.wikisource.org/wiki/Working_Together_to_Realize_ Rejuvenation_of_the_Chinese_Nation_and_Advance_China%E2%80%99s_Peaceful_ Reunification.

33. Taiwan Affairs Office of the State Council, "台湾问题与新时代中国统一事业," *The Taiwan Issue and China's Reunification in the New Era*, August 2022, https://www.gov. cn/zhengce/2022-08/10/content_5704839.htm.

34. Sean Cooney, "Why Taiwan Is Not Hong Kong: A Review of the PRC's 'One Country Two Systems' Model for Reunification with Taiwan," *Washington International Law Journal* 6, no. 3 (January 1, 1997): 497, https://digitalcommons.law.uw.edu/cgi/viewcontent.cgi?article=1124&context=wilj; Ho-fung Hung and Huei-Ying Kuo, "'One Country, Two Systems' and Its Antagonists in Tibet and Taiwan," *China Information* 24, no. 3 (October 29, 2010): 317–337, https://journals.sagepub.com/doi/abs/10.1177/0920203X10382710?journalCode=cina.

35. Lindsay Maizland and Clara Fong, "Hong Kong's Freedoms: What China Promised and How It's Cracking Down," *Council on Foreign Relations*, updated March 19, 2024, https://www.cfr.org/backgrounder/hong-kong-freedoms-democracy-protests-china-crackdown.

36. Xi Jinping, "在《告台湾同胞书》发表40周年纪念会上的讲话," *Speech at the Meeting Marking the 40th Anniversary of the Issuance of the Message to Compatriots in Taiwan*, *Xinhua*, January 2, 2019, http://www.xinhuanet.com/tw/2019-01/02/c_1210028622.htm.

37. Yiyao Alex Fan and Bonnie S. Glaser, *Interpreting Xi Jinping's "'Two Systems' Taiwan Plan"* (Washington, DC: German Marshall Fund of the United States, August 2024), 8–10, https://www.gmfus.org/sites/default/files/2024-08/Interpreting%20Xi%20Jinping%E2%80%99s%20%E2%80%9C%E2%80%98Two%20Systems%E2%80%99%20Taiwan%20Plan%E2%80%9D%20-%20Final.pdf. For the conservative position, see Weifeng Guo, Jianmin Zhou, Ping Wang, and Weimin Guo, eds., 一国两制台湾方案初论 *A Preliminary Discussion on the One Country, Two Systems Taiwan Plan* (China Review Academic Publishers Limited, 2023), 29, 104, 249–252, 288–290, 339, 415.

38. Fan and Glaser, *Interpreting Xi Jinping's "Two Systems" Taiwan Plan*, 5–6. For the progressive position, see Guo et al., eds., *A Preliminary Discussion on the One Country, Two Systems Taiwan Plan*, 195–196, 227, 283–284, 367.

39. Fan and Glaser, *Interpreting Xi Jinping's "Two Systems" Taiwan Plan*, 11.

40. Lyle Morris, "Listen to Xi Jinping about Taiwan," *War on the Rocks*, November 18, 2022, https://warontherocks.com/2022/11/listen-to-xi-jingping-about-taiwan/.

41. John Pomfret, "Beijing Warns of a 'Calamity' for Taiwan," *Washington Post*, July 18, 1999, https://www.washingtonpost.com/archive/politics/1999/08/04/beijing-warns-of-a-calamity-for-taiwan/3a63623b-97aa-48db-b84d-c8df31ec6fa1/.

42. National People's Congress of the People's Republic of China, "反分裂国家法," *Anti-Secession Law*, March 14, 2005, https://www.gov.cn/ziliao/flfg/2005-06/21/content_8265.htm; Keyuan Zou, "Governing the Taiwan Issue in Accordance with Law: An Essay on China's Anti-Secession Law," *Chinese Journal of International Law* 4, no. 2 (January 1, 2005): 455–463; Jing You, "China's Anti-Secession Law and the Risk of War in the Taiwan Strait," *Contemporary Security Policy* 27, no. 2 (August 1, 2006): 237–257; Sui Sheng Zhao, "Conflict Prevention across the Taiwan Strait and the Making of China's Anti-Secession Law," *Asian Perspective* 30, no. 1 (January 1, 2006): 79–94.

43. Li Zhanshu, "坚决反对'台独'分裂，坚定推进祖国和平统一——在《反分裂国家法》实施15周年座谈会上的讲话," *Resolutely Oppose "Taiwan Independence" Secession and Firmly Promote the Peaceful Reunification of the Motherland—Speech at the Symposium on the 15th Anniversary of the Implementation of the "Anti-Secession Law,"* *National People's Congress of the People's Republic of China*, May 29, 2020, http://www.gwytb.gov.cn/wyly/202005/t20200529_12278461.htm.

44. Bureau of East Asian and Pacific Affairs, "U.S. Relations with Taiwan: Fact Sheet," *U.S. Department of State*, May 28, 2022, https://www.state.gov/u-s-relations-with-taiwan/.

45. On August 17, 1945, Douglas MacArthur, Supreme Commander for the Allied Powers, instructed Japanese commanders in "China . . . Formosa and French Indo-China" to surrender to Chiang Kai-Shek, President of the Republic of China. In October, U.S. naval vessels ferried Nationalist troops to Taiwan to accept the Japanese surrender. The ROC and PRC both officially claim that the ceremony handed Taiwan to "China." However, the U.S. position was slightly different. MacArthur's order listed "Formosa" separately from "China," implying that the U.S. government did not necessarily believe that the former was an appendage of the latter. Notably, MacArthur also let Chiang accept Japan's surrender of French Indo-China, even though that colony belonged to France. Washington had no interest in changing this position after Communist forces expelled the ROC government from the mainland in 1949. In the Treaty of San Francisco (September 1951), Japan legally "renounce[d] all right, title and claim to Formosa and the Pescadores." However, neither this document nor the Potsdam and Cairo declarations *transferred* control of Taiwan to China. This would typically require a treaty between China and Japan. As a 1961 State Department memo noted, "the most tenable theory regarding the status of Formosa . . . is that sovereignty over the islands has not yet been finally determined." See "Directive by President Truman to the Supreme Commander for the Allied Powers in Japan (MacArthur): Instruments for the Surrender of Japan, General Order No. 1, Military and Naval," *Office of the Historian*, August 15, 1945, https://history.state.gov/historicaldocuments/frus1945v07/d390; "San Francisco Peace Treaty," *Ministry of Foreign Affairs of Japan*, accessed December 29, 2023, https://www.mofa.go.jp/region/europe/russia/territory/edition92/period4.html; Lung-chu Chen and W. M. Reisman, "Who Owns Taiwan: A Search for International Title," *The Yale Law Journal* 81, no. 4 (March 1972): 599–671.

46. A total of 181 countries currently recognize Beijing as the sole legal government of China. Fifty-one of these accept Beijing's formulation of the "One China Principle"; the rest take ambiguous positions, which come in several varieties. Thirteen countries recognize Taiwan as a sovereign state, and Taiwan is not itself a member of the United Nations. See Ian Ja Chong, "The Many 'One Chinas': Multiple Approaches to Taiwan and China," *Carnegie Endowment for International Peace*, February 9, 2023, https://carnegieendowment.org/2023/02/09/many-one-chinas-multiple-approaches-to-taiwan-and-china-pub-89003.

47. See "Kissinger Transcripts and Related Material," *National Security Archive*, n.d., https://nsarchive2.gwu.edu/nsa/publications/DOC_readers/kissinger/docs/index.html.

48. In Chinese: 美国方面声明:美国认识到,在台湾海峡两边的所有中国人都认为只有一个中国,台湾是中国的一部分。美国政府对这一立场不提出异议。它重申它对由中国人自己和平解决台湾问题的关心. For the English version, see U.S. Department of State, *Foreign Relations of the United States, 1969–1976, Volume XVII, China, 1969–1972*, Document 203, "Joint Statement Following Discussions with Leaders of the People's Republic of China," February 17, 1972, https://history.state.gov/historicaldocuments/frus1969-76v17/d203. For the Chinese version, see Ministry of Foreign Affairs of the People's Republic of China, "中美联合公报(摘录)," *Sino-US Joint Communique (Excerpt)*, February 28, 1972, updated June 6, 2022, https://www.mfa.gov.cn/web/ziliao_674904/zt_674979/dnzt_674981/qtzt/zmlhgb/202206/t20220606_10699039.shtml.

49. Rosemary Foot, "Prizes Won, Opportunities Lost: The US Normalization of Relations with China, 1972–1979," in *Normalization of US-China Relations*, eds. William Kirby, Robert Ross, and Gong Li (Harvard University Asia Center, 2005), 90–115; Hong N. Kim and Jack L. Hammersmith, "U.S.-China Relations in the Post-Normalization Era, 1979–1985," *Pacific Affairs* 59, no. 1 (January 1, 1986), https://doi.org/10.2307/2759004.

50. "U.S.-PRC Joint Communique (1979)," *American Institute in Taiwan*, May 12, 2022, https://www.ait.org.tw/u-s-prc-joint-communique-1979.

51. The Second Communiqué was negotiated in English, but in the final days, Beijing introduced a Chinese-language translation that altered a critical word. As Michael Oksenberg of the National Security Council noted, Carter's team "never saw the Chinese translation. . . . We worked entirely from the English." Beijing replaced *renshidao* (acknowledge) with *chengren* (accept) in the sentence: "The U.S. acknowledges the Chinese position that there is but one China and Taiwan is a part of it." Oksenberg warned that *chengren* implied stronger agreement, calling it a tampering with the "holy writ" of the Shanghai Communiqué. The Carter administration dismissed the Chinese text as nonauthoritative, but Beijing claimed it signaled U.S. acceptance of its "One China Principle." As Oksenberg pointed out, "both Peking and the U.S. worked from the English text," which mirrored the Shanghai Communiqué. Still, it is remarkable that the "political foundation" of U.S.–China relations rests on a deliberate translation discrepancy. See Michel Oksenberg, Memorandum to Zbigniew Brzezinski, "A Translation Problem in the Joint Communique," January 3, 1979, in *Foreign Relations of the United States, 1977–1980, Volume XIII, China*, ed. David P. Nickles (Washington, DC: United States Government Printing Office, 2013), Document 186, https://history.state.gov/historicaldocuments/frus1977-80v13/d186.

52. "Joint Communiqué of the People's Republic of China and the United States of America (August 17, 1982)," *Embassy of the People's Republic of China in the United States of America*, July 1, 2012, http://us.china-embassy.gov.cn/eng/zmgx/zywj/lhgb/201207/t20120701_4917626.htm.

53. The U.S. side never violated its lawful commitments to Taiwan under the Mutual Defense Treaty. Article 10 outlined the provision for either party to terminate it by providing a one-year notice. Consequently, the treaty concluded on January 1, 1980, one year after the establishment of diplomatic relations between the United States and the People's Republic of China.

54. Steven M. Goldstein and Randall Schriver, "An Uncertain Relationship: The United States, Taiwan, and the Taiwan Relations Act," *The China Quarterly* 165 (March 1, 2001): 147–172; Shelley Rigger, "The Taiwan Relations Act: Past, Present, Future," *Asia Policy* 26, no. 4 (January 1, 2019): 11–17.

55. "Taiwan Relations Act (Public Law 96-8, 22 U.S.C. 3301 Et Seq.)," *American Institute in Taiwan*, March 30, 2022, https://www.ait.org.tw/taiwan-relations-act-public-law-96-8-22-u-s-c-3301-et-seq.

56. *American Institute in Taiwan*, "Taiwan Relations Act."

57. Jacques deLisle, "The Enduring—If Troubled—Genius of the Taiwan Relations Act, 45 Years On," *Global Taiwan Brief* 9, no. 7 (2024), https://globaltaiwan.org/wp-content/uploads/2024/04/GTB-Volume-9-Issue-7-2.pdf.

58. Hass, Glaser, and Bush, *U.S.-Taiwan Relations*, 155.

59. 中共中央台办、国务院台办 [Taiwan Affairs Office of the CPC Central Committee, Taiwan Affairs Office of the State Council], "国台办:美方所谓'与台湾关系法'及'六项保证'非法无效," *Taiwan Affairs Office: The So-Called 'Taiwan Relations Act' and 'Six Assurances' of the United States Are Illegal and Invalid*, April 10, 2024, http://www.gwytb.gov.cn/m/fyrbt/202404/t20240410_12612361.htm.

60. "Declassified Cables: Taiwan Arms Sales & Six Assurances (1982)," *American Institute in Taiwan*, March 30, 2022, https://www.ait.org.tw/declassified-cables-taiwan-arms-sales-six-assurances-1982.

61. Christensen, "PRC Security Relations with the United States"; Michael D. Swaine, "Trouble in Taiwan," *Foreign Affairs*, March 1, 2004, https://www.foreignaffairs.com/articles/asia/2004-03-01/trouble-taiwan.

62. "国民党全代会通过坚持'九二共识'," *KMT Congress Backs '1992 Consensus'*, *Taipei Times*, September 7, 2020, https://www.taipeitimes.com/News/front/archives/2020/09/07/2003742939.

63. Wang et al., "The Non-Consensus 1992 Consensus."

64. Yang Kuang-shun, "'Troublemaker' and 'Pawn': U.S.-Related Narratives Amid Taiwan's Presidential Election," *The Diplomat*, January 9, 2024, https://thediplomat.com/2024/01/troublemaker-and-pawn-us-related-narratives-amid-taiwans-presidential-election.

65. Zaki Atia, "KMT Factional Divisions and Their Implications for the 2024 Election," *Global Taiwan Institute*, March 8, 2023, https://globaltaiwan.org/2023/03/kmt-factional-divisions-and-their-implications-for-the-2024-election.

66. Jono Thompson, "Tainan Legislator Says China, Taiwan Share 'Same Blood, Culture' While Calling for Cross-Strait Peace," *Taiwan News*, March 31, 2024, https://www.taiwannews.com.tw/news/5133759; Russell Hsiao, "KMT Vice Chairman's PRC Tour Highlights Party's Difficult Balancing Act," *Global Taiwan Institute*, September 7, 2022, https://globaltaiwan.org/2022/09/kmt-vice-chairmans-prc-tour-highlights-partys-difficult-balancing-act; Ben Blanchard and Yimou Lee, "Taiwan Presidential Frontrunner Accuses Opposition Party of Being 'Pro-Communist'," *Reuters*, December 26, 2023, https://www.reuters.com/world/asia-pacific/taiwan-presidential-frontrunner-accuses-opposition-party-being-pro-communist-2023-12-26.

67. Kharis Templeman, "How Taiwan Stands Up to China," *Journal of Democracy* 31 (2020): 91–93, https://dx.doi.org/10.1353/jod.2020.0047.

68. Lev Nachman and Brian Hioe, "No, Taiwan's President Isn't 'Pro-Independence'," *The Diplomat*, April 23, 2020, https://thediplomat.com/2020/04/no-taiwans-president-isnt-pro-independence.

69. This policy is based on an internal DPP resolution, adopted in 1999, called the "Resolution on Taiwan's Future" (台灣前途決議文).

70. Brian Hioe and Lev Nachman, "Taiwanese Presidents Will Not and Can Not Unilaterally Change Taiwan's Status," *The Diplomat*, September 21, 2021, https://thediplomat.com/2021/09/taiwanese-presidents-will-not-and-can-not-unilaterally-change-taiwans-status.

71. Courtney Donovan Smith, "We're All Pro-Taiwan Independence Now," *Taiwan News*, January 16, 2023, https://www.taiwannews.com.tw/en/news/4782886.

72. Yi Zhang, "'Taiwan Independence' Ideology Condemned," *China Daily*, May 21, 2024, https://www.chinadaily.com.cn/a/202405/21/WS664cbb01a31082fc043c85d8.html.

73. During Chen Shui-bian's presidency (2000–2008), Chen and other DPP officials provocatively flirted with the prospect of offering ballot referenda that many analysts

saw as a first step toward eventually declaring independence. The Bush administration publicly admonished Chen for disrupting peace and stability. Keith Bradsher, "Taiwan's Leader Tones Down Referendum Opposed by Beijing," *New York Times*, January 17, 2004, https://www.nytimes.com/2004/01/17/world/taiwan-s-leader-tones-down-referendum-opposed-by-beijing.html.

74. As President George Bush said at the time: "We oppose any unilateral decision by either China or Taiwan to change the status quo. . . . [The] comments and actions made by the leader of Taiwan indicate that he may be willing to make decisions unilaterally, to change the status quo, which we oppose." Brian Knowlton, "Bush Warns Taiwan to Keep Status Quo: China Welcomes U.S. Stance," *New York Times*, December 10, 2003, https://www.nytimes.com/2003/12/10/news/bush-warns-taiwan-to-keep-status-quo-china-welcomes-us-stance.html; "Bush Warns Taiwan to Keep Status Quo: China Welcomes U.S. Stance," *New York Times*, December 10, 2003, https://www.nytimes.com/2003/12/10/news/bush-warns-taiwan-to-keep-status-quo-china-welcomes-us-stance.html. See also Thomas J. Christensen, "A Strong and Moderate Taiwan" (speech, U.S.-Taiwan Business Council Defense Industry Conference, Annapolis, Maryland, September 11), 2007, *U.S. Department of State*, https://2001-2009.state.gov/p/eap/rls/rm/2007/91979.htm.

75. Office of the President, Republic of China (Taiwan), "Inaugural Address of ROC 16th-term President Lai Ching-te," May 20, 2024. https://english.president.gov.tw/News/6726.

76. Office of the President, Republic of China (Taiwan), "President Tsai Interviewed by BBC," January 18, 2020. https://english.president.gov.tw/News/5962.

77. Yun Sun, "China's View of Lai Ching-te and the Pending Crisis in the Taiwan Strait," *China Leadership Monitor*, November 29, 2024, https://www.prcleader.org/post/china-s-view-of-lai-ching-te-and-the-pending-crisis-in-the-taiwan-strait, 4.

78. 中央通訊社 [Central News Agency], "賴清德:不會另行宣布台灣獨立," *Lai Qingte: Taiwan's Independence Will Not Be Declared Separately*, September 26, 2017, https://www.cna.com.tw/news/firstnews/201709265011.aspx; "Lai Explains Approach to Independence," *Taipei Times*, April 16, 2018, https://www.taipeitimes.com/News/front/archives/2018/04/16/2003691399.

79. Eric Cheung, "Taiwan Faces a Flood of Disinformation from China Ahead of Crucial Election. Here's How It's Fighting Back," *CNN*, December 16, 2023, https://www.cnn.com/2023/12/15/asia/taiwanelection-disinformation-china-technology-intl-hnk/index.html.

80. 王英津, "賴清德 '就職演说'充斥着赤裸裸的'台独'挑衅," 光明网, May 23, 2024, https://news.gmw.cn/2024-05/23/content_37337954.htm; "专家:赖清德'双十'讲话极具欺骗性、挑衅性、危害性," 新华网, October 13, 2024, http://www.news.cn/tw/20241013/c3daec007b374e309adacf4620b6ecf1/c.html.

81. Lai referred to mainland China simply as "China" (中国) rather than Tsai's preferred formulations: the "opposite side of the strait" (对岸) or "mainland China" (大陆). See Office of the President, Republic of China (Taiwan), "總統發表就職演說宣示打造民主和平繁榮的新臺灣," *Presidential Inaugural Address: Declaring a New Democratic, Peaceful, and Prosperous Taiwan*, May 20, 2024, https://www.president.gov.tw/News/28428. For analysis, see Rush Doshi and David Sacks, "Analyzing Lai Ching-te's Inaugural Address: More Continuity Than Difference," *Council on Foreign Relations*, May 21, 2024, https://www.cfr.org/blog/analyzing-lai-ching-tes-

inaugural-address-more-continuity-difference; Hsiao, "President Lai's Inauguration Speech"; Ian Ja Chong, "Commentary: Reading Between the Lines of Taiwan President William Lai's Inauguration Speech," *Channel News Asia*, May 27, 2024, https://www.channelnewsasia.com/commentary/taiwan-new-president-william-lai-ching-te-inauguration-speech-china-ties-4361711.

82. Bonny Lin and Brian Hart, "How Is China Responding to the Inauguration of Taiwan's President William Lai?," *ChinaPower, Center for Strategic and International Studies (CSIS)*, May 2024, https://chinapower.csis.org/china-respond-inauguration-taiwan-william-lai-joint-sword-2024a-military-exercise.

83. Doshi and Sacks, "Analyzing Lai Ching-te's Inaugural Address; Hsiao, "President Lai's Inauguration Speech"; Chong, "Commentary: Reading Between the Lines."

84. "叶剑英进一步阐明关于台湾回归祖国, 实现和平统一的9条方针政策," *Ye Jianying Further Elaborated on the Nine Principles and Policies Regarding Taiwan's Return to the Motherland and the Realization of Peaceful Reunification, Chinese Communist Party News*, September 30, 1981, http://cpc.people.com.cn/GB/64162/64165/70293/70323/4877134.html.

85. Kristian McGuire, "The PRC's 'One Family' Concept and Taiwanese Views of a Cross-Strait Familial Bond," *Jamestown China Brief* 23, no. 15 (August 18, 2023).

86. In Chinese, 两岸一家人 or 两岸一家亲. See *Xinhua*, "President Xi Meets Taiwan Politician," April 8, 2013.

87. James Leibold, "New Textbook Reveals Xi Jinping's Doctrine of Han-Centric Nation-Building Publication," *Jamestown China Brief* 24, no. 11 (May 24, 2024).

88. This is the paraphrase published in *Xinhua*. The direct quote was not recorded. See *Xinhua*, "Xi Jinping Meets Ma Ying-jeou in Beijing," April 10, 2024, https://english.news.cn/20240410/a9b4a2c789904bf3b6983524efb934a6/c.html.

89. McGuire, "The PRC's 'One Family' Concept."

90. Richard C. Bush, "What Xi Jinping Said about Taiwan at the 19th Party Congress," *Brookings*, October 19, 2017, https://www.brookings.edu/articles/what-xi-jinping-said-about-taiwan-at-the-19th-party-congress.

91. *President of Russia*, "Article by Vladimir Putin 'On the Historical Unity of Russians and Ukrainians,'" *Kremlin.ru*, July 12, 2021, http://en.kremlin.ru/events/president/transcripts/articles/66181.

92. Michael Martina and David Brunnstrom, "CIA Chief Warns Against Underestimating Xi's Ambitions Toward Taiwan," *Reuters*, February 3, 2023, https://www.reuters.com/world/cia-chief-says-chinas-xi-little-sobered-by-ukraine-war-2023-02-02/. Notably, other U.S. officials had hinted at this assessment before. Admiral Phil Davidson, Commander of United States Indo-Pacific Command, told Congress in 2021 that China might try to take control of Taiwan "in the next six years." See Mallory Shelbourne, "Davidson: China Could Try to Take Control of Taiwan in 'Next Six Years,'" *USNI News*, March 9, 2021, https://news.usni.org/2021/03/09/davidson-china-could-try-to-take-control-of-taiwan-in-next-six-years.

93. "Transcript: CIA Director William Burns on 'Face the Nation,' Feb. 26, 2023," *CBS News*, February 26, 2023, https://www.cbsnews.com/news/william-burns-cia-director-face-the-nation-transcript-02-26-2023.

94. In October 2022, for example, Secretary of State Antony Blinken said that "there has been a change in the approach from Beijing toward Taiwan in recent years," and that China's leaders had decided that reunification had to happen on a "much faster timeline" than

previously thought. The same month, Admiral Michael Gilday famously commented that the Pentagon should be prepared for a conflict over Taiwan at any time. In January 2023, a leaked memo from Air Force General Michael Minihan noted that "I hope I am wrong. My gut tells me we will fight in 2025." The Defense Department responded that Minihan's opinion was "not representative of the department's view on China." Courtney Kube and Mosheh Gains, "U.S. General Predicts War with China in 2025, Tells Officers to Get Ready," *NBC News*, January 28, 2023, https://www.nbcnews.com/politics/national-security/us-air-force-general-predicts-war-china-2025-memo-rcna67967.

95. "Communique of 5th Plenary Session of 19th CPC Central Committee Released," *The State Council of the People's Republic of China*, October 30, 2020, https://english.www.gov.cn/news/topnews/202010/30/content_WS5f9b6f64c6d0f7257693ea0a.html; 习近平在中共中央政治局第三十二次集体学习时强调 坚定决心意志 埋头苦干实干 确保如期实现建军一百年奋斗目标 *Xi Jinping Stressed during the Thirty-Second Collective Study of the Political Bureau of the Chinese Communist Party Central Committee Firm Determination and Will to Work Hard to Ensure the Timely Achievement of the Centennial Military Building Goal*, 新华网 (Xinhua Net), July 31, 2021, http://www.xinhuanet.com/politics/leaders/2021-07/31/c_1127716278.htm; 习近平: 确保如期实现建军一百年奋斗目标 *Xi Jinping: Ensure That the Goal of Building the Military for 100 Years Is Achieved as Scheduled*, 新华社 (Xinhua News Agency), July 31, 2021, https://news.stcn.com/news/202107/t20210731_3496271.html; 习近平 (Xi Jinping), "加强党史军史和光荣传统教育 确保官兵永远听党话、跟党走" *Strengthen the Party's History and Military History and Glorious Tradition of Education to Ensure That Officers and Soldiers Always Listen to the Party, Follow the Party*, 求是 (Seeking Truth), July 31, 2021, http://www.qstheory.cn/dukan/qs/2021-07/31/c_1127715309.htm.

96. Xi Jinping, "决胜全面建成小康社会 夺取新时代中国特色社会主义伟大胜利——在中国共产党第十九次全国代表大会上的报告" ["Secure a Decisive Victory in Building a Moderately Prosperous Society in All Respects and Strive for the Great Success of Socialism with Chinese Characteristics for a New Era—Report to the 19th National Congress of the Communist Party of China"], *Xinhua*, October 27, 2017. www.xinhuanet.com/politics/19cpcnc/2017-10/27/c_1121867529.htm

97. "Yang Shangkun on China's Reunification," *Beijing Review*, November 26–December 2, 1990, 7, quoted in Qingguo Jia, "Changing Relations across the Taiwan Strait: Beijing's Perceptions," *Asian Survey* 32, no. 3 (1992): 277–289.

98. Kristen Welker, Courtney Kube, Carol E. Lee, and Andrea Mitchell, "Xi Warned Biden during Summit That Beijing Will Reunify Taiwan With China," *NBC News*, December 20, 2023, https://www.nbcnews.com/news/china/xi-warned-biden-summit-beijing-will-reunify-taiwan-china-rcna130087.

99. "习近平新年致辞:中国在风雨洗礼中成长 人民要充满信心," *Xi Jinping's New Year Address: China Grows Through Trials; The People Must Be Full of Confidence*, *Oriental Daily*, January 1, 2025, https://www.orientaldaily.com.my/news/international/2025/01/01/703014.

100. Renmin Ribao, "高举中国特色社会主义伟大旗帜 为全面建设社会主义现代化国家而团结奋斗——习近平同志代表第十九届中央委员会向大会作的报告摘登," *Hold High the Great Banner of Socialism with Chinese Characteristics and Work Together to Build a Modern Socialist Country in an All-Round Way: Excerpts From the Report Delivered by Comrade Xi Jinping to the General Assembly on Behalf of the 19th*

Central Committee, *cpcnews*, October 17, 2022, http://cpc.people.com.cn/20th/n1/2022/1017/c448334-32546343.html.

101. "像保护眼睛一样保护生态环境——习近平生态文明思想引领共建人与自然生命共同体," *Protecting the Ecological Environment Like Protecting Your Eyes—Xi Jinping's Ecological Civilization Thought Leads the Way to Build a Community of Life Between Man and Nature, People's Daily*, June 4, 2022, https://www.gov.cn/xinwen/2022-06/04/content_5693895.htm.

102. Xi's other remarks on Taiwan at the 20th Party Congress repeated his predecessors' language nearly verbatim. See Lyle Morris, "Listen to Xi Jinping about Taiwan," *War on the Rocks*, November 18, 2022, https://warontherocks.com/2022/11/listen-to-xi-jingping-about-taiwan/.

103. Morris, "Listen to Xi Jinping about Taiwan."

104. Demetri Sevastopulo and Joe Leahy, "Xi Jinping Claimed US Wants China to Attack Taiwan," *Financial Times*, June 15, 2024, https://www.ft.com/content/7d6ca06c-d098-4a48-818e-112b97a9497a.

105. Yasmeen Abutaleb, "Chinese Leader Asked Biden to Prevent Pelosi from Visiting Taiwan," *The Washington Post*, August 20, 2022, https://www.washingtonpost.com/politics/2022/08/20/nancy-pelosi-biden-taiwan.

106. *Center for Strategic and International Studies (CSIS)*, "Tracking the Fourth Taiwan Strait Crisis," *ChinaPower*, August 5, 2024, https://chinapower.csis.org/tracking-the-fourth-taiwan-strait-crisis.

107. Dean Cheng, "PLA Exercises after Pelosi Taiwan Visit Were Largely Pre-Planned," *The Heritage Foundation*, August 18, 2022, https://www.heritage.org/china/commentary/pla-exercises-after-pelosi-taiwan-visit-were-largely-pre-planned; Arthur Ding, "Buckle Up: PLA's Military Drills After Pelosi's Taiwan Visit," *The China Story*, October 20, 2022, https://www.thechinastory.org/buckle-up-the-plas-military-drills-after-pelosis-taiwan-visit/; Greg Torode and Yew Lun Tian, "Risks Mount from China Drills Near Taiwan During Pelosi Visit—Analysts," *Reuters*, August 3, 2022, https://www.reuters.com/world/china/risks-mount-china-drills-near-taiwan-during-pelosi-visit-analysts-2022-08-03.

108. See Milan W. Svolik, *The Politics of Authoritarian Rule* (Cambridge: Cambridge University Press, 2012); Bruce Bueno de Mesquita and Alastair Smith, *The Dictator's Handbook: Why Bad Behavior Is Almost Always Good Politics* (New York: PublicAffairs, 2011); Victor Shih, *Factionalism in Chinese Communist Politics* (Cambridge: Cambridge University Press, 2008); Minxin Pei, *China's Trapped Transition: The Limits of Developmental Autocracy* (Cambridge, MA: Harvard University Press, 2006); Susan L. Shirk, *China: Fragile Superpower* (Oxford: Oxford University Press, 2007); and Miroslav Krcmaric, *The Justice Dilemma: Leaders and Exile in an Era of Accountability* (Ithaca, NY: Cornell University Press, 2020).

109. Richard McGregor, "Xi Jinping's Quest to Dominate China," *Foreign Affairs*, August 14, 2019, https://www.foreignaffairs.com/china/party-man; Chang Che, "A Former Chinese Leader Was Ushered Out, Leaving Many Questions," *New York Times*, October 22, 2022, https://www.nytimes.com/2022/10/22/world/asia/hu-jintao-china-congress.html.

110. Andrew S. Erickson, Gabriel B. Collins, and Matt Pottinger, "The Taiwan Catastrophe," *Foreign Affairs*, February 16, 2024, https://www.foreignaffairs.com/united-states/taiwan-catastrophe.

111. Toshi Yoshihara, "China's Vision of Its Seascape: The First Island Chain and Chinese Seapower," *Asian Politics and Policy* 4, no. 3 (July 2012): 293–314, https://doi.org/10.1111/j.1943-0787.2012.01349; Ministry of Foreign Affairs of the People's Republic of China, "一个中国原则是台海和平的基石," *The One-China Principle Is the Foundation of Peace in the Taiwan Strait*, May 26, 2022, https://www.mfa.gov.cn/zwbd_673032/wjzs/202205/t20220526_10693197.shtml.

112. Andrew Erickson and Joel Wuthnow, "Barriers, Springboards, and Benchmarks: China Conceptualizes the Pacific 'Island Chains'," *The China Quarterly* 225 (2016): 1–22, https://doi.org/10.1017/S0305741016000011.

113. Peng Guangqian and Youzhi Yao, eds., *The Science of Military Strategy* (Beijing: Military Science Press, 2005).

114. Jennifer Rice and Erik Robb, *China Maritime Report No. 13: The Origins of "Near Seas Defense and Far Seas Protection"* (Newport, RI: China Maritime Studies Institute, 2021), 5, https://digital-commons.usnwc.edu/cgi/viewcontent.cgi?article=1012&context=cmsi-maritime-reports.

115. Rana Mitter, "China: Revolutionary or Revisionist?" *The Washington Quarterly* 45, no. 2 (2022): 7–21, https://doi.org/10.1080/0163660X.2022.2124017.

116. "Address by Chinese President Xi Jinping at Session II of 19th G20 Summit," *gov.cn*, November 19, 2024, https://english.www.gov.cn/news/202411/19/content_WS673bcfd9c6d0868f4e8ed26b.html; "携手构建人类命运共同体:中国的倡议与行动," *Working Together to Build a Community with a Shared Future for Mankind: China's Proposals and Actions, The State Council Information Office of the People's Republic of China*, September 2023, https://www.gov.cn/zhengce/202309/content_6906335.htm.

117. Economy, "China's Alternative Order."

118. Shen Dingli, "China's 'One Belt, One Road' Strategy Is Not Another Marshall Plan," *China-US Focus*, March 16, 2015, http://www.chinausfocus.com/finance-economy/china-advances-its-one-belt-one-road-strategy.

119. M. Taylor Fravel, "China's Global Security Initiative at Two: A Journey, Not a Destination," *China Leadership Monitor* 80 (Summer 2024), https://www.prcleader.org/post/china-s-global-security-initiative-at-two-a-journey-not-a-destination; Xi Jinping, "Towards a Community of Common Destiny and a New Future for Asia" (speech, Boao, March 28, 2015), *Xinhua*, http://www.xinhuanet.com/english/2015-03/29/c_134106145.htm; Xi Jinping, "Work Together to Build a Community of Shared Future for Mankind" (speech, Geneva, January 18, 2017), *CGTN*, https://america.cgtn.com/2017/01/18/full-text-of-xi-jinping-keynote-speech-at-the-united-nations-office-in-geneva; Xi Jinping, "Carrying Forward the Shanghai Spirit to Build a Community with a Shared Future" (speech, Qingdao, June 10,) 2018, *State Council Information Office of China*, http://english.scio.gov.cn/featured/xigovernance/2018-06/11/content_51986400.htm.

120. Economy, "China's Alternative Order."

121. Ivar Kolstad, "Too Big to Fault? Effects of the 2010 Nobel Peace Prize on Norwegian Exports to China and Foreign Policy," *International Political Science Review* 41, no. 2 (2019): 207–223, https://doi.org/10.1177/0192512118808610; Xianwen Chen and Roberto J. Garcia, "China's Salmon Sanction" (Working Paper, Oslo: Norwegian Institute of International Affairs, 2015), https://chen.ac/works/Chen-Garcia-2015-China_Salmon_Sanction-NUPI.pdf.

122. Aaron L. Friedberg, "Stopping the Next China Shock: A Collective Strategy for Countering Beijing's Mercantilism," *Foreign Affairs*, August 20, 2024, https://www.foreignaffairs.com/china/stopping-next-china-shock-friedberg.

123. On the Philippines, see Isaac B. Kardon, *China's Law of the Sea: The New Rules of Maritime Order* (New Haven, CT: Yale University Press, 2023), chap. 6. On Bhutan, see Robert Barnett, "China Is Building Entire Villages in Another Country's Territory," *Foreign Policy*, May 7, 2021, https://foreignpolicy.com/2021/05/07/china-bhutan-border-villages-security-forces.

124. Robert Jervis, *Perception and Misperception in International Politics* (Princeton, NJ: Princeton University Press, 1976); Charles L. Glaser, "The Security Dilemma Revisited," *World Politics* 50, no. 1 (1997): 171–201.

125. *Xinhua*, "Wang Yi: China-US Relations Not Zero-Sum Game," May 29, 2022, https://www.chinadailyasia.com/hk/article/273538.

126. Rudd's book usefully juxtaposes the U.S. and PRC narratives to show how each side's interpretation of the same events fuels blame for deteriorating relations. See Kevin Rudd, *The Avoidable War: The Dangers of a Catastrophic Conflict Between the US and Xi Jinping's China* (New York: Hachette, 2022).

127. On salami-slicing, see Richard W. Maass, "Salami Tactics: Faits Accomplis and International Expansion in the Shadow of Major War," *Texas National Security Review* 5, no. 1 (Winter 2021/2022): 33–54. The term is associated with Schelling but was coined by Hungarian Communist leader Mátyás Rákosi. See "Hungary: Salami Tactics," *Time Magazine*, April 14, 1952, http://content.time.com/time/magazine/article/0,9171,857130,00.html. On the fluidity of the "status quo," see Scott L. Kastner, *War and Peace in the Taiwan Strait* (New York: Columbia University Press, 2022), 14.

128. 郑永年 [Zheng Yongnian], "美国的台湾想象与台湾恐惧," *The US Imagination and Fear of Taiwan*, *Weixin*, May 17, 2024, https://mp.weixin.qq.com/s/CkP9WoNpilq5X1RoTO7bFg.

129. Graham Allison, *Destined for War: Can America and China Escape Thucydides's Trap?* (Boston: Houghton Mifflin Harcourt, 2017).

130. "Full Text of Xi Jinping's Speech on China-U.S. Relations in Seattle," Embassy of the People's Republic of China in the Kingdom of Bahrain, September 25, 2015, http://bh.china-embassy.gov.cn/eng/xwdt/201509/t20150925_1036961.htm.

131. Ministry of Foreign Affairs of the People's Republic of China, "President Xi Jinping Meets with U.S. President Joe Biden in Lima."

132. Classic studies are James Reilly, *Strong Society, Smart State: The Rise of Public Opinion in China's Japan Policy* (New York: Columbia University Press, 2012); Peter Gries, "Nationalism, Social Influences, and Chinese Foreign Policy," in *China and the World*, ed. David Shambaugh (New York: Oxford University Press, 2020), 64.

133. Jessica Chen Weiss, *Powerful Patriots: Nationalist Protest in China's Foreign Relations* (Oxford: Oxford University Press, 2014); Jessica Chen Weiss and Allan Dafoe, "Authoritarian Audiences, Rhetoric, and Propaganda in International Crises: Evidence from China," *International Studies Quarterly* 63, no. 4 (2019): 963–973.

134. "Xi Faces Dilemma as China Quietly Detains Young Covid Protestors," *Bloomberg*, January 16, 2023, https://www.bloomberg.com/news/articles/2023-01-15/xi-faces-dilemma-as-china-quietly-detains-young-covid-protesters; Michael Greenstone, Guojun He, Shanjun Li, and Eric Zou, "China's War on Pollution: Evidence from the First Five

Years" (Working Paper, Cambridge, MA: National Bureau of Economic Research, 2021), https://www.nber.org/system/files/working_papers/w28467/w28467.pdf.

135. Adam Y. Liu and Xiaojun Li, "Assessing Public Support for (Non-)Peaceful Unification with Taiwan: Evidence from a Nationwide Survey in China," *Journal of Contemporary China* 33, no. 145 (2023): 1–13, https://doi.org/10.1080/10670564.2023.2209524.

136. Jack S. Levy and William R. Thompson, *Causes of War* (London: John Wiley & Sons, 2011), 99–104.s

137. Eyck Freymann and Ralph Su, "The Matter of Xi's Succession," *Fair Observer*, April 21, 2021, https://www.fairobserver.com/region/asia_pacific/eyck-freymann-ralph-su-chinese-communist-party-xi-jinping-succession-news-12910; Chun Han Wong, "The Loss of Hu Chunhua, China's Liberal Champion," *The Wall Street Journal*, October 23, 2022, https://www.wsj.com/livecoverage/china-xi-jinping-communist-party-congress/card/the-loss-of-hu-chunhua-china-s-liberal-champion-Whc8DdJYu1ijAuEFSvO2.

138. Christopher Gelpi, "Democratic Diversions: Governmental Structure and the Externalization of Domestic Conflict," *Journal of Conflict Resolution* 41, no. 2 (1997): 255–282. For critiques of diversionary war theory, see Jack S. Levy, "The Diversionary Theory of War: A Critique," *Handbook of War Studies* 1 (1989): 259–288; M. Taylor Fravel, "The Limits of Diversion: Rethinking Internal and External Conflict," *Security Studies* 19, no. 2 (2010): 307–341.

139. Amy Oakes, *Diversionary War: Domestic Unrest and International Conflict* (Stanford, CA: Stanford University Press, 2012).

140. Michael Beckley, "The Peril of Peaking Powers: Economic Slowdowns and Implications for China's Next Decade," *International Security* 48, no. 1 (2023): 7–46; Michael Buckley and Hal Brands, *Danger Zone: The Coming Conflict with China* (New York: W.W. Norton, 2022).

141. Edward S. Miller, *Bankrupting the Enemy: The US Financial Siege of Japan Before Pearl Harbor* (Annapolis, MD: Naval Institute Press, 2007).

142. Minxin Pei, "Do Chinese Leaders and Elites Think Their Best Days Are Behind Them?," *China Leadership Monitor* 81 (Fall 2024), https://www.prcleader.org/post/do-chinese-leaders-and-elites-think-their-best-days-are-behind-them.

143. See discussion in Steve Tsang and Olivia Cheung, *The Political Thought of Xi Jinping* (London: Oxford University Press, 2023).

144. Smeltz et al., *America's Foreign Policy Future*, 28.

145. Craig Kafura, "On Taiwan, Americans Favor the Status Quo," *Chicago Council on Global Affairs*, October 8, 2024, https://globalaffairs.org/research/public-opinion-survey/taiwan-americans-favor-status-quo.

146. Scott L. Kastner, "Does Economic Integration Across the Taiwan Strait Make Military Conflict Less Likely?," *Journal of East Asian Studies* 6, no. 3 (2006): 319–346.

147. Erik Gartzke, Quan Li, and Charles Boehmer, "Investing in the Peace: Economic Interdependence and International Conflict," *International Organization* 55, no. 2 (Spring 2001): 391–438; Dale C. Copeland, "Economic Interdependence and War: A Theory of Trade Expectations," *International Security* 20, no. 4 (1996): 5–41.

148. Bromley and Freymann, *On Day One*.

149. Mira Rapp-Hooper and Rebecca Friedman Lissner, *An Open World: How America Can Win the Contest for Twenty-First Century* (New Haven, CT: Yale University Press, 2021).

150. China recognizes and resents this fact. See 央视网 [CCTV News], "澳媒:美国如何操纵全球市场获取经济霸权," *Australian Media: How the United States Manipulates the*

Global Market to Gain Economic Hegemony, June 21, 2024, https://news.cctv.com/2024/06/21/ARTIgriFg9geC2SzQoBRrwPW240621.shtml.

151. For a balanced perspective on this process, see Petros C. Mavroidis and Andre Sapir, *China and the WTO: Why Multilateralism Still Matters* (Princeton, NJ: Princeton University Press, 2021).

152. Leopold Aschenbrenner, "Situational Awareness: The Decade Ahead," *situational-awareness.ai*, June 2024, https://situational-awareness.ai/.

153. Philip Zelikow, Mariano-Florentino Cuéllar, Eric Schmidt, and Jason Matheny, *Defense Against the AI Dark Arts: Threat Assessment and Coalition Defense* (Stanford, CA: Hoover Institution, 2024), https://www.hoover.org/sites/default/files/research/docs/Zelikow_DefenseAgainst_web-241126.pdf.

154. Nathan Beauchamp-Mustafaga, Kieran Green, William Marcellino, Sale Lilly, and Jackson Smith, *Dr. Li Bicheng, or How China Learned to Stop Worrying and Love Social Media Manipulation: Insights into Chinese Use of Generative AI and Social Bots From the Career of a PLA Researcher* (Santa Monica, CA: RAND Corporation, 2024), https://www.rand.org/pubs/research_reports/RRA2679-1.html.

155. David Sacks, "Threatening to Destroy TSMC Is Unnecessary and Counterproductive," *Council on Foreign Relations*, May 9, 2023, https://www.cfr.org/blog/threatening-destroy-tsmc-unnecessary-and-counterproductive.

156. Matt Sheehan, "China's Views on AI Safety Are Changing—Quickly," *Carnegie Endowment for International Peace*, August 27, 2024, https://carnegieendowment.org/research/2024/08/china-artificial-intelligence-ai-safety-regulation?lang=en.

157. Dmitri Alperovitch, "How the Right U.S. Chip Strategy Can Keep Taiwan Free," *The Washington Post*, April 29, 2024, https://www.washingtonpost.com/opinions/2024/04/29/china-us-computer-chip-strategy-breakout-free-taiwan.

158. 央视新闻 [CCTV News], "'五眼联盟'建立'绝密云端'目的何在?," *What Is the Purpose of the 'Five Eyes Alliance' Establishing a 'Top Secret Cloud'?*, October 31, 2024, https://content-static.cctvnews.cctv.com/snow-book/index.html?item_id=1295735489402671289; 新华网 [Xinhua News], "外交部发言人:'五眼联盟'联手发布虚假信息报告很讽刺," *Foreign Ministry Spokesperson: It Is Ironic That the Five Eyes Alliance Jointly Released a False Information Report*, May 26, 2023, http://cn.chinadiplomacy.org.cn/2023-05/26/content_85623784.shtml.

159. Andrew Erickson, Gabriel Collins, and Matt Pottinger, "Taiwan: The Stakes," in *The Boiling Moat: Urgent Steps to Defend Taiwan* (Stanford, CA: Hoover Institution Press, 2024), 35–37.

160. *China Digital Times*, "马英九:谁说中国人不适合民主," *Ma Ying-jeou: Who Says Chinese People Are Not Suitable for Democracy?*, June 23, 2010, https://chinadigitaltimes.net/chinese/80369.html; 博闻社 [Bowen Press], "民联副主席吕京花:台湾的民主制度是中国大陆的榜样," *Vice Chairman of the China Democratic League, Lü Jinghua: Taiwan's Democratic System Is a Model for Mainland China*, January 16, 2016, https://bowenpress.com/news/bowen_57952.html; *Radio France Internationale*, "网络时评人张尧台湾观选印象:没有哪个文化不适合民主," *Internet Commentator Zhang Yao's Impression of Taiwan's Election: No Culture Is Unsuitable for Democracy*, February 2, 2024.

161. Thomas J. Christensen, "The Contemporary Security Dilemma: Deterring a Taiwan Conflict," *Washington Quarterly* 25, no. 4 (2002): 5–21, https://doi.org/10.1162/016366002760252509.

162. Mark R. Wilson, *Destructive Creation: American Business and the Winning of World War II* (Philadelphia: University of Pennsylvania Press, 2016).

163. Jennifer Welch, Jenny Leonard, Maeva Cousin, Gerard DiPippo, and Tom Orlik, "Xi, Biden and the $10 Trillion Cost of War over Taiwan," *Bloomberg*, January 9, 2024, https://www.bloomberg.com/news/features/2024-01-09/if-china-invades-taiwan-it-would-cost-world-economy-10-trillion; Charlie Vest, Agatha Kratz, and Reva Goujon, "The Global Economic Disruptions From a Taiwan Conflict," *Rhodium Group*, December 14, 2022, https://rhg.com/research/taiwan-economic-disruptions/.

164. Tobias Burns, "How Trump and Biden Killed the Free-Trade Consensus," *The Hill*, September 25, 2023, https://thehill.com/business/4222035-how-trump-and-biden-killed-the-free-trade-consensus.

165. Alan O. Sykes, "The Utility of Appellate Review at the WTO and Its Optimal Structure," *Journal of International Economic Law* 27, no. 3 (2024): 422–440, https://www.law.columbia.edu/sites/default/files/2024-03/The%2520Utility%2520of%2520Appellate%2520Review%2520at%2520the%2520WTO%2520and%2520Its%2520Optimal%2520Structure_0.pdf; Inu Manak, Evan Rogerson, Daniel Gros, Jhanvi Tripathi, and Zhongmei Wang, "The WTO at a Crossroads: What the Failed Ministerial Conference Means," *Council of Councils*, March 6, 2024, https://www.cfr.org/councilofcouncils/global-memos/wto-crossroads-what-failed-ministerial-conference-means.

166. *World Trade Organization*, "General Agreement on Tariffs and Trade (GATT 1947)," accessed January 16, 2025, https://www.wto.org/english/docs_e/legal_e/gatt47_e.htm. The U.S. position is that national security interests are self-justifying—that is, they are what a state says they are, and they cannot be assessed by WTO jurists. See *World Trade Organization Panel, Russia—Measures Concerning Traffic in Transit* (Geneva: World Trade Organization, 2019), 51, https://doi.org/10.30875/9a582d67-en; James Bacchus, *The Black Hole of National Security: Striking the Right Balance for the National Security Exception in International Trade* (Washington, DC: Cato Policy Analysis, 2022), https://www.cato.org/sites/cato.org/files/2022-11/policy-analysis-936.pdf.

167. Among many excellent studies of the crisis of the 1930s, see Douglas A. Irwin, *Trade Policy Disaster: Lessons from the 1930s* (Cambridge, MA: MIT Press, 2011).

168. Robert D. Blackwill and Philip Zelikow, *The United States, China, and Taiwan: A Strategy to Prevent War* (New York: Council on Foreign Relations, 2021), 35–37.

169. Thomas Schelling, *Arms and Influence* (New Haven, CT: Yale University Press, 1966), 1–12.

170. Barry Eichengreen, "Sanctions, SWIFT, and China's Cross-Border Interbank Payments System," *Center for Strategic and International Studies*, May 20, 2022, https://www.csis.org/analysis/sanctions-swift-and-chinas-cross-border-interbank-payments-system.

171. Chris Anstey, "Dollar Faces Biggest Threat in Decades from 'Scary' Moves, Summers Says," *Bloomberg*, March 5, 2025 https://www.bloomberg.com/news/articles/2025-03-05/summers-sees-biggest-dollar-threat-in-decades-from-scary-moves; Barry Eichengreen, "Can the Dollar Remain King of Currencies?," *Financial Times*, March 21, 2025, https://www.ft.com/content/8a71dceb-806f-4681-80f9-416aa4c366ca.

172. Bromley and Freymann, *On Day One*, 22–25.

173. The most detailed discussion of China's options is Logan Wright, Agatha Kratz, Charlie Vest, and Matt Mingey, "Retaliation and Resistance: China's Economic Statecraft in a Taiwan Crisis," *Atlantic Council*, April 1, 2024, https://www.atlanticcouncil.org/in-

depth-research-reports/report/retaliation-and-resilience-chinas-economic-statecraft-in-a-taiwan-crisis/#g7-economic-statecraft. See also Bromley and Freymann, *On Day One*, 25.

174. On the logic of economic punishment, see Tami Davis Biddle, *Rhetoric and Reality in Air Warfare: The Evolution of British and American Ideas About Strategic Bombing, 1914–1945* (Princeton, NJ: Princeton University Press, 2009); Robert A. Pape, *Bombing to Win: Air Power and Coercion in War* (Ithaca, NY: Cornell University Press, 2014).

CHAPTER 2

1. "Chinese Coast Guard Boards Taiwan Tourist Boat, Triggers Panic," *Al Jazeera*, February 20, 2024, https://www.aljazeera.com/news/2024/2/20/chinese-coast-guard-boards-taiwan-tourist-boat-triggers-panic.

2. Nectar Gan and Kathleen Magramo, "'Only Pirates Do This': Philippines Accuses China of Using Bladed Weapons in Major South China Sea Escalation," *CNN*, June 20, 2024, https://www.cnn.com/2024/06/20/asia/philippines-footage-south-china-sea-clash-china-intl-hnk/index.html.

3. Aaron-Matthew Lariosa, "VIDEO: China Coast Guard Blasts Philippine Fisheries Vessel at Scarborough Shoal," *USNI News*, October 8, 2024, https://news.usni.org/2024/10/08/video-china-coast-guard-blasts-philippine-fisheries-vessel-at-scarborough-shoal.

4. Xin Liu and Yuandan Guo, "PLA Conducts Joint Drill Surrounding Taiwan Island to Send Stern Warning to 'Taiwan Independence' Separatists," *Global Times*, October 14, 2024, https://www.globaltimes.cn/page/202410/1321155.shtml; Ryan Chan, "China Deploys Coast Guard 'Monster' Ship in War Games to Surround Taiwan," *Newsweek*, October 14, 2024, https://www.newsweek.com/china-news-deploys-coast-guard-monster-ship-war-games-surround-taiwan-1968459.

5. Edward Wong, "Security Law Suggests a Broadening of China's 'Core Interests,'" *New York Times*, July 2, 2015, https://www.nytimes.com/2015/07/03/world/asia/security-law-suggests-a-broadening-of-chinas-core-interests.html; Joshua Kurlantzick and Abigail McGowan, "Why Tensions in the South China Sea Are Bolstering the U.S.-Philippines Alliance," *Council on Foreign Relations*, September 5, 2024, https://www.cfr.org/expert-brief/why-tensions-south-china-sea-are-bolstering-us-philippines-alliance.

6. Chapter 5, Section 2, Article 33 of the China Coast Guard's Administrative Law authorizes it to board vessels to conduct law enforcement. See 中国海警局 [China Coast Guard], "海警机构行政执法程序规定," *Administrative Law Enforcement Procedures of the Coast Guard Agency*, June 15, 2024, https://www.ccg.gov.cn/2024/xxgk_0515/2459.html.

7. Lauren Dickey and Matthew Kent, "This Is Not the Status Quo You're Looking For," *War on the Rocks*, November 27, 2024, https://warontherocks.com/2024/11/this-is-not-the-status-quo-youre-looking-for.

8. On the backlash, see the annual trends in opinion polling by the Taiwan government's Mainland Affairs Council; *Mainland Affairs Council*, "Opinion Polls," accessed January 16, 2025, https://www.mac.gov.tw/en/Content_List.aspx?n=2A0F1393B67987D2.

9. Blackwill and Zelikow, *The United States, China, and Taiwan*.

10. The term was coined by Gabriel Collins and Andrew Erickson and is widely used by my colleagues at the China Maritime Studies Institute at the U.S. Naval War College, though it is not an official term. See Gabriel Collins and Andrew Erickson, *Silicon Hegemon:*

Could China Take Over Taiwan's Semiconductor Industry Without Invading? (Houston: Baker Institute for Public Policy, 2023), https://www.bakerinstitute.org/research/silicon-hegemon-could-china-take-over-taiwans-semiconductor-industry-without-invading.

11. Alexander Bowe, *China's Overseas United Front Work: Background and Implications for the United States* (Washington, DC: U.S.-China Economic and Security Review Commission, August 24, 2018), https://www.uscc.gov/sites/default/files/Research/China%27s%20Overseas%20United%20Front%20Work%20-%20Background%20and%20Implications%20for%20US_final_0.pdf; Alex Joske, *The Party Speaks for You: Foreign Interference and the Chinese Communist Party's United Front System* (Canberra: Australian Strategic Policy Institute, June 9, 2020), https://ad-aspi.s3.ap-southeast-2.amazonaws.com/2020-06/The%20party%20speaks%20for%20you_0.pdf?VersionId=gFHuXyYMR0XuDQOs.6JSmrdyk7MralcN.

12. *CSIS Interpret*, "Transcript of the Press Conference on the Opinions on Punishing the Crimes of Secession and Incitement to Secession by 'Taiwan Independence' Diehards According to Law," June 21, 2024, https://interpret.csis.org/translations/transcript-of-the-press-conference-on-the-opinions-on-punishing-the-crimes-of-secession-and-incitement-to-secession-by-taiwan-independence-diehards-according-to-law.

13. 中国政府网 [Chinese Government Website], "反分裂国家法," *Anti-Secession Law*, June 21, 2005, https://www.gov.cn/zhengce/2005-06/21/content_2602175.htm.

14. 联合早报 [Lianhe Zaobao], "大陆国台办证实台民族党副主席杨智渊被判刑九年," *The Taiwan Affairs Office of Mainland China Confirmed That Yang Zhiyuan, Vice Chairman of the Taiwan National Party, Was Sentenced to Nine Years in Prison*, September 6, 2024, https://www.zaobao.com.sg/realtime/china/story20240907-4655294.

15. "China Jails Taiwanese Person on Separatism Charge for First Time," *Bloomberg*, September 6, 2024, https://www.bloomberg.com/news/articles/2024-09-06/china-jails-taiwan-activist-for-nine-years-on-separatism-charge.

16. 中共中央台办、国务院台办 [Taiwan Affairs Office of the CPC Central Committee, Taiwan Affairs Office of the State Council], "国台办: 制发台湾居民居住证是造福于台湾同胞的好事," *Taiwan Affairs Office of the State Council: Issuing Residence Permits for Taiwan Residents Is a Good Thing That Benefits Taiwan Compatriots*, September 12, 2018, http://www.gwytb.gov.cn/wyly/201809/t20180912_12058926.htm; Lawrence Chung, "Controversy over Popular Mainland Chinese ID Cards in Taiwan Prompts Crackdown," *South China Morning Post*, February 15, 2025, https://www.scmp.com/news/china/politics/article/3298706/controversy-over-popular-mainland-chinese-id-cards-taiwan-prompts-crackdown.

17. "Hundreds of Taiwanese Extradited to China, Says Report," *BBC News*, December 1, 2021, https://www.bbc.com/news/world-asia-59486286.

18. Che-Yuan Lin and Esme Yeh, "China-Friendly Countries Risky to Visit: Academic," *Taipei Times*, June 30, 2024, https://www.taipeitimes.com/News/taiwan/archives/2024/06/30/2003820110.

19. Chris Horton and Shuhei Yamada, "How Beijing Enlists Global Companies to Pressure Taiwan," *Nikkei Asia*, July 25, 2018, https://asia.nikkei.com/Spotlight/The-Big-Story/How-Beijing-enlists-global-companies-to-pressure-Taiwan.

20. For example: Sheng-ju Yang and James Lo, "Evergreen Apologizes over Chinese Flag Furor at Paris Hotel," *Focus Taiwan*, August 15, 2024, https://focustaiwan.tw/cross-strait/202408150021; Ming-yen Chiang, Wen-chi Liao, James Lo, and Francis Huang, "Evergreen Group Voices Support for '1992 Consensus' After Flag Furor in Paris," *Focus Taiwan*, August 24, 2024, https://focustaiwan.tw/cross-strait/20240824 0003.

21. Jacques DeLisle and Bonnie Glaser, "Exposing the PRC's Distortion of UN General Assembly Resolution 2758 to Press Its Claim over Taiwan," *German Marshall Fund of the United States*, April 30, 2024, https://www.gmfus.org/news/exposing-prcs-distortion-un-general-assembly-resolution-2758-press-its-claim-over-taiwan.

22. *Taiwan Affairs Office of the State Council, People's Republic of China, The Taiwan Question and the Reunification of China in the New Era*, sec. I, August 10, 2022, http://us.china-embassy.gov.cn/eng/zgyw/202208/t20220810_10740168.htm.

23. 国务院台湾事务办公室 [Taiwan Affairs Office of the State Council], "台湾问题与新时代中国统一事业," *The Taiwan Issue and China's Reunification in the New Era*, August 2022, https://www.gov.cn/zhengce/2022-08/10/content_5704839.htm.

24. Emily Rauhala, "Chinese Officials Note Serious Problems in Coronavirus Response. The World Health Organization Keeps Praising Them," *The Washington Post*, February 8, 2020, https://www.washingtonpost.com/world/asia_pacific/chinese-officials-note-serious-problems-in-coronavirus-response-the-world-health-organization-keeps-praising-them/2020/02/08/b663dd7c-4834-11ea-91ab-ce439aa5c7c1_story.html; Gerry Shih, "Taiwan Rejects WHO Chief's Claim of Racist Campaign Against Him," *The Washington Post*, April 9, 2020, https://www.washingtonpost.com/world/asia_pacific/taiwan-rejects-who-chiefs-claim-of-campaign-against-him-amid-coronavirus-pandemic/2020/04/09/ab1c8e8a-7a0e-11ea-a311-adb1344719a9_story.html. On the sloppy investigation into COVID's origins, see Smriti Mallapaty, "WHO Abandons Plans for Crucial Second Phase of COVID-Origins Investigation," *Nature*, February 14, 2023, https://www.nature.com/articles/d41586-023-00283-y; Michael R. Gordon and Warren P. Strobel, "Behind Closed Doors: The Spy-World Scientists Who Argued COVID Was a Lab Leak," *The Wall Street Journal*, December 26, 2024, https://www.wsj.com/politics/national-security/fbi-covid-19-pandemic-lab-leak-theory-dfbd8a51.

25. Shawn William Brennan, "Assessing the Legal Framework for Potential U.S. Conflict with China over Taiwan," *International Law Studies* 99, no. 1 (2022), https://digital-commons.usnwc.edu/cgi/viewcontent.cgi?article=3036&context=ils.

26. On the UFWD, see Alex Joske, *Spies and Lies: How China's Greatest Covert Operations Fooled the World* (London: Hardie Grant, 2022); Alex Joske, "The United Front and Technology Transfer," in *China's Quest for Foreign Technology: Beyond Espionage*, eds. William C. Hannas and Didi Kirsten Tatlow (London: Routledge, 2020), chap. 15; Anne-Marie Brady, "Magic Weapons: China's Political Influence Activities under Xi Jinping," *Wilson Center*, September 18, 2017, https://www.wilsoncenter.org/article/magic-weapons-chinas-political-influence-activities-under-xi-jinping.

27. Benjamin Sando, "Taiwan's Underworld, Part 2: The Chinese Communist Party and United Front Work," *Global Taiwan Institute*, September 18, 2024, https://globaltaiwan.org/2024/09/taiwans-underworld-part-2.

28. These allegations are widely believed in Taiwan but are not well documented. The ultranationalist mafia boss Chang An-lo is supposedly involved. See "The White Wolf of Taiwan: Chang An-lo and His Reunification Party," *The China Project*, August 16, 2018; Ko-lin Chin, *Heijin: Organized Crime, Business, and Politics in Taiwan* (London: Routledge, 2016), 37–38.

29. Chang Jiu-chen and Jason Pan, "Retired Officers Indicted over Collusion," *Taipei Times*, January 9, 2025, https://www.taipeitimes.com/News/front/archives/2025/01/09/2003829891.

30. Nathan Beauchamp-Mustafaga, "Cognitive Domain Operations: The PLA's New Holistic Concept for Influence Operations," *China Brief* 19, no. 16 (2019), https://jamestown.org/program/cognitive-domain-operations-the-plas-new-holistic-concept-for-influence-operations.

31. Joske, *The Party Speaks for You*.

32. June Teufel Dreyer, "A Weapon Without War: China's United Front Strategy," *Foreign Policy Research Institute*, February 8, 2018, https://www.fpri.org/article/2018/02/weapon-without-war-chinas-united-front-strategy.

33. Ben Westcott, "China Is Blaming the US for the Hong Kong Protests. Can That Really Be True?" *CNN*, July 31, 2019, https://edition.cnn.com/2019/07/31/asia/us-china-hong-kong-interference-intl-hnk/index.html.

34. Lynette H. Ong, "In Hong Kong, Are 'Thugs for Hire' Behind the Attacks on Protesters? Here's What We Know about These Groups," *The Washington Post*, July 24, 2019, https://www.washingtonpost.com/politics/2019/07/24/hired-guns-attacked-protesters-hong-kong-this-is-who-they-are-want-they-want; Lily Kuo, "'Where Were the Police?' Hong Kong Outcry After Masked Thugs Launch Attack," *The Guardian*, July 22, 2019, https://www.theguardian.com/world/2019/jul/22/where-were-the-police-hong-kong-outcry-after-masked-thugs-launch-attack.

35. "Money, Muscle, Media: How China Has Handled Hong Kong Protests," *France 24*, August 21, 2019, https://www.france24.com/en/20190821-money-muscle-media-how-china-has-handled-hong-kong-protests.

36. Yunh-yao Su and William Hetherington, "Beijing's New 26 Measures Condemned," *Taipei Times*, November 5, 2019, https://www.taipeitimes.com/News/front/archives/2019/11/05/2003725265; Emily Feng, "The Latest Thorn in Taiwan-China Tensions: Pineapples," *NPR*, March 7, 2024, https://www.npr.org/2024/03/07/1225536623/taiwan-china-tension-pineapple#:~:text=But%20in%20March%202021%2C%20China,fish%20and%20sugar%20apples%20followed.

37. Conor M. Kennedy and Andrew S. Erickson, *China Maritime Report No. 1: China's Third Sea Force, The People's Armed Forces Maritime Militia: Tethered to the PLA* (Newport, RI: China Maritime Studies Institute, March 2017).

38. The Central People's Government of the People's Republic of China, 中国武装力量的多样化运用, *The Diversified Employment of China's Armed Forces*, April 2013, https://www.gov.cn/jrzg/2013-04/16/content_2379013.htm. Quoted in Kennedy and Erickson, *China Maritime Report* No. 1.

39. Agnes Chang and Hannah Beech, "China's Maritime Militia," *New York Times*, December 9, 2023, https://nytimes.pressreader.com/article/281788518839486; Ben Blanchard and Ryan Woo, "Taiwan, China Trade Barbs over Undersea Cable Damage," *Reuters*, January 9, 2025, https://www.reuters.com/world/asia-pacific/taiwan-china-trade-barbs-over-undersea-cable-damage-2025-01-09.

40. Kennedy and Erickson, China Maritime Report No. 1; see also Lonnie D. Henley, China Maritime Report No. 21: Civilian Shipping and Maritime Militia: The Logistics Backbone of a Taiwan Invasion (Newport, RI: China Maritime Studies Institute, 2022), https://digital-commons.usnwc.edu/cmsi-maritime-reports/21/; Ryan D. Martinson, "Missing in the Gray Zone? China's Maritime Militia Forces Around Taiwan," *The Diplomat*, December 24, 2024, https://thediplomat.com/2024/12/missing-in-the-gray-zone-chinas-maritime-militia-forces-around-taiwan/; Andrew S. Erickson and Ryan D. Martinson, eds., *China's Maritime Gray Zone Operations* (Annapolis, MD: Naval Institute Press, 2023), 135–168.

41. Ben Lewis, "China's Recent ADIZ Violations Have Changed the Status Quo in the Taiwan Strait," *Council on Foreign Relations*, February 10, 2023, https://www.cfr.org/blog/chinas-recent-adiz-violations-have-changed-status-quo-taiwan-strait; Thomas J. Shattuck and Benjamin Lewis, "Breaking the Barrier: Four Years of PRC Military Activity Around Taiwan," *Foreign Policy Research Institute*, October 9, 2024, https://www.fpri.org/article/2024/10/breaking-the-barrier-four-years-of-prc-military-activity-around-taiwan.

42. Shattuck and Lewis, "Breaking the Barrier."

43. See Ivan Kanapathy, "Countering China's Gray Zone Activities," in *The Boiling Moat*, ed. Matt Pottinger, 112–16; Emily Feng and Connie Hanzhang Jin, "China Is Subtly Increasing Military Pressure on Taiwan. Here's How," *NPR*, December 18, 2023, https://www.npr.org/2023/12/18/1216317476/china-military-taiwan-air-defense; Thomas J. Shattuck and Benjamin Lewis, "How Taiwan's New President Should Respond to Chinese Coercion," *War on the Rocks*, January 31, 2024, https://warontherocks.com/2024/01/how-taiwans-new-president-should-respond-to-chinese-coercion/(which notes that intercepting Chinese planes had drained almost 9 percent of the Air Force's budget by October 2020).

44. Ryan Chan, "Map Shows Chinese Drones Surrounding Taiwan," *Newsweek*, September 2, 2024, https://www.newsweek.com/map-news-shows-chinese-drones-surrounding-taiwan-japan-1947348; Thomas Newdick, "Chinese TB-001 Scorpion Drone 'Encircled' Taiwan," *The Warzone*, April 28, 2023, https://www.twz.com/chinese-tb-001-scorpion-drone-encircled-taiwan.

45. "China-Linked Threat Group Targets Taiwan Critical Infrastructure, Smokescreen Ransomware," *CyCraft*, February 1, 2021, https://www.cycraft.com/en/post/smokescreen-ransomware; "Smokescreen Supply Chain Attack Targets Taiwan Financial Sector, A Deeper Look," *CyCraft*, March 1, 2022, https://www.cycraft.com/en/post/zero-day20220301.

46. Kenneth Ong, "China's Deviant Chip Strategy," *Foreign Policy Research Institute*, June 28, 2024, https://www.fpri.org/article/2024/06/chinas-defiant-chip-strategy.

47. Blackwill and Zelikow, *The United States, China, and Taiwan*, 36.

48. Blackwill and Zelikow, *The United States, China, and Taiwan*, 35.

49. 全国人民代表大会常务委员会 [Standing Committee of the National People's Congress], "中华人民共和国海上交通安全法," *Maritime Traffic Safety Law of the People's Republic of China*, April 29, 2021, https://www.gov.cn/xinwen/2021-04/30/content_5604045.htm.

50. *Airport Passenger Information Forecasting Platform*, "Commonly Asked Questions on Advance Passenger Information System for the Inbound/Outbound Aircraft to/from China," accessed January 16, 2025, https://iapi.nia.gov.cn/iAPI/files/cata/57/1210473118343110657.docx; *U.S. Customs and Border Protection*, "Fact Sheet:

APIS," accessed January 16, 2025, https://www.cbp.gov/sites/default/files/documents/apis_factsheet_3.pdf. On China's past efforts to coerce private airlines, see Tara Francis Chan, "China Wants to Dictate How Foreign Airlines Refer to Taiwan and the US Is Having None of It—This Is How Every Major Airline Is Responding," *Business Insider*, May 5, 2018, https://www.businessinsider.com/what-do-airlines-call-taiwan-china-2018-5.

51. For a history of this episode that includes careful assessment of the political context, not just military operations, see Avi Shlaim, *The United States and the Berlin Blockade 1948–1949: A Study in Crisis Decision-Making* (Berkeley: University of California Press, 2002).

52. Central Intelligence Agency, Review of the World Situation as It Relates to the Security of the United States (Independence, MO: Harry S. Truman Library, April 8, 1948), cited in Shlaim, *The United States and the Berlin Blockade*, 12.

53. *Office of the Historian*, "The Berlin Airlift, 1948–1949," accessed January 29, 2024, https://history.state.gov/milestones/1945-1952/berlin-airlift.

54. The Soviet Union did not acquire the bomb until summer 1949.

55. The literature on this crisis is enormous. The first volume to draw on Soviet archives and interviews with former Soviet officials was Aleksandr Fursenko and Timothy Naftali, *One Hell of a Gamble: Khrushchev, Castro, and Kennedy, 1958–1964* (New York: W. W. Norton, 1997).Shortly thereafter, the edited White House tapes were released in full. See Ernest R. May and Philip D. Zelikow, eds., *The Kennedy Tapes: Inside the White House during the Cuban Missile Crisis* (Cambridge, MA: Belknap Press, 1998). The most read-able account of the entire crisis, including both Berlin and Cuba, is Frederick Kempe, *Berlin 1961: Kennedy, Khrushchev, and the Most Dangerous Place on Earth* (New York: Penguin, 2011). However, Kempe's book, while exceptionally readable, is too critical of Kennedy. See Norman Birnbaum, "Book Review: 'Berlin 1961,'" *Columbia Magazine*, Spring 2012.

56. *Office of the Historian*, "Memorandum of Conversation Between Secretary of the Inte-rior Udall and Chairman Khrushchev (September 6, 1962)," accessed January 29, 2024, https://history.state.gov/historicaldocuments/frus1961-63v15/d112.

57. *U.S. Department of State*, "Message from Chairman Khrushchev to President Kennedy," accessed February 14, 2024, https://1997-2001.state.gov/about_state/history/volume_vi/exchanges.html.

58. *Office of the Historian*, "Memorandum of Conversation (October 18, 1962)," accessed January 29, 2024, https://history.state.gov/historicaldocuments/frus1961-63v15/d135.

59. The following section is adapted from Eyck Freymann and Harry Halem, *The Arsenal of Democracy*, chap. 4, "Logistics."

60. William P. Head, "The Berlin Airlift: First Test of the U.S. Air Force," *Air Power History* 68, no. 3 (2021): 33, https://www.jstor.org/stable/27086681.

61. Heavy-lift aircraft can move materiel and munitions to specific points very quickly, and they are invaluable for rapid deployment and for specific reserves and sustainment. The Civil Reserve Air Fleet (CRAF) program, which contracts civilian airlines to augment military airlift during crises, provides additional capacity but is unlikely to fully meet the logistics needs of a high-intensity conflict. Tanker aircraft are also essential for extending the range of U.S. bombers and fighters during wartime, so the United States might be wary of putting too many of them at risk in civilian resupply operations. China

is currently ramping up investments in its own tanker program to support sustained sorties off the east coast of Taiwan, which could harass incoming and outgoing resupply aircraft. See Air Mobility Command Public Affairs, "Civil Reserve Air Fleet," *U.S. Air Force*, July 2014, https://www.af.mil/About-Us/Fact-Sheets/Display/Article/104583/civil-reserve-air-fleet; Kris Osborn, "Chinese YU-20 Tanker Refuels Carrier-Based J-15, Massively Increases Pacific Threat," *Warrior Maven*, August 7, 2023, https://warriormaven.com/china/chinese-military-breakthrough-pla-y-20-tanker-refuels-carrier-based-j-15.

62. Paul Gucwa, "Increased Aerial Refueling Compatibility Facilitates True Joint Environment," *U.S. Navy*, October 3, 2022, https://www.navy.mil/Press-Office/News-Stories/Article/3178173/increased-aerial-refueling-compatibility-facilitates-true-joint-environment.

63. Richard L. Kilpatrick Jr., "Revisiting the Five Powers War Risk Exclusion," *International & Comparative Law Quarterly* 73, no. 3 (2024): 551–577, https://doi.org/10.1017/S0020589324000204.

64. John McCown, "What to Watch 2023: America Must Begin Growing Its Merchant Marine," *Center for Maritime Strategy*, January 10, 2023, https://centerformaritimestrategy.org/publications/what-to-watch-2023-america-must-begin-growing-its-merchant-marine.

65. U.S. Maritime Administration, "National Defense Reserve Fleet," *U.S. Department of Transportation*, accessed February 28, 2025, https://www.maritime.dot.gov/national-defense-reserve-fleet.

66. Seth Cropsey and Harry Halem, *A Strategic Concept for the United States Merchant Marine* (Bethesda, MD: Yorktown Institute, 2024).

67. For aging ships—particularly steam-powered RRF ships—finding spare parts can be a challenge, as is finding people who know how to operate and maintain the equipment. See Megan Eckstein, "Lack of Funds Hampers Emergency Naval Fleet from Growing Faster," *Defense News*, April 6, 2023, https://www.defensenews.com/naval/2023/04/06/lack-of-funds-hampers-emergency-naval-fleet-from-growing-faster.

68. John Grady, "MARAD Head 'Not at All Confident' Ready Reserve Fleet Could Be Crewed in a Crisis," *USNI News*, March 29, 2023, https://news.usni.org/2023/03/29/marad-head-not-at-all-confident-ready-reserve-fleet-could-be-crewed-in-a-crisis.

69. Blackwill and Zelikow, *The United States, China, and Taiwan*, 35–37.

70. The U.S. Merchant Marine is divided into distinct segments—Jones Act versus non-Jones Act and Section 2 owners versus non-Section 2 owners—that often compete, highlighting the absence of a cohesive maritime strategy or a central executive authority to align these differences for the national interest. Jones Act ships, which must be U.S.-built, are approximately four to five times more expensive to construct and take significantly longer to produce compared to foreign-built vessels, leading to an aging fleet in poor condition, as exemplified by the tragic sinking of the *El Faro* off Jacksonville, Florida, in 2015. These failures underscore why the United States needs a comprehensive maritime policy. See National Transportation Safety Board, *Sinking of the US Cargo Vessel* El Faro—*Illustrated Digest*, SPC-18-01 (Washington, DC: National Transportation Safety Board, 2018), 2024, https://www.ntsb.gov/investigations/AccidentReports/Reports/SPC1801.pdf.

71. The international fleet includes vessels in the Maritime Security Program, Tanker Security Program, and a handful involved in preference trade (e.g., food aid).

72. Hongshan Zhiyun, 美军后勤保障能力下降, 全球投送面临挑战, *Declining U.S. Military Logistical Support Capabilities and Challenges in Global Deployment*, May 28, 2024, https://www.hongshanzhiyun.com/hsdt/20240528_211.html.

73. Cropsey and Halem, *A Strategic Concept for the United States Merchant Marine.*

74. 阮佳琪 [Ruan Jiaqi], 中国主导物流业暴露美国弱点,'美军现在得搭便车', *China's Dominance in the Logistics Industry Exposes U.S. Weaknesses: 'The U.S. Military Now Has to Hitch a Ride'*, 观察者网 [The Observer], November 2, 2024, https://www.guancha.cn/internation/2024_11_02_753953_s.shtml.

75. Cropsey and Halem, *A Strategic Concept for the United States Merchant Marine.*

76. Isaac B. Kardon and Wendy Leutert, "Pier Competitor: China's Power Position in Global Ports," *International Security* 46, no. 4 (2022): 9–47.

77. Taiwan Relations Act (22 U.S.C. § 3301 et seq.).

78. The relevant law is: *Legal Information Institute*, "46 U.S. Code § 56301—General Authority," accessed February 20, 2025, https://www.law.cornell.edu/uscode/text/46/56301.

79. Japan is an example; since 2014, Japan's Self-Defense Forces (SDF) have conducted oil resupply exercises in the Southwestern Islands under the pretext of disaster readiness, though they could also serve as Taiwan contingency preparations. However, political and legal sensitivities continue to prevent Tokyo from explicitly acknowledging these exercises for what they are—or even hinting in public at how Japan might respond to a quarantine. As a result, based on open-source materials at the time of this writing in February 2025, it seems that U.S.–Japan joint preparations for quarantine are incomplete in scope and vastly insufficient in scale.

80. Austin Wang and his coauthors have gestured at this point: if China attacks Taiwan, the latter has no reason *not* to declare independence. See Austin Horng-En Wang, Charles K.S. Wu, Yao-Yuan Yeh, and Fang-Yu Chen, "Strategic Ambiguity, Strategic Clarity, and Dual Clarity," *Foreign Policy Analysis* 20, no. 3 (2024): orae010, https://doi.org/10.1093/fpa/orae010.

81. AFP, "Moscow Takes Measures in Response to 'Threatening' NATO Actions," *Moscow Times*, April 14, 2021, https://www.themoscowtimes.com/2021/04/13/moscow-takes-measures-in-response-to-threatening-nato-actions-a73581.

82. Matthew P. Funaiole, Joseph S. Bermudez Jr., et al., "Unpacking the Russian Troop Buildup Along Ukraine's Border," *CSIS*, April 22, 2021, https://www.csis.org/analysis/unpacking-russian-troop-buildup-along-ukraines-border.

83. Gianluca Mezzofiore, "Russia Accelerates Movement of Military Hardware Towards Ukraine, Satellite Images Show," *CNN*, February 7, 2022, https://edition.cnn.com/2022/02/07/europe/yelnya-russian-hardware-ukraine-border-intl/index.html.

84. Andriy Zagorodnyuk, "Putin's Ukraine War: Will Russia Attempt a Black Sea Blockade?" *Atlantic Council*, June 15, 2021, https://www.atlanticcouncil.org/blogs/ukrainealert/putins-ukraine-war-will-russia-attempt-a-black-sea-blockade/.

85. Erin Banco, Garrett M. Graff, Lara Seligman, Nahal Toosi, and Alexander Ward, "'Something Was Badly Wrong': When Washington Realized Russia Was Actually Invading Ukraine," *Politico*, February 24, 2023, https://www.politico.com/news/magazine/2023/02/24/russia-ukraine-war-oral-history-00083757.

86. President of Russia, "Article by Vladimir Putin: 'On the Historical Unity of Russians and Ukrainians,'" *Kremlin.ru*, July 12, 2021; for context, see Serhii Plokhy, *Lost Kingdom: The Quest for Empire and the Making of the Russian Nation* (New York: Basic Books, 2017).

87. Banco et al., "Something Was Badly Wrong."

88. Roberta Wohlstetter, *Pearl Harbor: Warning and Decision* (Palo Alto, CA: Stanford University Press, 1962).

89. *Henry Lewis Stimson Diaries*, November 25, 1941, Yale University Library, Manuscripts and Archives, microfilm edition, roll 7, vol. 36, pp. 48–49, quoted in Robert Joseph Charles Butow, "How Roosevelt Attacked Japan at Pearl Harbor: Myth Masquerading as History," *Prologue* 28, no. 3 (Fall 1996): 209.

90. Roland H. Worth Jr., *No Choice but War: The United States Embargo Against Japan and the Eruption of War in the Pacific* (Jefferson, NC: McFarland, 1995).

91. Wohlstetter, *Pearl Harbor*, 279–338.

92. John Culver, "How We Would Know When China Is Preparing to Invade Taiwan," *Carnegie Endowment for International Peace*, October 3, 2022, https://carnegieendowment.org/2022/10/03/how-we-would-know-when-china-is-preparing-to-invade-taiwan-pub-88053.

93. Lyle Goldstein, "The Hard School of Amphibious Warfare: Examining the Lessons of the 20th Century's Major Amphibious Campaigns for Contemporary Chinese Strategy," *Asian Security* 19, no. 1 (December 1, 2022): 26–42.

94. Thomas Shugart, "Mind the Gap, Part 2: The Cross-Strait Potential of China's Civilian Shipping Has Grown," *War on the Rocks*, October 12, 2022, https://warontherocks.com/2022/10/mind-the-gap-part-2-the-cross-strait-potential-of-chinas-civilian-shipping-has-grown/.

95. China could also arm more of its ballistic missile submarines with nuclear weapons as an indicator. Tong Zhao, *Tides of Change: China's Nuclear Ballistic Missile Submarines and Strategic Stability* (Carnegie Endowment for International Peace, 2018), 1–120, https://carnegieendowment.org/2018/10/24/tides-of-change-china-s-nuclear-ballistic-missile-submarines-and-strategic-stability-pub-77490.

96. Other Taiwan-controlled islands such as Pratas would have less value as potential staging points because major military construction would be necessary.

97. Ya Wang, Zongkui Wang, Bin Liu, Xiaoqian Huang, Wenhui Li, and Changqing Li, "Plasma Fractionation in China: Progress and Challenges," *Annals of Blood* 3 (February 2018): 15, https://aob.amegroups.org/article/view/4317/html; Grand View Research, *China Plasma Fractionation Market Size & Outlook, 2030*, accessed February 19, 2025, https://www.grandviewresearch.com/horizon/outlook/plasma-fractionation-market/china.

98. Deng's excuses were that Vietnam had been mistreating its Chinese minority and unlawfully occupying the Spratly Islands. See Xiaoming Zhang, *Deng Xiaoping's Long War: The Military Conflict Between China and Vietnam, 1979–1991* (Chapel Hill: University of North Carolina Press, 2015).

99. Meia Nouwens, "China's New Information Support Force," *International Institute for Strategic Studies*, May 3, 2024, https://www.iiss.org/online-analysis/online-analysis/2024/05/chinas-new-information-support-force.

100. Kobayashi Yuki, "Signs of China's Resumption of Nuclear Tests: Strong Determination to Bolster Nuclear Force and the Crisis of Nuclear Proliferation," *Sasakawa Peace Foundation*, April 4, 2023, https://www.spf.org/spf-china-observer/en/document-detail042.html.

101. James D. Fearon, "Signaling Foreign Policy Interests: Tying Hands versus Sinking Costs," *Journal of Conflict Resolution* 41, no. 1 (1997): 68–90, https://doi.org/10.1177/0022002797041001004.

102. On Austria's démarche, see Holger Afflerbach, *On a Knife Edge: How Germany Lost the First World War* (Cambridge: Cambridge University Press, 2022), 9–35. On crisis escalation and miscalculation dynamics, see Jack S. Levy, "Misperception and the Causes of War," *World Politics* 36, no. 1 (1983): 76–99.

103. On hand-tying, see Schelling, *Arms and Influence*, 35–43.

104. On the 1914 crisis and Russian mobilization, see Christopher Clark, *The Sleepwalkers: How Europe Went to War in 1914* (London: Allen Lane, 2012), 429–440; Margaret MacMillan, *The War That Ended Peace: The Road to 1914* (New York: Random House, 2013), 573–581.

105. Stephen Van Evera, "The Cult of the Offensive and the Origins of the First World War," *International Security* 9, no. 1 (1984): 58–107, https://www.jstor.org/stable/pdf/2538636.pdf.

106. Lawrence Freedman, *Strategy: A History* (Oxford: Oxford University Press, 2013), 555–561.

107. U.S. officials and experts generally believe that Japanese and South Korean nuclearization would be bad for regional stability, but the circumstances might change quickly if a Chinese military operation against Taiwan seemed imminent. See Kurt M. Campbell, Robert J. Einhorn, and Mitchell Reiss, *The Nuclear Tipping Point: Why States Reconsider Their Nuclear Choices* (Washington, DC: Brookings Institution Press), 243–246; Sigfried S. Hecker, "The Disastrous Downsides of South Korea Building Nuclear Weapons," *38 North*, January 20, 2023, https://www.38north.org/2023/01/the-disastrous-downsides-of-south-korea-building-nuclear-weapons.

108. For a disturbing but controversial discussion of the World War I analogy, see Graham Allison, *Destined for War: Can America and China Escape Thucydides's Trap?* (New York: Houghton Mifflin, 2017), 55–91. For a deeper exploration of the underlying history, see T. G. Otte, *July Crisis: The World's Descent into War, Summer 1914* (Cambridge: Cambridge University Press, 2015).

109. *Ministry of the Interior National Immigration Agency, Republic of China (Taiwan)*, "Statistics," accessed October 23, 2023, https://www.immigration.gov.tw/5475/5478/141478/141380.

110. *Ministry of the Interior National Immigration Agency*, "Statistics." The largest numbers are from Indonesia (roughly 234,000), the Philippines (234,000), Vietnam (154,000), Thailand (72,000), and Malaysia (24,000).

111. *U.S. Taiwan Defense*, "Taiwan in the National Defense Authorization Act (NDAA), 2024," July 14, 2023, https://www.ustaiwandefense.com/taiwan-in-the-national-defense-authorization-act-ndaa-2024.

112. Jeffrey W. Hornung, "Taiwan and Six Potential New Year's Resolutions for the U.S.-Japanese Alliance," *War on the Rocks*, January 5, 2022, https://warontherocks.com/2022/01/taiwan-and-six-potential-new-years-resolutions-for-the-u-s-japanese-alliance.

113. Daniel L. Haulman, "Vietnam Evacuation: Operation Frequent Wind," in *Short of War: Major Air Force Contingency Operations*, ed. Edward A. Warnock (Washington, DC: Air University Press, 1983), 83–93.

114. Nicole Gaouette, Jennifer Hansler, Barbara Starr, and Oren Liebermann, "The Last U.S. Military Planes Have Left Afghanistan, Marking the End of the United States' Longest War," *CNN*, August 31, 2021, https://edition.cnn.com/2021/08/30/politics/us-military-withdraws-afghanistan/index.html.

115. Michael Crowley, "U.S. Warns Americans Abroad Not to Count on a Rescue," *New York Times*, February 16, 2022, https://www.nytimes.com/2022/02/16/us/politics/us-evacuation-ukraine-kabul.html.

116. Tim Kelly, Kaori Kaneko, and Yukiko Toyoda, "Japan's Frontier Islanders Decry Lack of Plan to Aid Taiwanese Fleeing Attack," *Reuters*, December 5, 2023, https://www.reuters.com/world/asia-pacific/japans-frontier-islanders-decry-lack-plan-aid-taiwanese-fleeing-attack-2023-12-05.

117. U.S. Department of Defense, *Joint Publication 3–68: Noncombatant Evacuation Operations (NEO)* (Washington, DC: Department of Defense, 2022), V25–V28, https://www.afpc.af.mil/Portals/70/documents/CRISIS%20SUPPPORT/JP3_68%20Joint%20Noncombatant%20Evacuation%20Opeations%20(Leadership).pdf; for a historical example of a failed NEO, see Frank Snepp, *Decent Interval* (New York: Random House, 1977).

118. *Office of the Under Secretary of Defense for Personnel & Readiness*, "Memorandum of Agreement Between the Departments of State and Defense on the Protection and Evacuation of U.S. Citizens and Nationals and Designated Other Persons from Threatened Areas Overseas," July 14, 1998.

119. Bill Chappell, "Biden Tells U.S. Citizens to Leave Ukraine, Saying Military Wouldn't Rescue Them," *NPR*, February 11, 2022, https://www.npr.org/2022/02/11/1080060546/biden-us-citizens-leave-ukraine.

120. U.S. Congress, Senate, *DETER Act of 2023*, S. 2761, 118th Congress, introduced in Senate September 11, 2023, https://www.congress.gov/bill/118th-congress/senate-bill/2761.

CHAPTER 3

1. The head of Taiwan's military is the chief of the General Staff; the chief of intelligence is the director-general of the National Security Bureau.

2. The 66th Brigade was established in 2005 and is responsible for defending Taipei against decapitation strikes. Cindy Hurst, "China Rehearsing Possible Taiwan Decapitation Operation," *Foreign Military Studies Office*, July 19, 2024, https://fmso.tradoc.army.mil/2024/china-rehearsing-possible-taiwan-decapitation-operation; Aaron Tu and Jake Chung, "Counterdecapitation Plan in Place," *Taipei Times*, October 12, 2017, https://www.taipeitimes.com/News/taiwan/archives/2017/10/12/2003680188.

3. Taiwan has several underground air bases and bunkers. The details of contingency plans are classified, but the president would likely use the Heng Shan Command Center in the Taipei suburb of Taichih as the wartime command center. See *Taiwan News Formosa TV*, "President Tsai Visits Hengshan Command Center, Demonstrates Real-Time Battlefield Intel System," produced by *Taiwan News Formosa TV*, June 9, 2016, video, 1:42, https://www.youtube.com/watch?v=YEsrUSrTTXQ; Emma Helfrich, "Extremely Rare Photos Inside Taiwan's Underground Fighter Jet Caves," *The Warzone*, July 27, 2022, https://www.twz.com/extremely-rare-photos-inside-taiwans-underground-fighter-jet-caves.

4. For example, Deputy Secretary of Defense Bob Work stated after his retirement in 2017 that in all the most realistic wargames the Pentagon has run simulating war over Taiwan, China has beaten the United States every time. Work's point was not that the defense of Taiwan is a lost cause, but that the U.S. military should make high-tech investments to improve its menu of options.

5. Jacquelyn Schneider, "What War Games Really Reveal," *Foreign Affairs*, December 26, 2023, https://www.foreignaffairs.com/united-states/what-war-games-really-reveal.

6. I also assume that PRC strategic planning is professionalized, sophisticated, and highly centralized. The PLA seems basically to understand what capabilities the various Taiwan conflict scenarios would require, what capabilities it still lacks, and what U.S. and Taiwanese capabilities could complicate its missions. Notably, all open-source wargames make similar assumptions. See, for example, Mark F. Cancian, Matthew Cancian, and Eric Heginbotham, *The First Battle of the Next War: Wargaming a Chinese Invasion of Taiwan* (*CSIS*, January 2023), https://www.naval.com.br/blog/wp-content/uploads/2023/01/Wargaming-a-chinese-invasion-of-Taiwan.pdf.

7. Oriana Skylar Mastro, "The Challenges of Deterrence in the Taiwan Strait: Recommendations for U.S. Policy," *American Enterprise Institute*, April 26, 2023, https://selectcommitteeontheccp.house.gov/sites/evo-subsites/selectcommitteeontheccp.house.gov/files/evo-media-document/oriana-skylar-matro-scc-042623.pdf.

8. Easton, *The Chinese Invasion Threat*, 129–152.

9. Ian Easton, "Why a Taiwan Invasion Would Look Nothing Like D-Day," *The Diplomat*, May 26, https://thediplomat.com/2021/05/why-a-taiwan-invasion-would-look-nothing-like-d-day.

10. Easton, *The Chinese Invasion Threat*, 145–146.

11. Harry Halem and Eyck Freymann, "Ukraine Shows Why Taiwan Needs More Air Defense," *War on the Rocks*, April 7, 2022, https://warontherocks.com/2022/04/ukraine-shows-why-taiwan-needs-more-air-defense.

12. Michael J. Lostumbo, David R. Frelinger, James Williams, and Barry Wilson, *Air Defense Options for Taiwan: An Assessment of Relative Costs and Operational Benefits* (Santa Monica, CA: RAND Corporation, 2016), https://www.rand.org/content/dam/rand/pubs/research_reports/RR1000/RR1051/RAND_RR1051.pdf.

13. Matthew Revels, "Denying Command of the Air: The Future of Taiwan's Air Defense Strategy," *Journal of Indo-Pacific Affairs* 6, no. 3 (2023): 135–144, https://www.airuniversity.af.edu/JIPA/Display/Article/3371516/denying-command-of-the-air-the-future-of-taiwans-air-defense-strategy.

14. China has similar submarines and continues to build them despite being able to build nuclear-powered submarines. See Sarah Kirchberger, "China Maritime Report No. 31: China's Submarine Industrial Base: State-Led Innovation with Chinese Characteristics" (Newport, RI: 2023), 16–17.

15. *In Their Own Words: The Science of Military Strategy 2013* (Montgomery, AL: China Aerospace Studies Institute, 2021), 343, https://airuniversity.af.edu/Portals/10/CASI/documents/Translations/2021-02-08%20Chinese%20Military%20Thoughts-%20In%20their%20own%20words%20Science%20of%20Military%20Strategy%202013.pdf.

16. Gordon Harrison, *Cross-Channel Attack* (Washington, DC: U.S. Army Center of Military History, 1951), https://history.army.mil/books/wwii/7-4/7-4_Contents.htm; Martin Blumenson, *Breakout and Pursuit* (Washington, DC: U.S. Army Center of Military History, 1961), https://history.army.mil/html/books/007/7-5-1/index.html.

17. For amphibious operations and the preparation for Operation Neptune, see Stephen E. Ambrose, *D-Day, June 6, 1944: The Climactic Battle of World War II* (New York: Simon & Schuster, 1994), 25–36; Gordon A. Harrison, *Cross-Channel Attack* (Washington, DC: Office of the Chief of Military History, 1951), 268–274. On the Luftwaffe's degradation and strategic bombing, see Richard Overy, *The Bombing War: Europe 1939–1945* (London: Allen Lane, 2013), 442–445.

18. Roger Hesketh, *Fortitude: The D-Day Deception Campaign* (London: St. Ermin's Press, 1999), 235–241.

19. For operational challenges and securing beachheads, see Max Hastings, *Overlord: D-Day and the Battle for Normandy* (London: Pan Books, 1984), 139–147; Carlo D'Este, *Decision in Normandy* (New York: HarperCollins, 1994), 272–277.

20. Dennis Blasko, *China Maritime Report No. 20: The PLA Army Amphibious Force* (*China Maritime Studies Institute*, April 2022), https://digital-commons.usnwc.edu/cgi/viewcontent.cgi?article=1019&context=cmsi-maritime-reports.

21. "Taiwan Seeks to Strengthen Its Artillery Capabilities with Acquisition of US M109A7 Howitzers," *Global Defense News*, December 18, 2024, https://www.armyrecognition.com/news/army-news/army-news-2024/taiwan-seeks-to-strengthen-its-artillery-capabilities-with-acquisition-of-us-origin-m109a7-paladin-self-propelled-howitzers; "New Stage in US Military Support for Taiwan: $567 Million to Counter Beijing," *Global Defense News*, September 30, 2024, https://www.armyrecognition.com/news/army-news/army-news-2024/new-stage-in-us-military-support-for-taiwan-567-million-to-counter-beijing.

22. *PRC and Taiwanese Bases*, Bloomberg, n.d., https://www.bloomberg.com/toaster/v2/charts/2a1fb12a801548c0971a9eb0c0e43f52.html.

23. For a summary of various PRC speculations about Taiwan's port defenses, see Ian Easton, "Hostile Harbors: Taiwan's Ports and PLA Invasion Plans," in *Study No. 8, Chinese Amphibious Warfare: Prospects for a Cross-Strait Invasion*, eds. Andrew S. Erickson, Conor M. Kennedy, and Ryan D. Martinson (*China Maritime Studies Institute*, 2024), 349–350, https://digital-commons.usnwc.edu/cgi/viewcontent.cgi?article=1000&context=cmsi-studies.

24. Author's calculations based on tonnage of PLA vessels. See Cristina L. Garafola, *China Maritime Report No. 19: The PLA Airborne Corps in a Joint Island Landing Campaign* (Newport, RI: *China Maritime Studies Institute*, 2022), https://digital-commons.usnwc.edu/cgi/viewcontent.cgi?article=1018&context=cmsi-maritime-reports.

25. Surface combatants—such as destroyers, frigates, and cruisers—are primarily designed for engaging enemy ships, aircraft, and submarines, among other combat operations. Amphibious warfare ships are sometimes capable of defensive and support actions in combat scenarios, but they are primarily focused on the transportation and deployment of troops and equipment. Amphibious Assault Ships (LHD/LHA) can be considered as hybrids, but Dock Landing Ships (LSD), Amphibious Transport Docks (LPD), and Amphibious Cargo Ships (LKA/AKA) are of little use in combat.

26. The People's Maritime Militia would help in this effort, but it does not have enough tonnage to replace the need for civilian ferries. Lonnie Henley, *China Maritime Report*

No. 21: Civilian Shipping and Maritime Militia: The Logistics Backbone of a Taiwan Invasion (China Maritime Studies Institute, May 2022), https://digital-commons.usnwc.edu/cmsi-maritime-reports/21/;Michael Dahm, *China Maritime Report No. 25: More Chinese Ferry Tales: China's Use of Civilian Shipping in Military Activities, 2021–2022 (China Maritime Studies Institute*, January 2023), https://digital-commons.usnwc.edu/cmsi-maritime-reports/25/; Kevin McCauley, *China Maritime Report No. 22: Logistics Support for a Cross-Strait Invasion: The View from Beijing (China Maritime Studies Institute*, July 2022), https://digital-commons.usnwc.edu/cmsi-maritime-reports/22.

27. Carter Malkasian, "Charting the Pathway to OMFTS: A Historical Assessment of Amphibious Operations from 1941 to the Present" (Center for Naval Analyses, July 2002), https://www.cna.org/reports/2002/D0006297.A2.pdf.

28. Ian Easton, for example, speculates that up to 400,000 troops would be necessary if a prior PRC decapitation strike was successful, but as many as 2 million would be needed against a well-mobilized defense; Easton, "Hostile Harbors," 345–346.

29. McCauley, *China Maritime Report No. 22*, 23.

30. On Russia's failed attack on Hostomel Airport, see Andrew McGregor, "Russian Airborne Disaster at Hostomel Airport," *Aberfoyle International Security*, March 8, 2022, https://www.aberfoylesecurity.com/?p=4812; Jeremy Kofsky, "An Airfield Too Far: Failures at Market Garden and Antonov Airfield," *Modern War Institute*, May 5, 2022, https://mwi.westpoint.edu/an-airfield-too-far-failures-at-market-garden-and-antonov-airfield/. Open sources provide many fewer details about the PLA's airborne lift capacity, but a ballpark estimate is that China could deploy two airborne brigades at a time, totaling around 10,000 additional men.

31. Easton, "Hostile Harbors," 352–354.

32. Yimou Lee and David Lague, "Chinese Spies Have Penetrated Taiwan's Military, Case Documents Reveal," *Reuters*, December 20, 2021, https://www.reuters.com/investigates/special-report/taiwan-china-espionage/.

33. On planning for Market Garden, see Cornelius Ryan, *A Bridge Too Far* (New York: Simon & Schuster, 1974), 162–170; Sebastian Ritchie, *Arnhem: Myth and Reality* (London: Robert Hale, 2011), 127–135. On the operation itself, see Ryan, *A Bridge Too Far*, 185; Ritchie, *Arnhem*, 193–248.

34. William Fox and Roderick Lee, "Assessing the PLA's Confidence in Its Ability to Achieve Air and Sea Control Around Taiwan," in *Study No. 8, Chinese Amphibious Warfare: Prospects for a Cross-Strait Invasion*, eds. Andrew S. Erickson, Conor M. Kennedy, and Ryan D. Martinson (*China Maritime Studies Institute*, 2024), https://digital-commons.usnwc.edu/cgi/viewcontent.cgi?article=1000&context=cmsi-studies. See also: 肖天亮 [Tianliang Xiao], ed., 战略学 [*Science of Strategy*] (Beijing: National Defense University, 2015), 241–251; 张玉良 [Zhang Yuliang], ed., 战役学 [*Science of Campaigns*] (Beijing: National Defense University Press, 2006), 351–374. For Chinese scholarly articles assessing this challenge, see 王慕鸿 [Wang Muhong] et al., 两栖攻击舰对空自防御作战火力分配模型, *Amphibious Assault Ship Air Self-Defense Combat Firepower Distribution Model*, 火力与指挥控制 [Fire Control and Command Control] 45, no. 12 (2020): 127–31.; 王慕鸿 [Wang Muhong], 张浩 [Zhang Hao], and 徐圣良 [Xu Shengliang], "两栖攻 击舰对空自防御作战软硬武器火力冲突检测及消解" *Amphibious Assault Ship Antiair Self-defense Combat Soft- and Hard-Weapons Firepower Conflict Detection and Resolution*, 指挥控制与仿真 [Command Control &

Simulation] 42, no. 6 (2020): 122–26; 王慕鸿 [Wang Muhong], 张文娟 [Zhang Wenjuan], and 徐圣良 [Xu Shengliang], "基于对抗全过程仿真的两栖攻击舰对自防御作战能力评估" *Amphibious Assault Ship Antiair Self-defense Operational Capability Analysis Based on Confrontation Whole-Process Simulation*, 舰船电子工程 [Ship Electronic Engineering] 40, no. 11 (2020): 132–136.

35. Conor M. Kennedy, "The New Chinese Marine Corps: A 'Strategic Dagger' in a Cross-Strait Invasion," in *Study No. 8, Chinese Amphibious Warfare: Prospects for a Cross-Strait Invasion*, eds. Andrew S. Erickson, Conor M. Kennedy, and Ryan D. Martinson (*China Maritime Studies Institute*, 2024), 94–95, https://digital-commons.usnwc.edu/cgi/viewcontent.cgi?article=1000&context=cmsi-studies; U.S. Department of Defense, *2020 Report on Military and Security Developments Involving the People's Republic of China: Annual Report to Congress* (Washington, DC: U.S. Department of Defense, 2020), 114; Zhang, *Science of Campaigns*, 293, 298.

36. Tom Fox, "The PLA Ground Forces' New Helicopters: An 'Easy Button' for Crossing the Taiwan Strait?" in *Study No. 8, Chinese Amphibious Warfare: Prospects for a Cross-Strait Invasion*, eds. Andrew S. Erickson, Conor M. Kennedy, and Ryan D. Martinson (China Maritime Studies Institute, 2024), 178, https://digital-commons.usnwc.edu/cgi/viewcontent.cgi?article=1000&context=cmsi-studies; 张硕 [Zhang Shuo], "为飞行员'私人订制'训练计划, '指标清单'里有什么?" *What Is the "List of Indicators" for a Pilot's "Personalized" Training Program?*, 中国军网 [China Military Network], April 28, 2021, http://www.81.cn/ysym/ssjgy/index.html.

37. Fox and Lee, "Assessing the PLA's Confidence," 199, 206.

38. Cristina L. Garafola, "The PLA Airborne Corps in a Joint Island Landing Campaign," in *Study No. 8, Chinese Amphibious Warfare: Prospects for a Cross-Strait Invasion*, eds. Andrew S. Erickson, Conor M. Kennedy, and Ryan D. Martinson (*China Maritime Studies Institute*, 2024), 164–166, https://digital-commons.usnwc.edu/cgi/viewcontent.cgi?article=1000&context=cmsi-studies.

39. Leigh Ann Luce and Erin Richter, "Handling Logistics in a Reformed PLA: The Long March toward Joint Logistics," in *Chairman Xi Remakes the PLA: Assessing Chinese Military Reforms*, ed. Phillip C. Saunders et al. (Washington, DC: NDU Press, 2019), 278–280.

40. On the PLA's assessment of its capabilities and experience, see *Testimony to U.S.-China Economic and Security Review Commission Hearing on "PLA Weaknesses and Xi's Concerns about PLA Capabilities,"* 116th Cong. (2019) (statement of Dennis J. Blasko, Lieutenant Colonel, U.S. Army, Retired, Independent Analyst), 4–10.

41. "台军进行多种型号导弹试射" ["Taiwan Military Conducts Test Launch of Various Missile Types"], *Xinhua News*, August 21, 2024, http://www.news.cn/milpro/20240821/afe84cf80cac42c59d14cadb691c7897/c.html.

42. Lostumbo et al., *Air Defense Options for Taiwan*, 14–16.

43. "肩負運輸動脈及軍事運輸重任的高路公路-戰備跑道" ["Highways Shouldering the Important Task of Transportation Artery and Military Transportation-Combat Readiness Airstrips"], *Highway Administration, Ministry of Transportation, Taiwan*, May 6, 2019, https://www.freeway.gov.tw/Southernarchives/Publish.aspx?NID=3332&P=12889.

44. Erickson and Collins, "Deterring (or Defeating) a PLA Invasion," 462.

45. Fox, "The PLA Ground Forces' New Helicopters," 186–187.

46. Revels, "Denying Command of the Air"; Lostumbo et al., *Air Defense Options for Taiwan*, 11–18.

47. "Q & A, All-Out Defense Mobilization Agency, M.N.D.," *All-Out Defense Mobilization Agency, Ministry of National Defense*, January 6, 2025, https://adma.mnd.gov.tw/unit/100010/197.

48. John Chen and Joel Wuthnow, *Chinese Special Operations in a Large-Scale Island Landing, China Maritime Studies Institute Report No. 18* (Newport, RI: U.S. Naval War College, January 2022).

49. Xiao, *Science of Military Strategy*, 355, cited in Chen and Wuthnow, *Chinese Special Operations in a Large-Scale Island Landing*, 3.

50. *CBC News*, "Ukraine President Denounces Bucha Killings as 'Genocide,'" April 5, 2022, video, 5:49, https://www.youtube.com/watch?v=Kq--RzAbTHc.

51. Emile Simpson, *War from the Ground Up: Twenty-First Century Combat as Politics* (Oxford: Oxford University Press, 2018).

52. Max Hastings, *Vietnam: An Epic History of a Tragic War* (London: William Collins, 2019).

53. U.S. operations were complicated by the fact that Vietnam is roughly ten times as large as Taiwan and had twice the population.

54. David Yi, "Counterinsurgency Force Ratios: An Investigation into Military Logic" (Master's thesis, U.S. Army Command and General Staff College, 2018), https://apps.dtic.mil/sti/pdfs/AD1071542.pdf.

55. Quinlivan's troop density model recommends between ten and twenty-five troops per 1000 population; see John McGrath, *Boots on the Ground: Troop Density in Contingency Operations* (Fort Leavenworth, KS: Combat Studies Institute Press, 2006), 94. This implies a force of 500,000 troops for pacification and post-invasion stabilization—in addition to the landing operation.

56. Elsa B. Kania and Ian Burns McCaslin, *The PLA's Evolving Outlook on Urban Warfare: Learning, Training, and Implications for Taiwan* (Institute for the Study of War, April 2020), 1–43.

57. Ryo Nakamura, "U.S. Expands Training of Taiwanese Military with National Guard," *Nikkei Asia*, January 20, 2023.

58. "New Mobilization Agency Formed to Show Taiwan's Resolute All-Out Defense: Tsai," *CNA English News*, December 30, 2021, https://focustaiwan.tw/politics/202112300004.

59. "Our Mission," *Forward Alliance*, accessed January 8, 2025, https://www.forward.org.tw/about/us; "In Brief with Enoch Wu, Founder of Forward Alliance," *9DashLine*, April 5, 2023, https://www.9dashline.com/article/in-brief-with-enoch-wu-founder-of-the-forward-alliance.

60. "Taiwan's Military Says Capacity Sufficient to Train One-Year Conscripts," *Focus Taiwan*, January 5, 2023, https://focustaiwan.tw/politics/202301050012.

61. Mike Stokes, Yang kuang-shu, and Eric Lee, *Preparing for the Nightmare: Readiness and Ad Hoc Coalition Operations in the Taiwan Strait* (Arlington, VA: Project 49 Institute, 2020).

62. Fox and Lee, "Assessing the PLA's Confidence," 276–277.

63. Wayne P. Hughes, "Naval Tactics and Their Influence on Strategy," *Naval War College Review* 39, no. 1 (1986): 2–17, http://www.jstor.org/stable/44636482.

64. Zhang Yuliang, ed., Science of Campaigns (2006), 2nd ed., trans. *In Their Own Words* (China Aerospace Studies Institute, 2020), https://www.airuniversity.af.edu/

CASI/Display/Article/2421219/in-their-own-words-plas-science-of-campaigns;   Xiao
Tianliang, ed., "The Science of Military Strategy" (2020), trans. *In Their Own Words*
(China Aerospace Studies Institute, 2022), https://www.airuniversity.af.edu/Portals/
10/CASI/documents/Translations/2022-01-26%202020%20Science%20of%20Military
%20Strategy.pdf, 227.

65. Thomas Shugart, "Has China Been Practicing Preemptive Missile Strikes against U.S.
Bases?" *War on the Rocks*, February 6, 2017, https://warontherocks.com/2017/02/has-
china-been-practicing-preemptive-missile-strikes-against-u-s-bases.

66. U.S. Department of Defense, *Military and Security Developments Involving the People's
Republic of China: 2024* (Washington, DC: U.S. Department of Defense, 2024).

67. Caitlin Talmadge, "Beijing's Nuclear Option: Why a U.S.-Chinese War Could Spiral Out
of Control," *Foreign Affairs*, October 15, 2018, https://www.foreignaffairs.com/articles/
china/2018-10-15/beijings-nuclear-option.

68. Dennis C. Blair and Caitlin Talmadge, "Would China Go Nuclear?" *Foreign Affairs*,
December 11, 2018, https://www.foreignaffairs.com/articles/china/2018-12-11/would-
china-go-nuclear.

69. Blair and Talmadge, "Would China Go Nuclear?"

70. Dahlia Anne Goldfeld, Nathan Beauchamp-Mustafaga, Shawn Cochran, et al., "Denial
Without Disaster—Keeping a U.S.-China Conflict over Taiwan under the Nuclear
Threshold," Vol. 1, *An Overview of Ideas for U.S. Conventional Joint Long-Range Strike
in Support of Escalation Management* (Santa Monica, CA: RAND Corporation, 2024),
https://www.rand.org/pubs/research_reports/RRA2312-1.html.

71. U.S. Department of Defense, *Space Policy Review and Strategy on Protection of Satellites*
(Washington, DC: U.S. Department of Defense, September 2023), 5, https://media.
defense.gov/2023/Sep/14/2003301146/-1/-1/0/COMPREHENSIVE-REPORT-
FOR-RELEASE.PDF.

72. Michael McDevitt, "If China Invades, How Should the U.S. Navy Respond?" in *Study
No. 8, Chinese Amphibious Warfare: Prospects for a Cross-Strait Invasion*, eds. Andrew
S.Erickson, Conor M. Kennedy, and Ryan D. Martinson (Newport, RI: China Maritime
Studies Institute, 2024), 350–351, https://digital-commons.usnwc.edu/cgi/viewcontent.
cgi?article=1000&context=cmsi-studies.

73. As the 2013 *Science of Military Strategy* puts it: "Under the conditions of informatization [信息化] a local war is a system-to-system confrontation, and its basic form
of combat is integrated joint operations.Sun, *Science of Military Strategy*, 124–127,
cited in David M. Finkelstein, *The PLA's New Joint Doctrine: The Capstone of the
New Era Operations Regulations System* (CNA, September 2021), 37. See also Dean
Cheng, "PLA Perspectives on Network Warfare in 'Informationized Local Wars,'" *Testimony before U.S.–China Economic and Security Review Commission*, February 17,
2022.

74. China has missiles that have a longer range, but the targeting problem becomes more
difficult at extended distances. Attrition on China's strike network will reduce this range.

75. Clayton Swope, "No Place to Hide: A Look at China's Geosynchronous Surveillance Capabilities," *Center for Strategic and International Studies*, January 19, 2024,
https://www.csis.org/analysis/no-place-hide-look-chinas-geosynchronous-surveillance-
capabilities.

76. Stacie Pettyjohn, Andrew Metrick, and Becca Wasser, "The Kadena Conundrum:
Developing a Resilient Indo-Pacific Posture," *War on the Rocks*, December 1, 2022,

https://warontherocks.com/2022/12/the-kadena-conundrum-developing-a-resilient-indo-pacific-posture/.

77. Pettyjohn, Metrick, and Wasser, "The Kadena Conundrum.

78. U.S. Department of Defense, *Pacific Deterrence Initiative* (Washington, DC: U.S. Department of Defense, April 2022).

79. This includes reserve squadrons and Air National Guard squadrons.

80. Curtis E. LeMay, *Center Air Force Doctrine Note 1-21: Agile Combat Employment* (Maxwell AFB, AL: Curtis E. LeMay Center for Doctrine Development and Education, August 23), 2022, https://www.doctrine.af.mil/Portals/61/documents/AFDN_1-21_ACE.pdf.

81. Cancian, *First Battle of the Next War*, 83.

82. Eric Tegler, "The Boeing-Kratos PJDAM Is a 300-Mile Smart Bomb," *Forbes*, October 25, 2023, https://www.forbes.com/sites/erictegler/2023/10/25/the-boeing-kratos-pjdam-is-a-300-mile-smart-bomb.

83. Pottinger, *Boiling Moat*, 138–41.

84. Many of the current bombers are equipped with advanced stealth technologies, and the future B-21 Raider will have even more advanced stealth technology. Moreover, the longer the range of the air-launched missiles that the bombers carry, the further back from China's RSC they can operate.

85. U.S. Marine Corps, *Force Design 2030: Annual Update* (Washington, DC: U.S. Marine Corps, 2023), https://www.marines.mil/Portals/1/Docs/Force_Design_2030_Annual_Update.pdf.

86. Ronald O'Rourke, *Defense Primer: Navy Distributed Maritime Operations (DMO) Concept* (*Congressional Research Service*, October 2, 2024), https://sgp.fas.org/crs/natsec/IF12599.pdf.

87. Ronald O'Rourke, *Navy Force Structure and Shipbuilding Plans: Background and Issues for Congress* (Washington, DC: Congressional Research Service, August 31, 2023), 5, https://crsreports.congress.gov/product/pdf/RL/RL32665/386; "Long-Range Anti-Ship Missile (LRASM)," *Defense Advanced Research Projects Agency*, accessed October 18, 2024, https://www.darpa.mil/about-us/long-range-anti-ship-missile.

88. Megan Eckstein, "Navy's 2024 Plan Backs Long-Range Weapons, Shrinks Amphibious Fleet," *Defense News*, March 13, 2023, https://www.defensenews.com/naval/2023/03/13/navys-2024-plan-backs-long-range-weapons-shrinks-amphibious-fleet.

89. "SSN Seawolf Class," *Naval Technology*, accessed February 21, 2025, https://www.naval-technology.com/projects/seawolf.

90. Mike Sweeney, "Submarines Will Reign in a War with China," *Proceedings* 149, no. 3 (March 2023), https://www.usni.org/magazines/proceedings/2023/march/submarines-will-reign-war-china.

91. Brent Eastwood, "U.S. Navy Submarines vs. China: We Say the Quiet Part Out Loud," *1945*, November 27, 2024, https://www.19fortyfive.com/2024/11/u-s-navy-submarines-vs-china-we-say-the-quiet-part-out-loud.

92. Polina Lemenkova, "Visualization of the Geophysical Settings in the Philippine Sea Margins by Means of GMT and ISC Data," *ResearchGate*, 2020, https://www.researchgate.net/figure/Bathymetric-map-of-the-Philippine-Sea-Basin-Bathymetry-GEBCO-Global-Relief-Model-15-arc_fig1_340262054.

93. Michael J. Dahm and Alison Zhao, *China Maritime Report No. 28: Bitterness Ends, Sweetness Begins: Organizational Changes to the PLAN Submarine Force Since 2015* (Newport, RI: China Maritime Studies Institute, 2023); Alastair Gale, "The Era of Total

U.S. Submarine Dominance over China Is Ending," *The Wall Street Journal*, November 20, 2023, https://www.wsj.com/world/china/us-submarine-dominance-shift-china-8db10a0d; Rajeswari Pillai Rajagopalan, "China's Growing Submarine Capabilities," *The Diplomat*, October 31, 2023, https://thediplomat.com/2023/10/chinas-growing-submarine-capabilities/; "China Submarine Capabilities," *Nuclear Threat Initiative*, August 13, 2024, https://www.nti.org/analysis/articles/china-submarine-capabilities.

94. Toshi Yoshihara, "Chinese Views of Taiwan's Geostrategic Value," *SPF China Observer* 45 (December 4, 2023).

95. *U.S. Naval Institute News*, "Advanced Russian Attack Submarine Operating in the East China Sea," *USNI News*, December 3, 2024, https://news.usni.org/2024/12/03/advanced-russian-attack-submarine-operating-in-the-east-china-sea; Peter Aitken, "Samuel Paparo Warns Russia Could Help China Cut U.S. Military Dominance," *Newsweek*, December 3, 2024, https://www.newsweek.com/samuel-paparo-warns-russia-help-china-cut-military-dominance-1990633.

96. Jim Garamone, "Hicks Discusses Replicator Initiative," *DoD News*, September 7, 2023, https://www.defense.gov/News/News-Stories/Article/Article/3518827/hicks-discusses-replicator-initiative.

97. Josh Rogin, "The U.S. Military Plans a 'Hellscape' to Deter China from Attacking Taiwan," *Washington Post*, June 9, 2024, https://www.washingtonpost.com/opinions/2024/06/10/taiwan-china-hellscape-military-plan.

98. Eric Tegler, "A Defense Startup CEO Says There's Too Much Negativity on Replicator," *Forbes*, February 21, 2024, https://www.forbes.com/sites/erictegler/2024/02/21/a-defense-startup-ceo-says-theres-too-much-negativity-on-replicator; Noah Robertson, "Replicator: An Inside Look at the Pentagon's Ambitious Drone Program," *Defense News*, December 19, 2023, https://www.defensenews.com/pentagon/2023/12/19/replicator-an-inside-look-at-the-pentagons-ambitious-drone-program; Matt Berg, "'Disorganized and Confusing': Lawmakers, Industry Rip Pentagon Plans for Drones," *Politico*, December 17, 2023, https://www.politico.com/news/2023/12/17/pentagon-drones-replicator-program-funding-00132092; Chris Jenks, "YEAR AHEAD—The U.S. DoD Replicator Initiative and the Acquisition Process for Autonomous Weapons," *Lieber Institute at West Point—Articles of War*, January 9, 2024, https://lieber.westpoint.edu/us-dod-replicator-initiative-acquisition-process-autonomous-weapons.

99. Jeffrey W. Hornung, Kristen Gunness, Bryan Rooney, Dan McCormick, Lydia Grek, Ryan A. Schwankhart, Gian Gentile, and Marisa R. Lino, *Fighting Abroad from an Ally's Land* (Santa Monica, CA: RAND Corporation, 2024), https://www.rand.org/pubs/research_reports/RRA1985-1.html.

100. China Aerospace Studies Institute (CASI), *Science of Campaigns (2006), In Their Own Words: Foreign Military Thought* (Montgomery, AL: Air University, November 23, 2020), 329–351, https://www.airuniversity.af.edu/Portals/10/CASI/documents/Translations/2020-12-02%20In%20Their%20Own%20Words-%20Science%20of%20Campaigns%20(2006).pdf; for the original Mandarin, see: 张玉良 (Zhang Yuliang), 战役学 (*The Science of Campaigns*) (Beijing: National Defense University Press, 2006), 292–310, https://taiwan-in-perspective.com/wp-content/uploads/2015/12/the-science-of-campaigns-e68898e5bdb9e5ada6-2006.pdf.

101. Thomas Shattuck, "Breaking the Barrier: Four Years of PRC Military Activity Around Taiwan," *Foreign Policy Research Institute*, October 9, 2024, https://www.fpri.org/article/2024/10/breaking-the-barrier-four-years-of-prc-military-activity-around-taiwan.

102. Henley, *China Maritime Report No. 26.*

103. It is unclear how sustainably China could disrupt Taiwan's electrical grid using cyberattacks alone.

104. "Russia's Disregard for Nuclear Safety and Security in Ukraine," *U.S. Department of Energy*, accessed January 8, 2025, https://www.energy.gov/nnsa/russias-disregard-nuclear-safety-and-security-ukraine#:~:text=One%20year%20ago%2C%20on%20March,before%20and%20after%20its%20capture.

105. Henley, *China Maritime Report No. 26,* 6.

106. William Yang, "Taiwan Unveils Plans to Cope with Potential Chinese Military Blockade," *Voice of America*, October 23, 2024, https://www.voanews.com/a/taiwan-unveils-plans-to-cope-with-potential-chinese-military-blockade-/7835984.html; Yimou Lee and Ben Blanchard, "Preparing for a Chinese Blockade, Taiwan Maps Out Wartime Food Plans," *Reuters*, October 22, 2024, https://www.reuters.com/world/asia-pacific/preparing-chinese-blockade-taiwan-maps-out-wartime-food-plans-2024-10-22/; Su Tzu-yun (蘇紫雲), "緊急時期能源與電力供應韌性　確保政府與社會持續運作" (*Resilience of Energy and Power Supply in Emergencies: Ensuring Continuity of Government and Society*), *Institute for National Defense and Security Research*, February 25, 2022, https://indsr.org.tw/respublicationcon?uid=12&resid=1855&pid=1102; Cheng You-han (鄭佑漢), "憂中國封控台灣引發能源危機　政院持續研議增加安全存量" (*Concerned about China's Blockade of Taiwan Triggering an Energy Crisis, the Executive Yuan Continues to Deliberate on Increasing Safety Stockpiles*), *Radio Taiwan International*, October 29, 2024, https://www.rti.org.tw/news/view/id/2225910; Taiwan Power Company (台灣電力公司), "我國電價相較各國緩漲　台電努力改善財務　也需千億補貼民生用電虧損" (*Taiwan's Electricity Prices Rise More Slowly Compared to Other Countries; Taipower Strives to Improve Finances but Also Needs 100 Billion Subsidy for Residential Electricity Losses*), October 18, 2024, https://www.taipower.com.tw/2289/2323/2324/58568/normalPost.
Ministry of Economic Affairs, Republic of China (中华民国经济部), "相關物資儲備有固定機制且持續改良　未雨綢繆有備無患" (*Relevant Material Reserves Have a Fixed Mechanism and Are Continuously Improved to Prepare for Rainy Days*), October 7, 2022, https://www.moea.gov.tw/Mns/populace/news/News.aspx?kind=1&menu_id=40&news_id=103052; Ministry of Economic Affairs, Republic of China (中华民国经济部), "我國能源供應與儲備之現況及未來規劃方向" (*The Current Situation and Future Planning Directions of Taiwan's Energy Supply and Reserves*), Special Report, March 16, 2023, https://ppg.ly.gov.tw/ppg/SittingAttachment/download/2023030989/02291301002301567002.pdf.

107. Bureau of Energy, Ministry of Economic Affairs, Republic of China (中华民国经济部能源局), "2021年能源平衡表" (*2021 Energy Balance Sheet*), December 2021, https://www.esist.org.tw/publication/annually?tab=%E8%83%BD%E6%BA%90%E5%B9%B3%E8%A1%A1%E8%A1%A8 #.

108. "Q-Max," *Trefin Tankers*, accessed January 8, 2025, https://trefintankers.com/en/fleet/q-max.

109. Chaouki Ghenai and Eugene Chausovsky, "Taiwan's Semiconductor Sustainability and Global Implications," *New Lines Institute*, August 27, 2024, https://newlinesinstitute.org/geo-economics/taiwans-semiconductor-sustainability-and-global-implications/; Charlotte Trueman, "TSMC Could Account for 24% of Taiwan's Electricity Consumption by 2030," *Data Center Dynamics*, October 7, 2024, https://www.

datacenterdynamics.com/en/news/tsmc-could-account-for-24-of-taiwans-electricity-consumption-by-2030.

110. As of August 2022, the government of Taiwan reported that its strategic energy reserves contained 146 days' worth of crude oil, 39 days of coal, and 10 days of gas. Roughly 40 percent of Taiwan's power plants are gas-powered, but if necessary they could be easily converted to burn oil.

111. Industry represents 32 percent of Taiwan's power consumption. In a war, manufacturing for export would probably fall to close to zero, reducing Taiwan's total energy demand by around 20 percent. Civilian flights (another 7 percent of power consumption) would probably be grounded to conserve fuel. The household sector and services make up just 13 percent of Taiwan's total energy demand. If the situation resembled that of COVID lockdowns in developed countries, residential energy demand would probably increase, but services demand would decrease. There might also be periodic blackouts.

112. Under blockade, Taiwan's naval operations would be far more constrained than that of the Royal Navy in World War II. The PLA would intensify operations around the island to exhaust Taiwan's military ships and aircraft, depleting their spare parts and fuel reserves. See Department for Energy Security and Net Zero and Department for Business, Energy & Industrial Strategy, "Crude Oil and Petroleum Products: Imports by Product," *gov.uk*, accessed January 30, 2024; see also David Edgerton, *Britain's War Machine: Weapons, Resources, and Experts in the Second World War* (Oxford: Oxford University Press, 2011), 182.

113. Eyck Freymann, Nicholas Kumleben, and Will Taylor, *Taiwan in the Blockade Contingency* (Working Paper, July 2023).

114. At the peak in the 1980s, Taiwan drew around half its total energy from nuclear power, but the DPP is committed to phasing out nuclear as existing reactors reach the end of their operational lives. The Taiwan People's Party (TPP) and KMT have called for a referendum on nuclear power. As of this writing in April 2025, the remaining reactors in Maanshan Nuclear Power Plant are still planned to be decommissioned, but if necessary they could be kept online without grave safety risks.

115. Oscar Lin, *Taiwan Food Security Situation Overview* (Taipei: USDA Foreign Agricultural Service, 2024), 2, https://apps.fas.usda.gov/newgainapi/api/Report/DownloadReport ByFileName?fileName=Taiwan%20Food%20Security%20Situation%20Overview_ Taipei_Taiwan_TW2024-0030.pdf.

116. "Government Soothes Fears, Says Taiwan Has 6 Months of Food Supplies," *Taiwan News*, May 14, 2021, https://www.taiwannews.com.tw/news/4203406.

117. Troy Lai and Erik Syngle, *Taiwan Confident of Basic Food Supply Amid Second Wave of COVID Infection* (USDA Foreign Agricultural Service, June 7, 2021), 2–3; Jackson Rice, *The Resilience of Taiwan's Energy and Food Systems to Blockade* (San Diego, CA: Center for Excellence in Disaster Management and Humanitarian Assistance, August 2023).

118. Ministry of Agriculture and Fisheries Administration (農業部漁業署), *Overview of the Fisheries*, accessed November 22, 2024, https://en.fa.gov.tw/view.php?theme=web_ structure&id=110.

119. Lin, *Taiwan Food Security Situation Overview*, 4.

120. Henley, *China Maritime Report No. 26*, 1–2.

121. "Remarks by Assistant Secretary Ely Ratner at Center for Strategic and International Studies Conference on 'China's Power: Up for Debate 2023,'" *U.S. Department of Defense*, October 5, 2023.

122. Beijing has many other options to cut Taiwan off from the world. It could sever the undersea communications cables connecting Taiwan to the rest of the world, cutting the island off from the Internet. It could use cyberattacks to knock out Taiwan's communications, electricity grid, and airports. If China persisted with these attacks, it could make a quarantine much harder for Taiwan to bear. However, the United States could also respond by damaging China's own connections to the outside world, which could cause substantial economic and financial disruption. These measures are therefore not cost-free for China and would probably not be undertaken outside the context of conflict.

123. "美国智库猜测大陆如何封锁台湾的选项,统一过程可能很简单" (American Think Tank Speculates on Mainland China's Options to Blockade Taiwan; Unification Process May Be Simple), Tencent News (腾讯新闻), September 9, 2024, https://news.qq.com/rain/a/20240909A03WCM00.

124. The U.S. military does not have an acknowledged anti-satellite program, as China does, but if a general war with China escalated into the space domain, it is reasonable to assume that the U.S. military has various capabilities to deal with China's satellites.

125. "The Need for SEAD / DEAD," *Northrop Grumman*, accessed February 21, 2025, https://www.northropgrumman.com/what-we-do/advanced-weapons/the-need-for-sead-dead.

126. Jude Blanchette and Gerard DiPippo, "'Reunification' with Taiwan through Force Would Be a Pyrrhic Victory for China," *Center for Strategic and International Studies*, November 22, 2022, https://www.csis.org/analysis/reunification-taiwan-through-force-would-be-pyrrhic-victory-china.

127. Eric Milstein and David Wessel, "What Did the Fed Do in Response to the COVID-19 Crisis?," *Brookings*, December 17, 2021, https://www.brookings.edu/articles/fed-response-to-covid19; Board of Governors of the Federal Reserve System, "Coronavirus Disease 2019 (COVID-19): Funding, Credit, Liquidity, and Loan Facilities," *U.S. Federal Reserve*, July 7, 2023, https://www.federalreserve.gov/funding-credit-liquidity-and-loan-facilities.htm.

128. Nicholas Lambert, *Planning Armageddon: British Economic Warfare and the First World War* (Cambridge, MA: Harvard University Press, 2012), 190.

129. Eyck Freymann and Calvin Heng, "The Logic of Partial RMB Internationalization: PRC Perspectives on 'Financial War,'" *The China Quarterly*, published online February 20, 2025, 1–16, https://doi.org/10.1017/S0305741025000037.

130. The impact could vary by region: manufacturing-heavy East Asian economies might struggle with disrupted supply chains and competitive pressures from a weaker yuan, while commodity-exporting nations in Latin America or Africa could face rising debt burdens and reduced demand for their products. Coordinated policy interventions, including expanded Federal Reserve swap lines and emergency IMF lending, could mitigate some of these challenges. However, their effectiveness would depend on the crisis's severity and the willingness of major powers to cooperate.

CHAPTER 4

1. National Security Council and NSC Records Management System, "Declassified Documents Regarding President Jiang Zemin of China," *Clinton Digital Library*, accessed January 5, 2025, https://clinton.presidentiallibraries.us/items/show/118735.

2. U.S. Congress, House. *Expressing the Sense of the Congress Regarding a Private Visit by President Lee Teng-hui of the Republic of China on Taiwan to the United States.* H. Con. Res.53, 104th Cong. (1995).

3. National Security Council and NSC Records Management System, "Declassified Documents Concerning the 1996 Taiwan Election," *Clinton Digital Library*, accessed January 8, 2025, https://clinton.presidentiallibraries.us/items/show/101116. Among many excellent works on the complex politics of U.S.–Taiwan relations in the 1990s, see Robert L. Suettinger, *Beyond Tiananmen: The Politics of U.S.-China Relations 1989–2000* (Washington, DC: Brookings Institution Press, 2003), 238–243; Robert S. Ross, "The 1995–96 Taiwan Strait Confrontation: Coercion, Credibility, and the Use of Force," *International Security* 25, no. 2 (Fall 2000): 87–123; Nancy Bernkopf Tucker, *Strait Talk: United States-Taiwan Relations and the Crisis with China* (Cambridge, MA: Harvard University Press, 2009), 259–263; John W. Garver, *Face Off: China, the United States, and Taiwan's Democratization* (Seattle: University of Washington Press, 1997), 67–90; and Richard C. Bush, *At Cross Purposes: U.S.-Taiwan Relations Since 1942* (New York: M. E. Sharpe, 2004), 219–238.

4. National Security Council, "Declassified Documents Regarding President Jiang."

5. *Tampa Bay Times*, "U.S. Is Non-Committal on Defense of Taiwan," February 7, 1996, https://www.tampabay.com/archive/1996/02/07/u-s-is-non-committal-on-defense-of-taiwan/.

6. Douglas Porch, "The Taiwan Strait Crisis of 1996," *Naval War College Review* 52, no. 3 (1999): 19–20, https://digital-commons.usnwc.edu/cgi/viewcontent.cgi?article=2673&context=nwc-review.

7. Thomas J. Christensen, "PRC Security Relations with the United States: Why Things Are Going So Well," *China Leadership Monitor* 8 (Fall 2003): 1–10; Michael D. Swaine, "Trouble in Taiwan," *Foreign Affairs* 83, no. 2 (March/April 2004): 39–49, https://www.foreignaffairs.com/articles/asia/2004-03-01/trouble-taiwan.

8. Scott L. Kastner, "Ambiguity, Economic Interdependence, and the U.S. Strategic Dilemma in the Taiwan Strait," *Journal of Contemporary China* 15, no. 49 (2006): 651–669, https://doi.org/10.1080/10670560600836705; Timothy W. Crawford, *Pivotal Deterrence: Third-Party Statecraft and the Pursuit of Peace* (Ithaca, NY: Cornell University Press, 2003), 187–201.

9. "Share of Respondents Who Recognize Themselves as Taiwanese or Taiwanese and Chinese in Taiwan in 2020, by Affiliated Political Party," *Statista*, May 2020, https://www.statista.com/statistics/1118324/taiwan-national-identity-affiliation-by-political-party/; "2024 Taiwan Election: Pre-election Telephone Surveys—Research Data," *Medium*, January 19, 2024, https://medium.com/doublethinklab/2024-taiwan-elections-pre-election-telephone-surveys-research-data-23ed084fd60e.; Courtney Donovan Smith, "Donovan's Deep Dives: Big Shifts in Support for Ko and the TPP," *Taipei Times*, December 31, 2024, https://www.taipeitimes.com/News/feat/archives/2024/12/31/2003829393.

10. Bush, *At Cross Purposes*, 90–124.

11. U.S. officials have commented publicly that if Taiwan's chipmaking factories (known as "fabs") were not destroyed in an initial exchange, U.S. forces might destroy them to prevent Beijing from taking possession of them. Taiwanese officials have strenuously denied that this would be necessary, but they take the U.S. threat very seriously. Indeed, the understanding that Washington would rather see Taiwan destroyed

than let China take control has become a source of quiet resentment, both within TSMC and among some of the public, particularly on the KMT side. See Brittney Nguyen, "U.S. Would Destroy Taiwan's Semiconductor Factories Rather Than Letting Them Fall into China's Hands, a Former National Security Advisor Says," *Business Insider*, March 14, 2023, https://www.businessinsider.com/us-would-destroy-taiwan-semiconductor-factories-avoid-china-trump-adviser-2023-3?op=1; David Sacks, "Threatening to Destroy TSMC Is Unnecessary and Counterproductive," *Council on Foreign Relations*, May 9, 2023, https://www.cfr.org/blog/threatening-destroy-tsmc-unnecessary-and-counterproductive; Jason Wilick, "Blow Up the Microchips? What a Taiwan Spat Says about U.S. Strategy," *Washington Post*, May 12, 2023, https://www.washingtonpost.com/opinions/2023/05/12/microchips-us-taiwan-strategy; Sarah Zheng and Cindy Wang, "No Need to Blow Up TSMC in China War, Taiwan Security Chief Says," *Bloomberg*, October 12, 2022, https://www.bloomberg.com/news/articles/2022-10-12/no-need-to-blow-up-tsmc-in-china-war-taiwan-security-chief-says.

12. Didi Tang and Dake Kang, "Far Fewer Young Americans Now Want to Study in China. Both Countries Are Trying to Fix That," Associated Press, April 13, 2024, https://apnews.com/article/china-american-students-universities-f5f6e53cd5d3bc686590f2f961165281; Bo Gu, "Decline of American Students in China Could Mean Fewer Experts," *Voice of America*, June 24, 2024, https://www.voanews.com/a/decline-of-american-students-in-china-could-mean-fewer-experts/7668461.html.

13. Notable exceptions to this rule include Courtney Donovan Smith's essential blog and columns for the *Taipei Times*, as well as Nathan Batto's Frozen Garlic bloc. Lev Nachman and Brian Hioe also publish regular thoughtful commentary. See "The Frozen Garlic Manifesto," *Frozen Garlic*, accessed January 9, 2025, https://frozengarlic.wordpress.com/about/the-frozen-garlic-manifesto/; Jonathan Sullivan and Lev Nachman, *A Contested Democracy Under Threat* (Newcastle: Agenda Publishing, 2024).

14. Kuan-chen Lee, "Release of the 2024 Third Wave of the 'Taiwan Defense Security Public Opinion Survey' by the INDSR for External Use," INDSR, accessed January 29, 2025, https://indsr.org.tw/en/focus?typeid=42&uid=7&pid=2733.

15. *Deutsche Welle*, "Most Taiwanese Would Defend Island Against China, Poll Finds," October 9, 2024, https://www.dw.com/en/most-taiwanese-would-defend-island-against-china-poll-finds/a-70440750.

16. Richard Allen Green, "Half of Russians Say It Would Be Right to Use Military Force to Keep Ukraine Out of NATO," *CNN*, February 23, 2022, https://edition.cnn.com/interactive/2022/02/europe/russia-ukraine-crisis-poll-intl/index.html.

17. Katherine Koretsky, "Vivek Ramaswamy Defends Positions on Ukraine and Taiwan," *NBC News*, August 30, 2023, https://www.nbcnews.com/meet-the-press/meetthepressblog/vivek-ramaswamy-defends-positions-ukraine-taiwan-rcna102408.

18. John Dotson, *Chinese Information Operations against Taiwan: The 'Abandoned Chess Piece' and 'America Skepticism Theory'* (Washington, DC: Global Taiwan Institute, August 2023), https://globaltaiwan.org/wp-content/uploads/2023/08/OR_ASTAW0807FINAL.pdf.

19. Jacques DeLisle and Bonnie Glaser, "Exposing the PRC's Distortion of UN General Assembly Resolution 2758 to Press Its Claim Over Taiwan," *German Marshall Fund of the United States*, April 30, 2024, https://www.gmfus.org/event/exposing-prcs-distortion-un-general-assembly-resolution-2758-press-its-claim-over-taiwan.

20. Government of Saint Lucia, "Taiwan, U.S. Enhance Partnership with Saint Lucia," *Government of Saint Lucia*, April 12, 2024, https://www.govt.lc/news/taiwan-u-s-enhance-partnership-with-saint-lucia; John Hennessey-Niland, "U.S.-Taiwan Partnership with the Pacific Islands," *Global Taiwan Institute*, March 22, 2023, https://globaltaiwan.org/2023/03/us-taiwan-partnership-with-the-pacific-islands.

21. Erin Baggott Carter, "The 'Revolution from Below': The Voice of America and US Democracy Promotion in China" (Working Paper).

22. Riley Walters, "U.S.-Taiwan Relations: Towards a Second Agreement of the U.S.-Taiwan 21st Century Trae Initiative," *Global Taiwan Institute*, May 15, 2024, https://globaltaiwan.org/2024/05/towards-a-second-agreement-of=the-us-taiwan-21st-century-trade-initiative.

23. Evan A. Feigenbaum and Jen-yi Hou, "Overcoming Taiwan's Energy Trilemma," *Carnegie Endowment for International Peace*, April 27, 2020, https://carnegieendowment.org/2020/04/27/overcoming-taiwan-s-energy-trilemma-pub-81645.

24. Brad W. Setser, "What Does Taiwan's Hidden Forward Book Mean for Taiwan's Financial Stability and U.S. Currency Policy?" *Council on Foreign Relations*, October 15, 2019, https://www.cfr.org/blog/what-does-taiwans-hidden-forward-book-mean-taiwans-financial-stability-and-us-currency-policy.

25. Elbridge Colby (@ElbridgeColby), "American Officials and Experts Are Essentially Uniform on What Taiwan Needs to Defend Itself. Yet Taiwan Is Lagging," *X* (formerly Twitter), June 1, 2023, https://x.com/ElbridgeColby/status/1664107388339912704?mx=2.

26. Mark Montgomery and Bradley Bowman, "Beijing Is Listening as Americans Threaten Taiwan," *Foundation for Defense of Democracies*, September 12, 2024, https://www.fdd.org/analysis/op_eds/2024/09/12/beijing-is-listening-as-americans-threaten-taiwan.

27. Michael A. Hunzeker, Enoch Wu, and Kobi Marom, "A New Military Culture for Taiwan," in *The Boiling Moat: Urgent Steps to Defend Taiwan*, ed. Matt Pottinger (Stanford, CA: Hoover Institution Press, 2024), ch. 4.

28. Hunzeker, Wu, and Marom, "A New Military Culture for Taiwan.

29. *House Select Committee on the Strategic Competition Between the United States and the Chinese Communist Party, 118th Cong., 7 (2023) (statement of Matt Pottinger, China Program Chairman, Foundation for the Defense of Democracies).*

30. The discussion below rehashes decades-old arguments in favor of strategic ambiguity. For a few examples, see Steven M. Goldstein, "In Defense of Strategic Ambiguity in the Taiwan Strait," *National Bureau of Asian Research*, October 15, 2021, https://www.nbr.org/publication/in-defense-of-strategic-ambiguity-in-the-taiwan-strait/; Nancy Bernkopf Tucker, "Strategic Ambiguity or Strategic Clarity?" in *Dangerous Strait: The U.S.–Taiwan–China Crisis*, ed. Nancy Bernkopf Tucker (New York: Columbia University Press, 2005)

31. For more on the debate over strategic ambiguity, see: Michael Cunningham, "Should the USA Maintain Its Policy of Strategic Ambiguity Towards Taiwan?" *The Heritage Foundation*, June 24, 2024, https://www.heritage.org/china/commentary/should-the-usa-maintain-its-policy-strategic-ambiguity-towards-taiwan; Raymond Kuo, "'Strategic Ambiguity' Has the U.S. and Taiwan Trapped," *Foreign Policy*, January 18, 2023, https://foreignpolicy.com/2023/01/18/taiwan-us-china-strategic-ambiguity-military-strategy-asymmetric-defense-invasion; Ethan D. Chaffee, "Strategic Ambiguity on Taiwan Has Run Its Course," *Proceedings, U.S. Naval Institute*, March 2023, https://www.usni.org/magazines/proceedings/2023/march/strategic-ambiguity-taiwan-has-run-its-course;

Tim Willasey-Wilsey, "US Policy on Taiwan and the Perils of 'Strategic Ambiguity'," *Royal United Services Institute* (RUSI), September 26, 2022, https://rusi.org/explore-our-research/publications/commentary/us-policy-taiwan-and-perils-strategic-ambiguity; Michael E. O'Hanlon, Ivan Kanapathy, Rorry Daniels, and Thomas Hanson, "Should the United States Change Its Policies Toward Taiwan?" *Brookings Institution*, April 16, 2024, https://www.brookings.edu/articles/should-the-united-states-change-its-policies-toward-taiwan.

32. Amy Mackinnon and Anna Weber, "Biden Struggles to Stick to the Script on Taiwan," *Foreign Policy*, November 17, 2021, https://foreignpolicy.com/2021/11/17/biden-taiwan-china-misspoke-policy-mistake.

33. Vincent Ni, "China Warns Against 'Wrong Signals' as Biden Suggests U.S. Would Defend Taiwan," *The Guardian*, October 22, 2021, https://www.theguardian.com/world/2021/oct/22/biden-suggests-us-would-defend-taiwan-against-china-forcing-fresh-white-house-clarification.

34. David Brunnstrom and Trevor Hunnicutt, "Biden Says U.S. Forces Would Defend Taiwan in the Event of a Chinese Invasion," *Reuters*, September 19, 2022, https://www.reuters.com/world/biden-says-us-forces-would-defend-taiwan-event-chinese-invasion-2022-09-18.

35. "Department Press Briefing—May 24, 2022," *U.S. Department of State*, accessed December 29, 2023, https://www.state.gov/briefings/department-press-briefing-may-24-2022.

36. "A Bristling China Says Biden Remarks on Taiwan 'Severely Violate' U.S. Policy," *CBS News*, September 19, 2022, https://www.cbsnews.com/news/china-biden-taiwan-remarks-angry-reaction.

37. Trevor Hunnicutt, "Trump Declines to Answer Question about China and Taiwan," *Reuters*, February 26, 2025, https://www.reuters.com/world/trump-declines-answer-question-about-china-taiwan-2025-02-26.

38. "Strategic Clarity and the Future of U.S.–Taiwan Foreign Relations: Interview with Raymond Kuo," *The National Bureau of Asian Research*, February 3, 2022, https://www.nbr.org/publication/strategic-clarity-and-the-future-of-u-s-taiwan-foreign-relations.

39. Michael Cunningham, "Is Taiwan About to Declare Independence? Not Exactly," *The Heritage Foundation*, March 18, 2024, https://www.heritage.org/china/commentary/taiwan-about-declare-independence-not-exactly.

40. Ankit Panda, "Seoul's Nuclear Temptations and the U.S.-South Korea Alliance," *War on the Rocks*, February 3, 2023, https://warontherocks.com/2023/02/seouls-nuclear-temptations-and-the-u-s-south-korea-alliance.

41. Unconditional commitments are very rare, and states have many ways to avoid commitments. Their counterparts in turn understand and respond to that. See Tongfi Kim, *The Supply Side of Security: A Market Theory of Military Alliances* (Oxford: Oxford University Press, 2016); Brett Benson, *Constructing International Security: Alliances, Deterrence, and Moral Hazard* (Cambridge: Cambridge University Press, 2012); Michael Beckley, *The Myth of Entangling Alliances: Reassessing the Security Risks of U.S. Defense Pacts* (Ithaca, NY: Cornell University Press, 2021); Erik Lin-Greenberg, "Backing Up Instead of Backing Down: Casualty Aversion and the Fate of Military Interventions," *International Studies Quarterly* 65, no. 3 (2021): 771–82; Keren Yarhi-Milo, *Who Fights for Reputation? The Psychology of Leaders in International Conflict* (Princeton, NJ: Princeton University Press, 2018); Roseanne McManus, *Statements of Resolve: Achieving Coercive Credibility in International Conflict* (Cambridge: Cambridge University Press, 2017); Austin Carson, *Secret*

Wars: Covert Conflict in International Politics (Princeton, NJ: Princeton University Press, 2018).

42. Richard Haass and David Sacks, "American Support for Taiwan Must Be Unambiguous: To Keep the Peace, Make Clear to China That Force Won't Stand," *Foreign Affairs*, October 4, 2023, https://www.foreignaffairs.com/articles/united-states/american-support-taiwan-must-be-unambiguous.

43. "Bush Says U.S. Will Defend Taiwan if China Starts a War," *Taipei Times*, June 10, 2005, https://www.taipeitimes.com/News/front/archives/2005/06/10/2003258664.

44. Brett V. Benson, *Constructing International Security: Alliances, Deterrence, and Moral Hazard* (Cambridge: Cambridge University Press, 2012).

45. Other proposals for conditional clarity include framing Taiwan as a Chinese democracy, with the hope that mainland China might one day join Taiwan in a united democratic China. While thought-provoking, this idea would face significant challenges in today's political and strategic context. See Christensen, "Contemporary Security Dilemma," 19–20.

46. "Joint Communique of the Government of Japan and the Government of the People's Republic of China," *Ministry for Foreign Affairs of Japan*, accessed December 29, 2023, https://www.mofa.go.jp/region/asia-paci/china/joint72.html.

47. Adam P. Liff, "Has Japan's Policy toward the Taiwan Strait Changed?" *Brookings Institution*, August 23, 2021, https://www.brookings.edu/articles/has-japans-policy-toward-the-taiwan-strait-changed.

48. Julian Ryall, "Aso Walks Back Claim Japan Would Join U.S. in Defence of Taiwan if Mainland Chinese Forces Invade," *South China Morning Post*, July 6, 2021, https://www.scmp.com/week-asia/politics/article/3139995/aso-walks-back-claim-japan-would-join-us-defence-taiwan-if.

49. Ofek Riemer and Daniel Sobelman, "Coercive Disclosure: The Weaponization of Public Intelligence Revelation in International Relations," *Contemporary Security Policy* 44, no. 2 (2023): 276–307.

50. Demetri Sevastopulo, "US Demands to Know What Allies Would Do in Event of war over Taiwan," *Financial Times*, July 12, 2025, https://www.ft.com/content/41e272e4-5b25-47ee-807c-2b57c1316fe4.

51. *Ministry for Foreign Affairs of Japan*, "Joint Communique."

52. Rather than replicating the U.S. TRA wholesale, Japan may consider a phased, carefully structured approach. First, it could pass a basic law on Japan–Taiwan exchanges, explicitly reaffirming the one-China language of 1972, while codifying nonmilitary areas of cooperation such as humanitarian relief, civil defense training, supply-chain security, and information sharing. This would provide a legal roof over existing practice without appearing to shift Tokyo's official position. Second, Japan could adopt a Diet resolution declaring cross-strait stability a "vital interest" for Japan's security, thereby framing any Taiwan-related action as consistent with constitutional interpretations of collective self-defense. Third, to avoid economic blowback, Tokyo could pair any Taiwan legislation with broader economic security initiatives, including incentives for reshoring critical industries.

53. Wilson Beaver, "Strengthening the U.S.–Australian Alliance," *The Heritage Foundation*, October 28, 2024, https://www.heritage.org/defense/report/strengthening-the-us-australian-alliance; Sang Hun Seok, "Expanding AUKUS Pillar 2: An Inclusive Indo-Pacific Alliance Structure," *Royal United Services Institute*, July 16, 2024, https://www.rusi.org/explore-our-research/publications/commentary/expanding-aukus-pillar-2-inclusive-indo-pacific-alliance-structure.

54. Victor D. Cha, *Powerplay: The Origins of the American Alliance System in Asia* (Princeton, NJ: Princeton University Press, 2016).

55. "Signing of the Japan-Philippines Reciprocal Access Agreement," *Ministry of Foreign Affairs of Japan*, July 8, 2024, https://www.mofa.go.jp/s_sa/sea2/ph/pageite_000001_00432.html; "Signing of Japan-UK Reciprocal Access Agreement," *Ministry of Foreign Affairs of Japan*, January 11, 2023, https://www.mofa.go.jp/erp/we/gb/page1e_000556.html; "United States-Japan-Australia Trilateral Defense Ministers' Meeting (TDMM) 2024 Joint Statement, May 2, 2024," *U.S. Department of Defense*, May 3, 2024, https://www.defense.gov/News/Releases/Release/Article/3764063/united-states-japan-australia-trilateral-defense-ministers-meeting-tdmm-2024-jo; Sebastian Strangio, "France, Philippines to Begin Negotiating Reciprocal Access Agreement," *The Diplomat*, April 26, 2024, https://thediplomat.com/2024/04/france-philippines-to-begin-negotiating-reciprocal-access-agreement; "Japan, France Begin Informal Talks on Access Deal for Joint Drills," *Kyodo News*, December 13, 2021, https://english.kyodonews.net/news/2021/12/c5a71dda1d3c-japan-france-begin-informal-talks-on-access-deal-for-joint-drills.html; "Japan-France Foreign Ministers' Telephone Talk," *Ministry of Foreign Affairs of Japan*, October 11, 2024, https://www.mofa.go.jp/press/release/pressite_000001_00643.html.

56. *NATO 2022 Strategic Concept* (Brussels: North Atlantic Treaty Organization, 2022), https://www.nato.int/strategic-concept.

57. Stuart Lau and Laura Kayali, "Macron Blocks NATO Outpost in Japan Amid Chinese Complaints," *Politico*, July 7, 2023, https://www.politico.eu/article/emmanuel-macron-block-nato-outpost-japan-china-complaints.

58. Jamil Anderlini and Clea Caulcutt, "Europe Must Resist Pressure to Become 'America's Followers,' Says Macron," *Politico*, April 9, 2023, https://www.politico.eu/article/emmanuel-macron-china-america-pressure-interview.

59. Nan Tian, Diego Lopes da Silva, Xiao Liang, and Lorenzo Scarazzato, *Trends in World Military Expenditure, 2023* (Stockholm: Stockholm International Peace Research Institute, 2024), https://doi.org/10.55163/BQGA2180, 2.

60. "拜登批中国在印太咄咄逼人 中国外交部吁美放下'维霸遏华'执念" *Biden Criticizes China's Aggressiveness in the Indo-Pacific; Chinese Foreign Ministry Urges U.S. to Abandon 'Hegemonic Containment' Mentality*, 联合早报 (Lianhe Zaobao), September 23, 2024, https://www.zaobao.com.sg/realtime/china/story20240923-4817174.

61. Alyssa Chen, "China–India talks: Narendra Modi Praises 'Stable, Predictable, Constructive Ties'," *South China Morning Post*, August 20, 2025, https:www.scmp.com/news/china/diplomacy/article/3322471/china-india-talks-narendra-modi-praises-stable-predictable-constuctive-ties.

CHAPTER 5

1. Pottinger, *The Boiling Moat*.

2. Ivan Kanapathy, "Countering China's Use of Force" and "Countering China's Gray Zone Activities," in *The Boiling Moat: Urgent Steps to Defend Taiwan*, ed. Matt Pottinger, 83–129.

3. For a thorough discussion, see Gabriel Collins and Andrew Erickson, *Annexation of Taiwan: A Defeat from Which the US and Its Allies Could Not Retreat* (Houston: Baker Institute for Public Policy, Rice University, July 2024), https://www.bakerinstitute.org/

sites/default/files/2024-07/CES-Collins-China%20Taiwan%20Annexation%20Paper-FINAL-073024.pdf.

4. Michael J. Mazarr, "Beating the Ossification Trap: Why Reform, Not Spending, Will Salvage American Power," *War on the Rocks*, February 15, 2024, https://warontherocks.com/2024/02/beating-the-ossification-trap-why-reform-not-spending-will-salvage-american-power; U.S. Department of Defense, *Military and Security Developments Involving the People's Republic of China: 2023*.

5. Collins and Erickson, *Annexation of Taiwan*, 89.

6. On Trafalgar, see Wayne P. Hughes, "Naval Operations: A Close Look at the Operational Level of War at Sea," *Naval War College Review* 65, no. 3 (Summer 2012): 22–46; National Defense University, *Horatio Nelson and the 1798 Mediterranean Campaign* (Norfolk, VA: National Defense University Joint Forces Staff College, January 2006); Joseph F. Callo, "Lasting Lessons of Trafalgar," *U.S. Naval Institute Naval History*, October 1, 2005, https://www.usni.org/magazines/naval-history-magazine/2005/october/lasting-lessons-trafalgar.

7. On Jutland, see Robert K. Massie, *Castles of Steel: Britain, Germany, and the Winning of the Great War at Sea* (New York: Vintage Books, 2007); Edmund B. Hernandez, "The Fundamental Naval Tactical Problem," *Proceedings* 148, no. 11 (November 2022).

8. Thomas Hone, Norman Friedman, and Mark David Mandeles, *Innovation in Carrier Aviation, Newport Paper* 37 (Newport, RI: Naval War College Press, 2011).

9. U.S. Naval History and Heritage Command, *Battle of Midway, June 3–6, 1942* (Washington, DC: U.S. Naval History and Heritage Command, 2017).

10. *Stanford Emerging Technology Review 2025*, 131–133.

11. John F. Lehman, *Oceans Ventured: Winning the Cold War at Sea*, 1st ed. (New York: W. W. Norton, 2018). Robert G. Angevine, "Hiding in Plain Sight—The U.S. Navy and Dispersed Operations under EMCON, 1956–1972," *Naval War College Review* 64, no. 2 (Spring 2011): 79–95; Andrew Krepinevich, *Maritime Competition in a Mature Precision-Strike Regime* (Washington, DC: Center for Strategic and Budgetary Assessments, 2014), 43; Brendan Rittenhouse Green and Austin G. Long, "Signaling with Secrets: Evidence on Soviet Perceptions and Counterforce Developments in the Late Cold War," in Gartzke and Lindsay, *Cross-Domain Deterrence*, 205–233.

12. U.S. Space Force, *Space Threat Fact Sheet* (Washington, DC: Headquarters Space Force Intelligence, July 16, 2024), https://www.andrewerickson.com/wp-content/uploads/2024/09/20240716-S2-Space-Threat-Fact-Sheet-v5-RELEASE.pdf.

13. Travis Sharp, Thomas G. Mahnken, and Tim Sadov, *Extending Deterrence by Detection: The Case for Integrating Unmanned Aircraft Systems into the Indo-Pacific Partnership for Maritime Domain Awareness* (Washington, DC: Center for Strategic and Budgetary Assessments, 2023); Amila Prasanga, "The Strategic Impact of Military Drone Proliferation on Indo-Pacific Maritime Security," Center for International Maritime Security, November 7, 2023.

14. The Wing Loong II is roughly comparable to the Reaper, albeit with lower speed, endurance, and payload. The precise unit cost of the Reaper is hard to ascertain. U.S. figures ($27–33 million per unit in FY2019–2020) include R&D and ground systems, whereas Wing Loong costs likely exclude such expenses. See Tom Risen, "China Plays Catch-Up to U.S. Drones," *Aerospace America*, October 2017, https://aerospaceamerica.aiaa.org/departments/china-plays-catch-up-to-u-s-drones/; J. Michael Dahm, *Special Mission Aircraft and Unmanned Systems* (Laurel, MD: Johns Hopkins University

Applied Physics Laboratory, 2020), 19–25, https://apps.dtic.mil/sti/pdfs/AD1128646.
pdf; U.S. Department of Defense, *Program Acquisition Cost by Weapons Systems* (Washington, DC: U.S. Department of Defense, February 2020), 1–6, https://comptroller.
defense.gov/Portals/45/Documents/defbudget/fy2021/fy2021_Weapons.pdf.

15. The WZ-7's range is far shorter than the Global Hawk's (7000 km versus 23,000 km),
but this limitation is less significant given that potential U.S.-China conflicts would
occur close to China's shores. See Elsa Kania, *The People's Liberation Army's Unmanned
Aerial Systems* (Maxwell Air Force Base, AL: China Aerospace Studies Institute,
Air University, 2018), https://www.airuniversity.af.edu/Portals/10/CASI/documents/
Research/PLAAF/2018-08-29%20PLAs_Unmanned_Aerial_Systems.pdf.; Dahm, *Special Mission Aircraft*, 19–25.

16. On China's UAS scouting assets, see Kania, *The PLA's Unmanned Aerial Systems*; Dahm,
Special Mission Aircraft; Ian Burns McCaslin, *Red Drones Over Disputed Seas: A Field
Guide to Chinese UAVs/UCAVs Operating in the Disputed East and South China Seas*
(Arlington, VA: Project 2049 Institute, April 2018); Stacie Pettyjohn, Hannah Dennis,
and Molly Campbell, *Swarms over the Strait: Drone Warfare in a Future Fight to Defend
Taiwan* (Washington, DC: Center for a New American Security, June 20, 2024), 53,
https://www.cnas.org/publications/reports/swarms-over-the-strait.

17. Joseph Clark, "Defense Innovation Official Says Replicator Initiative Remains on Track,"
DoD News, January 26, 2024, https://www.defense.gov/News/News-Stories/Article/
Article/3657609/defense-innovation-official-says-replicator-initiative-remains-on-track.

18. U.S. Department of Defense, *Military and Security Developments Involving the People's
Republic of China: 2024* (Washington, DC: U.S. Department of Defense, 2024), 63–67.

19. See: Sam Tangredi, "Replicate Ordnance, Not Cheap Drones," *Proceedings*, March
2024, https://www.usni.org/magazines/proceedings/2024/march/replicate-ordnance-
not-cheap-drones; Jack Montgomery, "The Navy Must Build More Missiles Now,"
Proceedings, August 2023, https://www.usni.org/magazines/proceedings/2023/august/
navy-must-build-more-missiles-now; Seth G. Jones, "The U.S. Defense Industrial Base Is
Not Prepared for a Possible Conflict with China," *Center for Strategic and International
Studies*, 2023, https://features.csis.org/preparing-the-US-industrial-base-to-deter-
conflict-with-China/; Dmitry Filipoff, "Fighting DMO Pt. 2: Anti-Ship Firepower and
the Major Limits of the American Naval Arsenal," *Center for International Maritime
Security (CIMSEC)*, February 27, 2023, https://cimsec.org/fighting-dmo-pt-2-anti-ship-
firepower-and-the-major-limits-of-the-american-naval-arsenal/.

20. Pettyjohn, Metrick, and Wasser, "The Kadena Conundrum."

21. U.S. Department of Defense, *Military and Security Developments*, 64–66, 88; CSIS,
"YJ-18. Missile Threat"; Andrew Erickson, "What the Pentagon's New Report on
Chinese Military Power Reveals About Capabilities, Context, and Consequences,"
War on the Rocks, December 19, 2024, https://warontherocks.com/2024/12/what-the-
pentagons-new-report-on-chinese-military-power-reveals-about-capabilities-context-
and-consequences/. For more on China's anti-ship capabilities, see U.S. Department of
Defense, *Military and Security Developments*, 64–65, 88.

22. Center for Strategic and International Studies, *How Are China's Land-Based Conventional
Missile Forces Evolving? China Power*, accessed January 2025, https://chinapower.csis.org/
conventional-missiles/.

23. China has missiles that have a longer range, but the targeting problem becomes more
difficult at extended distances. Attrition on China's strike network will reduce this
range.

24. Joseph Trevithick, "Special Operations C-130 Hits Target with a Rapid Dragon Pallet-Dropped Cruise Missile," *The War Zone*, November 10, 2022, https://www.twz.com/43550/special-operations-c-130-hits-target-with-a-rapid-dragon-pallet-dropped-cruise-missile; Air Force Research Laboratory, "Rapid Dragon," *Air Force Research Lab*, accessed February 2024, https://afresearchlab.com/technology/rapid-dragon.

25. David Hambling, "Why U.S. Air Force's CLEAVER Is a New Type of Bomb," *Forbes*, June 3, 2020, https://www.forbes.com/sites/davidhambling/2020/06/03/why-us-air-forces-cleaver-is-a-new-type-of-bomb.

26. CSIS Missile Defense Project, "Missiles of the United States," *Missile Threat*, March 3, 2021, https://missilethreat.csis.org/country/united-states.

27. CSIS Missile Defense Project, "JASSM/JASSM ER," *Missile Threat*, April 23, 2024, https://missilethreat.csis.org/missile/jassm.

28. Cancian, Cancian, and Heginbotham, *First Battle of the Next War*.

29. U.S. Department of Defense, *Military and Security Developments*, 149. For a pertinent example, see the DF-17 MRBM, equipped with a HGV, and the DF-27 ICBM, which can in theory combine HGV technology with a nuclear payload (U.S. Department of Defense, *Military and Security Developments*), 89.

30. Kelley M. Sayler, *Hypersonic Weapons: Background and Issues for Congress* (Washington, DC: Congressional Research Service, August 14, 2024), 5, https://sgp.fas.org/crs/weapons/R45811.pdf.; Gabriel Honrada, "AUKUS Supercharging Joint Hypersonic Weapon Drive," *Asia Times*, November 22, 2024, https://asiatimes.com/2024/11/aukus-supercharging-joint-hypersonic-weapon-drive; Josh Luckenbough, "Testing Top of Mind as U.S. Lags China in Hypersonics Race," *National Defense Magazine*, July 24, 2024, https://www.nationaldefensemagazine.org/articles/2024/7/24/testing-top-of-mind-as-us-lags-china-in-hypersonics-race; Stephen Losey, "Air Force Budget Backs Raytheon Hypersonic, No Lockheed Missile Funds," *Defense News*, March 13, 2024, https://www.defensenews.com/air/2024/03/12/air-force-budget-backs-raytheon-hypersonic-no-lockheed-missile-funds.

31. Lawrence "Sid" Trevethan, "The PLA Rocket Force's Conventional Missiles," *U.S. Naval Institute*, April 1, 2023, https://www.usni.org/magazines/proceedings/2023/april/pla-rocket-forces-conventional-missiles.

32. Associated Press, "Israel Says 99% of Drones and Missiles Launched by Iran Were Intercepted," *AP News*, April 14, 2024, https://apnews.com/live/israel-iran-drone-attack-live-updates; Associated Press, "Iran Fires at Least 180 Missiles into Israel as Regionwide Conflict Grows," *AP News*, October 1, 2024, https://apnews.com/article/israel-lebanon-hezbollah-gaza-news-10-01-2024-eb175dff6e46906caea8b9e43dfbd3da.

33. Halem and Freymann, "Ukraine Shows Why Taiwan Needs More Air Defense."

34. Nancy A. Youssef and Gordon Lubold, "Pentagon Runs Low on Air-Defense Missiles as Demand Surges," *Wall Street Journal*, October 29, 2024, https://www.wsj.com/politics/national-security/pentagon-runs-low-on-air-defense-missiles-as-demand-surges-7fc9370c.

35. Aaron-Mathew Lariosa, "US Navy Looks to Drastically Increase Missile Production," *Naval News*, April 5, 2023, https://www.navalnews.com/event-news/sea-air-space-2023/2023/04/navy-looks-to-drastically-increase-missile-production.

36. Aaron-Mathew Lariosa, "US Navy Looks to Drastically Increase Missile Production."

37. Mari Yamaguchi, "US-Japan Security Talks Focus on Bolstering Military Cooperation, Underscores Threat from China," *AP News*, July 28, 2024, https://apnews.com/article/japan-us-military-command-missile-china-4e97f4cb01cfef7b6db8fb1a5df771e4.

38. Henry E. Eccles, *Logistics in the National Defense* (Newport, RI: Naval War College, 1959), 42–57.

39. On triangulated fighting in the Philippine Sea, see Scott Tait and Anthony LaVopa, "It All Comes Down to Sea Control," *Proceedings*, December 2023, https://www.usni.org/magazines/proceedings/2023/december/it-all-comes-down-sea-control; Paul Giarra, Bill Hamblet, and Gerard Roncolato, "War in 2026: Phase III Scenario," *Proceedings*, December 2023, https://www.usni.org/magazines/proceedings/2023/december/war-2026-phase-iii-scenario.

40. On logistics and strategy, see Salvatore Mercogliano, "Logistics Wins—and Loses—Wars," *Proceedings*, February 2024, https://www.usni.org/magazines/proceedings/2024/february/logistics-wins-and-loses-wars.

41. Zachary S. Hughes, "Giving Our 'Paper Tiger' Real Teeth: Fixing the U.S. Military's Plans for Contested Logistics Against China," *Joint Force Quarterly*, National Defense University, no. 115 (4th Quarter 2024): 34, https://digitalcommons.ndu.edu/cgi/viewcontent.cgi?article=1148&context=joint-force-quarterly.

42. The most common heavy transport airlifter, the U.S. Air Force C-17 Globemaster, can carry around 85 tons. The most common maritime transports, including the T-AKE Dry Cargo ships and the T-AOE Fast Combat Support Ships, have capacities of around 11,000 tons and 29,000 tons respectively. See Paul Gucwa, "Increased Aerial Refueling Compatibility Facilitates True Joint Environment," *U.S. Navy*, October 3, 2022, https://www.navy.mil/Press-Office/News-Stories/Article/3178173/increased-aerial-refueling-compatibility-facilitates-true-joint-environment/; U.S. Air Force, "C-17 Globemaster," *U.S. Air Force Fact Sheets*, https://www.af.mil/About-Us/Fact-Sheets/Display/Article/1529726/c-17-globemaster-iii/; U.S. Navy, "Fact Files," *U.S. Navy*, accessed February 24, 2025, https://www.navy.mil/resources/fact-files.

43. "Ship Inventory," *Military Sealift Command*, accessed February 24, 2025, https://www.msc.usff.navy.mil/Ships/Ship-Inventory; Sam LaGrone, "Navy Could Sideline 17 Support Ships Due to Manpower Issues," *USNI News*, August 22, 2024, https://news.usni.org/2024/08/22/navy-could-sideline-17-support-ships-due-to-manpower-issues.

44. Isaac B. Kardon and Wendy Leutert, "Pier Competitor: China's Power Position in Global Ports," *International Security* 46, no. 4 (2022): 9–47.

45. The United States does preposition supplies in some allied states. However, prepositioning exposes these stores to direct strikes, necessitating hardening forward deployments with bunkers, reinforced warehouses, covered piers, backup generators, and the like.

46. Luke A. Nicastro, *The Pacific Deterrence Initiative* (Washington, DC: Congressional Research Service, November 25, 2024), https://crsreports.congress.gov/product/pdf/IF/IF12303.

47. U.S. Navy, *Unmanned Campaign Framework*, March 16, 2021, https://www.navy.mil/Portals/1/Strategic/20210315%20Unmanned%20Campaign_Final_LowRes.pdf?ver=LtCZ-BPlWki6vCBTdgtDMA%3D%3D.

48. John Geddie and Tim Kelly, "U.S. Wants Japanese Shipyards to Help Keep Warships Ready to Fight in Asia," *Reuters*, January 19, 2024, https://www.reuters.com/world/asia-pacific/us-eyeing-japanese-shipyards-warship-overhauls-says-us-ambassador-2024-01-19/; Brian T. DiMascio, "Foreign Shipyards Can Help the U.S. Navy Build Its Fleet," *Proceedings* 150, no. 10 (October 2024), https://www.usni.org/magazines/proceedings/2024/october/foreign-shipyards-can-help-us-navy-build-its-fleet; "U.S. Navy Partners with South Korea's Hanwha to Strengthen Its Shipbuilding Capabilities," *Marine*

Insight, September 23, 2024, https://www.marineinsight.com/shipping-news/u-s-navy-partners-with-south-koreas-hanwha-to-strengthen-its-shipbuilding-capabilities.

49. Andrea Magi, "The Role of Aircraft Carriers in a Contested Age," *Joint Air Power Competence Centre*, July 2022, https://www.japcc.org/articles/the-role-of-aircraft-carriers-in-a-contested-age.

50. O'Rourke, *Navy Force Structure and Shipbuilding Plans*.

51. For instance, the Navy is developing the unmanned MQ-25 Stingray refueler to extend the range of carrier-based aircraft, thus allowing carriers to operate from further away. The Navy is also integrating more long-range strike capabilities into the air wing and improving missile defense systems and electronic warfare. See Jan Tegler, "Despite Delays, Navy to Accelerate Delivery of Unmanned Tanker," *National Defense Magazine*, January 26, 2024, https://www.nationaldefensemagazine.org/articles/2024/1/26/despite-delays-navy-to-accelerate-delivery-of-unmanned-tanker; Sam Lagrone, "MQ-25A Stingray IOC Pushed to 2026 Following Manufacturing Delays," *USNI News*, April 4, 2023, https://news.usni.org/2023/04/04/mq-25a-stingray-ioc-pushed-to-2026-following-manufacturing-delays; Joseph Trevithick, "Navy's HALO Hypersonic Anti-Ship Missile Planned for Ships, Submarines, as Well as Jets," *The War Zone*, June 5, 2024, https://www.twz.com/air/navys-halo-hypersonic-anti-ship-missile-planned-for-ships-submarines-as-well-as-jets.

52. CSIS Missile Defense Project, "DF-21 (CSS-5)," *Missile Threat*, April 23, 2024, https://missilethreat.csis.org/missile/df-21/; Peter Suciu, "China's Carrier Killers: How DF-21D and DF-26B Missiles Threaten the U.S. Navy," *The National Interest*, September 21, 2024, https://nationalinterest.org/blog/buzz/chinas-carrier-killers-how-df-21d-and-df-26b-missiles-threaten-us-navy-207372.

53. CSIS Missile Defense Project, "DF-26," *Missile Threat*, April 23, 2024, https://missilethreat.csis.org/missile/dong-feng-26-df-26.

54. Henk Warnar, "Ukraine and Russia in the Black Sea: A Naval War of Mutual Denial," *Atlantisch Perspectief* 47, no. 4 (2023): 12–16, https://www.jstor.org/stable/48761735; Justin Bronk and Jack Watling, *Mass Precision Strike: Designing UAV Complexes for Land Forces* (Whitehall, London: Royal United Services Institute, April 11, 2024), https://www.rusi.org/explore-our-research/publications/occasional-papers/mass-precision-strike-designing-uav-complexes-land-forces.

55. Ronald O'Rourke, *China Naval Modernization: Implications for U.S. Navy Capabilities—Background and Issues for Congress* (Congressional Research Service, August 16, 2024), https://sgp.fas.org/crs/row/RL33153.pdf.

56. H. I. Sutton, "Uncrewed Platforms Have Been Critical to Ukraine's Success in the Black Sea," *Royal United Services Institute (RUSI)*, August 20, 2024, https://www.rusi.org/explore-our-research/publications/commentary/uncrewed-platforms-have-been-critical-ukraines-success-black-sea.

57. O'Rourke, *Defense Primer: Navy Distributed Maritime Operations (DMO) Concept*.

58. Arthur Burke, *Torpedoes and Their Impact on Naval Warfare* (Newport, RI: Naval Undersea Warfare Center Division, Defense Technical Information Center, 2017), https://apps.dtic.mil/sti/tr/pdf/AD1033484.pdf.

59. On the impact of the torpedo, see Burke, *Torpedoes and Their Impact on Naval Warfare*; Frank Hoffman, "What We Can Learn from Jackie Fisher," *Proceedings*, April 2004, https://www.usni.org/magazines/proceedings/2004/april/what-we-can-learn-jackie-fisher; Rindert Zinderen Bakker, "The Development of the Destroyer,"

in *Warship 6: Destroyer HMCS Haida* (Amsterdam: Amsterdam University Press, 2016), https://doi.org/10.1515/9789086163212-003, 12–13.

60. On the carrier transition, see Thomas C. Hone, "Replacing Battleships with Aircraft Carriers in the Pacific in World War II," *Naval War College Review* 66, no. 1 (2013): Article 6, https://digital-commons.usnwc.edu/nwc-review/vol66/iss1/6; Geoffrey Till, "Adopting the Aircraft Carrier: The British, American, and Japanese Cases," in *Military Innovation in the Interwar Period*, eds. Williamson Murray and Allan R. Millett (Cambridge: Cambridge University Press, 1998), 191–226.

61. On the general value of legacy systems, see Marine Corps History Division, *The Legacy American Naval Power: Reinvigorating Maritime Strategic Thought* (Quantico, VA: U.S. Marine Corps University, 2020), https://www.usmcu.edu/Portals/218/LegacyAmericanNavalPower_WEB2.pdf, 28; Mackenzie Eaglen, "Give Legacy Weapons a New Lease on Life," *American Enterprise Institute*, January 23, 2023, https://www.aei.org/foreign-and-defense-policy/give-legacy-weapons-a-new-lease-on-life; Cameron M. Rountree, "The Final Countdown?—Charting a New Course for Capital Ships," *Naval War College Review* 76, no. 1 (Winter 2023): 18–21, https://digital-commons.usnwc.edu/cgi/viewcontent.cgi?article=8326&context=nwc-review; Tim Sweijs, *Reinvigorating NATO's Edge: Military Innovation and the Strategic Concept* (Bratislava, Slovakia: GLOBSEC, 2022), 4, https://www.globsec.org/sites/default/files/2022-05/Reinvigorating-NATOs-Edge-ver3-spreads.pdf.

62. IAMD systems are designed to provide protection against HGVs, HCMs, and traditional cruise missiles. The Navy's current IAMD system is the Aegis Combat System. There are limitations to these defenses, however. Each Aegis-equipped ship operates independently and is unable to share data with other ships. The Navy is working on data-sharing networks. See Thomas C. Hone, Douglas V. Smith, and Roger C. Easton Jr., "The Politics of Developing the Aegis Combat System: Pt. 1," *Center for International Maritime Security*, April 24, 2023, https://cimsec.org/the-politics-of-developing-the-aegis-combat-system-pt-1/; Todd South, "New Navy Contracts Boost Battle Command, Electronic Warfare Potential," *Army Times*, September 17, 2024, https://www.armytimes.com/air/2024/09/17/new-navy-contracts-boost-battle-command-electronic-warfare-potential/.

63. Ghost Fleet Overlord is developing large USVs that field anti-ship and land-targeted missiles. The Orca is a large UUV that can carry mines, torpedoes, and various electronic warfare capabilities. See O'Rourke, *Navy Large Unmanned Surface and Undersea Vehicles*. On China's equivalent programs, see Ryan Fedasiuk, "Leviathan Wakes: China's Growing Fleet of Autonomous Undersea Vehicles," *CIMSEC*, August 17, 2021, https://cimsec.org/leviathan-wakes-chinas-growing-fleet-of-autonomous-undersea-vehicles/; Joseph Trevithick, "China's New Stealthy Trimaran Drone Ship: Our Best Look Yet (Updated)," *The Warzone*, November 9, 2024, https://www.twz.com/news-features/our-best-look-yet-chinas-new-stealthy-trimaran-drone-ship; Global Defense News, "DSA 2024: China Unveils New UUV-300CD Unmanned Underwater Vehicle Capable of Launching Torpedoes," *Global Defense News*, May 8, 2024, https://www.armyrecognition.com/news/navy-news/2024/dsa-2024-china-unveils-new-uuv-300cd-unmanned-underwater-vehicle-capable-of-launching-torpedoes; Lyle J. Goldstein, "China's Underwater Unmanned Vehicles: How They'll Dominate Undersea Combat," *The National Interest*, January 29, 2022, https://nationalinterest.org/blog/reboot/chinas-underwater-unmanned-vehicles-how-theyll-dominate-undersea-combat-200098.

64. Ronald O'Rourke, *Navy Force Structure and Shipbuilding Plans: Background and Issues for Congress* (Washington, DC: Congressional Research Service, September 24, 2024), https://crsreports.congress.gov/product/pdf/RL/RL32665/330, 2.

65. Alexander Palmer, Henry H. Carroll, and Nicholas Velazquez, "Unpacking China's Naval Buildup," *Center for Strategic and International Studies*, June 5, 2024, https://www.csis.org/analysis/unpacking-chinas-naval-buildup"; U.S. Department of Defense, *Military and Security Developments Involving the People's Republic of China: 2024*, 48.

66. The debate about fleet size is ongoing. For examples, see Rob Wittman, "The Nation Needs a Real Plan to Grow the Navy," *U.S. Naval Institute Proceedings* 148, no. 3 (March 2022), https://www.usni.org/magazines/proceedings/2022/march/nation-needs-real-plan-grow-navy; Matthew Olay, "CNO: Investing in Industrial Base, Growing the Fleet Are Top Priorities," *U.S. Department of Defense*, April 8, 2024, https://www.defense.gov/News/News-Stories/Article/Article/3734545/cno-investing-in-industrial-base-growing-the-fleet-are-top-priorities; Jeremy Greenwood and Emily Miletello, "To Expand the Navy Isn't Enough. We Need a Bigger Commercial Fleet," *Brookings Institution*, November 4, 2021, https://www.brookings.edu/articles/to-expand-the-navy-isnt-enough-we-need-a-bigger-commercial-fleet.

67. The LCS does not have sufficient defensive technology onboard to protect itself. The *Constellation*-class frigate is over half the price of an *Arleigh Burke*-class destroyer and just a quarter smaller by tonnage, but it cannot field even half the number of missiles. See Sam LaGrone, "All Freedom Littoral Combat Ships in Commission Tapped for Early Disposal," *USNI News*, March 29, 2022, https://news.usni.org/2022/03/29/all-freedom-littoral-combat-ships-in-commission-tapped-for-early-disposal.

68. Big-deck amphibious assault ships (such as the *Wasp*-class and the *America*-class), are designed to carry Marines and their air support. However, they can launch and recover only aircraft capable of vertical landing, and they have comparatively little air defense technology. They probably could not come close enough to Taiwan to contribute usefully.

69. On the Reagan buildup, see Joseph Sims, "Lessons from the 600-Ship Navy," *Naval History* 36, no. 4 (August 2022), https://www.usni.org/magazines/naval-history-magazine/2022/august/lessons-600-ship-navy.

70. The six are Boeing, General Dynamics, Huntington Ingalls, Lockheed Martin, Northrop Grumman, and RTX, formerly known as Raytheon. On the failures of DIB consolidation, see U.S. Government Accountability Office, *State of Competition within the Defense Industrial Base* (Washington, DC: Government Printing Office, 2022); David Thornton, "Consolidating the Defense-Industrial Base in the Post-Cold War Era: Budgetary Priorities & Procurement Policies in the U.S. & Western Europe," *Public Finance and Management* 7, no. 3 (2007); Nicastro, *The U.S. Defense Industrial Base*.

71. Sam Skove, "US to Sextuple 155mm Production, Improve Arms Factories," *Defense One*, March 28, 2023, https://www.defenseone.com/policy/2023/03/us-sextuple-155mm-artillery-shell-production-replenish-stocks-sent-ukraine/384542.

72. The shipbuilding industry is particularly affected. The average age of a worker at BAE Systems Ship Repair is fifty-five years old, and shipbuilders are struggling to recruit workers. In the submarine industrial base alone, approximately 140,000 jobs need to be filled in the next decade. See Richard Burgess, "SECNAV: Frigate Delay Due to 'Atrocious' Shipyard Worker Retention," *Sea Power Magazine*, May 16, 2024, https://seapowermagazine.org/secnav-frigate-delay-due-to-atrocious-worker-retention; Carten Cordell, "Inflation, Workforce Issues Challenge Defense Contractors Amid Security

Pivot," *Nextgov.com*, February 10, 2023, https://www.nextgov.com/defense/2023/02/inflation-workforce-issues-challenge-defense-contractors-amid-security-pivot/382822/; "U.S. Navy Celebrates Expanding Talent Pipeline for Submarine Industrial Base," *Naval Sea Systems Command*, May 3, 2024, https://www.navsea.navy.mil/Media/News/Article-View/Article/3764598/us-navy-celebrates-expanding-talent-pipeline-for-submarine-industrial-base.

73. "10 U.S. Code § 4171—Operational Test and Evaluation of Defense Acquisition Programs," *Legal Information Institute*, accessed January 10, 2025, https://www.law.cornell.edu/uscode/text/10/4171.

74. Otto Kreisher, "Shipbuilding Industry Struggles to Recruit and Retain Workforce," *USNI News*, June 21, 2019, https://news.usni.org/2019/06/21/shipbuilding-industry-struggles-to-recruit-and-retain-workforce.

75. Mark A. Milley, "Strategic Inflection Point: The Most Historically Significant and Fundamental Change in the Character of War Is Happening Now—While the Future Is Clouded in Mist and Uncertainty," *Joint Forces Quarterly* 110 (2023): 6–15.

76. "ACQuipedia," *Defense Acquisition University* (DAU), accessed [date], https://www.dau.edu/acquipedia.

77. "Multiyear Procurement Authority for Virginia Class Submarine Program," *Office of General Counsel (Office of the Secretary of Defense)*, May 18, 2023, https://ogc.osd.mil/Portals/99/OLC%20FY%202024%20Proposals/18May2023Proposals.pdf?ver=delei6MXUUCc-zuCIOgBLg%3D%3D.

78. On the DPA's history, see Douglas I. Bell, *"A Little-known Bill of Great National Significance": The Uses and Evolution of the Defense Production Act, 1950–2020* (Carlisle, PA: U.S. Army Heritage and Education Center, 2020), https://ahec.armywarcollege.edu/documents/Defense_Production_Act_1950-2020.pdf.

79. William Casey Biggerstaff, "The Defense Production Act: Assessing the Ukraine Arms Shortage," *Lieber Institute*, August 3, 2022, https://lieber.westpoint.edu/defense-production-act-assessing-ukraine-arms-shortage.

80. Warren Katz, "The Cost-Plus Boondoggle That Hobbles US Defense," *Breaking Defense*, October 2024, https://breakingdefense.com/2024/10/the-cost-plus-boondoggle-that-hobbles-us-defense.

81. Jaspreet Gill, "From Prototypes to Operations: In Record-Breaking Year, DIU Transitioned 17 New Tech," *Breaking Defense*, January 25, 2023, https://breakingdefense.com/2023/01/from-prototypes-to-operations-in-record-breaking-year-diu-transitioned-17-new-tech.

82. Steve Escavarage and Adam Hammer, "To Stay Competitive, US Military Complex Must Hurdle 'Valley of Death,'" *Marine Corps Times*, September 27, 2023, https://www.marinecorpstimes.com/opinion/2023/09/27/to-stay-competitive-us-military-complex-must-hurdle-valley-of-death.

83. Michael Sion, John Wenzel, and Blaine Pellicore, "Rethinking Defense: The Role of Private Capital," *Bain & Company*, December 2024, https://www.bain.com/insights/rethinking-defense-the-role-of-private-capital; Dylan Thomas and Neel Hiteshbhai Bharucha, "Rise in Defense Sector Funding Defies Broader Venture Capital Slump," *S&P Global*, September 11, 2024, https://www.spglobal.com/marketintelligence/en/news-insights/latest-news-headlines/rise-in-defense-sector-funding-defies-broader-venture-capital-slump-83265012.

84. On procurement reform proposals, see U.S. Department of Defense, *Terraforming the Valley of Death, Defense Innovation Board* (Washington, DC: U.S. Department of Defense, July 2023), https://innovation.defense.gov/Portals/63/DIB_Terraforming%20the%20Valley%20of%20Death_230717_1.pdf.

85. Rob Murray, *Europe and the United States Need to Revolutionize Their Defense Industrial Bases and How They Cooperate* (Washington, DC: Atlantic Council, December 10, 2024), https://www.atlanticcouncil.org/in-depth-research-reports/report/europe-and-the-united-states-need-to-revolutionize-their-defense-industrial-bases-and-how-they-cooperate; Kristen Taylor and Luka Ignac, "NATO Needs a Defense-Industrial Strategy That Prioritizes Being Strong, Smart, and Together," *Atlantic Council*, November 1, 2024, https://www.atlanticcouncil.org/blogs/new-atlanticist/nato-needs-a-defense-industrial-strategy-that-prioritizes-being-strong-smart-and-together; Jeffrey W. Hornung and Zack Cooper, "Shifting the U.S.-Japan Alliance from Coordination to Integration," *War on the Rocks*, August 2, 2024, https://warontherocks.com/2024/08/shifting-the-u-s-japan-alliance-from-coordination-to-integration; Bo Ram Kwon, "Policy Brief: U.S.-South Korea Defense Industrial Cooperation—Drivers, Developments, and Tasks Ahead," *Korea Economic Institute of America*, December 17, 2024, https://keia.org/the-peninsula/policy-brief-us-south-korea-defense-industrial-cooperation-drivers-developments-and-tasks-ahead.

86. Rheinmetall, "Rheinmetall Supplies Light Artillery Cannon to U.S. Army," News release, May 25, 2022. https://www.rheinmetall.com/en/media/news-watch/news/2022/2022-05-25_rheinmetall-supplies-light-artillery-cannon-to-u.s.-army; *Maritime Executive*, "South Korea's Rise as a Global Shipbuilder," June 23, 2024, https://maritime-executive.com/article/south-korea-s-rise-as-a-global-shipbuilder; Hoshik Nam and Wilder Alejandro Sánchez, "South Korea's Growing Role as a Major Arms Exporter: Future Prospects in Latin America," War on the Rocks, August 21, 2024, https://warontherocks.com/2024/08/south-koreas-growing-role-as-a-major-arms-exporter-future-prospects-in-latin-america.

87. Brian T. Di Mascio, "Foreign Shipyards Can Help the U.S. Navy Build Its Fleet," *Proceedings* 150, no. 10 (October 2024), https://www.usni.org/magazines/proceedings/2024/october/foreign-shipyards-can-help-us-navy-build-its-fleet.

88. U.S. Department of State, "Directorate of Defense Trade Controls," Bureau of Political-Military Affairs, https://www.state.gov/bureaus-offices/under-secretary-for-arms-control-and-international-security-affairs/bureau-of-political-military-affairs/directorate-of-defense-trade-controls-pm-ddtc/; John Schaus and Elizabeth Hoffman, "Is ITAR Working in an Era of Great Power Competition?" Center for Strategic and International Studies, February 24, 2023, https://www.csis.org/analysis/itar-working-era-great-power-competition.

89. On ITAR's detrimental effects on alliances, see Tom Corben, "Even with Intended Reforms, US Defence Trade Rules Threaten AUKUS Cooperation," *The Strategist*, June 18, 2024, https://www.aspistrategist.org.au/even-with-intended-reforms-us-defence-trade-rules-threaten-aukus-cooperation. On the subsequent rule change, see U.S. Department of State, "Key Elements of the International Traffic in Arms Regulations Exemption for Defense Trade and Cooperation among Australia, the United Kingdom, and the United States: Fact Sheet," January 20, 2025, https://www.state.gov/key-elements-of-the-international-traffic-in-arms-regulations-exemption-for-defense-trade-and-cooperation-among-australia-the-united-kingdom-and-the-united-states. However, key items relating

to hypersonics, electronic warfare, and undersea warfare remain restricted—as well as relevant data and manufacturing know-how. See Federal Register, "International Traffic in Arms Regulations: Exemption for Defense Trade and Cooperation among Australia, the United Kingdom, and the United States: A Rule by the State Department," FR Doc. 2024-18043, August 20, 2024, https://www.federalregister.gov/documents/2024/08/20/2024-18043/international-traffic-in-arms-regulations-exemption-for-defense-trade-and-cooperation-among.

90. James Carouso, Thomas Schieffer, et al., "ITAR Should End for Australia," Center for Strategic and International Studies, December 7, 2022, https://www.csis.org/analysis/itar-should-end-australia.

91. Kari Bingen, "How to Deepen U.S.-Japan Space Cooperation to Meet the Urgent Security Challenges Ahead," Center for Strategic and International Studies, March 29, 2024, https://www.csis.org/analysis/how-deepen-us-japan-space-cooperation-meet-urgent-security-challenges-ahead; Jeff Foust, "U.S. Government Plans Review of Space Technology Export Controls," *Space News*, April 10, 2024, https://spacenews.com/u-s-government-plans-review-of-space-technology-export-controls.

92. Richard Burgess, "SECNAV: Frigate Delay Due to 'Atrocious' Shipyard Worker Retention," *Sea Power Magazine*, May 16, 2024, https://seapowermagazine.org/secnav-frigate-delay-due-to-atrocious-worker-retention.

93. Lisbeth Perez, "Hill Witnesses Spotlight DIB Workforce Retention Challenges," *Meritalk.com*, February 28, 2024, https://www.meritalk.com/articles/hill-witnesses-spotlight-dib-workforce-retention-challenges.

94. Jack Watling and Nick Reynolds, *Meatgrinder: Russian Tactics in the Second Year of Its Invasion of Ukraine* (London: Royal United Services Institute, May 19, 2023), https://static.rusi.org/403-SR-Russian-Tactics-web-final.pdf. Today, there are likely significantly more UAS being used in Ukraine at any given time, simply because of increased production scale and the diversity of systems employed.

95. Radar tracking relies on terrain and line-of-sight conditions, making it vulnerable to exploitation by skilled operators or advanced AI. Radio frequency (RF) analysis facilitates the identification of control signals and classification of UAS aiding in the selection of countermeasures. Sophisticated UAS can evade RF analysis by frequently changing frequencies. Acoustic detection identifies UAS through sound signatures. It is prone to environmental interference and is most effective on elevated terrain or mounted on a drone. Optical sensors use camera-based systems to classify UAS by detecting wavelengths across the visible and infrared spectrum. See *Dedrone*, "Counter-Drone: The Comprehensive Guide to Counter-UAS/C-UAS/CUAS," https://www.dedrone.com/white-papers/counter-uas; and Bhargav Patel and Dmitri Rizer, *Counter-Unmanned Aircraft Systems: Technology Guide* (New York: National Urban Security Technology Laboratory, September 2019).

96. One effective CUAS technique is to target UAS components on the ground. When the adversary has redundant ground control stations or communications equipment, focusing on the launch and recovery units is often more effective. See United States Army, *Counter-Unmanned Aircraft System (C-UAS)* (Washington, DC: Department of the Army, August 2023), https://irp.fas.org/doddir/army/atp3-01-81.pdf.

97. Miriam McNabb, "Has the U.S.-China Trade War Changed DJI's Drone Market Share? The Latest from Drone Industry Insights," *Drone Life*, March 5, 2021, https://dronelife.com/2021/03/05/has-the-u-s-china-trade-war-changed-djis-drone-market-share-the-latest-from-drone-industry-insights.

98. Siladitya Ray, "Largest U.S. Drone Manufacturer Says It Will Need to Ration Batteries for Customers after Sanctions by China," *Forbes*, October 31, 2024, https://www.forbes.com/sites/siladityaray/2024/10/31/largest-us-drone-manufacturer-says-it-will-need-to-ration-batteries-for-customers-after-sanctions-by-china.

99. See Joseph Trevithick, "Super-Quiet Special Operations Drones May Migrate to Pacific Theater," *The War Zone*, August 13, 2024, https://www.twz.com/air/super-quiet-special-operations-drones-may-migrate-to-pacific-theater; interview with U.S. Special Operators in 5th SFG.

100. Jennifer DiMascio, *U.S. Air Force Collaborative Combat Aircraft (CCA)* (Washington, DC: Congressional Research Service, August 15, 2024), https://crsreports.congress.gov/product/pdf/IF/IF12740.

101. CCAs could take on higher-risk missions and could undertake a variety of tasks including electronic warfare, scouting, and precision strike. Eventually, the goal is to make CCA aircraft attritable. For more on their role, see Gregory Allen and Isaac Goldston, *The Department of Defense's Collaborative Combat Aircraft Program: Good News, Bad News, and Unanswered Questions* (Washington, DC: Center for Strategic and International Studies, August 6, 2024), https://www.csis.org/analysis/department-defenses-collaborative-combat-aircraft-program-good-news-bad-news-and; Benjamin Jensen, Christopher Koeltzow, et al., *Cockpit or Command Center? C2 Options for Collaborative Combat Aircraft* (Washington, DC: Center for Strategic and International Studies, October 29, 2024), https://www.csis.org/analysis/cockpit-or-command-center-c2-options-collaborative-combat-aircraft.

102. DiMascio, *U.S. Air Force Collaborative Combat Aircraft (CCA)*; Allen and Goldston, *The Department of Defense's Collaborative Combat Aircraft Program*.

103. For more discussion of the limitations of CCAs, see Heather R. Penney, *Five Imperatives for Developing Collaborative Combat Aircraft for Teaming Operations* (Arlington, VA: Mitchell Institute for Aerospace Studies, October 2022), https://mitchellaerospacepower.org/wp-content/uploads/2022/10/Five-Imperatives-for-Developing-Collaborative-Combat-Aircraft-FINAL.pdf.; Allen and Goldston, *The Department of Defense's Collaborative Combat Aircraft Program*.

104. *Military and Security Developments Involving the People's Republic of China: 2024*, 62.

105. For more on the threats that spoofing and AAI pose, see David Hambling, "Ukraine Is Spoofing Russian Drones Out of the Sky," *Forbes*, April 21, 2023, https://www.forbes.com/sites/davidhambling/2023/04/21/ukraine-is-spoofing-russian-drones-out-of-the-sky; U.S. Department of Homeland Security, *Risks and Mitigation Strategies for Adversarial Artificial Intelligence Threats: A DHS S&T Study* (Washington, DC: Department of Homeland Security, June 2023), https://www.dhs.gov/sites/default/files/2023-12/23_1222_st_risks_mitigation_strategies.pdf.

106. Military UAS defend against AAI and spoofing with layered defense systems that include multi-modal sensors and anomaly detection algorithms. However, these can be compromised, and encrypted communications can be bypassed. See U.S. Department of Homeland Security, Risks and Mitigation Strategies for Adversarial Artificial Intelligence Threats: A DHS S&T Study.

107. 118th Congress, *National Defense Authorization Act for Fiscal Year 2024*, H.R. 2670, Sections 1823–1829, https://www.congress.gov/bill/118th-congress/house-bill/2670/text.

108. *Dedrone*, "Counter-Drone: The Comprehensive Guide to Counter-UAS/C-UAS/CUAS."

109. Submarines are hard to detect because electromagnetic radiation does not travel well through water. The United States only operates nuclear-powered submarines, which are quiet and particularly difficult to track.

110. Nuclear-armed ballistic missile submarines house the U.S. sea-based strategic nuclear deterrent. Conventional armed fast-attack submarines, including the *Virginia* class and *Los Angeles* class, can deploy cruise missiles, torpedoes, and mines.

111. Seth Cropsey, "The Sorry State of America's Submarine Fleet," *Wall Street Journal*, September 29, 2023, https://www.wsj.com/articles/the-sorry-state-of-americas-submarine-fleet-japan-korea-alliance-taiwan-invasion-china-c29203bd.

112. On the readiness crisis, see Edward Bartlett, "The Navy's Submarine Maintenance Crisis Needs Ready, Affordable Solutions," *Proceedings*, January 2024, https://www.usni.org/magazines/proceedings/2024/january/navys-submarine-maintenance-crisis-needs-ready-affordable; "Report on Virginia-Class Attack Submarine Program," *USNI News*, July 4, 2023, https://news.usni.org/2023/07/04/report-on-virginia-class-attack-submarine-program-12; Seth Cropsey, "Delayed Repairs Shrink the U.S. Submarine Fleet," *Wall Street Journal*, September 14, 2022, https://www.wsj.com/articles/delayed-repairs-shrink-the-submarine-fleet-taiwan-china-navy-amphibious-assault-aircraft-private-shipyards-deployable-boats-materials-11663162266.

113. Tony Shepherd, "US Virginia Class Submarines Hit Further Two-Year Delay as Australia Awaits 2030 Delivery," *The Guardian*, June 8, 2023, https://www.theguardian.com/world/2023/jun/09/us-virginia-class-submarines-hit-further-two-year-delay-as-australia-awaits-2030-delivery.

114. Gale, "The Era of Total U.S. Submarine Dominance over China Is Ending."

115. Attack submarines carry the same munitions as surface ships. The industrial base for torpedos, the classic undersea combat weapon, faces industrial bottlenecks. See Megan Eckstein, Joe Gould, and Bryant Harris, "How the US Plans to Expand Its Submarine Industrial Base for AUKUS," *Defense News*, March 15, 2023, https://www.defensenews.com/naval/2023/03/15/how-the-us-plans-to-expand-its-submarine-industrial-base-for-aukus; Scott Gourley, "Manufacturing the Very Lightweight Torpedo: A Key Factor in Next Gen Defense Technology," *Northrop Grumman*, accessed November 15, 2024, https://www.northropgrumman.com/what-we-do/sea/manufacturing-the-very-lightweight-torpedo; U.S. Naval Institute, "Torpedoes Get Smaller, Think Bigger," *Proceedings*, March 2024, https://www.usni.org/magazines/proceedings/2024/march/torpedoes-get-smaller-think-bigger.

116. For more on China's growing anti-submarine capability, see *Asia Maritime Transparency Initiative*, "Exploring China's Unmanned Ocean Network," June 16, 2020, https://amti.csis.org/exploring-chinas-unmanned-ocean-network/; Eli Tirk and Daniel Salisbury, *China Maritime Report No. 38: PLAN Anti-Submarine Warfare Aircraft—Sensors, Weapons, and Operational Concepts* (Newport, RI: China Maritime Studies Institute, May 2024), https://digital-commons.usnwc.edu/cmsi-maritime-reports/38.

117. U.S. Department of Defense, *Military and Security Developments Involving the People's Republic of China: 2024*, 52.

118. U.S. Naval War College, "CMSI Conference: Chinese Undersea Warfare: Development, Capabilities, Trends," *China Maritime Studies Institute*, April 2023, https://usnwc.edu/News-and-Events/Events/CMSI-Conference-Chinese-Undersea-Warfare; H. I. Sutton, "First Image of China's New Nuclear Submarine Under Construction," *Naval*

News, February 1, 2021, https://www.navalnews.com/naval-news/2021/02/first-image-of-chinas-new-nuclear-submarine-under-construction.

119. U.S. Department of Defense, *Military and Security Developments Involving the People's Republic of China: 2024*, 52.

120. Ronald O'Rourke, *Navy Virginia-Class Submarine Program and AUKUS Submarine (Pillar 1) Project: Background and Issues for Congress* (Washington, DC: Congressional Research Service, February 11, 2025), 55; Sam Lagrone, "Senators Question SecNav, OMB on Submarine Funding Ahead of 17 Attack Boat Buy," *USNI News*, October 28, 2024, https://news.usni.org/2024/10/28/senators-question-secnav-omb-on-submarine-funding-ahead-of-17-attack-boat-buy; David Axe, "US Navy Submarines Are Expensive. Check Out This Graph," *Forbes*, December 15, 2020, https://www.forbes.com/sites/davidaxe/2020/12/15/us-navy-submarines-are-expensive-check-out-this-graph; O'Rourke, *Navy Force Structure and Shipbuilding Plans*.

121. Michael Walker and Austin Krusz, "There's a Case for Diesels," *Proceedings*, June 2018, https://www.usni.org/magazines/proceedings/2018/june/theres-case-diesels; on Korean submarines, see Eric Wertheim, "South Korea's Sophisticated KSS-III Submarines," *Proceedings*, June 2023, https://www.usni.org/magazines/proceedings/2023/june/south-koreas-sophisticated-kss-iii-submarines.

122. For more on these technologies, see Mizuho Kajiwara, "Maritime Security and Underwater Surveillance Technology: Lessons from the Cold War," *Indo-Pacific Outlook* 1, no. 3 (January 24, 2024), https://manoa.hawaii.edu/indopacificaffairs/article/maritime-security-and-underwater-surveillance-technology-lessons-from-the-cold-war; Katarzyna Kubiak, *Quantum Technology and Submarine Near-Invulnerability*, Global Security Policy Brief (London: European Leadership Network, 2020); Matthew Cancian, "An Offensive Minelaying Campaign Against China," *Naval War College Review* 75, no. 1 (Winter 2022).

123. "Orca XLUUV, USA," *Naval Technology*, April 19, 2024, https://www.naval-technology.com/projects/orca-xluuv; Prakash Panneerselvam, "Unmanned Systems in China's Maritime 'Gray Zone Operations,'" *The Diplomat*, January 23, 2023, https://thediplomat.com/2023/01/unmanned-systems-in-chinas-maritime-gray-zone-operations; Julian Kerr, "Australia's Future Extra-Large UUV Named 'Ghost Shark,'" *Janes*, December 12, 2022, https://www.janes.com/osint-insights/defence-news/defence/australias-future-extra-large-uuv-named-ghost-shark; "MSubs Wins UK Royal Navy Contract For Cetus XLUUV," *Naval News*, December 1, 2022, https://www.navalnews.com/naval-news/2022/12/msubs-wins-uk-royal-navy-contract-for-cetus-xluuv.

124. On the role of space assets in the Russia-Ukraine war, and implications for the U.S. military, see U.S. Department of Defense, *Space Policy Review and Strategy on Protection of Satellites* (Washington, DC: U.S. Department of Defense, September 2023), https://media.defense.gov/2023/Sep/14/2003301146/-1/-1/0/COMPREHENSIVE-REPORT-FOR-RELEASE.PDF, 5; Adam Satariano, Scott Reinhard, Cade Metz, Sheera Frenkel, and Malika Khurana, "Elon Musk's Unmatched Power in the Stars," *New York Times*, July 28, 2023, https://www.nytimes.com/interactive/2023/07/28/business/starlink.html; Theodora Ogden, Anna Snack, Melusine Lebret, James Black, and Vasilios Mavroudis, *The Role of the Space Domain in the Russia-Ukraine War* (Centre for Emerging Technology and Security, February 2023), https://cetas.turing.ac.uk/publications/role-space-domain-russia-ukraine-war.

125. Richard Manson et al., *Analyzing a More Resilient National Positioning, Navigation, and Timing Capability* (RAND Corporation, May 17, 2021), 35, https://www.rand.org/pubs/research_reports/RR2970.html.

126. *Space Threat Fact Sheet* (Washington, DC: Headquarters Space Force Intelligence, July 16, 2024), http://www.andrewerickson.com/wp-content/uploads/2024/09/20240716-S2-Space-Threat-Fact-Sheet-v5-RELEASE.pdf.

127. *Space Threat Fact Sheet* (2024).

128. U.S. Department of Defense, *Military and Security Developments Involving the People's Republic of China: 2024*, 99.

129. PRC theoretical writings are clear on this, particularly Xiao, *Science of Military Strategy (2020)*. See also Mark Stokes, Emily Weinstein, Gabriel Alvarado, and Cody Daniel, *China's Space and Counterspace Activities* (Project 2049 Institute and Pointe Bello, March 30, 2020).

130. Bart Hendrickx, "Kalina: a Russian Ground-Based Laser to Dazzle Imaging Satellites," *The Space Review*, July 5, 2022, https://www.thespacereview.com/article/4416/1; Ken Moriyasu, "China Can 'Grapple' US Satellites with Robotic Arm, Commander Says," *Nikkei Asia*, April 21, 2021, https://asia.nikkei.com/Politics/International-relations/US-China-tensions/China-can-grapple-US-satellites-with-robotic-arm-commander-says; Brian Weeden, *2007 Chinese Anti-Satellite Test Fact Sheet* (Secure World Foundation, November 23, 2010), https://swfound.org/media/9550/chinese_asat_fact_sheet_updated_2012.pdf.

131. Herbert S. Lin, ed., *Stanford Emerging Technology Review 2025* (Stanford, CA: Stanford University, 2025), 137; Mark A. Gubrud, "Chinese and US Kinetic Energy Space Weapons and Arms Control," *Asian Perspective* 35, no. 4 (2011): 617–641, http://www.jstor.org/stable/42704774.

132. The United States is quietly developing anti-satellite capabilities. One notable system is the Boeing X-37B orbital spaceplane. See U.S. Space Force, "X-37B Begins Novel Space Maneuver," October 20, 2024, https://www.spaceforce.mil/News/Article-Display/Article/3932137/x-37b-begins-novel-space-maneuver.

133. Lin, *Stanford Emerging Technology Review 2025*, 133.

134. Ria Urban, "Space Systems Command Facilitates Multiple Contract Awards for Proliferated Low Earth Orbit Satellite-Based Services," *Space Impulse*, July 24, 2023, https://spaceimpulse.com/2023/07/28/space-systems-command-facilitates-multiple-contract-awards-for-proliferated-low-earth-orbit-satellite-based-services.

135. Amy Thompson, "SpaceX Sets a New Reusability Record," *The Hill*, July 11, 2023, https://thehill.com/homenews/space/4090715-spacex-sets-a-new-reusability-record/; Kate Duffy, "Elon Musk Says He's 'Highly Confident' That SpaceX's Starship Rocket Launches Will Cost Less Than $10 Million Within 2–3 Years," *Business Insider India*, February 11, 2022, https://www.businessinsider.in/tech/news/elon-musk-says-hes-highly-confident-that-spacexs-starship-rocket-launches-will-cost-less-than-10-million-within-2-3-years/articleshow/89507371.cms.

136. John Olson et al., *State of the Space Industrial Base 2022* (U.S. Space Force, August 2022), 39, https://assets.ctfassets.net/3nanhbfkropc/6L5409bpVlnVyu2H5FOFnc/7595c4909616df92372a1d31be609625/State_of_the_Space_Industrial_Base_2022_Report.pdf.; Citigroup Global Perspectives and Solutions, *Space: The Dawn of a New Age* (Citigroup Global Perspectives and Solutions, May 9, 2022), https://ir.citi.com/gps/829sRzYY4sQ%2BOhctTEs%2B1WWLgPbyZktiZpoz3QRCC6ToaLgXov4Kxy852czeh38jOi72XKhJGpo%3D.

137. Sandra Erwin, "Space Force Changed Launch Procurement Plan Due to Concerns about Capacity," *SpaceNews*, July 19, 2023, https://spacenews.com/space-force-changed-launch-procurement-plan-due-to-concerns-about-capacity.

138. For more on nuclear power and propulsion, see Defense Advanced Research Projects Agency (DARPA), "DARPA, NASA Collaborate on Nuclear Thermal Rocket Engine," January 24, 2023, https://www.darpa.mil/news-events/2023-01-24; Katherine McAlpine, "Space Force Funds $35M Institute for Versatile Propulsion," *University of Michigan Record*, October 16, 2024, https://record.umich.edu/articles/space-force-establishes-35m-institute-for-versatile-propulsion; Roxana Bardan, "NASA, DARPA Will Test Nuclear Engine for Future Mars Missions," *NASA News Release*, January 24, 2023, https://www.nasa.gov/news-release/nasa-darpa-will-test-nuclear-engine-for-future-mars-missions.

139. On ISAM, see Sandra Erwin, "Lockheed Martin Declares Success Demonstrating Tech for In-Orbit Satellite Servicing," *SpaceNews*, April 17, 2023, https://spacenews.com/lockheed-martin-declares-success-demonstrating-tech-for-in-orbit-satellite-servicing; SpaceLogistics, *Mission Extension Vehicle (MEV) Fact Sheet* (Northrop Grumman, 2021), https://cdn.northropgrumman.com/-/media/wp-content/uploads/Mission-Extension-Vehicle-MEV-fact-sheet.pdf?v=1.0.0.

140. John Costello, *The Pacific War 1941–1945* (New York: HarperCollins, 1982), 67–76.

141. Craig Symonds, *American Naval History: A Very Short Introduction* (Oxford: Oxford University Press, 2018), 80–96.

142. U.S. Department of Defense, "Senior Defense Official Briefs on 2024 China Military Power Report," transcript, December 18, 2024, https://www.defense.gov/News/Transcripts/Transcript/Article/4009708/senior-defense-official-briefs-on-2024-china-military-power-report.

143. Franklin D. Roosevelt, "Fireside Chat," *The American Presidency Project*, December 29, 1940, https://www.presidency.ucsb.edu/node/209416.

CHAPTER 6

1. Shannon Bugos and Julia Masterson, "New Chinese Missile Silo Fields Discovered," Arms Control Association, September 2021, https://www.armscontrol.org/act/2021-09/news/new-chinese-missile-silo-fields-discovered.

2. Hans M. Kristensen, Matt Korda, Eliana Johns, and Mackenzie Knight, "Chinese Nuclear Weapons, 2024," *Bulletin of the Atomic Scientists*, January 15, 2024, https://thebulletin.org/premium/2024-01/chinese-nuclear-weapons-2024. For discussion of how China is explaining its buildup, see Tong Zhao, "What's Driving China's Nuclear Buildup?" *Journal of Strategic Studies* 36, no. 4 (2013): 579–614, https://doi.org/10.1080/01402390.2013.772510.

3. U.S. Department of Defense, *2024 Report on Military and Security Developments Involving the People's Republic of China*, 101.

4. U.S. Department of Defense, *2023 Report on Military and Security Developments Involving the People's Republic of China: Annual Report to Congress* (Washington, DC: U.S. Department of Defense, 2023), 104; U.S. Department of Defense, *2022 Report on Military and Security Developments Involving the People's Republic of China: Annual Report to Congress* (Washington, DC: U.S. Department of Defense, 2022), 94.

5. The classic text on China's nuclear posture in the pre-Xi era is Jeffrey Lewis, *Paper Tigers: China's Nuclear Posture* (London: Routledge, 2014). Also see Taylor M. Fravel,

Active Defense: China's Military Strategy since 1949 (Princeton, NJ: Princeton University Press, 2019); and Wu Riqiang, "Certainty of Uncertainty: Nuclear Strategy with Chinese Characteristics," *Journal of Strategic Studies* 36, no. 4 (2013): 579–614.

6. Zhao, "What's Driving China's Nuclear Buildup?"

7. Eric Heginbotham et al., *China's Evolving Nuclear Deterrent: Major Drivers and Issues for the United States* (Santa Monica, CA: RAND Corporation, 2017), https://www.rand.org/content/dam/rand/pubs/research_reports/RR1600/RR1628/RAND_RR1628.pdf.

8. U.S. Strategic Command, "Mission, Vision, & Intent," accessed February 27, 2025, https://www.stratcom.mil/About/Mission.

9. According to the Department of Defense, China "may" be developing a new conventionally armed missile system that could reach the continental United States. U.S. Department of Defense, *2024 Report on Military and Security Developments Involving the People's Republic of China*, 63.

10. On the Russian concept of strategic deterrence (*strategicheskoe sderzhivanie*), see Kristin Ven Bruusgaard, "Russian Strategic Deterrence," *Survival* 58, no. 4 (2016): 7–26, https://doi.org/10.1080/00396338.2016.1207945. Since the full-scale invasion of Ukraine in 2022, Russia has also expanded Soviet-era biological weapons labs. These efforts are likely linked to changes to its nuclear doctrine—an effort to revive biological attacks as an aspect of strategic deterrence. See Joby Warrick and Jarrett Ley, "Satellite Images Show Major Expansion at Russian Site with Secret Bioweapons Past," *Washington Post*, October 25, 2024, https://www.washingtonpost.com/national-security/interactive/2024/russia-biological-chemical-weapons-laboratory-expansion.

11. Terri Moon Cronk, "Hyten Discusses 21st Century Strategic Deterrence," *U.S. Strategic Command*, September 21, 2017, https://www.stratcom.mil/Media/News/News-Article-View/Article/1319337/hyten-discusses-21st-century-strategic-deterrence/.

12. An important exception is Robert Jervis, who highlighted the risk that states' perceptions and misperceptions could cause unintended threats to strategic stability. See Robert Jervis, *The Meaning of the Nuclear Revolution: Statecraft and the Prospect of Armageddon* (Ithaca, NY: Cornell University Press, 1989), 32.

13. Tong Zhao, "The Real Motives for China's Nuclear Expansion," *Foreign Affairs*, May 3, 2024, https://www.foreignaffairs.com/china/real-motives-chinas-nuclear-expansion.

14. The PRC literature on MAD draws extensively on Western Cold War concepts, generally defining MAD as the situation brought about by two states' "mutual vulnerability" (*xianghu cuiruo* 相互脆弱) to second strikes by the other. See Kaufman and Waidelich, *PRC Writings on Strategic Deterrence*, 15.

15. James F. Schnabel and Robert J. Watson, *The Joint Chiefs of Staff and National Policy, Volume III 1950–1951, The Korean War, Part One* (Washington, DC: Government Printing Office, 1998); Morton H. Halperin, *The 1958 Taiwan Straits Crisis: A Document History (U)* (Santa Monica, CA: RAND, 1975), https://www.rand.org/content/dam/rand/pubs/research_memoranda/2006/RM4900.pdf. On India, see "Galwan Valley: Image Appears to Show Nail-studded Rods Used in India-China Brawl," *BBC News*, June 18, 2020, https://www.bbc.com/news/world-asia-india-53089037.

16. Andrew S. Erickson, "China's Approach to Conventional Deterrence," in *Modernizing Deterrence: How China Coerces, Compels, and Deters*, ed. Roy D. Kamphausen (Washington, DC: National Bureau of Asian Research, 2023), 25–26.

17. Schelling, *Arms and Influence*, 70–71; Robert J. Art and Kelly M. Greenhill, "Coercion: An Analytical Overview," in *Coercion: The Power to Hurt in International Politics*, ed. Kelly M. Greenhill and Peter Krause (New York: Oxford University Press, 2018).

18. Jiang Tianjiao, "关于中国威慑理论自主知识体系构建的回顾与思考" Reflections on the Construction of China's Independent Knowledge System of Deterrence Theory, 国际安全研究 *International Security Studies*, no. 5 (2024): 3–20, https://www.secrss.com/articles/70430.

19. On compellence, see Tami Davis Biddle, "Coercion Theory: A Basic Introduction for Practitioners," *Texas National Security Review* 3, no. 2 (2020): 94–109, https://dx.doi.org/10.26153/tsw/8864.

20. Schelling, *Arms and Influence*, 91.

21. Schelling, *Arms and Influence*, 73.

22. See, for example, Robert Jervis, "Deterrence and Perception," *International Security* 7, no. 3 (Winter 1982/1983); Graham T. Allison and Philip Zelikow, *Essence of Decision: Explaining the Cuban Missile Crisis*, 2nd ed. (New York: Longman, 1999); Lawrence Freedman, *Deterrence* (Cambridge: Polity Press, 2004).

23. Alexander L. George and Richard Smoke, *Deterrence in American Foreign Policy: Theory and Practice* (New York: Columbia University Press, 1974).

24. Todd S. Sechser and Matthew Fuhrmann, "Crisis Bargaining and Nuclear Blackmail," *International Organization* 67, no. 1 (Winter 2013): 173–195, https://doi.org/10.1017/S0020818312000392.

25. Sechser and Fuhrmann, "Crisis Bargaining and Nuclear Blackmail," 182.

26. Sechser and Fuhrmann, "Crisis Bargaining and Nuclear Blackmail."

27. Sechser and Fuhrmann, "Crisis Bargaining and Nuclear Blackmail," 177.

28. Erin R. Mahan and Jeffrey A. Larsen, eds., *Evolution of the Secretary of Defense in the Era of Massive Retaliation: Charles Wilson, Neil McElroy, and Thomas Gates 1953–1961* (Washington, DC: Government Printing Office, 2012).

29. Albert Wohlstetter, *The Delicate Balance of Terror* (Santa Monica, CA: RAND, 1958), https://www.rand.org/pubs/papers/P1472.html.

30. Bernard Brodie, "The Anatomy of Deterrence," *World Politics* 11, no. 2 (January 1959): 173–191, https://doi.org/10.2307/2009527.

31. Rose Gottemoeller, "The Standstill Conundrum: The Advent of Second-Strike Vulnerability and Options to Address It," *Texas National Security Review* 4, no. 4 (2021): 115–124, https://tnsr.org/2021/10/the-standstill-conundrum-the-advent-of-second-strike-vulnerability-and-options-to-address-it.

32. For a thoughtful and up to date survey, see Ankit Panda, *The New Nuclear Age: At the Precipice of Armageddon* (New York: Polity, 2025).

33. Keir A. Lieber and Daryl G. Press, "The End of MAD? The Nuclear Dimension of U.S. Primacy," *International Security* 30, no. 4 (Spring 2006): 10, https://www.jstor.org/stable/4137528.

34. Fiona S. Cunningham and M. Taylor Fravel, "Assuring Assured Retaliation: China's Nuclear Posture and U.S.-China Strategic Stability," *International Security* 40, no. 2 (2015): 7–50, https://doi.org/10.1162/ISEC_a_00215.

35. Shou Xiaosong, 战略学 *Science of Military Strategy* (Beijing: Academy of Military Science Press, 2013), 148.

36. Michael D. Swaine, "China's Assertive Behavior. Part One: On 'Core Interests,'" *China Leadership Monitor* 34, no. 22 (2011): 1–25, https://carnegie-production-assets.s3.amazonaws.com/static/files/CLM34MS_FINAL.pdf.

37. James F. Schnabel and Robert J. Watson, *The Joint Chiefs of Staff and National Policy, Volume III 1950–1951, The Korean War, Part One* (Washington, DC: Government Printing Office, 1998).

38. Schnabel and Watson, *The Joint Chiefs of Staff and National Policy*, 239.

39. Graham A. Cosmas, *MACV: The Joint Command in the Years of Withdrawal, 1968–1973* (Washington, DC: U.S. Government Printing Office, 2007).

40. David E. Sanger and William J. Broad, "Obama Unlikely to Vow No First Use of Nuclear Weapons," *New York Times*, September 5, 2016, https://www.nytimes.com/2016/09/06/science/obama-unlikely-to-vow-no-first-use-of-nuclear-weapons.html.

41. On China's perspective, see Liping Xia, "China's Nuclear Doctrine: Debates and Evolution," *Carnegie Endowment for International Peace*, June 30, 2016, https://carnegieendowment.org/research/2016/06/chinas-nuclear-doctrine-debates-and-evolution?lang=en.

42. 陆军领导机构火箭军战略支援部队成立大会在京举行： 习近平向中国人民解放军陆军火箭军战略支援部队授予军旗并致训词 *Meeting to Establish the PLA Army General Command, Rocket Force, and Strategic Support Group Held in Beijing: Xi Jinping Confers Flag and Makes Address*, 人民日报 *People's Daily*, January 2, 2016, cited in Heginbotham et al., *China's Evolving Nuclear Deterrent*.

43. Xiao Tianliang, ed., 战略学 *Science of Military Strategy* (Beijing: National Defense University Press, 2020), 126–127, cited in Erickson, "China's Approach to Conventional Deterrence," 15–16.

44. 学习《决定》每日问答 | 如何理解构建武器装备现代化管理体系 *Daily Q&A on Studying the 'Decision' | Understanding the Construction of a Modernized Weaponry Management System*, 中国政府网 *The State Council of the People's Republic of China*, November 2024, https://www.gov.cn/zhengce/202411/content_6986137.htm.

45. Matt Korda and Hans Kristensen, "A Closer Look at China's Missile Silo Construction," *Federation of American Scientists*, November 2, 2023, https://fas.org/publication/a-closer-look-at-chinas-missile-silo-construction; U.S. Department of Defense, *Military and Security Developments Involving the People's Republic of China: 2024*, 101.

46. Kristensen et al., "Chinese Nuclear Weapons, 2024."

47. On the technology itself, see Ritwik Gupta, "Orbital Hypersonic Delivery Systems Threaten Strategic Stability," *Bulletin of the Atomic Scientists*, June 13, 2023, https://thebulletin.org/2023/06/orbital-hypersonic-delivery-systems-threaten-strategic-stability. On the U.S. government's surprise, see Demetri Sevastopulo and Kathrin Hille, "China Tests New Space Capability with Hypersonic Missile," *Financial Times*, October 17, 2021, https://www.ft.com/content/ba0a3cde-719b-4040-93cb-a486e1f843fb.

48. "Fact Sheet: China's Nuclear Inventory," *Center for Arms Control and Non-Proliferation*, October 19, 2023, https://armscontrolcenter.org/wp-content/uploads/2020/04/Chinas-Nuclear-Inventory-Fact-Sheet-2.pdf. For more on China's ICBM arsenal, see CSIS Missile Defense Project, "DF-41 (Dong Feng-41/CSS-X-20)," *Missile Threat*, July 31, 2021, https://missilethreat.csis.org/missile/df-41; *Military and Security Developments Involving the People's Republic of China: 2024*, 61.

49. U.S. Department of Defense, *Military and Security Developments Involving the People's Republic of China: 2024*, 61.

50. U.S. Department of Defense, *Military and Security Developments Involving the People's Republic of China: 2024*, 53.

51. U.S. Department of Defense, *Military and Security Developments Involving the People's Republic of China: 2024*, 56

52. U.S. Department of Defense, *Military and Security Developments Involving the People's Republic of China: 2024*, 88; Kristensen et al., "Chinese Nuclear Weapons, 2024"; Patrick Tucker, "Russian Submarine Tech Could Help China Outpace U.S.: INDOPACOM," *Defense One*, November 23, 2024, https://www.defenseone.com/threats/2024/11/russian-submarine-tech-could-help-china-out-pace-us-says-indopacom-chief/401270.

53. U.S. Department of Defense, *Military and Security Developments Involving the People's Republic of China: 2023*, 89.

54. According to the Pentagon, the DF-26 is the most likely system to field a low-yield nuclear warhead. U.S. Department of Defense, *Military and Security Developments Involving the People's Republic of China: 2024*, 110.

55. U.S. Department of Defense, *Military and Security Developments Involving the People's Republic of China: 2024*, 101.

56. Between 1988 and 2018, the United States abided by the Intermediate-range Nuclear Forces (INF) Treaty, which precluded it from developing ground-launched theater nuclear weapons. China was not a party to the treaty, a key reason why the Trump administration withdrew.

57. Kyle Balzer and Dan Blumenthal, "The True Aims of China's Nuclear Buildup," *Foreign Affairs*, November 21, 2024, https://www.foreignaffairs.com/china/true-aims-chinas-nuclear-buildup.

58. Heather Williams, Kelsey Hartigan, Lachlan MacKenzie, and Reja Younis, "Russian Nuclear Calibration in the War in Ukraine," *CSIS Briefs*, February 2024, https://www.csis.org/analysis/russian-nuclear-calibration-war-ukraine.

59. Scott D. Sagan, "Lessons of the Yom Kippur Alert," *Foreign Policy*, no. 36 (1979): 169–171, https://www.jstor.org/stable/pdf/1148213.pdf?casa_token=xG-9XoWsPUM AAAAA:uyQ983VmmLM1tIXwH_iZCBf7zSMsMeQ63Lcg56gXbkkVa2lq1wO sIbOZABzr9pzSwQxtWVcXvZtFFDyAKvm3T9xEmWvx_IV_amx_TISkXF 3xozgrobS6.

60. Wei Fan and Siqi Cao, "China Debuts Container-Type Missile Launch System; Weapon Can 'Effectively Improve Defense Capabilities of Coastal Countries,'" *Global Times*, November 12, 2022, https://www.globaltimes.cn/page/202211/1279349.shtml.

61. U.S. Department of Defense, *Military and Security Developments Involving the People's Republic of China: 2024*, 54, 88; "#36—China's Container-Launched Cruise Missiles," *Vermilion China*, February 23, 2023, https://www.vermilionchina.com/p/36-chinas-container-launched-cruise.

62. "About Us," *COSCO Shipping*, accessed January 13, 2025, https://lines.coscoshipping.com/home/About/about/Profile.

63. Tom Shugart (@tshugart3), "If only, say, 10% of those containers were used for munitions, they could for example field 144 cruise missiles and 252 quadcopters, more than enough to devastate every warship at Norfolk, and able to reach land targets across the mid-Atlantic and well past DC," *X*, August 22, 2024, 8:29 p.m., https://x.com/tshugart3/status/1826597569813676146.

64. 中华人民共和国国防交通法 *National Defense Transportation Law of the People's Republic of China*, 共产党员网 *Communist Party Member*, September 3, 2016.

65. *LOGINK: Risks from China's Promotion of a Global Logistics Management Platform* (Washington, DC: U.S.-China Economic and Security Review Commission, 2022), https://www.uscc.gov/research/logink-risks-chinas-promotion-global-logistics-management-platform; Sean Lyngaas, "Congressional Probe Finds Communications Gear in Chinese Cranes, Raising Spying Concerns," *CNN*, March 8, 2024, https://edition.cnn.com/2024/03/07/politics/congressional-probe-communications-gear-chinese-cranes/index.html.

66. Raul Pedrozo, "China's Container Missile Deployments Could Violate the Law of Naval Warfare," *International Law Studies* 97 (2021): 1160–1170, https://digital-commons.usnwc.edu/cgi/viewcontent.cgi?article=2982&context=ils.

67. Office of the United States Trade Representative, "Proposed Action Pursuant to the Section 301 Investigation of China's Targeting of the Maritime, Logistics, and Shipbuilding Sectors for Dominance," Federal Register 90, no. 38 (February 26, 2025): 11234–11256, https://ustr.gov/sites/default/files/files/Press/Releases/2025/Ships%20Proposed%20Action%20FRN.pdf.

68. Vanda Felbab-Brown, "The China Connection in Mexico's Illegal Economies," *Brookings*, February 4, 2022, https://www.brookings.edu/articles/the-china-connection-in-mexicos-illegal-economies; U.S. Office of Public Affairs, "Federal Indictment Alleges Alliance Between Sinaloa Cartel and Money Launderers Linked to Chinese Underground Banking," June 18, 2024, https://www.justice.gov/opa/pr/federal-indictment-alleges-alliance-between-sinaloa-cartel-and-money-launderers-linked.

69. Eva Dou and Gerrit De Vynck, "Pagers Attack Brings to Life Long-Feared Supply Chain Threat," *The Washington Post*, September 19, 2024, https://www.washingtonpost.com/technology/2024/09/19/hezbollah-pager-attack-supply-chain.

70. "Christopher Wray on the Threat of China's Cyber Program," produced by *60 Minutes*, January 13, 2025, video, 1:15, https://www.youtube.com/watch?v=EXa5-5WuwNg.

71. For a compelling case that the United States botched response to COVID-19 was fundamentally a national security failure, which could happen again with even more dire results, see The Covid Crisis Group, *Lessons from the Covid War: An Investigative Report* (New York: PublicAffairs, 2023).

72. Lingling Wei, "Xi Jinping Is Betting It All on Zero-COVID," *The Wall Street Journal*, April 28, 2022, https://www.wsj.com/articles/xi-jinping-is-betting-it-all-on-zero-covid-lockdowns-mandates-china-pandemic-omicron-great-leap-forward-11651155033.

73. "习近平:在全国抗击新冠肺炎疫情表彰大会上的讲话" Xi Jinping: Speech at the National Commendation Conference for Fighting the New Coronavirus Epidemic, *Xinhua net*, September 8, 2020, https://www.xinhuanet.com/politics/leaders/2020-09/08/c_1126467958.htm3.

74. Jimmy Goodrich, " China's Evolving Fortress Economy" (Working Paper, Washington, DC: Institute on Global Conflict and Cooperation, 2024), https://ucigcc.org/wp-content/uploads/2024/07/2024_wp5_goodrich_v1-FINAL-2.pdf.

75. On the national climate adaptation strategy, see Eyck Freymann, "The Adaptation Advantage," *The Wire China*, July 17, 2022, https://www.thewirechina.com/2022/07/17/chinas-climate-adaptation-advantage/; on "financial war," see Freymann, "Logic of Partial RMB Internationalization."

76. Shao Sujun (邵素军) and Yang Xianming (杨先明), "多角度认识中国经济韧性" *Understanding China's Economic Resilience from Multiple Perspectives*, 求是网 QS Theory, September 4, 2023, https://www.qstheory.cn/2023-09/04/c_1129843783.htm.

77. On China's official claims, see 中华人民共和国外交部 Ministry of Foreign Affairs of the People's Republic of China, 中国关于互不首先使用核武器倡议的工作文件 China's Working Paper on the Initiative of Mutual No-First-Use of Nuclear Weapons, July 2024; 中华人民共和国外交部 Ministry of Foreign Affairs of the People's Republic of China, 中国倡议互不首先使用核武器 China Proposes No-First-Use of Nuclear Weapons, October 16, 2024, https://www.mfa.gov.cn/web/sp_683685/wjbfyrlxjzh_683691/202410/t20241016_11508421.shtml. For a critical perspective, see Sari Arho Havrén, "China's No First Use of Nuclear Weapons Policy: Change or False Alarm?" RUSI, October 13, 2023, https://www.rusi.org/explore-our-research/publications/commentary/chinas-no-first-use-nuclear-weapons-policy-change-or-false-alarm; Nicola Leveringhaus, "How China's Nuclear Past Shapes the Present: Ideological and Diplomatic Considerations in Nuclear Deterrence," in *Modernizing Deterrence: How China Coerces, Compels, and Deters*, ed. Roy D. Kamphausen (Seattle, WA: National Bureau of Asian Research, 2023).

78. Kaufman and Waidelich, *PRC Writings on Strategic Deterrence*, 45–46.

79. Adam Mount, "No First Use Can Still Help to Reduce US-China Nuclear Risks," *Journal for Peace and Nuclear Disarmament* 7, no. 1 (2024): 131–142, https://doi.org/10.1080/25751654.2024.2356333.

80. For the blending of Deterrence capability, see Zhang Yan (张岩), "战略威慑理论的历史演进" The Historical Evolution of the Theory of Strategic Deterrence, 军事历史 *Military History*, no. 2 (2018): 60–61; 战略威慑理论的历史演进), *Military History (Junshi lishi; 军事历史)*, no. 2 (2018): 60–61; Xiao, *Science of Military Strategy (2020)*, 128–131; Ling Shengyin (凌胜银), Sun Ying (孙英), and Chen Maoxia (陈茂霞), "论我国战略威慑能力建设" On Our Country's Strategic Deterrence Capability Building, 南京政治学院学报 *Journal of PLA Nanjing Institute of Politics*, no. 3 (2017): 103–105; Li Zhe (李喆), "核军控之路仍荆棘塞途" Path to Nuclear Arms Control Remains Beset with Difficulties, 解放军报 *PLA Daily*, February 6, 2021, https://www.81.cn/jfjbmap/content/2021-02/06/content_282330.htm. For a new concept of coercion, see Hu Wenlong (胡文龙), "准战争"思想给新的历史起点上军事斗争的深刻启示" *Deep Insights of 'Quasi-War' Thinking for Military Struggle at a New Historical Starting Point*, 铁军 *Iron Soldier*, no. 12 (2016): 35–36; Liu Ziye (刘子夜), "论网络胁迫成功的条件" On the Conditions for Successful Cyber Coercion, 国际政治科学 *Quarterly Journal of International Politics*, no. 2 (2020): 148–183; Gaoyang Yuxi (高杨予兮), "美国太空威慑战略调整及其影响" The Adjustment of US Space Deterrence Strategy and Its Impact, 和平与发展 *Peace and Development*, no. 3 (2018).

81. The best English-language articulation of this argument—that China's buildup is reactive and largely defensively motivated—is Taylor M. Fravel, Henrik Stålhane Hiim, and Magnus Langset Trøan, "China's Misunderstood Nuclear Expansion," *Foreign Affairs*, November 10, 2023, https://www.foreignaffairs.com/china/chinas-misunderstood-nuclear-expansion.

82. Kaufman and Waidelich, *PRC Writings on Strategic Deterrence*, iii.

83. Heginbotham et al., *China's Evolving Nuclear Deterrent*, 24.

84. Li Bin, "Differences Between Chinese and U.S. Nuclear Thinking and Their Origins," in Li Bin and Tong Zhao, eds., *Understanding Chinese Nuclear Thinking* (Washington, DC: Carnegie Endowment for International Peace, 2016), 9–10.

85. Li Bin, "中美 对 '核威慑' 理解的差异" *The Difference in Chinese and American Understandings about 'Nuclear Deterrence'*, 世界经济与政治 *World Economics and Politics*, no. 2 (2014): 8; cited in Kaufman and Weidelich, *PRC Writings on Strategic Deterrence*, 10.

86. Zou Zhibo and Liu Wei, "构建中美核战略稳定性框架:非对称性战略平衡的视角" *Constructing the Sino-US Nuclear Strategic Stability Framework: An Asymmetric Strategic Balance Approach,* 国际安全研究 *Journal of International Security Studies,* no. 1 (2019), cited in Kaufman and Waidelich, *PRC Writings on Strategic Deterrence,* 24.

87. Anonymous U.S. government official, quoted in Erickson, "China's Approach to Conventional Deterrence," 26.

88. "The 1983 War Scare: 'The Last Paroxysm' of the Cold War Part II," *The National Security Archive,* May 21, 2013, https://nsarchive2.gwu.edu/NSAEBB/NSAEBB427; Jonathan M. DiCicco, "Fear, Loathing, and Cracks in Reagan's Mirror Images: Able Archer 83 and an American First Step toward Rapprochement in the Cold War," *Foreign Policy Analysis* 7, no. 3 (2011): 253–274, https://www.jstor.org/stable/24909797

89. Simon Miles, "The War Scare That Wasn't: Able Archer 83 and the Myths of the Second Cold War," *Journal of Cold War Studies* 22, no. 3 (Summer 2020): 93, https://doi.org/10.1162/jcws_a_00952.

90. Miles, "The War Scare That Wasn't," 93.

91. The White House, Memorandum of Conversation, "Subject: U.S.-Soviet Relations," October 11, 1983, Secret, *Reagan Presidential Library, Matlock Files,* Chron October 1983 [10/11/1983–10/24/1983], Box 2, 90888, https://nsarchive2.gwu.edu/NSAEBB/NSAEBB426.

92. "Notes of WINTEX 83 Senior Level First Impressions Conference, 22 Mar 1983," *The National Security Archive,* May 21, 2013, https://nsarchive2.gwu.edu/NSAEBB/NSAEBB427; "The 1983 War Scare: 'The Last Paroxysm' of the Cold War Part II," *The National Security Archive,* May 21, 2013, https://nsarchive2.gwu.edu/NSAEBB/NSAEBB427.

93. Thomas Fraise and Kjølv Egeland, "Able Archer: How Close of a Call Was It?" *Bulletin of the Atomic Scientists,* May 9, 2023, https://thebulletin.org/premium/2023-05/able-archer-how-close-of-a-call-was-it.

94. Robert Michael Gates, *From the Shadows: The Ultimate Insider's Story of Five Presidents and How They Won the Cold War* (New York: Simon and Schuster, 1997), 273.

95. For China, another salient anecdote from history is the accidental NATO bombing of the PRC embassy in Belgrade in 1999. Despite NATO's apologies, CCP propaganda claims that the bombing illustrates the U.S. willingness to strike first and without provocation should the opportunity arise.

96. James G. Blight and David A. Welch, *On the Brink: Americans and Soviets Reexamine the Cuban Missile Crisis* (New York: Hill and Wang, 1989), 100.

97. "Inside Able Archer 83: The Nuclear War Game That Put U.S.-Soviet Relations on Hair Trigger," *The National Security Archive,* December 6, 2016. https://nsarchive.gwu.edu/briefing-book/foia/2016-12-06/inside-able-archer-83-nuclear-war-game-put-us-soviet-relations-hair.

98. Among many excellent studies, I recommend Serhii Plokhy, *Nuclear Folly: A History of the Cuban Missile Crisis* (New York: W. W. Norton, 2021), which draws on Soviet sources, unearths new details about the internal operations of Kennedy's team, and presents the most nuanced portrait of Khrushchev's personal insecurities.

99. Raymond Garthoff, "The NATO Decision on Theater Nuclear Forces," *Political Science Quarterly* 98, no. 2 (1983): 197–214. https://doi.org/10.2307/2149415.

100. Garthoff, "The NATO Decision on Theater Nuclear Forces," 199; Susan Colbourn, *Euromissiles: The Nuclear Weapons That Nearly Destroyed NATO* (Ithaca, NY: Cornell

University Press, 2022), chap. 2. https://search.ebscohost.com/login.aspx?direct=true&db=nlebk&AN=3165626&site=ehost-live.

101. Tom Nichols, Douglas Stuart, and Jeffrey D. McCausland, eds., *Tactical Nuclear Weapons and NATO* (Carlisle, PA: U.S. Army War College, Strategic Studies Institute, April 2012), 5–6.

102. Nichols et al., *Tactical Nuclear Weapons and NATO*, 25–30.

103. Cold War International History Project, *Document Reader Part II: The Euromissiles Crisis and the End of the Cold War, 1977–1987* (Washington, DC: Wilson Center, December 10–12, 2009), https://www.wilsoncenter.org/sites/default/files/media/uploads/documents/Euromissiles_Reader_PartII.pdf.

104. Washington's initial answer was the "Dual-Track Decision" of 1979: (1) the deployment of 108 Pershing IIs and 464 Gryphon ground-launched cruise missiles across Western Europe, and (2) a commitment to arms control negotiations with the Soviets to limit intermediate-range nuclear weapons. However, the Soviets played on antinuclear sentiment in the European left to spread the narrative that a warmongering Washington was turning Europe into a nuclear target. The crisis was not fully resolved until the 1987 INF Treaty, which eliminated an entire category of nuclear missiles from the region. See Garthoff, "The NATO Decision on Theater Nuclear Forces"; Nichols et al., *Tactical Nuclear Weapons and NATO*, 57; and Colbourn, *Euromissiles*.

105. Washington neither confirms nor denies having nukes in Japan and the Philippines. Voters in both countries would be strongly opposed if it turned out that U.S. forces had nukes deployed on their soil.

106. Andrew Erickson, "Good Riddance to the INF Treaty: Washington Shouldn't Tie Its Own Hands in Asia," *Foreign Affairs*, August 29, 2019, https://www.foreignaffairs.com/articles/china/2019-08-29/good-riddance-inf-treaty.

107. Adam Mount and Toby Dalton, "America's Ironclad Alliance with South Korea Is a Touch Rusty," *Foreign Policy*, April 27, 2023, https://foreignpolicy.com/2023/04/27/biden-yoon-summit-north-south-korea-nuclear-assurances.

108. Toby Dalton, Karl Friedhoff, and Lami Kim, *Thinking Nuclear: South Korean Attitudes on Nuclear Weapons* (Chicago: Chicago Council on Global Affairs, February 21), 2022, https://globalaffairs.org/sites/default/files/2022-02/Korea%20Nuclear%20Report%20PDF.pdf.

109. Dasl Yoon and Timothy W. Martin, "South Korea's Interest in Nuclear Weapons Hasn't Gone Away—It's Just on Hold," *The Wall Street Journal*, September 16, 2023, https://www.wsj.com/world/asia/south-koreas-interest-in-nuclear-weapons-hasnt-gone-awayits-just-on-hold-7c91cf8a.

110. Martha Raddatz and Luis Martinez, "ABC News Exclusive: Inside the US Nuclear Ballistic Missile Submarine in South Korea," *ABC News*, July 20, 2023, https://abcnews.go.com/International/abc-news-exclusive-us-nuclear-ballistic-missile-submarine/story?id=101615235.

111. Anya Fink, *Nuclear-Armed Sea-Launched Cruise Missile (SLCM-N)* (Congressional Research Service, October 17), 2024, https://crsreports.congress.gov/product/pdf/IF/IF12084.

112. "Japan's Efforts on Nuclear Disarmament and Non-Proliferation," *Ministry of Foreign Affairs of Japan*, accessed November 15, 2024, https://www.mofa.go.jp/policy/un/disarmament/nnp/index.html.

113. *The 1987 Constitution of the Republic of the Philippines*, Article II, Section 8, ratified February 2, 1987.

114. Fink, *Nuclear-Armed Sea-Launched Cruise Missile (SLCM-N)*.

115. Air-launched nuclear-armed Long Range Stand-Off (LRSO) weapons are advanced cruise missiles designed to be launched from aircraft and deliver nuclear warheads over distances of more than 1,500 miles while remaining outside the range of enemy defenses. These weapons enhance a nation's strategic deterrence capability by allowing precise, long-range nuclear strikes without putting the launching aircraft at risk; Center for Arms Control and Non-Proliferation, *Fact Sheet: Nuclear Sea-Launched Cruise Missiles* (Washington, DC: Center for Arms Control and Non-Proliferation, May 2024), https://armscontrolcenter.org/wp-content/uploads/2021/06/Nuclear-Sea-Launched-Cruise-Missiles-Fact-Sheet-v3.pdf; Bryant Harris, "GOP Moves to Instate Sea-Launched Cruise Missile Nuclear Program," *Defense News*, June 21, 2023, https://www.defensenews.com/congress/budget/2023/06/22/gop-moves-to-instate-sea-launched-cruise-missile-nuclear-program.

116. Eric Heginbotham and Richard J. Samuels, "Vulnerable U.S. Alliances in Northeast Asia: The Nuclear Implications," *Washington Quarterly* 44, no. 1 (2021): 170; Brad Roberts, *Living with a Nuclear-Arming North Korea: Deterrence Decisions in a Deteriorating Threat Environment* (Washington, DC: Stimson Center, November 2020), https://www.38north.org/wp-content/uploads/pdf/38-North-SR-2011-Brad-Roberts-Nuclear-North-Korea-Deterrence.pdf, 14, 17.

117. Hans M. Kristensen, Matt Korda, Eliana Johns, and Mackenzie Knight, "Nuclear Weapons Sharing, 2023," *Bulletin of the Atomic Scientists*, November 8, 2023, https://thebulletin.org/premium/2023-11/nuclear-weapons-sharing-2023.

118. U.S. nuclear sharing was more permissive in the early years of the Cold War, but the Kennedy administration tightened the rules in the early 1960s. Joshua Byun and Do Young Lee, "The Case Against Nuclear Sharing in East Asia," *Washington Quarterly* 44, no. 4 (October 2021): 71; Peter Douglas Feaver, *Guarding the Guardians: Civilian Control of Nuclear Weapons in the United States* (Ithaca, NY: Cornell University Press, 1992), 183–198.

119. Jesse Johnson, "Japan Should Consider Hosting U.S. Nuclear Weapons, Abe Says," *Japan Times*, February 27, 2022, https://www.japantimes.co.jp/news/2022/02/27/national/politics-diplomacy/shinzo-abe-japan-nuclear-weapons-taiwan.

120. Yuki Tatsumi, Pamela Kennedy, and Kenji Nagayoshi, *Japan's Strategic Future and Implications for the U.S.-Japan Alliance* (Washington, DC: Stimson Center, February 28), 2024, https://www.stimson.org/2024/japans-strategic-future-and-implications-for-the-us-japan-alliance.

121. Jennifer Ahn, "The Evolution of South Korea's Nuclear Weapons Policy Debate," *Council on Foreign Relations*, August 16, 2022, https://www.cfr.org/blog/evolution-south-koreas-nuclear-weapons-policy-debate; Kim Soo-yeon, "Yoon Says He Will Request Redeployment of U.S. Tactical Nukes in Case of Emergency," *Yonhap*, September 22, 2021, https://en.yna.co.kr/view/AEN20210922005300320.

122. Ministry of Foreign Affairs of the Republic of Korea, "Joint Declaration on the Denuclearization of the Korean Peninsula," January 20, 1992, https://www.mofa.go.kr/eng/brd/m_5476/view.do?seq=305870&multi_itm_seq=0&itm_seq_1=0&itm_seq_2=0&page=6.

123. Robert E. Kelly and Min-hyung Kim, "Why South Korea Should Go Nuclear," *Foreign Affairs*, January 31, 2024, https://www.foreignaffairs.com/north-korea/why-south-korea-should-go-nuclear

124. Congressional Commission on the Strategic Posture of the United States, *America's Strategic Posture* (Washington, DC: Congressional Commission on the Strategic Posture of the United States, 2023), 7.

125. Congressional Commission on the Strategic Posture of the United States, *America's Strategic Posture*, 7.

126. Congressional Commission on the Strategic Posture of the United States, *America's Strategic Posture*, 33.

127. Congressional Commission on the Strategic Posture of the United States, *America's Strategic Posture*, 60.

128. William Hennigan, "Inside the Mission to Modernize America's Nuclear Missiles," *TIME*, September 13, 2022, https://time.com/6212698/nuclear-missiles-icbm-triad-upgrade.

129. The White House, "Fact Sheet: An Enduring Commitment to the U.S. Nuclear Deterrent," November 17, 2010, https://obamawhitehouse.archives.gov/the-press-office/2010/11/17/fact-sheet-enduring-commitment-us-nuclear-deterrent.

130. Air Force Nuclear Weapons Center, "Sentinel ICBM," n.d., https://www.afnwc.af.mil/Weapon-Systems/Sentinel-ICBM-LGM-35A.

131. Based on limited public information, the B-21 looks like a very long-range stealth bomber, akin to the B-2, the only aircraft in U.S. service that can remain stealthy while carrying air-launched standoff weapons—missiles with long-enough ranges that the attacker can evade defensive fire. However, the B-21 will have a number of conventional missions alongside nuclear delivery, particularly in a China conflict, where it would be used alongside U.S. submarines to penetrate and break China's reconnaissance network; Aerotech News, "B-21 Bomber to Be Unveiled First Week in December," September 21, 2022, https://www.aerotechnews.com/blog/2022/09/21/b-21-bomber-to-be-unveiled-first-week-in-december; Maya Carlin, "The U.S. Air Force's B-21 Raider Problem Gives Me the Chills," *The National Interest*, May 16, 2024, https://nationalinterest.org/blog/buzz/b-21-nightmare-numbers-problem-air-force-cant-fix-208059.

132. A "dial-a-yield" weapon is an explosive device whose power can be adjusted before use, allowing military planners to tailor the explosion to specific targets. This capability applies to both nuclear and conventional weapons; Andrea Howard, "Tactical Nuclear Weapons Are Back," *Proceedings* 144, no. 4 (April 2018): 1382, https://www.usni.org/magazines/proceedings/2018/april/tactical-nuclear-weapons-are-back.

133. While a submarine can quickly submerge and move away after launching a missile, the initial launch still reveals its location, making it temporarily vulnerable to detection and potential counterattack. Additionally, the use of a strategic asset like an SSBN for a non-strategic strike could compromise its primary role in ensuring a credible second-strike capability.

134. Chinese theoretical writings are clear on this, particularly Xiao, *Science of Military Strategy*, 2022. See also Stokes et al., *China's Space and Counterspace Activities*.

135. Colin Demarest, "Electronic Warfare in Ukraine Has Lessons for US Weapons, Navigation," *DefenseNews*, May 6, 2024, https://www.defensenews.com/electronic-warfare/2024/05/06/electronic-warfare-in-ukraine-has-lessons-for-us-weapons-navigation; Lara Seligman, "Russia Jamming U.S. Smart Bombs in Ukraine, Leaked Docs Say," *Politico*,

April 12, 2023, https://www.politico.com/news/2023/04/12/russia-jamming-u-s-smart-bombs-in-ukraine-leaked-docs-say-00091600.

136. Cyber operations also require significant planning and persistence. Thus, initial disruptions at the outbreak of a war could be significant. Over time, both belligerents might adapt and build more resilient space-based arrays, but this would happen only in a long war.

137. Ria Urban, "Space Systems Command Facilitates Multiple Contract Awards for Proliferated Low Earth Orbit Satellite-Based Services," *Space Impulse*, July 24, 2023, https://spaceimpulse.com/2023/07/28/space-systems-command-facilitates-multiple-contract-awards-for-proliferated-low-earth-orbit-satellite-based-services.

138. U.S. Space Force, *Space Threat Fact Sheet*.

139. David E. Hoffman, "Mutually Assured Misperception on SDI," *Arms Control Association*, October 2010, https://www.armscontrol.org/act/2010-10/mutually-assured-misperception-sdi.

140. U.S. ballistic missile defenses rely on a layered architecture of complementary systems. The Aegis Ballistic Missile Defense (BMD) is a naval-based system that uses shipboard interceptors to detect, track, and destroy short- to intermediate-range ballistic missiles during their midcourse phase in space. The Patriot missile system, a ground-based platform, counters tactical ballistic missiles, cruise missiles, and advanced aircraft at medium to long ranges. The Terminal High Altitude Area Defense (THAAD) system, also ground-based, intercepts short- to intermediate-range ballistic missiles during their terminal phase with a hit-to-kill approach. For homeland defense, the Ground-Based Interceptor (GBI) program deploys interceptors in Alaska and California to neutralize long-range ballistic missiles during their midcourse phase in space.

141. *Fact Sheet: U.S. Ballistic Missile Defense* (Washington, DC: Center for Arms Control and Non-Proliferation, June 12), 2023, https://armscontrolcenter.org/wp-content/uploads/2021/04/U.S.-Ballistic-Missile-Defense-Fact-Sheet-June-2023.pdf.

142. Gao Wen, 抢抓人工智能发展的历史性机遇 [Seize the historic opportunity for the development of artificial intelligence], Renmin Ribao, February 24, 2025, p. 9. For an English translation, see Bill Bishop, *Notion*, accessed March 3, 2025, https://abalone-taleggio-85c.notion.site/Seizing-the-Historic-Opportunity-for-the-Development-of-Artificial-Intelligence-1a41b804835280a78b44d17e0ef92a04.

143. Jeffrey Ding and Allan Dafoe, "Engines of Power: Electricity, AI, and General-purpose, Military Transformations," *European Journal of International Security* 8, no. 3 (2023): 377–394.

144. See, for example, Aschenbrenner, "Situational Awareness."

145. Dario Amodei and Matt Pottinger, "Trump Can Keep America's AI Advantage," *Wall Street Journal*, January 6, 2025, https://www.wsj.com/opinion/trump-can-keep-americas-ai-advantage-china-chips-data-eccdce91;
Dario Amodei, "Machines of Loving Grace: How AI Could Transform the World for the Better,"; *darioamodei.com*, October 2024, https://darioamodei.com/machines-of-loving-grace; Sam Altman, "The Intelligence Age," ia.samaltman.com, September 23, 2024, https://ia.samaltman.com; George Hammond, "Elon Musk Predicts AI Will Overtake Human Intelligence Next Year," *Financial Times*, April 9, 2024, https://www.ft.com/content/027b133f-f7e3-459d-95bf-8afd815ae23d. For a counter-argument, see Billy Perrigo, "Meta's AI Chief Yann LeCun on AGI, Open-Source, and AI Risk," *Time*, February 13, 2024, https://time.com/6694432/yann-lecun-meta-ai-interview.

146. Nick Bostrom, *Superintelligence: Paths, Dangers, Strategies* (Oxford: Oxford University Press, 2016).

147. For a forceful rebuttal of the AGI concept, see https://time.com/6694432/yann-lecun-meta-ai-interview.

148. Richard Danzig, *Machines, Bureaucracies, and Markets as Artificial Intelligences* (Washington, DC: Center for Security and Emerging Technology, 2022), https://cset.georgetown.edu/wp-content/uploads/Machines-Bureaucracies-and-Markets-as-Artificial-Intelligences.pdf.

149. Amodei, "Machines of Loving Grace."

150. See, for example, Benjamin Jensen, Yasir Atalan, and Dan Tadross, " It Is Time to Democratize Wargaming Using Generative AI," Center for Strategic and International Studies, February 22, 2024, https://www.csis.org/analysis/it-time-democratize-wargaming-using-generative-ai.

151. Jacquelyn Schneider, Benjamin Schechter, and Rachael Shaffer, "Hacking Nuclear Stability: Wargaming Technology, Uncertainty, and Escalation," *International Organization* 77, no. 3 (2023): 633–667, https://doi.org/10.1017/S0020818323000115; Keir A. Lieber and Daryl G. Press, "The New Era of Counterforce: Technological Change and the Future of Nuclear Deterrence," *International Security* 41, no. 4 (2017): 9–49, https://doi.org/10.1162/ISEC_a_00273. See also Robert Jervis, *Perception and Misperception in International Politics* (Princeton, NJ: Princeton University Press, 1976); Ariel Levite, George Perkovich, and Jinghua Lyu et al., "China-U.S. Cyber-Nuclear C3 Stability" (Working Paper, Carnegie Endowment for International Peace, 2021); Rose Gottemoeller, "The Standstill Conundrum: The Advent of Second-Strike Vulnerability and Options to Address It," *Texas National Security Review* 4, no. 4 (2021): 115–124, https://dx.doi.org/10.26153/tsw/17496.

152. David Rothwell, *The Impact of Artificial Intelligence on Undersea Warfare Tactics* (Newport, RI: Naval War College, 2023), 3–6.

153. Henry Kissinger, Eric Schmidt, and Craig Mundie, *Genesis: Artificial Intelligence, Hope, and the Human Spirit* (New York: Little, Brown, 2024).

154. Sam Altman, Reflections, January 5, 2025 https://blog.samaltman.com/reflections

155. James Black, Mattias Eken, Jacob Parakilas et al., *Strategic Competition in the Age of AI: Emerging Risks and Opportunities from Military Use of Artificial Intelligence* (Santa Monica, CA: RAND, 2024), https://www.rand.org/content/dam/rand/pubs/research_reports/RRA3200/RRA3295-1/RAND_RRA3295-1.pdf.

156. For a trenchant criticism of the concept of "human-in-the-loop," see Richard Danzig, *Technology Roulette: Managing Loss of Control as Many Militaries Pursue Technological Superiority* (Washington, DC: Center for a New American Security, 2018), https://s3.amazonaws.com/files.cnas.org/documents/CNASReport-Technology-Roulette-Final.pdf. See also *Stanford Emerging Technology Review 2025*, ed. Herbert S. Lin (Stanford, CA: Stanford University, 2025), 33. For U.S. doctrine, see U.S. Department of Defense, *2022 National Defense Strategy of the United States of America*. On Russian thinking, see Samuel Bendett, "The Role of AI in Russia's Confrontation with the West," Center for a New American Security, May 3, 2024, https://www.cnas.org/publications/reports/the-role-of-ai-in-russias-confrontation-with-the-west. On the U.S.–China dialogue on this issue, see Jarrett Renshaw and Trevor Hunnicutt, "Biden, Xi Agree That Humans, Not AI, Should Control Nuclear Arms," *Reuters*, November 17, 2024, https://www.reuters.com/world/biden-xi-agreed-that-humans-not-ai-should-control-nuclear-weapons-white-

house-2024-11-16/. See "Readout of President Joe Biden's Meeting with President Xi Jinping of the People's Republic of China," U.S. Mission China, November 17, 2024, https://china.usembassy-china.org.cn/readout-of-president-joe-bidens-meeting-with-president-xi-jinping-of-the-peoples-republic-of-china-3.

157. Danzig, *Technology Roulette*.

158. Charles Perrow, *Normal Accidents: Living with High-Risk Technologies* (Princeton, NJ: Princeton University Press, 1999); Scott D. Sagan, *The Limits of Safety: Organizations, Accidents and Nuclear Weapons* (Princeton, NJ: Princeton University Press, 1993).

159. As Danzig notes, "What appear to be two separate systems—the machine and the human—are interdependent, and the greater influence on the decision resides in the machinery. This is a common situation in the modern age. Human decisionmakers are riders traveling across obscured terrain with little or no ability to assess the powerful beasts that carry and guide them." Danzig, *Technology Roulette*, 16; Hannah Kelley and Bill Drexel, "China Is Flirting with AI Catastrophe," *Foreign Affairs*, May 17, 2023, https://www.foreignaffairs.com/china/china-flirting-ai-catastrophe. On the counterargument that existential risk from AI is exaggerated, see Marc Andreessen, "Why AI Will Save the World," *Andreessen Horowitz*, June 6, 2023, https://a16z.com/ai-will-save-the-world.

160. On China's views on AI safety, see Matt Sheehan, "China's Views on AI Safety Are Changing—Quickly," *Carnegie Endowment for International Peace*, August 27, 2024, https://carnegieendowment.org/research/2024/08/china-artificial-intelligence-ai-safety-regulation.

161. In a February 2025 interview, Amodei called for U.S. policymakers to aim for a stable two-year lead over China in cutting-edge models: "Let's say we're two years ahead. Maybe we can spend six months of those two years to ensure that the things we build ourselves are safe. In other words, we're still ahead and we're able to make things safe. If things are evenly matched, then we have to worry that what they build isn't safe, and at the same time we have to worry about them dominating us with the technology. That puts us in a very bad dilemma where there are no options; Jordan Schneider and Lily Ottinger, "Anthropic's Dario Amodei on AI Competition," *ChinaTalk*, February 5, 2025, https://www.chinatalk.media/p/anthropics-dario-amodei-on-ai-competition. Others have argued that China is more likely to produce AI accidents because of a general cultural attitude toward risk in scientific innovation; Kelley and Drexel, "China Is Flirting with AI Catastrophe."

162. Jake Sullivan, "The Biden Administration's International Economic Agenda: A Conversation with National Security Advisor Jake Sullivan," *Brookings Institution*, April 27, 2023, https://www.brookings.edu/events/the-biden-administrations-international-economic-agenda-a-conversation-with-national-security-advisor-jake-sullivan.

163. White House, "Removing Barriers to American Leadership in Artificial Intelligence," January 23, 2025 https://www.whitehouse.gov/presidential-actions/2025/01/removing-barriers-to-american-leadership-in-artificial-intelligence.

164. Diego Mendoza, "China Is Falling Behind US in AI Race, Chinese Premier Warned," *Semafor*, March 16, 2024, https://www.semafor.com/article/03/15/2024/china-is-falling-behind-us-in-ai-race-chinese-premier-warned.

165. Xingwu Sun, Yanfeng Chen, Yiqing Huang, et al., "Hunyuan-Large: An Open-Source MoE Model with 52 Billion Activated Parameters by Tencent," *ArXiv* 2411.02265, Version 3 (2024), https://doi.org/10.48550/arXiv.2411.02265.

166. "Christophe Fouquet, CEO ASML: 'Je moest eens weten hoeveel fuck-ups er nodig zijn om de meest complexe machine ter wereld te maken'," *NRC*, December 18, 2024, https://www.nrc.nl/nieuws/2024/12/18/christophe-fouquet-ceo-asml-je-moest-eens-weten-hoeveel-fuck-ups-er-nodig-zijn-om-de-meest-complexe-machine-ter-wereld-te-maken-a4877089.

167. Alexander Ward and Asa Fitch, "Raimondo Says Holding Back China in Chips Race Is a 'Fool's Errand'," *Wall Street Journal*, December 22, 2024, https://www.wsj.com/politics/national-security/china-biden-chip-manufacturing-gina-raimondo-b98c2606.

168. Yoko Kubota, "China Tells Its AI Leaders to Avoid U.S. Travel over Security Concerns," *WSJ*, March 1, 2025, https://www.wsj.com/world/china/china-ai-us-travel-advisory-ff248349.

169. Helen Toner, Jenny Xiao, and Jeffrey Ding, "The Illusion of China's AI Prowess," *Foreign Affairs*, June 2, 2023, https://www.foreignaffairs.com/china/illusion-chinas-ai-prowess-regulation-helen-toner; Jeffrey Ding, *Technology and the Rise of Great Powers: How Diffusion Shapes Economic Competition* (Princeton, NJ: Princeton University Press, 2024).

170. Eleanor Olcott and Wenjie Ding, "DeepSeek spreads across China with Beijing's Backing," *Financial Times*, February 26, 2025, https://www.ft.com/content/5684fb1f-1a84-4542-8fe9-2fcae9653f87.

171. Amodei and Pottinger, "Trump Can Keep America's AI Advantage." On the high energy demands of AI models, see *Stanford Emerging Technology Review 2025*, 23.

172. Annie Jacobsen, *Operation Paperclip: The Secret Intelligence Program that Brought Nazi Scientists to America* (New York: Little, Brown, 2014).

173. For two clever ideas, see Tom Fist and Erich Grunewald, "Preventing AI Chip Smuggling to China," *CNAS*, October 24, 2023, https://www.cnas.org/publications/reports/preventing-ai-chip-smuggling-to-china; Onni Aarne, Tim Fist and Caleb Withers, "Secure, Governable Chips," *CNAS*, January 8, 2024, https://www.cnas.org/publications/reports/secure-governable-chips

174. Zelikow et al., *Defense Against the AI Dark Arts*.

175. Initiatives like the Hoover Institution's SECURE program could play a key role in this effort. Glenn Tiffert, "The Hoover Institution Launches NSF-Backed SECURE Initiative, Building Data and Tools to Analyze Research Security Risks and Opportunities," *Hoover Institution*, September 8, 2024, https://www.hoover.org/press/hoover-institution-launches-nsf-backed-secure-initiative-building-data-and-tools.

176. *Business Times*, "TSMC Supplier's CEO Dismisses AI Concerns after Nvidia Wipeout," September 5, 2024, https://www.businesstimes.com.sg/international/global/tsmc-suppliers-ceo-dismisses-ai-concerns-after-nvidia-wipeout

177. See, for example, comments by U.S. Air Force Secretary Frank Kendall in John A. Tirpak, "Kendall: In US-China 'Race for Technological Superiority,' AI May Be the Key," *Air & Space Forces Magazine*, October 29, 2024, https://www.airandspaceforces.com/kendall-us-china-race-technological-superiority-ai.

178. Aaron Bateman, "The Enduring Impact of Reagan's Strategic Defense Initiative," *Arms Control Association*, September 2023, https://www.armscontrol.org/act/2023-09/features/enduring-impact-reagans-strategic-defense-initiative. For an account of how SDI shaped Chinese perceptions of U.S. intentions in space, see Alexis A. Blanc, Nathan Beauchamp-Mustafaga, Khrystyna Holynska, M. Scott Bond, and Stephen J. Flanagan, *Chinese and Russian Perceptions of and Responses to U.S. Military Activities in the Space*

Domain (Santa Monica, CA: RAND, 2022), https://www.rand.org/content/dam/rand/pubs/research_reports/RRA1800/RRA1835-1/RAND_RRA1835-1.pdf, 9–13

179. The best analysis of this case, using the theoretical framework of cross-domain deterrence, is Brendan Rittenhouse Green and Austin Long, "Signaling with Secrets: Evidence on Soviet Perceptions and Counterforce Developments in the Late Cold War," in Gartzke and Lindsay, *Cross-Domain Deterrence*, 205–233.

180. Anton Shilov, "Nvidia's Defeatured H20 GPUs Sell Surprisingly Well in China—50% Increase Every Quarter in Sanctions-Compliant GPUs for Chinese AI Customers," *Tom's Hardware*, December 30, 2024, https://www.tomshardware.com/tech-industry/artificial-intelligence/nvidias-defeatured-h20-gpus-in-china-sell-surprisingly-well-50-percent-increase-every-quarter-in-sanctions-compliant-gpus-for-chinese-ai-customers; "Google, Microsoft Offer Nvidia Chips to Chinese Companies, *The Information* Reports," *Reuters*, July 17, 2024, https://www.reuters.com/technology/google-microsoft-offer-nvidia-chips-chinese-companies-information-reports-2024-07-17.

181. Rebecca Arcesati and Caroline Meinhardt, "China Bets on Open-Source Technologies to Boost Domestic Innovation," *MERICS*, May 19, 2021, https://merics.org/en/report/china-bets-open-source-technologies-boost-domestic-innovation; Paul Triolo, "The Evolution of China's Semiconductor Industry under U.S. Export Controls," *American Affairs*, November 20, 2024, https://americanaffairsjournal.org/2024/11/the-evolution-of-chinas-semiconductor-industry-under-u-s-export-controls.

182. James Pomfret and Jessie Pang, "Exclusive: Chinese Researchers Develop AI Model for Military Use on Back of Meta's Llama," *Reuters*, November 1, 2024, https://www.reuters.com/technology/artificial-intelligence/chinese-researchers-develop-ai-model-military-use-back-metas-llama-2024-11-01; Gabriel Honrada, "China's People's Liberation Army Weaponizing Meta's AI," *Asia Times*, November 2, 2024, https://asiatimes.com/2024/11/chinas-peoples-liberation-army-weaponizing-metas-ai.

183. Mark Zuckerberg, "Open Source AI Is the Path Forward," *Meta*, July 23, 2024, https://about.fb.com/news/2024/07/open-source-ai-is-the-path-forward; *AI in America: OpenAI's Economic Blueprint* (San Francisco, CA: OpenAI, 2025), https://cdn.openai.com/global-affairs/ai-in-america-oais-economic-blueprint-20250109.pdf.

184. For one example, see Ben Thompson, "AI Promise and Chip Precariousness," *Stratechery*, February 25, 2025, https://stratechery.com/2025/ai-promise-and-chip-precariousness.

185. Alexander Downes's meta-analysis of the literature finds that compellent threats succeed around 35 percent of the time; Alexander Downes, "Step Aside or Face the Consequences: Explaining the Success and Failure of Compellent Threats to Remove Foreign Leaders," in *Coercion: The Power to Hurt in International Politics*, eds. Kelly Greenhill and Peter Krause (Oxford: Oxford University Press, 2018), 97.

186. As Schelling notes, threats without deadlines, or with overly loose deadlines, make compliance unnecessary. But overly tight deadlines make compliance impossible. Neither is credible. See Schelling, *Arms and Influence*, 72.

187. "Uproar over a Brink," *Time*, January 23, 1956, https://time.com/archive/6799334/foreign-relations-uproar-over-a-brink.

CHAPTER 7

1. This chapter is adapted from Bromley and Freymann, *On Day One*, and Bromley and Freymann, "The Malacca Myth."

2. For a contrarian argument that World War I did not represent a failure of economic interdependence, see Erik Gartzke and Yonatan Lupu, "Trading on Preconceptions: Why World War I Was Not a Failure of Economic Interdependence," *International Security* 36, no. 4 (Spring 2012): 115–150, https://doi.org/10.1162/ISEC_a_00078.

3. Norman Angell, *The Great Illusion: A Study of the Relation of Military Power in Nations to Their Economic and Social Advantage* (New York: G. P. Putnam, 1910), 33.

4. Angell, *The Great Illusion*, 33.

5. Nicholas A. Lambert, *Planning Armageddon: British Economic Warfare and the First World War* (Cambridge, MA: Harvard University Press, 2012), 2.

6. Avner Offer, "The Blockade of Germany and the Strategy of Starvation, 1914–1918," in *Great War, Total War: Combat and Mobilization on the Western Front, 1914–1918*, eds. Roger Chickering and Stig Förster (Cambridge: Cambridge University Press, 2013), 169–88.

7. Lambert, *Planning Armageddon*.

8. Some of the details of Lambert's analysis are contested, but the basic point stands. For a contrary view, see David G. Morgan-Owen, "An 'Intermediate Blockade'? British North Sea Strategy, 1912–1914," *War in History* 22, no. 4 (2015): 478–502.

9. David Stevenson, *With Our Backs to the Wall: Victory and Defeat in 1918* (Cambridge, MA: Belknap Press of Harvard University Press, 2011). For the role of American finance, see Adam Tooze, *The Deluge: The Great War, America, and the Remaking of the Global Order, 1916–1931* (New York: Viking, 2014), 38–45.

10. Annie Linskey, "Trump Says He Did Tariff Pause Because of 'Yippy' Reaction," *Wall Street Journal*, April 9, 2025, https://www.wsj.com/livecoverage/stock-market-trump-tariffs-trade-war-04-09-25/card/trump-says-he-did-tariff-pause-because-yippee-reaction-4Y6So9Q4WhgSovWY8li1.

11. Jeff Mason and Andrea Shalal, "Amid Turmoil over Tariffs, Bessent Rises in Trump Trade World," *Reuters*, April 11, 2025.

12. Select Committee on the Strategic Competition Between the United States and the Chinese Communist Party, *Reset, Prevent, Build* (Washington, DC: U.S. House of Representatives, 2024).

13. The political science literature shows that costly economic signaling plays a key role in communicating resolve, thereby deterring militarized disputes. See Erik Gartzke, Quan Li, and Charles Boehmer, "Investing in the Peace: Economic Interdependence and International Conflict," *International Organization* 55, no. 2 (2001): 391–438, https://doi.org/10.1162/00208180151140612.

14. Mariya Grinberg, "Wartime Commercial Policy and Trade between Enemies," *International Security* 46, no. 4 (Summer 2021), https://doi.org/10.1162/isec_a_00412.

15. Barry Eichengreen, the preeminent expert on the history of dollar hegemony, has been arguing for over a decade that the most likely alternative to dollar hegemony is a multicurrency system, not the replacement of the dollar with another hegemonic currency. See Barry Eichengreen, "Can the Dollar Remain King of Currencies?," *Financial Times*, March 21, 2025; Barry Eichengreen, *Exorbitant Privilege: The Rise and Fall of the Dollar and the Future of the International Monetary System* (New York: Oxford University Press, 2012).

16. 刁大明、王丽, "中美关系中的'脱钩':概念、影响与前景" *"Decoupling" in China-U.S. Relations: Concept, Impact, and Prospects*, 中国智库网 *China Think Tanks Network*, 2019, https://www.chinathinktanks.org.cn/content/detail/id/jhzrdu48.

17. Jeff Mason, Chris Sanders, and David Brunnstrom, "Trump Again Raises Idea of Decoupling Economy from China," *Reuters*, September 7, 2020.

18. "President Biden Takes Action to Protect American Workers and Businesses from China's Unfair Trade Practices," *The White House*, May 14, 2024, https://bidenwhitehouse. archives.gov/briefing-room/statements-releases/2024/05/14/fact-sheet-president-biden-takes-action-to-protect-american-workers-and-businesses-from-chinas-unfair-trade-practices/.

19. Brenda Goh, "EU Does Not Want to Decouple from China but Must Protect Itself, Says EU Trade Chief," *Reuters*, September 22, 2023.

20. "Remarks by National Security Advisor Jake Sullivan on Renewing American Economic Leadership at the Brookings Institution," *White House*, April 27, 2023.

21. *Testimony Before the U.S.-China Economic and Security Review Commission: Key Economic Strategies for Leveling the U.S.-China Playing Field: Trade, Investment, and Technology*, 118th Cong. (2024) (Statement of Jamieson L. Greer).

22. Bruce Crumley, "Congress Delays Threatened DJI Drone Ban for a Year," *Inc.*, December 23, 2024, https://www.inc.com/bruce-crumley/congress-delays-threatened-dji-drone-ban-for-a-year/91069950; "Biosecure Act Fails to Be Enacted," *MichBio*, December 31, 2024, https://michbio.org/biosecure-act-fails-to-be-enacted/; Anna Swanson and Tripp Mickle, "Biden Administration Ignites Firestorm With Rules Governing A.I.'s Global Spread," *New York Times*, January 9, 2025, https://www.nytimes.com/2025/01/09/business/economy/biden-ai-chips-rules.html.

23. 闻伟英，"美国对华制裁的影响与中国的反制路径" *The Impact of U.S. Sanctions on China and China's Countermeasures*, 腾讯新闻 *Tencent News*, November 6, 2024, https://news.qq.com/rain/a/20241106A08U1Y00.

24. "Employment in Industry (% of Total Employment) (Modeled ILO Estimate)—China," *The World Bank*, accessed January 19, 2024, https://data.worldbank.org/indicator/SL.IND.EMPL.ZS?locations=CN.

25. Matthew C. Klein and Michael Pettis, *Trade Wars Are Class Wars: How Rising Inequality Distorts the Global Economy and Threatens International Peace* (New Haven, CT: Yale University Press, 2020).

26. Klein and Pettis, *Trade Wars Are Class Wars*.

27. For how this could be weaponized in a crisis, see Charlie Vest and Agatha Kratz, *Sanctioning China in a Taiwan Crisis: Scenarios and Risks, Atlantic Council/Rhodium Group Report*, https://www.atlanticcouncil.org/in-depth-research-reports/report/sanctioning-china-in-a-taiwan-crisis-scenarios-and-risks/#introduction.

28. Zhang Han, "Xi Stresses Irreversible Trend of Economic Globalization to Dutch PM Rutte," *Global Times*, March 27, 2024. For an illuminating view of how prominent Chinese scholars are grappling with this problem, see Danube Institute, "Counter Globalization and China's Foreign Policy—Lecture by Professor Yan Xuetong," *YouTube*, April 22, 2024.

29. Susan Gordon, Michael Mullen, and David Sacks, *U.S.-Taiwan Relations in a New Era: Responding to a More Assertive China* (New York: Council on Foreign Relations, 2023), 82.

30. Gordon, Mullen, and Sacks, *U.S.-Taiwan Relations in a New Era*, 82.

31. Kaush Arha, Peter Harrell, and Clete Willems, "A New U.S. Economic Playbook to Lead the World Economy and Counter China," *Atlantic Council*, May 7, 2024; Jack Connolly, *The Fourth Fighting Service: The Early Development of British Economic Statecraft, Blavatnik School of Government*, Working Paper, January 2024, 1–40.

32. The authoritative survey of China's resilience is Logan Wright, Agatha Kratz, Charlie Vest, and Matthew Mingey, "Retaliation and Resilience: China's Economic Statecraft in a Taiwan Crisis," *Rhodium Group*, April 2, 2024. On intermediate sanctions, see Emily Kilcrease, "No Winners in This Game: Assessing the U.S. Playbook for Sanctioning China," *Center for a New American Security*, December 2023; Agatha Kratz and Charlie Vest, *Sanctioning China in a Taiwan Crisis: Scenarios and Risks, Rhodium Group*, June 22, 2023.

33. Henry Farrell and Abraham L. Newman, *Underground Empire: How America Weaponized the World Economy* (New York: Henry Holt and Co., 2023); Daniel Drezner, Henry Farrell, and Abraham L. Newman, *The Uses and Abuses of Weaponized Interdependence* (Washington, DC: Brookings Institution Press, 2021).

34. More broadly, weaponized interdependence can involve denying adversaries access to critical resources, manipulating access to information, or allowing target states to participate in the network only under specific conditions.

35. The best study of how the Obama, Trump, and Biden administrations have operationalized these ideas is Edward Fishman, *Chokepoints: American Power in the Age of Economic Warfare* (New York: Penguin, 2025).

36. Henry Farrell and Abraham Newman, who proposed the weaponized interdependence concept, do not discuss its relevance to a Taiwan crisis. Indeed, they have called for U.S.–China cooperation in developing strategies of weaponized interdependence to advance a global agenda on climate change and other issues of global concern. See Farrell and Newman, *Underground Empire*.

37. Emily Kilcrease, "No Winners in This Game: Assessing the U.S. Playbook for Sanctioning China," *Center for a New American Security*, December 1, 2023. For a high-level discussion of strategic implications, see Emily Kilcrease, "America's China Strategy Has a Credibility Problem," *Foreign Affairs*, May 7, 2024.

38. Gordon, Mullen, and Sacks, *U.S.-Taiwan Relations in a New Era*, 82, 93.

39. Blackwill and Zelikow, *A Strategy to Prevent War*, 45.

40. For a thorough discussion of potential U.S. sanctions options, see Kilcrease, "No Winners in This Game."

41. "Sullivan Introduces S.T.A.N.D. with Taiwan Act," *Sullivan Senate*, January 20, 2022, https://www.sullivan.senate.gov/newsroom/press-releases/sullivan-introduces-stand-with-taiwan-act#:~:text=Madam%20President%2C%20today%20I%20introduce, People's%20Liberation%20Army%20initiates%20a.

42. The Committee has endorsed the STAND with Taiwan Act (H.R. 2372). See Select Committee on the Strategic Competition Between the United States and the Chinese Communist Party, *Reset, Prevent, Build*, 19.

43. Philip Zelikow, "A Fresh Look at the Russian Assets: A Proposal for International Resolution of Sanctioned Accounts," January 9, 2025, https://www.hoover.org/research/fresh-look-russian-assets-proposal-international-resolution-sanctioned-accounts.

44. This section is adapted from Bromley and Freymann, "The Malacca Myth." For arguments in favor of a Malacca blockade, see Charles L. Glaser, "A U.S.-China Grand Bargain? The Hard Choice Between Military Competition and Accommodation," *International Security* 39, no. 4 (2015): 49–90, https://www.jstor.org/stable/24480607; Llewelyn Hughes and Austin Long, "Is There an Oil Weapon?: Security Implications of Changes in the Structure of the International Oil Market," *International Security* 39, no. 3 (2014): 152–189, https://doi.org/10.1162/ISEC_a_00188; Michael Beckley, "The Emerging Military Balance in East Asia: How China's Neighbors Can Check Chinese

Naval Expansion," *International Security* 42, no. 2 (2017): 93, https://doi.org/10.1162/ISEC_a_00294.

45. See, for example, Thomas X. Hammes, "Offshore Control: A Proposed Strategy for an Unlikely Conflict," *Strategic Forum* 278 (2012): 1; Arzan Tarapore, "Building Strategic Leverage in the Indian Ocean Region," *The Washington Quarterly* 43, no. 4 (2020): 207–237, https://ndupress.ndu.edu/Portals/68/Documents/stratforum/SF-278.pdf?ver=2014-08-21-140306-147.

46. If ordered, U.S. bombers could probably lay between 840 and 3,880 mines at a time and reseed them faster than China could clear them. The PLAN has only twenty minesweeper vessels, and comparable historical case studies suggest that each could clear an average of just 0.8 to 2 mines per day. However, China has its own offensive mine-laying capabilities. Obviously, a U.S. turn to unrestricted mine warfare would represent a massive escalation against the Chinese people and would risk equally devastating Chinese retaliation against U.S. civilians. See Matthew Cancian, "An Offensive Minelaying Campaign against China," *Naval War College Review* 75, no. 1 (2022): 2, https://www.jstor.org/stable/48733089.

47. Eric Heginbotham and Richard J. Samuels, "Active Denial: Redesigning Japan's Response to China's Military Challenge," *International Security* 42, no. 4 (2018): 146, https://doi.org/10.1162/isec_a_00313.

48. Fiona S. Cunningham, "The Maritime Rung on the Escalation Ladder: Naval Blockades in a U.S.-China Conflict," *Security Studies* 29, no. 4 (2020): 730–768, https://doi.org/10.1080/09636412.2020.1811462.

49. UK cooperation would likely be necessary given UK control over the key Indian Ocean base at Diego Garcia. For analyses of the operational feasibility of a Malacca blockade, see Sean Mirski, "Stranglehold: The Context, Conduct and Consequences of an American Naval Blockade of China," *Journal of Strategic Studies* 36, no. 3 (2013): 385–421, https://doi.org/10.1080/01402390.2012.743885; Llewelyn Hughes and Austin Long, "Is There an Oil Weapon? Security Implications of Changes in the Structure of the International Oil Market," *International Security* 39, no. 3 (2014/15): 152–189, https://doi.org/10.1162/ISEC_a_00188; Jennifer Lind and Daryl G. Press, "Markets or Mercantilism? How China Secures Its Energy Supplies," *International Security* 42, no. 4 (2018): 170–204, https://doi.org/10.1162/isec_a_00310; Bruce Jones, *Temperatures Rising: The Struggle for Bases and Access in the Pacific Islands* (Washington, DC: Brookings, 2023), 1–7, https://www.brookings.edu/wp-content/uploads/2023/02/FP_20230207_pacific_basing_jones.pdf; Derek Grossman and John Speed Meyers, "Minding the Gaps," *Strategic Studies Quarterly* 13, no. 4 (2019): 105–121, https://www.jstor.org/stable/26815048. See also Cunningham, "The Maritime Rung on the Escalation Ladder."

50. Their critique is that the operation would degrade China's warfighting capability more slowly than its supporters assume, based on an analysis of the oil market. See Gabriel Collins, "A Maritime Oil Blockade against China," *Naval War College Review* 71, no. 2 (2018): 49–78.

51. Marc Lanteigne, "China's Maritime Security and the 'Malacca Dilemma,'" *Asian Security* 4, no. 2 (2008): 143.

52. For examples of Chinese scholars' concerns, see Lind and Press, "Markets or Mercantilism?" Notable primary sources expressing concern about a Malacca blockade include

Zhang Yuncheng, "The Malacca Strait and World Oil Security," *Huanqiu Shibao*, December 5, 2003; Shi Hongtao, "China's 'Malacca Straits,'" *Qingnian Bao*, June 15, 2004; Lin Yun, "The Dragon's Arteries," *Modern Ships* (2006): 8–19. The quote on China's "Achilles Heel" comes from Zhang Wenmu, "Sea Power and China's Strategic Choices," *China Security* (2006): 22. Zhang is a professor of Aeronautics and Astronautics at Beijing University.

53. Liang Fang (梁芳), *Haishang zhanlüe tongdaolun (海上战略通道论) On Maritime Strategic Access* (Beijing: Current Affairs Press, 2011). See also Eyck Freymann, *One Belt One Road: Chinese Power Meets the World* (Cambridge, MA: Harvard University Press, 2020).

54. Goodrich, "China's Evolving Fortress Economy," Testimony to *U.S.-China Economic and Security Review Commission Hearing on "China's Stockpiling and Mobilization Measures for Competition and Conflict,"* 118th Cong. (2024) (Statement of Gabriel Collins, J.D., Fellow in Energy & Environmental Regulatory Affairs, Rice University's Baker Institute for Public Policy).

55. Aaron L. Friedberg, "Competing with China," *Survival* 60, no. 3 (2018): 36.

56. The following discussion is adapted from Bromley and Freymann, "The Malacca Myth."

57. For a few examples of this point, see Eugene Gholz and Daryl G. Press, "The Effects of Wars on Neutral Countries: Why It Doesn't Pay to Preserve the Peace," *Security Studies* 10, no. 4 (2001): 1–57; Nicholas Mulder, *The Economic Weapon: The Rise of Sanctions as a Tool of Modern War* (New Haven, CT: Yale University Press, 2022); Lambert, *Planning Armageddon*; Edward Fishman, "How to Fix America's Failing Sanctions Policy," *Lawfare*, June 4, 2020, https://www.lawfaremedia.org/article/how-fix-americas-failing-sanctions-policy.

58. Bromley and Freymann, "The Malacca Myth," forthcoming.

59. Peter Reuter and Mark A. R. Kleiman, "Risks and Prices: An Economic Analysis of Drug Enforcement," *Crime and Justice* 7 (1986): 289–340.

60. If the target economy is relatively small, the incentives to cheat are not so great. If the neutral community is relatively small, then the coercing power can safely risk escalation to enforce compliance. Alternatively, it can "buy off" the neutral actor by offering to purchase goods at elevated prices. Britain and America took this approach in World War II when they negotiated "compulsory purchase agreements" for key commodities with several South American countries.

61. Patricia Clavin, *Securing the World Economy: The Reinvention of the League of Nations, 1920–1946*, 1st ed. (Oxford: Oxford University Press, 2013); Mulder, *The Economic Weapon*.

62. Gordon, Mullen, and Sacks, *U.S.-Taiwan Relations in a New Era*, 83.

63. Blanchette and DiPippo, "'Reunification' with Taiwan through Force."

64. Ian Ja Chong, "The Many 'One Chinas'."

65. On March 2, 2022, 141 countries voted to condemn Russia's invasion of Ukraine; 7 voted against; and 32 abstained; G.A. Res. ES-11/1, U.N. Doc. A/ES-11/L.1 (March 1, 2022).

66. Ivan Kanapathy, "Countering China's Grey-zone Activities" in Pottinger, ed., *The Boiling Moat*, 120–123.

67. Agatha Kratz and Charlie Vest, "Sanctioning China in a Taiwan Crisis: Scenarios and Risks" (June 22, 2023), 22–29, https://rhg.com/research/sanctioning-china-in-a-taiwan-crisis-scenarios-and-risks.

68. Anton Shilov, "U.S. Asks Malaysia to 'Monitor Every Shipment' to Close the Flow of Restricted GPUs to China," *Tom's Hardware*, March 24, 2025, https://www.tomshardware.com/tech-industry/artificial-intelligence/u-s-asks-malaysia-to-monitor-every-shipment-to-close-the-flow-of-restricted-gpus-to-china

69. CECIMO Global Machine Tool Report, 2022, 2–3, https://www.mta.org.uk/wp-content/uploads/2023/08/CECIMO-Global-Machine-Tool-Report-2022-May-23.pdf.

70. Brian Hioe, "Will the KMT Seek to Expand Legislative Power over TSMC?," *New Bloom Magazine*, March 2025, https://newbloommag.net/2025/03/12/kmt-ly-tsmc.

71. Statista, "EV Lithium-Ion Battery Production Capacity Shares Worldwide 2021–2025, by Country," October 24, 2023, https://www.statista.com/statistics/1249871/share-of-the-global-lithium-ion-battery-manufacturing-capacity-by-country.

72. Bonnie S. Glaser and Abigail Wulf, *China's Role in Critical Mineral Supply Chains* (German Marshall Fund of the U.S., August 2, 2023), https://www.gmfus.org/news/chinas-role-critical-mineral-supply-chains.

73. Select Committee on the Strategic Competition Between the United States and the Chinese Communist Party, *Reset, Prevent, Build*, 48.

74. *A Profile of U.S. Importing and Exporting Companies, 2020–2021* (Washington, DC: U.S. Census Bureau, 2023), 6, https://www.census.gov/foreign-trade/Press-Release/edb/edbrel2021.pdf.

75. *Soystats 2020: A Reference Guide to Important Soybean Facts and Figures* (Saint Louis, MO: American Soybean Association, 2022), 2, https://soygrowers.com/wp-content/uploads/2022/06/22ASA-002-Soy-Stats-Final-WEB.pdf.

76. Anshu Siripurapu, "What Happened to Supply Chains in 2021?," *Council on Foreign Relations*, December 13, 2021, https://www.cfr.org/article/what-happened-supply-chains-2021.

77. Yasuyuki Todo and Inoue Hiroyasu, "The Economic Effects of Import Disruption Can Be Magnified by Domestic Supply Chains," *CEPR*, December 5, 2022, https://www.rieti.go.jp/en/columns/v01_0195.html; see Hiroyasu Inoue and Yasuyuki Todo, *Propagation of Overseas Economic Shocks through Global Supply Chains: Firm-Level Evidence* (Tokyo: Research Institute for Economy, Trade and Industry, 2022), https://www.rieti.go.jp/jp/publications/dp/22e062.pdf.

78. "UN Comtrade Database," *United Nations*, 2022, https://comtradeplus.un.org, cited in Hiroyasu Inoue and Yasuyuki Todo, "Disruption of International Trade and Its Propagation through Firm-Level Domestic Supply Chains: A Case of Japan," *PLOS One* 18, no. 11 (2023): 18, https://doi.org/10.1371/journal.pone.0294574.

79. Japan is particularly vulnerable to losing access to chemicals, plastics, production machinery, business machinery, electronics and electrical machinery and equipment, and information and communication electronics equipment from China—essential critical inputs for a broad range of products produced by Japanese manufacturers; Inoue and Todo, "Disruption of International Trade," 14, 16.

80. Bree Neff et al., "Australia China Decoupling," *S&P Global*, December 14, 2020, https://www.spglobal.com/marketintelligence/en/mi/research-analysis/australia-china-decoupling.html.

81. Kandy Wong, "Australia Concludes China Decoupling 'Impossible' after Carrying Out Series of Classified Studies," *South China Morning Post*, October 6, 2023, https://www.scmp.com/economy/china-economy/article/3236860/australia-concluded-china-decoupling-impossible-after-series-classified-studies.

82. David Baqaee et al., "What If? The Effects of a Hard Decoupling from China on the German Economy" (Kiel: Kiel Institute for the World Economy, December 2023), https://www.ifw-kiel.de/fileadmin/Dateiverwaltung/IfW-Publications/fis-import/1012569b-7b3f-4a52-991a-1a4a7af556c2-KPB_EN_14-12.pdf.

83. Guy Chazan and Yuan Yang, "Germany Struggles with Its Dependency on China," *Financial Times*, November 1, 2022, https://www.ft.com/content/be082c77-1f9c-409f-86e8-eeb2bd9d1418.

84. Riham Alkoussa, "German Finance Minister Warns Against Quick Decoupling from China," *Reuters*, January 21, 2023, https://www.reuters.com/markets/german-finance-minister-warns-against-quick-decoupling-china-2023-01-22.

85. Clyde Russell, "China's Record Crude, Coal, Iron Ore Imports Don't Tell the Whole Story," *Reuters*, January 15, 2024, https://www.reuters.com/markets/commodities/chinas-record-crude-coal-iron-ore-imports-dont-tell-whole-story-russell-2024-01-15/#:~:text=Crude%20oil%20imports%20rose%2011,at%20the%20end%20of%202022.

86. The early COVID pandemic illustrates the potential risk to Saudi government finances of a permanent loss of PRC demand. When the first lockdowns were imposed in the West in March 2020, global oil demand plummeted. Saudi Arabia and Russia were initially unable to agree on coordinated production cuts to balance the market, which resulted in a global oil glut. By April, the future contract price of West Texas Intermediate (WTI) oil had fallen to $37 per barrel, while the Brent benchmark was down to $9.12. Thankfully for Riyadh, oil prices recovered over the summer as countries began to ease lockdowns and the Organization of the Petroleum Exporting Countries (OPEC) agreed to cut production by 9.7 million barrels per day for two months starting on May 1, OPEC's largest output cut in history. Ultimately, global oil consumption fell by a total of 9.1 million barrels per day in 2020, but demand recovered steadily into the second half of the year, so prices recovered; Jeff Barron, "EIA Estimates That Global Petroleum Liquids Consumption Dropped 9% in 2020," *U.S. Energy Information Administration (EIA)*, January 29, 2021, https://www.eia.gov/todayinenergy/detail.php?id=46596#:~:text=The%20U.S.%20Energy%20Information%20Administration,that%20dates%20back%20to%201980.

87. Abeer Abu Omar, "Saudi Budget's Oil Needs Take Another Leap in Fresh IMF Snapshot," *Bloomberg*, October 12, 2023, https://www.bloomberg.com/news/articles/2023-10-12/saudi-budget-s-oil-needs-take-another-leap-in-fresh-imf-snapshot#:~:text=Using%20a%20measure%20of%20fiscal,the%20IMF's%20estimates%20in%20May.

88. Naser Al-Tamimi, "Saudi Arabia's Once Marginal Relationship with China Has Grown into a Comprehensive Strategic Partnership," *MERICS*, August 18, 2022, https://merics.org/en/saudi-arabias-once-marginal-relationship-china-has-grown-comprehensive-strategic-partnership.

89. For a detailed modeling analysis, see Charlie Vest, Agatha Kratz, and Reva Goujon, "The Global Economic Disruptions from a Taiwan Conflict," *Rhodium Group*, December 14, 2022, https://rhg.com/research/taiwan-economic-disruptions.

90. The Bloomberg model is based on some dubious assumptions, including a total shut-off in Taiwan trade, a near-total collapse of U.S.–China trade, the immediate imposition of 50 percent tariffs on China by U.S. allies, an 80 percent reduction in Japanese, South Korean, and ASEAN trade, and a 40-point jump in the VIX financial market volatility index. Still, these figures are indicative of which countries would suffer greater relative pain than others; Jennifer Welch et al., "Xi, Biden and the $10 Trillion Cost of War over Taiwan,"

Bloomberg, January 9, 2024, https://www.bloomberg.com/news/features/2024-01-09/if-china-invades-taiwan-it-would-cost-world-economy-10-trillion.

91. Blackwill and Zelikow, *A Strategy to Prevent War*, 45.

92. "Financial Sanctions May Not Deter China from Invading Taiwan," *The Economist*, June 29, 2023, https://www.economist.com/finance-and-economics/2023/06/29/financial-sanctions-may-not-deter-china-from-invading-taiwan.

93. Bromley and Freymann, "The Malacca Myth."

94. U.S.-watchers in top Chinese think tanks and universities also follow the U.S. debate about Taiwan policy and integrated deterrence in a truly staggering level of detail. For two illuminating recent surveys in Chinese, see Zhou Wenxing (周文星), "Meiguo zhanluejie duitaizhengce bianlun ji qi yingxiang 美国战略界对台政策辩论及其影响" (*The U.S. Strategic Community's Taiwan Policy Debates and Their Implications*), *Xiandai Guoji Guanxi* 2 (2022): 54–62. Zhou is a special assistant researcher at the School of International Relations, and a researcher at the Huazhi Institute of Global Governance, both in Nanjing University; Wang Shushen (汪曙申), "Zhongmei jingzheng shijiaoxia Meiguo jieru Taihai de zhengce tanxi 中美竞争视角下美国介入台海的政策探析" (*An Analysis on U.S. Intervention in the Taiwan Strait from the Perspective of China-U.S. Competition*), *Dangdai Meiguo Pinglun* 4 (2022): 112–13.

95. Zhu Hongda (朱洪达), "Guojia anquanzhanlüe yu woguo jinrong anquan 国家安全战略与我国金融安全" (*National Security Strategy and China's Financial Security*), *Junshi Jingji Yanjiu* 7 (2011): 5–7. Zhu was the chief of Air Force Logistics and a member of the National Committee of the 12th Chinese People's Political Consultative Conference; Huang Zhiling (黄志凌), "Guanyu jinrongzhan de lijie 关于金融战的理解" (*Understanding Financial Warfare*), *Quanqiuhua* 3 (2020): 27–30. Huang is the chief economist of China Construction Bank and previously held positions in the State Planning Commission's Economic Research Center; Niu Wenxin (钮文新), "Jinrongzhan shijian shilishi, shixianshi, gengshi weilai 金融战史鉴是历史、是现实,更是未来" (*Financial Warfare History Is History, Reality, and the Future*), *Zhongguo Jingji Zhoukan*, April 15, 2022, 16–36. Niu is an expert member of the State Council's Financial Stability Committee and vice-president of the China Institute of Foreign Exchange, among many other government, party, and academic titles.

96. Freymann and Heng, "The Logic of Partial RMB Internationalization."

97. Gao Xingwei (高惺惟), "Zhongmei maoyi mocaxia renminbi guojihua zhanlüe yanjiu 中美贸易摩擦下人民币国际化战略研究" (*Study on RMB Internationalization Strategy under China-U.S. Trade Frictions*), *Jingji Xuejia* 5 (2019): 66. Gao is an associate professor at the Economics Department of Central Party School. He is also a researcher at Renmin University's International Monetary Institute.

98. Gao, "Zhongmei maoyi mocaxia renminbi guojihua zhanlüe yanjiu," 66.

99. See Raymond Yeung and Khoon Goh, "Petroyuan Will Not Bring about a Regime Shift Soon," *ANZ Research*, April 6, 2022, cited in Barry Eichengreen, "Sanctions, SWIFT, and China's Cross-Border Interbank Payments System," *CSIS Briefs*, May 2022, https://www.csis.org/analysis/sanctions-swift-and-chinas-cross-border-interbank-payments-system.

100. For a thoughtful perspective on barriers to CIPS's expansion by a prominent PRC economist, see Fred Gao, "Can CIPS Replace SWIFT? Insights from Bank of China's Former Vice President," *Inside China*, December 5, 2024, https://www.fredgao.com/p/can-cips-replace-swift-insights-from.

101. Russia's agreement with India is significant, allowing over $2 billion of backlogged transactions to be settled. India and Russia had already agreed to settle payments through Russian-owned, rupee-denominated "Special Rupee Vostro Accounts" in Indian banks. However, Indian banks were afraid to operationalize these accounts for fear of Western sanctions. The currency of settlement was another and related contested issue. Russia also wanted to be paid in RMB or Emirati dirhams, which are pegged to the dollar. India did not want to use RMB, and the Emiratis were wary of Western sanctions. Ultimately, the Indian government decided that by accepting SPFS, it could restart trade and give cover to domestic banks to settle their trade with Russia in rubles. See "India Signs Deal to Adopt Moscow's SPFS System for Banking Payments to Russia: Report," *The Wire*, April 25, 2023, https://thewire.in/diplomacy/india-signs-deal-to-adopt-moscows-spfs-system-for-banking-payments-to-russia-report. See also "Iran, Russia Link Banking Systems amid Western Sanction," *Reuters*, January 30, 2023, https://www.reuters.com/business/finance/iran-russia-link-banking-systems-amid-western-sanction-2023-01-30.

102. George Glover, "Russia Is Using China's Yuan to Settle 25% of Its Trade with the Rest of the World, Report Says," *Yahoo Finance*, September 28, 2023, https://finance.yahoo.com/news/russia-using-chinas-yuan-settle-193805731.html.

103. China's foreign loans are generally denominated in CNY, not CNH. Bradley C. Parks et al., *Belt and Road Reboot: Beijing's Bid to De-Risk Its Global Infrastructure Initiative* (Williamsburg, VA: AidData, November 2023), 78, https://docs.aiddata.org/reports/belt-and-road-reboot/Belt_and_Road_Reboot_Full_Report.pdf.

104. In a sense, China is exploiting the reality that many developing countries are trapped in a de facto debt trap. The Belt and Road seems to be evolving in the direction that its critics feared prior to the pandemic. See Freymann, *One Belt One Road*.

105. Fanhua Zeng, Wei-Chiao Huang, and James Hueng, "On Chinese Government's Stock Market Rescue Efforts in 2015," *Modern Economy* 7, no. 4 (2016): 411–18, https://doi.org/10.4236/me.2016.74045.

106. Zhou Hanmin 周汉民 and Huang Hua 黄骅, "Meiguo duiwai jinrongzhicai de falifenxi 美国对外金融制裁的法理分析 [Legal Analysis of American Foreign Financial Sanctions]," *Haiguan yu jingmao yanjiu* 43, no. 1 (2022): 11.

107. Zongyuan Zoe Liu and Mihaela Papa, *Can BRICS De-dollarize the Global Financial System?* (Cambridge: Cambridge University Press, 2022).

108. This chapter is adapted from Bromley and Freymann, *On Day One*. See also "Statement from President Biden on United Nations Security Council Meeting," *The White House*, January 31, 2022, https://bidenwhitehouse.archives.gov/briefing-room/statements-releases/2022/01/31/statement-from-president-biden-on-united-nations-security-council-meeting/.

109. Chris Miller, "Russia Thinks America Is Bluffing: To Deter a Ukraine Invasion, Washington's Threats Need to Be Tougher," *Foreign Affairs*, July 13, 2023, https://www.foreignaffairs.com/articles/russia-fsu/2022-01-10/russia-thinks-america-bluffing; Adam M. Smith, "SWIFT and Certain Punishment for Russia? There Are Better Ways to Deter Moscow than Threatening Its Banking Access," *Foreign Affairs*, July 13, 2023, https://www.foreignaffairs.com/articles/ukraine/2022-01-04/swift-and-certain-punishment-russia.

110. Edward Fishman and Chris Miller, "The Russia Sanctions That Could Actually Stop Putin," *Politico*, January 21, 2022, https://www.politico.com/news/magazine/2022/01/21/russia-sanctions-stop-putin-energy-markets-us-invasion-527524.

111. Edward Fishman, "A Tool of Attrition: What the War in Ukraine Has Revealed about Economic Sanctions," *Foreign Affairs*, June 26, 2023, https://www.foreignaffairs.com/ukraine/tool-attrition.

112. Elizabeth Wishnick, "The Xi-Putin Summit: A Display of China-Russia Resilience on Victory Day," *The Diplomat*, May 17, 2025.

113. "In an Effort to Choke Russian Economy, New Sanctions Target Russia's Central Bank," *NPR*, February 28, 2022, https://www.npr.org/2022/02/28/1083580974/in-an-effort-to-choke-russian-economy-new-sanctions-target-russias-central-bank.

114. "The West Declares Economic War on Russia," *Politico*, February 28, 2022, https://www.politico.com/newsletters/morning-money/2022/02/28/the-west-declares-economic-war-on-russia-00012208.

115. "'Panicked' Russians Withdrew $9.8 bln in FX from Banks in March," *Reuters*, April 20, 2022, https://www.reuters.com/business/finance/panicked-russians-withdrew-98-bln-fx-banks-march-2022-04-20.

116. Alexandra Prokopenko, "The Risks of Russia's Growing Dependence on the Yuan," *Carnegie Endowment for International Peace*, February 2, 2023, https://carnegieendowment.org/politika/88926.

117. Russia's other moves included (1) ordering Russian firms to swap 80 percent of their FX revenues into rubles; (2) banning Russian financial institutions from helping foreigners sell Russian assets: (3) demanding that foreign countries pay in rubles for their purchases of Russian energy, even if the contracts were priced in dollars or euros; and (4) restricting imports to increase Russia's current account surplus. See Paddy Hirsch, "How Russia Rescued the Ruble," *NPR*, April 5, 2022, https://www.npr.org/sections/money/2022/04/05/1090920442/how-russia-rescued-the-ruble.

118. "Turkey Faces Scrutiny as Exports to Russia Surge, Fuelling Concerns of Sanctions Evasion," *Euronews Digital*, November 27, 2023, https://www.euronews.com/business/2023/11/27/turkey-faces-scrutiny-as-exports-to-russia-surge-fuelling-concerns-of-sanctions-evasion.

119. Among many other examples, Ana Swanson and Niraj Chokshi, "U.S.-Made Technology Is Flowing to Russian Airlines, Despite Sanctions," *New York Times*, May 15, 2023, https://www.nytimes.com/2023/05/15/business/economy/russia-airlines-sanctions-ukraine.html.

120. *Bank of Russia Annual Report for 2021* (Moscow: Bank of Russia, April 8, 2022), 102, https://d1e00ek4ebabms.cloudfront.net/production/uploaded-files/Bank%20of%20Russia%20Annual%20Report_2021_e-1be447a6-c70f-4c45-8cf0-eocf45de13bb.pdf.

121. Brad W. Setser, "How to Hide Your Foreign Exchange Reserves—A User's Guide," *Council on Foreign Relations*, June 29, 2023, https://www.cfr.org/blog/how-hide-your-foreign-exchange-reseserves-users-guide.

122. "Country List Government Debt to GDP| G20," Trading Economics, accessed March 3, 2025, https://tradingeconomics.com/country-list/government-debt-to-gdp?continent=g20.

123. "Russia's Hidden War Debt: Full Report," *Navigating Russia* (Substack), accessed March 3, 2025, https://navigatingrussia.substack.com/p/russias-hidden-war-debt-full-report.

124. Alexander Marrow, "Russia's New Car Sales Up 47% in 2024, Agencies Cite Industry Ministry," *Reuters*, January 4, 2025, https://www.reuters.com/business/autos-transportation/russias-new-car-sales-up-47-2024-agencies-cite-industry-ministry-2025-01-04/

125. Jeffrey A. Sonnenfeld et al., "Business Retreats and Sanctions Are Crippling the Russian Economy," *SSRN Scholarly Paper* No. 4167193, Social Science Research Network, July 20, 2022, https://papers.ssrn.com/sol3/papers.cfm?abstract_id=4167193.

126. See Ibrahim Al-Marashi, "Russia's Looming Economic Crisis Will Be Worse Than 1991," *Al Jazeera*, March 4, 2022, https://www.aljazeera.com/opinions/2022/3/4/russias-looming-economic-crisis-will-be-worse-than-1991; Sergei Guriev, "The Cost of War: Russian Economy Faces a Decade of Regress," Carnegie Endowment for International Peace, December 2022, https://carnegieendowment.org/russia-eurasia/politika/2022/12/the-cost-of-war-russian-economy-faces-a-decade-of-regress?lang=en; European Council, "The Impact of Sanctions on the Russian Economy," *Council of the European Union*, 2023, https://www.consilium.europa.eu/en/infographics/impact-sanctions-russian-economy/; Brendan Cole, "Russian Banks Are Sounding the Alarm on Economy as Inflation Surges," *Newsweek*, January 9, 2024, https://www.newsweek.com/russia-bank-inflation-economy-crisis-1922208; Andrei Movchan, "Russia's Economy: Difficulties Ahead," *Carnegie Endowment for International Peace*, December 2024, https://carnegieendowment.org/russia-eurasia/politika/2024/12/russia-economy-difficulties?lang=en; Wilson Center, "The Risks of Russia's Two-Speed Economy in 2025," *Wilson Center*, January 2025, https://www.wilsoncenter.org/blog-post/risks-russias-two-speed-economy-2025; Mikhail Fishman, "Quagmire or Catastrophe?" *Novaya Gazeta Europe*, December 26, 2024, https://novayagazeta.eu/articles/2024/12/26/quagmire-or-catastrophe-en.

127. Zhao Hongtu 赵宏图, "马六甲困局与中国能源安全再思考" (*"Malacca Dilemma" and China's Energy Security*), 现代国际关系 (*Contemporary International Relations*) 6 (2007): 36–37. Zhao is the deputy director and associate researcher at the Institute of World Economic Studies at the influential China Institutes of Contemporary International Relations, a bureau of the Ministry of State Security; see also Xue Li 薛力, "马六甲困境内涵辨析与中国的应对" (*Analyzing Different Interpretations of the "Malacca Dilemma" and China's Countermeasures*), 世界与政治 (*World and Politics*) 10 (2010): 117–140. Xue is a researcher at the Institute of World Economics and Politics of the Chinese Academy of Social Sciences; Chen Tenghan 陈腾瀚, "马六甲困局再思考: 被'过度解释'的风险" (*Rethinking the "Malacca Dilemma": The Risk of "Over-Interpreting"*), 东南亚研究 (*Southeast Asian Studies*) 6 (2018): 131–146. Chen is a postdoctoral fellow in theoretical economics at Fudan University; Chen Shaofeng, "Has China's Foreign Energy Enhanced Its Energy Security?" *China Quarterly* 207 (2011): 600–625; Chen Shaofeng, "Motivations behind China's Foreign Oil Quest: A Perspective from the Chinese Government and the Oil Companies," *Journal of Chinese Political Science* 13, no. 1 (2018): 79–104. Chen Shaofeng (陈绍锋) is an Associate Professor at the Department of International Political Economy, School of International Studies, Peking University. Chen writes dismissively of the "so-called 'Malacca Dilemma.'"

128. Bai Jun 白俊 and Zhang Xiongjun 张雄君, "中国天然气供应安全形势及建议" (*China's Natural Gas Supply Security Situation and Recommendations*), *Natural Gas Technology and Economy* 14, no. 1 (2020): 1. See also Chen, "'马六甲困局'再思考." Bai and Zhang are senior researchers at the Beijing Gas Group Research Institute, a state industry think tank.

129. Lind and Press, "Markets or Mercantilism?"

130. For a systematic presentation, see Chen Shaofeng, "China's Self-Extrication from the 'Malacca Dilemma' and Implications," *International Journal of China Studies* 1, no. 1 (2010): 1–24; Goodrich, "China's Evolving Fortress Economy."

131. "China Likely Buying Oil for SPR at Low Prices, Energy Aspects Says," *Bloomberg*, September 9, 2024, https://www.bloomberg.com/news/articles/2024-09-09/china-likely-buying-oil-for-spr-at-low-prices-energy-aspects.

132. Zhao, "'马六甲困局'与中国," 37.

133. These estimates come from the U.S. Department of Agriculture. See Shin Watanabe and Aiko Munakata, "China Hoards over Half the World's Grain, Pushing up Global Prices," *Nikkei Asia*, December 23, 2021.

134. "China Soybean Oilseed Imports by Year," *IndexMundi*, accessed February 27, 2025.

135. Yujie Xue, "China's Appetite for Protein Developed through Fermentation Grows, amid Drive to Boost Demand for Meat Alternatives, Net-zero Goal," *South China Morning Post*, June 23, 2022.

136. The U.S. and its allies could narrow the oil price differential somewhat by buying up surplus production and stashing it in their own SPRs, but these would eventually fill up.

137. Zhao, "'马六甲困局'与中国," 38.

138. Zhao, "'马六甲困局'与中国," 38.

139. Collins, "A Maritime Oil Blockade Against China."

140. "Russia Using Ship-to-Ship Diesel Transfers for Transatlantic Exports," *Reuters*, April 5, 2023, https://www.reuters.com/markets/commodities/russia-using-ship-to-ship-diesel-transfers-transatlantic-exports-2023-04-05.

141. Xue, "马六甲困境内涵辨析," 137.

142. Jun Nie, "How Has the Current Lockdown in China Affected the Global Supply Chain?" *Federal Reserve Bank of Kansas City Economic Bulletin*, May 20, 2022.

143. Arguments attempting to justify a Malacca blockade under UNCLOS would rest on shaky political and legal ground. Close U.S. allies such as the UK or Australia that are signatories to UNCLOS may be reluctant to support an operation for which they would be legally liable after the conflict.

144. The National Archives of the UK (TNA): CAB 21/5.

145. Xue, "马六甲困境内涵辨析," 137.

146. Cunningham, "The Maritime Rung on the Escalation Ladder."

147. Xue, "'Maliujia kunjing' neihanbianxi," 137.

148. Adam Biggs, Dan Xu, Joshua Roaf, and Tatana Olson, "Theories of Naval Blockades and Their Application in the Twenty-First Century," *Naval War College Review* 74, no. 1 (2021): 1–31, https://digital-commons.usnwc.edu/nwc-review/vol74/iss1/9.

149. For example, Britain's "Pacific Blockade" of 1827 confined the Ottoman fleet to harbor so it could not interfere in the Greek war of independence. Close blockades were used coercively to expand market access in the Pastry War of 1838–1839, to negotiate prices for raw materials in the Sulfur Crisis of 1840, to enforce debt repayment in the Venezuela Crisis of 1895, and to demand redress for alleged wrongs in the Paraguay Expedition of 1858–1859. In 1982, Britain successfully used a close blockade to starve out Argentine positions in the Falkland Islands.

150. Henley, *China Maritime Report* No. 26, 7.

151. Bromley and Freymann, "The Malacca Myth."

CHAPTER 8

1. This chapter is adapted from Bromley and Freymann, *On Day One*.

2. Douglas G. Brinkley and David Facey-Crowther, eds., *The Atlantic Charter* (Basingstoke: Palgrave Macmillan, 1994).

3. The phrase "due respect for their existing obligations" was inserted at Churchill's request to cover Commonwealth and Empire preference. "Atlantic Charter," *The Avalon Project*, accessed January 19, 2024, https://avalon.law.yale.edu/wwii/atlantic.asp.

4. Jeff Stein, "Trump Aides Ready 'Universal' Tariff Plans—with One Key Change," *The Washington Post*, January 6, 2025, https://www.washingtonpost.com/business/2025/01/06/trump-tariff-economy-trade.

5. Randy Thanthong-Knight, "Canada Trade Surplus with US Narrows as Tariff Fight Looms," *BNN Bloomberg*, December 5, 2024, https://www.bnnbloomberg.ca/business/2024/12/05/canada-trade-surplus-with-us-narrows-as-tariff-fight-looms.

6. "Foreign Trade: Export Control," *German Federal Office for Economic Affairs and Export Control*, https://www.bafa.de/EN/Foreign_Trade/Export_Control/export_control_node.html.

7. See Alan Milward, *The Reconstruction of Western Europe, 1945–1951* (Los Angeles: University of California Press, 1984); Douglas Irwin, *Clashing over Commerce* (Chicago: University of Chicago Press, 2017), chap. 10.

8. Revoking PNTR would not automatically raise tariffs on goods from China. Rather, it would eliminate legal protections that prevent the president from raising tariffs rapidly. Most economic analyses of this issue do not make that point clear. For example, a notable Oxford Economics study assumes that revoking PNTR would involve automatically hiking the average tariff on nonfuel goods imports from China from 19 percent to 61 percent. It estimates that this would reduce U.S. GDP by 1.4 percent in the first year, costing hundreds of thousands of jobs and raising inflation. If Congress revoked PNTR in order to implement the Day One Plan, tariffs would almost certainly ratchet up much more slowly than the Oxford Economics team predicts, so the disruption to the U.S. economy would be significantly smaller. See Oxford Economics, *The Impact of China PNTR Repeal and Increased Tariffs on the U.S. Economy and American Jobs* (Oxford: Oxford Economics, November 2023), 13.

9. Bryce Baschuk, "Why There Are Calls in U.S. to Revoke China's Preferred Trade Status," *Bloomberg*, August 22, 2023, https://www.bloomberg.com/news/articles/2023-08-22/what-is-china-s-permanent-normal-trade-relations-or-pntr-quicktake.

10. Section 232 works like this. First, the president or any department, agency head, or "interested party" can ask Commerce to initiate an investigation, which can take up to 270 days. If Commerce finds that certain imports threaten U.S. national security, the president has an additional 90 days to impose whatever remedy he or she thinks is most appropriate. Rachel F. Fefer, *Section 232 of the Trade Expansion Act of 1962* (Washington, DC: Congressional Research Service, 2022), https://crsreports.congress.gov/product/pdf/IF/IF10667.

11. James Bacchus, *The Black Hole of National Security: Striking the Right Balance for the National Security Exception in International Trade* (Washington, DC: Cato Policy Analysis, 2022), https://www.cato.org/sites/cato.org/files/2022-11/policy-analysis-936.pdf.

12. To strengthen the political legitimacy of the Core's legal claim, Taiwan, a WTO member in its own right, could also bring suits against China.

13. Legally speaking, use of the national security exemption would only become relevant if China chose to challenge it; Bacchus, *The Black Hole of National Security*, 3.

14. The current U.S. position is that national security interests are self-justifying—that is, they are what a state says they are, and they cannot be assessed by WTO jurists. There is a strong argument for this position in principle. However, in the unique context of a Taiwan crisis,

it might be a mistake to continue to insist upon it. See WTO Panel, *Russia—Measures Concerning Traffic in Transit* (Geneva: World Trade Organization, 2019), 51, https://doi.org/10.30875/9a582d67-en.

15. Congress would ideally amend Section 232 to take control over the avalanche decoupling process. The decision to trigger avalanche decoupling is too significant to give to a single person, unless Congress authorizes that person to decide. Bipartisan groups in the House and Senate have already proposed legislation restricting the president's future authority to use Section 232 against U.S. treaty allies. See Senate Foreign Relations Committee, "Senators Introduce Legislation to Require Congressional Approval of National Security-Designated Tariffs," June 6, 2018, https://www.foreign.senate.gov/press/rep/release/senators-introduce-legislation-to-require-congressional-approval-of-national-security-designated-tariffs.

16. Hunter L. Clark and Anna Wong, "Did the U.S. Bilateral Goods Deficit with China Increase or Decrease during the U.S.-China Trade Conflict?" *Board of Governors of the Federal Reserve System*, June 21, 2021, https://www.federalreserve.gov/econres/notes/feds-notes/did-the-us-bilateral-goods-deficit-with-china-increase-or-decrease-during-the-us-china-trade-conflict-20210621.html.

17. "America's Tariff Wall on Chinese Imports Looks Increasingly Like Swiss Cheese," *The Economist*, February 24, 2022, https://www.economist.com/finance-and-economics/americas-tariff-wall-on-chinese-imports-looks-increasingly-like-swiss-cheese/21807816.

18. Albert Veenstra and Frank Heijmann, "The Future Role of Customs," *World Customs Journal* 17, no. 2 (September 2023): 13–30, https://doi.org/10.55596/001c.88415.

19. Two states within the ESCB could still in theory use the national security exemption to implement discriminatory trade against each other. However, the ESCB would not be in the business of enforcing these policies.

20. J. Bradford DeLong and Barry Eichengreen, "The Marshall Plan: History's Most Successful Structural Adjustment Program" (Working Paper, Cambridge, MA: National Bureau of Economic Research, 1991), https://doi.org/10.3386/w3899; William Hitchcock, "The Marshall Plan and the Creation of the West," in *The Cambridge History of the Cold War*, eds. Melvyn P. Leffler and Odd Arne Westad (Cambridge: Cambridge University Press, 2010), 154–174; Alan S. Milward, review of *The Marshall Plan: America, Britain, and the Reconstruction of Western Europe, 1947–1952*, by Michael J. Hogan, *Diplomatic History* 13, no. 2 (1989): 231–253.

21. For labor in particular, see Michael J. Hogan, *The Marshall Plan: America, Britain and the Reconstruction of Western Europe, 1947–1952* (Cambridge: Cambridge University Press, 2009). See also J. Bradford DeLong and Barry Eichengreen, "The Marshall Plan: History's Most Successful Structural Adjustment Program" (Working Paper, Cambridge, MA: National Bureau of Economic Research, 1991), https://www.nber.org/papers/w3899.

22. Raw materials and machinery combined represented 67 percent of French Marshall Plan spending. See Hogan, *The Marshall Plan*; Milward, review of *The Marshall Plan*, 231.

23. British Library, IOR/L/E/8/6880.

24. "Convention Establishing a Customs Co-operation Council (CCC)," University of Oslo, accessed December 14, 2024, https://www.jus.uio.no/english/services/library/treaties/09/9-04/wco_customs_council.html.

25. M. M. Parthiban, T. Samaya Murali, and G. Kanaga Subramanian, "World Customs Organization and Global Trade: Imprints and Future Paradigms," *World Customs Journal* 14, no. 2 (September 2020), https://doi.org/10.55596/001c.116425.

26. DeLong and Eichengreen, "The Marshall Plan"; William Hitchcock, "The Marshall Plan and the Creation of the West," in *The Cambridge History of the Cold War*, eds. Melvyn P. Leffler and Odd Arne Westad (Cambridge: Cambridge University Press, 2010), 154–174; Alan S. Milward, Review of *The Marshall Plan: America, Britain, and the Reconstruction of Western Europe, 1947–1952*, by Michael J. Hogan, *Diplomatic History* 13, no. 2 (1989): 231–253.

27. For a discussion of PRC history textbooks' bitter treatment of the history of the Marshall Plan, see Eyck Freymann, *One Belt One Road*, 35–37.

28. Hitchcock, "The Marshall Plan and the Creation of the West."

29. DeLong and Eichengreen, "The Marshall Plan"; Alan S. Milward, "Was the Marshall Plan Necessary?," *Diplomatic History* 13, no. 2 (April 1989): 231–253, https://www.jstor.org/stable/24911817.

30. Core allies would be sorely tempted to use ESCB data as a legal basis for enforcing unilateral export controls on dual-use products. It would be a mistake to do so. The ESCB must be an independent body not associated with dollar sanctions. This would be important to protect both its independence and its legitimacy.

31. Claas Mertens, "Carrots as Sticks: How Effective Are Foreign Aid Suspensions and Economic Sanctions?," *International Studies Quarterly* 68, no. 2 (June 2024), https://doi.org/10.1093/isq/sqae016.

32. Burt Braverman and Edlira Kuka, "China's Newest Anti-Foreign Sanctions Blocking Law: What We Know, What We Don't Know, and What U.S. Companies Can Do," Davis Wright Tremaine LLP, August 30, 2021, https://www.dwt.com/blogs/broadband-advisor/2021/08/anti-foreign-sanctions-law-china.

33. As of the end of 2022, it declared $2.8 trillion in FDI assets, $1 trillion in overseas portfolio assets, and $2.1 trillion in other investment assets. See "SAFE Releases China's International Investment Position as at the End of 2022," *State Administration of Foreign Exchange (SAFE)*, March 31, 2023, https://www.safe.gov.cn/en/2023/0331/2063.html.

34. "China Gallium, Germanium Export Curbs Kick in; Wait for Permits Starts," *Reuters*, August 1, 2023, https://www.reuters.com/markets/commodities/chinas-controls-take-effect-wait-gallium-germanium-export-permits-begins-2023-08-01; Joe McDonald, "China Restricts Civilian Drone Exports, Citing Ukraine and Concern about Military Use," *AP News*, August 1, 2023, https://apnews.com/article/china-ukraine-russia-drone-export-dji-e6694b3209b4d8a93fd76cf29bd8a056.

35. The Fischer-Tropsch process designed to turn Ruhr coal into fuel oil, created in Nazi Germany, is the most famous example of this process; Adam Tooze and Jamie Martin, "The Economics of the War with Nazi Germany," in *The Cambridge History of the Second World War*, eds. Michael Geyer and Adam Tooze (Cambridge: Cambridge University Press, 2015), 47–48.

36. When China embargoed exports of rare earth magnets in 2025, all the G7 countries and other major economies like India scrambled to build stockpiles and de-risk their supply chains.

37. In 2010, China restricted imports of Norwegian salmon after dissident Liu Xiaobo won the Nobel Peace Prize. In 2017, it arranged a "grassroots" boycott of South Korean products in retaliation for the government's decision to install the American THAAD missile defense system. Between 2017 and 2021, China took a variety of similar measures against Australia, targeting lobster, wine, and other goods. In 2021, it imposed a sudden ban on

pineapples from Taiwan. See Justin Ng and Lei Dijie, trans., "The Sugar-Coated Poison of the Chinese Market: How Will Taiwanese Pineapples Fight Against Their Fate?," *Baodaozhe* (報導者), March 1, 2021, https://www.twreporter.org/a/china-bans-taiwanese-pineapples-english.

38. If China kept import levels of commodities constant, it would not affect long-term price levels or the economies of affected countries if it shifted its imports from one supplier to another. The global market would simply rebalance. The shift in global oil and gas markets after Russia's invasion of Ukraine provides an analogy. As a result of sanctions, Russian oil and gas exports that once flowed to Europe began to flow to China, India, and other non-G7 countries instead. Suppliers that previously sold oil and gas to China, India, and others then had excess supply to sell to Europe. Lengthening supply routes added only marginally to the global price level.

39. By 2023, 80 percent of South Koreans had a negative opinion of China, the second-highest in all countries surveyed by Pew; Laura Silver, Christine Huang, and Laura Clancy, "How Global Public Opinion of China Has Shifted in the Xi Era," *Pew Research Center*, September 28, 2022, https://www.pewresearch.org/global/2022/09/28/how-global-public-opinion-of-china-has-shifted-in-the-xi-era.

40. Ann M. Simmons, "What Is Novichok, the Poisoning Agent Used on Russia's Alexei Navalny?," *Wall Street Journal*, February 2, 2021, https://www.wsj.com/articles/what-is-novichok-the-nerve-agent-used-to-poison-alexei-navalny-11599072960; Bojan Pancevski, Thomas Grove, Max Colchester, and Daniel Michaels, "Russia Suspected of Plotting to Send Incendiary Devices on U.S.-Bound Planes," *Wall Street Journal*, November 4, 2024, https://www.wsj.com/world/russia-plot-us-planes-incendiary-devices-de3b8c0a; Michelle Nichols, "Russia, US Clash at UN over Nuclear Weapons in Space," *Reuters*, April 25, 2024, https://www.reuters.com/science/russia-blocks-us-move-un-nuclear-weapons-space-2024-04-24.

41. Sophia Besch and Erik Brown, "A Chinese-Flagged Ship Cut Baltic Sea Internet Cables. This Time, Europe Was More Prepared," *Carnegie Endowment for International Peace*, December 3, 2024, https://carnegieendowment.org/emissary/2024/12/baltic-sea-internet-cable-cut-europe-nato-security?lang=en.

42. Jonathan Kirshner, *Currency and Coercion: The Political Economy of International Monetary Power* (Princeton, NJ: Princeton University Press, 1995), 64–86.

43. Although the scale of the intervention has been debated, its intention has not. See Diane B. Kunz, *The Economic Diplomacy of the Suez Crisis* (Chapel Hill: University of North Carolina Press, 1991); Kirshner, *Currency and Coercion*, 69.

44. Cited in Kirshner, *Currency and Coercion*, 69.

45. Kirshner makes a compelling argument that financial considerations were the decisive factor in London's decision to capitulate.

CONCLUSION

1. *Renmin Ribao* (人民日报), 习近平在参观《复兴之路》展览时强调:承前启后 继往开来 继续朝着中华民族伟大复兴目标奋勇前进 [When visiting the "Road to Rejuvenation" exhibition, Xi Jinping stressed: "We must build on the past and forge ahead into the future, and continue to forge ahead toward the goal of the great rejuvenation of the Chinese nation"], November 29, 2012.

2. Andrew S. Erickson, Conor M. Kennedy, and Ryan D. Martinson, eds., *Chinese Amphibious Warfare: Prospects for a Cross-Strait Invasion* (Newport, RI: Naval War College Press, November 7, 2024), https://digital-commons.usnwc.edu/cmsi-studies/8/. For a two-part summary, see Andrew S. Erickson, "China's Amphibious Warfare: History, Doctrine, and Forces," *The Diplomat*, December 14, 2024, https://thediplomat.com/2024/12/chinas-amphibious-warfare-history-doctrine-and-forces/; Andrew S. Erickson, "Chinese Amphibious Warfare: Taiwan Targeted, Scenarios Swirling," *The Diplomat*, December 14, 2024, https://thediplomat.com/2024/12/chinese-amphibious-warfare-taiwan-targeted-scenarios-swirling/.

APPENDIX A

1. This was the only one of the four conversations conducted in Chinese. Chang and his staff have approved the translation. Thanks to Karl Lai and Qi Siang Ng for their help and advice on the transcription.
2. CMP Staff, "Sneaky Visit (窜访)," *China Media Project*, September 5, 2022, https://chinamediaproject.org/the_ccp_dictionary/sneaky-visit/.

APPENDIX B

1. If the U.S. Treasury attacked the HKD, backstopping the HKD's peg to the U.S. dollar could become another drain on Beijing's reserves. The HKMA holds FX reserves several times the size of the Hong Kong monetary base, which has enabled it to maintain the peg even in moments of great strain, such as the 2019 protests and 1997 Asian Financial Crisis. As of April 2023, the HKMA's total foreign currency reserve assets were $430.7 billion—over five times the currency in circulation, or about 41 percent of Hong Kong dollar M3. However, in a Taiwan crisis, Hong Kong would face a grim combination of forces: existential risk to short- and long-term viability of its financial sector, forced selling of real estate, an exodus of foreign residents, and a collapse in its export facilitation sector. Foreign hedge funds have already eyed the peg for decades as a potential target for a speculative attack. Given that the HKD is the world's ninth-most traded currency, the HKMA's reserves are small relative to the potential firepower that global capital markets could put behind a short trade; Robin Harding, "Hong Kong's Dollar Peg Is on Increasingly Thin Ice," *Financial Times*, December 29, 2022, https://www.ft.com/content/a045f068-7639-4d75-ba71-63a1f62d6767. See also Bromley and Freymann, *On Day One*.
2. The PBoC and HKMA already have swap lines established, and these could be expanded in a crisis. Nevertheless, depending on the extent of selling pressure, a simultaneous speculative attack on the HKD and CNH could force China to bleed enormous quantities of reserves. If the HKD peg broke, capital would flood out of Hong Kong, the HKD would depreciate sharply, and international investors would be even less inclined to hold or take payment in CNH. Notably, the Federal Reserve and allied central banks such as the Bank of England and Bank of Japan would have to rescue their own financial institutions from the general meltdown in Hong Kong. But they could attach conditions—including, for example, a requirement to dump all RMB assets. See "Enhanced Currency Swap Agreement between People's Bank of China and Hong Kong Monetary Authority," *Hong Kong Monetary Authority*, July 20, 2022, https://www.hkma.gov.hk/eng/news-and-media/press-releases/2022/07/20220704-5/. See also Bromley and Freymann, *On Day One*.

3. Yiye Liu, Liyan Han, and You Wu, "Can Skewness Predict CNY-CNH Spread?," *Finance Research Letters* 46 (May 2022), https://doi.org/10.1016/j.frl.2021.102392.

4. Suppose that capital controls and government intervention cause the onshore exchange rate to stabilize at 10 to the dollar, while the offshore exchange rate falls to 20 to the dollar. Suppose also that Taoli, a PRC firm, produces widgets in China and sells them overseas for $1. If PRC entities are allowed to convert offshore back into CNY on a 1:1 basis, Taoli could receive $1 in payment for its exported widgets, convert them into 20 CNH, and then convert that into 20 CNY, which can theoretically be exchanged for $2 in the onshore market. If Taoli anticipated future CNH depreciation, it might prefer to take payment in FX, hold the cash offshore, and hope to convert it back into CNH later for a profit. Meanwhile, Taoli would want to convert as much CNY into dollars at the onshore exchange rate as possible, so that it could repeat the arbitrage process. These examples illustrate the risk that China would face if it failed to enforce capital controls effectively, as well as the difficulty of managing the incentives of domestic actors.

5. Zongyuan Zoe Liu, *Sovereign Funds: How the Chinese Communist Party Finances Its Global Ambitions* (Cambridge, MA: Harvard University Press, 2023).

6. Here are a few examples. Beijing could instruct PRC state-owned banks and sovereign funds to buy CNH on the open market and hold it indefinitely. It could raise interest rates on CNH and CNY deposits to discourage bank withdrawals. It could shutter onshore exchanges and prohibit PRC financial institutions from helping foreigners liquidate assets onshore. It could tighten capital controls, potentially including physical limits on outbound travel. And it could demand that foreign countries buying PRC goods pay in CNH.

7. If China's export partners stopped paying in FX, but Beijing had to continue paying for most of its imports in FX, SAFE could potentially drain its FX reserves by over $2 trillion per year. China's imports in 2023 amounted to $2.56 trillion.

8. Brad Setser, "Power and Financial Interdependence," *Institut français des relations internationales* (IFRI), May 3, 2024, https://www.ifri.org/en/papers/power-and-financial-interdependence.

9. "Table 5: Major Foreign Holders of Treasury Securities," *U.S. Treasury*, accessed January 19, 2024, https://ticdata.treasury.gov/resource-center/data-chart-center/tic/Documents/slt_table5.html.

10. As of this writing, the Fed holds more than $4 trillion of Treasury securities on its balance sheet. See Tim Sablik, "The Fed Is Shrinking Its Balance Sheet. What Does That Mean?," *Federal Reserve Bank of Richmond, Econ Focus*, Third Quarter 2022, # https://www.richmondfed.org/publications/research/econ_focus/2022/q3_federal_reserve.

11. Brad W. Setser, "China Isn't Shifting Away from the Dollar or Dollar Bonds," *Council on Foreign Relations*, October 3, 2023, https://www.cfr.org/blog/china-isnt-shifting-away-dollar-or-dollar-bonds.

12. U.S. Treasury, "Table 5: Major Foreign Holders of Treasury Securities."

13. Here are three examples: (1) China could ban conversion between CNH and dollars, requiring that all CNH transactions take place on CIPS. However, the Treasury could respond by selling CNH in exchange for euros, yen, or any other currency for which CNH conversion was not banned. If necessary, the Treasury could conduct its currency intervention through proxies. (2) China could try to establish a cryptocurrency pegged to the dollar. However, the Treasury could simply short the cryptocurrency, draining FX reserves in the process. (3) China could hypothetically create a blockchain-enabled e-CNH that automatically demonetized itself when taken off the CIPS platform. However, it is not

clear that such a solution is technically possible. Even if it were, foreign central banks and private actors might not want to hold a currency that Beijing could demonetize at will.

14. The risks to the currency intervention would come from independent market participants, not just PRC counter-intervention. The further the CNH exchange rate fell below its fundamental value, the more attractive it would be to speculators.

15. PRC exporters might not want to accept payment in CNH if Beijing made it difficult or expensive to convert into the onshore equivalent, because these firms' foreign suppliers would not want to take payment in CNH.

16. Even if China temporarily allowed the onshore and offshore exchange rates to diverge and suspended 1:1 convertibility between them, it would still have a long-term interest in bringing the two currencies back into alignment in the long term and "reissuing" the CNH, if it were capable of doing so in the postwar era.

17. These IOUs would have some value as long as China had enough FX reserves to make repayment plausible and the potential capacity to earn hard currency in the future through exports. The more likely China appeared to favor terms of trade in a postwar settlement, the closer to par these IOUs would be valued. Historically, investors have treated IOUs from belligerent states in wartime as a form of financial option. If the borrower wins the war, it can be expected that it will pay as much of its loans as possible, to stabilize the financial system for the postwar period. By contrast, if the borrower loses the war, its ability and willingness to pay wartime debt may fade, so bond prices might trend toward zero. Global investors therefore tend to be happy to hold debt of the side that they expect to win the war, though sentiment will turn in real time as the war plays out. While the fighting continues, this can be a bumpy ride. During World War I, the bond market saw twenty-two turning points of sentiment. The market ultimately determined that the Allies would win after the Central Powers' 1918 spring offensive failed. See Tobias A. Jopp, "Contemporaries' Opinions of the Allied and Central Powers' Performance during the First World War: Measuring Turning Points in Perception with Sovereign Debt Prices," *European Review of Economic History* 20, no. 2 (2016): 242–273, https://www.jstor.org/stable/24806692.

18. Benham Gholipour, "Official Report: Iran Could Use Cryptocurrencies to Avoid Sanctions," *Iran Wire*, March 2, 2021, https://iranwire.com/en/features/69084.

19. Barry Naughton, "The Impact of the Tiananmen Crisis on China's Economic Transition," in *The Impact of China's 1989 Tiananmen Massacre* (London: Routledge, 2010), 166–190.

Index

For the benefit of digital users, indexed terms that span two pages (e.g., 52–53) may, on occasion, appear on only one of those pages.

Figures are indicated by an italic f.

Able Archer 83
  as benchmark for future escalation risks, 192
  NATO exercise and nuclear near-miss, 183
  retrospective acknowledgment by U.S. leaders, 184
  Soviet misinterpretation, 183–184
Admiralty (Royal Navy), 202–203, 207
Agile Combat Employment (ACE), 103
AI
  American AI policy and strategic stability, 174
  CCP's aim to dominate the deployment of, 1–2
  China's ability to produce advanced chips, 195–197
  comparison with strategic nuclear threats, 193
  contribution to strategic deterrence, 5–6, 10, 44, 201
  "human-in-the-loop" and challenges, 193–194
  integration with strategic deterrence capabilities, 167, 191–194, 196, 199, 201
  potential role in reaching audiences across the "Great Firewall," 131, 194
  relationship to mutually assured destruction (MAD), 192
  U.S. AI-backed deterrence initiatives, 195–199
all-domain pressure campaign
  aims of, 25, 56–58, 84, 124, 134
  excluding Taiwan from international organization as a goal of, 59
  extension to foreign companies and countries that engage with Taiwan, 58
  failure, so far, of, 56
  legal, cyber, and sociocultural avenues of attack of, 56–60
  offensive lawfare used to delegitimize Taiwan's claim to protection under international law, 59
  role of the UFWD in, 59–60, 86
All-out Defense Mobilization Agency (Taiwan)
  civil and military mobilization for occupation contingency, 99
Amodei, Dario, 194
amphibious invasion
  basic requirements for, 88–95
  challenges of holding together a U.S.-led coalition during, 118
  China's insecurity during the Third Taiwan Straits Crisis, 290–291
  early warning indicators, 75–77
  economic and political implications of, 113–117
  the economic dimensions of, compared to the outbreak of World War I, 114
  importance of Taiwan's air defenses in, 94–95
  mines and anti-ship missiles used to disrupt it, 150
  Operation Neptune (1944) as a historical benchmark for, 91
  the PLA Air Force (PLAAF), 90
  the PLAN amphibious fleet, 9, 90–91, 93–94, 96, 112, 331 n.25
  as a potential "Plan B" for China, 272
  potential decapitation of Taiwan's leadership, 97–98

rules of engagement and difficulty of
enforcing them, 97

Taiwan's preparedness for, 99–100, 282

Taiwan's reliance on Man-
Portable Air Defense Systems
(MANPADS), 96–97

Angell, Norman, 202

Anti-Access/Area Denial (A2/AD)

China's missile-based strategy and allied
countermeasures, 153

Anti-Foreign Sanctions Law (2021)

PRC legal basis for asset freezes and
escalation in economic warfare, 258

Anti-Secession Law (2005), 24

APEC (Asia-Pacific Economic Cooperation)

PRC leverage and exclusion of
Taiwan, 290

Arbitrage

in pressuring PRC capital controls, 294.
See also blockades

role in sanctions and blockade evasion by
neutral states and firms, 212

role in undermining oil embargoes against
China, 231

Arsenal of Democracy, The, 150–151, 278

Atlantic Charter, 237–238, 242, 388 n.3

AUKUS (Australia, UK, and US), 143, 154,
163–164, 243

Australia

AUKUS (Australia, UK, and US), 143,
154, 163–164, 243

China's economic coercion against, 391
n.37

China's exports to, 222*f*

expected GDP loss during hard
decoupling, 220

exports to China, 219, 221*f*

geographic significance, 149*f*

impact of a Day One economic crisis
on, 220, 242

ITAR and cooperation with, 160

need for stronger nuclear assurances, 173,
201

potential role in execution of a Malacca
blockade, 210

role as a Core ally, 5, 9, 71, 118, 125–126,
146

role in the Berlin airlift, 66

avalanche decoupling. *See also* Day One and
the Day One Plan

achieving consensus on how to phase
out noncritical dependencies on
China, 240, 244–245, 260

commitment of the American economic
contingency plan to, 238–239, 248,
260, 275

coordinated ratcheting of trade policies
against China to achieve avalanche
decoupling, 239–240, 246–247,
261, 275–276

establishing an ESCB as a policy pillar
of, 12, 239–240, 249–251, 254,
256–257, 259–260, 262, 266, 275

locking China inside the dollar system
during, 262

and Section 232 of the Trade Expansion
Act of 1962, 244–246, 389 n.10,
390 n.15

B-21 Raider

replacement bomber in U.S. nuclear
modernization program, 188

Bashi Channel

as a geographic chokepoint, 34, 35*f*, 36*f*

undersea cables in, 289

Battle of Jutland (1916)

naval scouting and fleet allocation, 151–152. *See also* intelligence,
surveillance, and reconnaissance
(ISR)

Battle of Midway (1942)

naval scouting and signals intelligence, 151–152. *See also* intelligence,
surveillance, and reconnaissance
(ISR)

Biden, Joe and the Biden administration

adherence to the One China Policy, 33

approach to evacuating U.S. citizens from
Ukraine, 81

AUKUS and incremental ITAR
reform, 160

communication of One China
Policy, 137–138

export controls on advanced
semiconductors, 162

imposition of sanctions on
Russia, 225–226

Biden, Joe and the Biden administration
      (*Continued*)
   intelligence on Putin's plans to invade
      Ukraine, 73
   Kabul evacuation, 80
   meeting in Lima with Xi Jinping
      (2024), 17–18
   nuclear assurances for South
      Korea, 185–186
   Pelosi's visit to Taiwan during his
      presidency (August 2022), 33–34,
      289
   Xi's comments about "reunification"
      being inevitable, 32
Blackwill, Robert D.
   on the "quarantine" or "indirect control"
      scenario, 5, 56–57, 63
   on strikes on PRC territory as risking
      escalation to general war, 101–102
Blanchette, Jude and Gerard DiPippo, 214
blockades and blockade scenarios. *See also*
      Malacca blockade
   blockades against Taiwan as, 232–233
   Britain's blockade of Germany in World
      War I, 232
   distinction from other forms of economic
      coercion, 212–213
   historic use against small
      islands, 232–233, 388 n.149
   impact on Taiwan's energy
      supplies, 108–112
   impact on Taiwan's food
      security, 110–112
   "joint blockade operation"
      (联合封锁战役) as Xi's pre-
      ferred operational concept, 3,
      107–108, 299 n.12
   "Joint Sword 2024B," 55
   need for deterrence by denial specifically
      for blockade, 9–10, 112
   as part of an invasion or a fallback after a
      failed invasion, 111
   potential political and strategic effects on
      Taiwan, 108–109
   risk that China might miscalculate about a
      sure path to checkmate, 112–113
   similarities and differences to Berlin
      blockade and Berlin Airlift, 64–68,
      84

   Taiwan Relations Act and, 71, 232
brinkmanship
   as the art of risking the loss of control, 194
   nuclear brinkmanship, 176, 183, 193, 200
   Thomas Schelling on, 175
Burns, William, 4–5, 31
Bush, George W. and the Bush
      administration
   communication of the One China
      Policy, 138–139
   criticism of Chen Shui-Bian's prospect of
      offering ballot referenda, 309 n.73
   Dec. 10, 2003, 310 n.74
Bush, Richard C., 5

Canada
   coercive treatment by the Trump
      administration, 245
   as a Core ally, 125–126, 146, 243,
      255–256
   expected GDP loss during hard
      decoupling, 220
   poaching of AI talent from China, 196
   role in political deterrence, 143, 275
   role in the Berlin airlift, 66
Capital controls
   limits of U.S. sanctions leverage if controls
      hold, 225
   role in PRC crisis management
      and financial stability during
      conflict, 115
   vulnerability to arbitrage and currency
      instability, 293–294
CCP propaganda. *See also* Road to
      rejuvenation
   claim that UN Resolution 2758 has
      defined Taiwan's status, 59, 130
   potential for the U.S. to reach audiences
      across the "Great Firewall," 131, 194
   the term "reunification" as, 1–2
Central Military Commission (CMC), 182
Chen Shui-Bian
   offering ballot referenda considered
      by, 309 n.73
Cheung, Olivia, 5
Chiang Kai-Shek. *See also* Kuomintang
      (KMT)
   acceptance of Japan's surrender, 25, 307
      n.45

China Institutes of Contemporary International Relations (CICIR)
views on Malacca blockade risk, 230
China's currency system. *See also* Cross-border Interbank Payments System (CIPS)
China's strategy for currency internationalization, 223–224
currency intervention against the RMB
attacks on the CNY and HKD as a means to maintain strategic deterrence in a post-Day One world, 262–263
China's currency system—CNH (offshore currency)
development of the offshore CNH market, 223
potential counter-strategies to a currency attack, 295
China's reconnaissance–strike complex, 100, 118, 152
Chinese Coast Guard (CCG), 86
coercive presence in the maritime space around Taiwan, 55, 61
Second Thomas Shoal episode (2024), 55–56
Taiwan's response to unlawful boarding of its vessels, 70–71
Chinese Communist Party (CCP). *See also* CCP propaganda
2049 as a Party deadline, 4–5
claim to authority over all Chinese globally, 31
claim to have restored China's unity, 18
"core" structural interests in Taiwan, 19–20, 32–33, 270
domestic and global ambitions, 1–2
formats for unification with Taiwan, 23–24
goals for world order, 37–38, 269–270
growing assertiveness, 37–38
historic patience on Taiwan issue, 30
hostility to freedom, 127
insecurity, 269–270
KMT's view of, 28
National Museum of China, 268–269
other countries' fear of, 236

as a potential target of U.S. strategic deterrence, 200–201, 210–212, 276–277
Taiwan and CCP legitimacy, 45–46, 101
Taiwan crisis and threat to regime survival, 111, 131, 140, 267
Taiwanese perspectives on, 282–285, 287–291
view of AI, 1–2, 44, 194
Xi's war on internal norms, 34
CHIPS (Clearing House Interbank Payments System)
contrasted with China's CIPS as alternative payments system, 223–224
U.S.-controlled payment settlement infrastructure underpinning dollar hegemony and sanctions enforcement, 48–49, 296
chokepoints
the efficacy of imposing export controls as problematic, 215–216
landing zones on Taiwan's Western coast as, 91–94, 92*f*
leveraging by the United States, 208–210, 215
Miyako Strait and Bashi Channel as, 34, 35*f*
"weaponized interdependence," 208
Christensen, Thomas J., 5
Churchill, Winston, 237, 388 n.3
civil–military fusion
integration of national defense and economic power under PLA modernization goals, 31–32
Clinton, Bill, handling of Third Taiwan Straits Crisis (1995–6), 123
coercive mobilization. *See under* military mobilization
cognitive domain operations, 60
Collaborative Combat Aircraft (CCA)
"loyal wingman" concept augmenting manned aircraft, 162
Collins, Gabriel B.
analysis of the Malacca blockade scenario, 210
on Xi's "all-domain pressure campaign," 57–58, 319 n.10
Columbia-class submarines, 188

combat readiness. *See also* People's Liberation
    Army Navy (PLAN)
    United States combat readiness
      basic requirements for an amphibious
        invasion, 88–95
command-and-control, communications,
    computers, intelligence, surveillance,
    and reconnaissance (C4ISR), 10,
    150–152, 168, 200–201. *See also*
    intelligence, surveillance, and
    reconnaissance (ISR)
Committee for the Defense of the Empire
    preauthorization of British economic
      warfare plans (1912), 202
"community of common des-
    tiny for mankind"
    (人类命运共同体), 32–33,
    37–38
Copeland, Dale C., 5
Core coalition
    aims of, 126
    five members of, 125–126, 146
    flexible membership in, 243–244
    holding together a U.S.-led coalition as
      essential and challenging during an
      invasion, 118
    mobilization during a quarantine, 71–72
    the need for establishing it, 124, 142–146
    revoking of permanent normal trading
      relations (PNTR), 244–245
    transport of liquefied natural gas from the
      U.S. to Taiwan, 131–132
COVID-19 pandemic
    effects on oil prices, 383 n.86
    Federal Reserve action during, 114
    Taiwan's world-leading response, 59
    the U.S. government's botched
      response, 181
    Xi's "zero-COVID" policy, 39–40, 181
Crawford, Timothy W., 5
critical minerals
    China's dominance in production and
      processing of, 217
    as leverage in economic coercion and
      export controls, 247
    role in decoupling, de-risking, and
      supply-chain vulnerability, 116, 206
    weaponization in response to sanctions or
      conflict over Taiwan, 258

Cross-border Interbank Payments System
    (CIPS)
    as an alternative to SWIFT and
      CHIPS, 223–224
    requirement that CNH take place on
      CIPS, 224, 295, 330 n.13
Cuban Missile Crisis (1962)
    lessons on miscalculation, misperception,
      and limits of crisis management, 184
    nuclear brinkmanship and escalation, 67
Cunningham, Fiona S., 101–102, 177
currency intervention against the RMB
    Beijing's options for deploying FX reserves
      in response, 293–296, 330 n.7, n.13,
      331 n.17
    effect on dollar prices, 296–297
    as a form of strategic deterrence, 262–264,
      293
    goals for HKD and CNH exchange
      rates, 293–294
    incentivizing capital outflows from
      China, 114–115, 297
    need for congressional authorization and
      sustained support, 296
    potential comparisons to the Suez Crisis
      (1956), 263–264
    proximate goals of, 293
    relationships between the CNY, CNH,
      HKD, and USD, 293–294
    risks to the United States, 294–295, 330
      n.14
    as a strategic deterrence threat to hold
      in reserve in a post-Day One
      world, 262–263, 297
    threat to trigger capital flight from the
      HKD and CNH, 293, 295–296
currency system in China. *See* China's
    currency system
cyberattacks
    and AI, 44
    backlash in Taiwan against, 339 n.122
    China's use for strategic
      deterrence, 61–62
    relationship to legal and information
      warfare, 56–58
    relationship to space domain, 113, 118
    role in China's gray-zone coercion, 2–3

Danzig, Richard, 5, 374 n.159

Day One and the Day One Plan. *See also* avalanche decoupling; currency intervention
   Australia's reliance on the U.S. for security assurance in a post-Day One world, 243
   China's dependence on neutral markets in a post-Day One world shaped by avalanche decoupling, 261–262
   the Day One plan as a means to strengthen U.S. integrated deterrence, 266–267
   discriminatory trade policy as the first pillar of, 242
   the role of the ESCB in a post-Day One world, 241
   and the U.S. affirmative vision for the global economy after a rupture, 275

decapitation strike
   PLA scenario and Taiwan's continuity-of-government response, 87

declassification of information
   before a potential PRC move against Taiwan, 77, 84–85
   before Putin's invasion of Ukraine, 77

decoupling of the U.S.–China trade relationship
   impact on the U.S. economy and those of its allies, 235
   PRC scholars' reflections on, 223, 384 n.95
   the United States lack of a coherent strategy regarding, 6, 11

defense industrial base (DIB)
   adaptation to emerging technologies, 150, 158–159, 168
   challenges of procuring from early-stage companies, 159–160
   definition, 157
   procurement system challenges and reforms, 157–161
   workforce challenges, 157–158, 161, 353 n.72

Defense Production Act (DPA)
   limits of coercive industrial mobilization, 159

Democratic Progressive Party (DPP). *See also* Lai Ching-te

characterization as "separatist" and "pro-independence," 17–18, 29
cross-Strait policy, 29–30, 124
policy on nuclear power, 339 n.114
view of the PRC, 22–23
views on status quo of Taiwan, 23

democratic Taiwan
   as an alternative pathway for China, 45–46
   U.S. engagement to strengthen, 46, 126–127, 130, 145–146

Deng Xiaoping
   depiction in the *Road to Rejuvenation* exhibit, 171
   justification for China's invasion of Vietnam, 77–78

Department of Defense. *See also* United States—Department of Defense (DOD)
   need to address gaps in the U.S. force structure, 5–6, 88, 158
   shift to Distributed Maritime Operations (DMO), 104–105, 154–156
   support for companies investing in emerging technologies, 166

De-risking
   contrasted with decoupling in U.S.-China policy debate, 206

deterrence—deterrence by denial
   the DoD's slow progress on, 5–6
   as necessary but not sufficient to deter an amphibious invasion and blockade, 118–119
   need for it extend to a blockade scenario, 9–10, 112
   as the second of four pillars of deterrence, 9–10, 273

deterrence—dual deterrence, 5–6, 124, 126, 135–136
   Thomas Schelling, 172, 174–176, 182

deterrence—integrated deterrence
   the Day One plan as a means to strengthen, 267
   economic and political deterrence as essential pillars of, 11–12, 145
   "integrated strategic deterrence" (综合性战略威慑), 269–270, 301 n.34

deterrence–integrated deterrence (*Continued*)
    PRC perceptions of, 384 n.97
    as a psychological warfare directed at Xi, 276–277
    the U.S. government's need for, 6
DF-21D/DF-26 missiles
    contribution to China's long-range precision-strike regime, 153
    dual-capable systems and escalation ambiguity in Taiwan conflict scenarios, 178–179
    role in China's anti-access/area-denial strategy against U.S. naval forces, 156
    threat to U.S. bases and logistics hubs, 37, 103
Diego Garcia base, 149*f*, 380 n.49
Ding, Jeffrey, 5
diplomatic relations
    countries with diplomatic relations with Taiwan, 22, 58
    the PRC's policy to not conduct diplomatic relations with countries that recognize Taiwan, 305 n.26
    U.S. diplomatic relations with the PRC, 25–27, 107, 308 n.53
Distributed Maritime Operations (DMO)
    dispersal of U.S. surface forces using stealth and long-range fires to counter missile and drone threats, 104
dollar hegemony
    in the context of an economic contingency plan for a Taiwan crisis, 238, 275
    as a core U.S. national interest, 48–49
    and ESCB, 251
    impact of a Taiwan crisis on, 49, 51
    impact of Trump's tariffs on, 203–204
    implications of a Taiwan crises on, 116–117
    imposition of secondary sanctions on Europe on, 214–215
    locking China inside the dollar system while avalanche decoupling proceeds, 262
    a multicurrency system as an alternative to, 49, 205, 377 n.15

trade settlement in currencies other than dollars triggered by hard decoupling, 235
Doshi, Rush, 5
drones/unmanned aerial systems (UAS)
    allied UAS production, 161
    China's DJI drones, 162, 258
    Collaborative Combat Aircraft (CCA), 162, 357 n.101
    counter-UAS (CUAS) technologies, 161, 163, 356 n.96
    rapid evolution of UAS during the war in Ukraine, 147, 161
    REPLICATOR program, 105–106, 152
    scouting drones, 152
    unmanned drones from China operating in Taiwan's airspace, 61
Dulles, John Foster, 200

Easton, Ian, 5, 89, 332 n.28
economic contingency planning
    commitment to avalanche decoupling, 238–239, 248, 260, 264, 275
    connection to dollar hegemony, 238, 275
    feasibility of execution, 265
    as the fourth pillar of deterrence, 11–13
    fundamental principles of an American economic contingency plan, 238–239
    impact of CCP responses on U.S. economy, 220, 274
    joint contingency planning and strategic communication among the core allies, 9, 236, 273
    the need for the U.S. to have a credible affirmative contingency plan, 7, 205
    political and economic deterrence as inseparable issues, 7–8
    possible economic and political implications of Taiwan crises, 113–117
    scholarly exploration, 5
Economic Cooperation Administration (ECA)
    administered Marshall Plan, 252
economic mutually assured destruction (EMAD)

currency intervention against the RMB
compared with, 264
logic of, 233
mutually assured destruction (MAD)
compared with, 10, 233–234
Economic Security Cooperation Board
(ESCB)
China's possible responses to the
formation of, 258–259
investigation of cases of transshipment, 241–242, 250–251,
254
key functions, 12, 241, 250
mandates, 239–240, 242, 255–256, 276
Marshall Plan and historical inspiration
for, 250
operational independence of, 255, 391
n.30
role in facilitating U.S.–China bilateral
decoupling, 12, 239–242, 249–251,
254, 256–257, 259–260, 262, 266,
275
role in safeguarding of a fair and honest
international trading system, 241,
249–251, 255, 258, 275
Russia, North Korea, Iran, and China
excluded from, 12, 241
treatment of third countries, 241–242,
250–251
Economy, Elizabeth, 5
Eichengreen, Barry, 377 n.15
Eisenhower, Dwight, 66–67, 176
consideration of nuclear use during the
first two Taiwan Straits Crises, 173,
177
Erickson, Andrew S., 5
evaluation of the Malacca blockade
scenario, 210
on Xi's "all-domain pressure
campaign," 57–58, 319 n.10
European Union
China's goals for, 43–44
cooperation with ESCB, 256–257
defense industrial cooperation, 273
expected GDP loss during hard
decoupling, 220
indirect effects of avalanche decoupling
on, 116

trade conflict with the Trump
administration, 214, 245
uncertain cooperation on
sanctions, 213–214, 248
evacuation of civilians
air evacuation as the only viable option for
Taiwan, 81
foreign residents in Taiwan, 79–80
imminent conflict and loss of control
signaled by, 80–81
the Kabul evacuation, 80
noncombatant evacuation operations
(NEO), 80–81
U.S. airlift out of Saigon, 80
U.S. plans to evacuate citizens from
Taiwan, 81–82, 84–85, 142–143,
272–273
export controls
allied coordination requirements, 196–197,
215–216
China's retaliatory export controls, 217,
239
as deterrence tool (benefits and limits), 40–41, 195, 197–198, 215, 216,
239
enforcement challenges and
evasion, 215–216
extraterritorial enforcement via dollar
system, 48–49
as perceived by China (security
dilemma), 38–39
risks of escalation and instability, 40–41,
197–198
semiconductor and AI controls, 162,
196–197
TSMC's perspective, 216
Extended deterrence
U.S. nuclear assurances to treaty allies
(Japan, Australia, Philippines) and
limits regarding Taiwan, 173

Farrell, Henry and Abraham L.
Newman, 208, n.36
February 28 Incident (1947), 284
Federal Reserve
coordination with Treasury and
Congress, 114, 240

Federal Reserve (*Continued*)
   crisis management in Taiwan
      contingency, 113–114
   currency intervention backstop (Treasurys;
      RMB/CNH), 295–297
   dollar swap lines, 114, 132
   historical precedent, 263–264
fentanyl, 63, 180
Financial repression
   role in sustaining China's export
      surplus, 206
First and Second Island Chains
   China's strategic perceptions of U.S. forces
      in, 34–37
   the First Island Chain viewed as both
      "barrier" and "springboard" by PLA
      strategists, 34–36
   location of, 34, 35*f*
   potential to screen transit into the First
      Island Chain, during a Malacca
      blockade, 210
   Taiwan's geographic position in the First
      Island Chain, 148
   U.S. facilities in the First Island Chain, 68,
      75, 149*f*, 163, 281
Five Eyes
   intelligence sharing and trust among U.S.,
      UK, Australia, and Canada, 143
Five Powers Clause
   commercial war-risk insurance pro-
      vision terminating coverage in
      conflicts involving major powers
      (U.S./China), 69
Foreign Direct Product Rule (FDPR)
   export-control tool in deterrence scenarios
      involving Taiwan and China, 215
Formosa Incident (Meilidao Incident,
      1979), 284
Forward Alliance, 99
France
   during the Berlin blockade, 64–65
   blocking of NATO's cooperation with
      Indo-Pacific partners, 143–144
   experience in Algeria and Indochina, 90
   fall to Nazi Germany, 166–167
   Japanese surrender of Indochina, 307
      n.45
   Macron, Emmanuel, 144
   Operation Neptune (1944), 91

potential interest in a diminished role for
      the dollar, 49
   role in Marshall Plan, 242, 252
   trade relationship with neutral United
      States during Revolutionary and
      Napoleonic Wars (1807), 213
Fravel, M. Taylor, 177

G7
   asset freezes and escalation risk in
      economic warfare with China, 258
   sanctions coordination after Russia's 2022
      invasion of Ukraine, 225–226
   venue and reference point for Core
      coalition coordination, 143–144
Gao Xingwei (高惺惟), 223–224, 384 n.97
Gates, Robert Michael, 184
General Agreement on Tariffs and Trade
      (GATT), 237
   Article XXI of, 47, 245, 318 n.166
George, Alexander L. and Richard
      Smoke, 175
Germany
   assassination of Archduke Franz
      Ferdinand, 202
   the Berlin blockade and Berlin
      Airlift, 64–68, 84
   big-gun fleets dedicated to scouting
      during the Battle of Jutland
      (1916), 151–152
   Britain's blockade of Germany
      (1915), 232
   the Fisher-Tropsch process created by Nazi
      Germany, 391 n.35
   German residents in Taiwan, 79–80
   impact of hard decoupling from China
      on, 219, 221*f*, 222*f*
   sinking of the *Lusitania* and political
      responses in the United States, 101
Glaser, Bonnie S., 5
gray-zone aggression. *See also* all-domain
      pressure campaign
   Beijing's work in international
      institutions, 59
   as a central element of the Taiwan
      question, 84
   goals of economic gray zone coercion, 60
   incremental redefinition of the status
      quo, 2–3, 19

"law enforcement" vessels in the maritime
	space around Taiwan, 55, 61
PLA violations of the median line in the
	Taiwan Strait as, 34, 56, 61
police actions as a form of gray zone
	activity, 55–57, 60, 61, 71, 107–108,
	111, 271–272
a quarantine scenario as gray-zone
	strategy, 62
relation to structured ambiguity, 125,
	140, 141–142
the Second Thomas Shoal episode
	(2024), 55–56
testing of U.S. red lines, 62, 264, 266
the U.S. government's lack of a coherent
	public strategy to deter gray-zone
	aggression, 5–6
U.S. preparation for, 83–85
Great Britain and the UK
AUKUS (Australia, UK, and US), 143,
	154, 163–164, 243
Battle of Trafalgar (1805), 151–152
during the Berlin blockade, 64–65
blockade of Germany (1915), 232
closing of the London Stock Exchange
	during the outbreak of World
	War I, 114
as a Core ally, 125–126, 146
ITAR reform and technology
	partnership, 160
poaching of AI talent from China, 196
potential role in the execution of a Malacca
	blockade, 210
residents in Taiwan, 79–80
scouting during the Battle of Jutland
	(1916), 151–152
tensions with the neutral United States
	during Napoleonic Wars (1807), 213
Grinberg, Mariya, 5
Guam
China's DF-26 "Guam-killer" missile, 37,
	103, 153, 156
location of, 35f
U.S. forces and weapons based in, 37, 185

H-20 bomber
as component of China's air-based nuclear
	triad, 178
Hass, Ryan, 5

Hellscape
unmanned deterrence concept for
	the Taiwan Strait, 106. *See also*
	deterrence; drones; REPLICATOR
Henley, Lonnie D., 109, 111, 112
Hong Kong
Hong Kong-style framework of One
	Country, Two Systems, 23–24
Hong Kong Monetary Authority (HKMA)
	the HKD's peg to the U.S. dollar, 329 n.1
as a vital provider of CHN
	liquidity, 293–294
Huang Zhiling (黄志凌), 384 n.95
human-in-the-loop
U.S. doctrine on nuclear decision-making
	amid AI integration, 193. *See also* AI
hypersonic missiles
challenges to missile defense and
	implications for strategic
	deterrence, 199
role in China's expanding conventional
	and nuclear strike capabilities, 178

import restrictions. *See also* tariffs
Beijing's fear of restricting bilateral
	trade that would drive Taiwan to
	strengthen economic ties with the
	U.S. and Japan, 60
Beijing's history of using import
	restrictions for geopolitical
	coercion, 259
China's restriction of Norwegian
	salmon, 38, 391 n.37
Russia's restrictions of imports to increase
	account surplus, 386 n.117
India
civilians in Taiwan, 79–80
conflict over Kashmir, 175–176
cooperation with BRICS, 144
expected GDP loss during hard
	decoupling, 220
redirected flows of Russian oil after
	sanctions, 392 n.38
relations with China as an early warning
	indicator, 79
responses to China's embargo of critical
	minerals, 391 n.36
role as a neutral in a Taiwan
	crisis, 213–214, 251

India (*Continued*)
  territorial dispute with China, 40, 56, 173
  trade settlement with Russia outside U.S. dollars, 49, 223–225, 384 n.101
  vulnerability to China's dumping during avalanche decoupling, 247–248
Indirect control scenario. *See* quarantine scenario
Indo-Pacific
  deployment of nuclear-capable intermediate-range delivery systems in, 273–274
  establishment of NATO-style structures, 143
  impact of a U.S.-China war over Taiwan on, 106–107
  U.S. interest in keeping the region free and open, 43–44
  U.S. military presence in, 42–43
  U.S. plans to stabilize the nuclear balance in, 186
integrated air defense system (IADS)
  China's IADS and implications for blockade and U.S. operations, 112
  as counter to missile advantage, 154
  PLA suppression of Taiwan's IADS, 90
  Taiwan's, 90
integrated deterrence. *See* deterrence—integrated deterrence
intelligence, surveillance, and reconnaissance (ISR). *See* command-and-control, communications, computers, intelligence, surveillance, and reconnaissance (C4ISR)
International Monetary Fund (IMF)
  procedural paralysis and limits during a Taiwan crisis, 250, 259
  Suez Crisis (1956), 263–264
  as template for ESCB governance model (voting shares, U.S. veto), 256
International Traffic in Arms Regulations (ITAR), 160
Iran
  dollar sanctions forcing it to sell oil at a discount, 296
  economic pressure used by the U.S. as a tool to push for long-term regime in, 49–50

effectiveness of U.S.-designed systems in protecting Israel from missiles from, 95, 154
  emboldening of, by a forceful takeover of Taiwan, 37–38, 43–45, 79, 186
  exclusion from ESCB, 12, 241
  expanding nuclear arsenal of, 187
  sanctioning of, by the U.S., 11, 49
  sanctions and export controls holding back the economic, technological, and military development of, 48–49
  sharing of advanced defense technologies with China, North Korea, and Russia, 147–148

Japan, 151–152. *See also* Battle of Midway (1942); Pearl Harbor
  blockade of Allied forces (1942), 167
  expected GDP loss during hard decoupling, 220
  growing nuclear threat from North Korea, China, and Russia faced by, 185–187
  impact of Day One on its trading relationships, 242
  impact of hard decoupling from China on, 219, 221*f*, 222*f*
  impact of United States-Taiwan relations on the U.S.-Japan alliance, 142
  Japanese residents in Taiwan, 79–80
  Japan's adoption of its own version of the TRA, 139, 142–143, 345 n.52
  NATO-style nuclear-sharing arrangements between the U.S. and, 273–274
  need for stronger nuclear assurances, 173, 201
  the need for the world's major democracies to build a joint allied defense industrial base with, 273
  oil resupply exercises in the Southwestern Islands by its Self Defense Forces, 326 n.80
  as one of five Core members, 125–126, 146
  poaching of AI talent from China, 196
  "three nonnuclear principles" as central to its national identity, 186
  the Vinson buildup and its failure to deter Japanese aggression, 7, 167

JASSM (Joint Air-to-Surface Standoff
        Missile)
    role in U.S. long-range standoff strike, 153
    stockpile limitations in Taiwan
        contingency, 153–154
Jervis, Robert, 362 n.12

Kastner, Scott L., 5
Kempe, Frederick, 324 n.55
Kennedy, Conor M., 5
Kennedy, John F. and the Kennedy
        administration
    Cuban Missile Crisis, 67
    exchanges with Khrushchev on the Berlin
        issue, 66–67, 324 n.55
    tightening of rules for U.S. nuclear
        sharing, 370 n.118
Khan, Sulmaan Wasif, 5
Khrushchev, Nikita
    Cuban Missile Crisis, 67
    exchanges with Kennedy on the Berlin
        issue, 66–67, 324 n.55
Kilcrease, Emily, 208
Kinmen and Matsu
    gray-zone coercion and crisis signaling, 55
    vulnerability as early-war seizure
        targets, 76
Kirshner, Jonathan, 392 n.45
Kissinger, Henry, 25
Kuomintang (KMT). *See also* Lee Teng-hui
    cross-Strait policy of, 28, 30
    government-in-exile in Taiwan established
        by, 22, 287
    the KMT pushed into China's inte-
        rior by Japan's expansionist
        ambitions, 166–167
    "One China" supported by, 27–28
    Su Chi's association with former KMT
        president Ma Ying-jeou, 280
    Taiwan assumed as part of China in the
        One China Principle disputed by, 23

Lai Ching-te
    association with the DPP, 17
    denial of his planned transit by the Trump
        administration (July 2025), 134
    election of, 280
    inaugural address, 29, 310 n.81
    Taiwanese independence supported
        by, 29, 281
    Xi's explicit mention of him by name, 17
Lee Teng-hui
    Chang Jung-feng as responsible for
        cross-Strait matters during his
        presidency, 288
    visit to Cornell University (1995), 123
Legal warfare (lawfare)
    use of legal instruments as coercive tools
        in cross-strait and international
        competition, 58–59
Lin, Hsiao-ting, 5
logistics
    basing, prepositioning, and logistics
        hubs, 155
    as bridge between economy and military
        operations, 154–155
    limits of airlift and missile
        exposure, 154–155
    rebuilding U.S. maritime logistics
        capacity, 155
    sealift shortfalls and maritime workforce
        crisis, 154–155
    U.S. vulnerabilities in Indo-Pacific
        conflict, 154–155
LRASM (Long-Range Anti-Ship Missile)
    limited stockpiles in Taiwan
        contingency, 153–154
    production capacity constraints, 154
    role in U.S. long-range standoff strike, 153
Lu Xun, "The True Story of Ah Q," 289

MacArthur, Douglas
    order to Japanese commanders in
        "China...Formosa and French
        Indo-China," 307 n.45
    Taiwan described as an "unsinkable
        aircraft carrier," 36
macroeconomic stability. *See also*
        deterrence—economic contingency
        planning
    impact of a crisis on, 11, 19
    as a strategic concern, 46–47
Malacca blockade
    arguments justifying a Malacca blockade
        under UNCLOS, 232, 388 n.143
    criticisms, 210

Malacca blockade (*Continued*)
  effects on cargo vessels, tankers and other
      ships, 35*f*, 211*f*
  as a *far blockade*, 232–233
  Hu Jintao's comments on the "Malacca
      dilemma," 210–212
  Japan's blockade of Allied forces
      (1942), 167
  political effects of supply chain disruptions
      and financial dislocations caused
      by, 232
  the U.S. Navy's operational capacity to
      execute a Malacca blockade, 210
MANPADS (Man-Portable Air Defense
    Systems)
  role in Taiwan's decentralized air
      defense, 96–97
Marshall Plan (1948–1952)
  economic logic of, 252–253
  the economic recovery of Western Europe
      as its objective, 251–253, 274–275
  as the inspiration for the ESCB, 250, 254
  as the paradigmatic success story of
      American capitalist imperialism, 253
  and the principles of the Atlantic
      Charter, 237, 242
Martinson, Ryan D., 5
Mastro, Oriana Skylar, 5
Ma Ying-jeou, 280, 285–286
McNamara, Robert S., 184
median line
  location of, 108*f*
  PLA violations of, 34, 56, 61, 291
  threats to cross it during the Taiwan Straits
      Crisis (1995–1996), 290–291
military mobilization
  coercive mobilization of PLA air-naval
      forces for a potential invasion, 2–3,
      57, 74–77, 84–85
  the impossibility for states to hide
      its preparations from its
      adversaries, 73–74
Miller, Chris, 5
Milley, Mark A., 73
Mullen, Michael, 208
Mutual Defense Treaty (U.S.–Taiwan)
  abrogation in 1979 following
      normalization with PRC, 26
mutually assured destruction (MAD)
  and AI-driven advances, 192
  economic mutually assured destruction
      (EMAD) compared with, 10,
      233–234
  logic of, 176
  and the 1972 Anti-Ballistic Missile
      Treaty, 176
  PRC literature on, 362 n.14

Nachman, Lev, 5
National Museum of China. See *Road to
    Rejuvenation* exhibit at the National
    Museum of China
National Party Congresses
  2027 as the date of the 21st National Party
      Congress, 32
  Xi's comments at the 20th Party
      Congress, 181–182
  Xi's remarks on reunification, at National
      Party Congresses, 32–33, 182, 313
      n.102
national rejuvenation
  aspiration to reshape regional and global
      order, 37–38
  economic tools the U.S. could use to put it
      at risk, 11–12
  encapsulation of CCP's domestic and
      global ambitions, 1–2
  necessary relationship to Taiwan's
      "reunification", 1–2, 32, 38, 270
  openness to a "grand bargain" with the
      United States, 39
  undermining by avalanche
      decoupling, 276
  Xi's suspicion that the U.S. is trying to
      derail, 18, 33
National security exemption (Article XXI)
  Norm set by the ESCB, 255
  use to justify decoupling and trade
      discrimination, 239–240
  under WTO/GATT rules, 47
naval mines
  as asymmetric defense against amphibious
      invasion, 93
  as component of U.S. and allied deterrence
      by denial, 106, 273
  role in Taiwan Strait denial and channeling
      PLA forces, 96

use in blockade and counter blockade
scenarios, 112–113
neutral states and third countries
China's dependence on neutral markets in
a post-Day One world, 261–262
impact of a U.S.–China war over
Taiwan on regional nonaligned
countries, 106–107
importance of fair and honest treatment of
neutrals in enforcing anti-PRC trade
policies, 237–238
the interest of all sovereign states in a fair
and honest international trading
system, 48, 145, 232, 237–238,
249–251, 275
threats to use military force against
neutrals during blockades, 232
trafficking of sanctioned goods
by, 212–214, 240
U.S. pitch to neutral states in a crisis, 9,
146
Xi's "Global Governance Initiative"
pitched to, 37
New Zealand
policy alignment with Core allies, 244
role in the Berlin airlift, 66
support for peace and stability in the
Taiwan Strait, 144
trade with China, 221f, 222f
"1992 Consensus"
Beijing's interpretation, 18–19, 23, 33
Jou Yi Cheng's discussion of it, 285
KMT perspectives on, 28
Su Chi's interpretation of, 280, 282–283
Su Chi's invention of the concept, 280,
285
No First Use (NFU)
China's nuclear use policy, 181–182
U.S. rejection of NFU policy, 177
Noncombatant evacuation operations
(NEO). See evacuation of civilians
North Korea
defense industrial integration with China,
Russia, and Iran, 147–148
exclusion from the ESCB, 12, 241
expanding nuclear arsenal of, 185–187
goal of U.S. sanctions on, 49–50
limited effects of sanctions on, 48–49

potential opportunistic responses to a
forceful takeover of Taiwan, 37–38,
43–45, 79, 186, 271
Norway
dispute with China, 38, 391 n.37
Nazi Germany's invasion of, 166–167
nuclear weapons. See also mutually assured
destruction (MAD)
B-21 Raiders, 188, 371 n.131
"Dial-a-Yield" gravity bombs, 188, 371
n.132
modernizing of the PLA's nuclear
arsenal, 177–178, 273–274
modernizing of the U.S. nuclear
arsenal, 187–189
nuclear brinkmanship, 176, 183, 193, 200
the Obama administration's consideration
and rejection of a "no first use"
nuclear policy, 177
tactical nuclear weapons, 113, 185–186,
188
U.S. Strategic Command
(STRATCOM), 170–171,
171f
nuclear weapons—nuclear proliferation
China's engagement in nuclear
buildup, 6, 10, 170, 171f, 178–179
DEFCON warnings, 179, 183–184
impact of a forced takeover of Taiwan
on, 4
nuclear competition, 176–177
nuclear sharing distinguished from, 187
nuclear weapons—nuclear sharing
involvement of South Korea and Japan in
nuclear deterrence operations, 10,
186–187
pathways to nuclear-sharing agreements
with the U.S. to allies expressing an
interest in, 201
potential arrangements with the South
Korea and Japan, 187, 273–274
tightening of rules during the Kennedy
administration, 370 n.118
U.S. nuclear sharing during early Cold
War, 370 n.118
nuclear weapons—strategic nuclear threats
AI models for strategic coercion compared
with, 193

nuclear weapons–nuclear proliferation
(*Continued*)
compellent nuclear threats, 175–176,
199–200, 376 n.185, n.186
No First Use (NFU) policy, 181–182
use by China in a possible invasion
scenario, 118, 199–200
nuclear weapons—U.S. nuclear assurances
extension of nuclear assurance to Taiwan,
likely viewed as escalation by
Beijing, 173
the need for, 185, 187, 201
U.S. plans to stabilize nuclear balance in
the Indo-Pacific, 186
Nye, Joseph, 123

Obama, Barack and the Obama
administration, 177
Office of Foreign Assets Control (OFAC)
U.S. Treasury agency enforcing sanctions;
potential role in blocking PRC access
to the dollar system, 209
Okinawa
Kadena Air Base, 101, 103, 149*f*
location of, 36*f*
Oksenberg, Michael, 308 n.51
One China Policy
Biden administration's communication
of, 137–138
under the Biden and Trump
administrations, 33
credible resolve and restraint, 8–9, 125,
139–140, 146, 200, 272–273
difference from Beijing's "One China
Principle", 23, 50–51
importance of, 25
reduced form, 27
Six Assurances, 3–4, 17–18, 24, 26–27,
136–137
Taiwan Relations Act, 17–18, 24, 26,
138–139
Three Joint Communiqués. *See* Three
Joint Communiqués
One China Principle (一中原则)
DPP opposition to, 29
One China Policy differentiated from, 23,
50–51
recognition of the legitimacy of, as a key
priority of, 18–19, 23

Xi's identification of it as the political foundation of China-U.S.
relations, 17
One Country, Two Systems
Hong Kong-style framework of, 23–24
as Xi's endgame for "peaceful
reunification," 2–3, 18–19,
269

Pacific Deterrence Initiative (PDI)
funding for Indo-Pacific basing and
logistics, 155
Paparo, Samuel, 106
peaceful reunification. *See*
reunification—peaceful reunification
Pearl Harbor, 167
as a *operational* surprise but not a *strategic*
surprise, 73–74
U.S. political response to, 101
Pelosi, Nancy, visit to Taiwan (August
2022), 33–34, 289
Penghu Islands
environmental constraints in the Taiwan
Strait, 89
vulnerability as early-war seizure
targets, 76
People's Armed Forces Maritime Militia
(PAFMM), 57–58, 61
People's Liberation Army Navy (PLAN), 55
amphibious fleet of, 9, 93–94, 96, 112,
331 n.25
preparations for an amphibious invasion
of Taiwan, 75–76
Permanent Normal Trading Relations
(PNTR)
revocation enabling U.S. trade decoupling
from China, 244–245
Philippines
geography of, 35*f*
need for stronger U.S. security
assurances, 173, 201
position on nuclear weapons, 186
PRC aggression against waters of, 38
Philippine Sea
logistical distance and strain on U.S.
Indo-Pacific operations, 154–155
undersea warfare and submarine
operations near the First Island
Chain, 105

PLA Air Force (PLAAF)
  contribution to China's nuclear triad and
    bomber modernization, 178
  coordination challenges with PLA
    Navy, 290–291
  role in suppression of Taiwan's air
    defenses, 90
PLA Rocket Force
  as conventional strike force targeting U.S.
    bases, 101
  corruption and force reliability, 168
  role in nuclear modernization and
    escalation dynamics, 177–178
political deterrence
  engagement with Taiwan as an essential
    component of, 124–127, 132–133,
    145–146
  as an essential pillar of integrated
    deterrence, 11–12, 145
  as the first pillar of deterrence, 8–9
  twofold goals of, 133–134
  U.S. partnerships in the developing world
    as a key element of, 144
porcupine strategy
  Taiwan's denial-based defense posture
    using mobile and survivable
    capabilities, 150
precision strikes
  China's missile arsenal and strike
    capabilities, 37, 68, 101, 103, 153,
    156
  China's reconnaissance-strike
    complex, 117–118
  PLA threat to Taiwan's air
    defenses, 94–95
  shift to satellite-based, C4ISR, 151–152
preparedness. *See also* Day One and the Day
    One Plan
  the "break-glass scenario," 82–84, 293
  Economic Security Cooperation Board
    (ESCB)
  joint contingency planning and strategic
    communication among Core
    allies, 9, 70, 236, 273
  need for targeted investments, 7, 168–169
  need to prepare for both a crisis and a
    war, 5
  Taiwan's state of preparedness for conflict

  joint allied decoupling from China in
    critical products, 12
  U.S. lack of preparedness for gray-zone
    aggression, 5–6, 83–85
  U.S. public statements on China's readi-
    ness for conflict over Taiwan, 31,
    311 n.94
Putin, Vladimir. *See also* Russian invasion of
    Ukraine
  essay "on the Historical Unity of Russians
    and Ukrainians," 31, 73

quarantine scenario
  Beijing's framing as routine law enforce-
    ment, 55–57, 71, 107–108, 111,
    271–272
  difficulty of deterring, 64, 204–205
  discussion by Blackwill and Zelikow, 5,
    56–57, 63
  escalation risks, 64–72 *passim*
  implications of the disruption of Taiwan's
    semiconductor exports, 70–71, 215
  mobilization of a Core coalition
    during, 71–72
  possible economic responses to, 244–245
  resupplying Taiwan during, 64, 67–72,
    272–273
  risks for China, 70–72
  stakes if the United States fails to
    deter, 43–44

Raimondo, Gina, 195
RAND Corporation, 101–102
Rapid Dragon
  palletized munitions concept enabling
    dispersed long-range strike, 153
ratcheting trade policies
  as a means of achieving avalanche
    decoupling, 239–240, 246–247,
    261, 275–276
  requirement to end permanent normal
    trading relations (PNTR), 244–245,
    389 n.8
  restructuring global trade after a Taiwan
    crisis, 116–117
  Section 232 of the Trade Expansion Act of
    1962, 244–246, 389 n.10, 390 n.15

Reagan, Ronald and the Reagan
    administration
    Able Archer crisis (1983), 183–185, 192,
        198
    communication of U.S. satellite and
        computing advantages to the Soviet
        Union, 174
    Six Assurances offered to Taiwan, 26–27
    Strategic Defense Initiative (SDI, i.e. "Star
        Wars"), 183–184, 189–190, 198
    strategic pressure on Moscow, 288
red lines
    China's red lines according to Chang
        Jung-feng, 290–291
    China's red lines according to Edward
        Lee, 288
    China's red lines according to Jou Yi
        Cheng, 285
    China's red lines according to Su Chi, 281
    economic Armageddon resulting from
        enforcing U.S. red lines, 204–234,
        264, 266, 274–275
    the PRC's 2005 Anti-Secession Law as
        articulation of, 24
    the "Taiwan question" identified as a red
        line by Xi Jinping, 17–19
    Taiwan's leaders respecting of, 29, 33
    U.S. redlines, 7–8, 55, 62, 71, 233, 264,
        266, 270, 271–272
    vagueness of, 24, 51
REPLICATOR
    DoD initiative for mass deploy-
        ment of attritable unmanned
        systems, 105–106
    role in scouting UAS and counter-scouting
        resilience, 152
Republic of China (ROC). See Taiwan
Republic of China Armed Forces
    (ROCAF), 20
    Su Chi's assessment of, 282
resilience
    China's potential resilience to economic
        shocks, 223–225
    need for collective allied
        resilience to PRC economic
        countermeasures, 258–259
    renxing (韧性, "resilience") as fun-
        damental to Xi's vision for
        China, 181
    resilience of nuclear deterrent, 273–274
    Russia's resilience to sanctions, 228–229
    Taiwan's need to invest in
        resilience, 124–125, 132–133
    U.S. engagement to strengthen-
        ing Taiwan's democracy and
        resilience, 145–146, 272
resupply operations
    resupplying Taiwan during a
        quarantine, 64, 67–72, 272–273
reunification
    Beijing's position that it began with the
        "1992 Consensus," 18–19, 23, 33
    as a propaganda term, 1–2
    the term "reunification" as PRC
        propaganda, 1–2
    viewed as "inevitable" in Xi's vision for
        national rejuvenation, 1–2, 32
    Xi's remarks on, at National Party
        Congresses, 32–33, 182, 313 n.102
reunification—peaceful reunification
    One Country, Two Systems as
        Xi's endgame for "peaceful
        reunification," 2–3, 18–19, 269
Rigger, Shelley, 5
RMB internationalization, 223–224
Road to Rejuvenation exhibit at the National
    Museum of China
    absence of Taiwan from, 269
    as the centerpiece of the museum, 170
    implicit narrative of, 271–272
    portrayal of Xi's leadership, 268–270,
        277
Roosevelt, Franklin Delano and the
    Roosevelt administration
    "arsenal of democracy" fireside chat, 169
    creation of the Atlantic Charter, 237–268
    Pearl Harbor, 73–74, 167
    prioritizing of preparations for a land war
        across the Atlantic over an air-naval
        war in the Pacific, 166–167
Rudd, Kevin, 5, 38–39, 315 n.126
Russia. See also Khrushchev, Nikita
    concept of strategic deterrence
        (strategicheskoe sderzhivanie), 171
    defense industrial integration with China,
        North Korea, and Iran, 147–148
    effects of U.S. sanctions on, 228–229

and the global oil glut during the early
COVID pandemic, 383 n.86
goals of U.S. sanctions against, 49–50
nuclear arms control and, 189
Putin, Vladimir
support for de-dollarization, 49
Russian invasion of Ukraine. *See also* Putin,
Vladimir; Russia; Ukraine
Declassification of information by Western
intelligence agencies before the
invasion, 77
differences between Taiwan and
Ukraine, 215
impact on global oil and gas markets, 217,
392 n.38
mobilization for invasion of Ukraine
(2021), 72–73
as a potential model for China's invasion
of Taiwan, 31, 70–71, 265
rapid evolution of UAS during, 147, 161
Russia's response to the imposition of
U.S. and EU sanctions (February
2022), 225–227, 229–230
transformation of Ukrainians society into
a determined and cohesive fighting
force, 12, 99–100, 128–129
U.S. citizens urged to leave Ukraine, 81

salami-slicing tactics
possible PRC perceptions that the United
States is using, 138
as a term, 39, 315 n.127
use by Moscow (1961), 66–67
Xi's use of, 72
sanctions
and blockades, 209–210. *See also*
Blockades; Malacca blockade
against China
limits and risks in Taiwan crisis (global
supply chains; credibility), 11, 50,
72, 115, 116
China's use of sanctions (example:
Norway), 38
de-dollarization/dollar weapon erosion, 48–49, 147–148, 205, 208,
223–224
default Washington "playbook" and why
it must be reimagined, 11
as deterrent threat (often implicit), 11–12

enforcement limits
neutrals, arbitrage, evasion, 205, 208,
212–213
institutions
OFAC; Treasury Department, 209,
223–224. *See also* CHIPS; CIPS;
SWIFT
Russia-2022 sanctions as baseline model
(debated), 208
secondary sanctions
coalition-fracturing risk, 214–215
Saudi Arabia, 221*f*, 222*f*
expected losses and potential reactions
during hard decoupling, 220, 383
n.86
Schelling, Thomas
on brinkmanship, 175
on deadlines for compellent nuclear
threats, 376 n.186
on deterrence and compellence, 172,
174–176
PRC questioning of, 182
on "salami-slicing" tactics, 315 n.127
on threats of "latent violence," 47–48,
174
U.S. reliance on his theories, 182–183
Science of Military Strategy, 36, 97–98,
177–178, 305 n.34, 314 n.113, 330
n.15, 334 n.49, n.64, 335 n.73, 360
n.129, 363 n.35, 364 n.43, 367 n.80,
371 n.134
scouting and counter-scouting. *See also*
intelligence, surveillance, and
reconnaissance (ISR)
changing role of naval scouting in
history, 151–152
PLA's anti-submarine warfare (ASW)
capabilities, 105
reliance on cross-domain
integration, 102–103, 151
scouting drones, 152
Section 232 (Trade Expansion Act of 1962)
legal authority for U.S. trade
decoupling following PNTR
revocation, 244–245
proposed reform to clarify congressional and executive roles in trade
policy, 246

Select Committee on the Chinese
Communist Party (House)
role in sanctions debates, 209
on U.S. economic unpreparedness for
China conflict, 11, 204
semiconductor manufacturing. *See also* Taiwan Semiconductor Manufacturing
Company (TSMC)
China's ability to produce its own
advanced chips, 195–197
CHIPS and Science Act, 20–22
comment by Vivek Ramaswamy on
defending Taiwan until the
U.S. achieves semiconductor
independence, 129
export controls by the Biden
administration on advanced
semiconductors, 162
implications of the disruption of Taiwan's
semiconductor exports during a
quarantine, 70–71
NVIDIA, 82–83, 197
the potential of Beijing to coerce the
United States by restricting the
supply of advanced chips, 44
weaponization of Taiwan's semiconductor
industry, 208, 215
Sentinel ICBM
replacement of Minuteman III in U.S.
nuclear modernization, 188
shipping. *See also* transshipment
China Ocean Shipping Company
(COSCO), 180
use of civilian ships for military
operations, 179–180
Silicon Shield
deterrent role of Taiwan's semiconductor
dominance, 22. *See also* semiconductor manufacturing; Taiwan
Semiconductor Manufacturing
Company (TSMC)
Six Assurances
case for Japan adopting its own version
of, 139, 142–143
role in One China Policy, 3–4, 17–18, 24,
26–27. 136–137
text of, 27
smuggling and smugglers. *See also*
transshipment
incentives for arbitrage, 111, 248
integration of criminal connections into
global supply chains, 180
need for harsher penalties to deter
smugglers, 196–197
of oil during a blockade, 231
triggering by hard decoupling, 235
of weapons via civilian ships, 180
Sonnenfeld, Jeffrey A., 229
South Korea
China's economic coercion of, 259, 391
n.37
defense industrial integration with, 273
expected GDP loss during hard
decoupling, 220
growing nuclear threat from North
Korea, China, and Russia faced
by, 185–187
Joint Declaration of the Denuclearization
of the Korean Peninsula (1991), 187
NATO-style nuclear-sharing arrangements
between the U.S. and, 273–274
potential impact of a Taiwan crises
on, 115
public opinion on China, 392 n.39
relationship with Core allies, 244
risks of North Korean aggression, 45
South Korean residents in Taiwan, 79–80
support for peace and stability in the
Taiwan Strait, 144
Taiwan's situation distinguished
from, 282
U.S. withdrawing of nuclear weapons
from (1991), 185
space power
China's anti-satellite (ASAT) systems, 165
escalation risks into cyberspace and outer
space during a blockade, 113, 118
Low Earth Orbit (LEO) satellite
constellations, 165–166, 189
maintaining U.S. technological leadership
in, 166, 189
positioning, navigation, and timing
(PNT), 102, 165
relation to strategic deterrence, 10, 13
Starlink
resilient LEO satellite constellation
and cost-imposition logic in space

deterrence, 165–166. *See also* space power

State Administration of Foreign Exchange (SAFE)
China's foreign exchange reserves and sanctions resilience, 227–228

status quo
China's understanding of, 2–3, 19, 135, 140
DPP's position on, 28–29
fluidity of, 39, 55, 176–177
One China Policy and, 24–25
relation to deterrence and compellence, 8–9, 17–18, 81–82, 84, 123–124, 172, 174–175, 237–238
Xi's possible view of, 270

Stimson, Henry, 73–74

strategic alignment
AUKUS (Australia, UK, and US), 143, 154, 163–164, 243
as a key part of strategic deterrence, 201
public communication of Core coalition, 142–144

strategic ambiguity
critics of, 138
as the de facto policy of the U.S., 8, 125, 134, 138–139, 145, 288
dual deterrence over Beijing and Taipei preserved by, 5–6, 124, 135–137
effect on U.S. credibility in a coercive mobilization scenario, 136–137
structured ambiguity compared with, 140–141

strategic deterrence. *See also* economic mutually assured destruction (EMAD); mutually assured destruction (MAD)
AI development and integration as a crucial part of, 274
command-and-control, communications, computers, intelligence, surveillance, and reconnaissance (C4ISR), 10, 150–151, 168, 200–201
contribution of AI to, 5–6, 10, 44, 201
contribution of semiconductor policies to, 5–6
currency intervention against the RMB as, 262–264, 293
as one of four essential pillars of deterrence, 7, 10, 13, 273–274

Russian concept of (*strategicheskoe sderzhivanie*), 171
U.S. Strategic Command (STRATCOM), 170–171, 171f
Xi Jinping's order to build a "strategic coercion system," not a "strategic deterrence system," 200

Strategic Petroleum Reserve (SPR)
role in China's response to the Malacca dilemma, 210–212

strategic stability
definition and MAD, 176
erosion through ambiguity, technology, and AI (Taiwan), 136, 176, 191–192, 194
PRC framing *vs.* U.S. view, 182

structured ambiguity
as a communication strategy to show credible resolve and restraint, 8–9, 125, 139–140, 146, 200, 272–273
deterrent logic of, 125, 140, 141–142
risks of, 141
selective intelligence disclosures as a tool of, 125, 141
strategic ambiguity compared with, 140–141
value in gray zone crisis scenarios, 141

submarines
nuclear second-strike bastions and escalation risks along the First Island Chain, 75–76
PLA submarine growth and breakout beyond the First Island Chain, 105
role in U.S.–China undersea balance and deterrence, 163–165
U.S.–PLA attack submarine balance, 106

Suez Crisis (1956)
limits of analogy to China, 264
U.S. use of currency pressure against the UK as coercive statecraft, 263–264

Sullivan, Jake, 73, 195, 206

Sunflower Movement, 284

SWIFT (Society for Worldwide Interbank Financial Telecommunication), 48–49, 208, 223–224, 296

systemic national security threat
definition, 47

systemic national security threat (*Continued*)
ESCB enforcement, 250–251
legal designation enabling
decoupling, 245

Taiwan question, the 3
China's desire to resolve it in accordance
with PRC law, 18–19
gray-zone pressure as a central element
of, 84
identified as a red line by Xi
Jinping, 17–19
U.S. interest in a peaceful settlement
of, expressed in the First Joint
Communiqué, 25
Taiwan Relations Act (TRA)
case for Japan adopting its own version
of, 139, 142–143, 345 n.52
commitment not to revise it in the Six
Assurances, 27
commitments to Taiwan, 26, 62, 71
position on blockades and embargoes, 71
role in guiding One China Policy, 17–18,
24, 26, 138–139
Taiwan Semiconductor Manufacturing
Company (TSMC)
cutting off access to TSMC chips as a
response to a quarantine or limited
blockade, 215
export controls on advanced chips
produced with U.S. intellectual
property, 20
incentives to build fabs outside of
Taiwan, 20–22, 196–197
investments in the United States, 131
risks of CCP control of, 44
role in U.S. and allied supply chains, 20
as a "Silicon Shield" for Taiwan, 22
U.S. and China's mutual dependence on
Taiwan's chipmaking, 197–198
U.S. threat to destroy them during a
confrontation between Taiwan and
the PRC, 341 n.11
use of U.S. intellectual property, 215–216
Taiwan's internal and territorial waters—Air
Defense Identification Zone (ADIZ)
location of, 108*f*
PLA fighter jets and bombers in, 93
Taiwan's state of preparedness for conflict

Chang Jung-Feng's assessment of, 291
combat training facilities, 99
military morale and willingness to
fight, 99–100, 127–129, 145–146
Talmadge, Caitlin, 101–102
tariffs. *See also* General Agreement on Tariffs
and Trade (GATT)
China's dumping behavior, 116, 247–248
impact of a U.S. comprehensive trade and
investment agreement with Taiwan
on, 131
impact of revoking permanent normal
trading relations (PNTR), 389 n.8
possible use as strategic deterrence, 10
Trump's "Liberation Day" tariffs (April
2025), 203–204, 206, 214, 217–218,
239–240, 248, 276
Terminal High Altitude Area Defense
(THAAD), 201, 372 n.140, 391
n.37
terms of trade
balance-of-payments risk and FX
constraints, 294–296
currency intervention and long-term
erosion, 263–264
degradation as strategic objective
(avalanche decoupling), 262, 267
third countries. *See* neutral states and third
countries
Three Joint Communiqués
as the basis of the One China Policy, 3–4,
8–9, 17–18, 25, 135, 272–273
diplomatic normalization (1979), 25–26
as the "political foundation" of China-U.S.
relations, 17
translation differences, 25–26, 308 n.51
U.S. interest in a peaceful settlement
of expressed in the First Joint
Communiqué, 25
Thucydides Trap, 39
transshipment
how neutral countries evade sanctions and
tariffs, 212–214, 240
investigation by the ESCB, 241–242,
250–251, 254
need for crisis planning, 240
Truman, Harry S.
and the Berlin blockade, 65–66

rejection of using nuclear weapons during the Korean War, 173, 177

Trump, Donald J.

adherence to the One China Policy, 33

coercive trade measures against U.S. allies, 245

comments on Taiwan, 129

communication of strategic ambiguity, 138

crackdown of PRC container ships docking at U.S. ports, 180

denial of planned transit by Lai Ching-te (July 2025), 134

goal of "AI dominance" and its limitations, 174, 195

"Liberation Day" tariffs (April 2025), 116–117, 203–204, 206, 214, 217–218, 239–240, 276

positive steps on AUKUS, 160

tariffs, 203–204, 240, 248

and the Trump administration, 27

Tsai Ing-wen, 29, 280, 281, 283, 286

Tsang, Steve, 5

Type 096 submarine

as next-generation SSBN enhancing PRC nuclear second-strike capability, 178

role in submarine modernization and fleet expansion, 164

2027

as a crucial date for Xi personally, 32

as the one-hundredth anniversary of the PLA's founding, 31–32

PLA Taiwan invasion readiness goal, 4–5, 31–32, 168, 270–271, 311 n.92

as a possible date for achieving artificial general intelligence (AGI), 191

scenario imagined in which in which strategic ambiguity is used, 136–137

scenario imagined in which structured ambiguity is used, 141

2049

CCP's broad global ambitions for, 1–2, 4

as the centennial of the People's Republic of China, 1–2

as the deadline for "reunification," 32

Two-Ocean Navy Act, 166–168. *See also* Vinson, Carl

UK. *See* Great Britain and the UK

Ukraine. *See also* Putin, Vladimir; Russia; Russian invasion of Ukraine

China's perceptions of U.S. resolve in, 31, 41

energy consumption and GDP during wartime, 110

geographic differences from Taiwan, why non-combatant evacuation would be harder in Taiwan, 81

lessons about fluidity of public opinion and morale, 12, 99–100, 128–129

other military lessons for Taiwan, 74, 91–93

risks to attacker of miscalculating defender's resolve, 70–71, 99–100

strategic bombing and national morale, 50

threats to Zaporizhzhia nuclear power plant, 108–109

use of air defenses, 90, 95

Use of drones, 96, 105–106, 147, 156

Xi–Biden discussion about, 17

UN Convention on the Law of the Sea (UNCLOS), 232, 388 n.143

undersea cables

in the Bashi Channel, 289

British-controlled undersea cables, 202

interference with Taiwan's undersea cables, 61, 86, 140, 261

undersea warfare

China's submarines and undersea technology, 164, 325 n.69

PLAN nuclear-armed submarines, 75–76

potential U.S. and PLA submarine bastions around Taiwan, 75–76, 76f

U.S. dominance undersea, 9, 102, 163–165, 358 n.114

United Front Work Department (UFWD)

the need for the U.S. to disclose intelligence about UFWD activity, 130

potential role in crisis scenarios or coups in Taiwan, 86

role in the PRC's all-domain pressure campaign, 59–60

United Nations (UN)

China's view as a legitimizing force, 101

collective self-defense and the UN Charter, 59

United Nations (UN) (*Continued*)
  possible General Assembly responses to a Taiwan crisis, 215
  Resolution 2758, 22, 59, 130
  and structured ambiguity, 9
  in the Suez crisis (1956), 263–264
United States—Department of Defense (DoD)
  cost-plus model of, compared with a productized-sales (VC model), 159–160
  long-term contracts for key systems, 159
  low progress on its strategy of "deterrence by denial," 5–6
United States—House Select Committee on the Chinese Communist Party
  the idea of automatically triggering sanctions endorsed by, 209
  on the lack of a contingency plan for the economic and financial impacts of conflict with the PRC, 11, 204
United States Navy—integrated air and missile defense (IAMD) systems
  adaptation by the U.S. Navy, 156–157
  Aegis Ashore and the Aegis Ballistic Missile Defense (BMD), 201, 372 n.140, 391 n.37
  decline of the U.S. maritime industry, 69–70
  estimated capacity of major U.S. sea/airlifts, 67–68, 68*f*
  Maritime Administration (MARAD), 69
  Merchant Marine, 69–72, 325 n.71
  missile capability, 103, 153–154
  Ready Reserve Force (RRF), 69, 325 n.68
  submarines and undersea technology, 163–165
  U.S. assets within striking range of Taiwan, 103
  U.S. facilities in the First Island Chain, 149*f*
United States–Taiwan relations
  impact of, on the U.S.-Japan alliance, 142
  mutual defense treaty (1979–1980), 26, 308 n.53
unmanned aerial systems (UAS). *See* drones/unmanned aerial systems (UAS)

Venezuela
  U.S. sanctions on, 49–50
Vietnam
  as a Core allies' trading partner during avalanche decoupling, 247–248
  as a diversionary war target, 40
  as example of waning U.S. resolve, 41
  as potential target of future Chinese blockade or quarantine, 47–48
  as potential target of U.S. nuclear attack, 177
  1979 invasion by China, 77–78, 327 n.98
Vinson, Carl, 7, 167
Virginia-class submarines
  production capacity constraints, 163–164
  role in U.S. attack submarine fleet and Taiwan contingency, 105
  transfer to Australia under AUKUS, 143

Wang, Austin Horng-En, 326 n.81
War on Drugs, 212
Wild Lily Student Movement, 283
World Bank
  procedural paralysis during a Taiwan crisis, 250, 259
World Trade Organization (WTO)
  accession of Russia and China, 43
  Appellate Body, 47
  China's repeated violations, 265
  current paralysis of, 245, 251
  establishment of, 37
  national security exceptions, 239–240, 245
  permanent normal trading relations (PNTR), 244–245
  principles of the Atlantic Charter, 237
  relationship to the ESCB, 251, 254, 256
  Taiwan as a member of, 84, 389 n.12
Wray, Christopher, 181
Wuthnow, Joel, 5

Xi Jinping
  defensive and offensive interests in seizing Taiwan, 34
  instructions to the PLA, 4–5, 31–32, 168, 270–271
  Jou Yi Cheng on his resolve, 284
  meeting in Lima with Joe Biden (2024), 17–18

as the primary target of U.S.
    deterrence, 276–277
prioritizing of nonnuclear strategic
    deterrence capabilities, 179–180
relationship with Putin, 225–226
remarks on reunification at National Party
    Congresses, 32–33, 182, 313 n.102
views of "strategic coercion," 200
visit to Zhurihe (2017), 1, 3f
"zero-COVID" strategy of, 39–40, 181
Xue Li (薛力), 231–232

Zelensky, Volodymyr, 87–88, 128–129
Zelikow, Philip

on the "quarantine" or "indirect control"
    scenario, 5, 56–57, 63
on strikes on PRC territory as risking
    escalation to general war, 101–102
Zhao Hongtu (赵宏图), 230–231
Zhou Enlai, 25
Zhou Hanmin (周汉民), 225
Zhou Wenxing (周文星), 384 n.97
Zhu Hongda (朱洪达) on decoupling the
    U.S.–China trade relationship, 384
    n.95
Zhurihe
    PLA training ground with replicas of
        Taiwan's official structures, 1, 2f
    Xi Jinping's visit to (2017), 1, 3f